Managing with Microsoft Project® 98

How to Order:

For information on quantity discounts, contact the publisher: Prima Publishing, P.O. Box 1260BK, Rocklin, CA 95677-1260; (916) 632-4400. On your letterhead, include information concerning the intended use of the books and the number of books you wish to purchase.

Managing with Microsoft Project® 98

Lisa A. Bucki

PRIMA PUBLISHING

Prima Publishing and colophon are registered trademarks of Prima Communications, Inc., Rocklin, California 95677.

Publisher: Matthew H. Carleson
Managing Editor: Dan J. Foster
Acquisitions Editor: Deborah F. Abshier
Project Editor: Kevin Harreld
Technical Reviewer: Richard Morgan
Copy Editor: Sydney Jones
Interior Layout: Shawn Morningstar
Cover Design: Prima Design Team
Indexer: Katherine Stimson

IMPORTANT: If you have problems installing or running Microsoft Project 98, contact Microsoft Corporation at (206) 635-7056. Prima Publishing cannot provide software support.

ISBN: 0-7615-1420-1
Library of Congress Catalog Card Number: 97-75645
Printed in the United States of America
98 99 00 BB 10 9 8 7 6 5 4 3 2

To my best friend and husband, Steve,
and our canine kids, Bojangles and Reggie,
who bring me coffee when I need it,
forgive my long nights at the computer,
and are always ready to snuggle.

Contents at a Glance

Contents

Acknowledgments

I appreciate the support of acquisitions editor Deb Abshier and publisher Matt Carleson of Prima, who asked me to continue as a member of the Prima team and update this book. Kevin Harreld, who served as Prima's primary shepherd for this book, deserves praise for the spit and polish he applied. Copy editor Sydney Jones ensured the clarity of the text, and technical reviewer Richard Morgan ensured its accuracy. I'm also grateful to the design and layout team members, who presented such a pleasing visual package here.

Finally, thanks to you, Prima's readers, who lend your interest and input to enliven publications like this one.

Lisa A. Bucki, bucki@mindspring.com

About the Author

Lisa A. Bucki has over eight years of experience in computer training and computer book publishing. She was Associate Publisher of Alpha Books, an imprint founded to address the needs of beginning users. Bucki has authored or co-authored several books, including the original *Managing with Microsoft Project*.

Introduction

The most sophisticated project management tool available to most managers 20 or so years ago was a large white paper pad, put up on an easel or hung on the wall, and a marker. The manager or supervisor would meet with a group, list tasks on the white paper, write down assignments and deadlines (usually after heavy pauses during which everyone contemplated who could handle the assignment and how long it would take), and (if the group was really lucky) scratch out a rough flow chart of how the project would progress. Then, everyone would go away to start working, and the manager would have to hang up the large pages all around an office to have any hope of checking to see whether the project was progressing as planned.

That clumsy, primitive approach won't cut it today. Computers and other forms of automation have increased precision in all aspects of business, project management included. Anyone leading a project in today's lean and mean business environment shoulders heavy responsibility and pressure, and must make the project happen on time and on budget despite a minimum of resources. Thus, project managers need tools to lend speed and precision to both the planning process and each project's execution.

In the last few years, the developers of the leading project management program, Microsoft Project, have taken great steps in honing this software tool into an effective management weapon. The new release, Project 98, covers all the bases, enabling you to review and control many facets of a project from start to finish.

With Project, there's a significant payoff for your time investment in learning how to use the software. Not only will you be more organized, but your team will be more effective, you'll be able to anticipate problems, and your ability to make resource estimates will improve, so that over time you'll become a stronger manager.

This book is designed to help you make the most of your company's financial investment in Project, as well as your professional investment—the time you'll spend learning to work with Project, and the impact Project will have on your performance.

Who Should Read This Book

This book assumes that you or your company have already purchased and installed the Project software and all the supporting tools needed to work effectively with Project. Therefore, you won't find information here designed to help you justify using Project 98 in business. Instead, this book is for anyone who suddenly needs to work with Project, such as:

- Managers and assistants whose company has adopted Project
- Managers beginning to use Project as a method to standardize the planning process
- Project or team leaders who need to use Project to create graphical printouts of task assignments, or to allocate resources between several projects
- Project or team leaders who want to take advantage of the company network, a company Intranet, or the Internet to communicate about tasks, progress, and completion
- Professional project managers who have purchased Project to implement an organized planning system for their companies or clients

How This Book Is Organized

Whether you review the chapters from start to finish or browse around to review specific subjects when you need information about them, *Managing with Microsoft Project 98* is structured for easy use. Here's a brief review of what you'll find in each part of the book:

Part I, "Project Management Basics," focuses on the minimum you need to know to set up a project. You'll learn how to create a file in Project, set the overall project parameters, define the tasks that must be completed, and indicate the resources that will be used to complete each task.

Part II, "Making Adjustments to Projects," helps you learn to work out project kinks. You'll look at identifying and resolving resource overcommitments, adjusting tasks, and tracking a project's progress.

Part III, "Viewing, Formatting, and Printing Projects," discusses using the information you so diligently captured in Project. You'll choose different display formats for a project, print, work with forms and reports, review costs, and use outlining features.

Part IV, "Handling Multiple Projects," builds on the skills you mastered previously, showing you how to move and copy information between projects, create and use project templates, combine projects and resources, and use master projects and subprojects.

Part V, "Sharing and Publishing Project Information," covers using information from Project in other Microsoft Office applications, exporting project information, and setting reminders in Microsoft Outlook. It also provides information on online features for sending assignments or updates to team members, publishing project information on the Web, and more.

Part VI, "Working with Advanced Features," shows you how to customize the way you work with Project and create macros to make your work in Project even more efficient.

Conventions Used In This Book

To make it easier for you to use this book, the following "shorthand," or conventions, are used to present different kinds of information. You should review these conventions before beginning Part I:

- Key combinations—Pressing and holding one key while pressing another key is called a key combination. In this book, key combinations are indicated by a plus sign (+) separating the keys you have to press. For example, Ctrl+O is a key combination that requires you to press and hold the Ctrl key while pressing the O key.
- Menu names, commands, and dialog box options—In virtually all Windows programs, each menu name, command name, and dialog box option name contains an underlined letter called a selection letter. The selection letter is used to make that particular selection via the keyboard, sometimes as part of a key combination. In this book, all selection letters are indicated as an underlined letter, as in View.
- Text you type—When you need to type some text to complete a procedure, the text appears in bold, as in the following:

  Type the name for the task, such as **Request Price Quotes**.

Special Features of This Book

At times, I'll provide you with information that supplements the discussion at hand. This special information is set off in easy-to-identify sidebars, so you can review or skip these extras as you see fit. You'll find the following features in this book:

Tips provide shortcuts or better ways to accomplish tasks that make your job easier.

Notes provide supplemental information to expand your knowledge on the subject at hand.

Cautions protect you from what can be your worst computing enemy—yourself. When particular operations are risky and might cause you to lose some of your work, I'll forewarn you in these boxes.

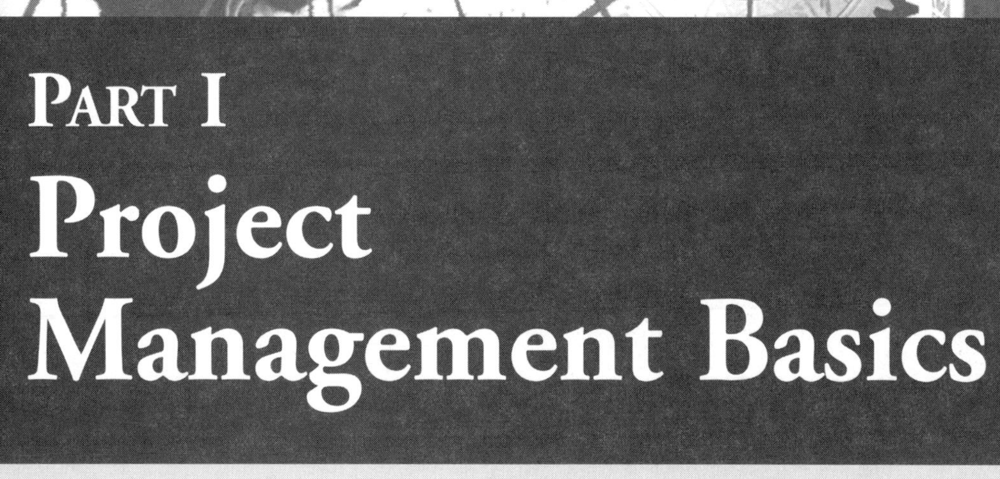

Part I
Project Management Basics

Microsoft Project 98

1

Getting Started with Project 98

In This Chapter

- The benefits of project management
- Key tools provided in Project
- How to start Project
- Online help resources
- How to exit Project

So, you've broken Microsoft Project 98 out of the box and installed it (or your MIS person has). You're all set up, but where do you go? With many applications, how to get started is obvious. To begin working in Microsoft Word, for example, you just start typing. In Microsoft Excel, you just click on and type numbers and formulas.

With Project, the starting point is not so obvious, but don't worry. This chapter and the next one introduce the steps you need to take to begin your work and set up a project.

Understanding Why You Need to Manage Projects

"Project management" used to be primarily a catch phrase adopted to flesh out a résumé. At best, in many cases, it involved keeping a long to-do list and dealing with problems after someone else had pointed them out. In its broadest sense, the label "project manager" could describe any individual who could complete most of his or her own work assignments.

In today's business climate, project management has emerged into a serious discipline, which is being incorporated into programs at technical schools and universities worldwide. For example, certain MBA programs include project management courses. You can earn undergraduate and graduate degrees in project management. Some international organizations, such as the Project Management Institute, train project management professionals, certify them with designations, such as Project Management Professional, and provide accreditation for project management courses. Finally, some consulting firms now specialize in providing project management services, and some businesses have developed formalized project manager positions.

Even if you don't have specific training in project management, you—like millions of others—might discover that project management skills are essential to career success. You need to have a precise handle on the steps involved in a project, how many resources you'll need, how long each portion of the project will last, and how much all of it will cost.

Business trends from the past decade are making those with project management skills increasingly valuable as managers or team leaders. Here are just a few examples:

- The dreaded corporate downsizing compels us all to accomplish more with fewer resources. As resources become more scarce, you have to plan further in advance and become more skilled at identifying and eliminating conflicts.
- In today's smaller workgroup or team environment, each team member's role has become less specialized. Thus, you must carefully define each person's role within the context of a particular project.

- The efficiency of online communication has lead to *virtual teams*—geographically dispersed individuals who need to work together as a cohesive unit. The fact that a team member is halfway across the country makes that person no less important to your overall mission. With virtual teams, you need to communicate frequently about deadlines and progress, and make sure you're getting feedback about issues and problems so that you can resolve them before they sidetrack your schedule or budget.
- To bring products to market more quickly, most companies distribute tasks across several departments so that different project phases can be handled concurrently. In such cross-departmental situations, tracking performance and communicating expectations has become more challenging and necessary.
- Companies that are under headcount restrictions, or that are unwilling to invest in specialized technology, increasingly rely on outside contractors for a variety of functions. Project management techniques and tools can help in keeping these outside resources on track.

Management Techniques Offered in Project

Even if you're just getting started with Project, you'll be surprised at how a little time spent with its features can make you look organized and impress your colleagues. Consider this true story. My husband took a job as a project manager with a large international manufacturer of audiocassettes and CDs. A month or so later, his primary client placed an order for several million units of product—one of the largest orders that the plant where my husband works had ever handled. The pressure was on my husband, both from the head honchos at the plant and from the client. So, to prepare, he launched Microsoft Project (which none of the other project managers ever bothered to start, let alone use). He typed in the list of tasks, start dates, and the approximate length of time each task could take. He indented some tasks to make the list a little clearer. Then, he printed only the list of tasks, called the task sheet. At the meeting to kick off the project, he handed out the task list and his other materials, and the clients and his bosses loved it. His company's president even said, "This is exactly what we should be doing for every job." The order went off like clockwork, and all my husband did to become the hero was type in some information. He didn't even use many of Project's most powerful features!

Keeping your arms around far-flung details and resources for big projects, such as a client order, previously required several tools. You outlined the project with a word processor, budgeted with a spreadsheet, plotted progress on paper timelines, and so on. Microsoft Project 98 handles all the key facets of project planning by blending traditional project management models, such as Gantt charts and critical path analysis with more contemporary techniques, such as printing custom calendars, importing information from other programs, and quickly e-mailing assignments. With Project, you can track the completion of various tasks, manage costs, reallocate resources, and more.

Overall, the process you follow when you use Project is to create a schedule by defining the tasks that need to be completed, determining the probable cost for each task, and determining what people, supplies, contractors, and other resources are needed to complete the task. After you establish the schedule, you can fine-tune it to decrease the total timeframe, deal with resource conflicts, and so on. Finally, you can track the team's progress, and communicate the schedule to others from start to finish by printing an overall chart, printing charts about individual resources, generating reports for your manager, and e-mailing information to other team members.

Thus, Project offers a variety of techniques for establishing, modifying, and managing the parameters for each project plan you pull together.

Key Benefits of Using Project

As with many other new types of software, users often wonder whether it's worth the time investment to learn the Project program and enter all the necessary information about a project. Why not simply stick with a word processor and spreadsheet to get the job done? Well, because you don't want to use a regular hammer when the job calls for a sledgehammer or jackhammer. Project not only makes the basic job of managing projects easier, but also offers features and capabilities that give you more control over the scope of the project.

You'll realize the following benefits if you use Project as a planning and management tool:

- **Manage more information**—Project can track thousands of tasks and resources per project, and more information about each task and resource. Only your computer's memory and other resources limit the amount of information you can enter in a Project file.
- **Automatically create project diagrams**—Project automatically generates Gantt and PERT charts, as well as calendars, to provide a look at how project tasks relate and a method to relay information to others.

- **Track specific aspects of the project and anticipate problems**—You can take a look at costs, the commitments, or available starting date of a particular resource.
- **Track overall progress**—As you enter task completion dates, you can compare progress with the original plan. In addition, you can add a status date to help you update progress more quickly and to clarify when you last updated the project.
- **Generate forms and reports to share information**—You can choose from a variety of predefined forms and reports, or create custom forms for particular situations.
- **Communicate via e-mail and the Web**—Project is optimized to enable you to share project information via existing e-mail tools, such as Microsoft Outlook. You can publish Project information as a Web page or develop a Web site to manage team messages, to give everyone involved in the project a central location to go for more information.

Starting Project

As with most other Windows 95 programs, the easiest way to start Project is via the Windows Taskbar:

1. Click the Start menu button; then point to Programs.
2. Click Microsoft Project.

If Project doesn't appear as a choice on the Start menu, follow these steps to add a shortcut icon to your desktop for starting the program:

1. Double-click the My Computer icon on your desktop to open the My Computer window.
2. Double-click the icon for the drive where Project 98 is installed, usually drive C:.
3. By default, Project installs to a subfolder in the Program Files folder, along with other Microsoft Office applications. Thus, first double-click the icon for the Program Files folder to open it, and then double-click the icon for the Microsoft Office subfolder. If you chose to install Project in a different folder, you should open that folder instead.
4. In the Microsoft Office folder, point to the Microsoft Project shortcut icon, press and hold the right mouse button, and drag the icon over the desktop. When you release the mouse button, a shortcut menu appears. Click on Copy Here, as shown in Figure 1.1.

Figure 1.1 After you release the right mouse button, click on Copy Here to create a shortcut icon for Project on the desktop.

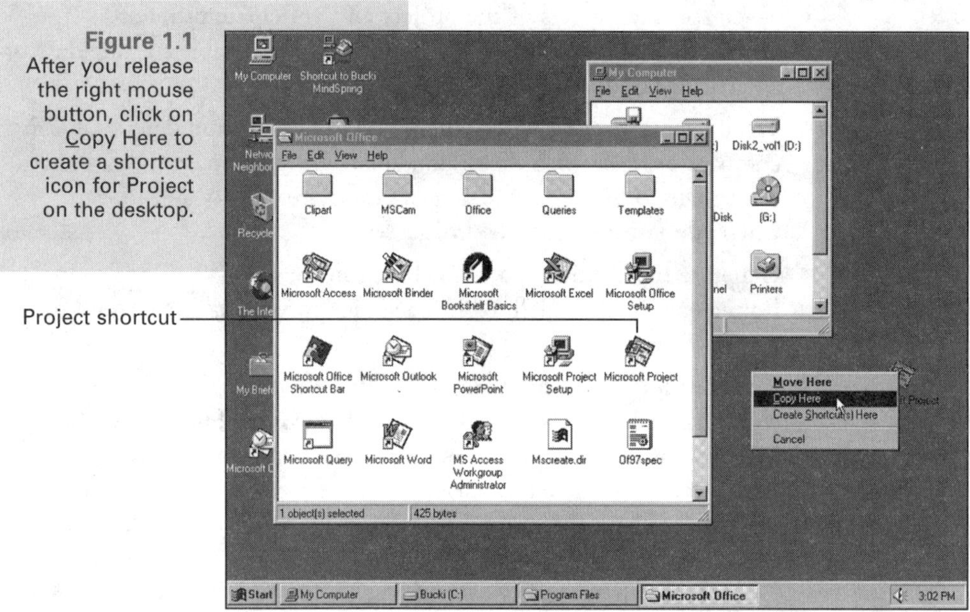

After you add a Microsoft Project shortcut to the desktop, you can double-click on it at any time to start Project.

No matter what method you use to start Project, by default you'll see the Welcome! startup screen shown in Figure 1.2. This screen offers three choices for how to proceed, as well as a check box:

- **Learn While You Work**—Click this button to use the Getting Started: Create Your Project tutorial, which offers brief lessons that walk you through the process of creating a project schedule.
- **Watch a Quick Preview**—Click this button to view onscreen information about Project and its benefits.
- **Navigate with a Map**—Click this button to view an interactive map (see Figure 1.3) that outlines the process of creating and monitoring a project schedule. When you click on a large circle, a pop-up box displays with information. Click outside the box when you finish reading it. Click a small circle to display a Help window with steps for a procedure. Click a yellow Hint box to receive more interactive help.
- **Don't Display this Startup Screen Again**—Click this box to check it before clicking any of the other buttons to have Project skip the Welcome! screen and go directly to a blank project file during subsequent startups.

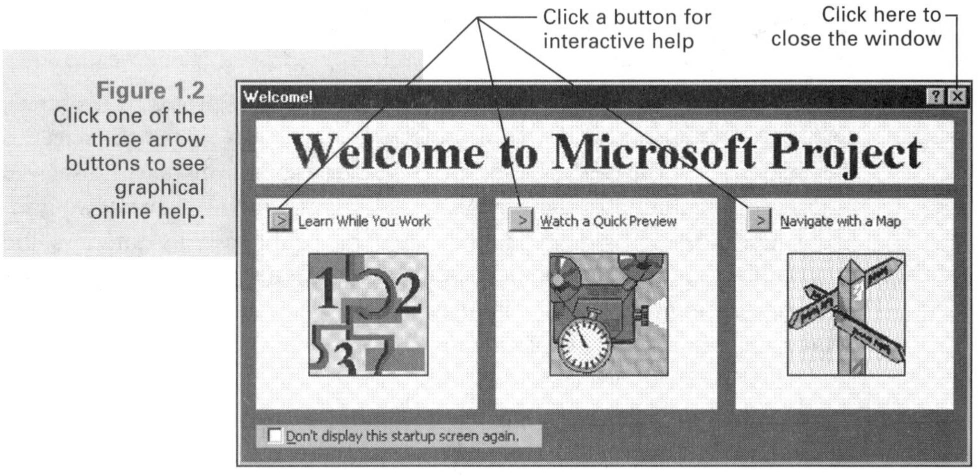

Figure 1.2 Click one of the three arrow buttons to see graphical online help.

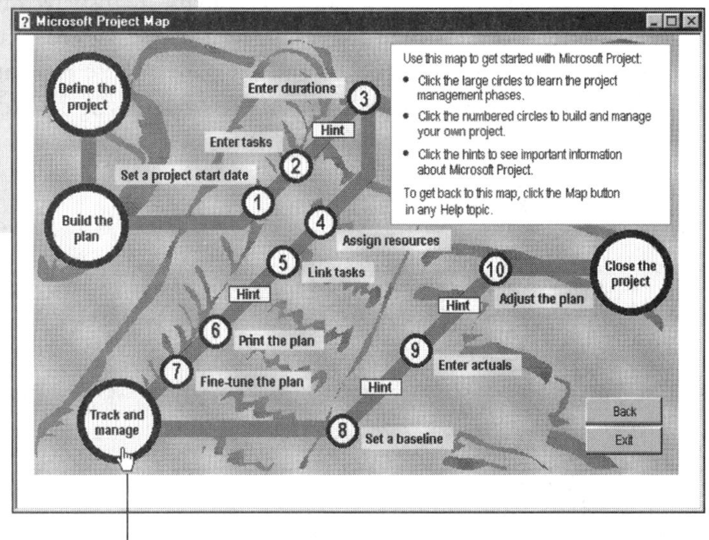

Figure 1.3 The large and small circles and Hint boxes on this map lead to additional types of help when you click them.

If you prefer not to work with interactive help and want to display a blank project file, click the Close button in the upper-right corner of the Welcome! screen. This takes you to the Project application window and a new, blank project file. You can display interactive help after you begin working (see "Accessing Interactive Help Features" later in this chapter).

Understanding the Project Screen

When Project displays a new, blank project, the screen looks like Figure 1.4. By default, you'll see the Gantt Chart view for the new project. This screen enables you to enter tasks for your project. At the far-left side of the screen is the View Bar, which you can use to change the way information is displayed in Project. In addition to the View Bar, the Project window features two grid-like panes. In the left pane, you enter the name of the task, its duration, and other columns of task information. (Chapter 2, "Setting Up a Project," covers creating tasks in more detail.) The right pane displays each task you create as a graphical bar in a weekly schedule, so you can see at a glance how long a task lasts, or where tasks overlap in time.

Project 98 looks even more like the Microsoft Office applications (Word, Excel, PowerPoint, Access, and Outlook), so the Project application feels familiar and you learn quickly to find and use Project features. The top of the screen displays a title bar and menu bar with commands, as in other Windows applications. Below the menu bar, two toolbars are displayed by default; each toolbar button is a shortcut for executing a particular command. A text entry box appears between the toolbars and the panes where you enter data; you use this box to enter and edit task entries. The box changes in appearance when you use it, as you learn in the next chapter.

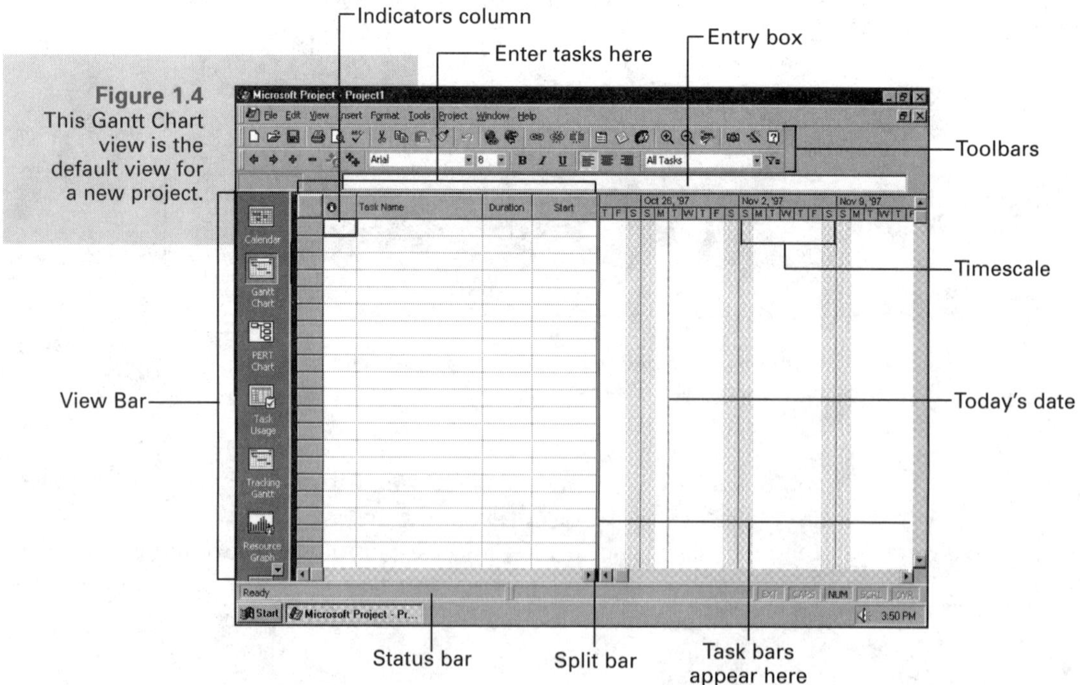

Figure 1.4 This Gantt Chart view is the default view for a new project.

For more information about Project and other Microsoft Products, visit the Microsoft home page on the Web at **http://www.microsoft.com**.

Looking at the View Bar

Project 98 offers a new onscreen feature called the View Bar. As its name suggests, the View Bar enables you to select a different onscreen layout or view for the various types of information stored in a Project file. For example, a particular view might show a graph you're looking for, and another view might make it easier to enter a certain type of information, such as information about a resource (a person who will be working on a project). Some views are graphical, some provide information about tasks, and so on. Don't worry about what each view looks like for now. You learn more about the various views in chapters where they apply and in Chapter 9, "Working with the Different Project Views."

Each icon in the View Bar represents a particular view in Project. Click the icon for the view you want in order to switch to that view. To scroll the View Bar and see additional view icons, click the down-arrow button at the bottom-right corner of the View Bar. After you click the down-arrow button once, an up-arrow button appears in the upper-right corner of the View Bar, as shown in Figure 1.5.

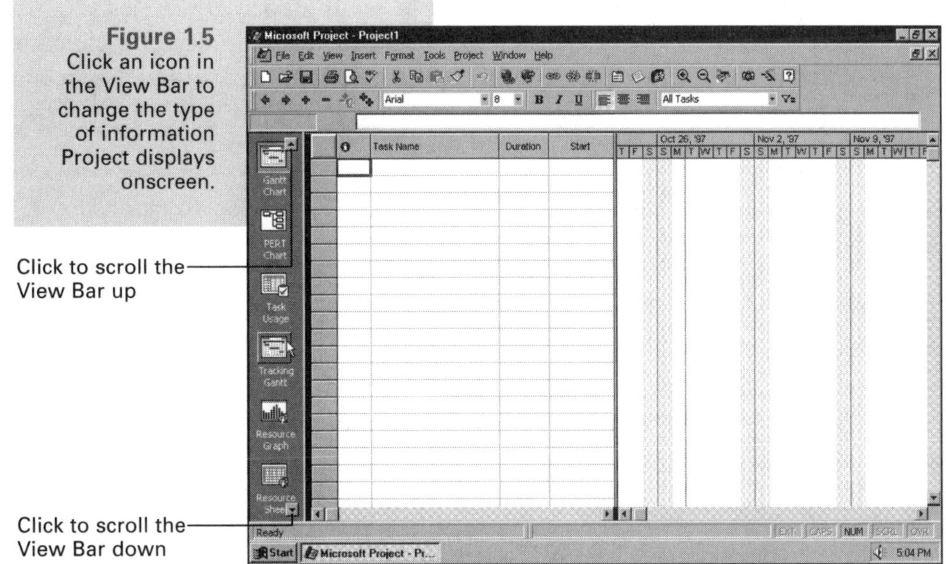

Figure 1.5 Click an icon in the View Bar to change the type of information Project displays onscreen.

When you move the mouse pointer over the icon for a particular view, the icon takes on a 3-D appearance. Then, you can click the icon to change to the view.

Note

If you use Microsoft Outlook 97 to manage your e-mail, to-do list, contact list, and other information, you're familiar with the Outlook Bar, which you use to view various types of information in Outlook. The View Bar in Project looks and works like the Outlook Bar.

Looking at the Toolbars

Project by default displays two toolbars, Standard (top) and Formatting. To discover what a particular toolbar button does, simply place the mouse pointer on it to display a yellow ScreenTip describing the button (see Figure 1.6).

Project enables you to control the toolbar display, to select the shortcuts you prefer to work with, and to control how much of your screen the toolbars use. As shown in Figure 1.7, you can drag a toolbar to another location onscreen, which automatically places the toolbar in a floating window that you can resize by dragging any of its borders.

The fastest way to choose which toolbars appear onscreen is to right-click a toolbar to display the toolbar's shortcut menu. A check beside a toolbar name in the list indicates that the toolbar is presently displayed (toggled on). To select or deselect a toolbar, click its name on this shortcut menu. To close the shortcut menu without changing a toolbar selection, click outside the menu (or press Esc).

If you worked with the previous version of Project, Project 95, you may find it easier to work in Project 98 if you hide its Standard toolbar. In its place, display the Project 95 toolbar, which offers the same buttons as the Standard toolbar in Project 95.

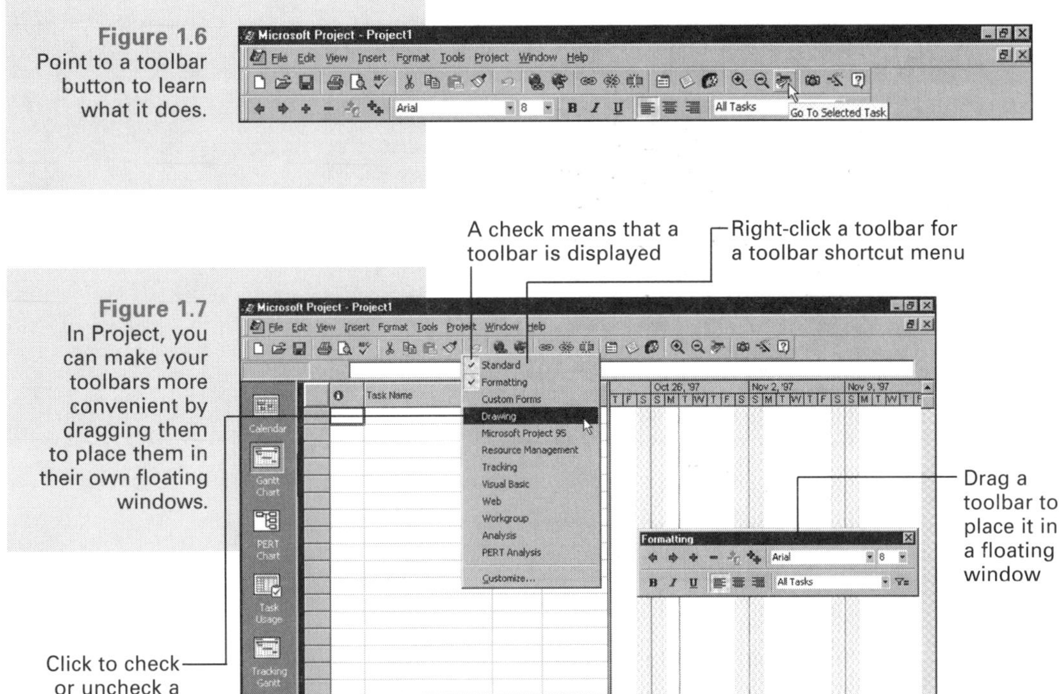

Figure 1.6 Point to a toolbar button to learn what it does.

Figure 1.7 In Project, you can make your toolbars more convenient by dragging them to place them in their own floating windows.

Getting Help When You Need It

Project offers several different "flavors" of help, via the Help menu. The most common way to start working with the Help system is to access the list of available Help topics. To do so, click the Help menu to open it, and click Contents and Index.

Displaying the Help Topics: Microsoft Project (see Figure 1.8) dialog box enables you to choose from among three tabs, each offering a different kind of help:

- **Contents**—The Contents tab lists several "books" or topic areas within the Help system. To view the topics within a book, double-click the book so that its icon changes to an open book and its contents (additional books and topics) are displayed. A question mark icon indicates specific topics. Double-click any topic to view it. To close a book, if needed, also double-click it. This tab is ideal for browsing through the available help.

Figure 1.8 After you access the Help Topics: Microsoft Project dialog box, you can click a tab to select the kind of help you need.

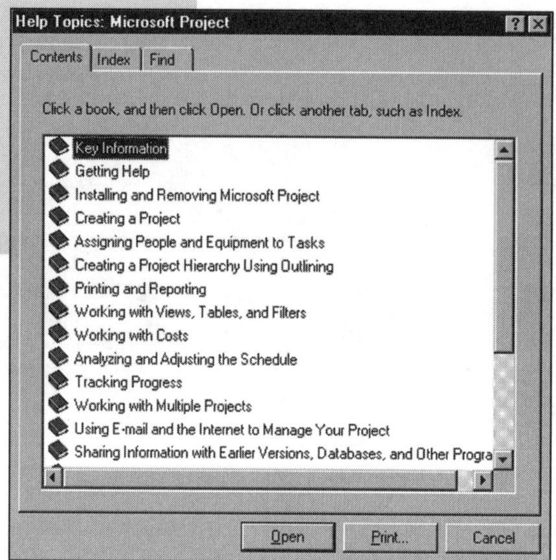

- **Index**—If you have a rough idea of the topic you're searching for and how it might be referenced in Help, click the Index tab. The top text box prompts you to type all or part of the topic you want information about. The list at the bottom scrolls to display the topics that most closely match your entry. Whenever you see an entry you want to view in the bottom list, double-click it (or click it, and then click Display).
- **Find**—The Find tab enables you to search to find terms used within Help topics, so you can zero in on pertinent details. The first time you choose the Find tab, the Find Setup Wizard dialog box appears. This dialog box lets you control how many terms appear in the Find database. You can leave the Minimize Database Size (Recommended) option button selected, which is the default. This choice ensures that the database doesn't consume too much disk space. Then click Next. Then click Finish to build the Find database. After the Find tab becomes active, type the word(s) you want to search for in the top text box. To narrow the search further, click on a choice in the second box, which presents a scrolling list of terms similar to those you typed. If the term you want to view appears in the bottom scrolling list, double-click it. Otherwise, click the Find Similar button (which, when available, finds topics that are associated with the selected topic, but not necessarily direct matches) or the Find Now button to display a list of possible matches in the bottom list box.

If you want to expand the number of terms in the Find database at a later time, click the Rebuild button on the Find tab in the Help Topics: Microsoft Project dialog box. Click Maximize Search Capabilities, click Next, and then click Find. Keep in mind that the expanded database may make the Find tab operate a bit more slowly.

After you display a Help topic in its own window (by selecting the topic from one of the tabs in the Help Topics: Microsoft Project dialog box), you can click the Options button in that window to display a menu with options for working with the help topic information. Choosing Annotate from the menu, for example, displays a window where you can add your own comments to the Help topic. Choose Copy to copy the Help topic contents to the Windows Clipboard, so you can paste that information into another document. If you select part of the Help topic by dragging over it before you choose Copy, only the selection is copied. Print Topic enables you to print the Help topic for easy reference. Font enables you to adjust the text size in the Help topic display. Keep Help on Top enables you to control whether the Help window remains in the foreground as you continue to work in Project and other applications. Use System Colors lets you toggle between the default help colors (when this menu choice is unchecked) and the currently selected Windows 95 colors (when this menu choice is checked). You can use the Define Bookmarks choice to mark the current Help topic as a bookmark, giving it the name of your choice. Use the Bookmarks choice to display the Bookmarks dialog box, which lists bookmarks you've previously created; double-click a bookmark name to redisplay the bookmarked Help topic.

Another Help menu choice can provide instant help for the task at hand. Click the Help menu to open it, and then click What's This?; alternately, press Shift+F1. The mouse pointer turns into a question mark pointer. Click the onscreen item that you're curious about, and Project displays a pop-up description of it. Click outside the description to close it.

The new Project version also offers a few more forms of help. One Help menu choice displays a submenu of different types of help and current information on the World Wide Web; Chapter 19 covers how to use Web help. I describe the other two types of new help next.

Note

If you see a Question Mark button next to the Close button at the right end of a dialog box title bar, you can click the Question Mark button, and then click an item in the dialog box for pop-up help about it. If the dialog box doesn't offer a Question Mark button, right-click the dialog box option you want help with, and then click What's This? in the shortcut menu.

Using the Office Assistant

The Office Assistant enables you to ask for help in plain English. You type in a question, and the Office Assistant searches the Help system and displays a list of topics that may answer your question. Follow these steps to display and work with the Office Assistant:

1. You can launch the Office Assistant in a few ways: by opening the Help menu and clicking Microsoft Project Help, by pressing F1, or by clicking the Office Assistant button on the Standard toolbar. No matter which method you use, the Office Assistant opens in its own small window onscreen, and its yellow question bubble opens. The bubble prompts you to type a question.
2. Type your question; it replaces the prompt in the bubble. Figure 1.9 shows an example question typed into the Assistant: "How do I save a project file?"
3. Click the Search button, located beneath the area where your question appeared when you typed. The Office Assistant searches all the Help topics, and lists topics that might answer your question in the yellow bubble. If there are more topics than can appear in the bubble at one time, a See More choice with a down-pointing triangle button appears at the bottom of the topic list; click it to review the additional topics. After you do so, a See previous choice appears at the top of the list so you can redisplay the initial list of topics.
4. When you see the Help topic you want, click the round button beside it. A Help window appears onscreen to give you steps, information, or links to more specific topics. Review the Help, and then click the Help window Close button to close the window.
5. If you are finished working with the Office Assistant, you can click the Close button on its window to remove the Office Assistant from your screen.

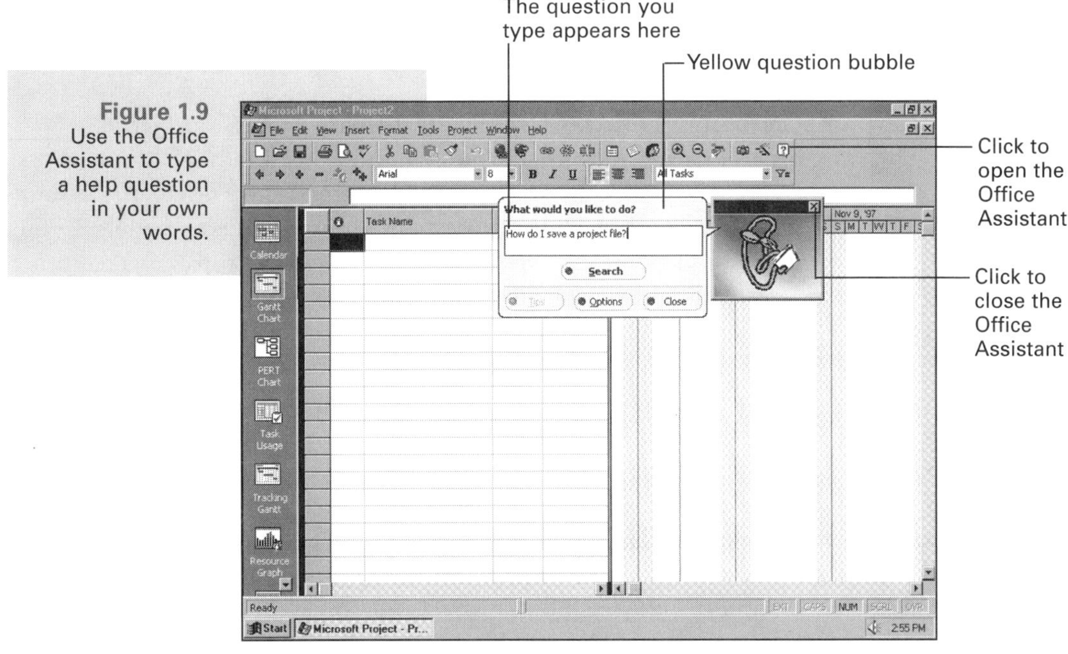

Figure 1.9 Use the Office Assistant to type a help question in your own words.

Rather than closing the Office Assistant after getting Help about a question, you can leave the Assistant onscreen as long as you need to. To redisplay the yellow question bubble at any time, click in the Office Assistant window. If you open the question bubble but decide not to ask a question, click the Close button in the bubble to close the bubble but leave the Office Assistant open.

Accessing Interactive Help Features

Earlier in this chapter, you learned that Project's Welcome! screen offers you the option of reviewing a few different types of interactive onscreen Help. If you choose not to view that interactive help and not to display the Welcome! screen each time you start Project, you can redisplay the interactive Help using the Help menu. If you click the Help menu and point to Getting Started, Project displays a submenu with three choices that lead you back to interactive Help:

- **Quick Preview**—Click this command, which displays the same Help as the Watch a Quick Preview choice in the Welcome! screen, to view an onscreen review of Project's key features and how they can help you. The Quick Preview window appears in Figure 1.10. To navigate in the Quick Preview window, click the Next and Back buttons to move through the screens consecutively. You also can click one of the numbers in the bar at the lower-left corner of the window to jump to a particular point in the preview. Click the window Close button or Exit button to close the Quick Preview.

- **Create Your Project**—This submenu choice displays the Getting Started: Create Your Project tutorial, just as the Learn While You Work choice in the Welcome! screen does. This interactive help offers lessons that walk you through the process of creating a project schedule. In the initial window for this type of help, there are three topics marked in green with dotted underlines. Click one of these topics to display pop-up help about the topic. You can use the Next and Back buttons in the lower-right corner of the window to navigate through the contents in the tutorial. When you click Next to display the second window for the tutorial, Project displays a list of several lessons. Click the blue underlined link to display the lesson you want to view. Each lesson screen displays a few more blue links to specific topics; clicking one of these links displays a Help window with steps or information. Each Help window you access in this way includes a button near the top for returning to the main lesson screen. You can close the Getting Started: Create Your Project tutorial by clicking the window Close button.
- **Microsoft Project 101: Fundamentals**—Click this button to view a Help window that offers six large buttons, each of which leads to help about a key concept in Project, such as where to enter project information. (It also offers Show Me a Map to Microsoft Project, which leads to the same choice as the Navigate with a Map choice in the Welcome! screen, and the Learn While I Build My Project choice, which displays the Getting Started: Create Your Project tutorial.) After you click one of the six large buttons, an initial Help window appears with brief information about the topic. Click the Show Me button in this type of Help window to display a window in which graphics appear, one at a time, to illustrate the steps for items within the topic. Click the yellow caption for a step or topic to display pop-up help; after reviewing the pop-up help, click outside it to close it. You can click the Back button at the top of the window to return to the previous window. Click the Project 101 Contents button to redisplay the initial window with the six Project 101 topic buttons. You can click the Map button to display the interactive Help map, which also appears (refer to Figure 1.3) if you click Navigate with a Map! in the Welcome! screen. Click the window Close button to finish working with this type of help.

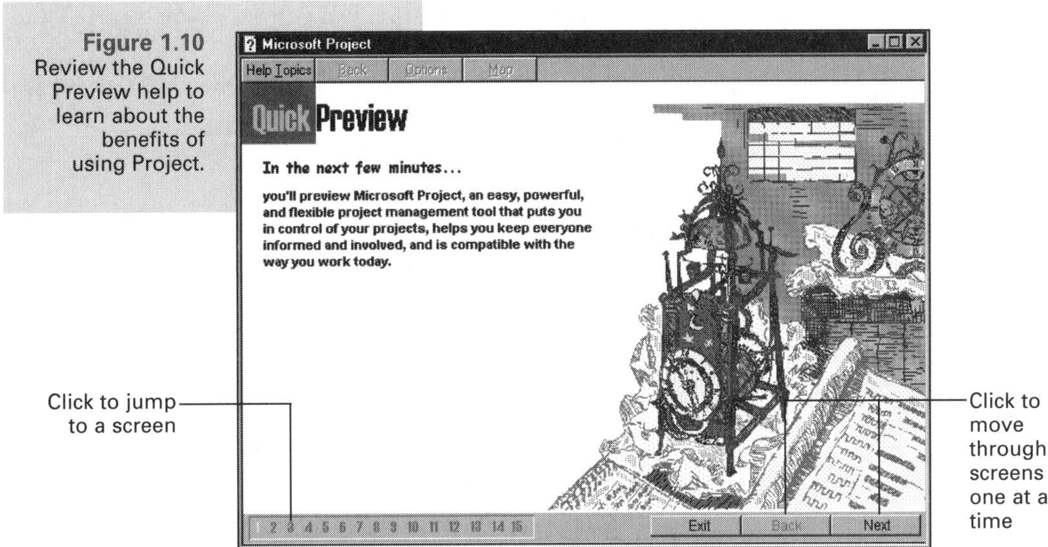

Figure 1.10 Review the Quick Preview help to learn about the benefits of using Project.

Working with Files

As in all other applications, in Project you must store your work by saving it to a file on your computer's hard disk. You won't be able to track your project's progress if you can't use your file repeatedly, so it's essential to be careful when saving your files and to choose file names that are specific and descriptive. This makes it easy to find the file you need. This section looks at preserving and organizing your work.

Starting a New File

As you learned earlier in this chapter, you can open a new, blank file when you launch the Project 98 application. There might be occasions, however, when you finish working with one file and then want to create a new file without exiting Project. Doing so is easy. Either click the New button on the Standard toolbar (it's at the far left and looks like a piece of paper), or open the File menu and click New. Project displays the Project Information dialog box for the new file, and gives the file the temporary name ProjectX, where X is a number sequentially assigned to each new file you open in a Project work session. The Project Information dialog box enables you to enter facts such as the starting and ending dates for the project. (You'll learn in detail how to work with this dialog box in Chapter 2, "Setting Up a Project.")

After you click OK to accept the information you entered for the new file, Project displays the empty file onscreen. It displays the file's temporary name in the title bar, until you save the file and assign a unique name to it. (See the section "Saving a File," later in this chapter.)

Opening an Existing File

If you ever opened files that have been previously created and saved in other Windows applications, you'll be relatively comfortable with Project's File Open dialog box. This dialog box enables you to open Project files you previously saved, so you can enter new information, change the view, print, and more.

To open a file, follow these steps:

1. Open the File menu and click on Open. Alternatively, you can press Ctrl+0, or click the Open button on the Standard toolbar. (It's second from the left, and looks like an open file folder.) The File Open dialog box appears (see Figure 1.11).

Note

On Windows 95 (or later) systems, the folder that appears by default in the Look In list is usually \My Documents\, which is located on drive C:. However, if you're running Project with Windows NT Workstation 3.51, the default folder is usually \Personal\, which is a subfolder of the folder that holds your Windows NT Workstation files. There isn't any option within Project for changing the default folder that appears.

2. Click the drop-down arrow beside the Look In list, and click the disk drive where your Project file is stored to select that drive and display its list of folders in the dialog box.

Select the Network Neighborhood icon from the Look In list if the file is on a drive connected to the network and doesn't initially appear in the Look In list.

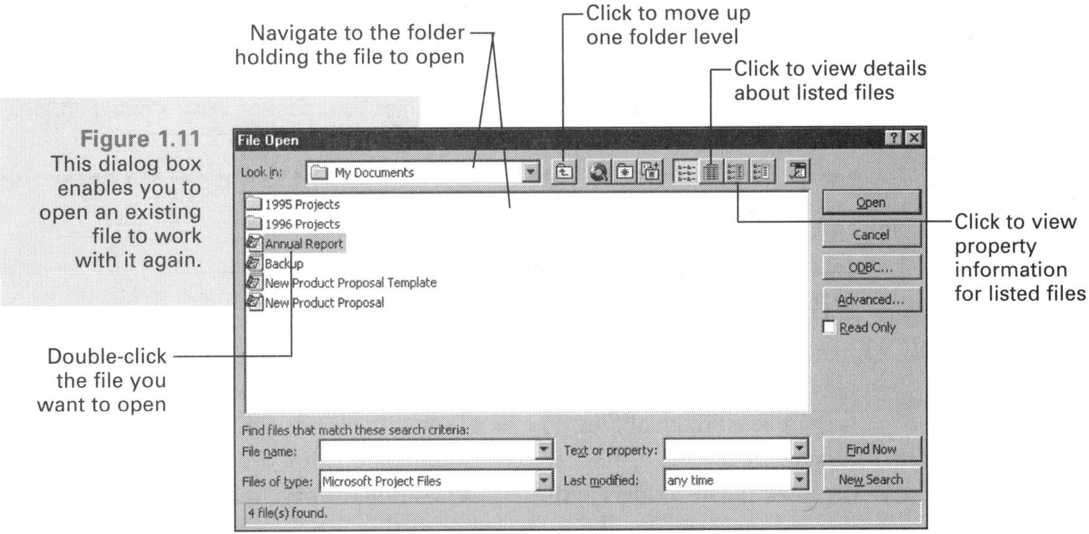

Figure 1.11 This dialog box enables you to open an existing file to work with it again.

3. Double-click a folder in the list of folders that appears; this displays the contents of that folder in the dialog box list. You might need to double-click subfolder icons to reach the file you want to open.
4. (Optional) If you want to view or print the file, but don't want to edit it, select the Read Only check box. This option prevents you from making unwanted changes to the file.
5. When the file you want to open appears in the list, double-click its name (or click its name, and then click Open) to load the file into Project.

After you select the file to open, Project displays it onscreen, ready for you to alter it, print, or whatever.

Note

If you are opening a file created in an earlier version of Project, Project may display a message telling you that some tasks may be scheduled a bit differently under Project 98. Click OK to close this dialog box. In addition, if a file contains macros and Project's virus protection features are enabled, you may see a dialog box asking whether you want to enable or disable the macros. Refer to Chapters 20 and 21 for more on working with macros and macro protection.

If you recently worked with a file and want to open it again, there's a shortcut; check the bottom of the File menu to see if the file name is listed there. By default, Project displays the names of the files you most recently worked on. If you see the name you want, click to open the file.

Finding a File with the File Open Dialog Box

As the sizes of hard disks on individual computer systems—and the sizes of networked drives—increase to several gigabytes each, it becomes harder for users to keep track of files. The best human memory can be challenged by hard disks with dozens of folders and thousands of files, even if you're diligent in organizing your folders and files. Or, you might have many files that are similar and need to use a Find feature to distinguish between them. To facilitate this, Microsoft has built file-finding help into the File Open dialog box in most of its applications.

When you perform a find, you can use wild-card characters if you remember part of a file name. Project will list files with names similar to the name you specified using wild cards. The asterisk (*) wild card stands in for any group of characters in the location where you use it within a file name. For example, entering **a*** in the File name text box results in a list of all file names that begin with the letter a, such as Annual Report and Accidents. The question mark (?) wild card stands in for any single character in the location where you use it. For example, entering **anders?n** in the File name text box finds files named Anderson and Andersen.

If you're working in the File Open dialog box and can't remember the exact location of the file you want to open, follow these steps to perform a basic find:

1. Navigate to the drive and folder where you think the file is located.
2. Use any one or a combination of the following entries (see Figure 1.12) to specify how Project should look for the file:
   - In the File name text box, enter the name of the file you're searching for (or use an approximation with wild cards).
   - In the Text or Property text box, enter any text that might appear in the project file or in the file's Properties dialog box. Be sure to enclose your entry in quotes. For example, enter **"1997"** for files that might include that year.

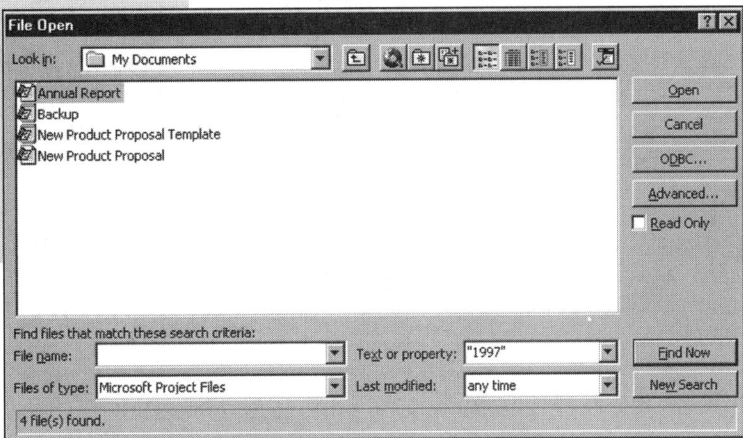

Figure 1.12 Use the text boxes at the bottom of this dialog box to narrow the search to files that meet specific criteria.

- Make a selection from the Last Modified list to search for a file depending on when you last saved changes to it. For example, if you know you made changes to the file recently, you can select "this month."

3. Click the Find Now button. Project searches the current folder for matching file(s). When the search is finished, Project displays a message in the lower-left portion of the dialog box that tells you how many files match the search criteria you specified. If only one file matches the criteria, that file is highlighted in the dialog box.
4. Double-click the name of the file you want to open (or click to select its name, and then click on Open).

Advanced Finds

To perform a basic find, you need to be familiar with a file, remembering where you saved it, its approximate name, and perhaps text that it contains. In some instances, though, you might not have that much information about the file. For example, if you have no idea where you saved the file, you need to use some more powerful searching capabilities to find the file. The advanced find features in the File Open dialog box will expand the search, enabling you to search more than one folder, more than one disk, and so on. Use the following steps to take advantage of the advanced search features after you open the File Open dialog box:

1. Specify any basic search criteria that apply, such as an approximate file name, as described in steps 1 and 2 of the preceding procedure.

2. Click on the Advanced button to display the Advanced Find dialog box (see Figure 1.13). Notice that the Find Files That Match These Criteria list displays any criteria you specified before clicking the Advanced button as well as additional criteria you add in the Advanced Find dialog box.

If you want to remove one of the criteria you defined, click it in the list of criteria, and then click Delete. To remove all the criteria, click New Search.

3. To add a new criterion to the list of criteria, start by selecting either the And or Or option button. And means that Find must match the original criteria (if any) and the new criterion you're specifying. In contrast, Or means that the file can match any one (or more) of the criteria you specified.
4. For the criterion you're creating, use the Property drop-down list to select the file property that will be used in the find operation, and use the Condition list to indicate how the Property and Value entries should correspond.
5. Finally, enter the Value that the Find operation should look for in that criterion. For example, if you have selected the Keyword Property, you might enter **report** as the value. If the Value entry contains more than one word, surround the entry with quotation marks, as in "**1997 report**."
6. Click the Add to List button to finish defining the criterion.
7. Repeat steps 3-6 to add more criteria based on file properties.
8. To fine-tune a single text criterion further, select it by clicking it in the list of criteria. Then select either the Match All Word Forms check box (when you want to match multiple tenses such as "run" and "ran") or the Match Case check box (when you want to match the exact capitalization you used).
9. Use the Look In drop-down list to specify a disk or folder to be searched. (If you want to search the current drive, but search all folders on the drive, make sure that the root directory is specified in the Look In list, rather than the current folder on that disk. To do so, double-click the Look In text box, and then edit the entry to specify the root of the disk, as in C:\. Select the Search Subfolders check box if you want to search subfolders within the selected disk or folder.

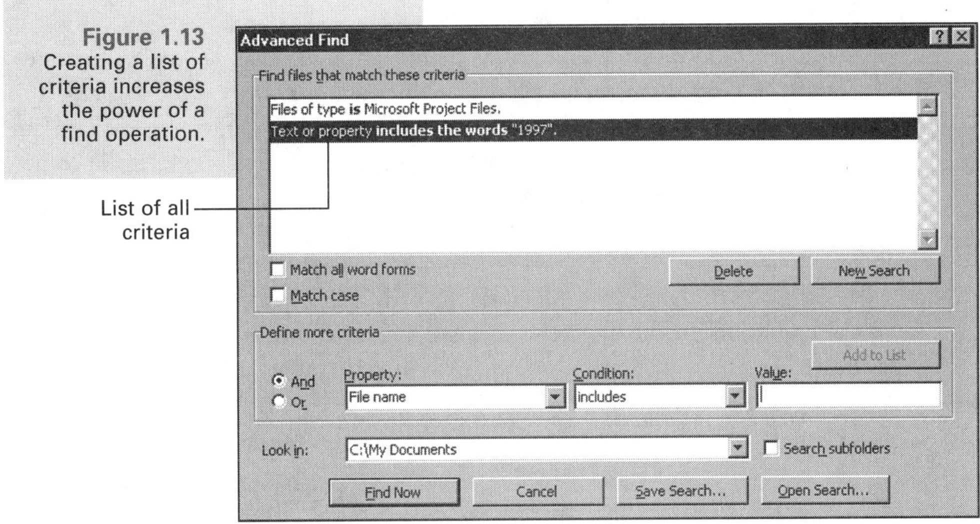

Figure 1.13 Creating a list of criteria increases the power of a find operation.

10. (Optional) To save the search (that is, all the criteria you specified), click the Save Search button, enter a name for this search in the Name text box, and then click OK.

To reuse a search you saved, click the Open Search button, select the named search in the Open Search dialog box, and click Open. You also can use Delete or Rename in the Open Search dialog box to delete or rename saved searches.

11. Click the Find Now button to execute the search. Project searches the specified folder(s) for the file(s). When the search is finished, Project displays a message in the lower-left portion of the Open File dialog box telling you how many files match the search criteria you specified. If only one file matches the specification, that file is highlighted in the dialog box.
12. Double-click the name of the file you want to open (or click to select its name, and then click Open).

Saving a File

Saving a file on disk preserves it (as permanently as possible, given the imperfections of electronic storage media) so that you can work with it again. The first time you save a file, you also have the opportunity to give the file a unique name. Project 98 enables you to take advantage of Windows 95 long file names. Previously, file names had to conform to the old DOS limitation of eight characters plus a three-character extension. Under Windows (95 and later versions), you can enter up to 255 characters, including spaces; however, keep in mind that the 255 characters must include the path, slashes, and so on. Therefore, the real limitation for the file name is closer to 230 characters. This enables you to create file names that are substantially more descriptive and useful.

To save a file for the first time and give it the name of your choice, perform the following steps:

1. Open the File menu and click on Save. Alternately, you can press Ctrl+S, or click the Save button on the Standard toolbar. (It's the third button from the left and looks like a floppy disk.) The File Save dialog box appears (see Figure 1.14).
2. Navigate to the drive and folder where you want to save the file, using the Save In drop-down list and the folders that appear below it. (Double-clicking a folder icon opens that folder so you can store the file there.)
3. Type a name for the file in the File name text box. Try to use something descriptive, even if it's lengthy, such as **Rider Bike Product Introduction**.
4. Click the Save button to save the file.

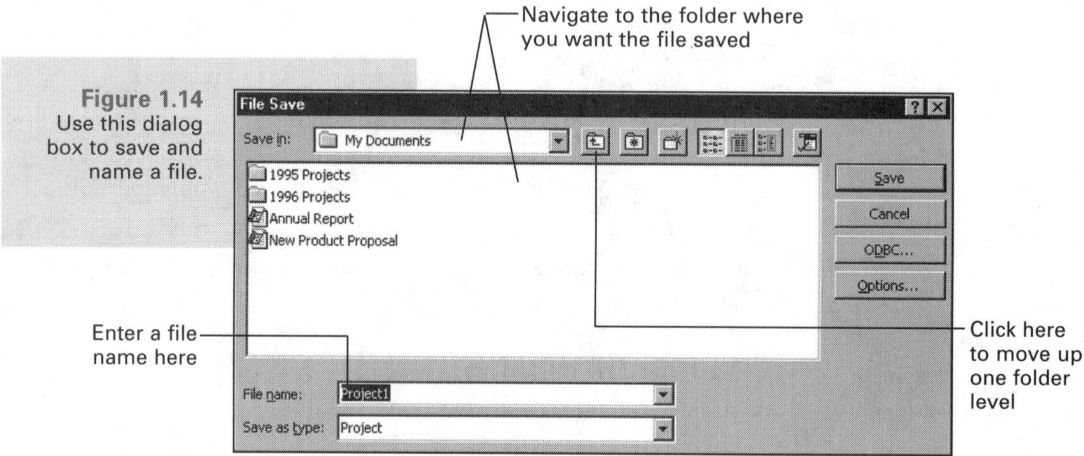

Figure 1.14 Use this dialog box to save and name a file.

After you save a file for the first time, you can save changes you make to it anytime in the future by pressing Ctrl+S (or clicking the Save button on the Standard toolbar).

There might be occasions, however, when you want to save a file with a new name. For example, if you have a lengthy project, you might want to save a version of the main project file at the end of each month, to keep a record of your progress and create a series of progressive "backup" copies of your file. In such a case, you must first save your file to ensure that the existing version reflects your most current changes. Next, redisplay the File Save dialog box by opening the File menu and clicking Save As. In the File Save dialog box, you can (but don't have to) change the selected folder to specify a new location for the renamed file. Then, type the new name, such as **March 97 Rider Bike Product Introduction**, and click Save to finish creating the new version of the file.

Each time you use Save As, you create a new copy of your file and leave the older version intact on disk. Because this tends to clutter your hard disk, use Save As sparingly. For example, you wouldn't want to use Save As daily to copy a file, but you might use it monthly to ensure you have a relatively up-to-date spare copy of the file.

File Protection and Backup Options

Part of the beauty of Project is that its files can be used easily in a networked environment. At any time, other team members can open the master plan for a project and review where things stand, or update information about tasks as they are completed. The downside to this, of course, is that it is difficult to control who can view the file and how changes are made.

Fortunately, the File Save dialog box provides a method for applying some protection to files; you can protect files the first time you save them or after the fact. Display the File Save dialog box by opening the File menu and clicking on Save the first time you save the file, or by opening the File menu and clicking on Save As for existing files. If necessary, specify the folder where the file should be saved, and then enter the file name. Next, click on the Options button to display the Save Options dialog box (see Figure 1.15).

If you want Project to automatically create a backup copy of the file each time you save it, select the Always Create Backup check box.

Figure 1.15 Protect your files, especially when they are on a network, by specifying password protection and backup protection.

Create a Protection password if you want users to enter a password to be able to open the file. Enter a Write reservation password if you want users to be able to view a read-only version of the file without a password but want to require a password for a user to be able to edit the file and save the edited version.

Passwords in Project are case sensitive. Therefore if happY is the password you create, it will not match user entries, such as Happy, happy, or HAPPY. Be careful to record the correct password and its capitalization in a secure location. Also, steer clear of using passwords that others might be able to guess or discover, such as your birthdate, your Social Security number, names (your spouse's, pet's, or child's), and so on.

Click the Read-only recommended check box if you want Project to display a dialog box giving the user the option of opening a read-only version of the file each time it is opened.

After you specify any desired save options, click OK. If you specify a new password (or change a password), Project asks you to enter the password again to verify it. Do so, and then click OK. Click Save to close the File Save dialog box and put your protection options in place.

If you ever want to make changes to the specified protection options—for example, change a password—just open the file, redisplay the Save Options dialog box, and make whatever changes you want. To remove a password, double-click it to select the whole password, and then press Backspace or Delete. Click OK, and then Save to finalize the changes and return to your Project file.

Saving and Opening a Workspace

You might encounter situations where you regularly need to work with several Project files. For example, if you frequently copy information between two project files (such as one for all tasks in your group and one for a specific project), it might be more convenient to have them open automatically and appear side-by-side onscreen. You might even want to have each file appear in a particular view.

Luckily, you can save such an onscreen configuration of multiple files and settings as a workspace. To reopen multiple files, position them precisely onscreen, and specify the appropriate views and settings, all you have to do is open a single workspace file.

Note

Workspace files have a different file name extension, to help the File Open dialog box distinguish them from regular Project files.

To create a workspace file:

1. Open all the project files that you want to include in the workspace.
2. Arrange the files onscreen (as covered in the next section), and specify the appropriate view for each file. (Views are covered where they apply throughout the book. They are also covered in detail in Chapter 9, "Working with the Different Project Views.")
3. Open the File menu and click Save Workspace. The File Save dialog box appears, with Workspace automatically selected as the Save as type choice (see Figure 1.16).
4. Select the folder where you want to save the workspace file by using the Save In list and double-clicking folders as needed below the list.
5. Type a name for the workspace in the File name text box. (By default, Project suggests the name "Resume," but you can enter any name you want.)
6. Click Save to finish saving the workspace.

Opening a workspace is virtually identical to opening a file. Use any of three methods: open the File menu and click Open; press Ctrl+O; or click the Open button on the Standard toolbar. In the File Open dialog box, navigate to the folder where the workspace file is saved. Click the down arrow to open the Files of Type drop-down list, and select Workspaces from the list. When you see the name of the workspace file you want opened, double-click the name.

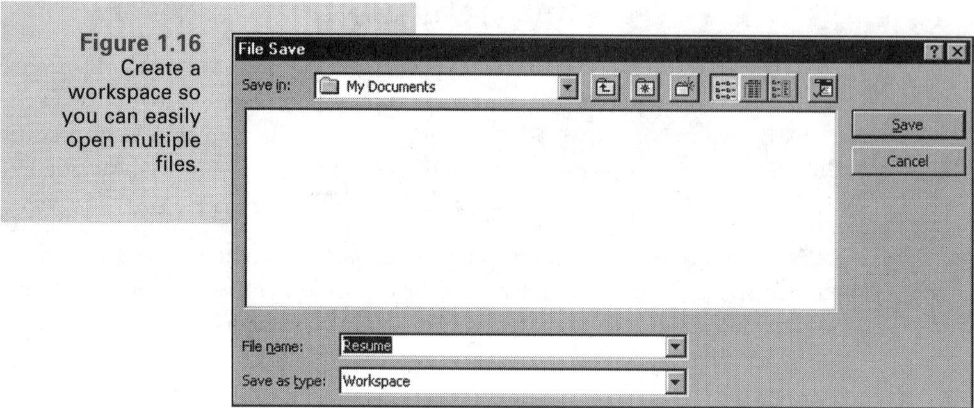

Figure 1.16 Create a workspace so you can easily open multiple files.

Selecting, Arranging, and Closing Files

Each time you open a file in Project, it remains open until you specifically close it after you finish working with it (and presumably after you save it). If you're viewing each open file at full-screen size (maximized), the easiest way to switch between open files is to use the Window menu. To choose which file to display, open the Window menu and click the name of the file you want to select (see Figure 1.17).

Notice that the Window menu offers some other useful options:

- New Window opens a new window of an open file. Doing so enables you, for example, to show two different views of the same file onscreen.
- Arrange All arranges all the open files and windows so that they fill the screen, with each file at least partially visible.
- Hide hides the currently selected file or window; this is handy if you want a file out of view during your lunch break, for example.
- Unhide displays a list of hidden windows so that you can redisplay one.
- Split breaks the current file into two panes so that you can display different areas of a file simultaneously.

After you finish working with a particular file and save it, you should close the file so that it is no longer consuming system memory. To close the current file, open the File menu and click Close.

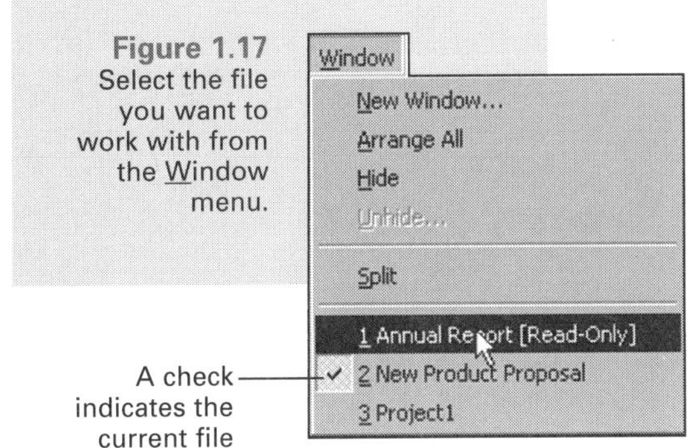

Figure 1.17 Select the file you want to work with from the Window menu.

Exiting Project

When you're finished with your work in Project, you can close the program in any of several ways:

- Press Alt+F4.
- Double-click the Close box (with the X in it) in the upper-right corner of the Microsoft Project application window.
- Open the File menu and click Exit.

If you haven't saved your work before you try to close Project, Project asks whether or not you want to save your changes. Click Yes to do so, or No to exit without saving.

2

Setting Up a Project

In This Chapter

- Establishing an overall schedule for your project
- Setting daily working hours for the schedule
- Defining each task in the schedule
- Working with the order of the tasks
- Setting up milestones
- Understanding file properties
- Controlling the base calendar schedule for the project

Traditionally, when you were assigned a new activity on the job, one of the first things you did was sit down with a yellow notepad and compile a to-do list. You made notes about steps you needed to take to complete the whole project and perhaps sketched out timeframes for individual assignments. As you completed each step, you simply scratched the item off your list and adjusted subsequent deadlines as needed.

The first step of the planning process in Project 98 resembles the yellow pad method. You begin by mapping out your timeframe and the tasks to be completed.

Managing Project Start and End Dates

As discussed in Chapter 1, "Getting Started with Project 98," the Project Information dialog box appears (see Figure 2.1) each time you start a new project file by opening the File menu and clicking on New. You use this dialog box to work with the overall time schedule for your project.

The first two text boxes in the dialog box are Start Date and Finish Date. Initially, the Start Date entry displays the current date, and the Finish Date entry is grayed out (disabled). That's because you enter only one of these dates; Project calculates the other one for you, based on the tasks you enter for the project and how long each task lasts. So, to determine how the duration of your schedule is calculated, you can use one of the following two methods:

- **Have Project calculate the Finish Date.** Leave Project Start Date as the Schedule From selection, and change the Start Date entry, if needed.
- **Have Project calculate the Start Date.** Click the arrow beside the Schedule From drop-down list, and select Project Finish Date. Then, edit the Finish Date entry.

Note

There might be instances where you want new tasks to be scheduled based on the current date rather than the project start or finish date. To override the Schedule From drop-down list choice in the Project Information dialog box, open the Tools menu and click Options. Click the Schedule tab. Select Current Date from the New Tasks Start On drop-down list, and then click OK.

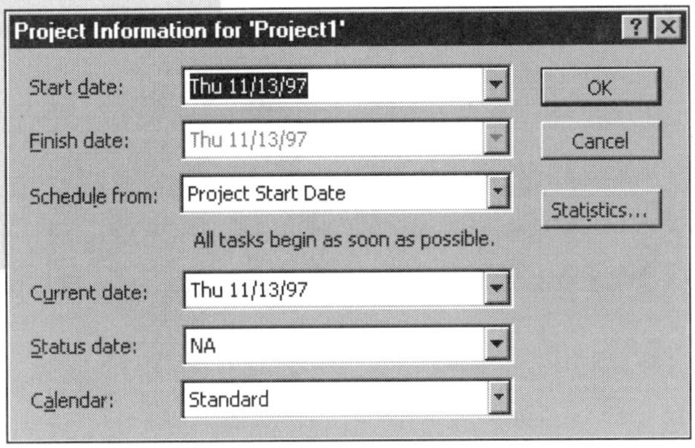

Figure 2.1 Use the Project Information dialog box to establish some overall timing issues for your project

When you enter or edit either Start Date or Finish Date, you can type the date in m/dd/yy or mm/dd/yy format in the appropriate text box. You don't need to enter the abbreviation for the day of the week; Project specifies it after you finish making changes to the Project Info settings.

If you type the date, however, you need to have a calendar at hand to ensure you type the correct date—for a Monday rather than a Sunday, for example. This new version of Project provides a method for entering dates more easily, though. When you see a drop-down arrow at the right end of any text box that holds a date (in the Project Information dialog box and others throughout Project), click the drop-down arrow to display a calendar you can use to select a date. For example, Figure 2.2 shows the calendar that opens when you click the drop-down arrow beside the Start Date text box. Click one of the arrows near the top of the calendar to display an earlier or later month, and then click a date to choose it and close the calendar.

The Current Date text box enables you to calibrate your project schedule with the actual calendar. By default, however, the starting date used for all new tasks you add to the project will be the Start Date or Finish Date you specified (depending on which of those entries Project is calculating for you). For example, if you chose Project Finish Date for the Schedule From entry and entered 6/12/98 as the Finish Date, the tasks you entered will be scheduled with a finish date of 6/12/98, regardless of the Current Date entry.

The last setting that you really need to adjust when you set up your new project is the Calendar setting. (For information on setting and working with a Status Date, see Chapter 7, "Comparing Progress versus Your Baseline Plan.") The Calendar setting determines the base calendar, or the working hours and days for the project. This calendar determines the number of hours per week

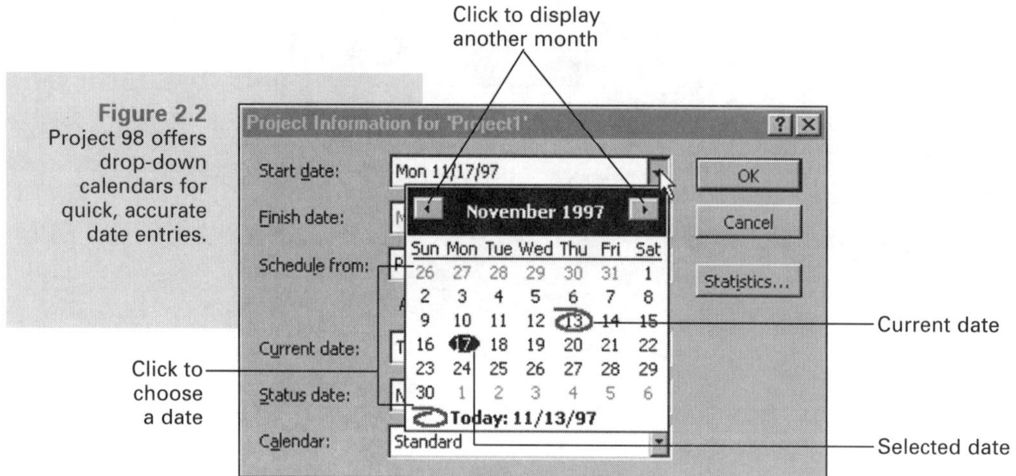

Figure 2.2 Project 98 offers drop-down calendars for quick, accurate date entries.

available in the project schedule. (You can change the working schedule for any particular resource, however, as explained in Chapter 4, "Managing Resources.") You can select one of the following choices from the Calendar drop-down list:

- **Standard**—This choice, the default, assigns corporate America's standard work week to the project. The project schedule is based on a Monday through Friday work week, with daily working hours of 8 a.m. to noon and 1 p.m. to 5 p.m.—thus, each workday is eight hours and each work week is 40 hours.
- **24 Hours**—If you make this selection, the schedule is continuous. Each workday is 24 hours long, and work is scheduled seven days a week.
- **Night Shift**—This option provides a schedule based on a 40-hour night shift week as scheduled in many companies, from Monday evening through Saturday morning:

Days	**Scheduled working hours**
Mondays	11 p.m. to 12 a.m.
Tuesday through Friday	12 a.m. to 3 a.m. 4 a.m. to 8 a.m. 11 p.m. to 12 a.m.
Saturdays	12 a.m. to 3 a.m. 4 a.m. to 8 a.m.

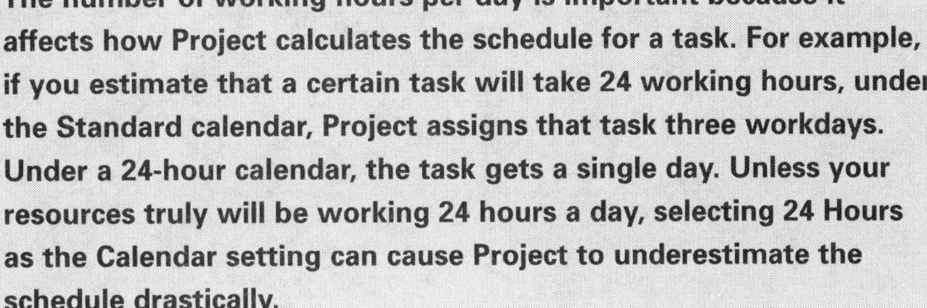
The number of working hours per day is important because it affects how Project calculates the schedule for a task. For example, if you estimate that a certain task will take 24 working hours, under the Standard calendar, Project assigns that task three workdays. Under a 24-hour calendar, the task gets a single day. Unless your resources truly will be working 24 hours a day, selecting 24 Hours as the Calendar setting can cause Project to underestimate the schedule drastically.

After you make your choice for the Calendar setting, click OK to close the Project Information dialog box.

Changing Project Information

After you create project information, it's by no means set in stone. You can redisplay the Project Information dialog box at any time to make changes to the options there. In addition, you might want to check the calculated Start Date or Finish Date for the schedule. To view or change schedule information, click to open the Project menu, and then click Project Information. When the Project Information dialog box appears, make any changes that you want, and then click OK to close the dialog box.

Be careful when making changes to the settings in the Project Information dialog box after you add tasks to the schedule. For example, selecting a different Calendar choice can have a drastic effect on your project's timeline. Also, if you make a change to the project Start Date or Finish Date, and have tasks that you marked as finished or that you set up to start or end on a specific date that falls outside the new overall schedule (see Chapters 7 and 3, respectively), Project will warn you after you click OK in the Project Information dialog box (see Figure 2.3). You can click OK and then reschedule individual tasks to fit within the new schedule, or click Cancel and choose a new start or finish date.

Viewing Project Statistics

Project provides numerous ways to review the information you entered for a project. In fact, it automatically tracks particular project statistics for you, so you can review the overall status at a glance. These statistics are displayed in the Project Statistics dialog box (see Figure 2.4).

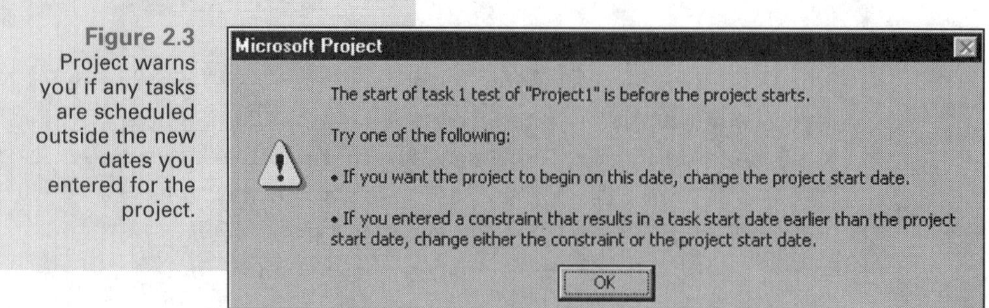

Figure 2.3 Project warns you if any tasks are scheduled outside the new dates you entered for the project.

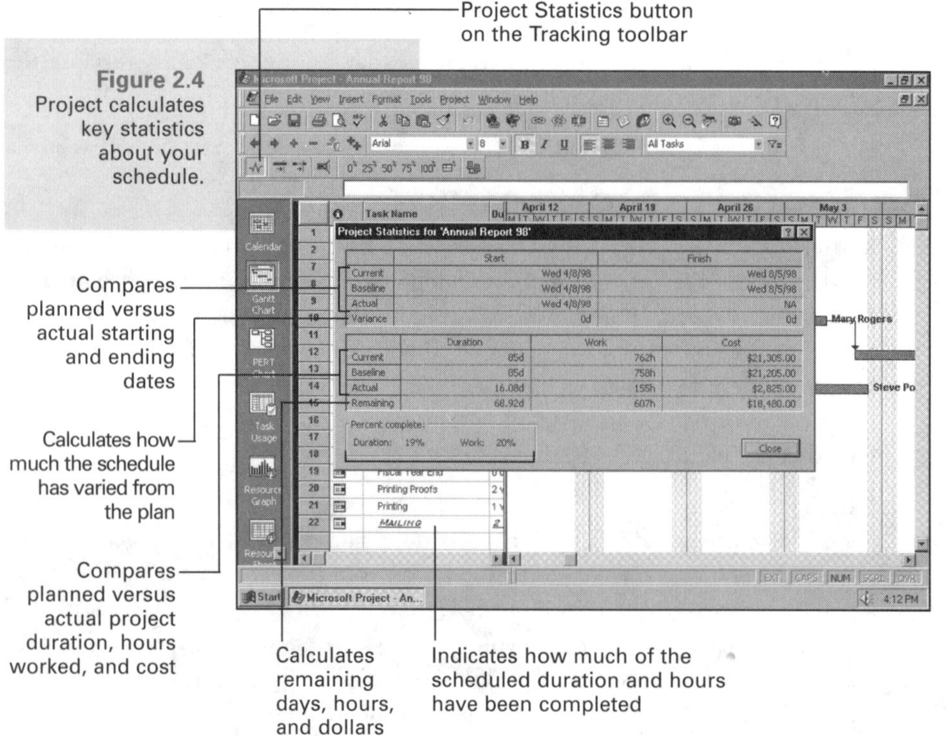

Figure 2.4 Project calculates key statistics about your schedule.

You can display the Project Statistics dialog box using either of two methods:

- Display the Tracking toolbar by right-clicking any onscreen toolbar and then clicking on Tracking. Click the Project Statistics button at the far left on the Tracking toolbar.
- Click the Project menu and click Project Information. Click the Statistics button in the Project Information dialog box.

Project does not allow you to edit or print the information in the Project Statistics dialog box. When you finish viewing the information, click the Close button to exit the dialog box.

Although Project doesn't enable you to print the Project Statistics dialog box information, you can use Windows to do so. With the Project Statistics dialog box open, press the Print Screen key. Click the Start button on the taskbar, point to Programs, point to Accessories, and click Paint. With Windows Paint open, choose Edit, Paste. If you're asked whether to enlarge the bitmap image, do so. Then, choose File, Print to print the image. You can then save the image if you want and close Paint.

Adding and Deleting Tasks

After you set up the overall parameters for the schedule, you're ready to begin entering the individual "jobs" that need to be done. This phase of building the project blueprint is most analogous to jotting down a to-do list, with each task roughly equating to a "to-do." Generally, you add tasks to the schedule in the default view, Gantt Chart view. In this view, enter basic information about each task in the Task Sheet, located just to the right of the View Bar.

As shown in Figure 2.5, the Task Sheet resembles a spreadsheet grid. You enter information about each task in a single row in the Task Sheet. You can use the scroll bar at the bottom of the Task Sheet to display more columns; each column, also called a field, holds a particular type of information.

- **Indicators (i)** —This column holds small icons, called indicators, which provide information about the current task. For example, if you add a note to a task, as described later in this section, a note indicator appears in the indicator field for the task. (You learn more about the various indicators later in this section and in later chapters where they apply.) You can't enter information in this column; Project automatically displays and removes applicable indicators as needed.
- **Task Name**—This column holds the descriptive label you want to identify each task. Use names that are unique enough to differentiate individual tasks. The name can include spaces as well as upper- and lowercase characters. And, although the name can include more than 100 characters, as a rule you should stick with names that are as brief and descriptive as possible.

- **Duration**—This column holds the time you're allowing for the completion of each task. If you enter no duration, Project assumes a default duration of one day (d). Project assumes other durations to be in days unless you specify otherwise (see "Using Differing Durations" later in this chapter).
- **Start**—This column holds the date that work is scheduled to begin on for a particular task. Unless you specify otherwise, Project assumes this date is the project Start Date or Finish Date specified in the Project Information dialog box. So, unless you want Project to use a default or calculated date, you need to enter a specific date in the Start field for a task.

When you change the date that Project is calculating (the date in either the Start or Finish column for the task in the Task Sheet, depending on whether the project is set up to calculate from the project start or finish date, as specified in the Project Information dialog box), Project automatically changes the Task Sheet Duration field for the task to reflect your change. For example, say that you enter a Duration of one day (1d) for a task that's being calculated from a Start of 2/9/98. If you change the date in the Finish column from 2/9/98 to 2/11/98, Project changes the duration to 3d.

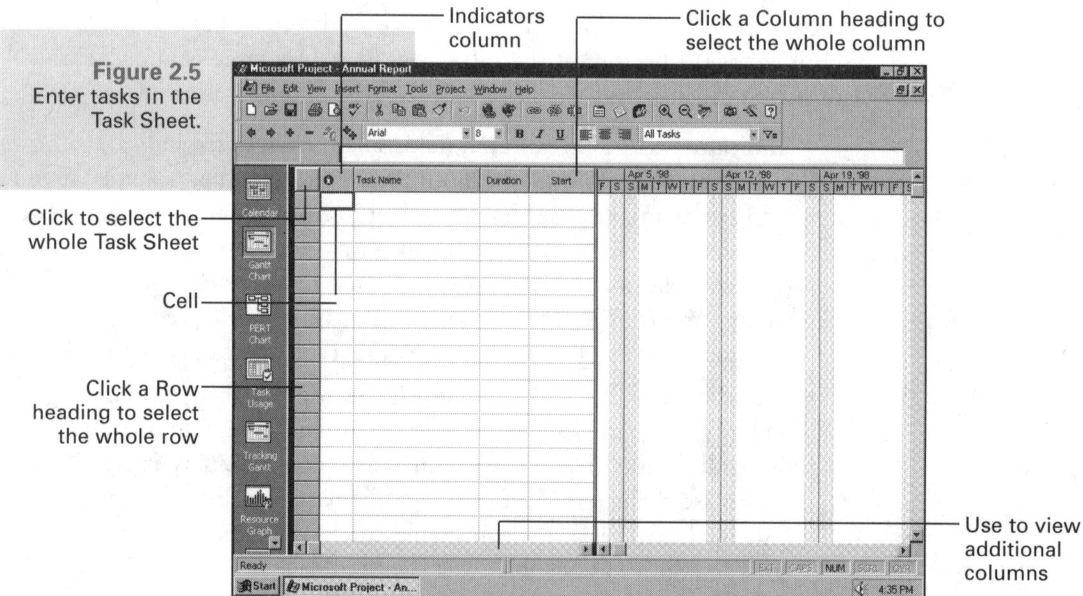

Figure 2.5 Enter tasks in the Task Sheet.

- **Finish**—This column holds the date when work on each task is to be completed. If you specified that Project should schedule tasks from the starting date in the Project Information dialog box, then the date in this column is automatically calculated based on the entries in the Duration and Start columns. On the other hand, if Project is scheduling tasks from the ending date, then the date in the Start column is calculated.
- **Predecessors**—This column indicates when a task is linked to one or more preceding tasks. Project can fill in this column for you, or you can use this column to establish links. Chapter 3, "Fine-Tuning Tasks," covers linking tasks.
- **Resource Names**—This column enables you to enter one or more resources (team member, outside contractor, and so on) responsible for completing a task. Chapter 4, "Managing Resources," explains how to create resources for use in your schedule.

Entering tasks in the Task Sheet works much like making spreadsheet entries. Although later chapters cover some of the entries for a task in more detail, here's an overview of the steps for creating a task:

1. Click the cell in the Task Name column of the first available row in the Task Sheet. Clicking selects the cell and prepares it for your entry. Alternately, you can press Tab to move from the Indicators column to the Task Name column.
2. Type the name of the task. For example, you might type a name such as **Develop Theme Proposal**. As you type, the text appears in the entry box above the Task Sheet, as shown in Figure 2.6. To complete the entry, press Tab, or click the Enter button with the green check mark, beside the Entry box above the Task Sheet; then click the next cell to the right in the Duration column. Clicking the Cancel button instead of the Enter button stops the entry altogether.

To quickly enter a list of tasks, press Enter after each task name you create. Project assigns each task a 1d (one day) duration and the default start date. You can then go back and adjust the duration and other entries.

3. Type a number, such as **3**, for the new duration entry. Alternately, click one of the spinner buttons (up and down-arrow buttons) that appear at the right side of the Duration cell to increase or decrease the value. The new entry appears in the Entry box as you type. Unless you include

more duration information, as described later in the section "Using Differing Durations," Project assumes the duration to be days. To finish the entry, press Tab; alternately, you can click the Enter button, scroll to the right, and then click the Start cell for the task.

4. The Start cell is selected. If Project is set to automatically calculate the Finish date, type the desired starting date in mm/dd/yy format and click the Enter button. Alternately, click the drop-down arrow that appears beside the Start cell to display a calendar, and click as needed on the calendar to choose a month and day. (See Figure 2.2 for a refresher of how a drop-down calendar works.) This finishes the basic task creation, and creates a bar for the task in the Gantt Chart pane on the right side of the screen (see Figure 2.7). If Project is set to automatically calculate backward (based on the ending date, which by default is the Project Finish Date in the Project Info dialog box), do not change the Start column entry; go to step 5.
5. Press Tab (or scroll, and then click the Finish cell for that task). Type the desired ending date in mm/dd/yy format and click the Enter button to complete it. Alternately, click the drop-down arrow that appears on the Finish cell to display a calendar, and then click the calendar to choose the month and day.

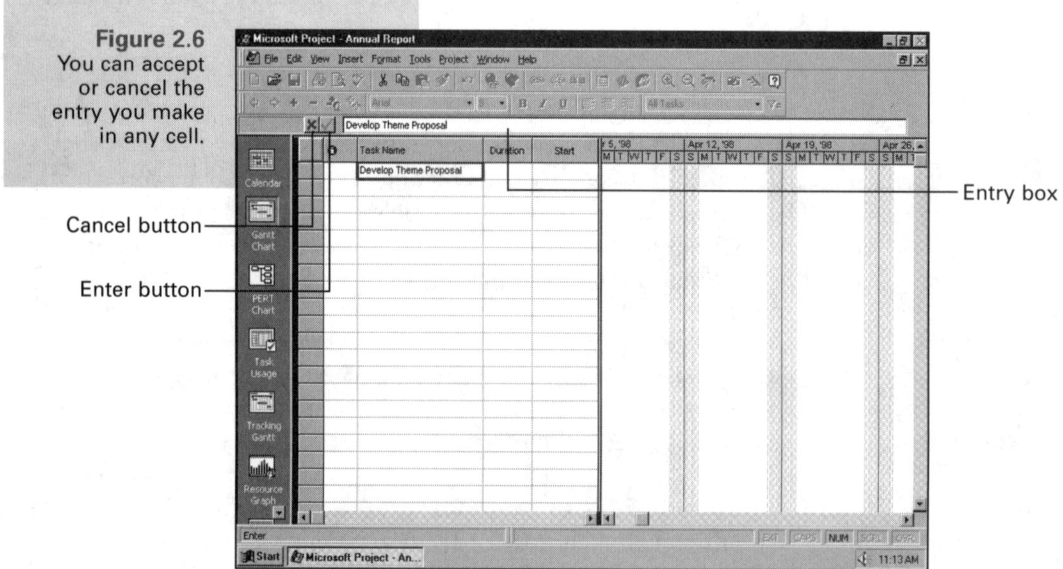

Figure 2.6 You can accept or cancel the entry you make in any cell.

6. (Optional) Make entries in the Predecessors and Resources cells, as described in Chapters 3 and 4. Press Tab or click the Resources cell after your Predecessors entry. Note that when you select a cell in the Resources column, a drop-down arrow appears. After you add resources to the project, as described in Chapter 4, you can simply click this drop-down arrow and click one of the available resources in the list to select that resource for the task. Go to step 7 after you make the Resources entry.
7. To create the next task, you need to move to the next row of the Task Sheet. To do so, scroll and click to select the first cell (the Task Name cell) in the next row; alternately, you can press Enter, and then press Ctrl+Left Arrow (or the Home key) to select that cell.
8. Repeat steps 2 through 7 as many times as needed to enter all the tasks for your project.

Based on all the tasks you create and the durations you enter for them, Project calculates the total schedule for the project. To check the total schedule, click the Project menu, and then click Project Information. The Project Information dialog box will then include the calculated Start Date or Finish Date, which will be grayed out to tell you it's a calculated value.

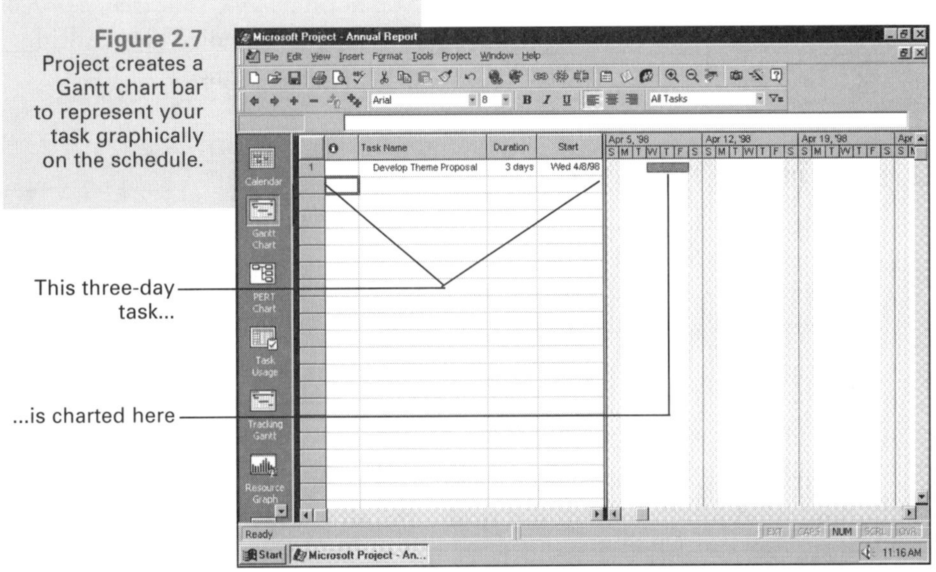

Figure 2.7 Project creates a Gantt chart bar to represent your task graphically on the schedule.

Editing a Task

No matter how well-formulated a business plan is, you can count on it to change. For example, you might start out using somewhat generic names for your tasks—or even code names. Later, after the project is announced, you might want to replace the temporary names with the real project names. Or, after consulting a particular resource, you might discover that you overestimated the time required to complete a particular task, so you might want to change the duration you specified for that task.

To edit any of the cell entries for a task, click to select the cell you want to edit. Use one of the following methods to make your changes:

- To replace the cell entry completely, start typing. Whatever you type completely replaces the previous entry. Click the Enter button when you are done making the replacement entry.
- If spinner buttons or a drop-down arrow appears, use them to change the entry as described earlier in the steps at the beginning of this section, "Adding and Deleting Tasks."
- To make changes to only part of an entry, click to position the insertion point in the entry box, or drag to highlight the text you want to replace. Type your changes. After you place the insertion point in the entry box, you can edit text as you would in most word processors, using the arrow keys, Backspace, and more. When you finish making your changes, click the Enter button. Or, press the F2 key to enter an Edit Mode (as with other Microsoft Products), so you can type your changes.

Using Differing Durations

As you've seen, when you assign a duration for a particular task, Project by default interprets that duration in terms of days. Each day consists of a full day's worth of working hours, depending on the base calendar you set for the schedule using the Calendar drop-down list in the Project Information dialog box. So, if your project is based on the 24 Hours calendar, each day of duration consists of 24 working hours; on the Standard calendar, each day of duration consists of eight working hours.

For the Night Shift base calendar, each "day" of duration is eight hours. Under this calendar, each working day spans two calendar days. For example, a task that begins on a Friday and is scheduled to last 1d, starts Friday at 11 p.m., when the working day starts, and spans to 3 a.m. on Saturday. After a one-hour lunch break, the workday and task continue from 4 a.m. to 8 a.m., which is the end of the shift.

Under the Night Shift calendar, keep in mind that when you enter a start date for a task, Project schedules the task for the workday that begins at 11 p.m. of that start date and runs over the next day. Thus, if you want work to be completed on a task during the early morning hours of a given day (12 a.m. to 3 a.m. and 4 a.m. to 8 a.m.), specify the preceding date as the start date for the task.

Obviously, not every task requires eight to 24 hours. Likewise, not every task is completed within the bounds of the workday hours (as much as we wish they all would be). For example, if you want to include a key meeting on your schedule, it's likely you only need to block out a few hours for it, not an entire day. On the other hand, if you expect a supplier to work during the weekend to deliver a product, or you know something will be shipped to you during a weekend, you need to schedule a task outside of normal working hours.

Project enables you to control the exact amount of time a task will take to finish, based on the abbreviation, or duration label, you include with the entry in the Duration column of the Task Sheet. Some duration abbreviations are for elapsed durations, where you specify work according to a 24-hour, seven-day-per-week calendar even though that isn't the base calendar for the project. To specify the new duration, enter the correct abbreviation along with your numeric entry. Table 2.1 lists the basic abbreviations or duration labels.

Project 98 offers a new feature called smart duration labels, making it even easier for you to enter durations. Basically, this feature enables you to make slight "mistakes" when you enter duration labels. For example, if you mistakenly include a space and enter **5 h** instead of **5h**, Project can still correctly interpret your entry as 5 hrs (5 hours).

When you enter an elapsed time, the Gantt chart bars at the right reflect how the task falls in terms of real time. For example, Figure 2.8 compares the actual scheduled time for a task entered as three working days (3d) and a task entered as 24 elapsed hours (24eh). When scheduled as standard workdays, a 24-hour period covers three days; as elapsed hours, however, a 24-hour period occupies a single day on the Gantt chart.

Table 2.1 Duration Labels (Abbreviations)

Time Unit	Abbreviations	Example
Minutes	M Min Mins	30m means 30 working minutes
Hours	H Hr Hrs Hour	30h means 30 working hours
Days	D Dy Day	30d means 30 working days
Weeks	W Wk Week	30w means 30 working weeks
Elapsed minutes	Em Emin Emins	30em means 30 consecutive, elapsed minutes
Elapsed hours	Eh Ehr Ehrs Ehour	30eh means 30 consecutive, elapsed hours
Elapsed days	Ed Edy Eday	30ed means 30 consecutive, elapsed days
Elapsed weeks	Ew Ewk Eweek	30ew means 30 consecutive, elapsed weeks

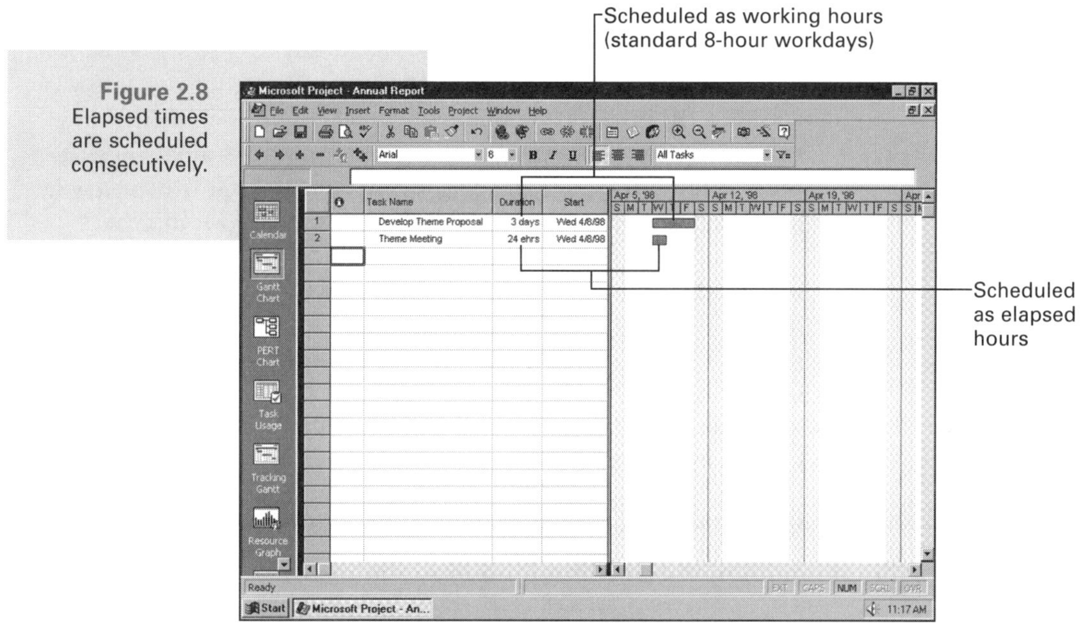

Figure 2.8 Elapsed times are scheduled consecutively.

Selecting, Inserting, and Deleting Tasks

When you're creating any kind of business plan, you start with the overall framework and refine it as you go along, adding details as you flesh out some ideas and discard others. You might discover the need to adjust the framework for your project by adding new tasks into the Task Sheet as you discover that they're necessary, or dropping them as you determine that they're extraneous or already included within the scope of other items. Project gives you total flexibility in determining which tasks appear on the Task Sheet.

Use the following steps to add a task to your Task Sheet:

1. Select any cell in the row above which you want to insert a new task. To select the cell, use the scroll bars at the far right and bottom of the screen to display the cell, and then click it. Alternatively, you can use the arrow keys to reach a cell in the appropriate row.
2. Press the Insert key (or open the Insert menu and then click New Task) to insert a new, blank row.
3. Enter information for the new task, as discussed previously in this section.

Use the following steps to delete a particular task:

1. Select the row in the Task Sheet that holds the task. To select the row, use the vertical scroll bar or the arrow keys to bring the row into view, and then click the row number. A highlight appears on the task row that is selected. To select additional consecutive rows after you select the first row, press Shift and click the row number for the last row in the group you want to delete. To select additional rows that are noncontiguous, press and hold down Ctrl while you click additional row numbers.

You can click the Select All button in the upper-left corner of the Task Sheet to select the entire Task Sheet.

2. Use one of the following methods to remove selected tasks:
   - Press the Delete key.
   - Open the Edit menu and click Delete Task.
   - Right-click the selected task to display a shortcut menu; then click Delete Task (see Figure 2.9).

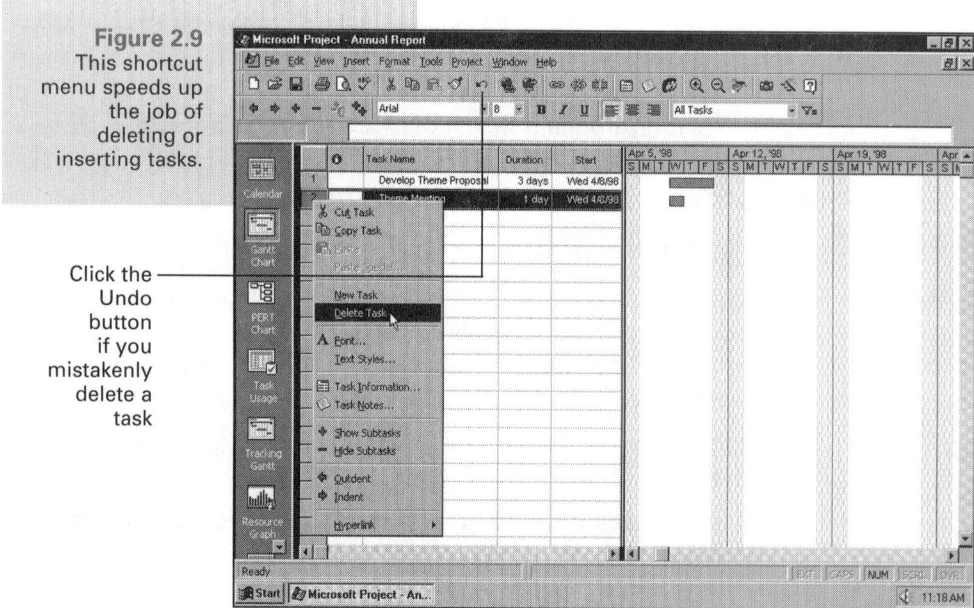

Figure 2.9 This shortcut menu speeds up the job of deleting or inserting tasks.

Project doesn't warn you about lost information when you choose to delete a task, even if other tasks are linked to the task you're deleting. If you mistakenly delete a task, immediately do any of the following: open the Edit menu and click Undo; press Ctrl+Z; or click the Undo button on the Standard toolbar.

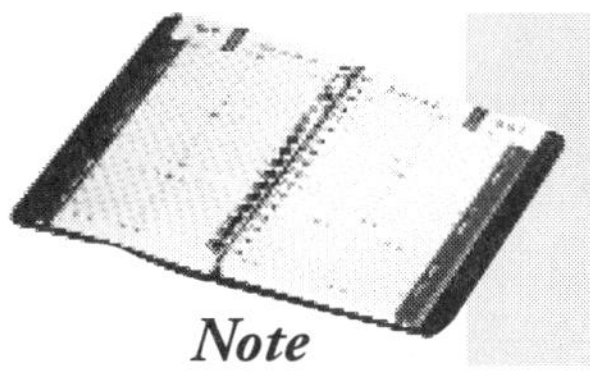

Notice that the task shortcut menu also offers an Insert Task command. You can choose that command to insert a new task row above the currently selected task row.

Moving and Copying Tasks

One of the many features that makes Project more efficient than a yellow pad for process planning is that you can easily change the order of the tasks on your list. There's no more endless renumbering or trying to figure out which arrow points where to indicate the final order of tasks.

The easiest way to move a task on the Task Sheet is by dragging the task information (see Figure 2.10). Click the row number for the task you want to move; this selects the whole task. Point to one of the selection borders until the mouse pointer turns into an arrow; then click and drag the row into its new position. As you drag, a gray insertion bar indicates exactly where the task row will be inserted if you release the mouse button.

You also can drag and drop cells to move their contents.

Dragging is convenient when the task you want to move is relatively close to the new location you want for it. It's a bit more difficult to drag a task into place, however, if you have to scroll other tasks to do so. Likewise, when you want to copy a task from one location to another, you need a different process to do the job. For example, if you have two tasks that will run on the same schedule and be completed by the same resource, it's much easier to copy the original task, and then edit the task name on the copy. In such cases, use the following steps to move or copy the task:

1. Click the row number for the task you want to move or copy to select the whole row.
2. If you want to move the task, open the Edit menu and click Cut Task. Alternatively, you can press Ctrl+X, click the Cut button on the Standard toolbar, or right-click the selection to display a shortcut menu, and then click Cut Task.

   If you want to copy the task, open the Edit menu and click Copy Task. Alternatively, you can press Ctrl+C, click the Copy button on the Standard toolbar, or right-click the selection to display a shortcut menu and then click Copy Task.
3. Click any cell in the row above where you want to insert the task you cut or copied.
4. Open the Edit menu and click Paste. Alternatively, you can press Ctrl+V, click the Paste button on the Standard toolbar, or right-click to display a shortcut menu, and then click Paste. Project pastes the task as a new row.

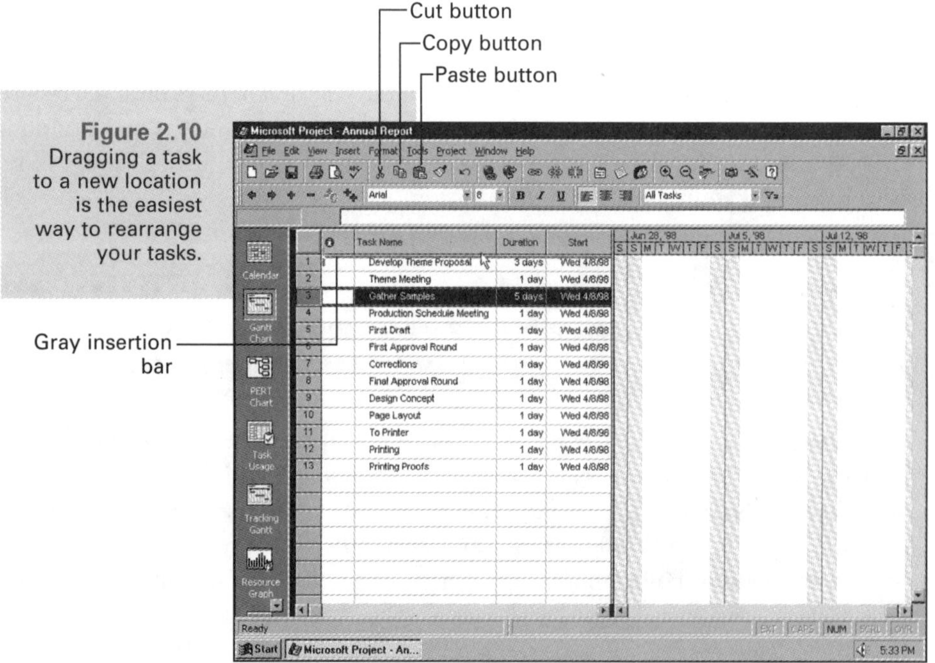

Figure 2.10 Dragging a task to a new location is the easiest way to rearrange your tasks.

Cut-and-paste (or copy-and-paste) operations also can be used to move or copy information in individual cells. When you select a cell, the Edit and shortcut menu commands change to Cut Cell and Copy Cell. After copying or cutting the selected cell, as just described for rows, select a destination cell and then paste the cut or copied information.

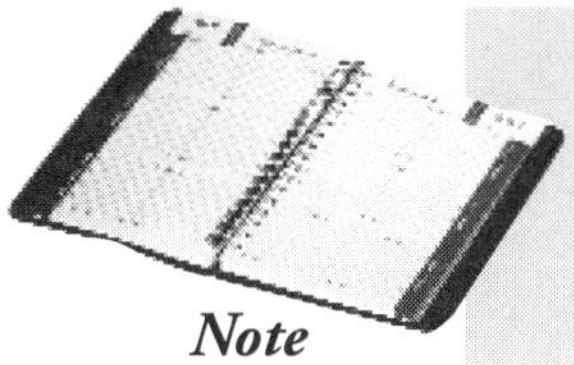

When you paste a cut or copied cell, the pasted information replaces any existing information in the selected destination cell. (It's not inserted above the cell you selected.)

You can select more than one row or cell to cut or copy by clicking and dragging over multiple row numbers or multiple cells.

Clearing Task Information

Cutting a task removes the task altogether from the Task Sheet. The remaining rows close the space vacated by the cut task. There might be instances, however, when you want to remove the information from a task, but want to keep the row that was occupied by that task in place. For example, you might know that you want to replace the old task with information about a new task. If you simply change the entries for the old task, however, you might neglect to edit one, resulting in a schedule error.

An alternative to cutting information in a task or cell is to clear the information. Clearing removes cell contents, but leaves all cells in place. Unlike cut information, however, cleared information can't be pasted, so you should clear material only when it's no longer needed.

Use these steps to clear information from your Task Sheet:

1. Select the task row or cell you want to clear.
2. Open the Edit menu and click Clear. A submenu appears (see Figure 2.11), offering you a choice of the kind of information to clear.

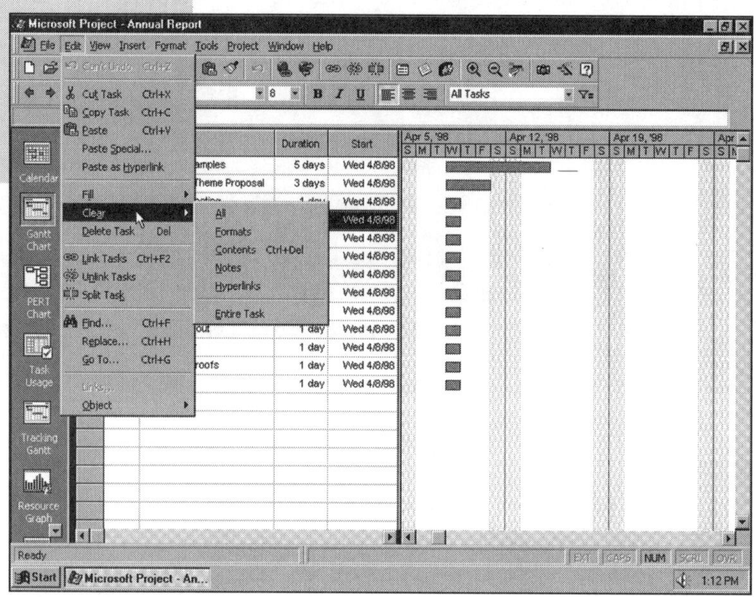

Figure 2.11 Choose the type of information to clear on the Edit, Clear submenu.

3. Choose the kind of information to clear by clicking the appropriate submenu item, as follows:
   - All—Choosing this item removes the task contents, formatting, and any note you added for the task (the next section explains how to add a note).
   - Formats—Choosing this item returns the selected task or cell contents to the default formatting, removing any formatting you added (such as a new font or color).
   - Contents—Choosing this item is equivalent to pressing Ctrl+Delete. It removes the contents of the selected task or cell.
   - Notes—Choosing this item clears any note you added for the task (as described in the next section).
   - Hyperlinks—Choosing this item removes any hyperlinks you created in a task to enable the user to jump to a Web page on the Internet or a company intranet. Chapter 19, "Taking Project Online," explains how to create hyperlinks.
   - Entire Task—Choosing this item clears the contents of the entire task when you haven't selected the entire task row.

Adding a Task Note

A *task note* enables you to capture information that doesn't need to appear within the Task Sheet, but does need to be recorded with the schedule. For example, you might create notes like these:

- If you have a task that is a reminder of a meeting, you can create a note listing materials you need to bring to the meeting.
- If a task relates to research gathering that will be completed by a resource other than yourself, you can include a note mentioning information sources that the designated researcher should check.
- If a task deals with proofreading or fact-checking, you can use a note to list the details that need to be reviewed.

Adding a note to a task is a straightforward process. Select the task row—or a cell in the task—for which you want to create a note. Right-click the selected area, or open the Project menu. Choose Task Notes. Alternately, click the Task Notes button on the Standard toolbar. The Task Information dialog box appears with the Notes tab selected. Click the Notes text entry area, and then type your note (see Figure 2.12). Press Enter to start each new line in the note. In Project 98, you can add special formatting to notes using the buttons at the top of the Notes text area. The first button enables you to change the font for any text you select by dragging over it in the note; it displays the Font dialog box, which Chapter 14, "Other Formatting," covers. The next three buttons align the current note line (which holds the blinking insertion point) left, center, and right, respectively. The fourth button adds or removes a bullet to the beginning of the current line of the note. The last button enables you to insert an embedded object into the note, such as information from Excel or a bitmap image; Chapter 18, "Using Project with Other Applications," provides more information on working with embedded objects.

When you finish typing the note, click OK to close the Task Information dialog box. Project inserts an icon in the Indicators column for the task to remind you that you added a note for that task. This section concludes with more information about indicators.

Understanding Indicators

As you saw earlier in this chapter, an Indicators column appears at the far-left side of the Task sheet in the default Gantt Chart view. The Indicators column remains blank until you begin entering information in other columns and changing the options for tasks. Then, depending on the settings you choose,

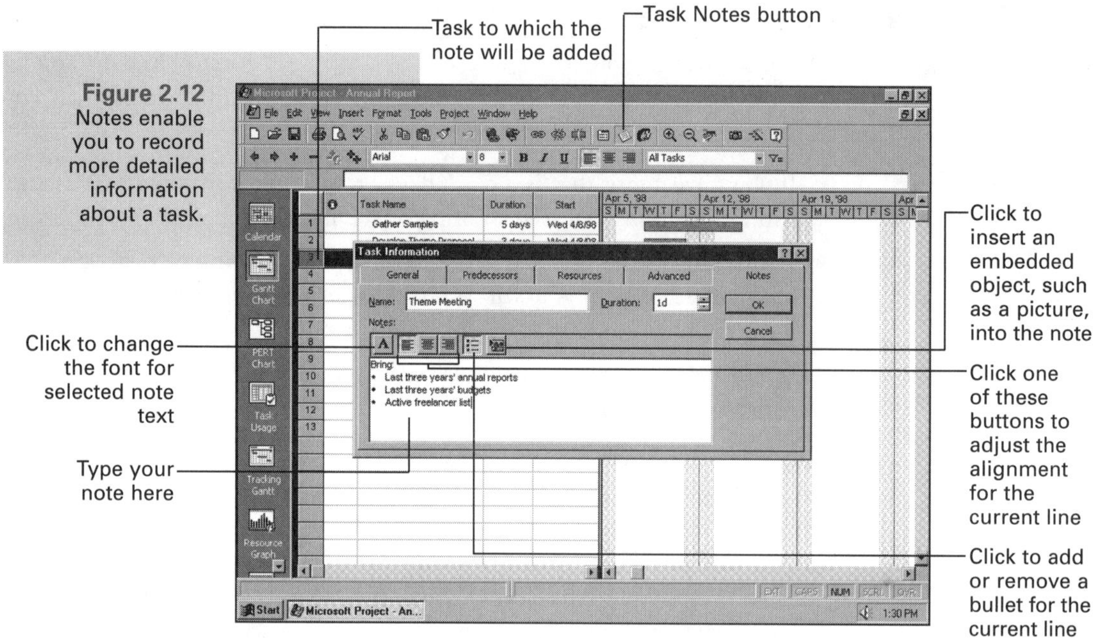
Task to which the note will be added
Task Notes button
Click to insert an embedded object, such as a picture, into the note
Click to change the font for selected note text
Click one of these buttons to adjust the alignment for the current line
Type your note here
Click to add or remove a bullet for the current line
Task Information
Name: Theme Meeting
Duration: 1d
Bring:
Last three years' annual reports
Last three years' budgets
Active freelancer list

Figure 2.12 Notes enable you to record more detailed information about a task.

indicator icons may appear in the Indicator column. Each indicator icon reminds you of a particular piece of information about a task. For example, the indicator icon in Figure 2.13 shows that a note has been added to task 3 in the Task Sheet.

Other indicator icons tell you whether a task has been completed; whether a task has been completed by a date you specified; whether you need to e-mail task information to the resource who will be completing the work, and so on. When you begin entering resource information as described in Chapter 4, you'll see that indicators also can give you more information about a particular resource's status. I'll identify particular indicators throughout the book as I describe settings that cause an indicator to appear. If you can't recall what a particular indicator beside a task means, move the mouse pointer over the indicator(s) beside that task to display pop-up help describing the indicators, as shown in Figure 2.14.

Adjusting the Task Sheet

By default, the Task Sheet occupies roughly the left third of the screen in Gantt Chart view, and offers six columns with preset names and sizes. The narrow screen area allocated for the Task Sheet means that you might spend more time

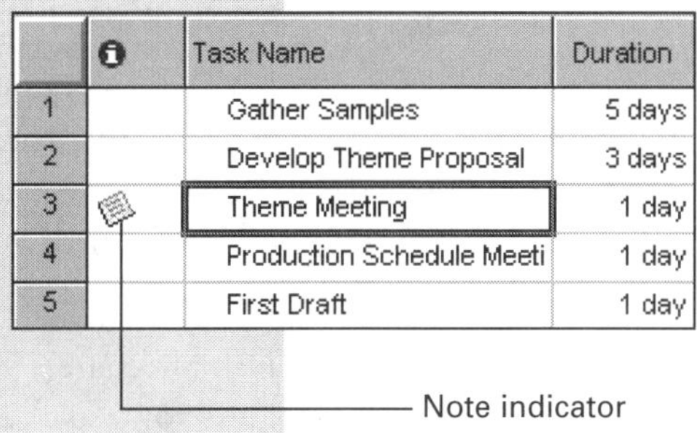

Figure 2.13 Indicator icons appear in the Indicator column to tell you that you specified particular task options or added information such as a note to a task.

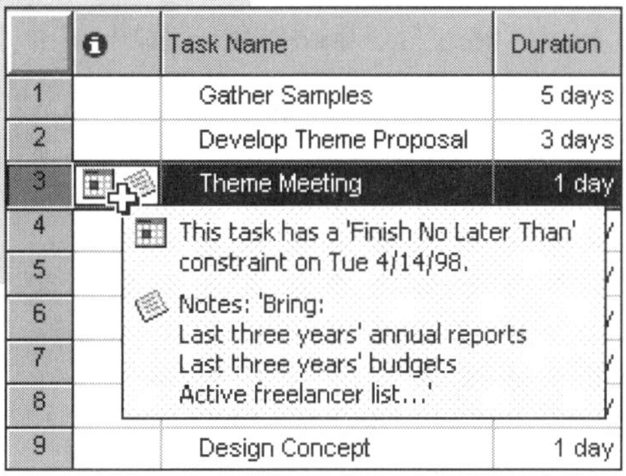

	ℹ	Task Name	Duration
1		Gather Samples	5 days
2		Develop Theme Proposal	3 days
3		Theme Meeting	1 day
4		Production Schedule Meeti	1 day
5		First Draft	1 day

Note indicator

Figure 2.14 Point to the indicators for a task or resource to see a pop-up description of each indicator.

	ℹ	Task Name	Duration
1		Gather Samples	5 days
2		Develop Theme Proposal	3 days
3		Theme Meeting	1 day
4			
5			
6			
7			
8			
9		Design Concept	1 day

This task has a 'Finish No Later Than' constraint on Tue 4/14/98.
Notes: 'Bring:
Last three years' annual reports
Last three years' budgets
Active freelancer list...'

than you prefer scrolling or tabbing back and forth to display particular cells or columns (fields). Or, if you have a column where the entries become rather lengthy, the column might be too narrow to display the column contents. Finally, the columns provided by default might not capture all the information you want to have available on the Task Sheet. As you'll see next, Project enables you to control the appearance of the Task Sheet to customize it for your project creation needs.

Sizing the Sheet and Columns

One of the first changes you might want to make is to display more of the Task Sheet to make editing easier. This change isn't permanent, so while you're entering information about various tasks in your schedule, for example, you can fill most of the Project application window with the Task Sheet. After you enter the task information, you can return the Task Sheet to its previous size so that the Gantt Chart pane of the window becomes visible again.

You can resize the screen area occupied by the Task Sheet by dragging it. A split bar separates the Task Sheet pane from the Gantt Chart pane on the right. Move the mouse pointer onto that split bar, and the pointer changes to a split pointer with a double-vertical line and left and right arrows. Press and hold the mouse button; then drag the split bar to move it. A gray, shaded line (see Figure 2.15) indicates where the bar will be repositioned; when this line reaches the location you want, release the mouse button.

Just as you can drag to resize the whole Task Sheet area, you can drag to resize the width of any column or the height of any row. To change a column width, point to the right border of the column heading, beside the column name. To change a row height, point to the bottom border of the row, below the row number. The mouse pointer changes to a resizing pointer with a line and a double-headed arrow. Press and hold the mouse button; then drag the border to change the size of the column or row. A dotted line indicates what the new size of the column or row will be; when the column or row reaches the new width or height you want, release the mouse button.

To resize a column to the optimum width for all its entries, double-click the right border of the column heading.

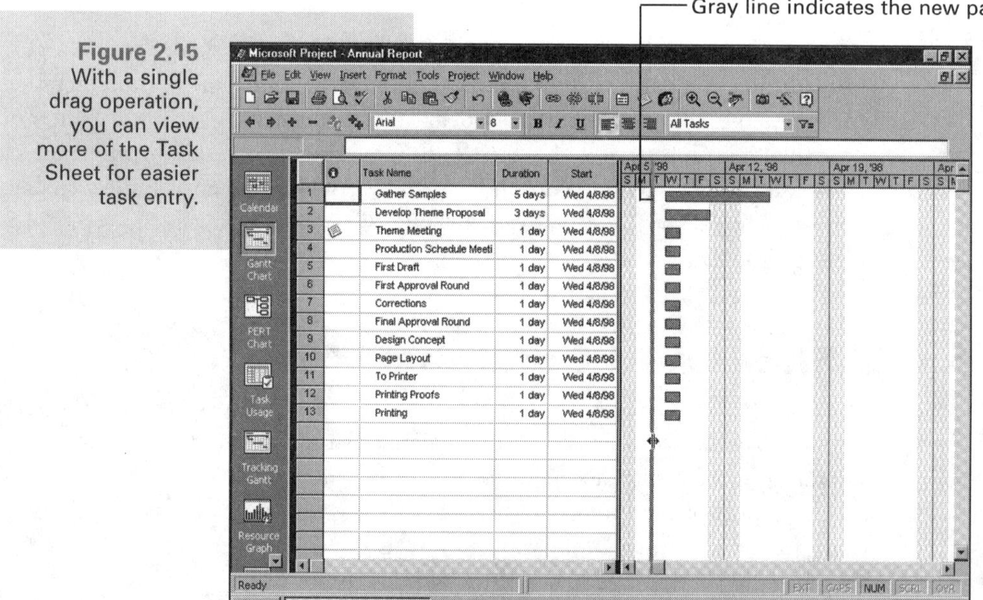

Figure 2.15 With a single drag operation, you can view more of the Task Sheet for easier task entry.

Adding Columns (Fields)

When there are many pieces of data to capture about a particular process, six or seven measly columns cannot do the job effectively. Furthermore, you might want to display some information that Project normally calculates for you. For example, if a given task is being completed by a particular resource at a certain hourly rate, and you entered the actual hours the resource spent to complete the task, you might want to see the resulting cost onscreen. You might even want the Task Sheet to display certain information that you can print and distribute to others. Table 2.2 lists several predefined *columns* (also called *fields*), many of which are self-calculating, that you can add to the Task Sheet. Project offers more than 100 fields that you can use for tasks, so Table 2.2 describes only the most significant ones. (If you consider fields that apply to resources and other uses as well as tasks, Project 98 offers twice as many fields as the preceding version!)

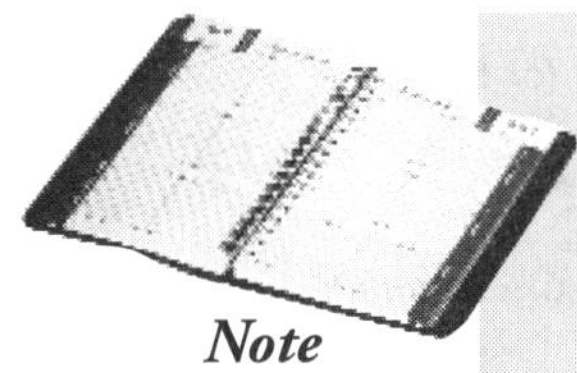
Note

Project's online help system contains a listing of all the Task Sheet field types, including a detailed description of each one. To view the list, open the Help menu and click Contents and Index. Click the Index tab, and then type fields, categories **in the upper text box. Double-click categories (which is indented under tasks) in the scrolling list box below; then click the double-arrow button beside the Task Fields choice in the Field Categories Help topic window. For more information on a particular field, click the double-arrow button beside its name. Project also considers certain fields to be *assignment* fields. (Chapter 5, "Resolving Overallocations and Overbooked Resources," explains what assignments are.) You can display assignment fields in the task sheet, as well. To learn about these fields, follow the process, described previously, to display the Field Categories Help topic window; then click the double-arrow button beside Assignment Fields.**

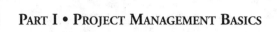

Table 2.2 Other Fields You Can Display in the Task Sheet

Field Name	Description
Actual Cost	Calculates the actual cost for the hours required to complete a project, or lets you enter an actual cost if the project was completed for a fee.
Actual Duration	Calculates the actual time that has elapsed since the scheduled start of the task, based on your entry in a Remaining Duration or Percent Complete field if displayed.
Actual Finish	Lets you enter the actual task completion date if it differs from the scheduled date.
Actual Overtime Cost and Actual Overtime Work	Calculates the actual overtime expenses or actual overtime work incurred to date for all resources.
Actual Start	Lets you enter the actual task starting date if it differs from the scheduled date.
Actual Work	Calculates or lets you enter the work completed for the task.
Baseline (various fields)	Displays the total planned cost, duration, finish, start, and work for the task.
BCWP	Baseline Cost of Work Performed—Displays the projected actual cost, calculated from the budgeted baseline cost and the percentage of work actually completed.
BCWS	Budgeted Cost of Work Scheduled—Lets you compare the cost of what has actually been accomplished (BCWP) versus the cost of what you planned to accomplish by a particular date.
Contact	Enables you to enter a contact name for the resource assigned to complete the task, if that contact person's name is different from the resource name. For example, you may list a consulting company as the overall resource, but your contact person in the contact column.
Cost Variance	Calculates the difference between the baseline cost and scheduled work cost for tasks in progress, and between the baseline and actual cost for finished tasks—negative values indicate that a cost came in under budget.
Critical	Indicates whether a task is critical or noncritical, via calculations based on the Total Slack field entry and some other dialog box entries for the task.
Duration Variance	Displays the difference between the planned duration for the task and the currently scheduled duration.
Finish Variance	Calculates the difference between the planned (baseline) finishing date for the task and the currently scheduled finishing date—negative values indicate that the task is now scheduled to finish earlier than initially planned.

Table 2.2 Other Fields You Can Display in the Task Sheet

Field Name	Description
Hyperlink	Contains the name for a hyperlink you can click to open a document on your hard disk, a network, or the World Wide Web. For example, you can edit the entry in this column so that it gives only the file name rather than the full path to the file. Hyperlink Address Contains the actual address for a hyperlink, no matter what name you assign in the hyperlink column; clicking the address in this column opens the hyperlinked document.
ID	Calculates a task's current position in the schedule, even if two tasks have the same name.
Overtime Cost and Overtime Work	Adds the actually incurred and remaining overtime costs or work for all resources assigned to the task.
Percent (%) Complete	Calculates or lets you enter the percentage of a task's duration that has passed.
Percent (%) Work Complete	Calculates or lets you enter the percentage of a task's work that has been completed.
Remaining (various fields)	Calculates or lets you enter the cost, duration, or work still available to complete a task.
Resource (various fields)	Displays the group, initials, or names for the resources assigned to the task.
Start Variance	Calculates the difference between the scheduled (baseline) starting date and the actual starting date.
Successors	Lists later tasks that depend on (are linked to) the current task.
Total Slack	Indicates, when the value is positive, that there is time in the schedule to delay the task.
Update Needed	Specifies when schedule changes need to be communicated to a resource via the TeamUpdate command.
Work	Calculates the total work that all resources are scheduled to dedicate to the task.
Work Variance	Calculates the difference between the baseline amount of work scheduled for the task and the work currently scheduled.

The process for adding a new column resembles adding a new task to the schedule. Here are the steps:

1. Click any cell in the column next to wherever you want to insert the new column. The inserted column will appear to the left of the column where you selected a cell.
2. Open the Insert menu and click Column. (As an alternative to steps 1 and 2, you can select an entire column, right-click it, and then click Insert Column). The Column Definition dialog box appears (see Figure 2.16).
3. Click the down arrow to display the Field name drop-down list. Use the scroll bar to display the name of the field you want to add, and then click the name to select it.
4. (Optional) If you want the inserted column to be identified with a name other than the built-in field name (say you want "Actual $" rather than "Actual Cost"), click to place the insertion point in the Title text box, and then type the name you want.
5. (Optional) If you want the title for the new column to be left- or right-aligned, rather than centered, click to open the Align Title drop-down list, and then click an alignment choice from the list that appears.
6. (Optional) If you want the entries you make in the new column to be left-aligned or centered automatically, rather than right-aligned, click the down arrow to display the Align data drop-down list, and then click to select the alignment you want.
7. (Optional) If you know that the entries in the new column will require many characters (for example, a long hyperlink address) or very few characters (for example, a one- or two-character ID number), double-click the value shown in the Width text box, then type the new number of characters you want the column to display. Alternately, you can click the up and down spinner buttons at the right side of the Width text box to use the mouse to increase or decrease the value.

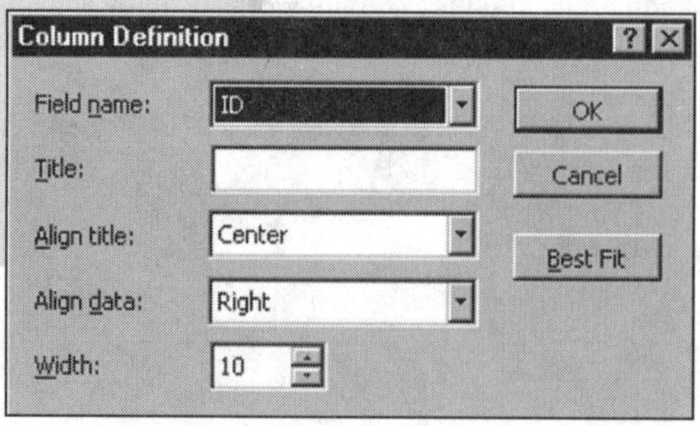

Figure 2.16 This dialog box enables you to create or edit the columns in the task sheet.

Column Definition
Field name: ID
Title:
Align title: Center
Align data: Right
Width: 10
OK
Cancel
Best Fit

8. Click OK to finish creating the column. The column you specified appears in the Task Sheet, as shown in the example in Figure 2.17.

Hiding, Deleting, and Editing Columns

In some instances, you might realize that you don't want to see a Task Sheet column, no longer need it, or need to make changes to it so that it's more useful and relevant to everyone using the project schedule you created.

Hiding a column removes it from display, but leaves its information intact. Therefore, you may want to hide a column after you have entered all the information for it, or when you'd prefer to focus on other columns. For example, you may decide that you really don't need to see the indicators column when you're entering basic task information, so you can hide that column. To hide a column, first click the column heading to select the entire column. Right-click the selected column or open the Edit menu, and click Hide Column. Alternately, you can drag the right border of the column heading all the way to the left, so that the column disappears. To redisplay the column and its contents, use the Insert, Column command as just described to add the column to the Task Sheet.

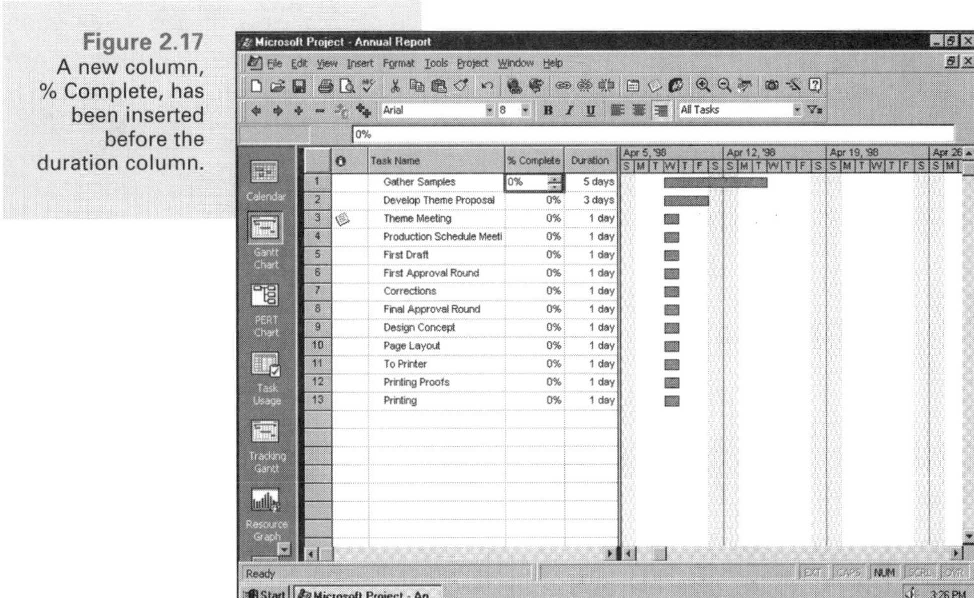

Figure 2.17 A new column, % Complete, has been inserted before the duration column.

If you hide the Task Name field column, you can redisplay it by inserting the Name column into the Task Sheet. When you do so, enter Task Name in the Title text box of the Column Definition dialog box, and choose Left as the Align Data choice.

In cases where a column is no longer needed, you can delete it, but Project hides this capability so you won't accidentally delete vital project information. To delete a column, click the column heading to select the column, and then press Delete.

When you delete a column, Project doesn't require you to confirm the deletion. If you mistakenly delete a column, you can immediately click the Undo button on the Standard toolbar to reinstate the column.

To edit an existing column, you need to display the Column Definition dialog box containing information about that particular column. To do so, double-click the column name in the column heading. Make the changes you want in the Column Definition dialog box, and then click OK to accept them. When you edit a column (as opposed to when you first create it), you might find it useful to click the Best Fit button in the Column Definition dialog box. Clicking this button resizes the column so that it's wide enough to fully display every entry already made in that column.

Dealing with the Planning Wizard

As you start entering information about tasks, you might discover that a Planning Wizard dialog box appears from time to time. The Planning Wizard pops up to point out situations where you might need to make a decision about the information you're entering; the dialog box prompts you with specific, easy choices (see Figure 2.18). For example, the Planning Wizard might ask whether you want to establish a link between tasks, or it might point out that you're about to create an error in your schedule.

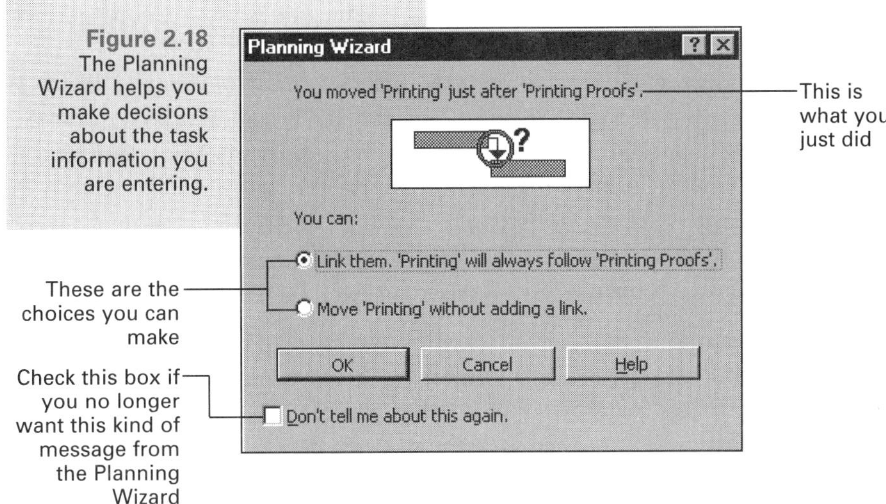

Figure 2.18 The Planning Wizard helps you make decisions about the task information you are entering.

To continue working after the Planning Wizard appears, click to select an option button to respond to the Planning Wizard's question. If the Planning Wizard has asked you this particular question previously and you no longer want to be reminded of the issue, click it to select the Don't tell me about this again check box. Click OK to finish working in the Planning Wizard.

Clicking Cancel closes the Planning Wizard and also cancels the task entry or edit you were making.

You can turn off all the Planning Wizard suggestions. Chapter 20, "Customizing Microsoft Project," explains how to use the Options dialog box to control certain Project features, including the Project Wizard.

Creating Milestones

Milestones were once stone markers used to identify one's relative position along a road—the particular distance to a certain city on that road. Figurative milestones enable you to gauge your progress through your life, through a particular phase of your career, or through a particular process. Milestones in your Project files enable you to mark a particular point of progress or a particular event during the course of a project.

For example, suppose that the project you're managing is the creation and production of your company's annual report, and the company's fiscal year ends June 30. Producing the annual report is tricky, because you want to release it as soon as possible after the close of the fiscal year. Yet you have to wait for the final, audited financial information for the year in order to compile the report. In this case, you might mark the end of the fiscal year with a milestone, to help you keep that key, approaching date in mind. In other cases, you might want to mark particular dates, such as the date when you're 25 or 50 percent through your total allotted schedule.

Creating a milestone isn't very different from creating a task. You insert a task into the Task Sheet, if needed, and then enter information about the task. To specify the task as a milestone, give it a duration of 0 days by entering **0** in the Duration column. Project then identifies the new task as a milestone, and displays a milestone marker for it in your schedule's Gantt chart (see Figure 2.19).

Looking at Project Properties

As with the files you create in other Microsoft applications, Project tracks certain properties, or details, to search for files more efficiently, and more. Some of the properties tracked for your Project files include statistics about the task scheduling and tracking information you enter in the file.

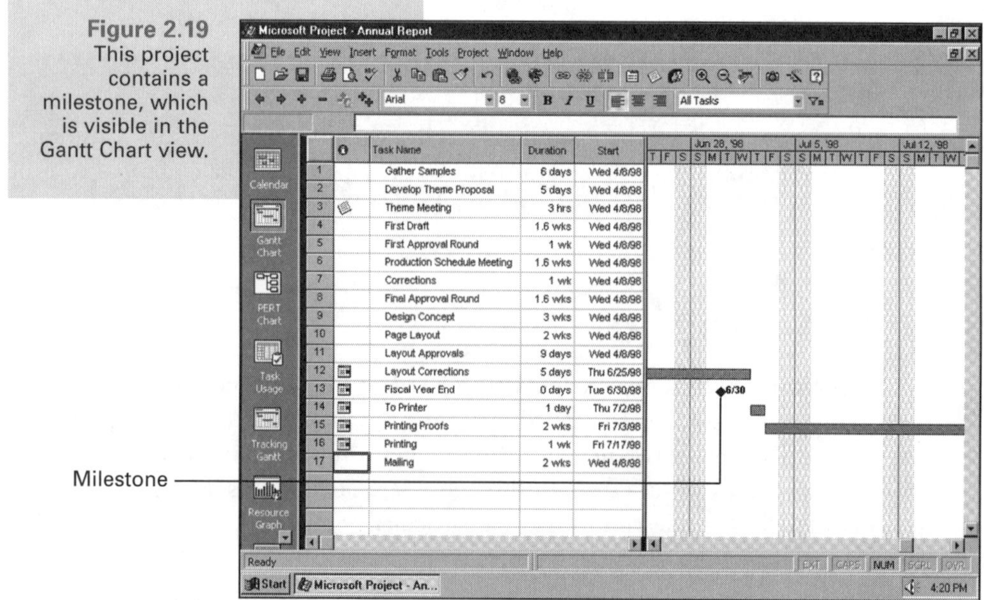

Figure 2.19 This project contains a milestone, which is visible in the Gantt Chart view.

You can review the properties for a particular file by opening the Properties dialog box. To do so, open the File menu and click Properties. This dialog box offers five tabs, some of which calculate and display information, and others that enable you to add details about the file:

- **General**—This tab displays the file type, creation date, date the file was last modified, DOS file name, and more.
- **Summary**—This tab is selected by default. It enables you to enter or edit information about your name, your company, your manager, a title for the file or project, a category to identify the file, keywords to uniquely identify the file if you're trying to find it using Windows search capabilities, and more.
- **Statistics**—This tab displays when the file was created and last modified, and also indicates when the file was last printed, who last saved it, how many times it has been revised, and how many total minutes have been spent editing the file.
- **Contents**—This tab displays some key facts about the scheduling information you entered, including the scheduled dates and total projected cost. Figure 2.20 illustrates what this tab looks like.

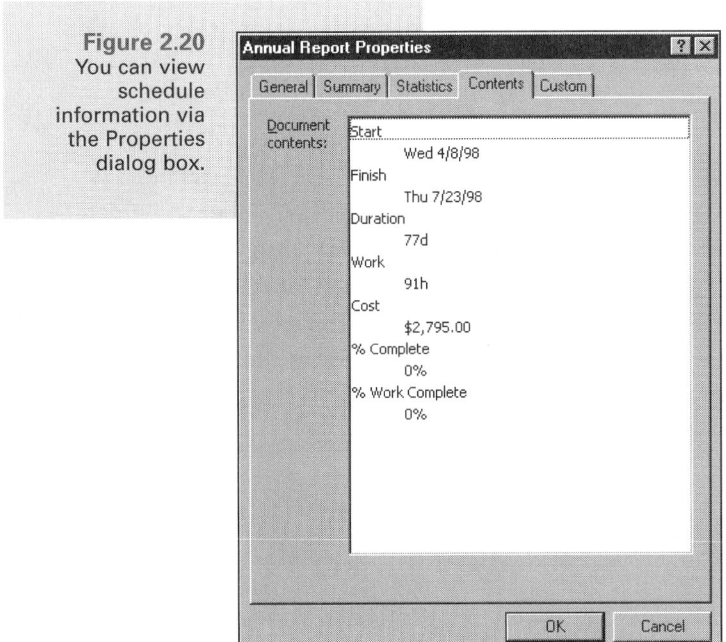

Figure 2.20 You can view schedule information via the Properties dialog box.

- **Custom**—This tab enables you to create a custom property to facilitate finding the file from Windows. For example, you can create a custom property to assign a unique number—such as the job number for the project—to the file. If you create a custom job number field for all your Project files, you can search for any project file by its job number. To create a custom property, specify values for the Name, Type, and Value text boxes, and then click the Add button.

Adjusting the Project Base Calendar

As you learned earlier in this chapter, when you create a new project file, you assign a base calendar for the schedule using the Calendar drop-down list in the Project Information dialog box. Thus, unless you select the 24 Hours base calendar, each workday in the schedule is eight hours long, and it takes three working days to complete a task that is 24 hours in duration.

There might be instances, however, when you want to change the working calendar slightly. For example, if the project you are tracking is a plan for some kind of special event, and the event takes place on a Saturday, you need to make that Saturday a working day. If you want certain workdays to be 10 hours long, you can make that change. This section explains how to alter the base calendar for your project schedule.

Make sure that you specify base calendar changes before you begin building your project schedule to ensure that a calendar change doesn't cause unpredictable results. In addition, under the default method of resource-driven scheduling, if you assigned a special calendar to a resource, that calendar overrides your base calendar. Thus, you need to be sure that you make the same changes to custom resource calendars, when needed, to keep them in sync with the base calendar.

Changing Working Hours or Adding a Day Off

Project gives you the flexibility to change the working hours for any day in any base calendar, or to specify any day as a nonworking day. To do so, follow these steps:

1. In Gantt Chart view, click to open the Tools menu; then click Change Working Time. The Change Working Time dialog box appears, as shown in Figure 2.21.
2. Use the scroll bar beside the calendar to display the month containing the date you want to adjust.
3. To specify a date as a nonworking day, click that date on the calendar. Then, in the For Selected Date(s) area of the dialog box, click Nonworking Time. Dates you specify as Nonworking should include holidays, vacation days, and other scheduled unavailabilities.

The Default choice returns a date to its default base calendar scheduling. This includes rescheduling the task as a working or nonworking day, as well as returning the Working Time entries to their defaults for the selected date.

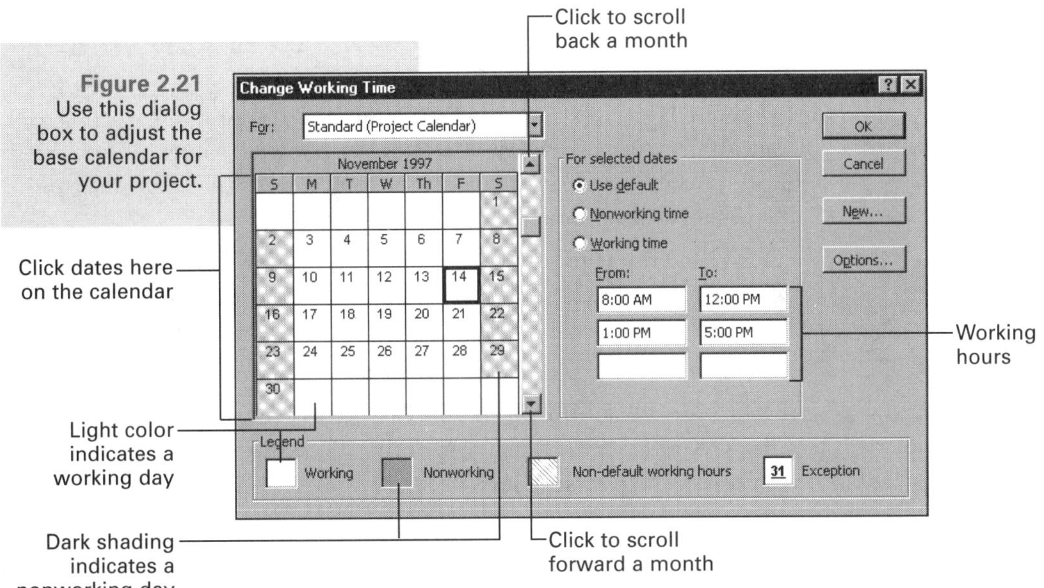

Figure 2.21 Use this dialog box to adjust the base calendar for your project.

4. To change the Working Time (daily working hours) for a date, select that date by clicking it in the calendar, and make sure that it's specified as a Working day or has the Default setting under For selected date(s). In the Working Time area, edit or delete the desired From and To entries.
5. Continue editing the calendar as needed, repeating steps 2 through 4 to change the schedule for additional dates. As you change the schedule for each date, Project marks the edited date in the calendar with bold and underlined lettering and light-gray shading.
6. Click OK to close the Change Working Time dialog box and implement the scheduling changes you made.

Creating a Custom Calendar

You might not want to make changes to the actual base calendar you selected for a project file. Instead, you might want to save your changes in a custom calendar for the project. (The resources you assign to the project also can use the custom calendar.) To create a custom calendar, follow these steps:

1. In Gantt Chart view, click to open the Tools menu; then click Change Working Time. The Change Working Time dialog box appears.
2. Click the New button. The Create New Base Calendar dialog box appears, as shown in Figure 2.22.
3. Because the Name text is highlighted, you can simply type a new name for the custom schedule.
4. Below the Name text box, click an option button to select whether you want to Create (a) New Base Calendar or Make (a) Copy Of (an existing base) Calendar. If you opt to copy a calendar, select one from the Calendar drop-down list.
5. Click OK. Project returns to the Change Working Time dialog box, where the custom calendar you created appears as the For drop-down list selection.
6. Make any schedule changes you want for your custom calendar, as described in the preceding set of steps.
7. Click OK to close the Change Working Time dialog box and implement the new schedule.

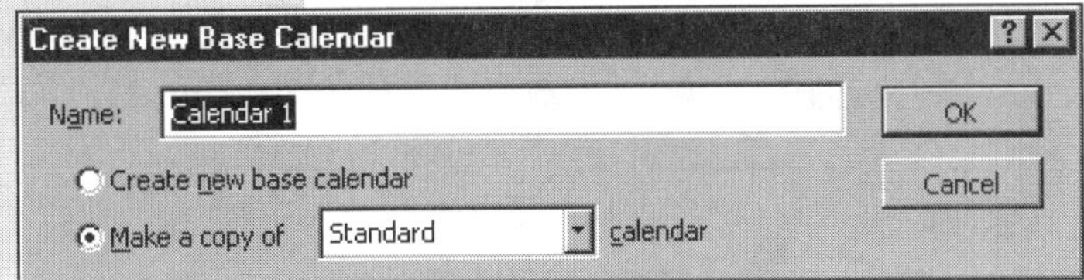

Figure 2.22 To create a new, custom base calendar for your project, use this dialog box.

Note

You can use Project's options to change the base calendar for the current project file globally. For example, you can specify a different day as the start of the work week. To access these settings (described in Chapter 20, "Customizing Microsoft Project,") click the Options button in the Change Working Time dialog box; or, click to open the Tools menu, click Options, and then click the Calendar tab.

3

Fine-Tuning Tasks

In This Chapter

- Graphically managing task schedules
- Identifying and creating tasks that you know will repeat
- Working with links that show relationships between tasks
- Understanding how lead times and lag times affect your schedule
- Applying constraints that further specify when the task should be performed
- Reviewing and changing other information stored about a task

Most designers and artists who create masterpieces don't start by creating subtle shading and fine lines, just as architects don't start a building design by selecting a brick color.

In putting the whole picture together, most of us—professionals and amateurs alike—start by sketching out a rough idea of what we want. Then, we go back and draw in the details.

In Chapter 2, "Setting Up a Project," you learned how to sketch out the schedule for your project in the default Gantt Chart view. This chapter helps you to continue working in the Gantt Chart view to begin the refinement process, making changes here and there, and starting to draw in some details to make your plan clear.

Creating and Editing Tasks with the Mouse

The last chapter focused on becoming comfortable working in the Task Sheet to create and edit task information. You learned to change the schedule for a task by editing the duration, start date, and finish date. In many cases, to change the schedule for a task, you simply have to change an entry in one of the columns in the Task Sheet.

There are, however, a few limitations when you use the Task Sheet to schedule your tasks:

- By default, Project schedules each task's start or finish date on the same date as the project's Start Date or Finish Date, depending on the settings you selected in the Project Information dialog box. Thus, you have to change the start or finish date for virtually every task you enter.
- Typing might not be your strong suit. If you're not an ace typist, entering information cell by cell can be tedious.
- You might be more comfortable working on an actual calendar, rather than trying to count dates in your mind and visualize where weekends fall.

If any of the preceding points applies to you, then you might prefer to create and edit tasks directly on the Gantt Chart pane of the Gantt Chart view. Project enables you to define the schedule for a new task—or change the schedule for an existing task—by using the mouse directly on the Gantt chart.

Dragging to Create a New Task

When you create a new task by dragging, you place it on the schedule exactly where you want it to appear. Creating tasks in this way is akin to using a marker to draw a line through successive dates on a calendar to block them out

for a particular purpose. To use the mouse to add a task to your schedule, do the following:

1. Scroll the Gantt Chart pane to display the approximate dates where you want to schedule the new task. (Use the scroll bar at the bottom of the pane.)
2. If needed, scroll down to display the task row where you want to place the new task.
3. Point to the location that is roughly where the row for the task and your desired start date for the task intersect.
4. Press and hold down the mouse button—the mouse pointer changes to a crosshair. Drag to the right to begin defining the task. As you drag (see Figure 3.1), the outline for the Gantt chart bar appears, and an informational Create Task pop-up box shows you the dates you are establishing for the task.
5. When the bar for the task is the length you want it, and the Create Task pop-up box displays the dates you want to schedule for the task, release the mouse button. Depending on where you draw the new task in relation to other tasks, the Planning Wizard might appear to ask you whether to link the task with another (more on linking later in this chapter). Click the appropriate option, and then click OK to finish creating the task. The new task bar appears on the Gantt chart, and the new start date, finish date, and duration appear in the appropriate columns in the corresponding row of the Task Sheet.

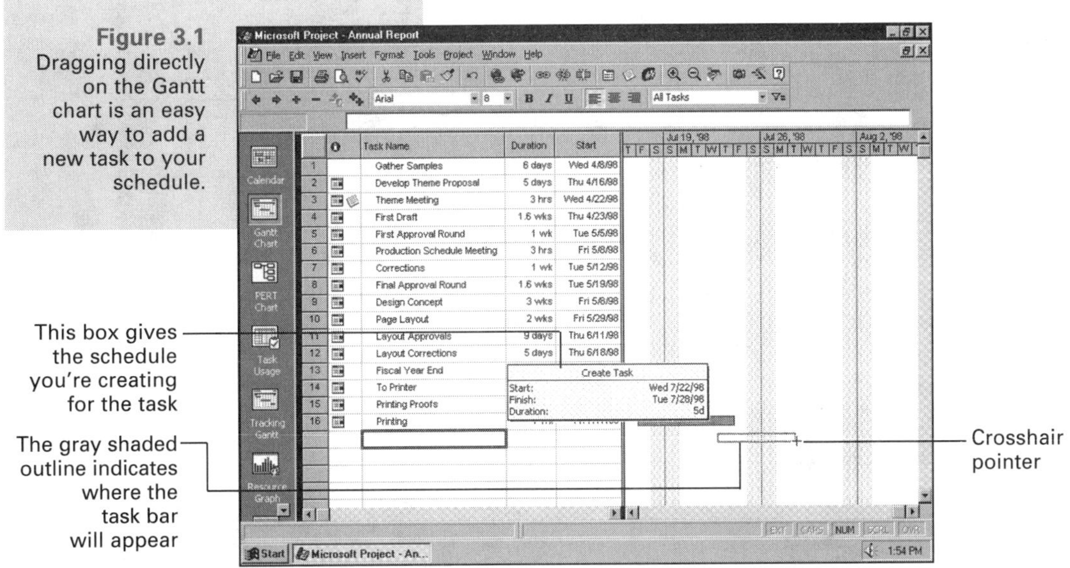

Figure 3.1 Dragging directly on the Gantt chart is an easy way to add a new task to your schedule.

6. Click to select the Task Name cell for the new task, and enter a name (see Figure 3.2).
7. Enter any other information that's needed for the task on the Task Sheet.

Note

Notice that when you create a task by dragging, an icon appears in the Indicator column for this task. This indicator appears because Project automatically assigns a constraint to the start date for the task. For more about what constraints are and how they work, see the section "Setting Task Constraints" later in this chapter.

Note

You can drag from left to right (start to finish) or from right to left (finish to start) when you're creating a task.

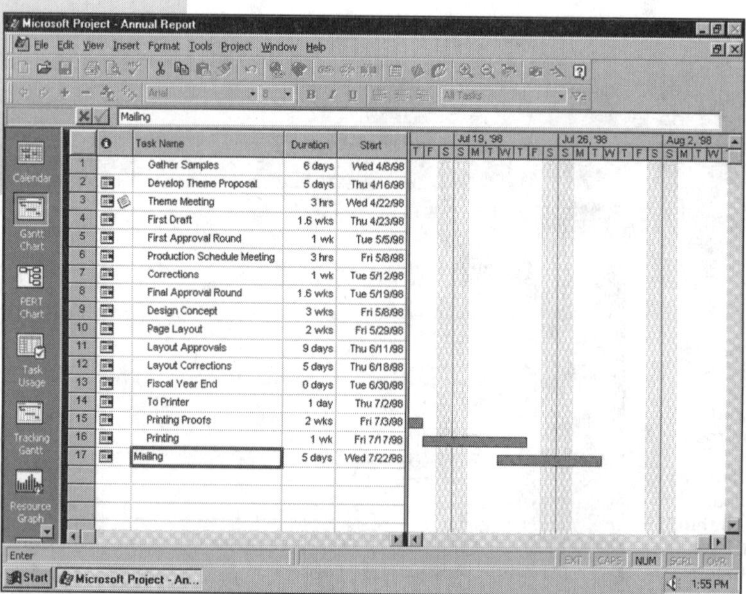

Figure 3.2 After you add the new task, give it a meaningful name.

Dragging to Move or Reschedule a Task

If you're inclined to work with the schedule via the Gantt chart, you also can use the mouse to move and change the schedule for a task.

When you move a task using the mouse, the duration for the task never changes; in effect, dragging the task simply changes the start and finish dates. To move a task on the Gantt chart, point to the task bar until the mouse pointer changes to a four-headed arrow. Press and hold down the mouse button; Project displays a Task pop-up box containing information about the task (see Figure 3.3). Drag the task to its new location; when you drag, the mouse pointer changes to a two-headed arrow, a gray outline appears to indicate the bar's position, and the changing task dates are reflected in the Task box. You can drag the task to the left to schedule it earlier, or to the right to schedule it later. Release the mouse button when the dates you want appear in the Task box. Again, if the Planning Wizard appears to ask whether you want to link the moved task, select the option you prefer and click OK to finish moving the task.

When you're using the mouse to move or otherwise work with a task, you might notice that at times the text in the Task pop-up box or other pop-up box becomes bold. This means that releasing the mouse button would return the task to its dates, with no changes.

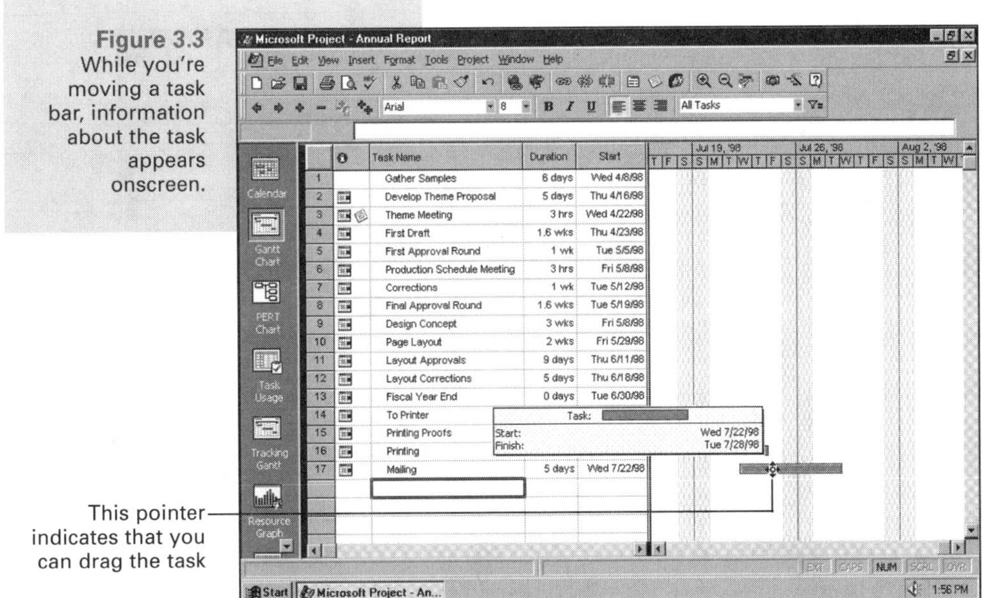

Figure 3.3 While you're moving a task bar, information about the task appears onscreen.

This pointer indicates that you can drag the task

If you selected Project Start Date for the Schedule From option in the Project Information dialog box, you need to reset the Start Date in that dialog box if you drag a task before the present start date. If you're scheduling the project from the Finish Date, you need to reset that date if you drag a task past the present finish date.

You can change the finish date, and thus alter the task's duration, by dragging the right end of the task bar. (You can't resize the task bar from its left end.) Simply point to the right end of the bar on the Gantt chart so that the mouse pointer changes to a right-pointing arrow. Press and hold down the mouse button; the Task box appears as shown in Figure 3.4. Drag to the left to make the task shorter or to the right to make the task longer. When the Duration value in the Task pop-up box is the duration you want, release the mouse button to complete the change. When you drag to change the duration, the control you have might not be as precise as it would be if you made the change in the Duration column of the Task Sheet. For example, in the Task Sheet you can enter small increments of duration, such as **7.25d.** When you drag, however, you can only reset the duration in increments of .5d, so you can choose **7.0d** or **7.5d**, but not **7.1d** or **7.25d**.

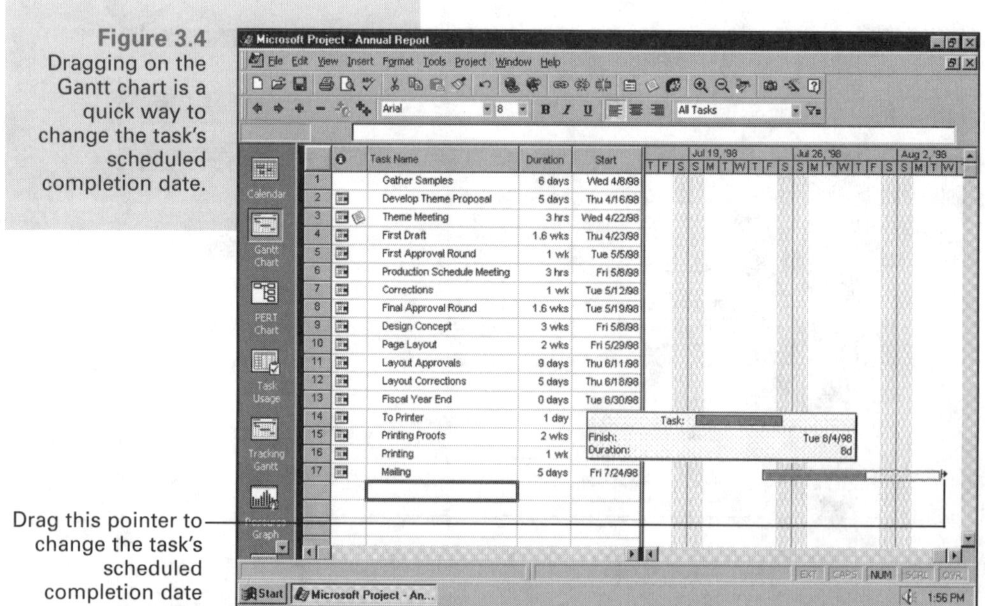

Figure 3.4 Dragging on the Gantt chart is a quick way to change the task's scheduled completion date.

If you try to drag the completion date to a time that's before the starting date, Project resets the task duration to 0 days and converts the task to a milestone. See Chapter 2, "Setting Up a Project," to learn more about milestones.

It's possible to use the mouse to change both the start date and duration for a task, but it requires two separate operations. First, drag the task's Gantt chart bar to reposition it at the correct start date. Second, resize the duration by clicking and dragging the right end of the bar.

Splitting a Task

Chapter 2 discussed how Project works with durations you enter. For example, if you enter a duration of 1 week (1 wk) for a task, Project assumes the task will take 40 hours of work to complete, assuming the project calendar uses a 40-hour workweek. However, there are instances where you might know that a task won't take 40 hours, even when the start and finish dates need to be a week apart. For example, if a resource spends all day Monday on the task, waits a few days for information to arrive from a supplier, and then spends Friday afternoon finishing the task, the resource worked only 1.5 days (12 hours) on the Project. If the resource is from an outside supplier or another department in your company that charges your department for time, it is in your best interest to hone in on the actual time spent on the task to accurately account for project costs, while keeping the true schedule dates intact.

In previous versions of Project this wasn't entirely possible, but Project 98 offers a new feature called task splitting to help you create an accurate picture of when tasks start and finish (the duration), while also tracking how much work (in person hours) occurs and when it occurs. When Project tracks working time accurately, it can then calculate costs accurately rather than overstating them. So, returning to the example, say you know a task will take about 1.5 days of work hours, and you want it to start on the morning of 5/5/98. Because of the delay while the resource is waiting to receive information, the finish date will be a week later, on 5/11/98. Therefore, you should enter the task with a 1.5 day duration and a start date of 5/5/98. Then, you can split the task and drag the last .5 of the task to the true finish date, 5/11/98. Then, the duration appears as 1 full week, while Project uses 1.5 days of work to calculate the resources commitment and costs for the work.

Follow these steps to use your mouse to split a task:

1. Scroll the Gantt Chart pane to display the task bar for the task that you want to split. Double-check to ensure the task start date is the date when all work will begin. This ensures that you have a more accurate picture of how long the split between tasks can be when you create the split, avoiding the need to repeatedly move around the split task or adjust the split.
2. Click the Split Task button on the Standard toolbar. Alternately, click to open the Edit menu, and then click Split Task. The Split Task pop-up box appears, and the mouse pointer changes to a split pointer, with two vertical lines to the left and a right-pointing arrow.
3. Point to the Gantt bar for the task you want to split. Move the pointer left or right until the date listed as the Start: date in the Split Task pop-up box is the date when you want the split (the nonworking period between the split portions of the task) to begin. Figure 3.5 shows the Split Task pop-up box.
4. When you see the correct Start: date in the Split Task pop-up box, press and hold the left mouse button, and drag the split portion of the task to the right. When you start dragging, the Split Task pop-up box changes to the Task pop-up box, which also appears when you drag to create a new task, and includes start: and finish: dates for the portion of the task you're moving.

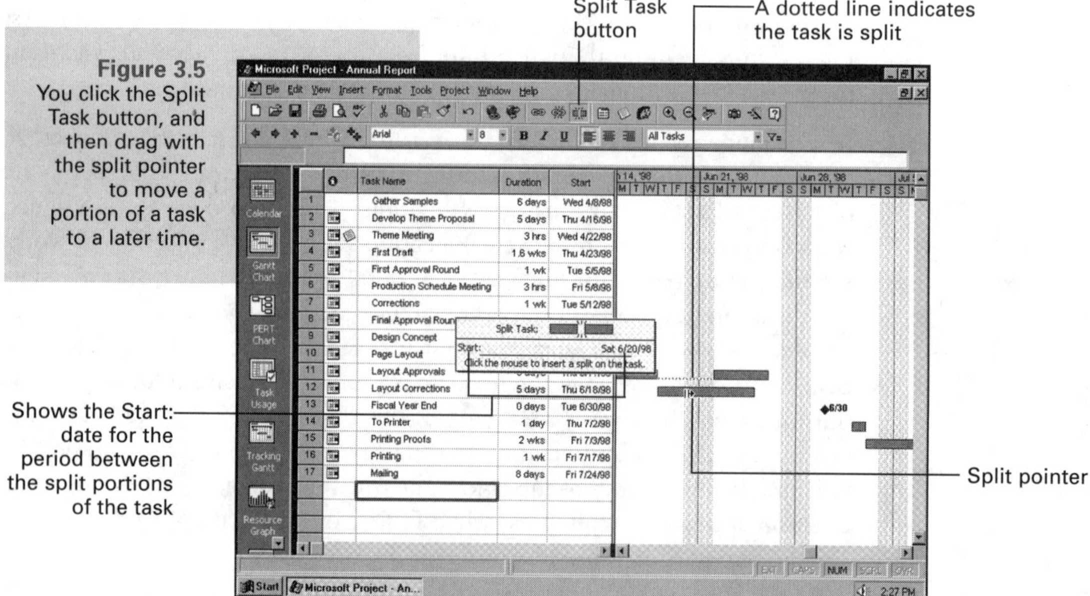
Split Task button
A dotted line indicates the task is split
Shows the Start: date for the period between the split portions of the task
Split pointer
Microsoft Project - Annual Report
Split Task:
Start: Sat 6/20/98
Click the mouse to insert a split on the task.

Figure 3.5
You click the Split Task button, and then drag with the split pointer to move a portion of a task to a later time.

5. When the Task pop-up box displays the correct start: date, and you want work to resume on the task, release the mouse button to drop the split portion of the task into place.

If you click the Split Task button, and then decide that you don't want to split a task, click the Split Task button again or press Esc.

You can split as many tasks as you want in a schedule, or even place multiple splits in the same task bar. In fact, if you double-click the Split Task button on the Standard toolbar, it remains turned on so that you can make as many splits as you want in the project. Click the Split Task button again to turn it off.

As you fine-tune your schedule, you may find a split task that no longer needs to be split. To remove the split in the task, point to the right-hand portion of the split task bar (that is, the Gantt bar for the split task). Press and hold the left mouse button, and drag the bar to the left; when it touches the left-hand portion of the split task bar, release the mouse button. The portions of the split task will merge back into a single task.

Similarly, if you want to adjust the length of the split, drag the right-hand portion of the split task and release the mouse button when it reaches the Start: date you want. Dragging the leftmost portion of a split task bar reschedules the entire task, leaving the split intact.

Creating Recurring Tasks

Splitting tasks is a great solution for breaking up work over a large span of time. There's an even better technique for brief tasks that occur regularly over a particular period of time, such as weekly team meetings, monthly reports to a client, and so on. Rather than entering a separate task for each one-hour meeting or each half-day of report preparation, you can automatically schedule tasks that will occur at set intervals; these are called recurring tasks.

You can schedule monthly team meetings, a weekly conference call, or a daily status report. You can even set tasks to occur more than once each week—for example, every Monday and Wednesday.

Although you can create recurring tasks from a few different views in Project, adding these tasks from the Gantt Chart view often works best, because there you get a clear picture of where the recurring task fits in.

To add a recurring task to your schedule, perform the following steps:

1. In the Task Sheet, click to select the row or a cell in the row that the first instance of the recurring task should precede. You do this because the recurring task will be inserted as a summary task on a single row of the Task Sheet, with the subtasks representing each recurrence hidden from view. (See Chapter 13, "Working with Outlining," to learn more about viewing subtasks.) Because the recurring tasks aren't dispersed throughout the task list by default, you need to place the summary recurring task early in the schedule, where it will be noticed by users of the file.
2. Open the Insert menu and click Recurring Task. The Recurring Task Information dialog box appears, as shown in Figure 3.6.
3. Enter the desired Name and Duration for the task by clicking in each text box and typing the desired entry. Remember that you can use abbreviations to specify the exact timing you want to assign, such as **2h** for a two-hour task.

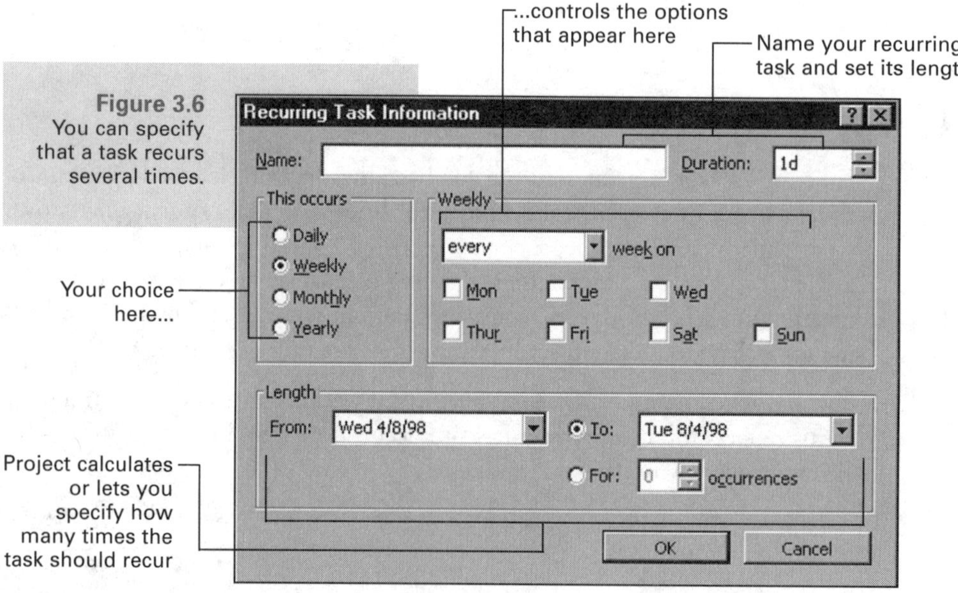

Figure 3.6 You can specify that a task recurs several times.

4. Click to select one of the choices in the This Occurs area of the dialog box: Daily, Weekly, Monthly, or Yearly.
5. Specify the interval between recurrences in the area to the right of This Occurs. The available choices vary depending on the This Occurs option you selected. Basically, you can choose from the following:
   - Daily—Use the drop-down list to specify whether the task appears every day, every second day, every third day, and so on, up to every twelfth day. The Day choice includes all days in the schedule, and the Workday choice only schedules the recurring task on days included in the calendar for the project.
   - Weekly—Use the Week On drop-down list to specify whether the task appears every week, every second week, and so on, up to every twelfth week. Next, select each day of the week on which you want the task to recur. Change the entry in the From text box (in the Length area of the dialog box) only if you want to schedule recurrences starting before—or a specified interval after—the project start date. Use the To option to specify an ending date for the recurrence; otherwise, click the For Occurrences option and specify the number of times that the task should be scheduled after the start date. Note that if you click the drop-down list arrow beside either the From or the To choices, a pop-up calendar palette appears so you can make sure you're selecting a working day (rather than a weekend or other nonworking date).
   - Monthly—Use the Day option button to specify the day of the month (by date number, such as the 25th of every month). Then use the corresponding drop-down list to specify whether to schedule the task in every month of the project timeframe. If you want to schedule the recurring task by a day of the week rather than a date within each month, click the The option button. Then use its drop-down lists to specify particular weekdays when the task should be scheduled, and whether to schedule the task every month. The Length options work exactly like the ones described under Weekly.

Whenever possible, schedule tasks by selecting a day of the week rather than entering a date. This helps you to avoid scheduling any instances of the recurring task on a nonworking date.

- Yearly—Click the option button beside the upper text box, and enter a single schedule date for the recurring task. Or, click the The button and use the drop-down lists to choose a month, weekday, and particular weekday in that month (first, second, and so on) for the task. Again, the Length options work as described previously.

6. Click OK to accept your choices. If, by chance, one or more of the recurrences you scheduled appears on a day that's not a working day according to the project calendar, Project asks if you want to reschedule the task (see Figure 3.7). To reschedule the task and continue, click Yes.

The recurring task appears in the Task Sheet in boldface, with a plus (+) outlining symbol to indicate that it's a summary task (see Figure 3.8). If you look at the row numbers to the left, you'll notice that some numbers no longer appear. For example, if the summary task appears in row 2, but the next row in the sheet is row 7, it's because rows 3–6 are hidden rows that each contain an individual recurrence. The duration, start date, and finish date for this summary task will span all the recurrences of the task, although you might not be able to see the Duration field entry at first. If you see a series of pound (#) signs filling the Duration column, double-click the right border of the Duration column heading to increase the column's size.

To adjust the schedule for the recurring task, click any cell in the summary task row. Press Shift+F2; alternately, open the Project menu and click Recurring Task Information. (You also could double-click a cell in the task, or right-click a cell in the task, and then click Recurring Task Information). Make the changes you want, and then click OK to complete your changes.

To delete the recurring task, select the summary task by clicking its row number; then press Delete (or open the Edit menu and click Delete Task). Alternately, right-click the heading for the summary task row and click Delete Task. If the planning wizard appears, click OK to confirm the deletion. This deletes the summary line and all the hidden rows that represent recurrences of the task.

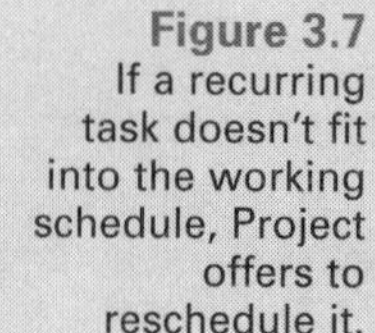

Figure 3.7
If a recurring task doesn't fit into the working schedule, Project offers to reschedule it.

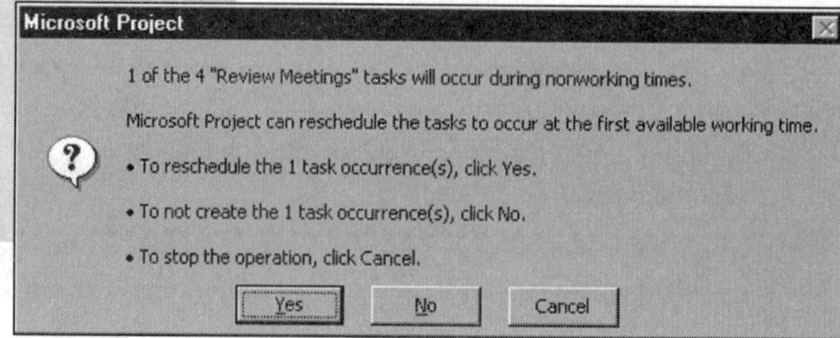

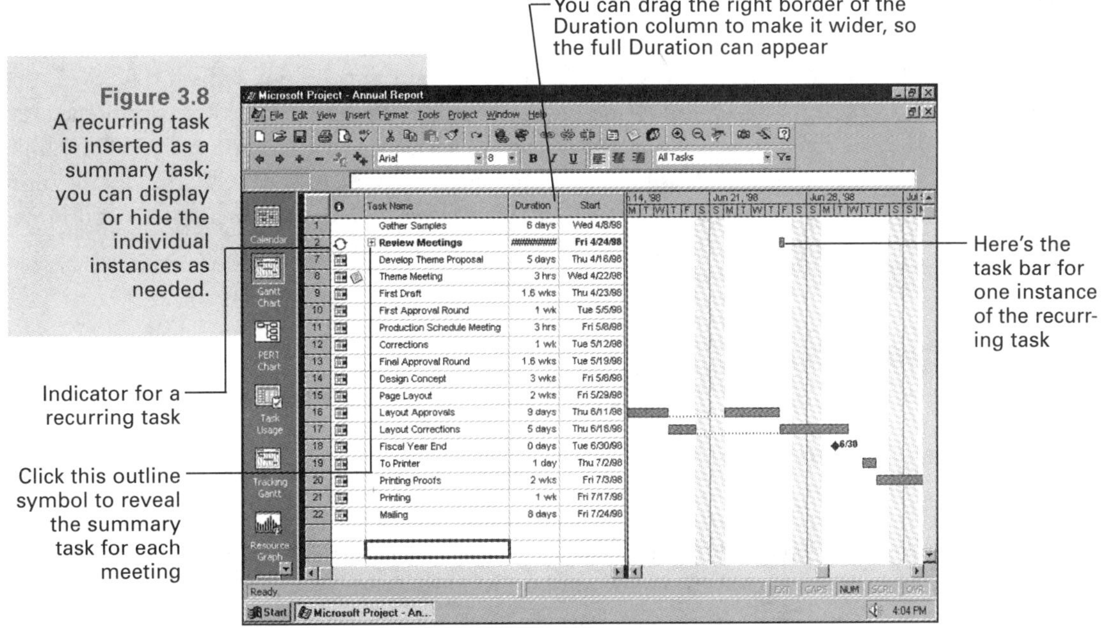
You can drag the right border of the Duration column to make it wider, so the full Duration can appear
Here's the task bar for one instance of the recurring task
Indicator for a recurring task
Click this outline symbol to reveal the summary task for each meeting

Figure 3.8 A recurring task is inserted as a summary task; you can display or hide the individual instances as needed.

Linking and Unlinking Tasks

One major drawback to the yellow pad method of project planning is that it forces you into a simplistic thinking. Because each task is on a separate line, it is separate and distinct from all other tasks on the list. That's perception, not reality.

Most projects don't progress in so neat a fashion. Many tasks are completely independent of one another, but sometimes tasks need to occur simultaneously. Other times, one task cannot start until another finishes. Some tasks need to start or finish simultaneously. Such a connection between the "destinies" of two tasks is called a task relationship. In Project, you define *task relationships* by creating *links*.

Links in your schedule define how tasks should proceed. The first task in a link, which usually must be completed before the other linked tasks can start, is called the *predecessor*. Tasks that follow and depend on predecessors are called *successors*. A predecessor can have more than one successor, and successors can serve as predecessors for other tasks, creating a "chain" of linked events. A successor task can even have multiple predecessors—for example, in a situation where three tasks must finish before one successor task can start.

One detail that might be difficult to get your arms around is that a predecessor task is identified by its ID number in the Predecessors field of the Task Sheet. The task ID is based on the task's current position (which row it's in) on the Task Sheet, not its individual schedule. It's perfectly okay to specify the task in row 20 as the predecessor to the task in row 12 in a Finish-to-Start link (described next), as long as the finish date for the row 20 task precedes the start date for the row 12 task. Task ID numbers change automatically if you move tasks to a new row, or sort the tasks in the Task Sheet.

Link Types

Project offers four types of links. Links are visually represented by lines and arrows between tasks in Gantt charts, calendars, and PERT charts that are based on your schedule. Each link is identified with a particular abbreviation:

- The most common kind of link is a *Finish-to-Start (FS) relationship*, where the first task must be finished before the next task can begin (see Figure 3.9). For example, a product prototype might need to be approved before prototype testing can begin. An FS relationship is the simplest type of link to create. It's the default link type, and Project creates an FS relationship if you don't specify a different link type.

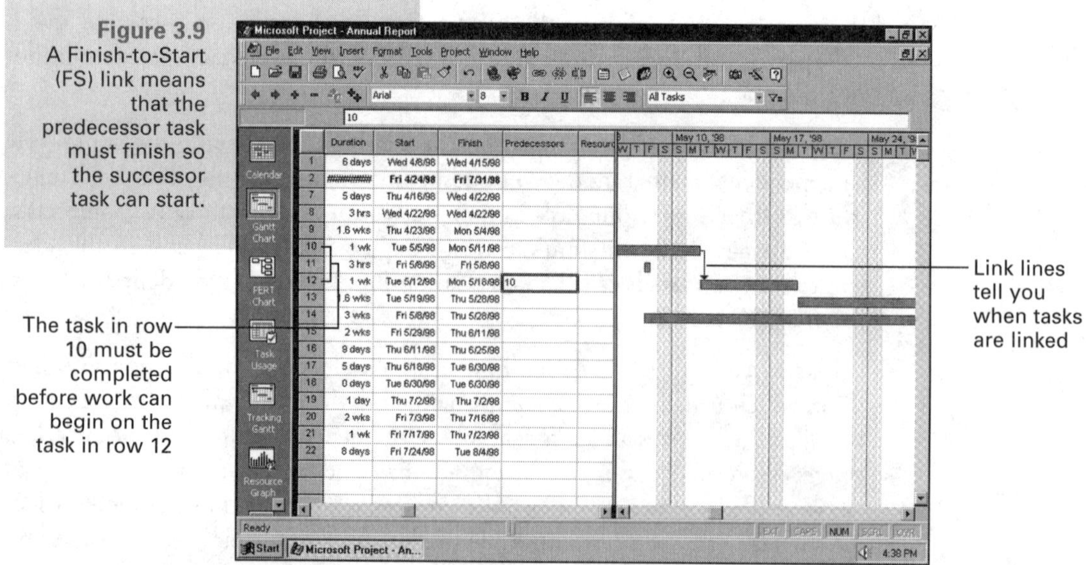
Microsoft Project - Annual Report
File Edit View Insert Format Tools Project Window Help
Duration
Start
Finish
Predecessors
Link lines tell you when tasks are linked
The task in row 10 must be completed before work can begin on the task in row 12

Figure 3.9 A Finish-to-Start (FS) link means that the predecessor task must finish so the successor task can start.

- A *Start-to-Start (SS) relationship* specifies that two tasks must start at the same time (see Figure 3.10). Use this type of relationship in situations where you want resources to work closely together, such as when an internal engineering department is working in concert with freelance resources. In this case, you're specifying that there can be no delay in the start of the successor task after the predecessor task starts; as soon as your engineering department's ready to go, the freelancer also must be ready to go.
- A *Finish-to-Finish (FF) relationship* means that two tasks must end at the same time (see Figure 3.11). Such a situation might arise when multiple tasks must be completed simultaneously, but the predecessor task is more lengthy or resource intensive than any successor task. For example, say that you're creating the first issue of a new magazine. When the page layout task (the predecessor) ends, it means an automatic end to the ad sales task (the successor), because, at that point, the magazine's page design is finalized, and no more time is available to incorporate new advertisements.
- A *Start-to-Finish (SF) relationship* is a bit more complex than the other relationships, and therefore is used less often. In such a relationship, the predecessor task cannot finish until the successor task begins (see Figure 3.12). Consider this accounting example: A company's quarterly or annual books have to remain "open" until the period-end closing procedures begin, no matter when that actually occurs.

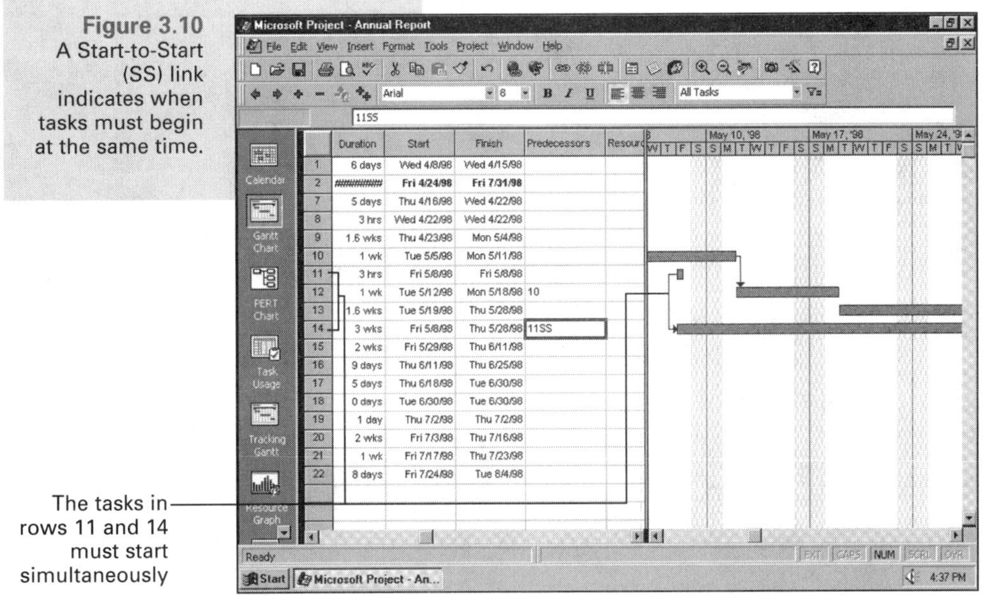

Figure 3.10
A Start-to-Start (SS) link indicates when tasks must begin at the same time.

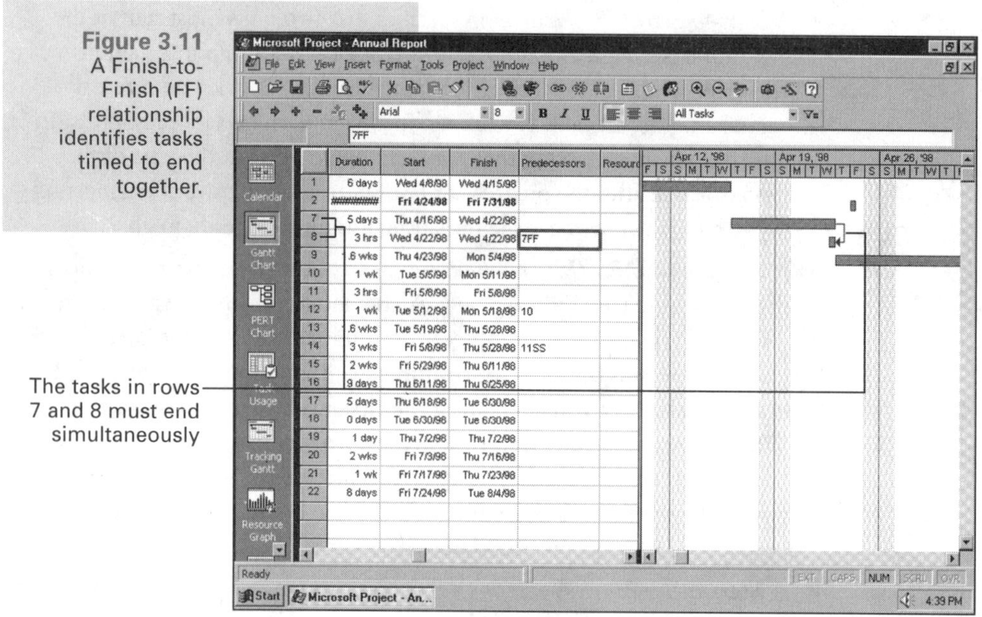

Figure 3.11 A Finish-to-Finish (FF) relationship identifies tasks timed to end together.

The tasks in rows 7 and 8 must end simultaneously

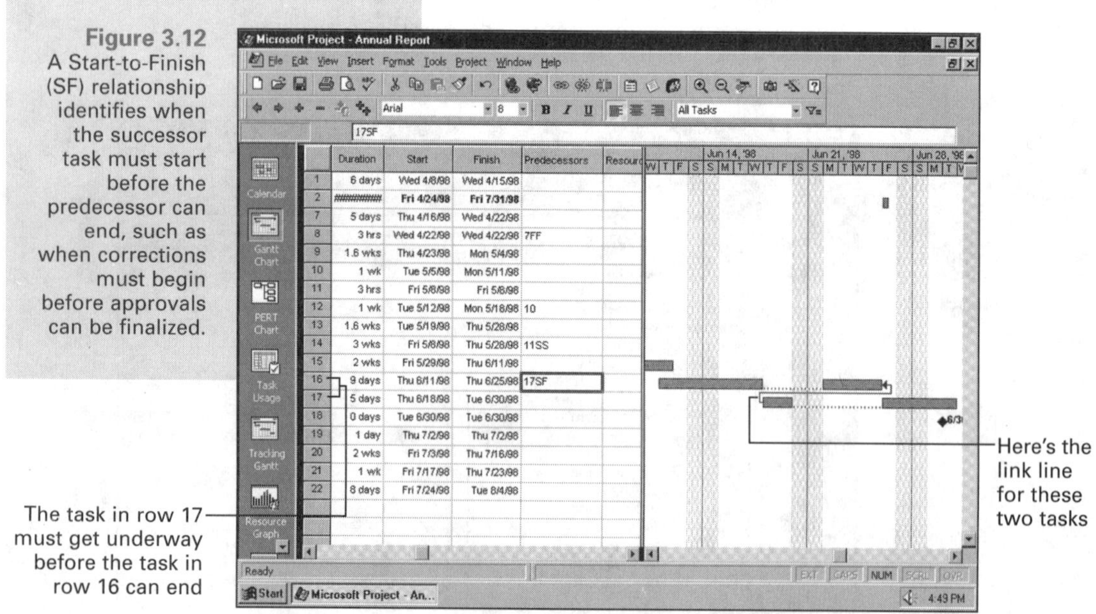

Figure 3.12 A Start-to-Finish (SF) relationship identifies when the successor task must start before the predecessor can end, such as when corrections must begin before approvals can be finalized.

Here's the link line for these two tasks

The task in row 17 must get underway before the task in row 16 can end

At times, when you create a particular relationship that requires it, Project might change the schedule for a successor task so that its schedule is consistent with a linked task. For example, if you create an FF relationship and the successor task's finish date is earlier than the predecessor's finish date, Project shifts the successor task's schedule so that it has the correct finish date, yet retains its original duration. Project might also shift successor tasks that are attached to any predecessor task you move, so don't be too surprised.

Linking Tasks on the Task Sheet

Recall from the description of the Task Sheet in Chapter 2, "Setting Up a Project," that one of the columns in the default Task Sheet is the Predecessors column. You can use this column to create links simply by typing; to do so, follow these steps:

1. Click to select the cell in the Predecessors column in the row holding the task that will be the successor task. For example, if you want the task in row 12 to start when the task in row 10 finishes, click the Predecessors cell in row 12.
2. Type the row number for the predecessor task.
3. If you want to designate a Start-to-Start, Finish-to-Finish, or Start-to-Finish link rather than the default Finish-to-Start link type, type its abbreviation using upper- or lowercase characters (for example, 10ff). You don't need a space between the predecessor's row number and the abbreviation. Your entry might resemble any of the ones shown in Figures 3.10, 3.11, and 3.12.
4. (Optional) To specify an additional predecessor, continue the entry by typing a comma followed by the task number and link type abbreviation (without any spaces).
5. (Optional) Repeat step 4 if you want to add other predecessors.
6. After you create all the links you want in the successor task's Predecessors cell, press Enter to finalize the link(s).

If you decide to make a change to a link, simply edit the link information by clicking the appropriate Predecessors cell and making your changes.

Linking Tasks with the Mouse

To create a default Finish-to-Start (FS) link, you can drag between task bars on the Gantt chart to create the link. Point to either of the task bars until you see the four-headed arrow pointer. Press and hold the mouse button, and drag to the other task bar. As you drag, a Finish-to-Start Link pop-up box appears as in Figure 3.13. Release the mouse button to finish creating the link.

You also can create links between tasks shown in Calendar view or in PERT Chart view by dragging between the tasks. You learn more about these views in Chapter 9, "Working with the Different Project Views."

Linking Tasks with the Toolbar

Using a toolbar button along with the Task Sheet can make even faster work of creating links between tasks—but only if you want to create the default type of link, an FS relationship. Also, links created with the method described next always assume that the task that's lower in the task list (with the higher row number) is the successor task; therefore, Project adjusts that successor task's schedule, if needed, to ensure that it follows the predecessor.

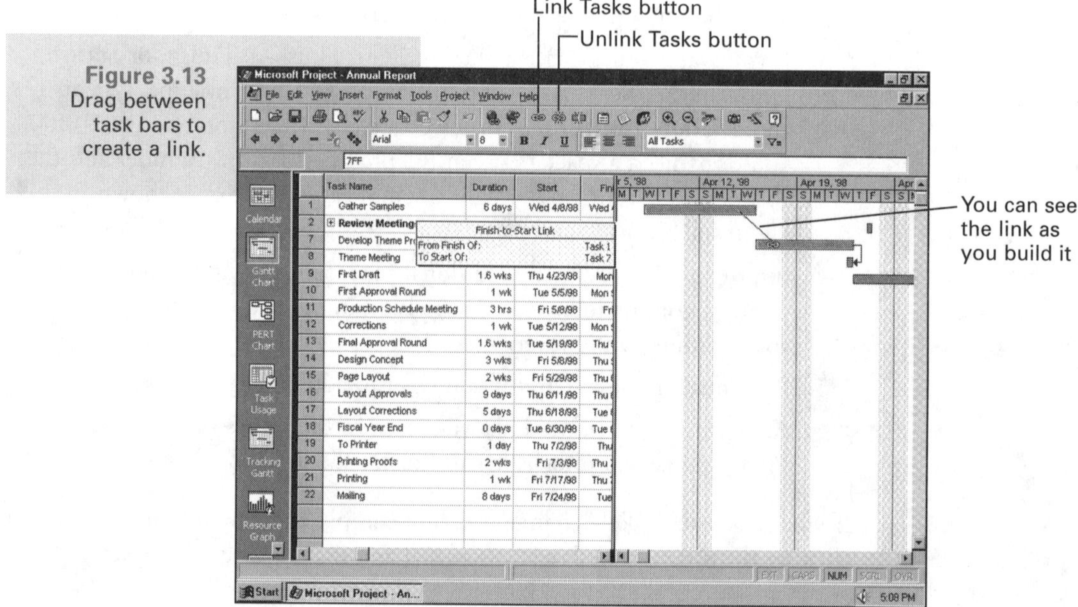

Figure 3.13 Drag between task bars to create a link.

One of the advantages to using the mouse to create your links is that you don't have to scroll right to the Predecessors column (which, at the default Task Sheet pane size, scrolls the Task Name column out of view), so you can see the task's name as well as the Gantt bar representing its schedule. The following steps also make it easy to link several tasks in a single operation:

1. Drag to select cells in two or more adjacent tasks. If you want to select noncontiguous tasks, click a cell in the predecessor task row, press and hold down Ctrl, and click a cell in the successor task row—both cells will be selected. If you want to select additional noncontiguous tasks, continue to hold down Ctrl and click cells in other rows.
2. Click the Link Tasks button on the Standard toolbar. Alternately, press Ctrl+F2, or open the Edit menu and click Link Tasks. Project creates the link(s) between the tasks in the rows you selected.

Linking via Task Information

The Task Information dialog box lets you view and alter numerous crucial details about a task. This dialog box offers five tabs of information, including the Notes tab that you learned about when creating task notes in Chapter 2, "Setting Up a Project," and the Predecessors tab, which enables you to create and edit links to predecessors for the selected task. The obvious disadvantage to this method is that you have to be familiar with details about the predecessor task you want to choose, or the schedule for the predecessor, because you might not be able to view that information while the dialog box is displayed.

To display the Predecessors tab in the Task Information dialog box, click a cell in the task for which you want to create or work with predecessors (that is, click a cell in the successor task row). Press Shift+F2; alternatively, click the Task Information button on the Standard toolbar, or if you prefer, open the Project menu and click Task Information (or right-click the task and then click Task Information). As another method, you can simply double-click a cell in the successor task row in the Task Sheet. When the Task Information dialog box appears, click the Predecessors tab.

To add a predecessor, type the ID (row) number for the predecessor task in the first cell of the ID column below the Predecessors choice. Press Enter or Tab, or click the Enter button (it looks like a checkmark) beside the Predecessors text box above the column heads. (The text entry area here operates just like the one above the Task Sheet.) Project enters the predecessor's task name.

Project 98 offers a second, easier method of specifying a predecessor task. Click the Task Name cell in the first empty row of the Task Name column of the Predecessors tab in the Task Information dialog box. A drop-down list arrow appears at the right side of the cell. Click the arrow to open a drop-down list giving the Task Name for each task in the schedule. Click the name of the predecessor task, as shown in Figure 3.14. Click the Enter button to finish choosing the predecessor.

Whether you specify the predecessor by ID or Task Name, by default Project enters `Finish-to-Start (FS)` in the Type column as the link type. To specify a different type, click the Type cell for a predecessor, and do one of the following:

- Select the type that currently appears in the text entry box, type the abbreviation for the preferred type of link, and click the Enter button (which looks like a checkmark).
- Click the down arrow at the right end of the text entry box to display a drop-down list of link types, and click the preferred type of link.

You can add additional predecessor tasks in lower rows of the tab. To edit any link, click the appropriate cell in the predecessor row, and then edit it in the text entry box or use a drop-down list for the cell, if available, to make another choice. To remove a predecessor, click the ID cell for it; then drag over the ID number that appears in the text entry box, press Backspace to remove it, and click the Enter button. When you finish using the tab to add or edit predecessors, click OK to close the task information dialog box.

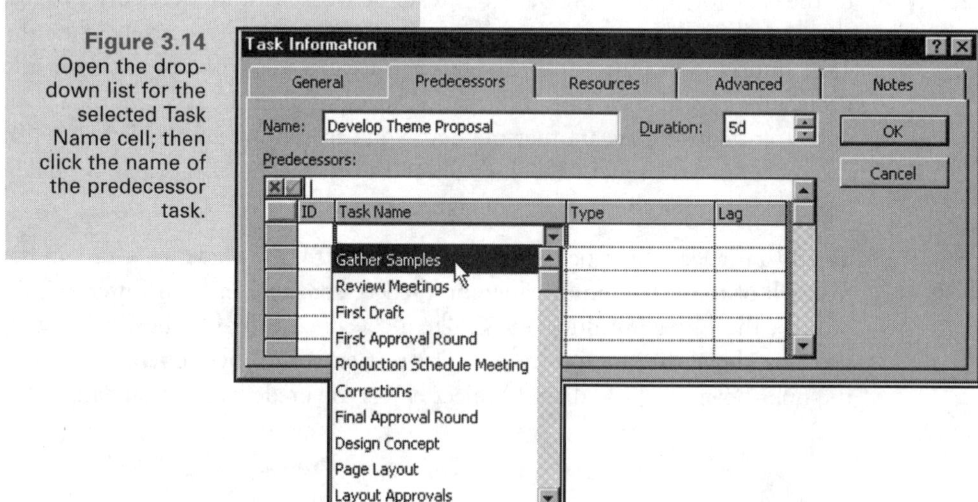

Figure 3.14 Open the drop-down list for the selected Task Name cell; then click the name of the predecessor task.

For information about the Lag column for predecessor tasks, see the "Working with Lead Times and Lag Times" section later in this chapter.

Unlinking Tasks or Changing the Link Type

To remove a link between tasks or change the type of link, you have to work from the successor task, not the predecessor task. Removing a link does not change the schedule for the successor task, unless that schedule was changed by Project when the link was created. If Project did automatically adjust the successor task schedule based on a link you added, then when you remove the link, Project returns the successor task to its original schedule.

Use any of the following methods to break a link or change the link type:

- Click any cell in the successor task row to select it; then click the Unlink Tasks button on the Standard toolbar. (This technique applies to breaking the link only.)
- Click to select the Predecessors cell in the successor task row of the Task Sheet. To remove the link, right-click the cell, then choose Clear Contents. Otherwise, click in the Entry box above the task sheet, edit the link type abbreviation, and click Enter to finish changing the link.

Do not press Delete to clear the contents of the Predecessors cell! Doing so deletes the entire task rather than the task link. Click the Undo button on the Standard toolbar immediately if you mistakenly delete a task.

- Click the Task Information button on the Standard toolbar (or use the method of your choice) to display the Task Information dialog box, then click the Predecessors tab. Delete the ID number for the predecessor to remove the link. Or, change the Type column entry for a predecessor to change the link type.

- Double-click the appropriate link line between two tasks in the Gantt chart. Choose Delete in the Task Dependency dialog box that appears to remove the link. Or, open the Type drop-down list, click a different link type; then click OK. Note that the (None) choice in the Type drop-down list removes the link, too.

Working with Lead Times and Lag Times

Reality dictates the way your schedule must progress, and how Project enables you to define task relationships. Time is analog, or continuous. Although it can be expressed in discrete units, such as minutes and seconds, it flows and blends together. Moreover, events blend together in time; even though tasks might seem to follow one after another, they, in fact, might flow together more loosely, overlapping or occurring after a delay.

Project accounts for this flexibility of time by enabling you to schedule *lead time* and *lag time* for linked tasks. Adding lead time causes the successor task to overlap with the predecessor task; this means that even though the task link is, for example, Finish-to-Start, the successor task can start before the predecessor task is finished. Adding lag time on a Finish-to-Start relationship enables you to insert a delay between the finish of the predecessor task and the start of the successor task. For example, if a predecessor task is scheduled to end on a Wednesday, you can schedule the successor task to begin the following Wednesday, without breaking the link between the two tasks.

You can schedule lead or lag time by entering the proper code for it in the Predecessor column entry (by appending it to the predecessor task number and task type specification), or by entering the code in the Lag column of the Predecessors tab of the Task Information dialog box, or in the Lag text box of the Task Dependency dialog box. You specify lead time using a minus sign (-) and lag time using a plus sign (+). You can specify the timing in terms of duration intervals (2h for two hours, 2d for two days, and so on) or as a percentage of the predecessor task's duration.

For example, if you want to create a Finish-to-Start link to task 7 with a two-day lead time, enter **7FS-2d** on the Task Sheet in the Predecessors cell for the successor task. If you're entering the lead time in the Lag column (Task Information dialog box) or Lag text box (Task Dependency dialog box), you only have to enter **-2d**. A Lag entry using percentages might be **7FS-50%** (on the Task Sheet) or -25% (in either of the dialog boxes), which respectively would insert lead time equivalent to 50% or 25% of the predecessor task's duration before the start date of the successor task. To specify lag time (a pause) rather than lead time, you simply use a plus sign rather than a minus sign in your entries. Figure 3.15 shows lead time and lag time added to tasks in an example schedule.

Even though the abbreviation for a Finish-To-Start (FS) relationship doesn't appear by default in the Predecessors column of the Task Sheet, you must type that abbreviation when specifying lead time or lag time.

However, there's a glitch when you're creating lead time. Project might not automatically reschedule the successor task to an earlier start date when you create lead time. Just as it won't let you drag the left end of a Gantt chart bar to adjust the start date of a task. In such a case, which occurs when Project is not set to automatically recalculate schedule changes, you have to adjust the start date for the successor task in the Start column of the Task Sheet, or press F9 if you see Calculate in the status bar. This tells Project to move the successor task's Gantt chart bar to the left to show the lead time. You can reduce lead time by dragging the successor task bar right, but you can't increase lead time by dragging it left. In general, dragging the Predecessor task bar moves both tasks.

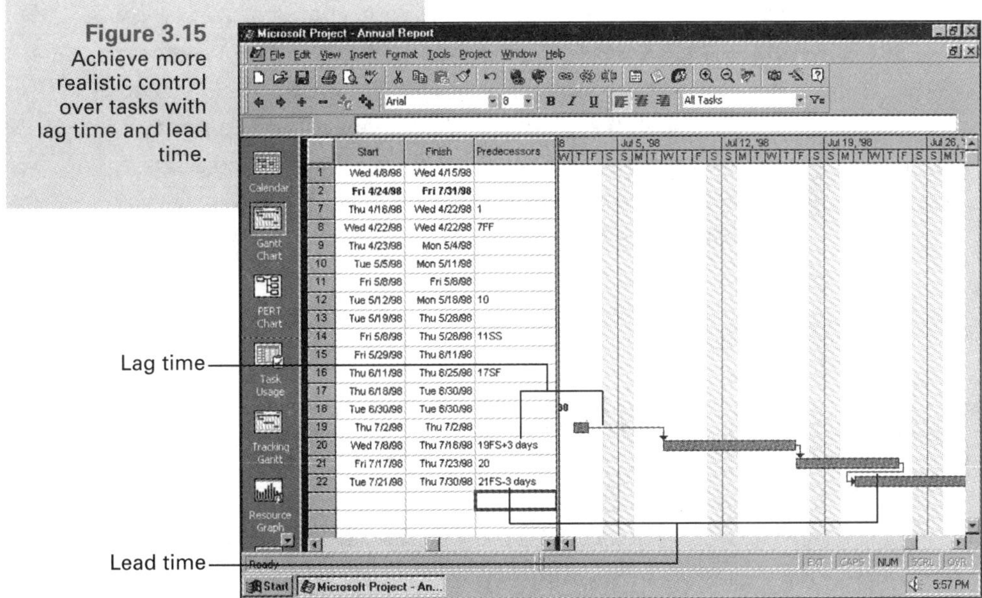

Figure 3.15 Achieve more realistic control over tasks with lag time and lead time.

By contrast, you can create lag time by dragging the Gantt chart bar for an existing successor task to the right. As soon as you release the mouse button, Project adds the lag time. Likewise, you can reduce the amount of lag time between tasks by dragging the Predecessor task bar to the right or increasing its duration by dragging its right end to the right. You can increase the lag time in either direction by dragging the successor task bar in either direction.

Note

In real life, problems arise, resources are detained, and other delays gum up the works. You should always include a bit of "cushion time" in your schedule to allow for such problems.

Note

Project offers you two ways to build this cushion into your project schedule. The first is to schedule extra time for some tasks, especially those for which you're less confident about estimating a duration. The second is to assign the anticipated duration for a task, but to build in some lag time after the task. I prefer the latter method, especially when I need to accurately track costs or when I'm dealing with a resource outside my company. I give the outside resource a task deadline (finish date) that is at least a couple of days before the real (internal) date when I require the task to be completed. This technique not only provides cushion time, but allows you, as manager of the project, some time to review the work from the outside resource, which is especially prudent if you haven't previously dealt with that resource.

Setting Task Constraints

As you learned elsewhere in this book, Project calculates a project Finish Date or Start Date for you depending on the duration and nature of the tasks you create. This book has focused quite a bit already on the flexibility you have in moving or rescheduling parts of tasks.

That flexibility is great if you're the only person able to edit the schedule. If, however, you want to make the schedule a bit more solid in most cases, you can establish constraints for tasks, just to make tasks a bit more difficult to move, and to control how the schedule progresses. Table 3.1 reviews the constraints.

Table 3.1 Constraints for Controlling Individual Task Scheduling

Constraint	Abbrev.	Description	Flexible/ Inflexible
As Soon As Possible	ASAP	Ensures that the task starts as soon as possible, based on the completion of any predecessors, and is the default constraint if you enter only the duration for the task.	Flexible
As Late As Possible	ALAP	Ensures that the task starts as late as possible when the project is being scheduled from its finish date, and is the default constraint if you enter only the duration for the task in this type of schedule.	Flexible
Finish No Earlier Than	FNET	Prevents a task from finishing when premature, and is the default if you edit or enter the task's finish date.	Inflexible when tasks are scheduled from the project finish date; Flexible when tasks are scheduled from the project start date.
Start No Earlier Than	SNET	Prevents a task from starting before the specified date, and is the default if you edit or enter the task's start date.	Inflexible when tasks are scheduled from the project finish date; Flexible when tasks are scheduled from the project start date.
Finish No Later Than	FNLT	Sets the drop-dead deadline for the task, but enables the task to start earlier if needed.	Inflexible when tasks are scheduled from the project start date; Flexible when tasks are scheduled from the project finish date.

Table 3.1 Constraints for Controlling Individual Task Scheduling

Constraint	Abbrev.	Description	Flexible/ Inflexible
Start No Later Than	SNLT	Sets the absolute latest date when the task can commence, but enables the task to start earlier if needed.	Inflexible when tasks are scheduled from the project start date; Flexible when tasks are scheduled from the project finish date.
Must Finish On	MFO	Specifies that a task must finish no sooner or later than a specified date.	Inflexible
Must Start On	MSO	Specifies that a task must start no sooner or later than a specified date.	Inflexible

To create constraints for a task, perform the following steps:

1. Click a cell in the Task Sheet row of the task you want to create constraints for.
2. Right-click the task or open the Project menu, and then click Task Information. Alternately, press Shift+F2 or click the Task Information button on the Standard toolbar. The Task Information dialog box appears.
3. Click the Advanced tab to display the advanced options (see Figure 3.16).
4. Click the down arrow beside the Type drop-down list to display a list of constraint types. Select the type of constraint you want for the selected task.
5. Click the drop-down list arrow beside the Date text box, and use the pop-up calendar to specify the new date to define the constraint.
6. Click OK to close the dialog box and finalize the constraint.

You may have noticed that as you moved tasks away from the date from which the project is being scheduled (the start date by default), a small, square, grid-like icon appeared in the Indicators column. This icon represents a particular type of constraint. By default, where you're moving a task from the beginning

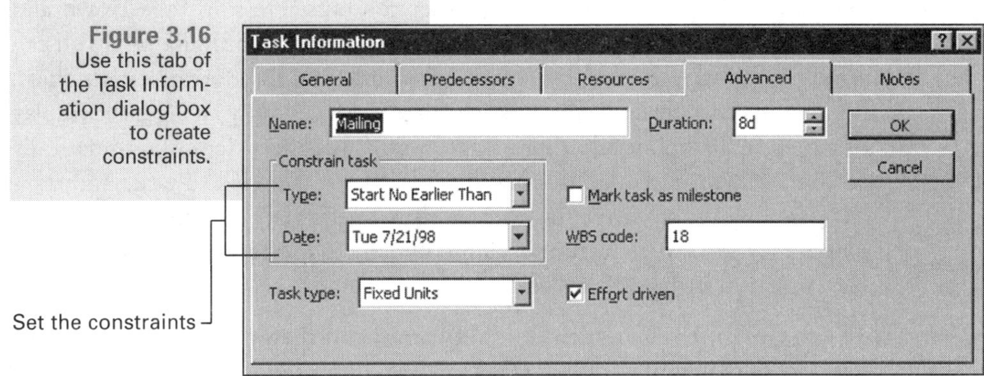

Figure 3.16 Use this tab of the Task Information dialog box to create constraints.

of the Project to a later date (that is, moving the start date for the task), the task has a Start No Earlier Than (SNET) constraint. You also may have noticed that this constraint isn't necessarily "enforced" by Project as you build links; successor tasks move as needed to honor the links. That's because SNET constraints are flexible in projects scheduled from the project start date (chosen from the Schedule From drop-down list in the Project Information dialog box).

Flexible constraints aren't anchored or restricted to a particular date; they can move as needed as you create links or add resources. In contrast, an inflexible constraint prevents a task from being rescheduled, unless you change the constraint. Some constraints can be flexible or inflexible, depending on the Schedule From choice for the Project. Table 3.1 also clarifies when particular constraints are flexible or inflexible. The indicator for an inflexible restraint is slightly different from that for a flexible constraint, as shown in Figure 3.17.

Using Go To to Find a Task

Scroll bars enable you to scroll through the various parts of each view. For example, you can scroll up and down to see different rows of the Task Sheet,

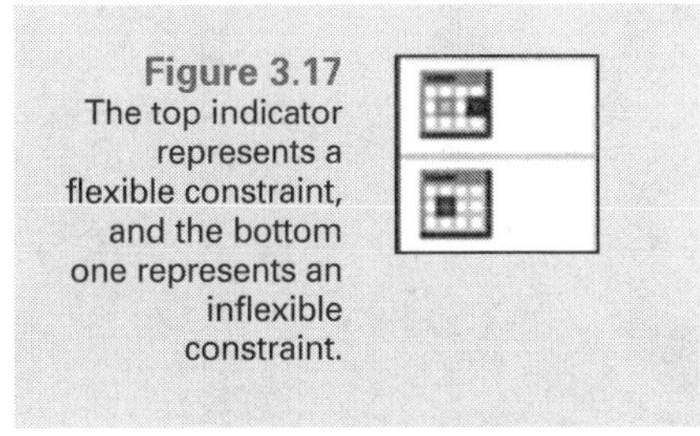

Figure 3.17 The top indicator represents a flexible constraint, and the bottom one represents an inflexible constraint.

and can scroll left and right to see other columns. Pressing Page Down and Page Up moves the display by one screenful of information. Likewise, you can scroll up, down, left, and right to display different areas of the Gantt chart. Moving the Task Sheet display and clicking a task certainly changes the display of the Task Sheet, but selecting a Task in the Task Sheet doesn't automatically scroll the Gantt chart and display the task bar for the selected task. Additionally, scrolling to the correct task bar on the Gantt chart could be slow. Instead, you can use the Go To features to jump directly to the Task Sheet task and task bar you want, or just the task bar.

To use Go To, click to open the Edit menu, and then click Go To (Ctrl+G). The Go To dialog box appears (Figure 3.18). Enter the ID number (row number) of the task you want to jump to in the Task Sheet and scroll the Gantt chart to display the task bar for the selected task. To simply scroll the Gantt chart to a particular date, click the drop-down arrow for the Date text box and select the date to scroll to in the Gantt chart. Click OK to finish your Go To selection and adjust the display.

If you already clicked a cell in a task in the Task Sheet and want to quickly display the task bar for that task, click the Go To Selected Task button on the Standard toolbar.

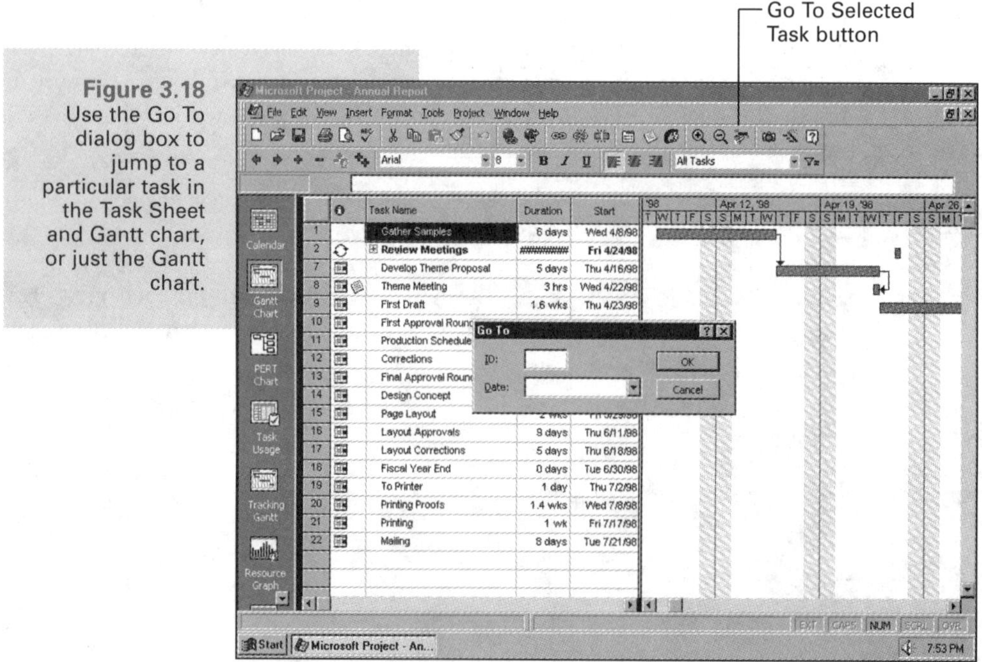

Figure 3.18 Use the Go To dialog box to jump to a particular task in the Task Sheet and Gantt chart, or just the Gantt chart.

Editing Other Task Information

So far, you worked in the Predecessors, Advanced, and Notes tabs of the Task Information dialog box. The fastest way to display this dialog box is to click a cell in the task that you want to learn more about or change information for, and then click the Task Information button on the Standard toolbar. You can click any tab in the Task Information dialog box to display its options, edit them as needed, and then click OK to close the dialog box. This section takes a brief look at the options not examined thus far.

The first tab in the Task Information dialog box is the General tab (see Figure 3.19). It lets you work with general parameters for the task, like its start and finish date, which you learned to adjust via other methods.

The Predecessors tab was described earlier in this chapter. It enables you to alter the task name and duration, as well as specify predecessors for the selected task to create links. The Resources tab is covered in Chapter 4, "Managing Resources." This tab enables you to assign one or more resources (coworkers, vendors, and so on) to complete the specified task.

In addition to the Constrain Task options you learned about in the preceding section, the Advanced tab (refer to Figure 3.16) offers a few more options of

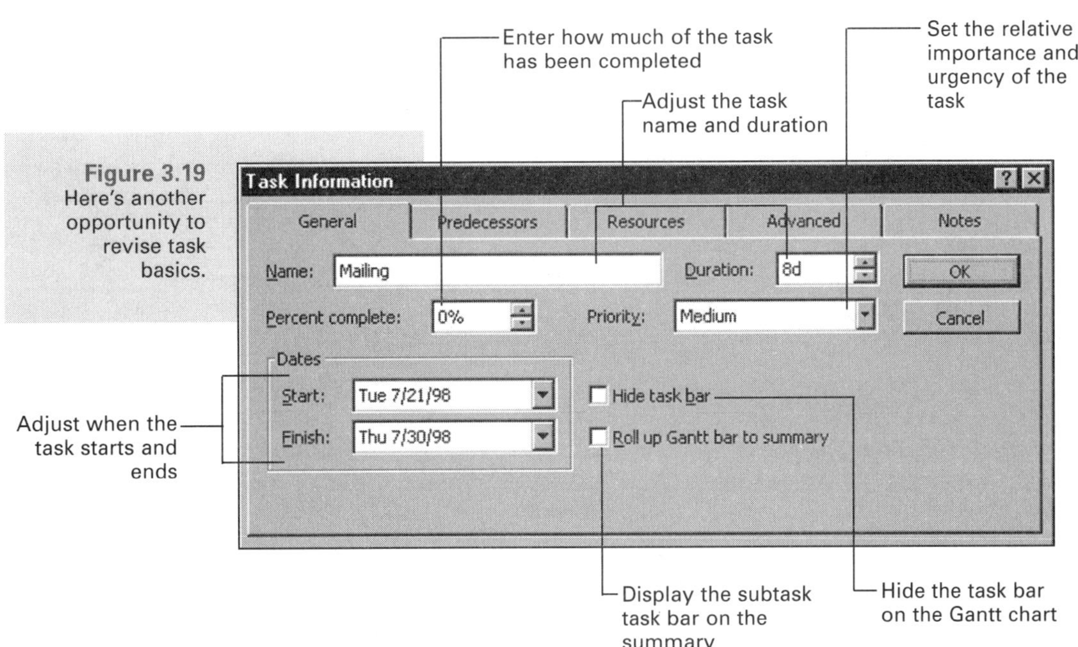

Figure 3.19 Here's another opportunity to revise task basics.

interest. The Mark Task As Milestone check box converts the task to a milestone. If you want to use a specialized coding system, enter the code to use for the task in the WBS Code text box. If you want the number of resources you add to a task to influence task durations, make sure the Effort Driven text box remains checked. The final tab, Notes, is where you enter and edit notes about the selected task.

Note

As an example, you might want to use WBS codes starting with 1000 (1001, 1002, and so on), or you might want to use the year as a code prefix (9801, 9802, and so on). This latter method can be useful if your project schedule falls into more than one calendar year.

4

Managing Resources

In This Chapter

- What resources are in Project
- How the resources you select affect the schedule
- Adding resources for your project
- Determining how much each resource will cost
- Controlling how a resource's time is scheduled
- Removing a resource
- Viewing and editing assignments

If you're a person who lives by your lists, then the first few chapters of this book might already have introduced you to the key concepts you need to be familiar with when using Project.

In those chapters, you learned the steps for building and scheduling the tasks associated with your plan. All the information you've compiled so far, however, doesn't answer the most critical question of all: How in the world is everything on the list going to be done?

What Is Effort-Driven (Resource-Driven) Scheduling?

Resources complete the tasks you specified in a plan or schedule, and can consist of more than simply the name of a coworker or team member. For example, a resource can be an outside freelancer or consulting firm; it can be a vendor that provides printing or manufacturing; it can be raw materials or supplies needed for a project, such as paper that needs to be purchased for a printing job; or, a resource can be a piece of equipment you might need to use during a project, whether that equipment exists in your company and is shared by others, or is leased from an outside firm. In a nutshell, resources include all the people and equipment used to complete tasks in a project.

You face several challenges when you try to assign resources to a project:

- You're generally limited in the number of resources available to you. That is, you can't just ask anyone in your company to handle a task for you. You have to work with the resources made available to you and figure out how to maximize the contribution made by each one.
- You're generally competing with others for each resource's time. For example, a resource from your company's marketing department might be handling items for you and five other colleagues in a given week.
- Even if money is no object, you generally can't just hand an entire project off to outside resources. It takes an insider—you or someone else—to coordinate with and manage contracted outside resources and ensure that your tasks don't suffer because of an external resource's commitments to other clients.
- Even in the most extreme circumstances, certain tasks require at least a minimum amount of a resource's time. For example, if a task requires that a resource fly from Los Angeles to your city with an approval mock-up of a new product, and the flight plus the commute from the airport always requires eight hours, you simply can't ask the resource to do it in six. People like to deliver excellent, timely work, but most haven't perfected the ability to warp time.

If you had any education in economics, you'll recognize that the preceding points sound a lot like the concept of scarcity. When resources in a marketplace are scarce, competition for the resources increases, so that people pay more for them and have to use them more wisely.

With scarcity of resources or anything else, what you can accomplish is limited by your access to the resources to do it. You can't make steel, for example, if scarcity makes coal so expensive that you can't afford to buy it for the furnace.

Project takes resource scarcity into account by using effort-driven scheduling (also called resource-driven scheduling) by default. Under effort-driven scheduling, Project may adjust a task's duration to take into account both the amount of work the task requires and the amount of resources assigned to it. For example, suppose that you have a task with a duration of three days, and the default calendar for the project calls for eight-hour workdays. This means that the project's duration in hours is 24. Suppose, however, that you assign a resource to the project, and the resource only works six hours per day. It'll take that resource four working days (6 hours times 4 days equals 24 hours) rather than three to finish the project, so Project adjusts the start or finish date for the task accordingly.

Note

You can override the effort-driven duration for any task. To learn how to do so, see the "Overriding an Effort-Driven Duration" section later in this chapter.

So, effort-driven scheduling results in the resources you select having a critical impact on your plan. As you create resources and make the related choices described in the remainder of this chapter, keep in mind how those choices might affect the overall schedule. If you encounter difficulties or conflicts as you create and work with resources, read Chapters 5, "Resolving Overallocations and Overbooked Resources," and 6, "Optimizing the Schedule," which provide techniques for addressing those difficulties.

Viewing and Using the Project Resource Sheet

The Task Sheet, which you learned to work with in earlier chapters, specifies *what* needs to happen in a project and *when* it needs to happen. (I'll assume that someone in your company also knows *why* it needs to happen.) The Resource Sheet for your schedule enables you to specify *who* will make it happen, and *how*.

Use the Resource Sheet to build the list of resources you'll need to complete all the tasks you listed on the Task Sheet for the schedule. To view the Resource Sheet, shown in Figure 4.1, open the View menu and click Resource Sheet. Or, scroll down the View Bar, and click the Resource Sheet icon. Just as each row in the Task Sheet holds information about a single task, each row in the Resource Sheet holds all the details about a single resource. Each column represents a particular field, or type of information. You can add columns that show information Project calculates, such as cost variances.

To select a cell in the Resource Sheet, click it, or drag to select (highlight) groups of cells. Alternatively, use the arrow keys to move the cell selector around. To select an entire column or row, click the column name or row number. Right-clicking any selection displays a shortcut menu with commands that you can perform on the selection. For example, you can select a row, right-click, and then click New Resource on the shortcut menu to insert a new, blank resource at the selected location in the Resource Sheet.

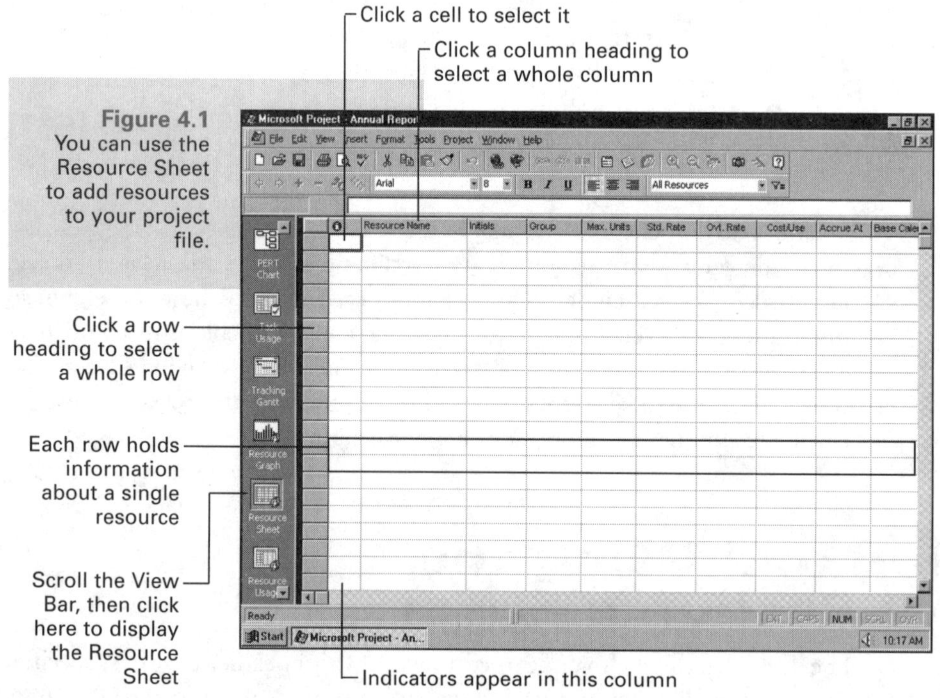

Figure 4.1 You can use the Resource Sheet to add resources to your project file.

You can make adjustments to the size and position of columns, or add columns, in the Resource Sheet just as you did in the Task Sheet. The steps are virtually the same in the Resource Sheet as they were in the Task Sheet. To learn more, see the section "Adjusting the Task Sheet" in Chapter 2, "Setting Up a Project." One important column you might want to add is for resources' e-mail addresses. Project 98 offers dozens of new fields for both the Task and Resource Sheet.

Setting Up a New Resource

By default, the Resource Sheet has 10 columns that enable you to enter information that might be crucial to your plan, plus a column where indicators appear. This section takes a look at the basic method for making entries in these columns, as well as the five columns that are most essential to use in defining the resource. Because the remaining columns deal with the resource calendars and costs, each of which requires a detailed discussion, I'll cover those columns in the next two sections of this chapter, after you get your feet wet here.

To start a new resource, click the Resource Name cell of a new, blank row in the Resource Sheet, and type the resource name. As you type, the Enter button and Cancel button appear beside the text entry box above the column headings (see Figure 4.2). To finish entering the name, click Enter. Project fills in some default information about the resource, such as entering a 1 in the Max. Units column. Then, you can press Tab to move to the next column to the right, or press Enter to move down to the next row and list all resources by name only.

To remove the contents of a cell in the Resource Sheet, do not simply click the cell and press Delete. Doing so removes the entire resource, not just the contents of the selected cell. Instead, right-click the cell, and then click Clear Contents to remove its contents.

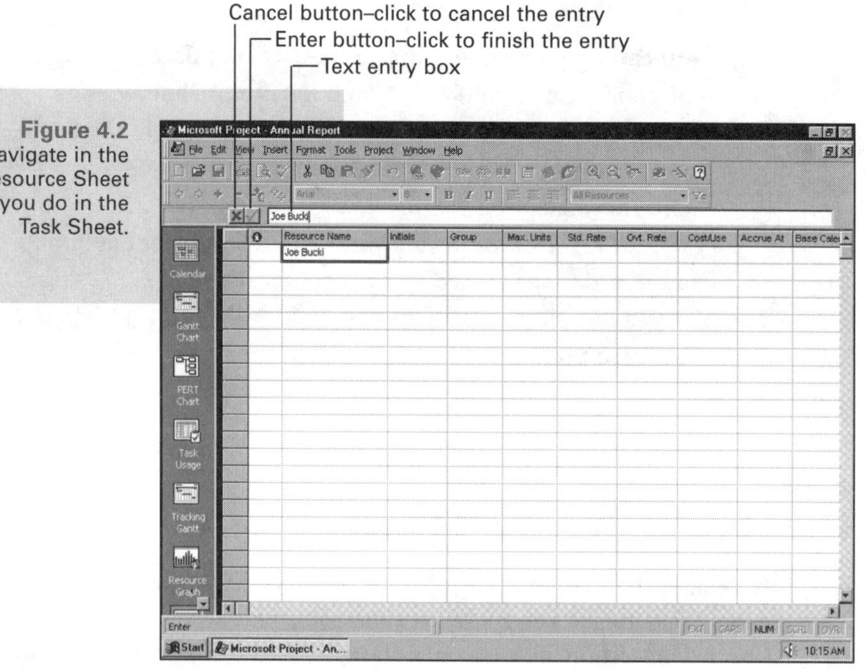

Figure 4.2 Navigate in the Resource Sheet as you do in the Task Sheet.

The style you use to create resources is up to you. You can use the Tab key after each entry to move across the row and complete each field entry for that resource. Or, you can simply enter all the resource names, and then come back to each row and fill in the details. As noted at the start of this section, five of the columns or fields are basic, yet essential in identifying each resource as you assign it to tasks in your plan:

- **Resource Name**—Enter the full name for the resource, such as the name of a team member, supply vendor, or independent contractor.
- **Initials**—Don't be afraid to use long resource names. Project also enables you to identify a resource by its initials, entered in this column. By default, Project uses the first initial of the first name of the Resource Name entry in the Initials column. You should, however, select the Initials entry and type another entry that's more specific. It is recommended that you make them more specific than a person's first and last initials, because it's pretty common to encounter people with the same initials. One approach is to use all or part of the first name, along with the last initial, as in JoeB, short for Joe Bucki.

- **Group**—When your resource belongs to a group, and it might be significant to identify that group for the purposes of your project, enter the group name in the Group column. For example, if your team members come from several departments in your company, and you want to track each department's contribution, enter the department name or tracking number. Or, if you're working with several different contractors for a project, each of whom needs to be entered as a separate resource, you can enter Contract in the Group column for each of them to be able to track their collective performance.
- **Max. Units**—The default entry for this column, 100%, means that for each scheduled workday, the resource offers one person (or machine, or so on) for the full duration of the workday; this is known as a single *assignment unit.* Entries of less than 100% indicate part-time work (more on that in Chapter 5), but entries of more than 100% don't assign overtime (more on overtime in Chapter 6). Entries of more than 100% mean that the resource might be offering additional people (or machines) for assignments. So, for example, if a resource offers four people to handle each task, you would change the Max. Units entry for the resource to 400%. When you select the Max. Units field in a row, spinner buttons appear at the right side of the cell, so you can use the mouse to increase or decrease the entry rather than typing. (Alternately, you can specify assignment units in the Max. Units column in decimal values, with 1 in decimal terms being equivalent to 100% in percentage terms. Use the Show Assignment Units As A drop-down list on the Schedule tab of the Options dialog box, described in Chapter 20, "Customizing Microsoft Project," to change this setting.)
- **Code**—This column at the far right side of the Resource Sheet enables you to enter an alphanumeric code to identify the resource. This code might be a department number that corresponds to your entry in the Group column, or a unique number, such as a Purchase Order number that you obtained for payment of the resource.

After you enter this basic information about several resources, your Resource Sheet might resemble the one shown in Figure 4.3.

Displaying Resource Information

If you're not comfortable working in the spreadsheet-like cells of the Resource Sheet, and would prefer a more convenient format in which to enter and edit the information about a resource, you can use the Resource Information dialog

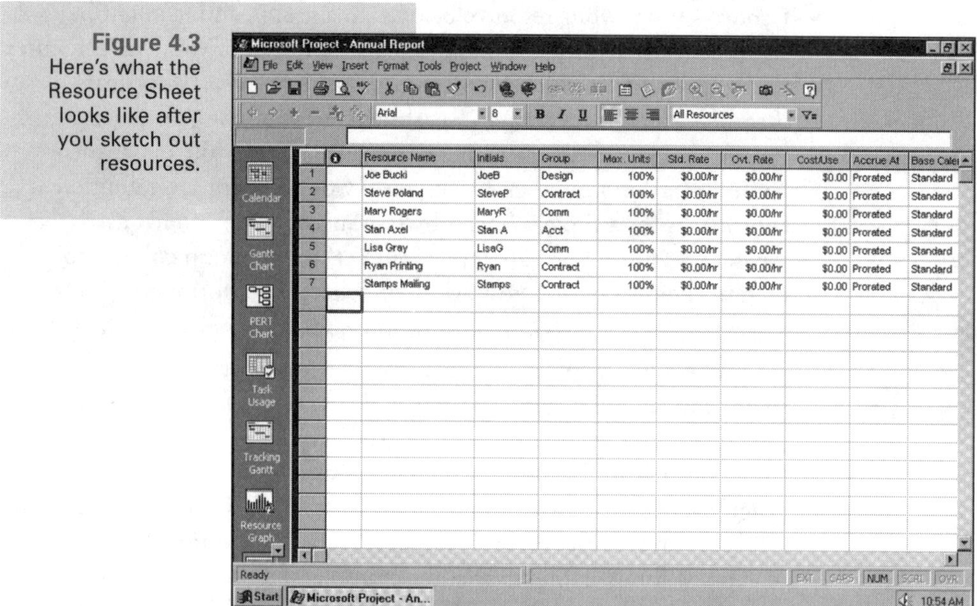

Figure 4.3 Here's what the Resource Sheet looks like after you sketch out resources.

box shown in Figure 4.4. The General tab of the Resource Information dialog box enables you to enter basic task information, as well as other schedule-related information. The dialog box also offers three other tabs, which are described where they apply in this chapter and the next.

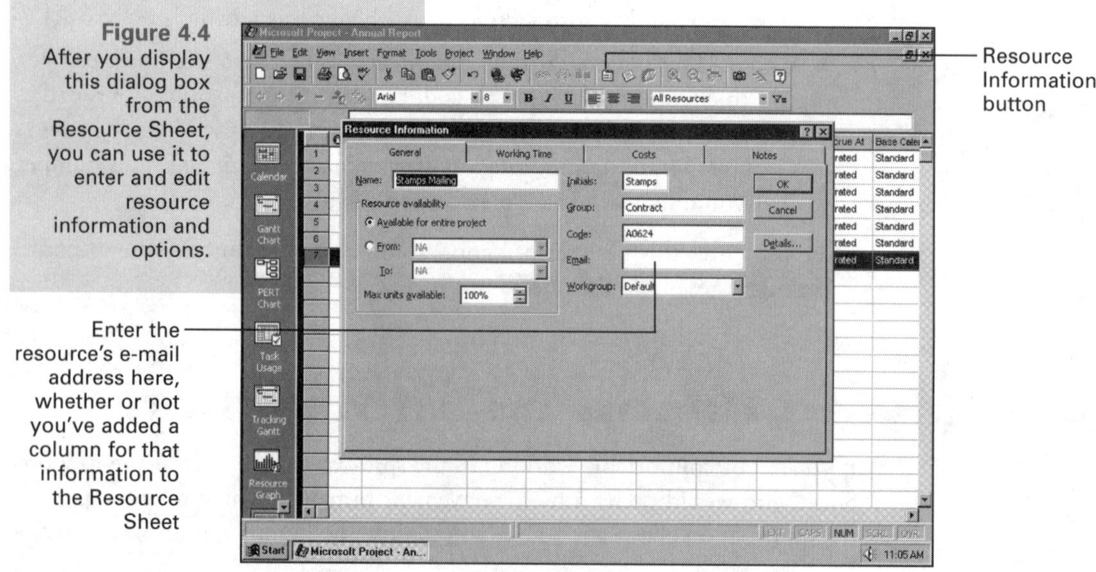

Figure 4.4 After you display this dialog box from the Resource Sheet, you can use it to enter and edit resource information and options.

To display the Resource Information dialog box for a resource in any view in Project that shows all or part of the Resource Sheet, start by clicking a cell in the row for the desired resource. Then, open the Project menu and click Resource Information (or right-click, and then click Resource Information). Alternately, press Shift+F2 or click the Resource Information button on the Standard toolbar. Enter or edit information about the resource in the dialog box, and then click OK to close the dialog box and accept the entries you made. Your changes appear in the appropriate columns for the selected task in the Resource Sheet.

You also can display information about a resource by double-clicking any cell in that resource's row in the Resource Sheet.

You can create a new resource by clicking a blank row of the Resource Sheet, displaying the Resource Information dialog box, entering information about the new resource, and clicking OK.

Assigning Resource Costs

There's a cost associated with every resource, even when the resource is seemingly free because it comes from within your company. In fact, tracking your use of internal resources throughout the year can be useful during year-end budgeting, when your company determines how costs from administrative or service departments are allocated to (charged to) departments that are profit centers. For example, you don't want your department to be charged for a third of the marketing department's time if your department only used about 10 percent of that time, while two other profit centers each used 45 percent.

Similarly, you want to be smart about using resources with the correct responsibility level for projects, and resource cost can help you make such decisions. For example, let's say that one task in a project is calling various companies for examples of annual reports to use as idea-starters for the project. A designer in your company is paid about $15 per hour, and an administrative assistant is paid $10 per hour, and both resources are capable of and have the time to make the calls. In this case, it's much more efficient to have the less-expensive resource, the administrative assistant, handle the calls. Such a strategy frees up more of the designer's time for true creative work, yielding better financial and design results on your project and more time for other projects.

If your company doesn't require you to track internal resource costs, then don't enter any cost information for the resource. This will simplify tracking for costs that you do have to report.

Three columns on the Resource Sheet enable you to assign default costs to the work performed by a resource. For most of these entries, you can simply select the cell and make your entry. Here are the fields that control costs on the Resource Sheet:

- **Std. Rate**—Enter the cost for work performed by the resource during normal working hours. To indicate an hourly rate, simply enter the hourly cost, such as 20 for $20 per hour. However, if the resource charges or will be paid by the minute (m), day (d), or week (w), enter the appropriate abbreviation along with your cost, such as 2000/w for $2,000 per week. You also can enter yearly salary amounts using the y abbreviation, and Project calculates the appropriate compensation for the actual length of the task.
- **Ovt. Rate**—If there's a possibility the resource will be working overtime on your project and your company is willing (or required by law, as for hourly, non-exempt workers) to pay a premium for the overtime, enter the overtime rate for the resource in this column, using the same method and abbreviations described above for the Std. Rate column.
- **Cost/Use**—A resource might have a set cost every time you use it; this cost might be the total cost for using the resource, or might supplement the hourly rate. For example, a courier service might charge you a set fee per delivery rather than an hourly rate. Or, a resource might charge you a set travel fee to your office in addition to an hourly rate. Enter an amount in this column (such as 15 for $15) to charge that fee to your project each time you assign the resource to a task and the task is completed.

If you're a consultant and need to provide both schedules and cost estimates for clients, assigning costs to every resource can help you build a reasonably accurate cost estimate. Build some cushion into the cost estimate you provide to your client, however, unless the client is willing to pay for budget overruns.

Setting How Costs are Calculated

As you just learned, the costs for a resource can be calculated based on units of work completed, a per use fee, or both. Most of us, however, aren't foolish enough to pay for work before it's completed—and doing so isn't a standard accounting practice. On the other hand, it's not reasonable to expect that all task costs for any given task will hit your project's bottom line after the work on the task is completed, especially if the task lasts more than a week or so.

To have a realistic picture of the costs incurred for your project at any given date, you need to specify the correct option for the resource's costs using the Accrue At column in the Resource Sheet or the Cost Accrual drop-down list on the Costs tab of the Resource Information dialog box. After you click a cell in the Accrue At column on the Resource Sheet, a drop-down list arrow appears at the right end of the cell. Click this arrow to display the Accrue At choices (see Figure 4.5), which are identical to the Cost Accrual drop-down list choices on the Costs tab of the Resource Information dialog box, and then click the method you want to select for the current resource:

- **Start**—Specifies that a resource's total cost for a task is expended as soon as work on the task starts. Use this method if you need to pay for contract work when the work begins. This choice also applies when a resource has only a per use cost that's due in advance, such as having to pay for a supply when you order it.
- **Prorated**—Under this method (the default), costs hit your project's bottom line as the work progresses. For example, if a resource charges $10 per hour and has completed 10 hours of work on a task, under this Accrue At method, the project shows $100 in expenses to date for the task. Use this method when tracking expenses for resources within your company, or for resources that you need to pay on a regular monthly basis.

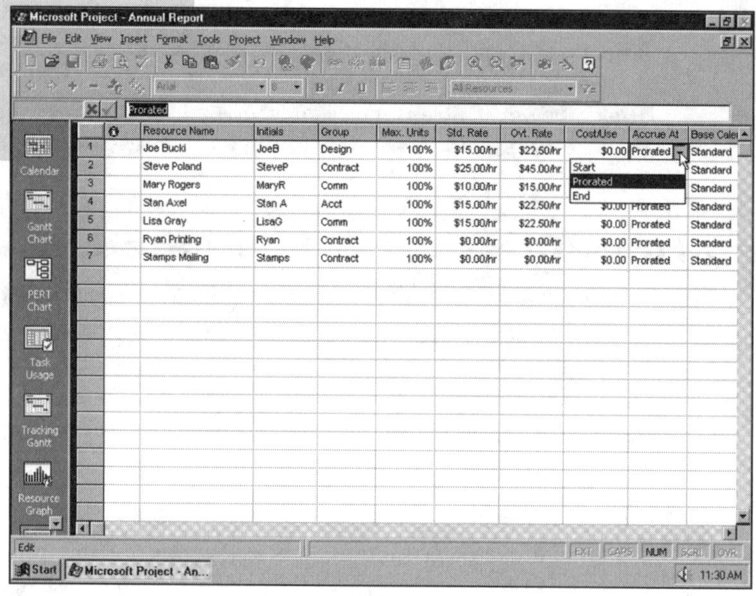

Figure 4.5 Use the drop-down list to select an Accrue At method.

Using the Prorated Accrue At method for resources that you work with only on a Per Use fee structure can lead to inaccurate reporting, because you might owe the full fee even if you need the resource for less time. For example, if you rent certain equipment, there might be a per-use minimum fee, due in advance. Make sure that you change the Accrue At method to Start or End for such resources.

- **End**—This method specifies that the expense will officially be charged to the project when the task is completed. Use this choice when you need to approve work before payment or when payment isn't due until work on a task is completed.

Creating Variable Pay Rates with Cost Rate Tables

The last version of Project assumed that cost values for a resource were set in stone for the duration of the project. However, business' ongoing pursuit to trim and accurately predict costs dictated that Project 98 offer more precise, flexible methods of tracking costs. In Project 98, you can set up *cost rate tables* to help you account for moving targets such as the following:

- **Scheduled pay rate increases or volume decreases.** If an internal resource's pay will increase on a particular date during the schedule, Project can automatically increase the Std. Rate and Ovt. Rate for the resource on the date you specify in the default cost rate table for the resource. Similarly, if an external resource's rates will increase or decrease (due to surpassing a minimum volume breakpoint) on a particular date (typically the start of a new calendar year) you can have Project automatically apply the rate increase when it kicks in by specifying the rate change on the resource's default cost rate table.
- **One resource, many rates.** For some resources, you might pay different rates depending on the nature of the work needed to complete different tasks. You'll typically encounter such a cost structure when you're working with an outside resource such as a consulting company. Such companies usually charge one rate for work by a partner or account manager, and another rate for work performed by assistants. Or, for example, the firm might charge one rate for research, another for designing a campaign or publication, and another for account administration. When a resource charges different rates for different tasks, you need to create a separate cost rate table for each rate, and then assign the appropriate cost table for each task you assign to the resource, as described later in this chapter under "Changing the Cost Table for an Assignment."

If a consulting firm doesn't provide a rate reduction for work handled by assistant-level folks, ask for such a reduction to reduce your costs.

- **Mixing hourly with per-use costs.** A resource might charge a per-use fee or other type of fee for some types of tasks, but not others. For example, if an outside consulting firm charges a fixed fee for preparing your monthly company newsletter but charges you an hourly fee for all other work, you'll need separate cost rate tables for the resource. One cost rate table would hold the per-use fee, and the other would hold the hourly rate. Then, you could assign the rate table that applies to each task assignment.

- **Periods with special rates.** If you have to convince a resource to work at a time when that resource wouldn't typically be working, that resource might charge a premium rate. For example, a resource might charge double the hourly rate for work during the week between Christmas and New Year's Day. In such a case, you would enter the increase starting date and rate on a row of the resource's default cost rate table, and then on the next row enter the date when the rate would return to normal, along with the normal rate.

You use the Resource Information dialog box to create cost rate tables for a resource. Follow these steps to edit or adjust a cost rate table:

1. In the Resource Sheet, click a cell in the row for the resource for which you want to create a cost rate table; then click the Resource Information button on the Standard toolbar. Or, double-click a cell in the resource row. The Resource Information dialog box appears.
2. Click the Costs tab to display its options. The Cost Rate Tables area of the dialog box offers five tabs, each of which represents a separate cost rate table. The A (Default) tab's rates will be used for the resource unless you create entries on another cost rate table tab (B-E) and specify that tab for an assignment as described later in the chapter.
3. To specify a rate change for the resource, enter an Effective Date on the next empty row of the tab—in this case, the A (Default) tab. Then, enter the new Standard Rate or Overtime Rate in the appropriate cell on that row, or a new Per Use Cost on that row. You have to change each rate; Project does not calculate a new Overtime Rate if you change the Standard Rate. You can enter positive or negative percentages to have Project calculate each rate increase or decrease respectively. For example, if you know an internal resource will receive a 4 percent pay increase on a particular date, you can enter that increase percentage as shown in Figure 4.6 rather than calculate dollars and cents.
4. Repeat step 3 as many times as needed to build the A (Default) cost rate table. Each cost rate table can hold up to 25 rate changes.
5. To create a new cost rate table, click another tab under Cost Rate Tables.
6. If you're working with the first row on another cost rate table tab, don't edit its Effective Date entry; this will designate the rate entries on that row as the "base" or "default" rates for the new cost table. Otherwise, create the rates on the table as described in steps 3 and 4.
7. Repeat steps 5 and 6 to specify additional cost rate tables. You can create up to five for each project file.

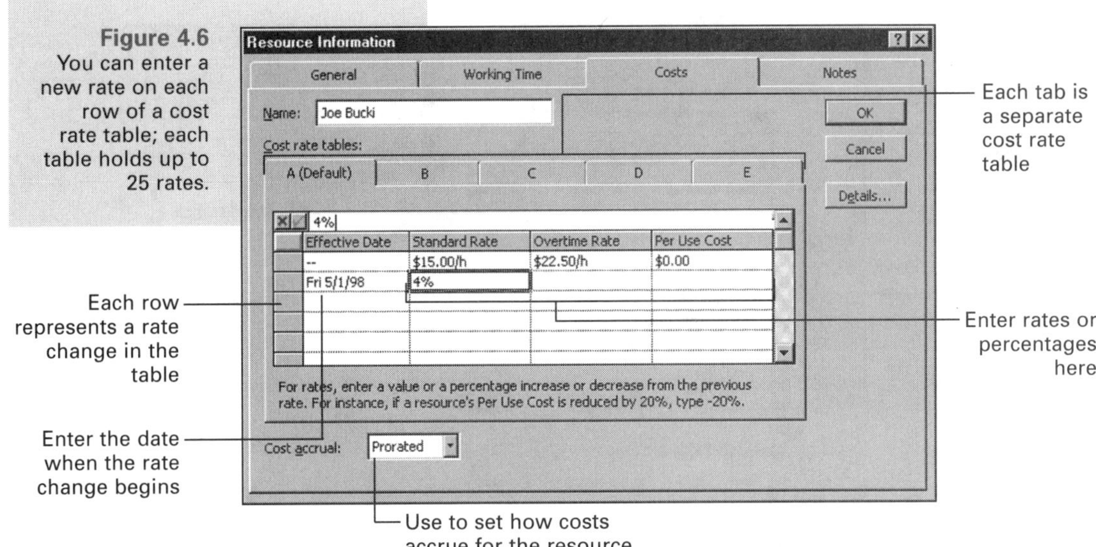

Figure 4.6 You can enter a new rate on each row of a cost rate table; each table holds up to 25 rates.

8. When you finish making cost rate table changes for the resource, click OK to close the Resource Information dialog box.

Working with Fixed Costs

Some tasks have a particular cost no matter which resource handles the work. For example, you might know from experience that the freight for a particular shipment of products costs approximately $1,000 if you use either of two shippers. Or, you might know what a particular type of material costs, or might have an accurate estimate of what it costs to complete the task.

In such a case, if the cost won't vary and you don't plan to assign a specific resource to the task, assign a fixed cost for the task rather than creating a resource entry with a per use or other cost assignment. You have to go back to Gantt Chart view to start this process, as indicated in the following steps:

1. Open the View menu and click Gantt Chart, if you're not already at the Gantt Chart view. Or, click the Gantt Chart icon in the View Bar.
2. Open the View menu, point to Table, and click Cost. The Task Sheet pane at the left side of the view changes to display columns specific to tracking costs for the tasks, as shown in Figure 4.7.

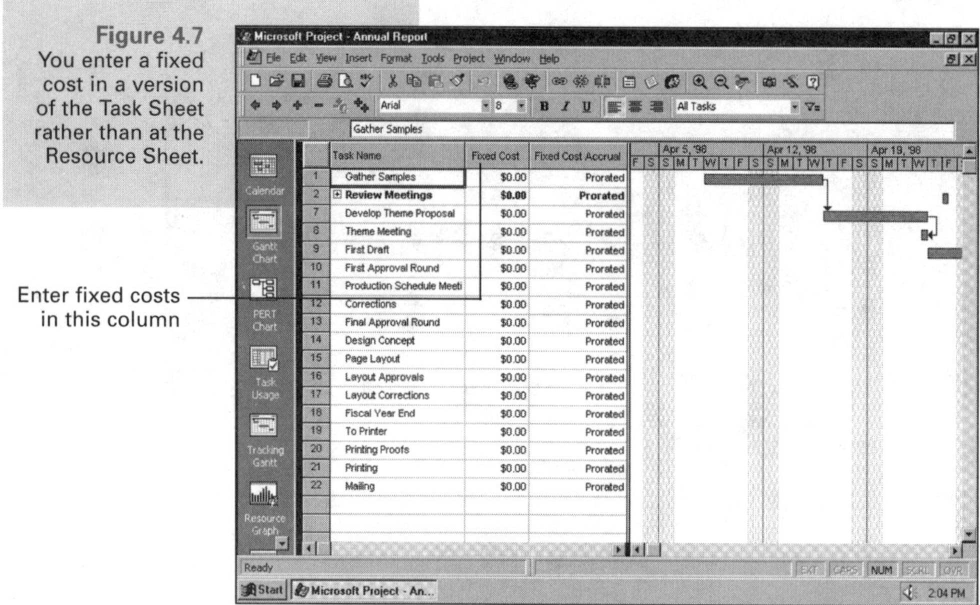

Figure 4.7 You enter a fixed cost in a version of the Task Sheet rather than at the Resource Sheet.

3. Click to select the Fixed Cost cell for the task for which you want to assign a fixed cost.
4. Type the amount (in dollars) of the fixed cost; for example, type 500 for $500. Press Enter or click the Enter button next to the text entry box to complete entering the fixed cost.
5. (Optional) Return to the view in which you were working by using a choice on the View menu; for example, open the View menu and click Resource Sheet or click the Resource Sheet icon in the View Bar. To simply change the Task Sheet pane of Gantt Chart view back to its normal entry mode, open the View menu, point to Table, and click Entry.

Working with Resource Calendars (Work Schedules)

By default, when you assign a resource to a task, Project assumes that the resource will follow the base calendar you established for the schedule (using the Calendar drop-down list in the Project Information dialog box, as discussed in Chapter 2, "Setting Up a Project"). Thus, if the normal workday is eight hours, the resource's typical workday is eight hours; under this scenario, it takes the resource three working days to complete a project that's 24 hours in duration. Sometimes, however, a resource's real working schedule differs from that of the project.

Under Project's effort-driven default scheduling method, you need to ensure that you specify the real working schedule for each resource to develop an accurate schedule. For example, if the base calendar for the project is set to 24 hours, but the resource works only eight hours per day, the durations for the tasks you assign to that resource need to be three times longer than you had anticipated.

Choosing a Calendar

Use the Base Calendar column of the Resource Sheet to select the appropriate working schedule for a resource. The base calendars available for resources are the same as those available for projects. The 24 Hours calendar runs round the clock, seven days a week. The Standard calendar provides 40 hours per week, scheduled 8 a.m. to noon and 1 p.m. to 5 p.m., Monday through Friday. The Night Shift schedule also offers 40 hours per week, scheduled from Monday evening through early Saturday morning.

To change the Base Calendar entry for a resource, click the Base Calendar cell for the resource. When you do so, a drop-down list arrow appears at the right end of the text entry box. Click this arrow to display the three choices, click the calendar you want, and then press Enter or click the Enter button next to the text entry box.

Setting Resource Availability

You may find yourself competing for a highly desirable resource. For example, a resource may be tied up with other projects until three weeks after your project starts. In such a case, rather than tediously marking nonworking days in the resource's base calendar (see the final part of this section, next), you should instead specify availability dates for the resource. Similarly, if you're sharing a resource with another department, Project offers an easy availability setting to account for that without adjusting the resource's working calendar. Project uses availability settings and the resource's base calendar together to determine whether a resource can take on a task and to calculate how long it will take the resource to complete the task.

Note

When you're working in the Gantt Chart view, Project will let you assign a resource a task that occurs during a period when you indicated that a resource isn't available. If you check the Resource Usage view (described later in this chapter) or other views that highlight when you assign too much work to a resource (see Chapter 5, "Resolving Overallocations and Overbooked Resources"), you'll clearly see that you assigned a task to a resource that's not available.

Follow these steps to change a resource's availability:

1. In the Resource Sheet, click a cell in the row for the resource for which you want to set availability; then click the Resource Information button on the Standard toolbar. Or, double-click a cell in the resource row. The Resource Information dialog box appears, with the General tab selected.
2. To specify the first date on which the resource becomes available, click the From option button; then enter a date in the From text box by clicking the drop-down arrow at the right end of the text box, and then choosing a date from the drop-down calendar. Figure 4.8 shows a From date entered for a resource.

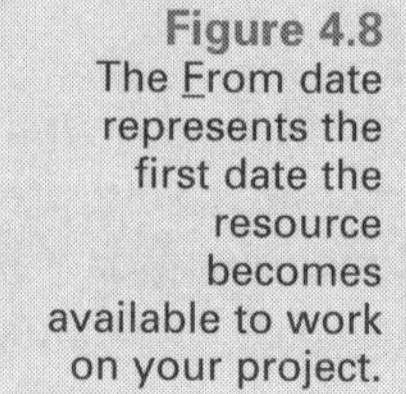

Figure 4.8
The From date represents the first date the resource becomes available to work on your project.

3. If the resource will become unavailable again after a certain date, specify that date by clicking the drop-down arrow at the right end of the To text box, and then choosing a date from the drop-down calendar. However, leave the To text box set to "NA" if the resource will remain available.

If you're removing availability dates you entered for a resource, click the Available for Entire Project option button, which removes From and To settings.

4. Use the Max Units Available text box or spinner buttons to specify how many work units the resource will provide for the task. For example, changing this value to 300% (or 3 if you're specifying work units as decimals) means the resource (such as an outside contractor) will provide three people to work full-time on the project. In contrast, if a resource can only work two hours per day (out of an eight-hour schedule) on your project, you would need to decrease this setting to 25% (.25 for decimals) to help Project accurately schedule the duration for any task the resource will be handling.
5. Click OK to finish changing the resource's availability settings.

Customizing a Resource Calendar

Sometimes you need to adjust the base calendar for a resource. For example, a resource might work two shifts per day, four days per week. Or, a resource might be unavailable on Wednesdays, or only available to work half-time for a few days during the schedule. To ensure that the effort-driven scheduling properly adjusts the durations of tasks to which you assign this resource, and to prevent you from scheduling the resource for times when it is unavailable, make sure that you adjust the selected base calendar for any resource that has special scheduling requirements.

To do so, follow these steps:

1. In the Resource Sheet, use the Base Calendar column to select the working schedule that most closely approximates the actual availability of the resource.
2. In the Resource Sheet, click a cell in the row for the resource for which you want to set availability; then click the Resource Information button on the Standard toolbar. Or, double-click a cell in the resource row.

When the Resource Information dialog box appears, click the Working Time tab to display it, as shown in Figure 4.9. Alternately, after you click a cell in the resource's row, choose Tools, Change Working Time.

3. To specify whether the resource works on a particular day, click on the date you want to change on the calendar. Then, in the For selected dates area of the dialog box, click on Working Time or Nonworking Time as needed. Dates to specify as Nonworking include holidays and vacation days.

The Use Default selection returns a date to its default scheduling according to the selected base calendar. This includes both rescheduling the task as a working or nonworking day and returning the Working Time entries to the defaults for the selected date.

4. To change the Working Time (daily working hours) for a date, select the date, and then make sure either the Working Time or the Use Default option button is selected for it under For selected dates. In the Working Time area, edit or delete the desired From and To entries.

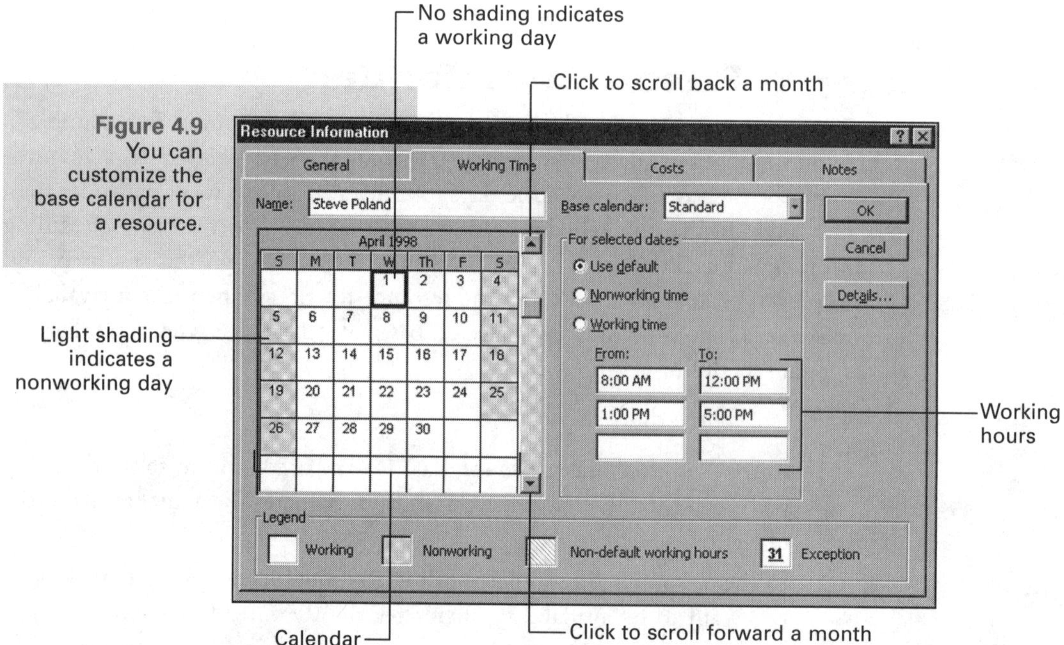

Figure 4.9 You can customize the base calendar for a resource.

5. Continue scrolling the Calendar view as needed, repeating steps 4 and 5 to change the schedule for additional dates. As you change the schedule for each date, Project indicates the edited date in the calendar, by marking the date with bold and underlining, and filling the date box with light-gray shading.
6. Click OK to close the dialog box and implement the scheduling changes you specified.

Adding a Resource Note

Just as you can add more detailed notes about a particular task you created, you can use a note to capture information about a specific resource. This feature can be particularly important when you're working with outside resources, or when a resource is handling especially complex tasks. For example, you can use a note to record detailed contact information for your contact at an external vendor. Or, you can add a note to a resource explaining why the resource has a per use fee in addition to an hourly rate. You can remind yourself of the names of key clients the resource has served in the past, in case someone working with your project file is interested in knowing more about the project resources.

To enter or edit note information about a resource in the Resource Sheet, do the following:

1. Click a cell in the row holding the resource for which you want to create a note.
2. Click the Project menu or right-click to display the resource shortcut menu. Click Resource Notes. Alternatively, click the Resource Notes button on the Standard toolbar. The Resource Information dialog box appears, with the Notes tab selected. (If you double-click the resource entry, instead, you can then click the Notes tab in the Resource Information dialog box.)
3. Click in the Notes text box, and then type or edit the text of your note (see Figure 4.10). Press Enter to start each new line in the note. You can add special formatting to notes using the buttons at the top of the Notes text area. The first button enables you to change the font for any text you select by dragging over it in the note; it displays the Font dialog box, which Chapter 14, "Other Formatting," covers. The next three buttons align the current note line (which holds the blinking insertion point) left, center, and right, respectively. The fourth button adds or removes a bullet at the beginning of the current line of the

note. The last button enables you to insert an embedded object into the note, such as information from Excel or a bitmap image; Chapter 18 provides more information on working with embedded objects. If you highlight and delete all of this text, Project removes the note altogether from the resource.

4. Click OK to close the Resource Information dialog box.

After you add a note to a resource, you can point to the note indicator on the Resource Sheet to display the note in a pop-up box.

Assigning a Resource to a Task

Until now, this book has described tasks and resources as somewhat separate, discrete entities. You enter information about tasks in one part of Project and information about resources in another. In this section, you learn to mesh these two forms of information in your schedule. Keep in mind that the resources you assign to a particular task might cause Project to adjust the start or finish date for the task, depending on the availability of the resource. If a resource assignment causes a schedule change you don't want, use one of the methods described later in this section to choose a different resource for the task.

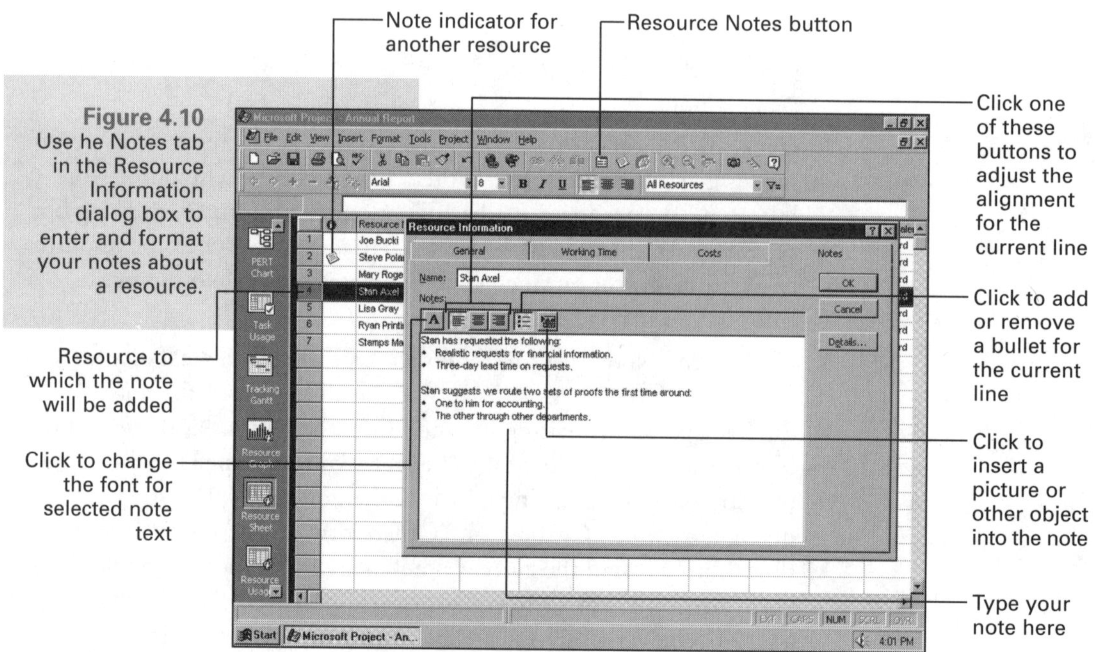
Note indicator for another resource
Resource Notes button
Click one of these buttons to adjust the alignment for the current line
Click to add or remove a bullet for the current line
Click to insert a picture or other object into the note
Type your note here
Resource to which the note will be added
Click to change the font for selected note text
Resource Information
Stan has requested the following:
Realistic requests for financial information.
Three-day lead time on requests.
Stan suggests we route two sets of proofs the first time around:
One to him for accounting.
The other through other departments.

Figure 4.10 Use he Notes tab in the Resource Information dialog box to enter and format your notes about a resource.

To assign resources to a particular task, you need to return to the location where you list the tasks for your schedule, the Task Sheet in the Gantt Chart view, or (in most cases) another view, the Task Entry view. To speed your work with resources, you might also want to display the Resource Management toolbar. To do so, right-click any toolbar onscreen and click Resource Management.

Note

You also can work with task and resource information in other views. Chapter 9, "Working with the Different Project Views," introduces more of the available views and helps you work with task and resource information. Most of the options in other views, however, work like the ones described here. Therefore, after you learn to display the views discussed in Chapter 9, you can apply the techniques you learn here to working in those views, as well.

If you're most comfortable working in the Task Sheet, you might prefer to assign resources there by using the Resource Names column, which provides a drop-down list of available resources. Switch to the Task Sheet, if necessary, by opening the View menu and clicking Gantt Chart; or click the Gantt Chart icon in the View Bar. Scroll the Task Sheet pane so that it shows the Resource Names column. Click the cell for the task to which you want to assign a resource. If you remember the full resource name, type it in the selected cell and press Enter. Otherwise, click the drop-down list arrow that appears at the right end of the cell; click the name of the resource you want (see Figure 4.11), and then press Enter or click the Enter button.

If you type the name of a resource in the Resource Names column of the Task Sheet in Gantt Chart view, and the name is for a brand-new resource, Project adds a new row for that resource in the Resource Sheet. You then can open the View menu and click Resource Sheet or click the Resource Sheet icon in the View Bar to switch to the Resource Sheet, where you can enter the remaining information about the resource.

If you're not comfortable with a lot of typing, or plan to enter multiple resources and want a faster method, you can display and use the Assign Resources dialog box. (You can't use this method to assign a resource to a sum-

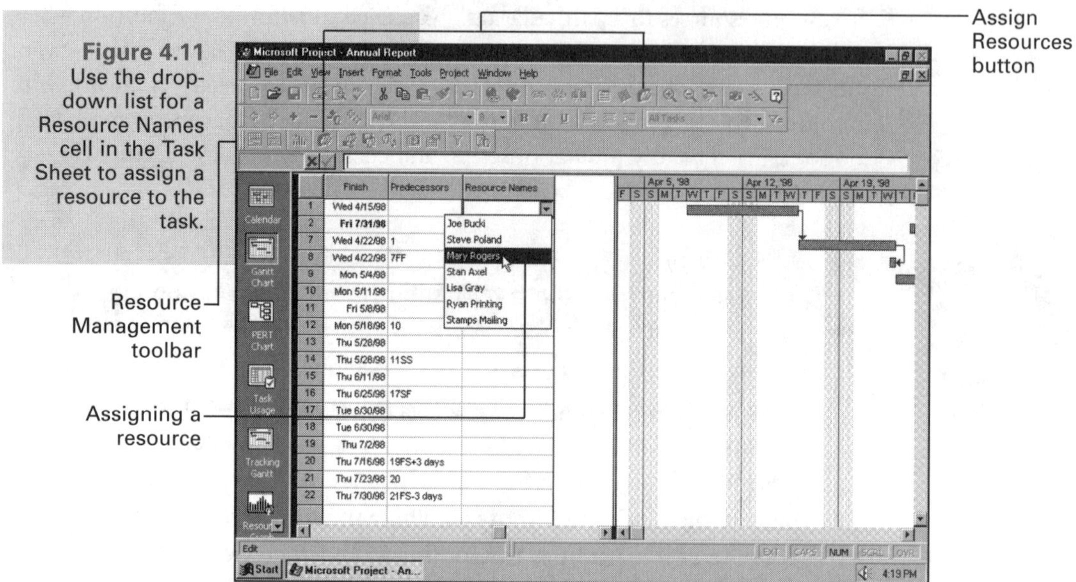

Figure 4.11 Use the drop-down list for a Resource Names cell in the Task Sheet to assign a resource to the task.

mary task; you can only use this method to assign resources to the tasks being summarized, if they're displayed.) To display this dialog box, click a cell in the task for which you want to add resources. Open the Tools menu, point to Resources, and click Assign Resources. Alternately, click the Assign Resources button on the Standard or Resource Management toolbar, or press Alt+F10. The Assign Resources dialog box appears, as shown in Figure 4.12.

To assign a resource to the cell you selected, click the desired resource name in the Resources From list, and then choose Assign. You can continue using this dialog box to assign resources to other tasks. Simply select the Resource Names cell for another task, and then use the Resource Assignment dialog box to select and Assign the resource. When you finish assigning resources, click Close to close the Resource Assignment dialog box.

A final way to assign a resource to a single task from the Task Sheet is to right-click the task, and then click the Task Information command (or click the Task Information button on the Standard toolbar). In the Task Information dialog box, click the Resources tab. Click the first blank Resource Name row, click the drop-down list arrow that appears beside the cell, click a resource name, and click the Enter button. Click OK to close the Task Information dialog box.

The biggest drawback to a couple of the resource assignment techniques just described is that unless you display the whole Task Sheet, you might not be able to see the name of the task to which you're assigning a resource. You can

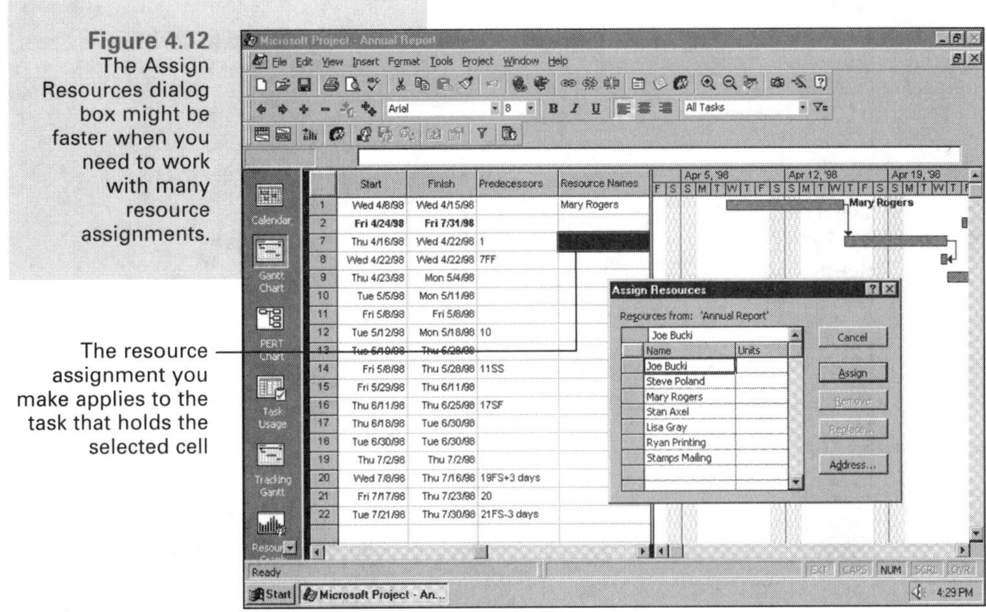

Figure 4.12 The Assign Resources dialog box might be faster when you need to work with many resource assignments.

The resource assignment you make applies to the task that holds the selected cell

use another view, Task Entry view, to enable you to be clear about which task you're entering a resource for. This view is sometimes referred to as the Task Form. To use this view to assign resources to tasks, do the following:

1. To switch to Task Entry view, click the Task Entry View button on the Resource Management toolbar. Alternately, open the View menu and click More Views or click the More Views icon in the View Bar; then, in the Views list, scroll down to display Task Entry, click it, and click Apply. The Task Entry view appears, as shown in Figure 4.13.
2. Select a task by choosing it from the Task Name column of the visible portion of the Task Sheet, or by using the Previous and Next buttons in the lower area of the view.
3. Click the first blank row of the Resource Name column of the lower portion of the view. A highlight appears on the name of the selected task in the Task Sheet.
4. Click the drop-down list arrow that appears at the right end of the selected cell under Resource Name, and then click the name of the resource you want to select. Click OK (which appears in place of the Previous button) to complete your entry. After you do so, information about the selected resource appears in the lower pane of the display, as shown in Figure 4.14.
5. Repeat steps 2–5 to assign resources to other tasks.

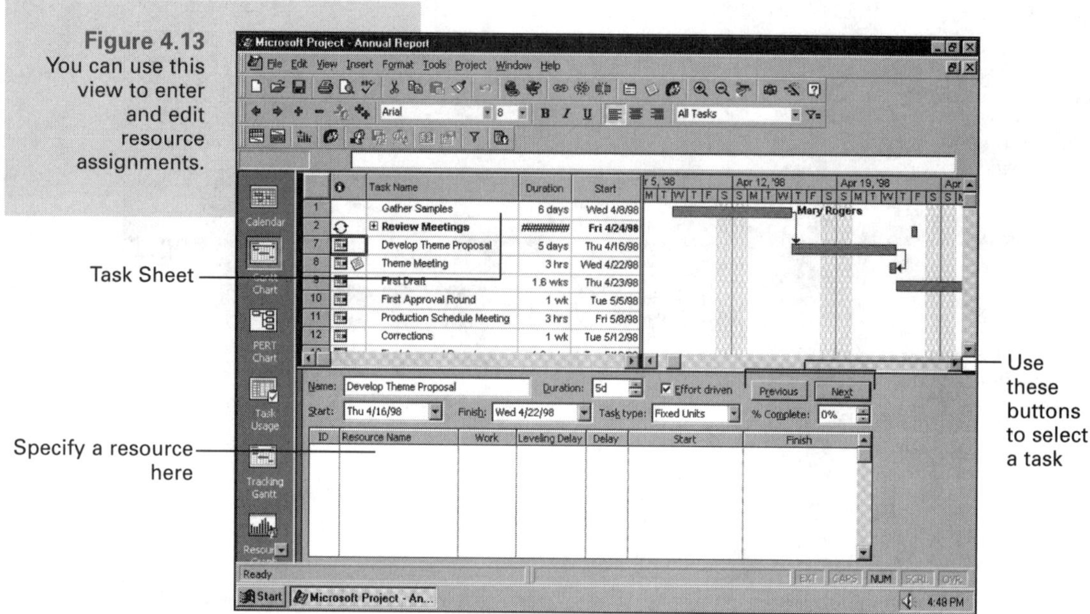

Figure 4.13 You can use this view to enter and edit resource assignments.

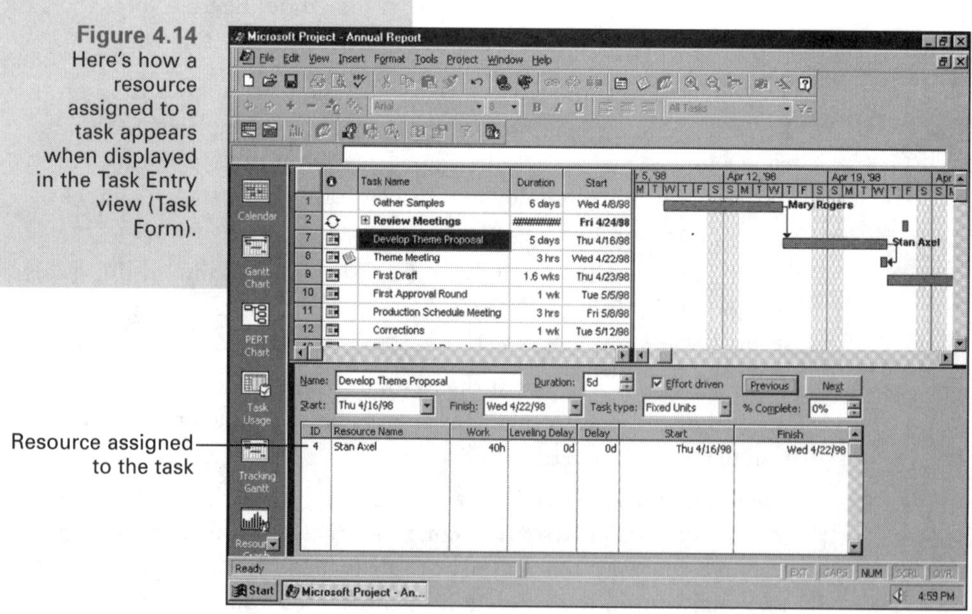

Figure 4.14 Here's how a resource assigned to a task appears when displayed in the Task Entry view (Task Form).

When you finish working in Task Entry view, open the View menu and click the appropriate menu command to return to another view, such as Gantt Chart. If the window remains divided into upper and lower panes, remove the split by opening the Window menu and clicking Remove Split.

Start Dates and Delays

As you can see in the lower pane of the Task Entry view in Figure 4.14, the view shows the task and resource names, task duration, number of work hours the resource will require to finish the project, and Start and Finish dates. Beside the Start column, however, you'll find the Delay column. You can use this column to specify that you don't want a resource to begin exactly when the start of the working day begins, or that you have more than one resource assigned to the task (see the next two chapters for more details) and want one to start a certain length of time after the first resource, perhaps to check the first resource's work.

To enter a delay for a resource, switch to Task Entry view, and display the task information by clicking the task in the Task Name column of the Task Sheet (or by using the Previous and Next buttons). Click the Delay column and enter the delay time period, along with a time unit specification such as **h** for hours or **d** for days. Figure 4.15 shows an example.

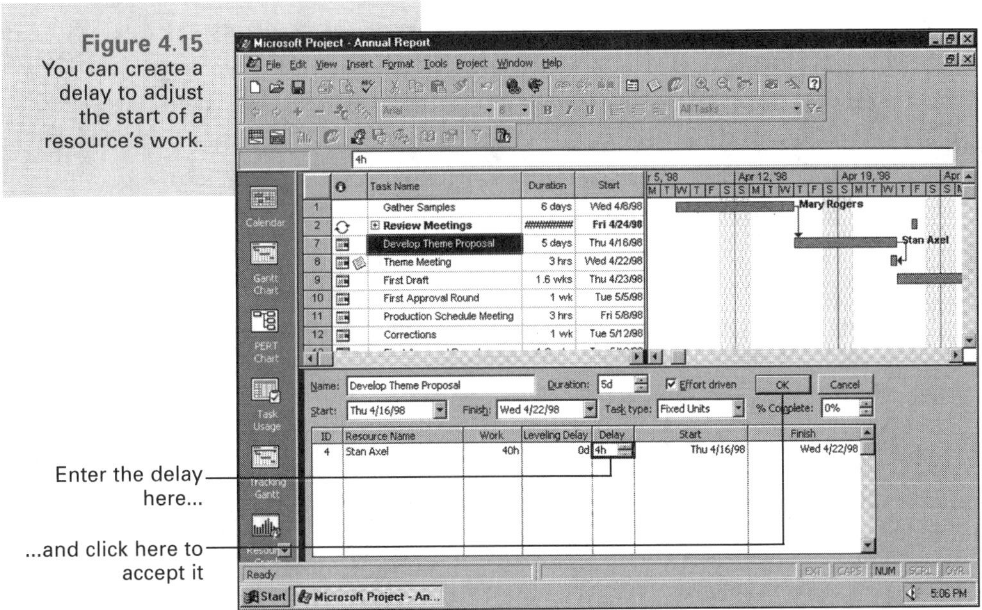

Figure 4.15
You can create a delay to adjust the start of a resource's work.

Click OK in the lower pane of the view to complete specifying the delay. If necessary—for example when you're creating a delay for the sole resource assigned to the task—Project adjusts the start and finish dates for the task. Keep in mind that such changes can introduce scheduling conflicts, particularly if other linked tasks depend on the scheduled completion of the task you're working with.

Overriding an Effort-Driven Duration

This chapter has noted repeatedly that under Project's default effort-driven method of scheduling tasks, the resource(s) you assign to a task might cause Project to adjust the schedule for the task depending on the resource's availability (Max Units Available on the General tab of the Resource Information dialog box, where each *unit* represents one person working full-time on the task, as determined by the resource's base calendar, compared with the calendar for the task). By default, the total number of hours allocated to the task (called the *work*) remains constant as you add more resources (*units*), with the *duration* being adjusted accordingly. For example, if a four-day task has the Standard eight-hour calendar, and a resource also uses the Standard eight-hour calendar as its working calendar but has 200% Max Units Available (two people working full-time on the task), applying that resource to the task reduces its duration to 2 days.

Note

The equation Duration*Units=Work establishes the relationship between the duration, units, and work for a task. So, Project does a little algebra to arrive at the equation that keeps work constant and adjusts the duration under the default effort-driven scheduling settings: Duration=Work/Units.

You can stop Project from making duration, work, or units changes for selected tasks, if you want, by changing the Task Type setting:

- **Fixed Units.** This is the default when effort-driven scheduling is enabled. Adding more resources makes the duration shorter, and removing resources increase the duration.
- **Fixed Work.** This setting disables effort-driven scheduling, and in most cases has the same effect as changing a task type to fixed units: adding resources shortens the duration, and removing resources increases the

duration. There's an exception, though. Each resource can't provide more work (hours) per day than the task's schedule allows. For example, if you create a four-day task and select Fixed Work as the Task Type, then, you assign a resource with 200% set as its Max Units Available setting on the General tab of the Resource Information dialog box. For a Fixed Unit task, Project would decrease the task duration to two days, but for a Fixed Work task the duration remains at four days, because a single resource can't work more than the allotted number of working hours per day on the task. Project halves the available units so that the work setting and duration can remain constant.

- **Fixed Duration.** This setting keeps the duration constant when you apply resources to the task. For example, if your project requires filing accounting information by a particular federal filing deadline, you'll want the duration and schedule for the task to remain fixed. Adding resources to this task decreases the amount of work each resource contributes on each day. For example, if you apply two full-time resources to a four-day task, Project doesn't cut the duration in half; it cuts the number of hours (work) each resource supplies each day in half.

You can specify the task type for a task in the Task Entry view by selecting the task in the visible portion of the Task Sheet. Then click the Task Type drop-down list in the bottom area of the view, and click the desired task type. You also can specify a task type for a task from any view that shows the Task Sheet. Right-click the task you want to fix, and then click Task Information; alternately, click the task, and then click the Task Information button on the Standard toolbar. The Task Information dialog box appears. Click the Advanced tab. Click to open the Task Type drop-down list (see Figure 4.16), and then click the task type you want. Click OK to close the dialog box.

Figure 4.16 Use the drop-down list shown in this dialog box to control whether Project adjusts the task's schedule.

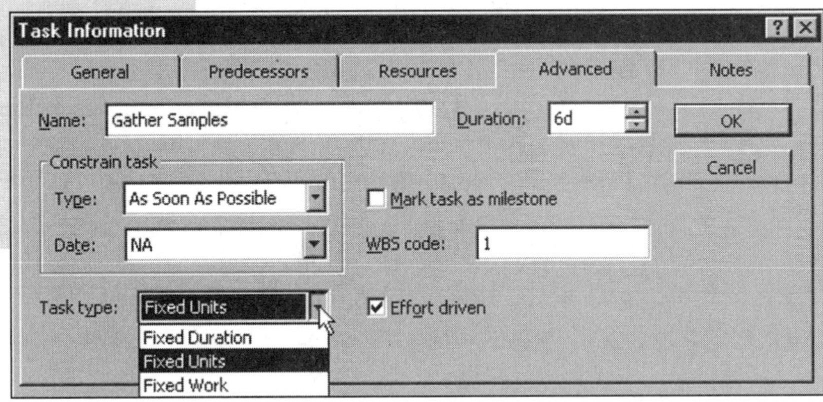

If you want all new tasks to be scheduled with the task type you select, use the Default Task Type drop-down list on the Schedule tab of the Options dialog box. Chapter 20, "Customizing Microsoft Project," explains how to change this and other default settings.

Turning Off Effort-Driven Scheduling

You also can turn off the effort-driven scheduling feature for a task to "disable" the Duration*Units=Work equation, so that adding more resources doesn't automatically increase the duration, but instead adds more units and work. In the Task Entry view, click the check beside the Effort Drive check box to clear it. Or, on the Advanced tab of the Task Information dialog box, clear the check mark beside Effort Driven.

Deleting Resources

There are instances when a resource is no longer needed, either within a task assignment or within the Resource Sheet. At that point, you'll want to delete it.

From a Task

To delete a resource from a task, you can use any of a number of methods, depending on the current view. From the Task Sheet view, click any cell in the task for which you want to remove the resource. Display the Assign Resources dialog box by clicking on the Assign Resources button on the Standard or Resource Management toolbar (or pressing Alt+F10). In the Assign Resources dialog box, click the resource to delete, which has a check mark beside it to indicate that it's assigned to the current task. Click Remove to remove the resource. From here, you can use the dialog box to add and remove resources for other tasks, or can simply click Close to close the dialog box.

You can use Task Entry view to make removing a resource from a task even easier. Simply click the name of the resource to delete in the Resource Name column of the bottom pane, then press Delete, and then click OK.

Selecting a cell in the Resource Names column and pressing Delete deletes the whole task entry, not just the resource. To delete the Resource Names entry only, right-click the appropriate cell and click Clear Contents.

From the Project

Just as you can use the Resource Sheet to add new resources to a project, you can use the Resource Sheet to remove entries for resources you no longer use. For example, say that you added the name of a person from another department to the resource list, but that person has been transferred to another city and is no longer available to work on the project. After you open the View menu and click Resource Sheet or click the Resource Sheet icon in the View Bar, use either of the following methods to remove the resource:

- Select any cell in the resource you want deleted, then press Delete.
- Click the row number for the resource you want deleted; this selects the whole row. Open the Edit menu and click Delete Resource (or right-click the selected row to access the shortcut menu, and then click Delete Resource).

Working with Assignments

Project 98 provides a new way of looking at the interplay between tasks and the resources assigned to complete them. A view that shows *assignments* lists each task in the Task Sheet as a summary task, with each resource assigned to the task listed in a subtask row below the task. Each resource listing under the task is an assignment—a specific task assigned to a specific resource. So, if you have a task to which you assigned three resources, that task has three assignments—one for each resource.

Assignments not only enable you to re-examine which resources will be handling which tasks, but they also provide an additional level of detail for adjusting your schedule. For example, you can adjust start and finish dates for one assignment (one resource working on a particular task) without adjusting the start and finish dates for the task as a whole or the other resources assigned to the same task.

Viewing Assigments

The Task Usage view offers a Task Sheet that includes both tasks and assignments. To switch to Task Usage view, click to open the View menu, and then click Task Usage. Or, click the Task Usage icon on the View Bar. The view, with tasks and assignments, appears onscreen, as shown in Figure 4.17.

You also can view assignments in the Resource Usage view, covered in the next chapter. The Resource Usage view lists each resource as a summary task, with individual assignments for that resource listed as subtasks.

In the Task Usage view, each task has a minus (-) symbol that you can use to display or hide the assignments for that task. Click the minus (-) symbol to hide the assignments and the plus (+) symbol to redisplay them. Or, you can use the outlining buttons on the Formatting toolbar (see Chapter 13, "Working with Outlining") to hide and display assignments for a task.

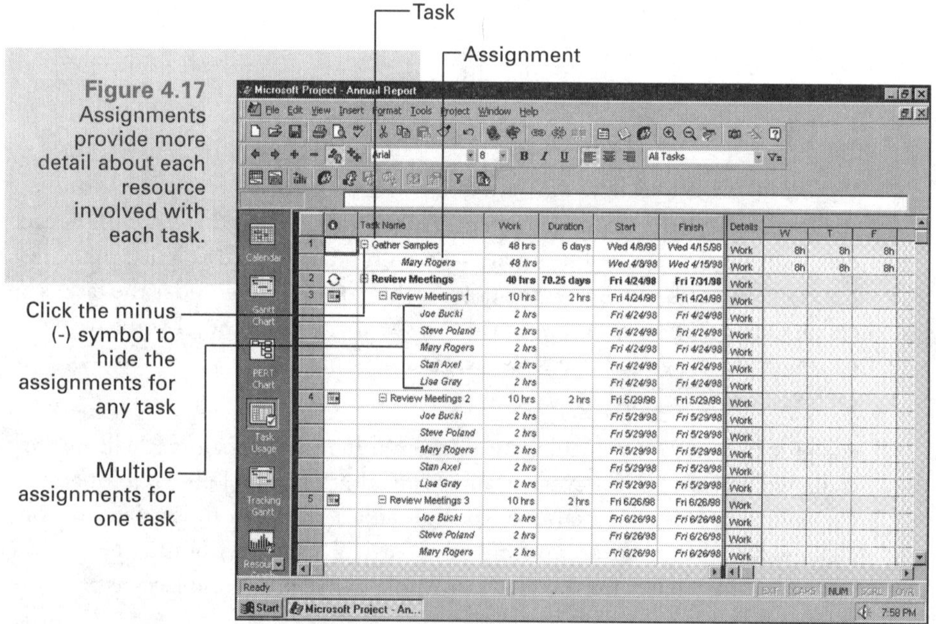

Figure 4.17 Assignments provide more detail about each resource involved with each task.

Displaying Assignment Information

The Assignment Information dialog box offers the settings for fine-tuning a selected assignment. To display the Assignment Information dialog box for an assignment, click a cell in the assignment row, and then click to open the Project menu or right-click the selected cell. In the menu or shortcut menu that appears, click Assignment Information. After you click a cell in an assignment row, you also can click the Assignment Information button on the Standard toolbar. Finally, you can simply double-click a cell in the assignment row. No matter which method you choose, the Assignment Information dialog box appears (see Figure 4.18).

I'll discuss specific settings in this dialog box where they apply later in the book, and simply touch on its three tabs here. After you make your changes in the Assignment Information dialog box, click OK to close it and make your changes take effect. Here's what you'll find on the three tabs:

- **General**—This tab enables you to adjust how much time the resource can spend on the assignment, such as when the resource can start work, how many units the resource can allocate to the assignment, and more.

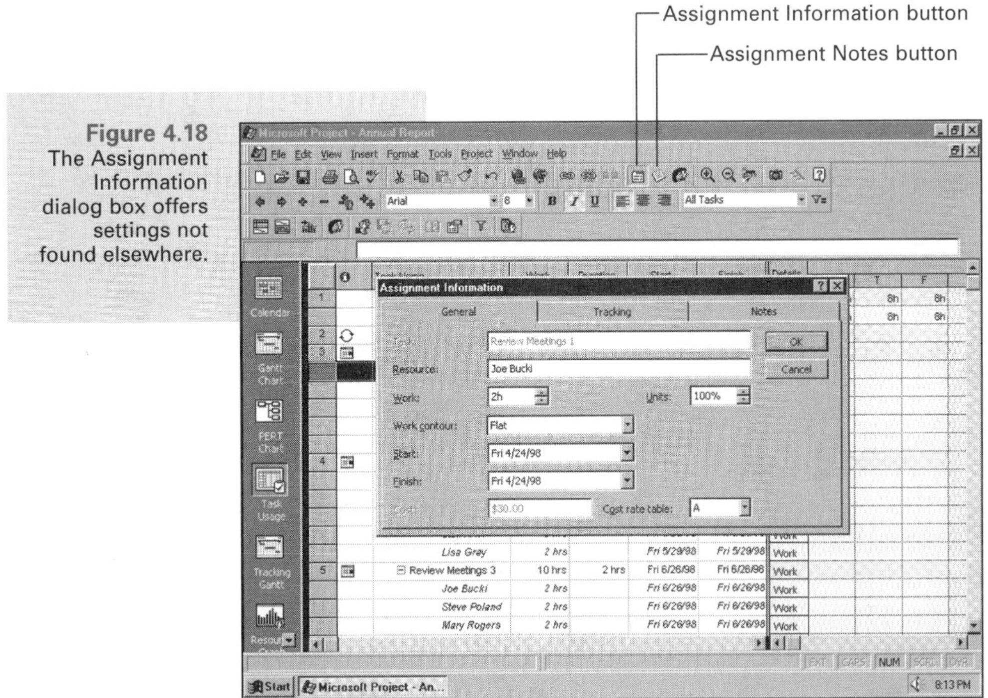

Figure 4.18 The Assignment Information dialog box offers settings not found elsewhere.

- **Tracking**—Use this tab to enter actual work the resource has completed on the assignment and the actual timing of that work.
- **Notes**—Use this tab to add a note for the assignment, using the same process described earlier under "Adding a Resource Note." You can display this tab directly for an assignment by clicking the Assignment Notes button on the Standard toolbar.

Changing the Cost Table for an Assignment

The section earlier in this chapter called "Creating Variable Pay Rates with Cost Rate Tables" explained how to create different cost rate tables for a resource, which you can use when a resource charges a different rate or fee for different types of work. Although rate changes within the A (Default) rate table apply automatically to all tasks on the dates that you specify, you must manually apply a different rate table to any assignment to which it applies. You do so by using the Assignment Information dialog box in the Task Usage view. Click a cell in assignment's row to specify the assignment; then click the Assignment Information button on the Standard toolbar or use one of the other methods described earlier for displaying the Assignment information dialog box. On the General tab, click to open the Cost Rate Table drop-down list, and then click on the cost rate table to use it. Click OK to close the dialog box and accept your change.

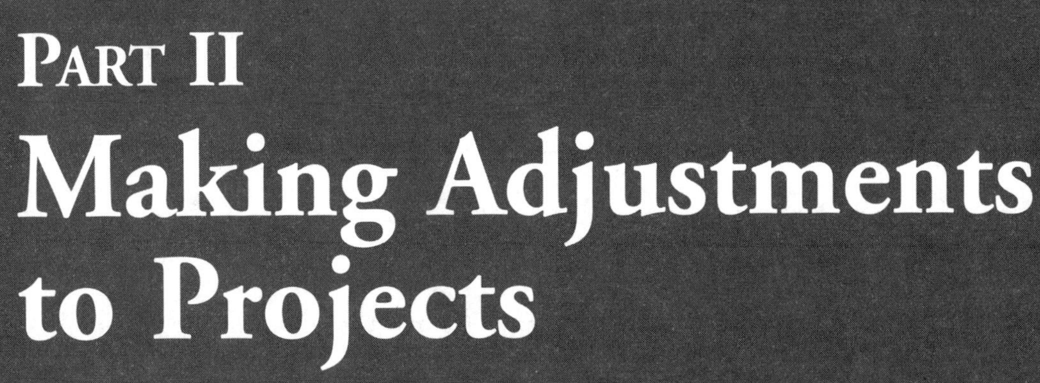

PART II
Making Adjustments to Projects

5

Resolving Overallocations and Overbooked Resources

In This Chapter

- What it means to overallocate a resource
- Finding overallocation problems in your plan
- Using automatic leveling to eliminate overbooked schedules
- Addressing overallocations on your own

I'm sure you've heard colleagues moan, "I wish there were more than 24 hours in a day, because I can't seem to get enough done." It might be a cliché, but only because it reflects our common tendency to cram too many activities into each and every day. As a leader under pressure, you'll need to fight this natural tendency when creating your project plans.

Project 98 provides features designed to help you make your schedule realistic and attainable. Some of the best of these features quietly point out to you when you've made a mistake such as assigning a resource 16 hours' worth of work on an eight-hour workday.

Discovering Overallocation

Early in the book, you learned to sketch out your schedule by simply listing the tasks to accomplish. Chapter 3 helped you make adjustments to the tasks you listed to help them flow together more cohesively. Chapter 4 focused on giving you the information you need to determine who handles what for your project, and now you need to go back and look at whether the resources you assigned to projects make sense.

Because Project uses effort-driven scheduling by default, you generally don't have to worry about having too few or too many resources assigned to a particular task. If the resource's working hours enable the resource to handle the task more quickly, Project shortens the task duration. Conversely, Project automatically lengthens the task if needed. For example, suppose that your schedule is based on a 24 Hours base calendar, but the resource you want to use follows the Standard calendar with eight-hour days. A task scheduled for one 24-hour day will be rescheduled to take three days if you assign the eight-hours-per-day resource to it.

Instead, what you need to be concerned about is assigning a resource to separate tasks that occur simultaneously. If your list includes 25 different tasks, then in theory, any number of them could partially occur during the same week. Let's say that the task in row 5 begins on the Monday of the third week of your project. The task in row 7 begins the same week, but on Thursday. You assigned the same resource to both tasks. Each of the tasks needs to be handled as quickly as possible, so it requires that the assigned resource give it full-time attention during the eight-hour workday defined for the project schedule. The problem is obvious; during Thursday and Friday, the resource needs to handle two full-time tasks. Thus, for Thursday and Friday, you've overallocated (overbooked) the selected resource.

You might be able to quickly spot overallocations in Gantt Chart view when tasks are close together in your list. Generally, though, you'll only be able to see 14 task rows onscreen at any time, so you can't visually compare the tasks in, let's say, rows 1 and 25 without scrolling back and forth. For that reason, Project provides a couple of other methods, described next, for quickly finding overallocations.

Finding Overallocations with the Resource Management Toolbar

If you need to identify an overallocation in the default Gantt Chart view, use the Resource Management toolbar. To display the Resource Management toolbar, right-click any toolbar onscreen; then select Resource Management. To go to a task in the Task Sheet that's assigned to an overallocated resource, click the Go To Next Overallocation button on the Resource Management toolbar. Project selects the indicator cell of the task with the overallocated resource, as shown in Figure 5.1. Clicking the Go To Next Overallocation button again takes you to the next task in the list with an overallocation. If you click the Go To Next Overallocation button when there are no more overallocated tasks in the list, you see a message telling you that there are no further overallocations. Click OK to close the message box and continue.

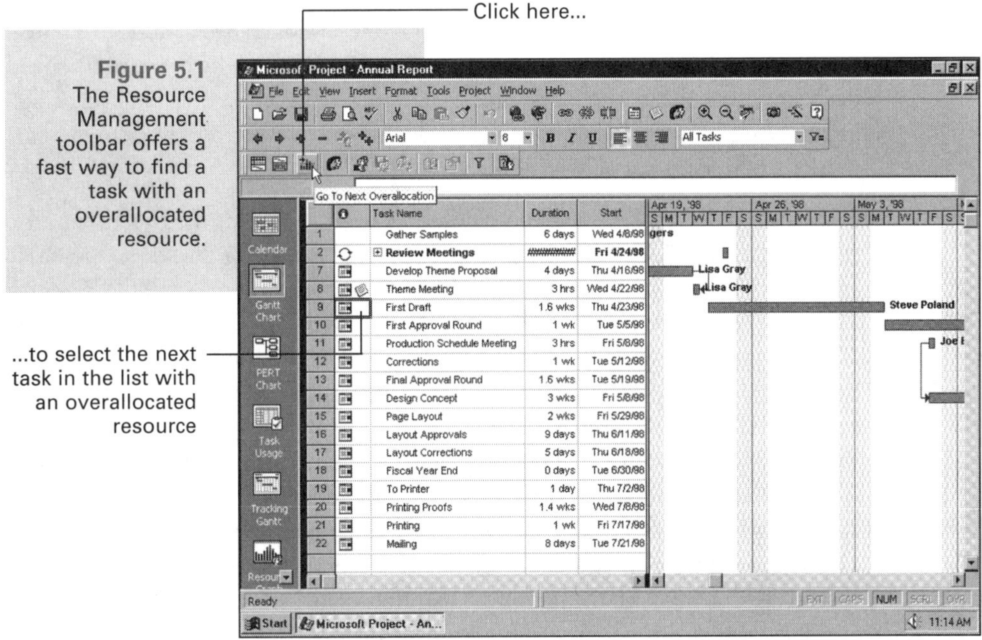

Figure 5.1 The Resource Management toolbar offers a fast way to find a task with an overallocated resource.

Looking at Resource Usage in Other Views

To make a good decision about how to fix an overallocation, you have to know the date(s) on which the overallocation occurs, and how extensive the overallocation is. Have you assigned 24 hours worth of work for an eight-hour day, or have you assigned only an extra hour or two? For more extensive schedules, you might have multiple overallocations, and might even have overallocated more than one resource on the same date.

Project offers a couple of options for getting a clearer overall picture of the overallocations in your schedule. (These are views, which you'll learn more about in Chapter 9, "Working with the Different Project Views.")

First, you can display the resource usage in a tabular format. To do so, open the View menu and click Resource Usage, or click the Resource Usage icon on the View Bar. The Resource Usage view appears onscreen, as shown in Figure 5.2. The Resource Name column in this view lists each resource you added to the schedule and lists each of the resource's assignments below the resource name. The Work column shows you the total amount of work (in hours) that you scheduled for the resource beside the resource name, as well as the amount of work scheduled for each assignment. The scrolling pane on the right side of the screen shows you the amount of work you assigned to each resource on each date. You can see which resources are overallocated at a glance, because Project displays the Resource Name and Work entries in bold, red text and displays an indicator telling you the resource needs leveling. Figure 5.2 shows overallocations for both the Steve Poland and Joe Bucki resources. If you look to the right along the row of an overallocated resource, you'll see that Project also highlights the particular dates on which you overbooked the resource according to the resource's work calendar. For example, on Friday during the week of April 19, Steve Poland is scheduled for 10 hours of work, two hours more than his calendar allows him to handle.

The Resource Allocation view combines the tabular layout for the Resource Usage view with a lower pane where you can see the assignments for the selected resource as a Gantt chart. To display the Resource Allocation view, you can click the Resource Allocation View button on the Resource Management toolbar. If you haven't displayed that toolbar, open the View menu and click More Views; then double-click Resource Allocation in the Views list of the More Views dialog box. Project displays your schedule in the Resource Allocation view. When you select a resource from the Resource Usage view in the upper pane, a Gantt chart in the lower pane shows you the tasks for the resource, so you can see which ones overlap (are scheduled for the same dates). Figure 5.3 shows that Steve Poland has overlapping tasks. This view is ideal for changing the schedule for overallocated resources, as you'll see later in the "Manually Cutting Back the Resource's Commitments" section; refer to that section for more information about working in this view.

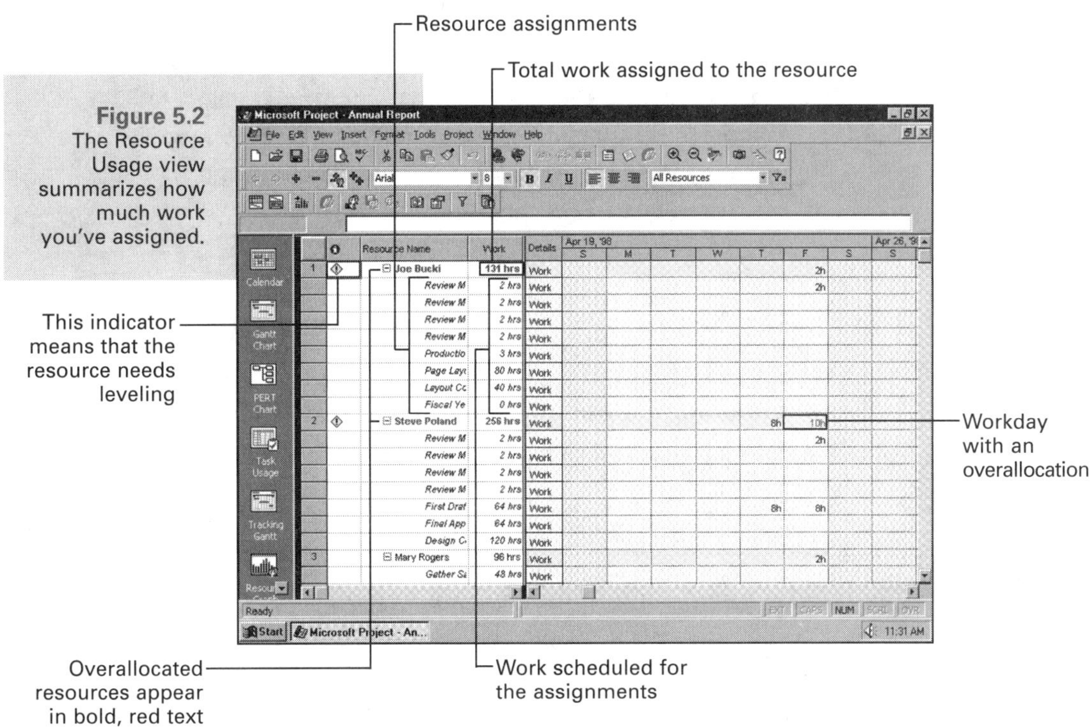

Figure 5.2 The Resource Usage view summarizes how much work you've assigned.

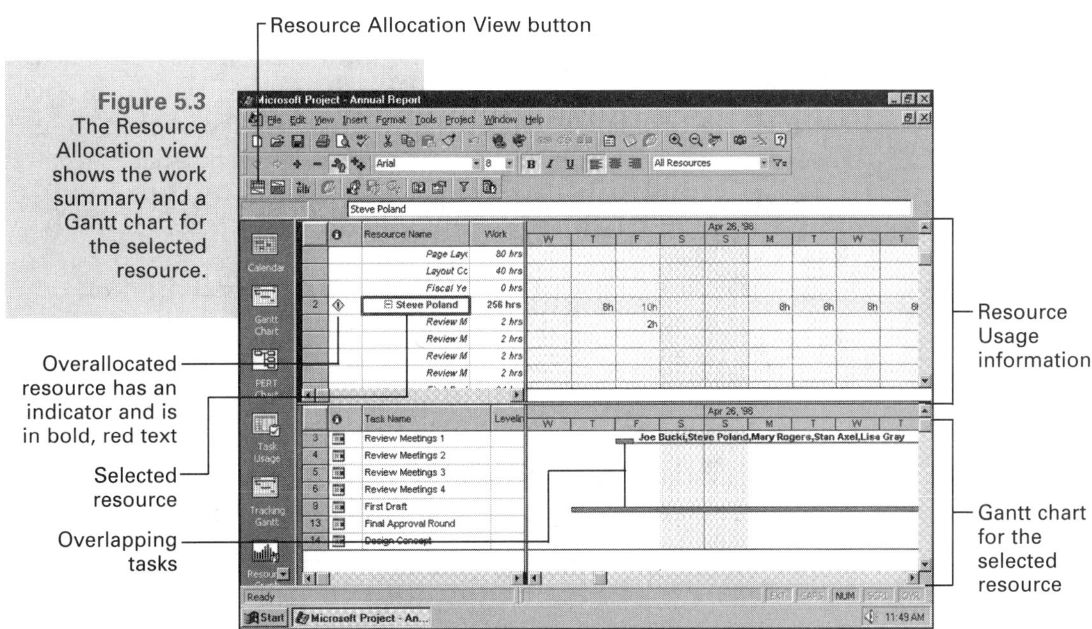

Figure 5.3 The Resource Allocation view shows the work summary and a Gantt chart for the selected resource.

If you switch back to the Resource Sheet (by opening the View menu and clicking Resource Sheet), overallocated resources are also indicated in bold, red text. You won't get any information, however, about where in the schedule the overallocation occurs.

When you display another view from the Resource Allocation view, the screen may remain split into upper and lower panes. Open the Window menu and click Remove Split to restore the view to Normal.

Creating and Printing an Overallocated Resources Report

Project can automatically create and print a report that lists each overallocated resource and the tasks assigned to that resource. Reports don't let you edit the information entered in your schedule, but they serve as a convenient tool for looking at particular types of information when decision-making. Although Chapter 12, "Creating and Printing a Report," provides more details about generating and printing the various types of reports in Project, here's a brief rundown of how to have Project compile an Overallocated Resources report:

1. Open the View menu and click Reports to access the Reports dialog box.
2. Double-click Assignments, or click it once, and then click Select. Project displays the Assignment Reports dialog box (see Figure 5.4).
3. Double-click Overallocated Resources, or click it once, and then click Select. Project creates a list of overallocated resources for you, and displays it onscreen.
4. To take a closer look at the information, as in Figure 5.5, click the report with the zoom pointer, which looks like a magnifying glass.
5. Click the Print button on the toolbar above the report to print the report.

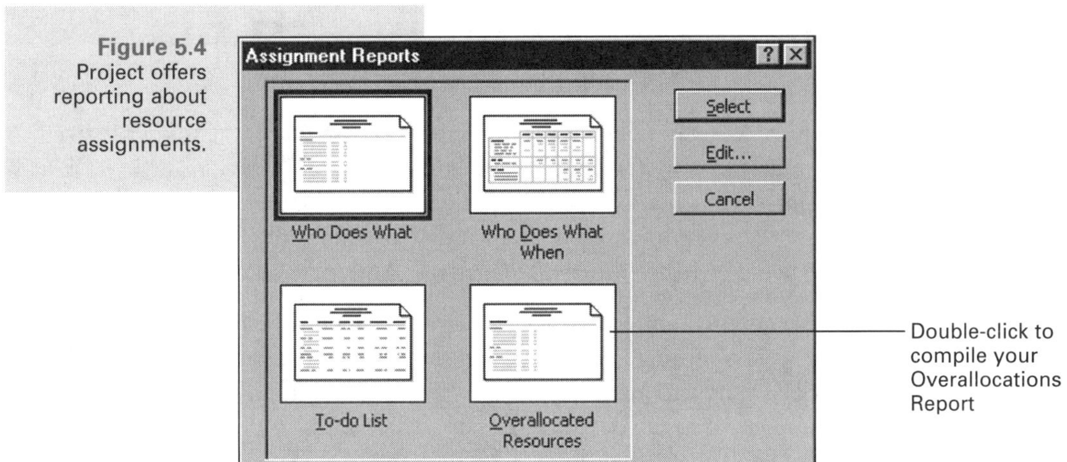

Figure 5.4 Project offers reporting about resource assignments.

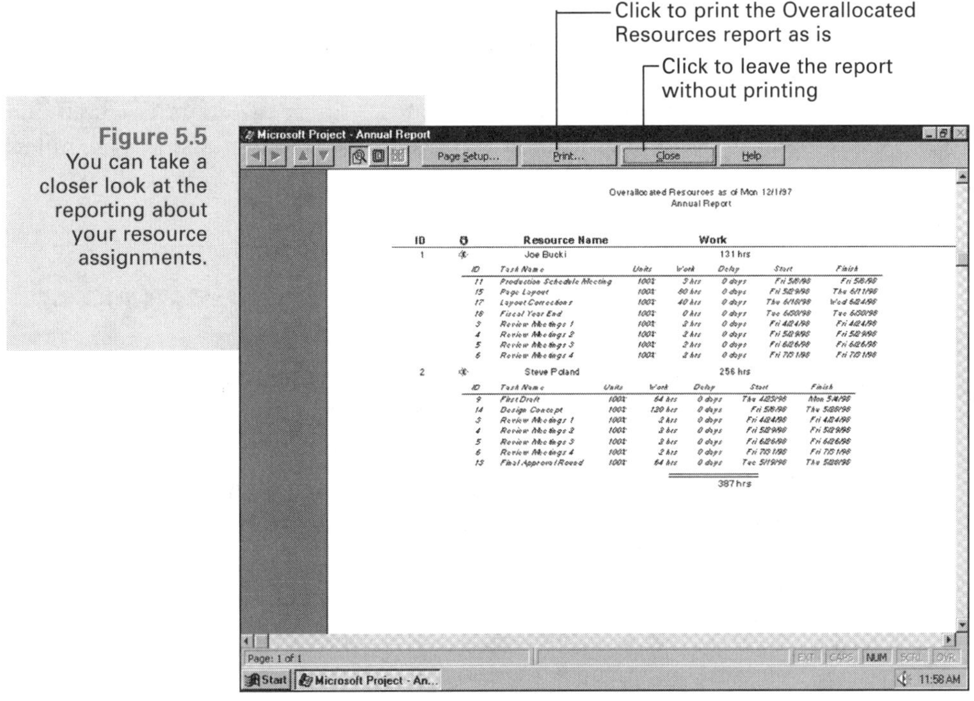

Figure 5.5 You can take a closer look at the reporting about your resource assignments.

Using Automatic Leveling to Fix Overallocations

When you've overbooked a resource, something has to give. You want to eliminate huge peaks in a resource's workload to achieve an even, realistic workload. The process of smoothing out the workloads for resources is called *resource leveling*. Project can level resource schedules automatically, when you specify, for any schedule where Project calculates the finish date automatically.

To level resources, Project basically delays a conflicting task, or splits the task and moves part of it, to a later time when the resource has available working hours. (You'll learn how to manually specify delay time later in this chapter, in the "Creating a Delay" section.) Project decides which tasks to delay by examining the information you entered about tasks, in particular looking for *slack*. Slack occurs when a task can be moved to a later date without delaying another task.

When tasks are linked, Project takes the links into consideration before delaying a particular task. This is important because linked tasks may be handled by different resources, and you don't want to create a problem for another resource as a result of the leveling. For example, if two tasks are linked using the default Finish-to-Start (FS) link type and there's no lag time between the two tasks, the first task can't be moved without the second task being moved as well, unless you change the nature of the link.

Note

The next chapter provides more detail about working with slack, but here's a quick example. Suppose that a resource is scheduled to handle a task that begins on Monday, 4/20/98, and has a duration of four days. The next task assigned to the resource begins on Monday, 4/27/98, and has the Start No Later Than (SNLT) constraint, meaning that it cannot move beyond its scheduled start date. Thus, there's one day of slack between the two tasks. The 4/20/98-4/23/98 task can only be delayed one day to a 4/21/98-4/24/98 schedule, because the resource must start working on the second task on the following Monday.

Here are a few more important issues to keep in mind before you level:

- Schedules built backwards from the finish date have no slack, so there's nowhere to move any tasks. You have to work manually to level resources for this type of schedule.
- By default, it's conceivable that Project may move a task that's listed earlier in the schedule, say in row 2, rather than the later conflicting one that's, say, in row 5. Project moves whichever task is easier to move based on links and other factors, regardless of its ID number or order in the Task Sheet. For example, compare the tasks for Steve Poland before and after leveling in Figure 5.6. Task 5 has a Must Start On constraint, so Project moved Task 1 and created a problem, because Steve needs to conduct research for the presentation before he can write the presentation. In some cases, such moves do not make sense. Be sure to double-check automatic leveling results carefully.
- Project can't change history. If a task has already started, Project can't move it when leveling a resource schedule.
- Automatic leveling can have a massive impact on the flow of your schedule. If your schedule is very complex, or you want to limit the scope of the changes made but still take advantage of automatic leveling, use automatic leveling for one resource at a time (see the following steps that explain how to use automatic leveling). Check the results after leveling each resource.

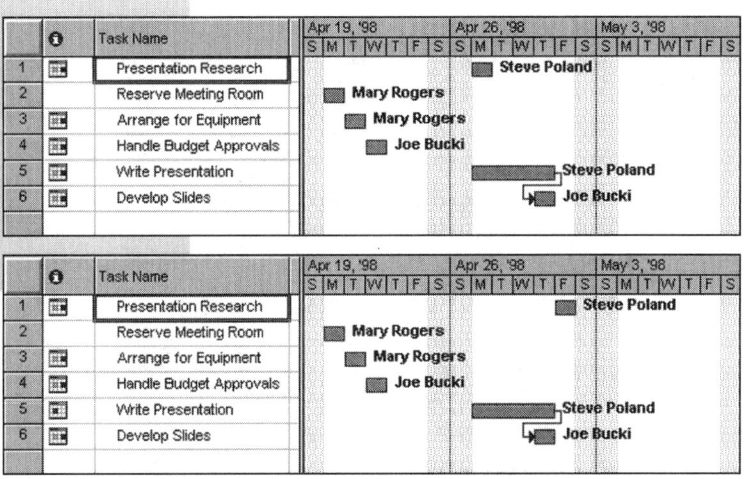

Figure 5.6 Leveling decisions aren't based on a task's order in the Task Sheet, as shown in this example of the same set of tasks before and after leveling.

	Task Name	Apr 19, '98 / Apr 26, '98 / May 3, '98
1	Presentation Research	Steve Poland
2	Reserve Meeting Room	Mary Rogers
3	Arrange for Equipment	Mary Rogers
4	Handle Budget Approvals	Joe Bucki
5	Write Presentation	Steve Poland
6	Develop Slides	Joe Bucki

	Task Name	Apr 19, '98 / Apr 26, '98 / May 3, '98
1	Presentation Research	Steve Poland
2	Reserve Meeting Room	Mary Rogers
3	Arrange for Equipment	Mary Rogers
4	Handle Budget Approvals	Joe Bucki
5	Write Presentation	Steve Poland
6	Develop Slides	Joe Bucki

Setting Options and Leveling

Project enables you to level resources with the Resource Leveling command on the Tools menu. As you proceed through the leveling process, Project gives you the opportunity to set numerous leveling options. To use automatic leveling, follow these steps:

1. Open the file with the resources you want to level, and make any desired adjustments to tasks, such as changing link types and priorities (see the "Reprioritizing Tasks Before Leveling" section later in this chapter).

If you want to level a schedule, but also be able to see the original dates, create a copy of the schedule file (by opening the File menu and clicking Save As, and then giving the file a new name). Then apply leveling to the copied file. Reopen the original file if you want to compare.

2. (Optional) If you want to level a single resource, change to Resource Sheet, Resource Usage, or Resource Allocation view; then click the resource name for the resource you want to level. (Press Ctrl and click other resource names if you also want to select those resources for leveling.)
3. Open the Tools menu and click Resource Leveling. The Resource Leveling dialog box appears (see Figure 5.7).

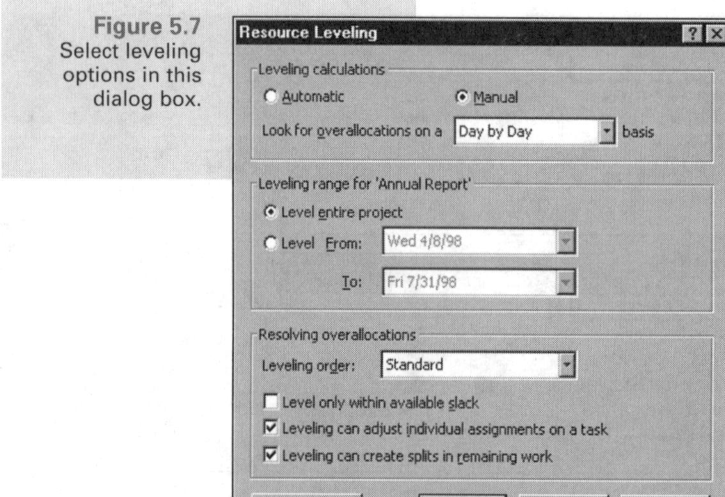

Figure 5.7 Select leveling options in this dialog box.

If you don't select a resource from one of the resource views, Project levels the whole schedule, and does not warn you before doing so.

4. If you want Project to automatically level the schedule each time you make a change in a task or resource assignment, select the Automatic option button in the Leveling Calculations area of the dialog box. Otherwise, you have to redisplay the Resource Leveling dialog box to level the schedule again after you make any changes. If, however, you want to retain control of when and how leveling occurs, leave the Manual option button selected.
5. The Look For Overallocations On A … Basis option specifies how precise leveling is. The default choice, Day by Day, compares the hours of work assigned to a resource on each day with the working hours available in the resource's calendar for that day. For the Standard calendar, then, any day with more than eight hours of work is marked as overallocated and will be leveled. Let's say, though, that you don't need to be that precise. If you assign a resource 12 hours of work that happens to fall on the same day, but that work really can be completed any time within the week, you can choose Week by Week so the work won't be leveled. The Look For Overallocations On A … Basis offers these choices, from most precise to most loose: Minute by Minute, Hour by Hour, Day by Day, Week by Week, and Month by Month.
6. If you don't want to level the entire project schedule, you can specify a range of dates to level in the Leveling Range for '(Current File)' area of the dialog box. To specify the schedule date when you want the leveling to start, click the Level From option button; then click the drop-down list arrow on the accompanying text box and select a date from the pop-up calendar that appears. Then, click the drop-down list arrow beside the To text box and use the pop-up calendar to select a date beyond which you don't want to level resources; if you want to level the remainder of the project, select a To date that is later than the project's finish date.
7. Use the Leveling Order drop-down list in the Resolving Overallocations area of the dialog box to tell Project how to choose which tasks to delay or split. This drop-down list offers three choices. The default is Standard, in which Project considers links, slack, dates, and priorities to determine which task to delay. If you select ID Only,

Project delays the overlapping task that appears latest in the Task Sheet and thus has the highest ID number. If you select the final choice, Priority, Standard, the priority you assigned to tasks takes precedence over other factors in determining which tasks to delay.

8. By default, the Level Only Within Available Slack option is not selected, meaning that Project can adjust the finish date of your schedule as needed when it moves tasks. However, this could lead to a delay of weeks or even months in your schedule, depending on the scope of your project. If you don't want the leveling operation to change the finish date, check this option so that Project moves tasks only within available slack time.
9. You may have several resources assigned to a task, and if only one of those resources is overallocated, Project can level only the overallocated resource. To have leveling work on individual resources in this way, leave the check mark beside Leveling Can Adjust Individual Assignments on a Task. Clear the check box if you would prefer that Project reschedule the entire task, even when only one of the resources handling the task is overbooked.
10. If you want Project to delay tasks and not split them, click to clear the check beside Leveling Can Create Splits in Remaining Work.
11. Click the Level Now button. If you selected a particular resource to level as described in step 2, or are displaying your schedule in one of the resource views, Project displays the Level Now dialog box (see Figure 5.8).
12. Leave the Entire Pool option selected to level all resources, or click Selected Resources to tell Project to level only the resource(s) you selected in step 2.
13. Click OK to complete the leveling operation. When a resource has been leveled, it no longer appears in bold, red type.
14. (Optional) If you're not happy with the leveling changes, immediately click the Undo button on the Standard toolbar, press Ctrl+Z, or open the Edit menu and click Undo Level.

Figure 5.8
Specify whether to level all resources in your project.

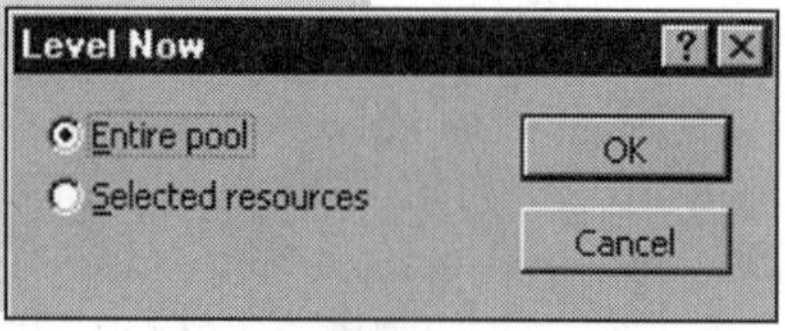

If you've leveled the resource and then view information about that resource in the Resource Allocation view, the Gantt chart pane at the bottom of the view clearly shows the effects of leveling. As shown in the example in Figure 5.9, each Gantt bar becomes a double-bar, with the top portion showing the original schedule for the task, and the bottom portion showing the leveled schedule.

Clearing Leveling

While you work with resources to add leveling, you work with tasks to remove leveling. Thus, you need to be in a view where you can select tasks, such as Gantt Chart view where the Task Sheet appears in the left pane, or Resource Allocation view where you can select task assignments for a particular resource in the lower pane of the view.

You can't select a resource name from any Resource Sheet and clear leveling. You have to be working from a task-oriented view or pane. You'll know you're in an incorrect place if the Clear Leveling button isn't available in the Resource Leveling dialog box.

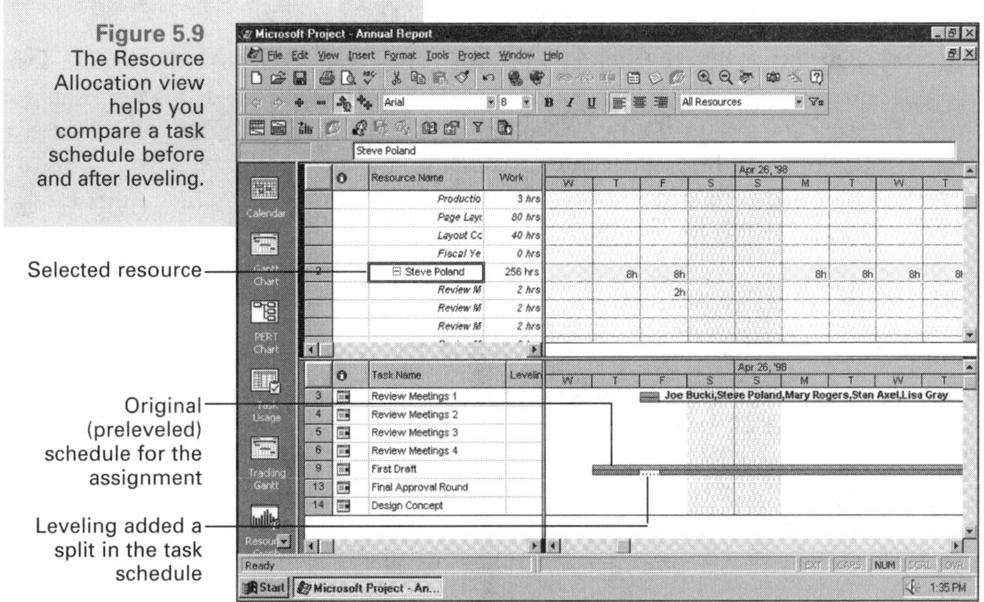

Figure 5.9 The Resource Allocation view helps you compare a task schedule before and after leveling.

Removing leveling removes any delay or split that Project inserted for a task or tasks during leveling. To remove leveling, perform the following steps:

1. Select a task-oriented view.
2. (Optional) If you only want to remove leveling from a particular task, click that task name. (If you select the Resource Allocation view, you'll also have to select a resource that has been leveled in the upper pane, and then click the task assignment to level in the lower pane.) To select more than one task, press and hold down the Ctrl key and click additional task names.
3. Open the Tools menu and click Resource Leveling. The Resource Leveling dialog box appears.
4. Click the Clear Leveling button. Project displays the Clear Leveling dialog box (see Figure 5.10).
5. If you chose one or more particular tasks to have leveling removed in step 2, make sure the Selected Tasks option button is selected. Otherwise, click Entire Project to remove all the leveling.
6. Click OK to remove the leveling. (Note that even after you clear leveling from a resource or task, the bottom pane of the Resource Allocation view will continue to show split bars for the tasks that were previously leveled.)

Reprioritizing Tasks Before Leveling

The last section of Chapter 3 provided an overview of the settings in the Task Information dialog box. To display the Task Information dialog box, double-click any task in the Task Sheet of the Gantt Chart view. The first tab in that dialog box, the General tab, enables you to enter and edit the basic information that defines the task, such as its name and duration. One of the settings in that dialog box is the Priority drop-down list, shown in Figure 5.11.

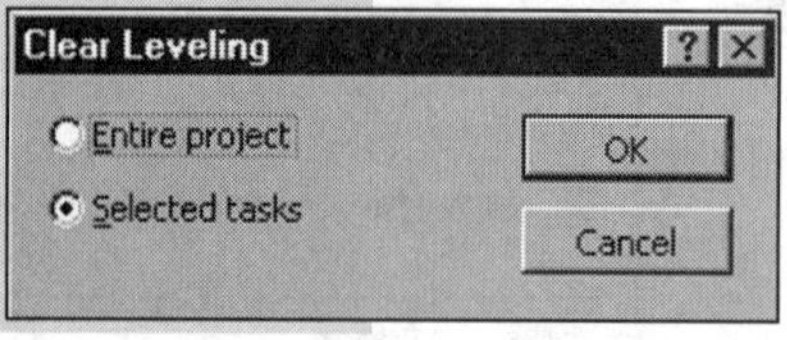

Figure 5.10 Choose whether to remove the delay from all or selected tasks.

Clear Leveling
Entire project
Selected tasks
OK
Cancel

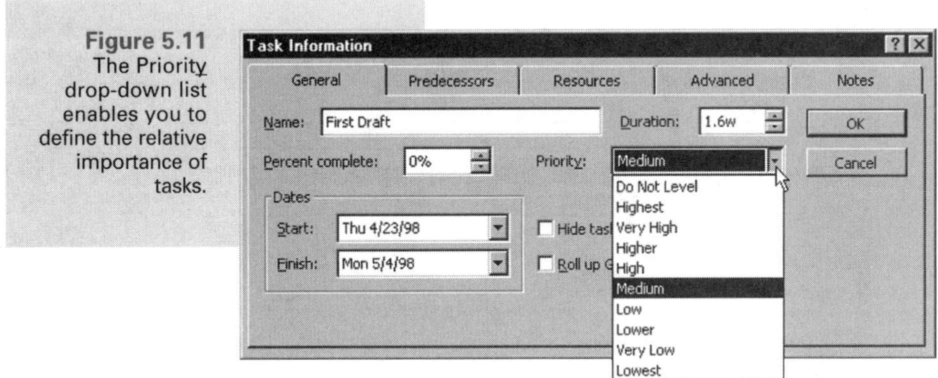

Figure 5.11 The Priority drop-down list enables you to define the relative importance of tasks.

By default, all tasks are assigned Medium priority, meaning that each task is equally important in the schedule. You can specify which tasks are more important by changing the Priority setting to any of the choices from Lowest through Highest, or to Do Not Level. (You can prevent Project from leveling a task at all by choosing Do Not Level.)

Project uses the priority settings as a factor in automatic leveling, and the priority is given even more precedence if you select the Priority, Standard choice in the Resource Leveling dialog box. Project moves tasks with lower priority settings before moving those with higher priority settings.

You can sort your list of tasks by priority. See Chapter 9, "Working with the Different Project Views," for details.

You should change task priorities before leveling, when necessary. Assuming that you'll be doing much of your leveling work in the Resource Allocation view, here's how to change a task's priority from that view:

1. In the upper pane of the Resource Allocation view, select the resource scheduled to handle the task for which you want to set the priority (usually an overallocated resource) by clicking it.
2. In the lower pane, right-click the task for which you want to set the priority—this displays the shortcut menu shown in Figure 5.12—and click Task Information. Alternately, double-click the Task Name in the lower pane or click the Task Information button on the Standard toolbar.

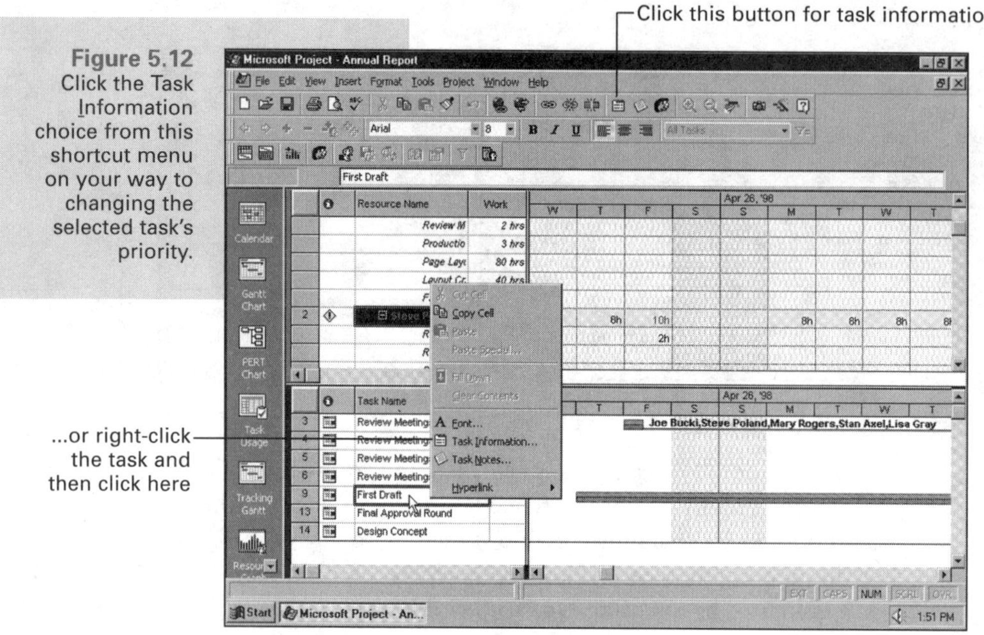
Click this button for task information...
...or right-click the task and then click here

Figure 5.12 Click the Task Information choice from this shortcut menu on your way to changing the selected task's priority.

3. On the General tab of the Task Information dialog box, click the drop-down list arrow for the Priority option; then click the setting you want.
4. Click OK to close the Task Information dialog box.

Use a similar approach to make such changes from other views that show a list of tasks.

Recurring tasks are automatically set with a Do Not Level priority. Changing this setting for a recurring task could have unwanted results.

Manually Cutting Back the Resource's Commitments

Although automatic leveling offers a no-brainer way to ensure that your resources can handle the work you assigned, some resource adjustment chores require thought. For example, as noted earlier in this chapter, if you set up your schedule file to have Project calculate its start date based on a finish date you entered, you can't use automatic leveling to deal with overallocations. Other instances where you might not want to use automatic leveling are if the tasks involved are high in priority, or if you need a solution that is more creative than simply delaying some tasks.

The methods described next enable you to resolve overallocations with precision and flexibility. To perform most of these adjustments, you work in Resource Allocation view. In the next chapter, you learn to adjust the schedule and make some resource adjustments from the Task Entry view.

Creating a Delay

Automatic leveling creates a delay for a task, so that tasks for a resource no longer overlap in the schedule. Without considering task linking, lead time, or lag time, this delay generally means that the second task starts after the first task ends, so the work flows in a continuous stream. If you enter a delay manually, you can create a delay of any length. For example, you might want to do the following:

- Build in extra delay time of a day or two (or more) between the tasks, in case the resource's first task takes longer than planned
- Enter a smaller delay that still lets the two tasks overlap by, let's say, one day; then you can use another method, such as adding another resource or specifying overtime, to take care of the smaller overallocation

To enter a delay of the length you prefer, do the following:

1. In Resource Allocation view, click the resource name for the overallocated resource in the upper pane.
2. In the lower pane, click the task name for the task you want to delay. Remember that entering the delay will move the task's start date; this technique doesn't work for schedules calculated backward from the project's finish date.
3. Press the right arrow or Tab key to scroll one column to the right (to the Leveling Delay column). You also can use the scroll bar below the Task Name column to scroll over; then click the desired cell in the Leveling Delay column.
4. Enter the delay that you desire (see Figure 5.13) and press Enter.

When you press Enter, Project pushes out the task. It adjusts the task's Start column entry, and moves the task to the right on the Gantt chart. For example, compare Figure 5.14 with Figure 5.13.

Figure 5.13 It's possible to manually enter a delay.

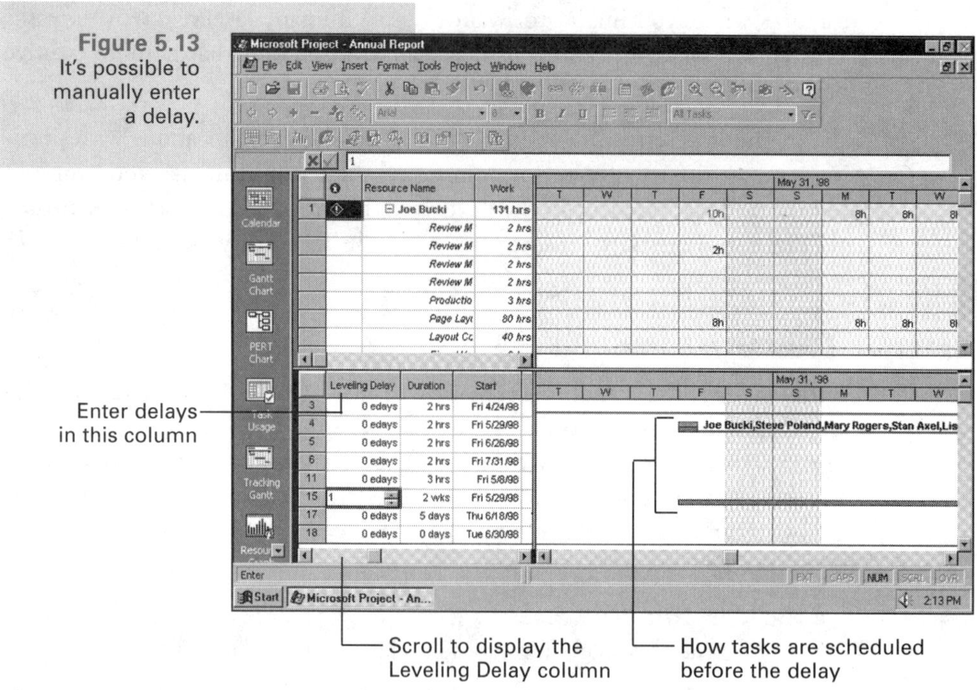

Figure 5.14 After you specify a delay value, Project moves the task based on that value.

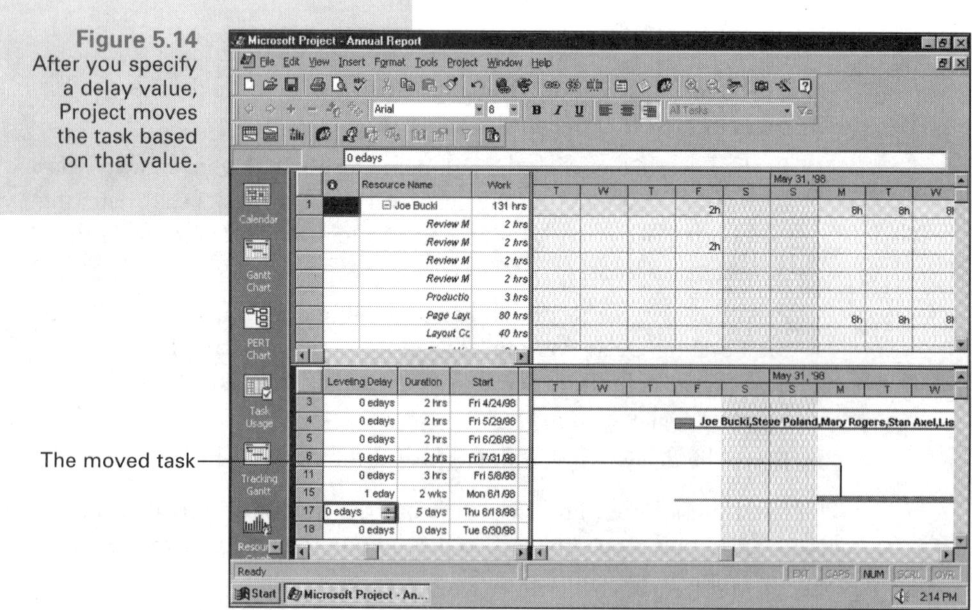

Delays are scheduled in elapsed days (edays), meaning that non-working days for the resource are included in the delay timeframe. You cannot schedule a delay in terms of workdays (d). If you enter a delay of 1w (one week), Project converts that entry to 7ed. Thus, after you enter a delay, make sure that it delays the task far enough based on the schedule's working days.

Removing or Replacing an Overbooked Resource

There will be times when delaying a task is not an option. For example, you might be required to finish a product by a particular date or else lose a customer's order. Additionally, certain tasks might need to be completed before the end of a financial period. Finally, a task might be so pivotal in your schedule, and linked to so many successor tasks down the line (see the next chapter to learn more), that delaying it will ruin your entire schedule.

In situations like this, you need to look closely at the resource you've assigned, rather than the schedule. You might be forced to remove a resource from a task (especially if you assigned more than one task to the resource) or to replace the resource with another one that's available to complete the task. Here's how to do so:

1. In Resource Allocation view, click the resource name for the overallocated resource in the upper pane.
2. In the lower pane, click the task name for which you want to remove or replace the resource.
3. Open the Tools menu, point to Resources, and click Assign Resources (or press Alt+F10). Alternately, click the Assign Resources button on the Standard toolbar or the Resource Management toolbar. The Assign Resources Assignment dialog box appears.
4. Click to select the assigned resource, which should have a check mark beside it.
5. To take the resource off the task, click the Replace button. Project immediately removes the resource from the task and changes the name of the Assign Resources dialog box to Replace Resource.
6. Click a new resource for the task in the With list, and then click OK. Project reassigns the task, removing it from the task list for the original resource and adding it to the task list for the newly selected resource.

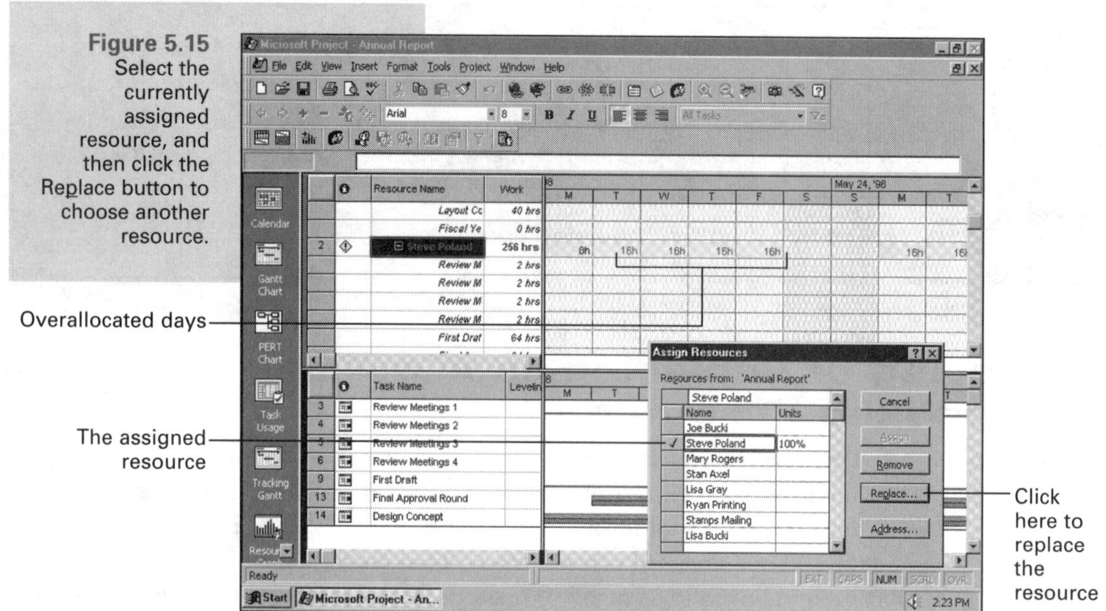

Figure 5.15 Select the currently assigned resource, and then click the Replace button to choose another resource.

Changing resource assignments in this way can fix one overallocation but create another; the new Resource Name entry changes to bold, red text to indicate a new overallocation. Pay careful attention to the results of your resource reassignment.

Click the Close button to put away the Resource Assignment dialog box when you're finished working with it.

Part-Time Work

There might be times when you're not in a position to delay one task or another altogether, perhaps because a third successor task is unable to start until its predecessor starts, as in an SS relationship. Or, there might be an instance where you don't want to remove a resource from a task altogether, but do want to scale back its commitment to the task and add another resource (as described in Chapter 6, "Optimizing the Schedule") to help finish the task in a timely fashion.

In such cases, you have the option of cutting back a resource to a part-time commitment to a task. Here's how:

1. In Resource Allocation view, click the resource name for the overallocated resource in the upper pane.
2. In the lower pane, click the task name for the task for which you want to reduce the resource assignment.
3. Open the Tools menu, point to Resources, and click Assign Resources (or press Alt+F10). Alternately, click the Assign Resources button on the Standard toolbar or the Resource Management toolbar. The Assign Resources dialog box appears (refer to Figure 5.15).
4. Click the Units cell for the assigned resource, which should have a check mark beside it. Begin typing to replace the existing Units entry, as shown in Figure 5.16. If the original number was a 100%, type a number that's less than 100% to indicate how much of each workday you want the resource to spend on the selected task. For example, if you want the resource to work on the task for half the day, type 50. If the original number was 1.00, type a decimal value, such as .5 for half-time work.
5. Press Enter to finish your entry; then click the Close button to close the Assign Resources dialog box. On the Gantt chart for the task, an indication beside the Resource label tells you what portion of the workday the resource will spend on the assignment (see Figure 5.17). If the task uses a resource-driven duration type, Project adjusts the task's duration (lengthening the Gantt chart bar) so that the resource works the same total hours on the task. For example, if a task originally has a one-week duration and you reduce the resource's commitment to half-time, the duration is extended to two weeks.

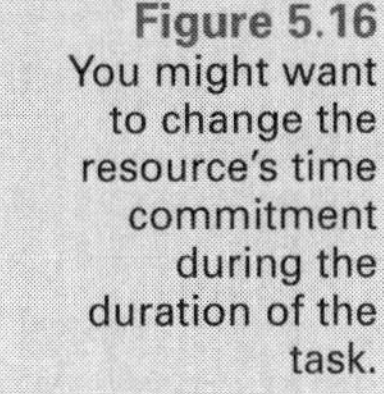

Figure 5.16 You might want to change the resource's time commitment during the duration of the task.

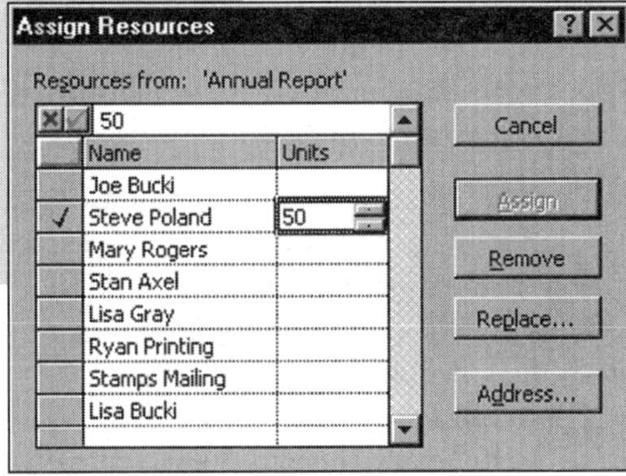

If you enter a number that's greater than 100%, Project does not assume that you want the resource to work overtime. It instead assumes that the resource has the proportion of extra time available within the bounds of the workday. For example, if the resource is a consulting firm you're working with, and you change the Units entry to 200%, Project assumes that two members of the firm will work on your task each day. To learn how to specify overtime for a task, see "Authorizing Overtime Work for a Task" in Chapter 6, "Optimizing the Schedule."

The resource will work half-time on this task

	Task Name	Levelin
3	Review Meetings 1	
4	Review Meetings 2	
5	Review Meetings 3	
6	Review Meetings 4	
9	First Draft	
13	Final Approval Round	
14	Design Concept	

Steve Poland[50%]

Figure 5.17 Check any Gantt chart bar for part-time resources.

Avoiding Underallocations

If you remove a resource from a task altogether in Resource Allocation view, that task no longer appears on the assignment list for any resource. Therefore, you should make a note of the task name and ID (row) number before you remove its resource. Make sure that you go back to Gantt Chart view or any other view where you can assign resources to tasks, and add a resource for the task. Otherwise, the task is completely underallocated and there's no resource scheduled to handle it.

An even trickier situation occurs if you change a resource from a full-time to a part-time commitment to a task. If the task has a fixed duration, Project will not increase the task's duration when you cut back the resource to a part-time commitment. In reality, the task still requires the same number of hours it initially did, but on the schedule there are fewer hours of work scheduled to get the task done. For example, suppose that you have a task with a 3d duration, which equates to 24 hours of work by the project's eight-hours-per-day base calendar. The duration type is Fixed, which means that the task's start and finish date don't change. If you cut back a resource assigned to this task to half-time work for the task, Project assumes that only 12 hours of work are now required on the task. In such a case, you need to add one or more additional part-time resources to the task to replace the 12 hours of work that the first resource no longer provides. (The "Adding More Resources" section in Chapter 6, "Optimizing the Schedule," covers how to do this.)

If you cut back a resource assignment to part-time but the task duration doesn't change, you should check the duration type. If it's Fixed, make sure that you add more resources for the task as needed.

Note

Remember that you can quickly check a task's duration type by clicking the task name in any task list, and then clicking the Task Information button on the Standard toolbar. Click the Advanced tab; then check the Task Type drop-down list. Click OK to close the dialog box.

Changing the Resource's Work Schedule

The "Working with Resource Calendars (Work Schedules)" section in Chapter 4, "Managing Resources," explains how to assign a calendar for a resource to determine how many hours per week the resource works and to set days the resource has off. Rather than cutting back a resource's commitment to a project, you can change a resource's schedule, adding more hours or days to remove the overallocations. Although you might not have much leeway to do this for resources within your company (you can't make certain people work extra hours without paying overtime, for example), there are instances when adjusting a resource's calendar, or selecting a new calendar, can resolve an overallocation. Consider the following examples:

- If a salaried employee is willing to give up a holiday or weekend day to complete a task, you can make that day a working day in the calendar. For example, if an employee has to attend a trade show on a weekend, you can specify those weekend days as working days.
- On a day that requires an evening or morning meeting, you can adjust the working hours for the resource.

- If you're working with a vendor that normally has a standard eight-hour workday, but can work around the clock when you request it, make the request and change that resource's schedule.

Although you can refer to Chapter 4, "Managing Resources," to review the details of making changes to the working days and hours for a resource, here's a quick way to select a different calendar for a resource:

1. Double-click the resource name in any view or resource list, or in the Resources From list in the Resource Assignment dialog box. The Resource Information dialog box appears.
2. Use the Base Calendar drop-down list on the Working Time tab to select another calendar, as shown in Figure 5.18.
3. Click OK to complete the change.

Using Contouring to Vary Workload

Project 98 offers another new feature intended to help you realistically plan workloads—workload *contouring*. Although contouring doesn't necessarily resolve all overallocations, it can help. Also, it does enable you to adjust how many hours per day a resource is scheduled to work on a task, so you can have more flexibility in working smaller tasks in around other tasks, or helping tasks overlap without creating an overallocation.

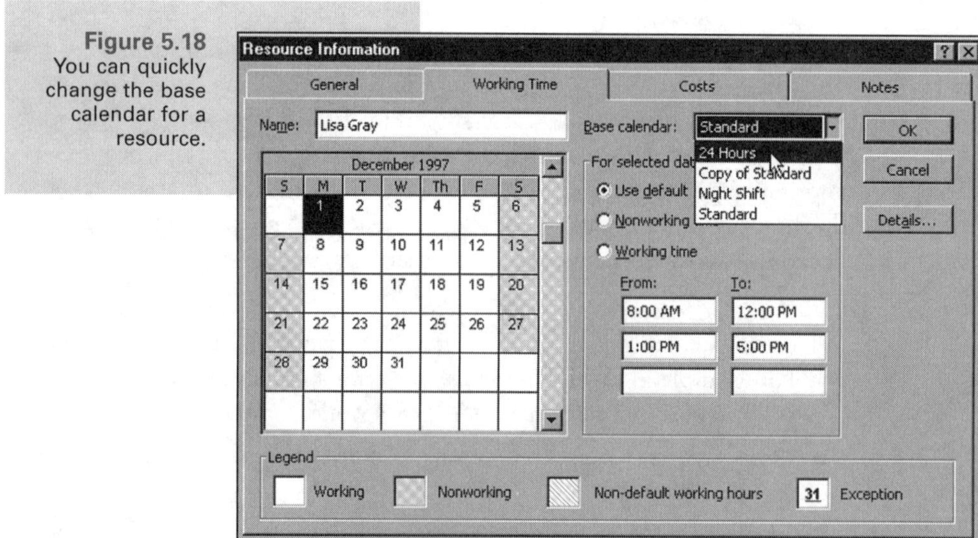

Figure 5.18 You can quickly change the base calendar for a resource.

Simply put, contouring an assignment adjusts the hours per day that a resource is scheduled to work on the assignment. You can choose one of several contouring patterns to automatically distribute the hours for an assignment. For example, say you have a two-week task, and you assign a single full-time resource handle it. If you apply a bell curve contour to that assignment, Project extends the task schedule to four working weeks, so it can redistribute the hours per day the resource works on the task in a bell-shaped pattern. The first two days, the resource is scheduled to work .8h on the task, the next two days 1.6 hours, and so on. The resource's work will peak at a full day during the middle of the task schedule, and then gradually drop back to .8h for the last two days. You can set these kinds of contouring for an assignment in the Resource Allocation, Resource Usage, Task Usage, or any other view where you can display the Assignment Information dialog box for an Assignment:

- **Front- or back-loaded.** This contour increases the hours per day from the start to the finish of the task, or decreases the hours per day form the start to the finish.
- **Early-, late, or double-peak.** The work peaks to a full eight-hour day near the start or finish of the project (but not on the first or last day, as under a front- or back-loaded schedule), or both.
- **Bell.** As just described, this contour smoothly allocates the hours per day to peak during the middle of the task. Generally, this contour doubles the task duration.
- **Turtle.** Similar to a bell curve, this schedule peaks in the middle, but allocates more full-time workdays, so the duration isn't extended as far as it would be under a bell contour.
- **Edited.** When you edit the hours for one or more days of the assignment in the Resource Usage or Task Usage view, you've created an edited or custom contour (described later in this section). This is the only type of contour that's not automatic or predefined.
- **Flat.** Choose this contour to return to the default, scheduling the same number of work hours per day through the completion of the task.

After you add a contour to an assignment, the indicator column displays a contour indicator. Figure 5.19 shows a Help window that displays the contour indicators.

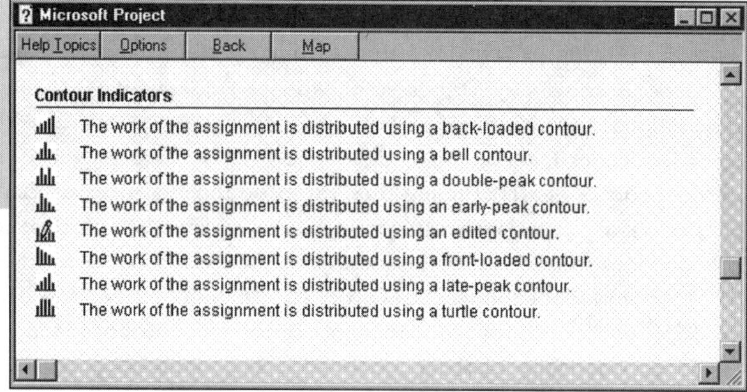

Figure 5.19 A specific indicator identifies a contoured assignment in Project.

To use the Assignment Information dialog box to assign an automatic or predefined contour to an assignment, follow these steps:

1. In the upper pane of the Resource Allocation view (or in the Resource Usage or Task Usage view), double-click the assignment to which you want to apply an automatic contour. Or, click the assignment, and then click the Assignment Information button on the Standard toolbar, which is the equivalent of clicking to open the Project menu and then clicking Assignment Information. The Assignment Information dialog box appears.
2. Click Work Contour to open the drop-down list, as shown in Figure 5.20. Then click the type of work contour you want to use.
3. Click OK to finish setting the contour.

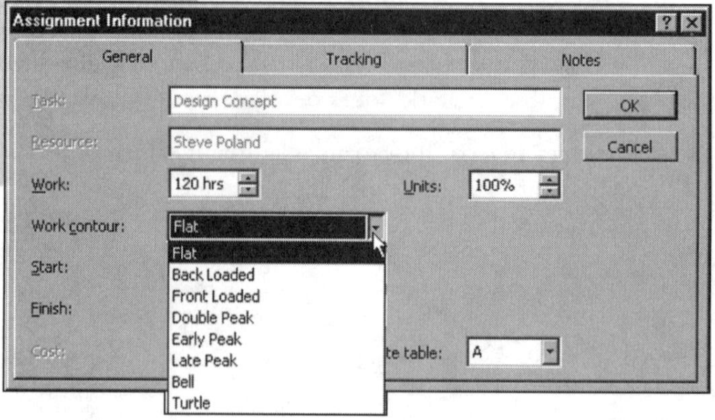

Figure 5.20 Set a work contour in the Assignment Information dialog box.

As I noted earlier, sometimes a contour doesn't seem to fix an overallocation the way it should. I've run into at least one instance where this is the case. For example, I created a recurring task for a two-hour Review Meeting. The first Review Meeting assignment created an overallocation with a second task, which I called First Draft. I tried applying an automatic contour to the First Draft task to reduce the hours for it on the day of the first Review Meeting, but found that even when the total hours for the day dropped below eight hours, the task was still overallocated. I did find a workaround, which involved working with the Units assigned to the first Review Meeting, and then creating an edited contour for the First Draft task.

First, for this example, I opened the Assignment Information dialog box for the first Review Meeting assignment for the overallocated resource. Because it was a two-hour meeting, I changed the Units setting on the General tab to clarify for Project that the meeting would use only part of the resource's day. Then, I created the edited contour.

To create an edited contour, click the cell for the day that you need to contour. As shown in Figure 5.21, I clicked the cell for F (Friday), Apr 24, '98 for the First Draft assignment. Type the new value for the cell, including the hours (h) abbreviation if you'd like (Project assumes the value you enter will be in hours), and then press Enter. Project reduces the work scheduled for that date of the assignment and displays an edited contour indicator for the assignment. In my example, it also removed the resource allocation as a result.

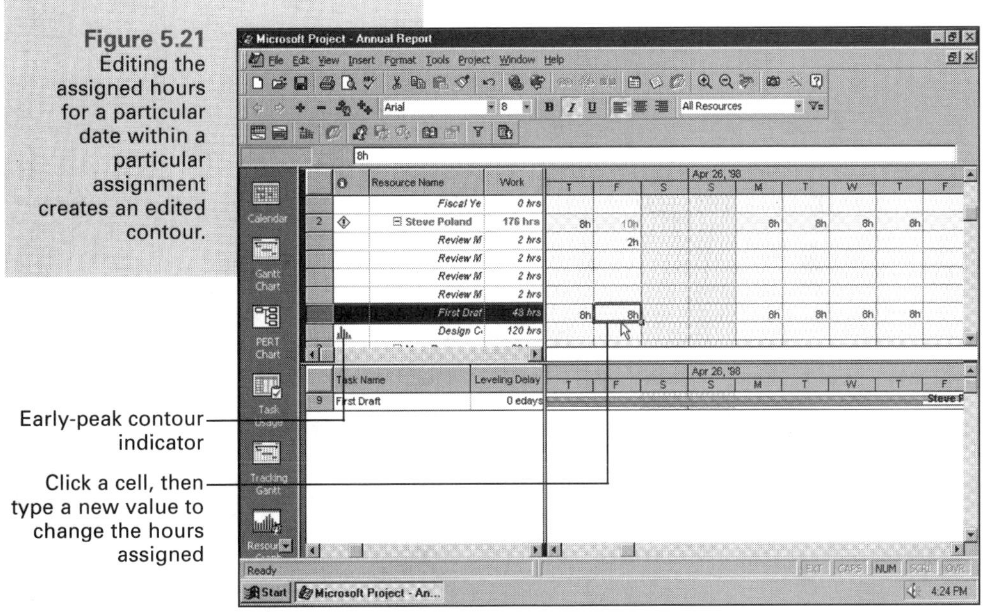
Microsoft Project - Annual Report
Early-peak contour indicator
Click a cell, then type a new value to change the hours assigned

Figure 5.21 Editing the assigned hours for a particular date within a particular assignment creates an edited contour.

6

Optimizing the Schedule

In This Chapter

- Understanding which tasks are critical and how they affect your schedule
- Looking for ways to finish critical tasks more quickly
- Finding "dead" time in the schedule and taking it out
- Giving yourself more room by adjusting the project base calendar

When you lead a project, you have to use a lot of creativity to bring everything together on time and within budget. You need to look at different ways to apply the resources you have, check for every place where you can trim back time, and do everything you can to ensure that as many tasks are moving along as simultaneously as possible.

In the last chapter, you looked at how to make your schedule attainable by ensuring that you didn't assign too much work to any particular resource. Now, you can apply your managerial creativity to tighten up your schedule to ensure that it gets the job done as quickly as possible.

Identifying and Tightening the Critical Path

In the Midwest and northern regions of the United States, the building industry is seasonal, because certain building tasks can't be completed under certain weather conditions. For example, if the weather isn't right, the foundation can't be constructed; if the foundation isn't constructed, the framing for the walls and roof can't be erected; without the framework, other key systems can't be installed. After the most important features of the building are in place, however, the schedules for many tasks are a bit more flexible; for example, work on finishing the exterior can proceed at the same time as work to complete the interior.

In the building example, the tasks that can't be delayed without drastically affecting the overall schedule—the foundation and framing work, for example—are called critical tasks.

Your schedule will have critical tasks, as well. If any of these tasks slip (either begin late or take more time than you allowed), the finish date for your project will move further out. Together, the critical tasks form the critical path for your schedule, the sequence of tasks that must happen on time for the project to finish on time. Although moving tasks that aren't on the critical path might even out resource assignments or help you improve milestones, such changes won't really affect the full schedule for your project.

The techniques covered in this chapter can introduce resource overallocations. After you make any of the changes you'll learn about in this chapter, check for resource overallocations as described in Chapter 5, "Resolving Overallocations and Overbooked Resources."

Thus, if you want to reduce the overall timeframe for your project, you need to reduce the length of time it takes to complete the critical path. You need to be able to identify which tasks comprise the critical path and make adjustments to compress the schedules for those tasks.

You can use a formatting technique to identify critical tasks in the Task Sheet in Gantt Chart or Task Entry view (you'll learn about the latter shortly), which is the easiest way to highlight critical tasks. You also can format critical tasks in the lower pane of Resource Allocation view, but that formatting won't appear if you switch back to Gantt Chart or Task Entry view. To highlight the critical tasks in your schedule, follow these steps:

1. Click the visible portion of the Task Sheet in whichever view you're presently using. For example, in Gantt Chart view, click the left pane of the screen, or in Task Entry View, click the upper pane.
2. Open the Format menu and click Text Styles. Project displays the Text Styles dialog box.
3. Click the drop-down list arrow to display the Item to Change choices, and click Critical Tasks (see Figure 6.1). This choice means that the formatting choices you make next will apply to any task that's part of the critical path.
4. In the scrolling Font list, display and click the name of a font to use for the critical task text.

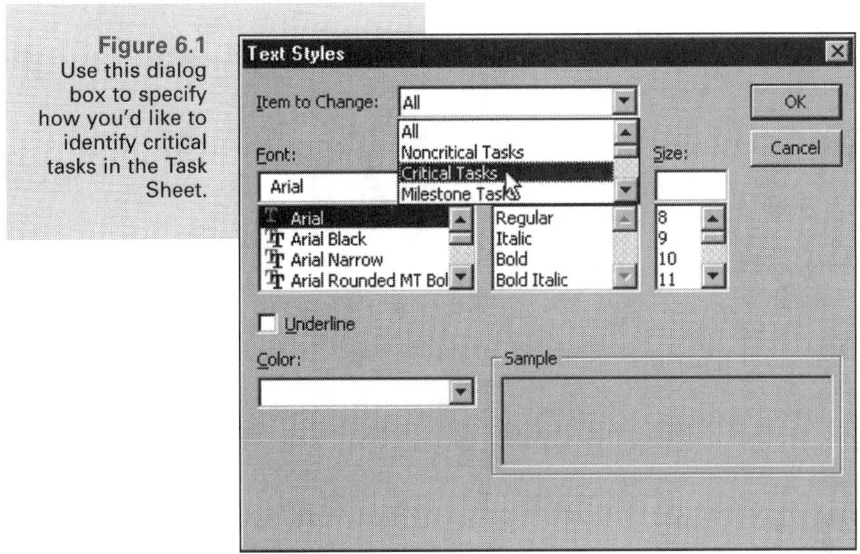

Figure 6.1 Use this dialog box to specify how you'd like to identify critical tasks in the Task Sheet.

5. Use the Font Style list to apply attributes such as bold or italic to the text. Depending on the font you chose; italic often is a better choice than bold, because it more clearly differentiates the text.
6. Use the Size list to select a size for the critical task names in the list. This further emphasizes the critical task names and makes them easier to read.
7. Click to select the Underline check box if you want to apply underlining to the critical path tasks.
8. Finally, click to open the Color drop-down list (see Figure. 6.2), and click the color you want to apply to the critical task text in the Task Sheet.
9. Click OK to apply your changes and close the Text Styles dialog box. The text formatting changes you specified now apply to all the tasks that are critical to your schedule. Figure 6.3 shows an example.

Your changes might cause a column in the Task Sheet to be filled with asterisks so that you can't see the data the column contains. If this happens, try repeating the preceding steps with different settings (especially the font size) until you find settings that work. Or, autofit the column width by double-clicking on the right border for the header of the column to be widened.

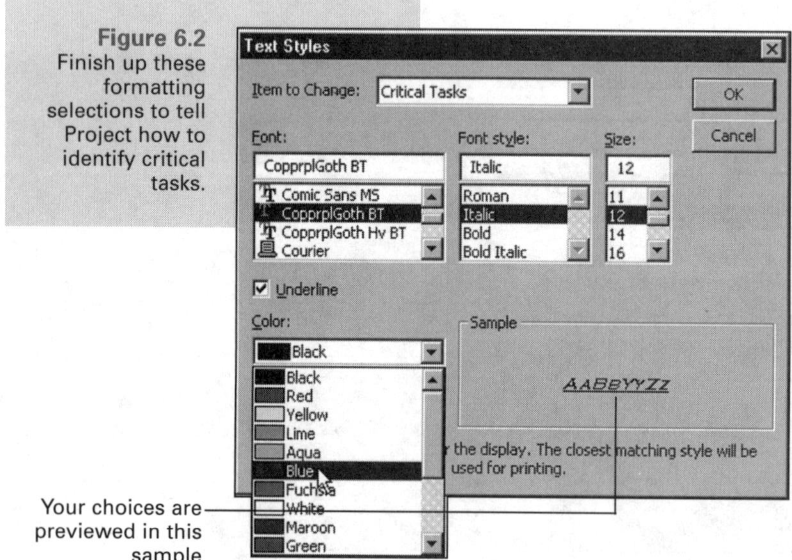

Figure 6.2 Finish up these formatting selections to tell Project how to identify critical tasks.

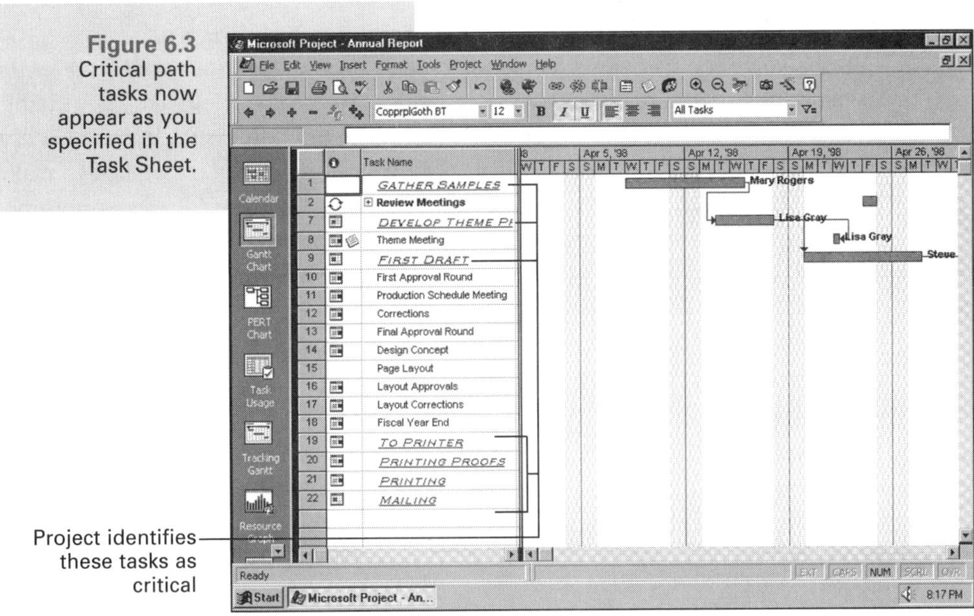

Figure 6.3 Critical path tasks now appear as you specified in the Task Sheet.

You can use filtering to limit the displayed lists of tasks to critical tasks only. To learn how to filter the Task Sheet, see "Filtering the Resource and Task Sheet" in Chapter 9.

If you use the preceding steps, and the only task that changes formatting in the list is the last one, Project isn't making an error. It simply means that you haven't built enough details into your schedule to define a true critical path. You can go back, however, and take the time to define task relationships (links) and add constraints to tasks (such as defining that a task should start no later than a particular date) using the Advanced tab of the Task Information dialog box. When you make alterations to task information that identify some tasks as critical, Project applies the critical path formatting.

To ensure that you can tighten up the schedule for critical tasks, make sure that the tasks have the effort-driven task type. Double-click the task in a Task Sheet, click the Advanced tab, and check the Effort Driven check box.

Using Task Entry View

After you identify which tasks are critical in your schedule, you can begin examining them one-by-one to look for areas where you can make adjustments to decrease the duration of each critical task. You could simply double-click each task in the Task Sheet to display the Task Information dialog box to make your changes, but that would be time-consuming, and wouldn't let you immediately see the effects of your changes on other tasks that were linked. It's better to use another view you haven't yet seen, Task Entry view, which displays Gantt Chart view in the upper pane, and an area for entering and changing task and resource information in the bottom pane. Switch to Task Entry view with one of the following ways:

- Click the Task Entry View button on the Resource Management toolbar, if that toolbar is displayed.
- Open the View menu and click More Views (or click the More Views icon in the View Bar). In the Views list of the More Views dialog box, double-click Task Entry.

No matter which method you use to reach it, Task Entry view appears onscreen as shown in Figure 6.4.

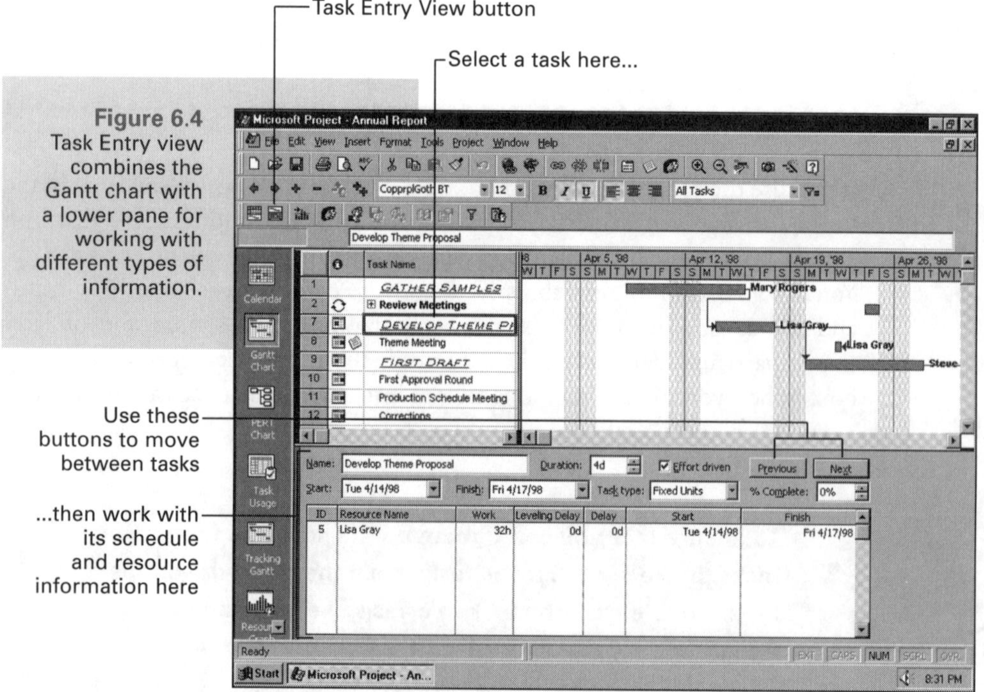
Task Entry View button
Select a task here...
Use these buttons to move between tasks
...then work with its schedule and resource information here

Figure 6.4 Task Entry view combines the Gantt chart with a lower pane for working with different types of information.

You can vary the details that appear in the lower pane of Task Entry view. In fact, some of the details you can modify here aren't available in other areas such as the Task Information dialog box. To change the information displayed in the lower pane of Task Entry view, right-click the pane to display its shortcut menu (see Figure 6.5). Then click one of the choices to change the pane. The top choice on the shortcut menu, Hide Form View, closes the bottom pane of Task Entry view, essentially returning to Gantt Chart view.

When you're working in Task Entry view, you can jump back and forth between panes, selecting a task in the upper pane, making changes in the lower pane, and then selecting a different task in the upper pane, changing its settings in the bottom pane, and so on.

Understanding Driving Resources

So far, for simplicity's sake, you've been looking at tasks with a single resource assigned to them. Imagine how restricted your options would be, though, if each task your team handles could only be assigned to one resource! Teams, by definition, mean that people work together to accomplish a goal. You can think of a goal in terms of the overall project, or in terms of any individual task. This means that you can use more than one resource (a mini-team, if you will) to accomplish each task in your schedule.

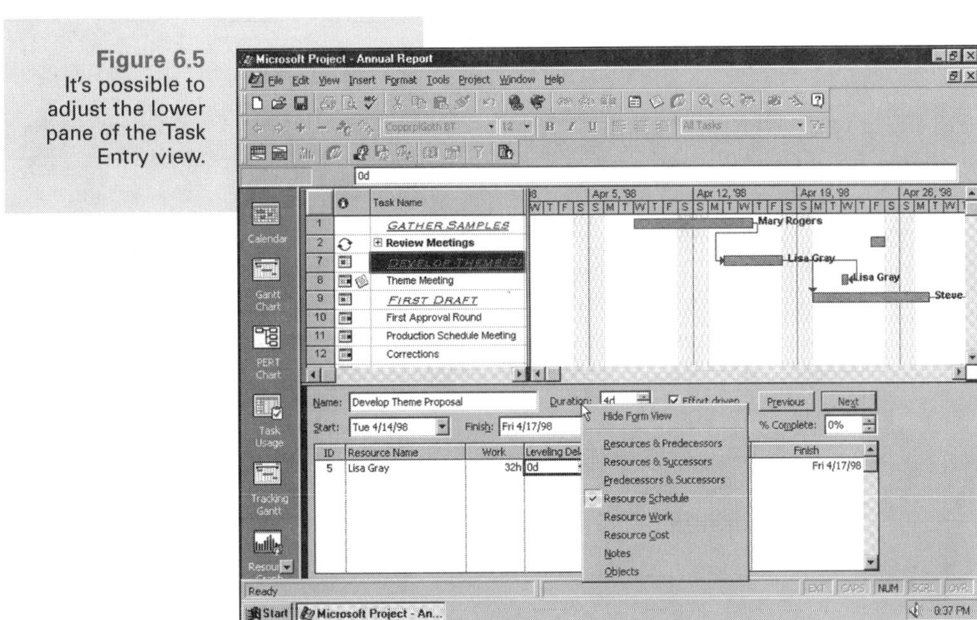

Figure 6.5 It's possible to adjust the lower pane of the Task Entry view.

Before I explain how to assign additional resources to a task, you need to understand that Project doesn't treat all resources assigned to a task the same. Rather, Project looks at the resource that's assigned to do the most work for the task, called the *driving resource*.

The time that the driving resource has available to work on the task determines the task's duration. If you want to shorten the task's duration, then, you must do one or more of the following things:

- Add more hours to the resource calendar, which you learned to work with in Chapter 4.
- Make more units available for the resource, indicating that the resource is adding more staff members to handle the task.
- Add another resource so that you can reduce the number of hours the driving resource needs to spend working on the task.

The latter two techniques are described next.

Adding Resources for a Task

If a critical task is being handled by a resource outside your company, you can start optimizing your schedule by asking that resource to assign more workers or equipment to the task to finish it more quickly. For example, the resource might be willing to assign three people or three pieces of equipment to your task to get it done in a third of the time originally planned.

Adding more resource units to a critical task can be tricky. Project always decreases the task duration directly in proportion to the number of additional resource units. Thus, if you increase the units from 100% or 1 (one full-time person) to 200% or 2 (two full-time people), Project automatically cuts the task duration in half; however, the two resource units might not get the task done in half the time. It might take a little longer, because the resources need to communicate amongst themselves. To allow for this possibility, consider building a lag time between the critical task and any successor tasks that depend on its completion.

To increase the number of units for a resource assigned to a critical task, follow these steps from Task Entry view:

1. Click the task name of the critical task in the top pane, or use the Previous and Next buttons in the bottom pane to display the information for the critical task.
2. Right-click the bottom pane of the Task Entry view; then click Resource Work.
3. Click the Units column of the bottom pane and type a new value, as shown in Figure 6.6.
4. Click the OK button in the bottom pane of the Task Entry view to finish the entry. Project adjusts the Duration for the task to reflect that the added resource units will finish the task more quickly.

You also can change the Units setting via the Assign Resources dialog box. To do so, click the critical task in the Task Sheet of Gantt Chart view or in the upper pane of Task Entry view. Click the Assign Resources button on the Standard toolbar or Resource Management toolbar. Or, open the Tools menu, point to Resources, and click Assign Resources. Click the Units column for the resource assigned to the task, type a new value (see Figure 6.7), and press Enter or click the Enter button to finish changing the entry. Then close the Assign Resources dialog box.

Figure 6.6 You can add more resource units to shorten the task duration.

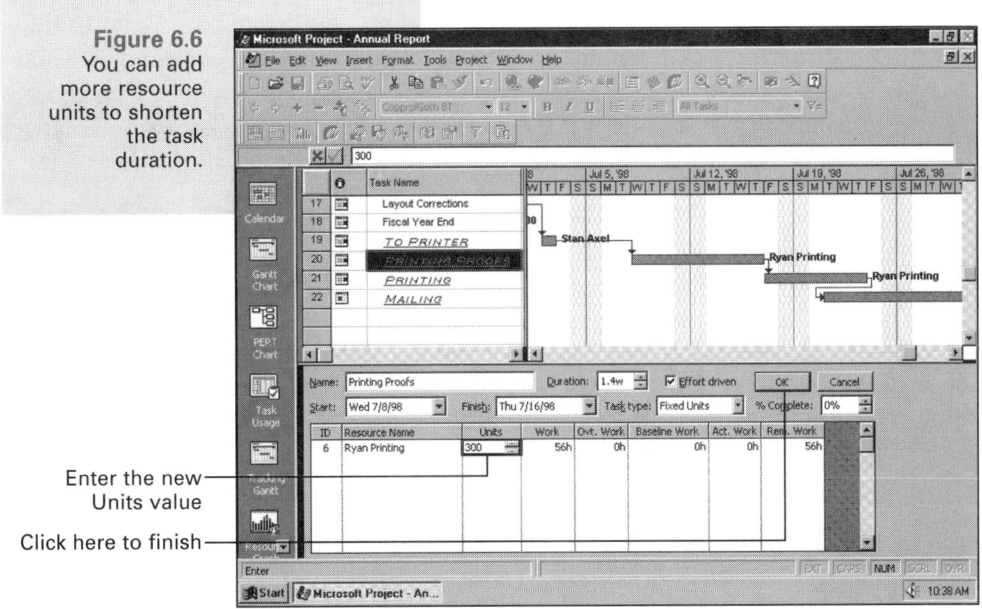

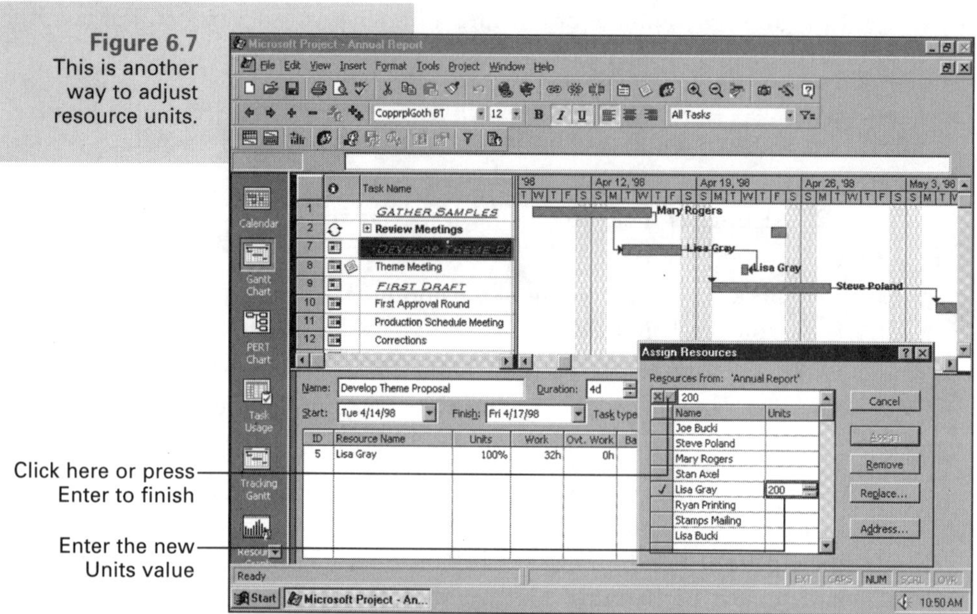

Figure 6.7 This is another way to adjust resource units.

If you don't have the option of increasing the number of resource units available to handle the task, you can add more resources to enable you to reduce the number of hours of work the driving resource must allocate to the task, thereby shortening the task's duration. For tasks with the default Fixed Units task type and for the Fixed Work task type, adding another resource automatically reduces the task duration. (Remember, Project uses the equation Duration= Work/Units to adjust the duration.) If you add one more resource, Project automatically gives each resource half of the work; Project assumes the resources will work concurrently, so the task can be completed in half the time.

Follow these steps to add more resources to a critical task and decrease the task's duration:

1. Change to Task Entry view.
2. In the upper pane, click a cell to select the critical task for which you want to add more resources.
3. In the lower pane, click in the first blank row of the Resource Name column. A drop-down list arrow appears at the far-right end of the text entry box.
4. Click to display the drop-down list; then click a resource in the list to select it (see Figure 6.8).

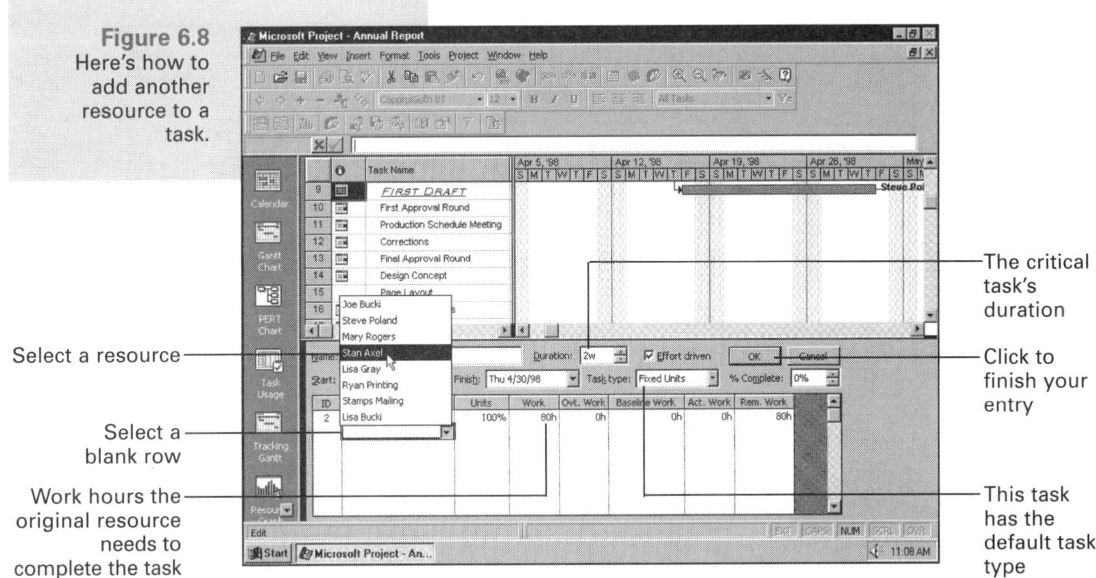

Figure 6.8 Here's how to add another resource to a task.

5. Click the OK button in the lower pane or the Enter button beside the text entry box to finish your entry. The new resource appears in the lower pane (see Figure 6.9). If you refer to Figure 6.8, you'll notice that the Work column for the original resource held 80h, for the 80 hours of work required to complete the task in the assigned duration. In Figure 6.9 you can see that these working hours have been adjusted in light of the new resource; the new resource offers 40h in the Work column, for a total of 80h between the two resources. The Duration entry drops from 2w in Figure 6.8 to 1w in Figure 6.9.

If the task has the Fixed Duration task type, adding an additional resource does not decrease the task duration. Instead, you need to manually adjust the Work hours for each resource so that their total matches the number of work hours available for only the original resource. You also can control the proportion of work each resource has, no matter what the task type by splitting the work evenly between the two resources or letting the driving resource retain the bulk of the work. Using the examples in Figures 6.8 and 6.9, we can specify 60 hours of work for the original resource, Steve Poland, and 20 hours of work for the new resource, Stan Axel. The total work given for the two resources then equals the 80 hours originally scheduled for Steve Poland (see Figure 6.10). To change each resource's Work entry, click in the Work column for the resource, type a new value (Project assumes you're specifying hours), and click on the OK button in the lower pane.

Figure 6.9 By default, adding a new resource decreases the task duration.

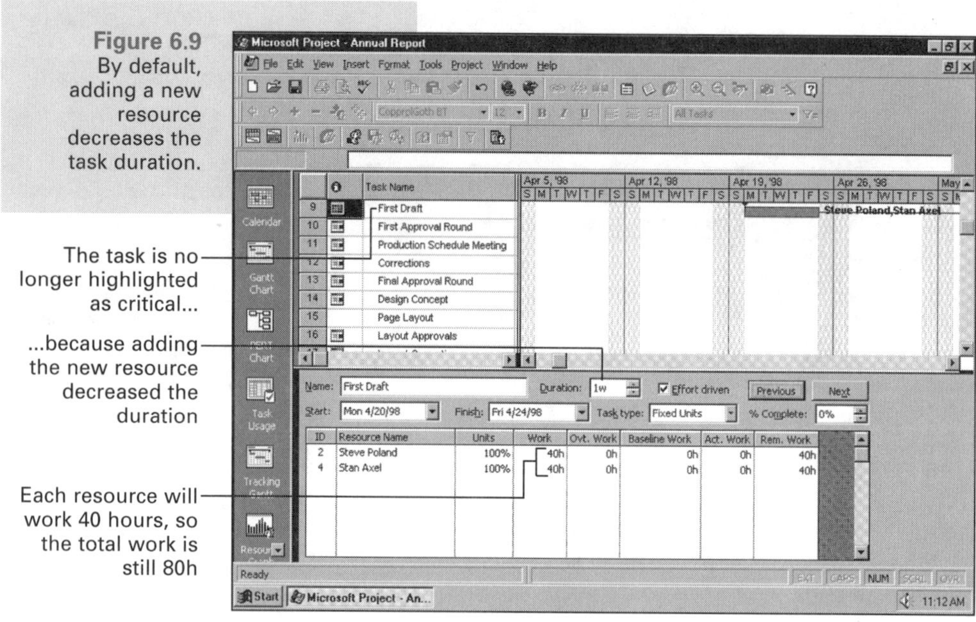

Figure 6.10 Here are the same two resources with the working hours adjusted.

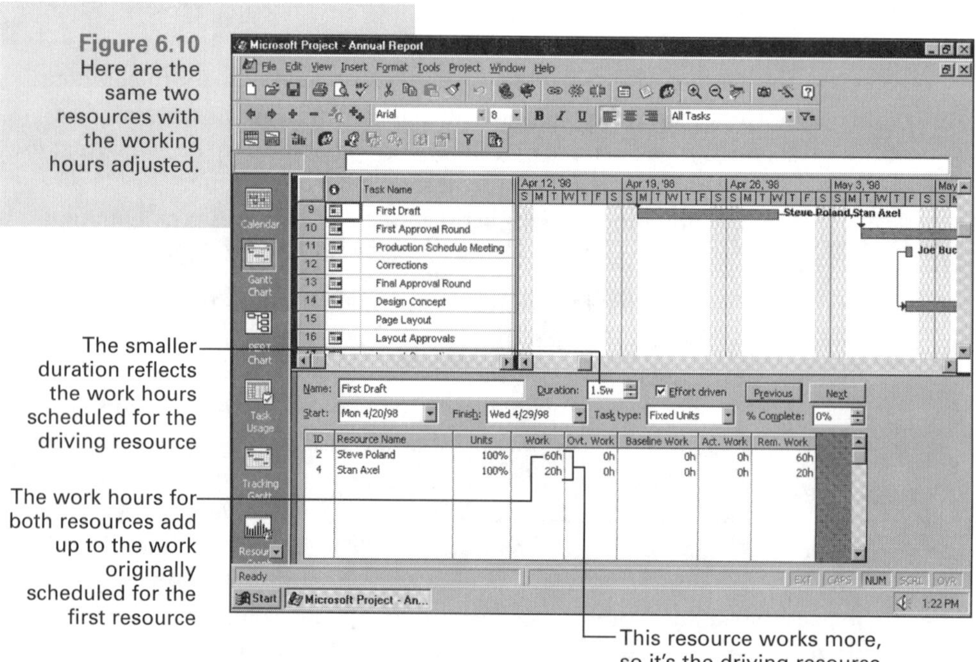

As an alternative to using the bottom pane of the Task Entry view to add resources, you can display the Assign Resources dialog box. (Click the Assign Resources button on the Standard toolbar after clicking the upper pane of Task Entry view.) Then you can drag new resources from the assignment box to the critical task. To do so, click the resource you want to drag, and then point to the gray box at the left of the resource name until you see the resource pointer (see Figure 6.11). Press and hold down the mouse button, and then drag the resource to the correct task name in the upper pane, and release the button.

You can add resources using the Resource Names columns of the Gantt Chart view by typing in additional resource names and separating the entries with a comma. Or, you can use the Resources tab of the Task Information dialog box to add more resources. These methods, however, don't let you adjust the hours each resource will spend on the task to tighten up the task duration. Your best bet, therefore, is to add more resources by using the techniques just described.

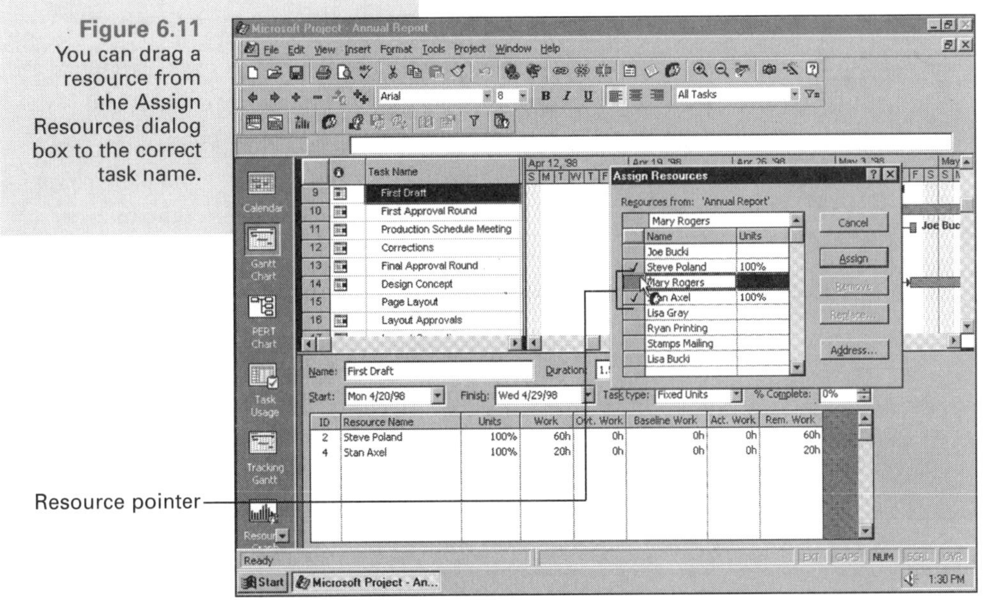

Figure 6.11 You can drag a resource from the Assign Resources dialog box to the correct task name.

Authorizing Overtime Work for a Task

Companies, particularly large ones, are obligated to compensate employees for overtime work. In some cases, you might also need to pay overtime charges for outside resources you bring in for your project. Overtime costs are required especially for any resources that are union workers. Thus, Project generally doesn't let you simply add extra shifts (overtime hours) for a resource by changing the Units entry to a value that's greater than 100% (or 1.00, if you're using decimal values). As you learned earlier, changing the Units entry assumes that more than one worker from the resource will work on the task simultaneously.

You also can't specify overtime by simply changing the working calendar so that a resource has more hours in the day. (You can use that technique, however, to resolve overallocations for salaried resources.) Project forces you to enter overtime hours in another way for two reasons:

- To ensure that overtime costs are calculated correctly, according to the overtime rate you entered when you added the resource to the file (see Chapter 4, "Managing Resources")
- To ensure that you approved the overtime work

The Task Entry view provides you the means to allocate overtime work for a task. After you add overtime, Project changes the task's duration to reflect the extra working hours, per day, provided by the overtime. Here's how to authorize overtime hours for a resource assigned to a critical task:

1. Change to Task Entry view.
2. In the upper pane of Task Entry view, click a cell in the critical task to which you want to assign overtime work. Information about the resource(s) assigned to the task appears in the lower pane.
3. Right-click the lower pane and click Resource Work. The pane changes to display more information about the resource's work schedule (see Figure 6.12).
4. Click the Ovt. Work cell belonging to the resource for which you want to specify overtime hours. Type the number of overtime hours you want to authorize, and then click the OK button in the lower pane. Project enters the overtime hours, and tightens the task's Duration entry accordingly (see Figure 6.13).

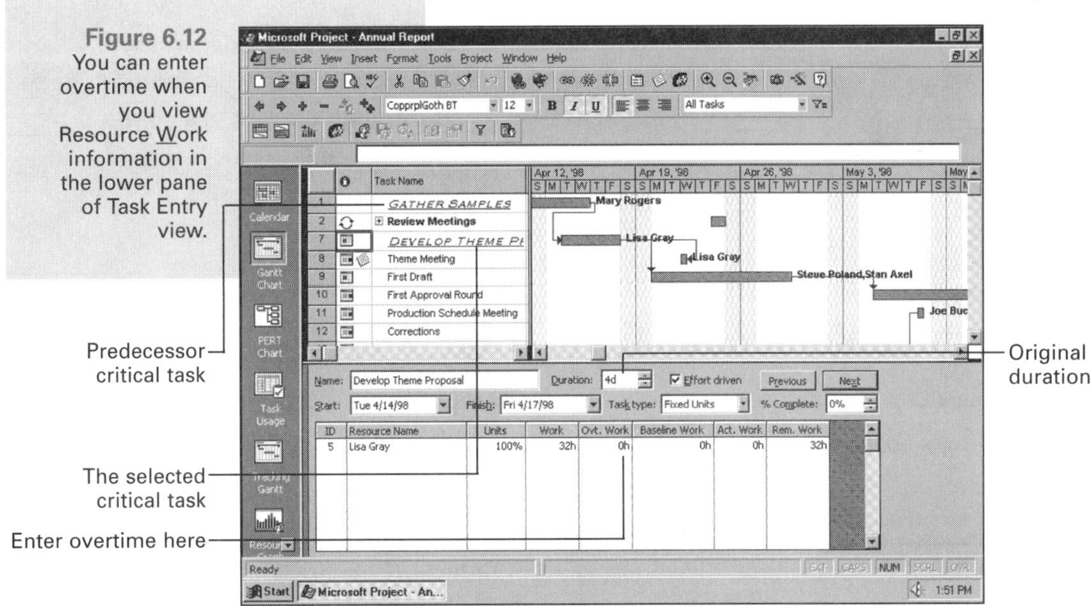

Figure 6.12 You can enter overtime when you view Resource Work information in the lower pane of Task Entry view.

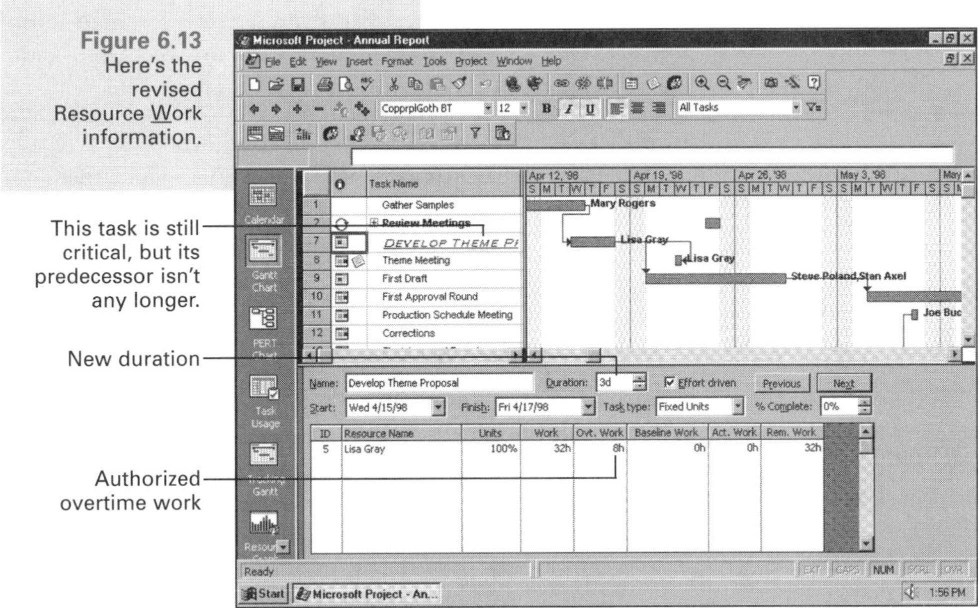

Figure 6.13 Here's the revised Resource Work information.

Adding overtime introduces slack in the schedule, which in turn might remove the critical designation for the task to which you add overtime, or (depending on task links and other task information) one or more predecessor tasks.

Using Multiple Critical Paths

In most instances, a task needs to have links to successor tasks (other tasks that cannot start or finish until the predecessor task starts or finishes, depending on the nature of the link) or have particular constraints set to be marked as critical and be part of the critical path. But that doesn't mean that tasks without successors or constraints can finish late without affecting the overall schedule. For example, if you set a project finish date of 4/30/98, *all* tasks must finish by that date for the project to finish on time.

Project 98 enables you to display *multiple critical paths* to mark more tasks as critical and help you identify potential trouble spots that could bog down your project. When you display multiple critical paths, Project resets certain information for tasks that have no constraints or successors, to make those tasks (and often any predecessors) critical.

Chapter 2 explained that even though a Task Sheet or Resource Sheet typically shows only a half-dozen or so fields (columns) in any given view, there are dozens of other fields you can display if needed. Many of these fields contain information that Project calculates to help it make decisions, such as determining which tasks are critical. Project uses two of these calculated fields to determine whether or not a task has slack and therefore whether or not it's critical: the *Late Finish Date* and the *Early Finish Date*.

A task cannot slip beyond its late finish date without delaying the finish of the whole project. When a task has no constraints or successors, Project sets the task's late finish date as the project finish date. This makes sense, because a task without constraints or links can move around in the schedule without affecting other tasks, but it still must finish by the project completion date. A task cannot finish before its early finish date, which Project calculates based on the task's duration, start date, resources, links, and so on. In other words, Project assumes that a task with a 2w duration requires a minimum of two weeks.

Therefore, if a task without successors or constraints falls in the middle of a lengthy project schedule, there could potentially be weeks between the early start date and the late finish date, time which Project considers *total slack* but which you might consider crucial lead time that you don't want to waste. When you turn on multiple critical paths, Project changes the late finish date for such tasks to the same date as the early finish date, eliminating that slack to make the tasks (and some predecessors) critical. Therefore, turning on multiple critical paths can highlight other groups of related tasks in the schedule to which you might want to add more resources or overtime, to ensure those tasks finish on time. To display multiple critical paths in Project, click the Tools menu; then click Options. Click the Calculation tab, and then click to place a check beside Calculate Multiple Critical Paths, as shown in Figure 6.14.

Working with Slack

Part of what defines a critical task is its impact on other tasks, depending on the relationships you established between tasks. Sometimes, there's room between related tasks, so the task scheduled first can slip (be delayed or take longer to finish than scheduled) without delaying the start or completion of the successor task. That room between tasks is called *float time* or *slack*. (As noted in the preceding section, if a task doesn't have a successor task, then the task's

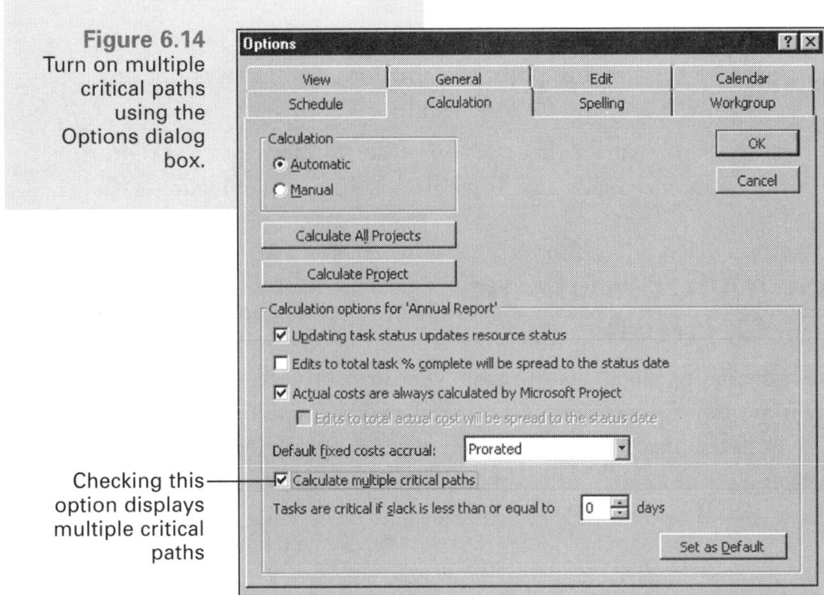

Figure 6.14 Turn on multiple critical paths using the Options dialog box.

slack is any time between the task's early start date and late finish date.) Slack between tasks is called *free slack*. Slack between a particular task and the project finish date is called *total slack*, and basically tells you how long the task can slip without impacting the project finish date.

Total slack measurements also can be negative. That happens when you have two linked tasks, both of which are constrained to start on particular dates. If you change the duration of the predecessor task to make it longer, and don't add any lead time for the successor task (so it can start before the finish of the predecessor), you'll create negative slack.

In optimizing your schedule, make sure that you look for negative slack measurements and make changes to eliminate them, to ensure that the critical path is realistic.

If the total slack for a task is less than a minimum amount you specified (which you'll learn to change shortly). Project identifies the task as a critical task.

You can display the free slack and total slack for the tasks in a schedule in the Task Sheet portion of Gantt Chart view or Task Entry view. Follow these steps to check the slack measurements for tasks:

1. Display Gantt Chart or Task Entry view.
2. Click anywhere in the Task Sheet portion of the view.
3. Open the View menu, point to Table for a submenu of options (see Figure 6.15), and click Schedule.
4. Use the scroll bar for that portion of the window to scroll right to display the Free Slack and Total Slack columns (see Figure 6.16).

Changing How Much Slack Makes a Task Critical

Although Chapter 20, "Customizing Microsoft Project," covers how to adjust many important Project features, one feature relating directly to slack and critical tasks bears mentioning here. You can change the minimum amount of slack that tasks must have to avoid being designated as critical tasks. By default, any task with 0 or fewer days of total slack is designated as a critical task.

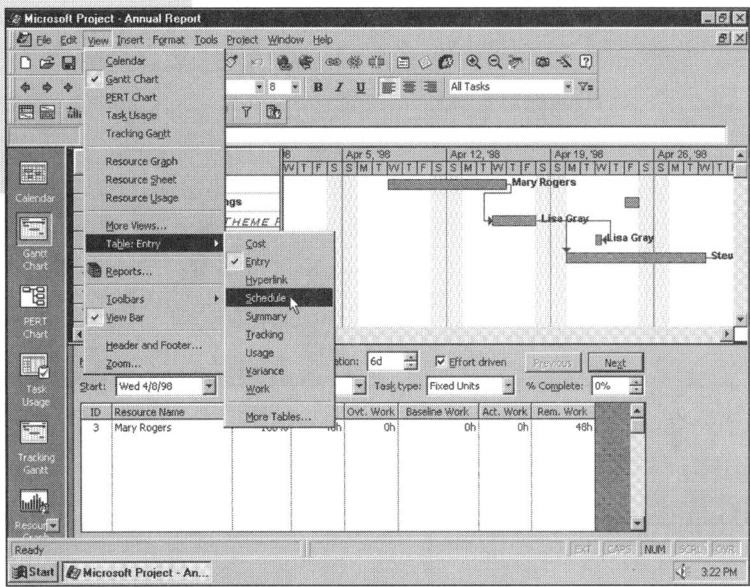

Figure 6.15 Select a way to see how much free slack and total slack your tasks have.

Slack measurements

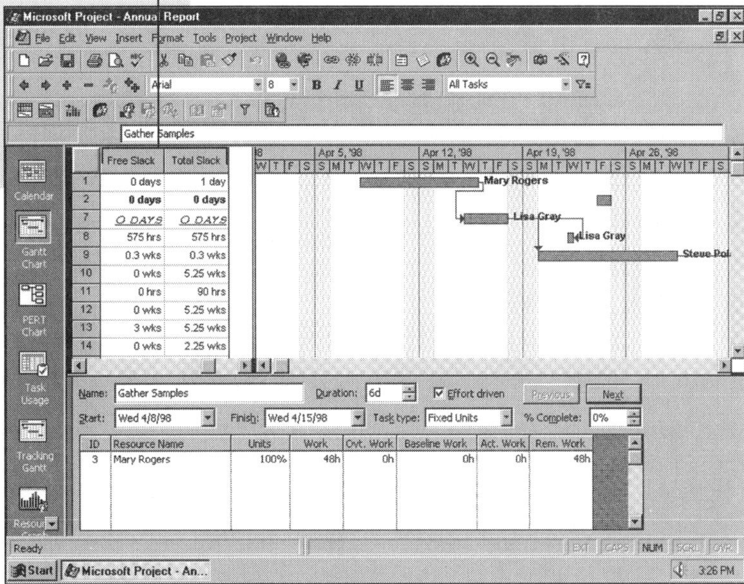

Figure 6.16 Here's what the slack columns look like when displayed in Task Entry view.

Increasing this setting designates more tasks as critical, giving you the opportunity to scrutinize them to look for ways to tighten the schedule. To change the option that controls which tasks are designated as critical, use these steps:

1. Open the Tools menu and click Options. The Options dialog box appears.
2. Click the Calculation tab to display its settings (see Figure 6.17).
3. Double-click the entry in the Tasks Are Critical If Slack Is Less Than or Equal To ... Days text box, and type a new entry. For example, type **3** to have Project designate any task with less than or equal to three days of slack as a critical task.
4. Click OK to close the dialog box. Project updates critical task designations in light of the new setting.

Adjusting Lead and Lag Times

Lead times and lag times can have a great impact on the slack available for a task as well as the critical path. (The "Working with Lead Times and Lag Times" section in Chapter 3 explains the basics of lead and lag times.)

You can, constraints allowing, add slack time by removing lead time or adding lag time. For example, you might change the Lag entry for a successor task from -2d to 0d to remove lead time. Adding slack time generally lengthens the

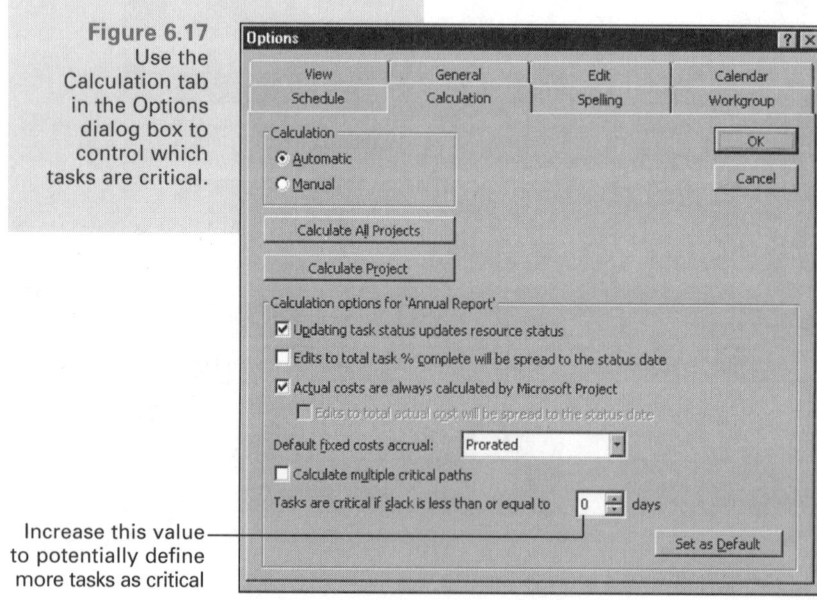

Figure 6.17 Use the Calculation tab in the Options dialog box to control which tasks are critical.

schedule to some degree. Depending how much slack you add, Project might remove a task from the critical path. This can be beneficial in your planning if you're really unsure how well you estimated the schedule for a task.

In contrast, to use lead and lag times to tighten the critical path, here are a few things you can do:

- Add lead time for a successor task where none exists, assuming that you can move up the start date of the successor task. For example, entering **-3d** creates three days' worth of lead time for a successor task.
- Add more lead time for a successor task with an FS link to its predecessor, as long as no constraint prohibits you from moving up the successor task.
- Cut back lag time, or eliminate it altogether, if constraints allow. For example, a 5d lag entry builds in five days of lag time; you might be able to change such an entry to **3d** or **2d**.

You can choose any of a number of techniques to adjust the lead and lag times for a task. For example, you can double-click a task name, click the Predecessors tab in the Task Information dialog box, and then edit the Lag column in the Predecessors list. Or, you can use the lower pane of Task Entry view to work with lead and lag time, as follows:

1. In the upper pane, click the name of the critical task for which you want to work with lead and lag times.
2. Right-click the lower pane; then click Predecessors & Successors on the shortcut menu that appears. The lower pane changes to show other tasks linked to the selected task, either as predecessors or successors (see Figure 6.18).
3. Click the cell in the Lag column for the link you want to edit. Type a new lag setting, and then click OK in the lower pane. Project adjusts any task schedule as needed, according to your change. For example, Figure 6.19 shows the result of eliminating the lag time assigned to row 9's predecessor task in row 7. The task in row 9 is no longer a critical task after the change.
4. To adjust lead and lag times for another task, select the task in the upper pane, and then make changes as needed in the lower pane.

Changing Constraints to Tighten the Schedule

Sometimes, constraints prohibit you from changing lead and lag time, or a schedule conflict arises if you try to do so. If you have Planning Wizard

Figure 6.18 The bottom pane has been adjusted to let you work with linked tasks.

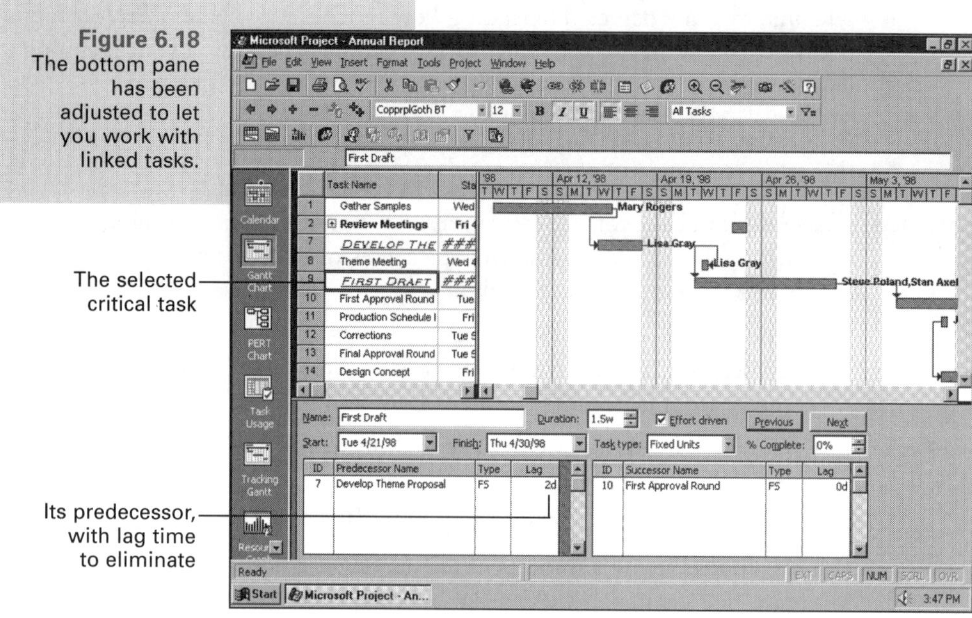
The selected critical task
Its predecessor, with lag time to eliminate

Figure 6.19 Here's an example of working with linked tasks.

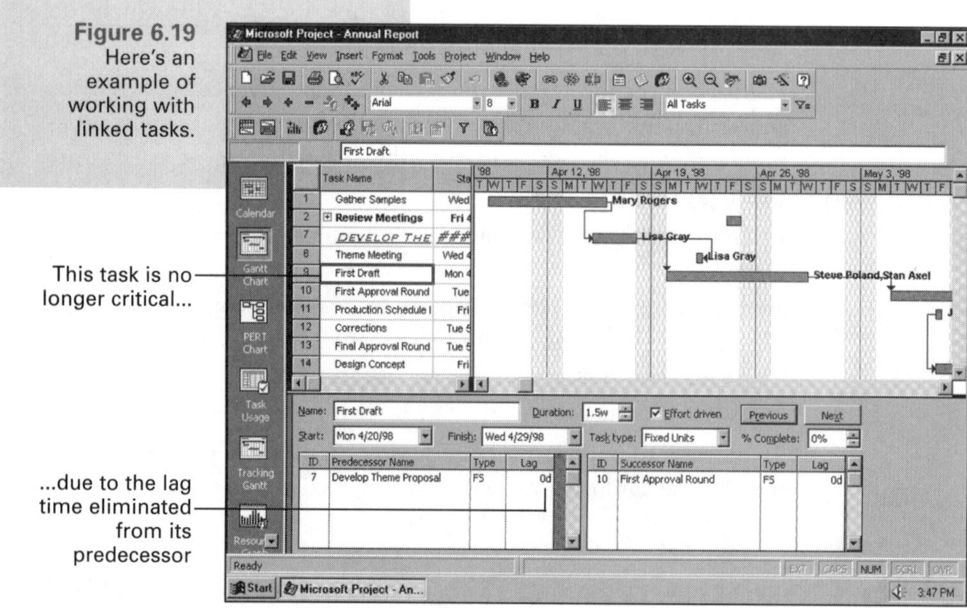
This task is no longer critical...
...due to the lag time eliminated from its predecessor

enabled, it warns you if a lead or lag time change will create such a conflict. For example, Figure 6.20 shows the message that appears if you try to add the lag time before a task that's constrained to Finish No Later Than (FNLT) a particular date.

As such, you should review all the constraints you assigned to tasks, looking for constraint changes that will allow you to tighten the schedule. In some cases, you might want to change constraints to ensure that a task stays on the critical path. Here are a few ideas of the types of constraint changes you can make:

- Change more tasks to As Soon As Possible (ASAP) constraints so that you can add lead times
- Remove Finish No Earlier Than (FNET) constraints for predecessor tasks, especially if they're linked to a successor with an FS link
- Use more Must Finish On (MFO) constraints to prevent predecessor tasks from slipping further out

To see a list of the constraints you assigned to tasks so that you can quickly identify which constraints you want to change, do the following:

1. Change to Gantt Chart view or Table Entry view and click a task name in the list.
2. Open the View menu, point to Table, and click More Tables.
3. In the Tables list (with the Task option button beside it selected), double-click Constraint Dates, or click it once and then click Apply. The Task Sheet changes to include Constraint Type and Constraint Date columns. You can drag the split bar from the upper pane, and use the scroll bar for the task list to display those columns (see Figure 6.21).

Figure 6.20 Constraints can keep you from making the schedule adjustments you want.

Planning Wizard

This action will cause a scheduling conflict. Task 7 of 'Annual Report' is linked to a task that cannot move, and as a result the link cannot be honored.

You can:

Cancel. Avoid the scheduling conflict.

Continue. Allow the scheduling conflict.

OK | Cancel | Help

Don't tell me about this again.

Chapter 3 covers the different types of task constraints in more detail. To quickly change constraints while the list of task constraints is onscreen, double-click the desired task name to display the Task Information dialog box. Click the Advanced tab. In the Constraint Task area, use the Type drop-down list and Date text box to specify a change to the constraint.

Ignoring Constraints to Remove Negative Slack

If your project has hundreds of tasks, manually reviewing and changing constraint types could take quite some time. Although you may want to use the manual route to really fine-tune your schedule, Project offers an alternative for situations where you only want to eliminate negative slack from the schedule. (As an example, negative slack occurs when a successor task can't start until its predecessor finishes, but the predecessor's finish date is after a Start No Later Than or Must Start On constraint date for the successor.) Basically, negative slack means that accomplishing both tasks within all the constraints is physically impossible, so you need to remove that negative slack. You can tell Project to ignore constraints and move tasks, where needed, to remove every instance of negative slack in the schedule, as follows. Click to open the Tools menu; then click Options. Click the Schedule tab; then click to clear the check mark beside the Tasks Will Always Honor Their Constraint Dates choice. Click OK.

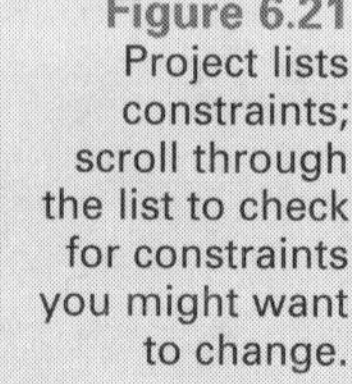

Figure 6.21 Project lists constraints; scroll through the list to check for constraints you might want to change.

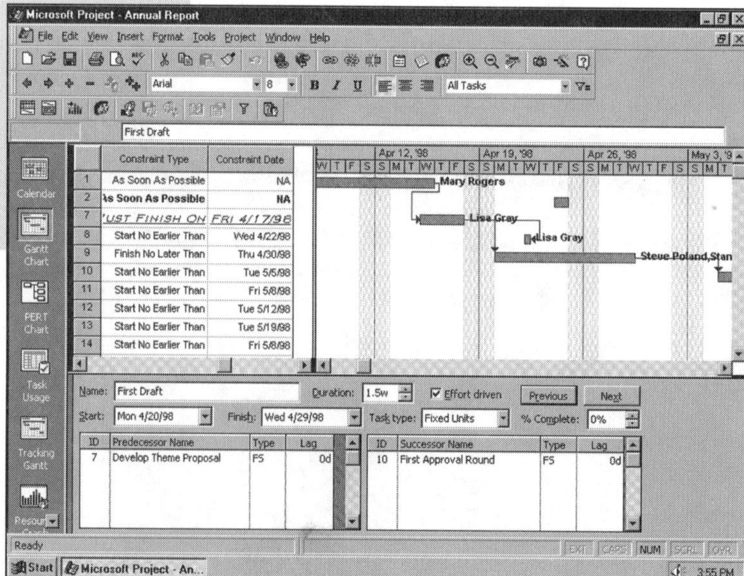

7

Comparing Progress versus Your Baseline Plan

In This Chapter

- Capturing the original project information and schedule
- Reporting work that has been completed
- Preserving the update information, and saving an interim plan
- Looking to see if your project's on time, ahead of schedule, or running behind

Because a project often calls on a varied combination of resources, tasks, and other factors, you need to act as a "deejay" to ensure that the right tune plays at the right time (tasks stay on schedule), that the volume is right (everything's done correctly), and that all the dancers stay in step (your resources remain available and capable to work when you need them).

This chapter shows you how to compare actual progress on a project with the schedule you had planned, so that you can make adjustments, if needed, to meet your project goals.

Creating the Baseline

When you're relatively young and the doctor puts you through your first thorough physical, the doc's not being paranoid and looking for imaginary illnesses. The physician's gathering your vital statistics while you're in good health, so that there will be a basis for comparison if you ever begin feeling ill. If your blood pressure is very low when you're healthy, a slight climb in the pressure can signal to your doctor that something serious is going on. However, if the doctor doesn't have your normal blood pressure reading, he or she might not catch the fact that your reading's higher than normal. Those original health measurements your doctor takes become the baseline, the starting point that your doctor uses for future comparison.

Project enables you to take a baseline reading of your schedule, too. Thus, you'll have a record of where you started that you can use to diagnose any problems that crop up in the schedule and budget. When you save a baseline for your schedule, Project records all the original details about your plan. Then you can compare information you entered about the actual work performed and actual costs with the plans you started with. (You'll learn how to do so later in this chapter.)

The first time you save any project file after adding information to it, Project displays the dialog box shown in Figure 7.1, which asks whether you want to save the baseline for your new file. To save the baseline information, click the bottom option button, and click OK. If you don't want to save the baseline (because you haven't added all the information for the schedule), leave the top option button selected, and then click OK.

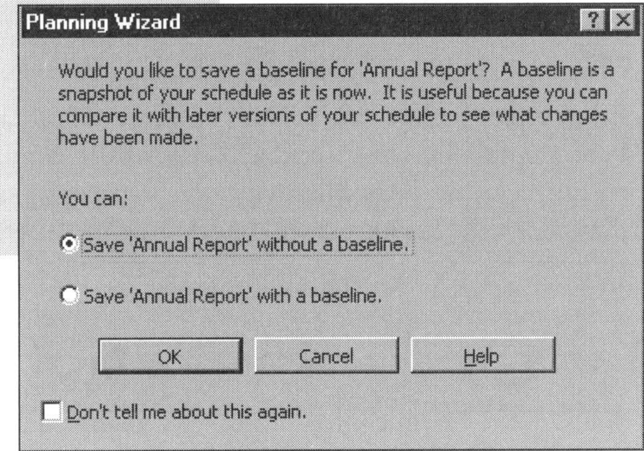

Figure 7.1 When you add information to your file and are trying to save it, Project asks if you want to add a baseline.

Every time you save the baseline, the save process overwrites any baseline information you saved previously. If you want to take a "snapshot" of your project at any given time and leave the baseline intact, save an *interim plan*. See the "Saving and Viewing an Interim Plan" section later in this chapter.

Don't worry if you opt not to create a baseline while saving. (In fact, there's really no point in entering a baseline until you enter all your task and resource information, as described in the first six chapters of this book.) You have the option of saving baseline information at any point during the plan development process. You also can save a baseline for only part of the project, by selecting certain tasks to track in detail. Here are the steps for creating your schedule baseline:

1. Enter all the task and resource information you want to save as part of the baseline. It doesn't hurt to double-check to make sure that everything's in place, including links and fixed task costs you might have overlooked.
2. (Optional) If you want to save only certain tasks, select the rows you want in the Task Sheet in Gantt Chart view. (Make sure that you're in Gantt Chart view by opening the View menu and clicking on Gantt Chart, or by clicking the Gantt Chart icon on the View Bar.) Select the tasks you want by pointing to the row number for the top row, and dragging down to highlight (select) the rows. To select noncontiguous rows, press and hold down Ctrl and then click each additional row.

3. Open the Tools menu and point to Tracking. A submenu of commands appears.
4. Click Save Baseline. The Save Baseline dialog box appears (see Figure 7.2).
5. If you saved baseline information for all the tasks, leave the Entire Project option button selected and click OK to continue. If you selected specific tasks for the baseline, click the Selected Tasks option button; then click OK. In either case, Project stores the baseline information.

Viewing Baseline Information

After you save the baseline information, you might want to look at the baseline values for reference, or print them out for others on the team. To view the baseline information, use a variation of the Task Sheet called the Baseline Table. Although the "Choosing a Table" section in Chapter 9, "Working with the Different Project Views," provides more details, here are the steps for viewing this table of baseline information:

The baseline information also appears in one of Project's reports, the Project Summary report in the Overview category. For more on project reports, see Chapter 12, "Creating and Printing a Report."

1. Make sure that you're in Gantt Chart view by opening the View menu and clicking Gantt Chart, or clicking the Gantt Chart icon in the View Bar. Gantt Chart view appears with a cell selected in the Task Sheet.
2. Open the View menu, point to Table, and click More Tables. Or, click the More Tables icon on the View Bar. The More Tables dialog box appears (see Figure 7.3).

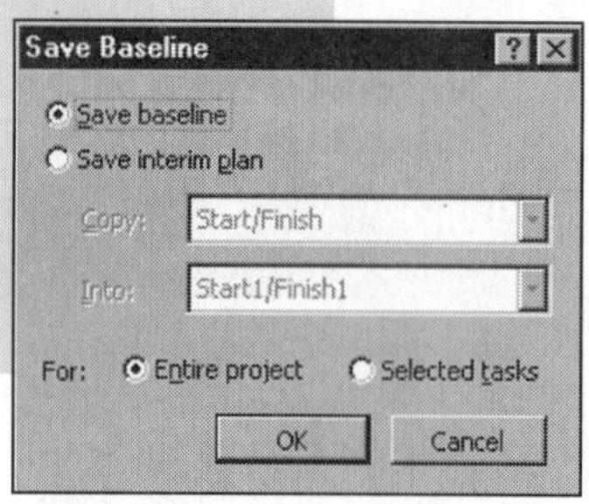

Figure 7.2 Using this dialog box, you can save baseline information easily at any time.

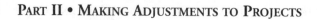

Figure 7.3 Selecting a table here changes the columns that appear in the Task Sheet.

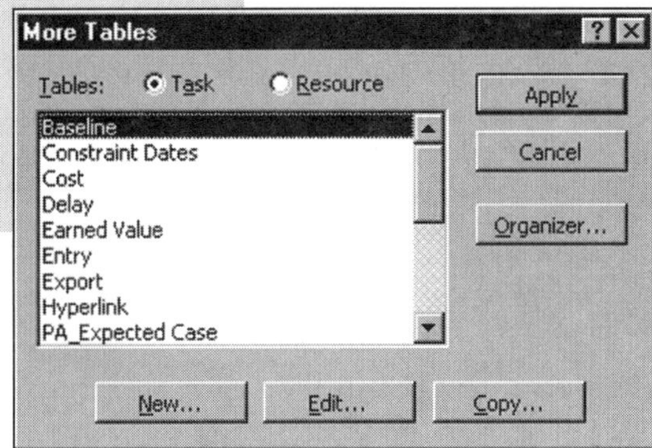

3. Make sure that you leave the Task option button selected at the top of the dialog box. From the Tables list, select Baseline by double-clicking it, or by clicking it once, and then clicking Apply. Project displays the baseline columns in the Task Sheet.
4. Scroll the Task Sheet to the right a bit, and drag the vertical split bar to the right to display more of the Task Sheet, so that you can see the baseline columns (see Figure 7.4).

If you want to return to the regular Task Sheet view at any time, open the View menu, point to Table, and click Entry.

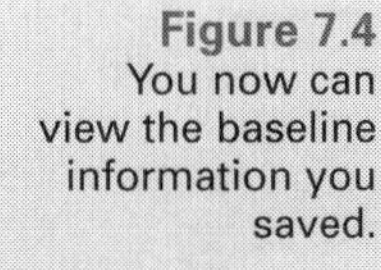

Figure 7.4 You now can view the baseline information you saved.

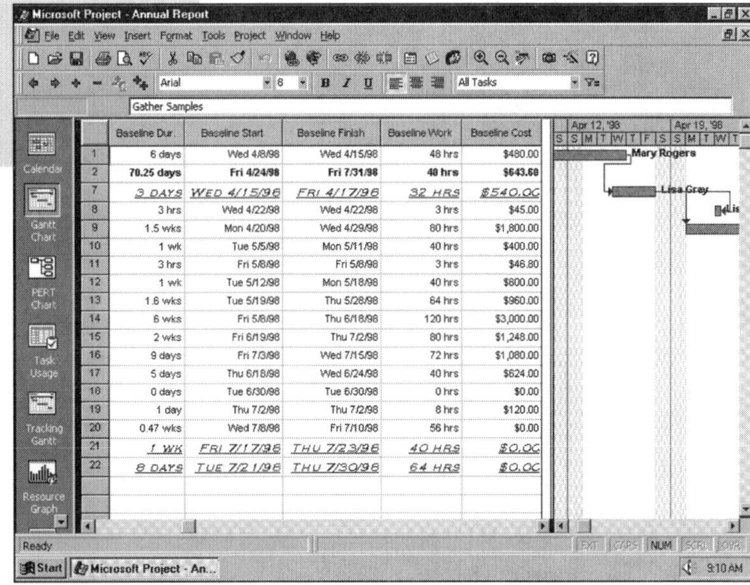

	Baseline Dur.	Baseline Start	Baseline Finish	Baseline Work	Baseline Cost
1	6 days	Wed 4/8/98	Wed 4/15/98	48 hrs	$480.00
2	70.25 days	Fri 4/24/98	Fri 7/31/98	40 hrs	$643.60
7	3 DAYS	WED 4/15/98	FRI 4/17/98	32 HRS	$540.00
8	3 hrs	Wed 4/22/98	Wed 4/22/98	3 hrs	$45.00
9	1.5 wks	Mon 4/20/98	Wed 4/29/98	80 hrs	$1,800.00
10	1 wk	Tue 5/5/98	Mon 5/11/98	40 hrs	$400.00
11	3 hrs	Fri 5/8/98	Fri 5/8/98	3 hrs	$46.80
12	1 wk	Tue 5/12/98	Mon 5/18/98	40 hrs	$600.00
13	1.6 wks	Tue 5/19/98	Thu 5/28/98	64 hrs	$960.00
14	6 wks	Fri 5/8/98	Thu 6/18/98	120 hrs	$3,000.00
15	2 wks	Fri 6/19/98	Thu 7/2/98	80 hrs	$1,248.00
16	9 days	Fri 7/3/98	Wed 7/15/98	72 hrs	$1,080.00
17	5 days	Thu 6/18/98	Wed 6/24/98	40 hrs	$624.00
18	0 days	Tue 6/30/98	Tue 6/30/98	0 hrs	$0.00
19	1 day	Thu 7/2/98	Thu 7/2/98	8 hrs	$120.00
20	0.47 wks	Wed 7/8/98	Fri 7/10/98	56 hrs	$0.00
21	1 WK	FRI 7/17/98	THU 7/23/98	40 HRS	$0.00
22	8 DAYS	TUE 7/21/98	THU 7/30/98	64 HRS	$0.00

Entering Completed Work

Project would be an even better product if you could attach a "work meter" to each and every resource that would automatically capture what the resource does, and report that information to Project. Because the world isn't that high-tech yet—and such an approach has the scary feeling of a "Big Brother" society—you'll have to tell Project what work has been completed on scheduled tasks.

Although Project offers you several means of entering information about actual work completed, one of the most convenient methods is the Tracking toolbar. To display the Tracking toolbar, right-click any onscreen toolbar, and then select Tracking. The Tracking toolbar appears, as shown in Figure 7.5. You'll use several of its buttons as you update and view information about completed work in the Gantt Chart view. I'll describe each button when you need it.

Choosing a Status Date

You'll learn in this chapter and the next one that Project automates some features for updating completed work. In addition, Project calculates how much work has been completed, costs that have accumulated, and whether the project is ahead or behind schedule and budget. Normally, when you're updating the work completed in a schedule, Project assumes that you're marking all the

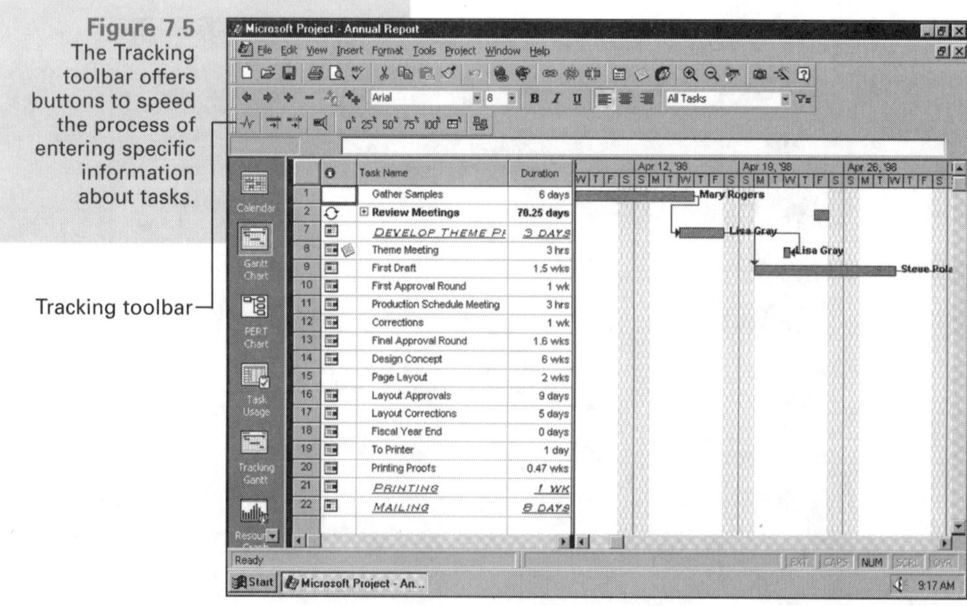

Figure 7.5 The Tracking toolbar offers buttons to speed the process of entering specific information about tasks.

work completed as of the current date (which is kept by your computer's clock). However, there may be instances where you want Project to use a different date when updating work and performing calculations regarding completed work and accumulated costs. For example, let's say that every Friday at 4 p.m. your group has a status meeting to discuss progress on individual tasks. Given your other commitments, you usually don't have time to enter that update information into the project file until Tuesday. The date that your status information really applies to is the previous Friday. So, to make it easier to use some methods to enter your updates and to ensure that Project's status calculations are accurate, you should enter the previous Friday's date as the *status date*.

To change the project status date before you enter completed work information, follow these steps:

1. Open the Project menu and click Project Information. The Project Information dialog box appears.
2. Click the drop-down list arrow for the Status Date option; then use the pop-up calendar to specify an alternate date. Alternately, if you want to use the current date as the status date, drag over the current entry in the Status Date text box, and then type **NA**.
3. Click OK to close the Project Information dialog box and finish setting the status date.

Updating Task by Task

There are three ways to tell Project about work that has been completed on a task or a selected set of tasks. The first method, updating completed work information with the mouse, is probably the most time-consuming, but enables you to have the greatest control over and familiarity with details about the completed work. With this method, you can update work using the calendar, indicating that, for example, someone has completed three out of five days of work scheduled for a task. Project calculates the percentage of work completed. To update task completion information using your mouse, work with the Gantt chart bars in Gantt Chart view. Point to the left end of the bar for the task you want to update, so that the mouse pointer changes to a percentage pointer. Press and hold the left mouse button and drag to the right (see Figure 7.6). As you drag, a Task information box appears, telling you how many days will be marked as completed. When you release the mouse button, Project indicates the percentage of the task that has been completed by placing a dark completion bar within the Gantt chart bar for the task you modified (see Figure 7.7). If a task has not started on time and you need to enter information about the actual starting date, use the method described next to update the task.

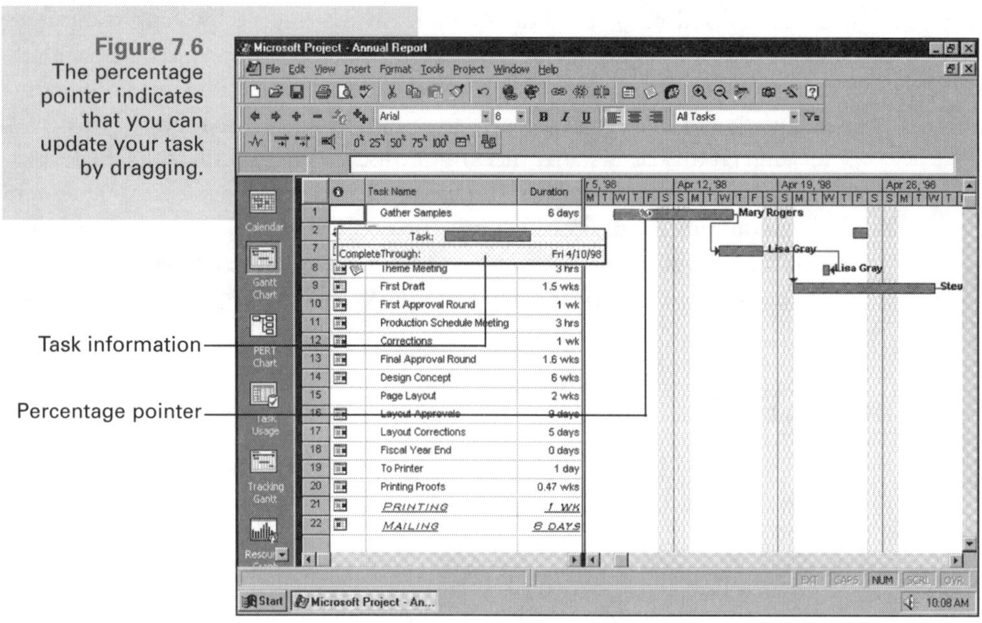
Task information
Percentage pointer

Figure 7.6 The percentage pointer indicates that you can update your task by dragging.

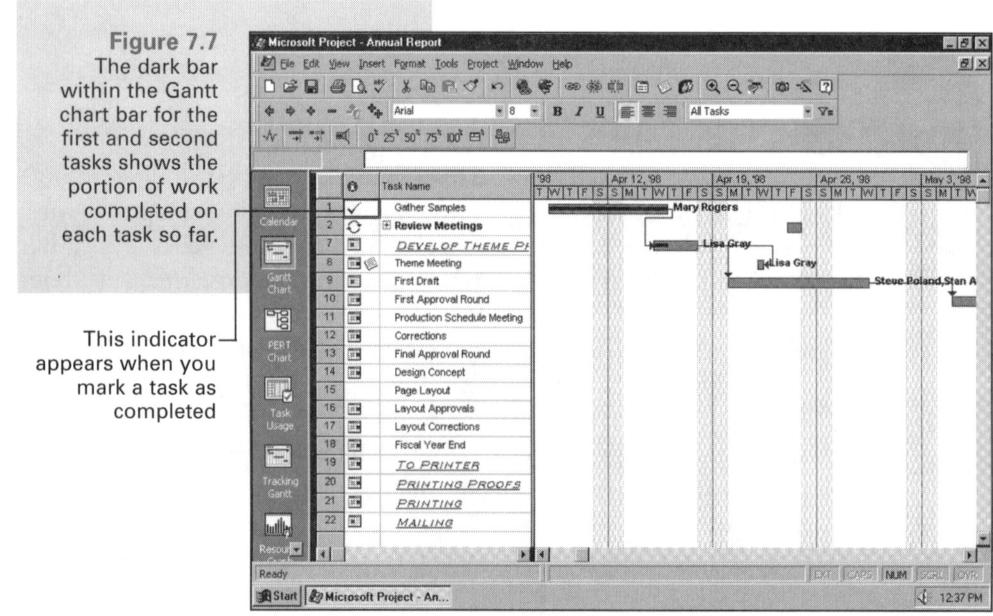
This indicator appears when you mark a task as completed

Figure 7.7 The dark bar within the Gantt chart bar for the first and second tasks shows the portion of work completed on each task so far.

The second method also enables you to update tasks one at a time, but gives you some options about how you specify that the work is completed. This method enables you to specify the actual start and finish dates for the task when those dates differ from the dates you scheduled. To use this method, follow these steps:

1. Select the task or tasks you want to update in the Task Sheet.

You can't select a summary task (the "master" task for a set of recurring tasks) to update it; you can only select the subtasks within a summary task. For more on working with summary tasks and subtasks, see Chapter 13, "Working with Outlining."

2. Open the Tools menu, point to Tracking, and click Update Tasks. Alternately, click the Update Tasks button on the Tracking toolbar. The Update Tasks dialog box appears (see Figure 7.8).
3. Enter information about the work that has been completed using one of the following three methods:

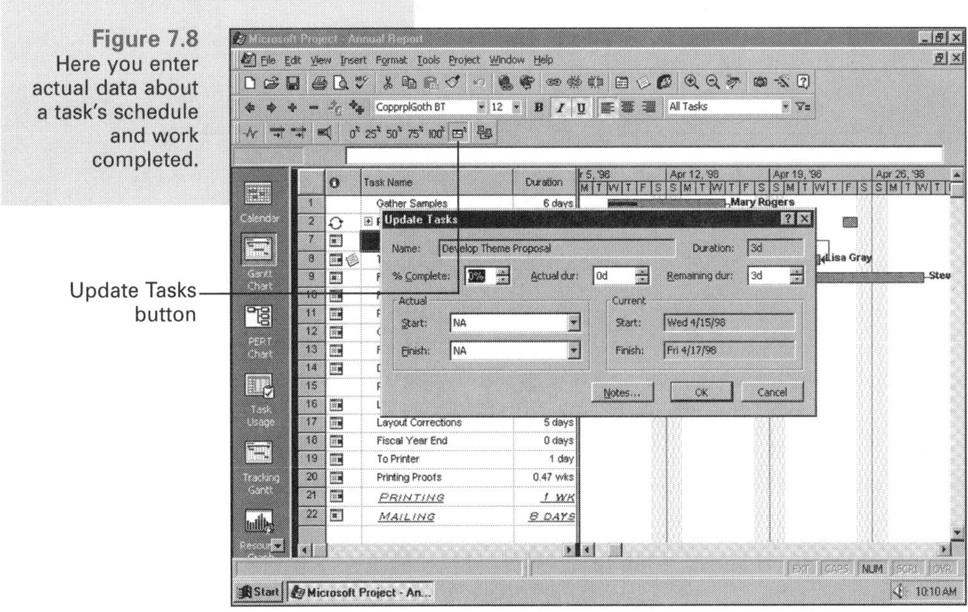

Figure 7.8 Here you enter actual data about a task's schedule and work completed.

- Enter a percentage value, such as 10 for 10%, in the % Complete text box, which is highlighted by default when you display the Update Tasks dialog box. Project changes the duration settings for you when you finish updating the task.
- Enter the number of days of work completed in the Actual Dur text box. If you want to use a duration other than the default (days), enter the duration abbreviation with the value you enter, such as **w** for weeks. Project calculates the percentage completed information and remaining duration information.
- Enter the number of days of work you estimate are remaining for the task in the Remaining Dur text box. Again, if you want to enter a duration that's not in days, include the appropriate duration abbreviation. When you specify work completed this way, Project calculates the percentage completed and duration.

4. If it looks like the actual starting or finishing date for the task will differ from those dates entered in the Current area of the Update Tasks dialog box, change the Start and Finish text box entries accordingly. Enter the new dates in mm/dd/yy format, or click the drop-down arrow beside either text box and use the pop-up calendar to specify the date. (By default, these text boxes contain NA if the actual date, according to your computer's date and time information, is later than the scheduled start date for the task.)
5. If you want to add notes describing special circumstances about why a task might be ahead of or behind schedule, click the Notes button, enter the information in the Notes dialog box that appears, and then click OK.
6. Click OK. Project updates the tasks, and will move and adjust any tasks as needed to reflect your changes in the Actual Start or Finish dates. It also uses a dark bar to mark the percentage of completed work you indicated for the selected task(s).

The final method for updating tasks is more "quick and dirty," and gives you less flexibility in specifying exact percentages or days of completed work. For this method, select the task or tasks you want to update in the Task Sheet, then click one of the five percentage buttons (0%, 25%, 50%, 75%, or 100%) on the Tracking toolbar. Project updates the Gantt bar(s) accordingly. Of course, you use the 0% button to remove any completed work that you previously specified. For example, if you thought an external resource had completed half a task, but you discover that no work has actually been completed (for instance, your contact person initially fibbed to you), you can select the task and click the 0% button to show the true percentage measurement.

If you select multiple tasks in the Task Sheet before displaying the Update Tasks dialog box, you can enter actual duration or actual start and finish information. Keep in mind, however, that these changes apply to all of the selected tasks. An instance where such a "global" change might be useful is if the project starting date becomes delayed, and you need to push out the actual starting dates for multiple tasks. Generally, you should select multiple tasks only when you want to enter the same % Complete value for all of them.

The Update As Scheduled button (second from the left on the Tracking toolbar) specifies work completed for the selected task(s) based on the scheduled start date(s) and the status date (or the current date, if you didn't specify a status date as described previously in this section). Project assumes that all work scheduled between those dates has been completed, and enters the work update information accordingly, adding dark tracking bars to the Gantt chart.

Updating Tasks by Resource

In some instances, you might not have information to enter about the work completed for all of the tasks that were underway recently. For example, say that in the last week, you received a progress report from only one resource, such as an outside contractor. However, other outside contractors and internal resources assigned to some of the same tasks have not reported. When such a situation arises, you need to be able to enter work completed on a resource-by-resource basis. You can use either the Task Usage view or Resource Usage view to enter actual work completed, by resource.

Using Task Usage View

If you still want to view tasks in order according to their ID or order in the Task Sheet, you can switch to the Task Usage view, which lists the tasks in order and then lists the resource assignments below each task. Then, you can find the task you need and enter a value for completed work for the resource assignment. Follow these steps to enter completed work for a resource in Task Usage view:

1. To change to Task Usage view, click to open the View menu; then click Task Usage, or click the Task Usage icon on the View Bar.

2. Click to open the View menu, point to Table; then click the Work choice. This changes which columns appear in Task Sheet portion of the view, including displaying the column where you enter completed work.
3. Drag the vertical split bar to the right so that you can see the Actual column of the Task Sheet portion of the view. You enter completed work values in this column.
4. Scroll to display the task for which you want to update resource work; then click the Actual column for the resource's assignment under the task.
5. Enter a completed work value in the cell, as shown in Figure 7.9. Project assumes that you're entering a value in hours.
6. Press Enter or click the green Enter button on the Entry box to complete the entry.

If you want to enter the total work completed on a task in Task Entry view, select the Actual cell for the row that holds the task information (rather than an assignment row below the task), and enter the work value.

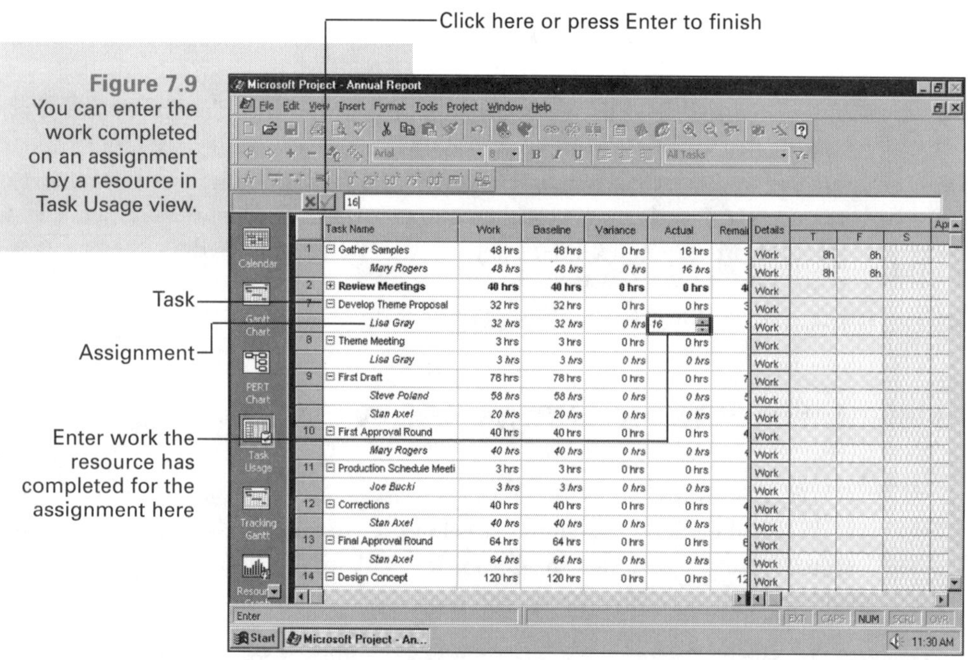

Click here or press Enter to finish
Task
Assignment
Enter work the resource has completed for the assignment here
Microsoft Project - Annual Report

Figure 7.9 You can enter the work completed on an assignment by a resource in Task Usage view.

Using Resource Usage View

If only one or two resources have reported completed work to you, you don't want to sift through the Task Sheet in Gantt Chart view or Task Usage view and hunt for each task handled by the resource to update it. Instead, you can use the Resource Usage view, which lists assignments by resource. To update completed work in Resource Usage view, follow these steps:

1. To change to Resource Usage view, click the View menu; then click Resource Usage, or click the Resource Usage icon on the View Bar.
   - Click the View menu, point to Table; then click the Work choice. This adds several more columns to the Resource Sheet portion of the view, including the column where you enter completed work.
2. If necessary, drag the column header for the Resource Name column to the right so that you can clearly see the assignment names indented beneath each resource. Then drag the vertical split bar to the right so you can see the Actual column for the Task Sheet portion of the view. You enter completed work values in this column.
3. Scroll to display the resource for which you want to update completed work; then click the Actual column cell for that assignment under the task.
4. Enter a completed work value in the cell, as shown in Figure 7.10. Project assumes that you're entering a value in hours.

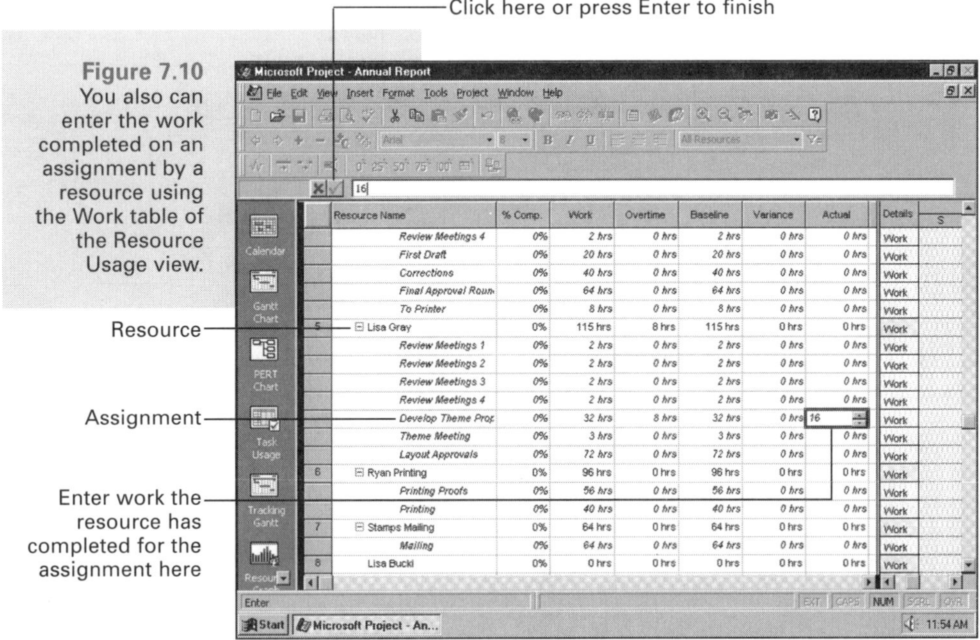
Click here or press Enter to finish
Resource
Assignment
Enter work the resource has completed for the assignment here
Microsoft Project - Annual Report

Figure 7.10 You also can enter the work completed on an assignment by a resource using the Work table of the Resource Usage view.

5. Press Enter or click the green Enter button on the Entry box to complete the entry.

Note

Don't forget that you can hide columns in the Task Sheet portion of the view to make data entry easier. For example, you might want to hide the % Comp., Work, Overtime, Baseline, and Variance columns in Figure 7.10. To hide a column, right-click the column heading; then click Hide Column.

Using Assignment Information

In either the Task Usage or Resource Usage view, you can double-click any assignment to display the Assignment Information dialog box. Click the Tracking tab to display its entries. Then, enter the completed work value (in hours) in the Actual Work text box (see Figure 7.11), or adjust the % Work Complete entry to use a percentage to specify how much work has been completed. If the assignment began early or late, change the Actual Start date, too. Click OK to finish entering the work.

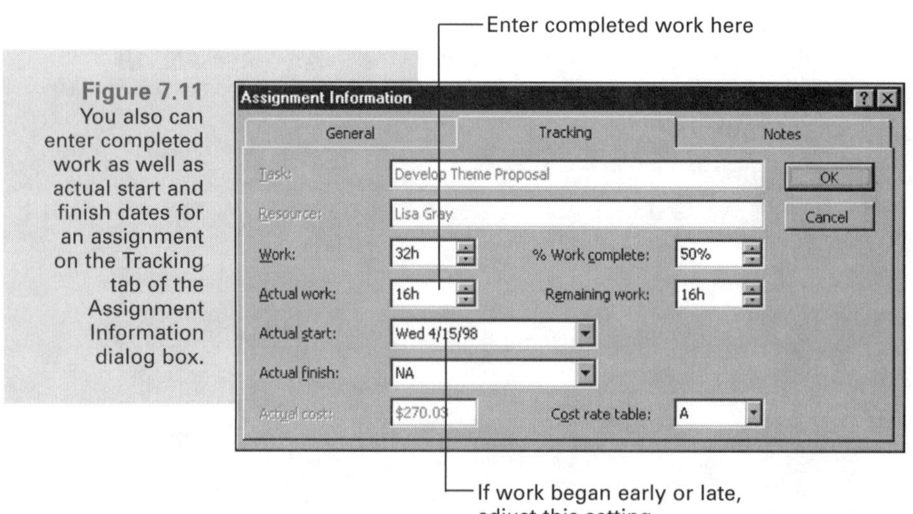

Figure 7.11 You also can enter completed work as well as actual start and finish dates for an assignment on the Tracking tab of the Assignment Information dialog box.

Entering Daily Values (Custom Time Period Tracking)

Chapter 5, "Resolving Overallocations and Overbooked Resources," explained how to use the new contouring feature in Project 98 to distribute hours worked on a task in the pattern of your choice. By default, when you assign a resource to a task, Project uses the flat contour and divides the work evenly over the duration of the project. That is, for a four-day task, the resource will be scheduled to work eight hours per day for four days. If you apply a contour to the assignment, however, Project extends the task duration and reallocates the daily work in a pattern such as a bell curve, in which the resource works fewer hours at the start and finish of the assignment, and full-time during the middle of the assignment. In addition, Chapter 5 explained how to create an edited contour so that you could control how many hours on a given day the resource is scheduled to work.

Similarly, you may need to have exact control over how you enter completed work for a resource to ensure your project tracking is accurate. For example, say a resource is assigned to work full-time on a task for five days, but actually only completes six hours of work per day for the first three days. Here's how to enter such precise settings for work completed:

1. Change to the Task Usage view or Resource Usage view.
2. Right-click the right pane of the view (the yellow area that displays work per day). Then click on Actual Work. Alternately, click the Format menu to open it, point to Details, and then click Actual Work. In the right pane, the schedule for each assignment is split into two rows. The top row, Work, holds scheduled entries. The bottom row, Act. Work (which may appear as "Act. W" unless you increase the width of the Details column), is where you enter actual work completed for the assignment.
3. Scroll to display the resource assignment for which you want to enter daily work values.
4. Click in the cell in the Act. Work row for the appropriate date, and type the work value. Figure 7.12 shows an example.
5. Press Enter or click the green Enter button on the Entry box to complete the entry.

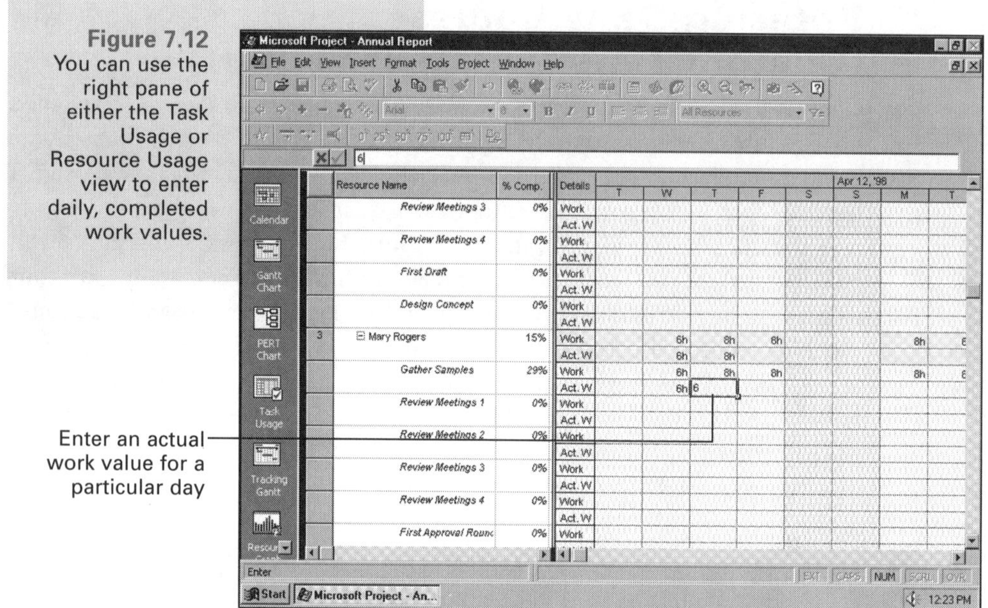

Figure 7.12 You can use the right pane of either the Task Usage or Resource Usage view to enter daily, completed work values.

Enter an actual work value for a particular day

Note

When you enter daily Act. Work values that are less than the scheduled values in the Work row, Project automatically extends the assignment duration (unless a constraint prevents it from doing so), adding an hour to the end of the resource assignment for each hour of shortfall.

Updating Project Information

As if the preceding methods weren't enough, Project offers one final path for indicating how much work has been completed for tasks you select, or for all the tasks in the project: the Update Project dialog box. To display and use this dialog box to update completed work information for the tasks in your schedule, follow these steps:

1. (Optional) If you want to update only selected tasks, select the tasks in the Task Sheet in Gantt Chart view by dragging over the task row numbers or dragging to select cells in the rows for the tasks you want.
2. Open the Tools menu, point to Tracking, and click Update Project. Project displays the Update Project dialog box (see Figure 7.13).

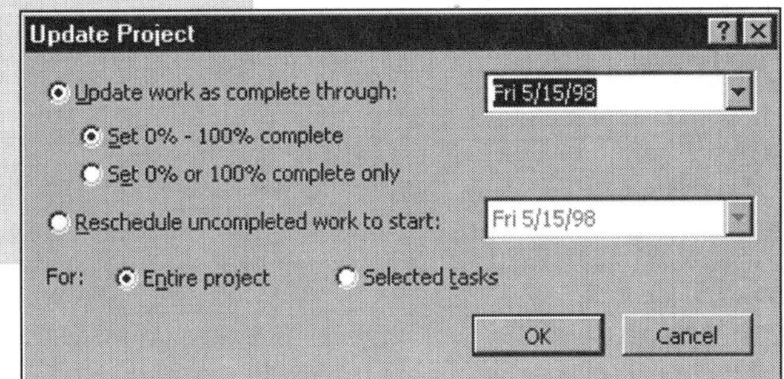

Figure 7.13 This is yet another method for updating information about work completed.

3. Leave the Update Work As Complete Through option button selected. By default, the date that appears here is the status date, described earlier, or the current date, if you haven't specified a status date for your project. If you don't have information that's absolutely current, you might want to change the date in the text box beside this option button to reflect the date through which you're certain work has been completed.
4. Choose among the following option buttons:
   - The Set 0%–100% Complete option button, which is selected by default and marks the work completed based on the percentage of work between the task's start date and the date specified in step 3.
   - The Set 0%–100% Complete Only option is an all-or-nothing choice. It marks the task as 0% completed if its finish date is after the date specified in step 3, or 100% if it was scheduled to finish on or before the date specified in step 3.
5. If you selected a range of tasks in step 1, click to select the Selected Tasks option button at the bottom of the dialog box.
6. Click OK. Project closes the dialog box and marks the appropriate tasks with indicators of how much work has been completed.

Rescheduling Work

Things happen, and work doesn't always start as planned. For example, if you schedule painters to handle some outdoor painting, and it rains, there's no choice but to start the painting on a later, drier day. You might also encounter situations in which a resource begins work on a task, but can't finish it on the scheduled date due to problems such as scheduling conflicts or unforeseen absences from work. In such instances, you need to reschedule the task to a timeframe that's realistic—which means moving all or some of the work after the current date in the schedule. When a task needs to be rescheduled, it has *slipped.*

Of course, you have the option of dragging the Gantt chart bar for the task into a new position, or dragging to reschedule the finish date for a partially completed task. However, Project also offers methods for quickly rescheduling all tasks for which work was to start (or finish) prior to the current date.

When you reschedule a task, if you indicate that no work has been completed on it, Project moves the task so that its start date becomes the status date or the current date. If you mark the task as partially complete, Project leaves the original start date in place but extends the task schedule so that the work yet to be done begins on the status date or current date. This is called *splitting* an in-progress task. The Gantt chart bar for the task displays the split. (Review the topic "Splitting a Task" in Chapter 3 to learn more about split tasks.)

Select the task(s) that you want to update in the Task Sheet, then choose one of the following methods to reschedule the task:

- Display the Update Project dialog box as just described. Click the Reschedule Uncompleted Work To Start option button (refer to Figure 7.13). Then enter the date when the rescheduled work should begin in the accompanying text box. Click on the Selected Tasks option button, and then click OK to let the work slip.
- Click the Reschedule Work button on the Tracking toolbar (the third button from the left) to move the selected task(s) so that uncompleted work begins on the status date or the current date.

Using Progress Lines

Progress lines on a Gantt chart mark a particular date and compare how in-progress tasks are advancing with relation to that date. They help you see at a glance how drastically a task may be lagging or exceeding its schedule. The mouse provides the fastest way to add a progress line to the schedule. Click the Add Progress Line button on the Tracking toolbar; then click the date for the progress line on the Gantt chart. The progress line appears, as shown in Figure 7.14.

If you want to add several progress lines that recur at regular intervals, or to control certain progress line settings, follow these steps:

1. Click the Tools menu to open it, point to Tracking, and click Progress Lines. The Progress Lines dialog box appears.

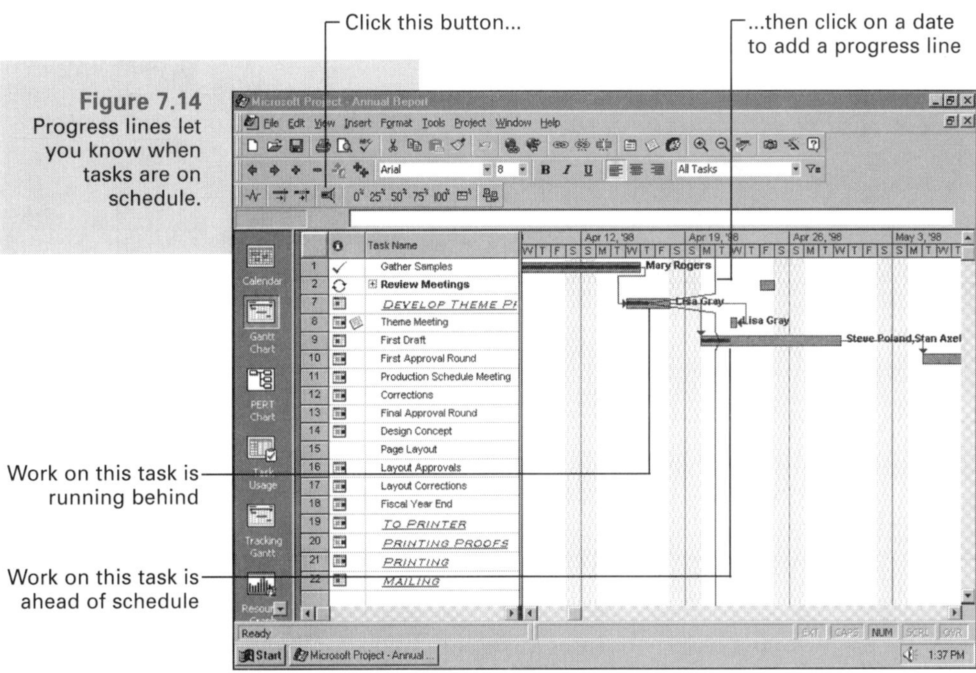
Click this button...
...then click on a date to add a progress line
Work on this task is running behind
Work on this task is ahead of schedule

Figure 7.14 Progress lines let you know when tasks are on schedule.

2. Click the Dates and Intervals tab, if it isn't selected.
3. To display a *current progress line*, which has special highlighting and is meant to highlight the current date (so you can have a daily look at where you stand) or a status date you set, click to check the Always Display Current Progress Line check box. Then, click an option button to specify whether you want that current progress line to appear At Project Status Date or At Current Date.
4. To add recurring progress lines to the schedule, click the Display Progress Lines at Recurring Intervals check box, activating the options below it, as shown in Figure 7.15. Choose whether to add the lines Daily, Weekly, or Monthly by clicking the appropriate option button. As with setting a recurring task, the choices that coincide with each option button are slightly different, but involve making schedule choices. For example, for the Weekly option, you need to select a day of the week and choose whether the lines should appear every week, every other week, or at intervals up to 12 weeks apart. Finally, beside Begin At, specify whether the progress lines should start appearing from the Project Start or a particular date that you specify.

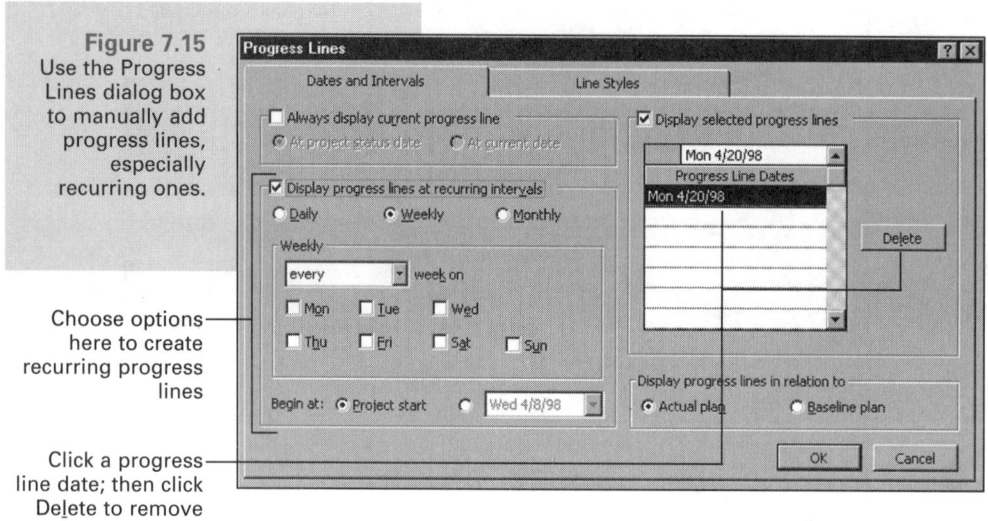

Figure 7.15 Use the Progress Lines dialog box to manually add progress lines, especially recurring ones.

5. Under Display Progress Lines in Relation To, specify whether the progress lines should compare project with the Actual Plan or Baseline Plan.
6. If you want to delete a progress line you added with the mouse, click the date in the Progress Line Dates list, and then click the Delete button.
7. Click OK to finish creating the progress line(s).

Saving and Viewing an Interim Plan

Baseline plans let you look at where you started with your schedule and resource plans. In contrast, an interim plan serves as a snapshot of changes you've made down the line, and shows how far you've come with a project. For example, you can set a milestone for the date when the project is 25 percent through its total schedule and get a record of how things stand at that point. If you save an interim plan, it captures the current information (or information from a previous interim plan) in the fields for the start and finish dates for tasks. Saving interim plans also can be thought of as saving "multiple baselines." You can save up to 10 interim plans for your project.

Consider a hypothetical situation. Your resource completed Task 1, but it took twice as long as you had anticipated. You can look at similar tasks later in your schedule, adjust them to reflect the new knowledge, and save an interim plan. Any changes you make after saving that interim plan are not added to the interim plan; they're added to the main scheduling fields for your project. You can save up to five interim plans to keep a record of where significant schedule changes occur.

If your company routinely uses follow-up meetings after the completion of a project to analyze what worked well and troubleshoot things that didn't work well, you should arm yourself for the discussion by creating interim plans and adding task notes about when and why key tasks slipped.

The initial steps for creating an interim plan resemble the initial steps for saving the baseline. Here are those initial steps and the rest of the steps needed to save your interim plan and view its information:

1. Enter all of the task and resource information you want to save as part of the interim plan.
2. (Optional) If you want to save selected tasks, select the rows you want in the Task Sheet in Gantt Chart view.
3. Open the Tools menu and point to Tracking. Click Save Baseline. The Save Baseline dialog box appears.
4. Click the Save Interim Plan option to select it; this enables the Copy and Into drop-down lists.
5. From the Copy drop-down list (see Figure 7.16), select the two fields of information from the Task Sheet you want to save in your interim plan. For the first interim plan, you should always select either (the default) Start/Finish or Baseline Start/Finish. For subsequent interim plans, choose the fields you specified in the Into drop-down list (see the next step) for the last interim plan you saved, so that the new interim plan gives you a record of which tasks have slipped more than once.
6. Use the Into drop-down list to specify what Project will call the fields in which it saves the interim plan dates. For your first interim plan, use Start1/Finish1, for your second interim plan, use Start2/Finish2, and so on.
7. If you want to save interim dates for only the tasks you selected in step 2, click to select the Selected Tasks option.
8. Click OK. Project saves the interim plan dates in new fields; you can add them to the Task Sheet to view their contents by completing the rest of these steps.
9. In the Task Sheet, click the column name of the column to the right of where you want to insert an interim plan field.

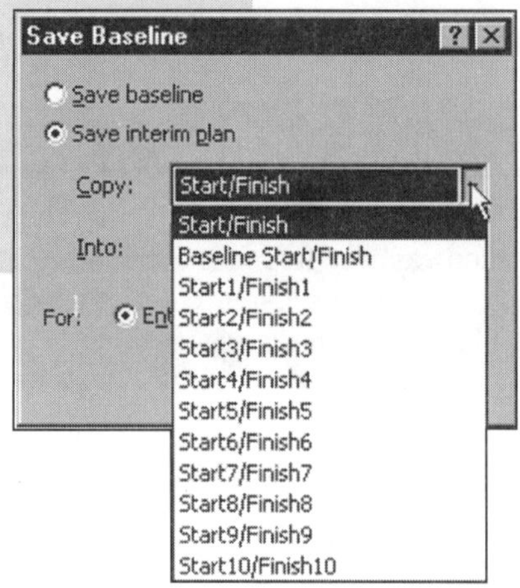

Figure 7.16 The interim plan captures information from two Task Sheet fields that you specify here.

10. Open the Insert menu and click Column (or right-click and then click Insert Column on the resulting shortcut menu). The Column Definition dialog box appears.
11. Click the drop-down list arrow to display the Field Name list; then scroll down and click the name of the interim plan field to be inserted at that location. For example, you would click Start1 to display the first field from your first interim plan (see Figure 7.17).
12. If needed, make changes to other fields in the Column Definition dialog box; then click OK to finish adding the field. It appears in the Task Sheet as shown in Figure 7.18.
13. Repeat steps 10–13 to add any other interim plan fields you want to view to the Task Sheet.

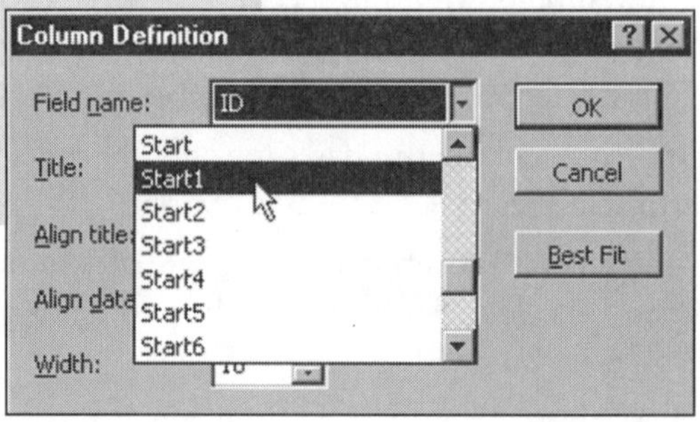

Figure 7.17 You can choose to add an interim plan field to the Task Sheet.

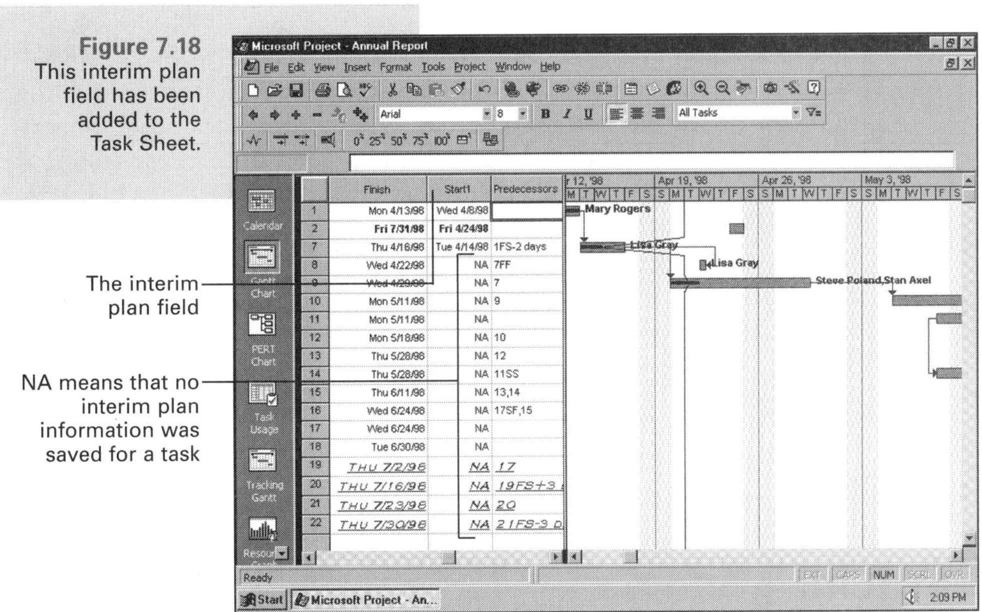

Figure 7.18 This interim plan field has been added to the Task Sheet.

Viewing Baseline versus Actual Information

Because there are so many different kinds of information captured in your Project file, the baseline information you store and the actual information you enter about work completed doesn't display automatically. To close this chapter, I'll show you a few different ways to view this information, depending how much and what kind of detail you want to see.

Using Tracking Gantt View

The Tracking Gantt view in Project lets you do virtually everything you can do in Gantt Chart view, such as dragging and moving tasks, updating links, or entering information about work that has been completed for a project. In addition, though, Tracking Gantt view uses Gantt bars that provide greater detail about work progress on tasks, so you can see at a glance which tasks are on schedule or falling behind. This is much more convenient than scrolling through various columns on the Task Sheet.

In this view, each Gantt bar is really two bars (see Figure 7.19). The lower portion, usually gray even on a color monitor, shows you the baseline schedule for the task, assuming you saved a baseline plan for the project. The top portion shows the current schedule for the project, in a lightly shaded bar. As you enter actual work information for the task, the portion of the bar representing the work completed becomes solid rather than shaded. By default, the top portion of the bar is blue if the task is on schedule or work has not yet begun on it. If the task is behind schedule (meaning that its finish date has passed but you haven't yet marked the task as 100% completed), the upper portion of the bar appears in red, a color commonly used to alert you that it's time to panic.

To display Tracking Gantt view, open the View menu and click More Views or click the More Views icon in the View Bar. In the More Views dialog box, scroll down the Views list to display the Tracking Gantt choice. Double-click this choice (or click it once and click Apply).

Other Tracking Views

If you want access to the baseline and tracking information in tabular form, you can change the Task Sheet display so that it displays the information you want. To do so in any view that contains the Task Sheet, click a cell in the Task Sheet; then open the View menu, point to Table, and click Tracking. The Task Sheet now displays tracking information (see Figure 7.20).

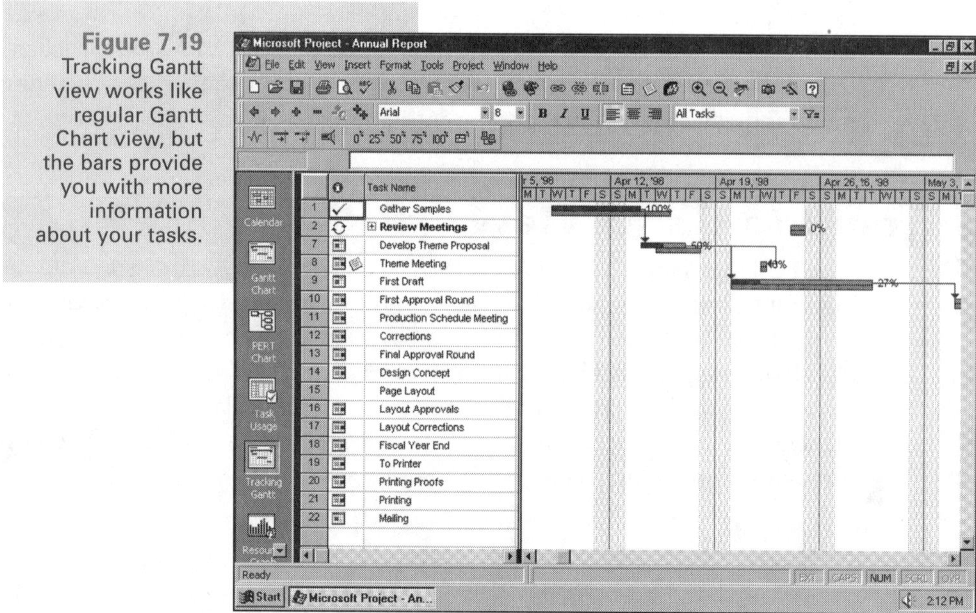

Figure 7.19 Tracking Gantt view works like regular Gantt Chart view, but the bars provide you with more information about your tasks.

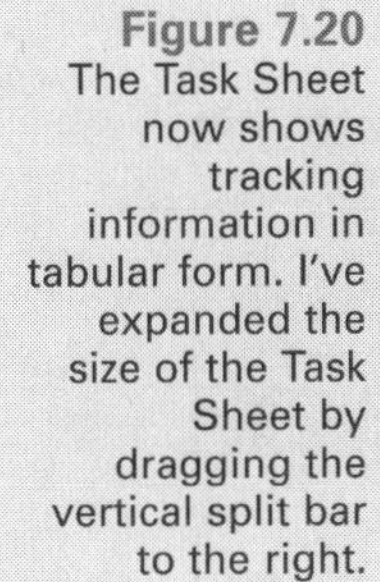

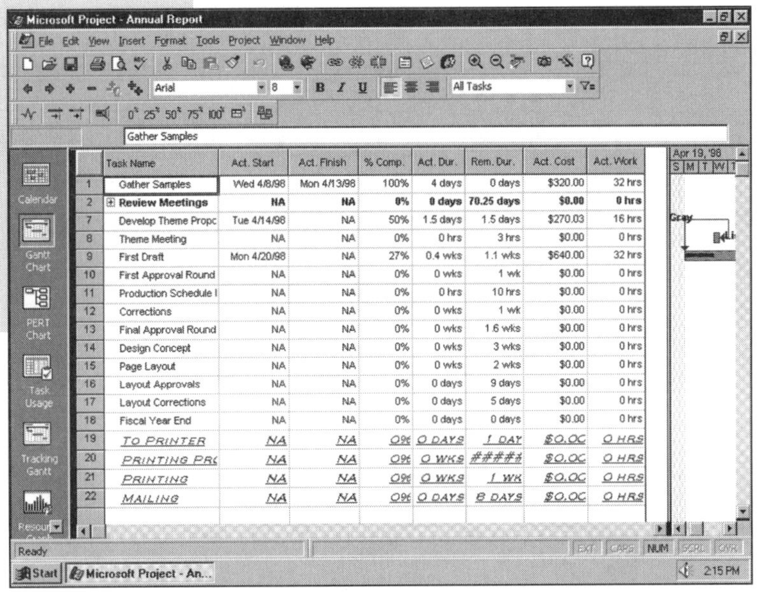

	Task Name	Act. Start	Act. Finish	% Comp.	Act. Dur.	Rem. Dur.	Act. Cost	Act. Work
1	Gather Samples	Wed 4/8/98	Mon 4/13/98	100%	4 days	0 days	$320.00	32 hrs
2	Review Meetings	NA	NA	0%	0 days	70.25 days	$0.00	0 hrs
7	Develop Theme Propc	Tue 4/14/98	NA	50%	1.5 days	1.5 days	$270.03	16 hrs
8	Theme Meeting	NA	NA	0%	0 hrs	3 hrs	$0.00	0 hrs
9	First Draft	Mon 4/20/98	NA	27%	0.4 wks	1.1 wks	$640.00	32 hrs
10	First Approval Round	NA	NA	0%	0 wks	1 wk	$0.00	0 hrs
11	Production Schedule I	NA	NA	0%	0 hrs	10 hrs	$0.00	0 hrs
12	Corrections	NA	NA	0%	0 wks	1 wk	$0.00	0 hrs
13	Final Approval Round	NA	NA	0%	0 wks	1.6 wks	$0.00	0 hrs
14	Design Concept	NA	NA	0%	0 wks	3 wks	$0.00	0 hrs
15	Page Layout	NA	NA	0%	0 wks	2 wks	$0.00	0 hrs
16	Layout Approvals	NA	NA	0%	0 days	9 days	$0.00	0 hrs
17	Layout Corrections	NA	NA	0%	0 days	5 days	$0.00	0 hrs
18	Fiscal Year End	NA	NA	0%	0 days	0 days	$0.00	0 hrs
19	TO PRINTER	NA	NA	0%	0 DAYS	1 DAY	$0.0C	0 HRS
20	PRINTING PR(	NA	NA	0%	0 WKS	#####	$0.0C	0 HRS
21	PRINTING	NA	NA	0%	0 WKS	1 WK	$0.0C	0 HRS
22	MAILING	NA	NA	0%	0 DAYS	8 DAYS	$0.0C	0 HRS

Figure 7.20 The Task Sheet now shows tracking information in tabular form. I've expanded the size of the Task Sheet by dragging the vertical split bar to the right.

At times, Tracking Gantt view can be a bit unpredictable. If you switch to this view and don't see *anything* in the Gantt chart pane at the right, first make sure that Project hasn't scrolled the displayed dates beyond the schedule for the project. Press Alt+Home to go to the beginning of the project in the Gantt Chart view. If that's not the solution, click the Go To Selected Task button on the Standard toolbar.

In Chapter 2, "Setting Up a Project," you learned how to display the Project Statistics box via the Project Information dialog box. The Project Statistics dialog box offers information about the baseline schedule for the project, including work and cost information, as well as the actual work completed and dollars spent. You also can display this dialog box by clicking the Project Statistics button (the first button) on the Tracking toolbar. The dialog box appears as shown in Figure 7.21.

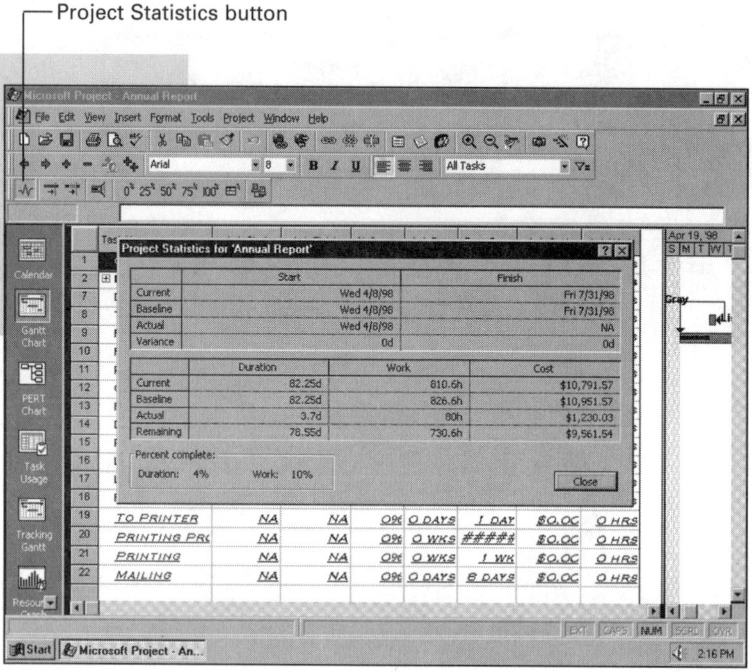

Project Statistics button

Figure 7.21 As you enter actual data about tasks using the methods covered in this chapter, the statistics for your project change.

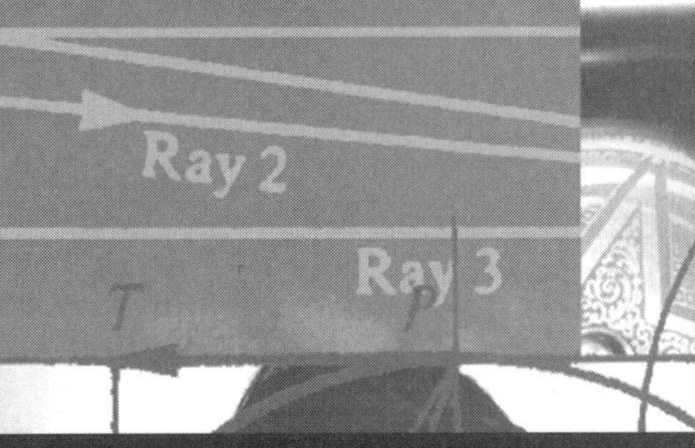

PART III
Viewing, Formatting, and Printing Projects

8

Viewing and Managing Costs

In This Chapter

- Viewing and finding task costs
- Looking at resource costs
- Previewing cost reports
- Reporting costs to others
- Managing costs and cash flow

When you're an independent contractor, you have to keep your eye on three key aspects of any project you manage for your client. First, you have to ensure that the work you deliver is of the highest quality. Second, you have get the job done on time—or even earlier. Finally, you have to track costs like a maniac to ensure that you not only charge the client a fair price but also make a fair profit.

Even a project manager within a company needs to think like an independent contractor. The work your team delivers has to be top quality and on time, and must be delivered at a cost that helps your company stay profitable.

This chapter shows you how to get crucial mileage from all the resource and task information you entered into Project. Specifically, this chapter shows you how to do the following:

Viewing and Finding Task Costs

Chapter 7, "Comparing Progress versus Your Baseline Plan," explains how to tell Project how much work has been completed on a task, and therefore how much of the task-duration time has elapsed. In addition, although you might not be able to see it immediately, Project can use the task completion information you entered to calculate the actual cost for that completed work, based on hourly rates for resources, and other cost information you entered.

You might not be able to see the costs immediately because Gantt Chart view doesn't display any cost information by default. You have to learn techniques for examining cost information in various ways, depending on what type of information you want to view. Project enables you to view accumulated costs (costs based on actual work completed plus any fixed and per-use costs) by task, by the whole project, or by the resource(s) completing the work. The remainder of this section describes how you can access each type of cost information and make sure that task costs are calculated for you.

Controlling Whether Costs Are Updated Based on Work Completed

By default, Project automatically updates the calculated costs for a task or resource when you update information about how much work has been completed on a task. Project calculates cost values by multiplying the number of hours of work completed for a task by the hourly rate for the resource completing the task.

You can turn calculation off, however, if you need to. The primary reason not to have Project calculate these values as you go is to avoid calculation delays while you're updating information about the work completed on various tasks. The other reason to turn off automatic calculation is if you want to enter actual cost information before you indicate that work has been completed on the project. (See the section later in this chapter called "Changing How Costs Add Up" to learn more about entering actual costs.)

To ensure that Project correctly calculates information about actual costs, based on the work you mark as completed, or to turn off automatic calculation, follow these steps:

1. Open the Tools menu and click Options. The Options dialog box appears, with many tabs.
2. Click the Calculation tab to display its options (see Figure 8.1).
3. Click the Actual Costs Are Always Calculated by Microsoft Project option if you want Project to update all calculated cost information whenever you update task completion information. Clear the check box if you prefer to enter actual cost information or calculate actual costs periodically.

After you enable this option, it's enabled for all files you open in Project.

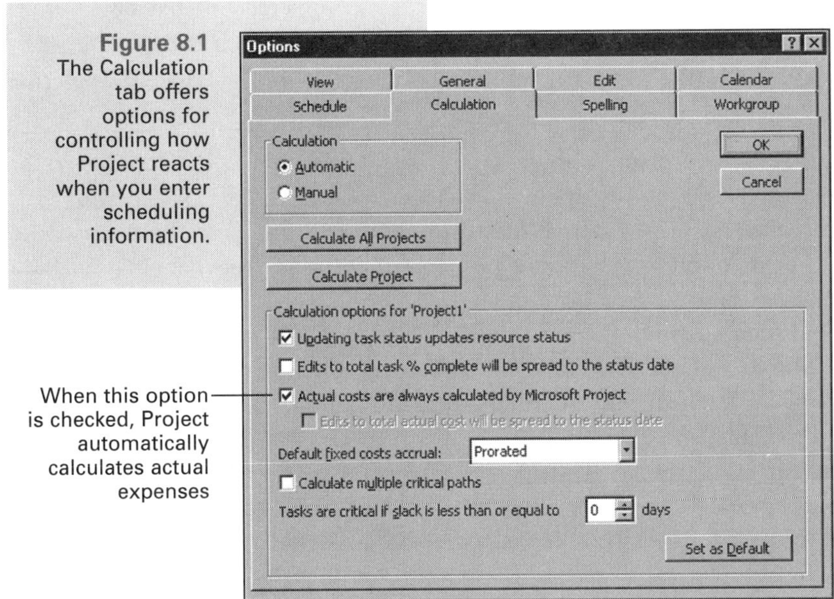

Figure 8.1 The Calculation tab offers options for controlling how Project reacts when you enter scheduling information.

If you've checked the Actual Costs Are Always Calculated by Microsoft Project box after you've already entered actual cost information, the calculated costs will wipe out those actual costs you previously entered.

4. Click OK to close the Options dialog box. If you turned on automatic calculation, a message box warns you that actual cost entries will be overridden. Click OK to close the message box. Your change takes effect immediately.

Viewing Task Costs

One way to look at the expenses associated with your project is task by task. For example, your plan might include particular tasks for which you really need to watch expenses, such as work handled by an outside contractor with a particularly high hourly rate. Or, you might need to provide information about the costs you estimated for a particular task to a team member negotiating to have that task completed, so the team member will know the highest price you're willing to pay to have the task completed.

Project offers a couple of methods by which you can take a look at how costs are adding up for a task based on the work completed for that task. Either method enables you to enter or edit cost information when you need to, such as when the actual fixed cost turns out to be less than the fixed cost you initially estimated.

The first method involves adjusting the columns shown in the Task Sheet; do this in any view that displays the Task Sheet, such as Gantt Chart view or Task Entry view. To display actual cost information in the Task Sheet, open the View menu, point to Table, and click Cost. The Task Sheet changes to include several columns with cost information. Drag the vertical split bar (if there is one) to the right to display additional columns of cost information, as shown in Figure 8.2. (The View Bar is hidden in the figure so that you can see all the columns.) To return the Task Sheet to its regular view, open the View menu, point to Table, and click Entry.

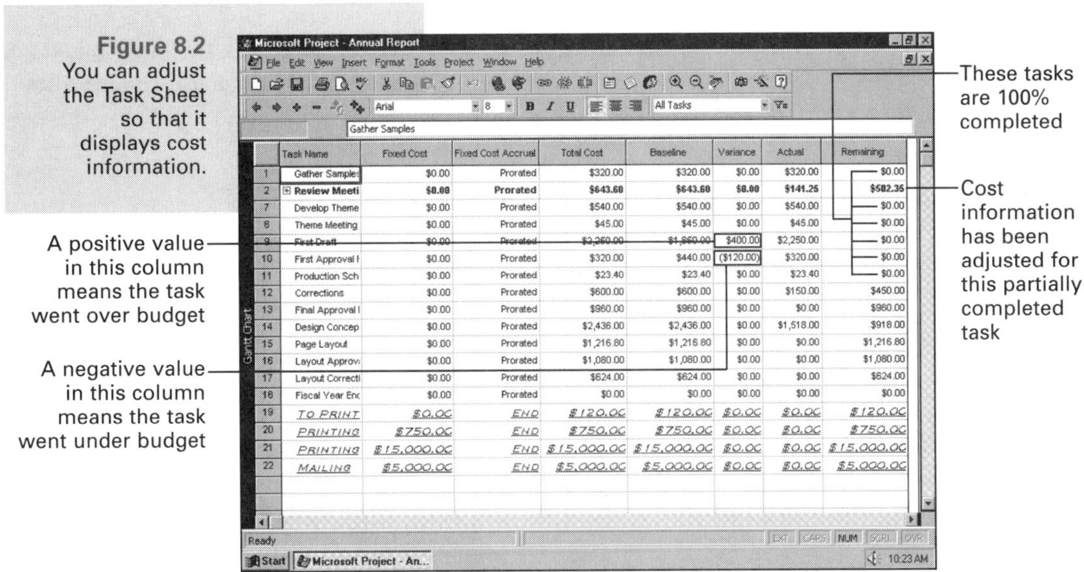
Microsoft Project - Annual Report
Task Name
Fixed Cost
Fixed Cost Accrual
Total Cost
Baseline
Variance
Actual
Remaining
These tasks are 100% completed
Cost information has been adjusted for this partially completed task
A positive value in this column means the task went over budget
A negative value in this column means the task went under budget

Figure 8.2 You can adjust the Task Sheet so that it displays cost information.

Tip

If Project doesn't automatically update actual cost information after you update task information, press Shift+F9 to manually recalculate the project information.

Tip

Before you save a project baseline or enter information about work completed, use the Task Sheet view shown in Figure 8.2 to enter a fixed cost for a task, such as the ones shown for tasks 20 through 22 in Figure 8.2.

Displaying cost information in the Task Sheet, as just described, is useful when you want to view the costs for many tasks. There might be instances, however, when you don't want to change the Task Sheet's appearance, but you do want to view the cost information for a particular task. You can do so by displaying the Cost Tracking form (you'll learn more detail about forms in Chapter 11, "Working with Forms"). Use one of the following methods to access the Cost Tracking form:

- Display the Custom Forms toolbar by right-clicking any toolbar onscreen and clicking on Custom Forms. Click the Cost Tracking button (second from the left) on this toolbar.

- Open the Tools menu, point to Customize, and click Forms. The Custom Forms dialog box appears (see Figure 8.3). Click the Task option button if it isn't already selected. In the Forms list, double-click Cost Tracking (or click it once, and then click Apply).

When you use either of the methods just described, the Cost Tracking form appears (see Figure 8.4). As you can see, this form offers several text entry boxes with various task cost information, including the baseline cost (how much you estimated the work on the task would cost), the actual cost of the work performed so far, and any remaining (Rem) budgeted cost. It also calculates the variance between the baseline cost and the actual cost. You can change several of the entries in this dialog box. Note, however, that if Project is calculating the task cost based on hourly cost rates you entered for a resource, any edits you make in the Total text box will revert to the calculated value as soon as you close the dialog box (unless you turn off automatic calculation). To close the dialog box after making the changes you want, click OK.

A positive variance means that a task has gone over budget. A negative variance means that the task costs remain under the baseline budget.

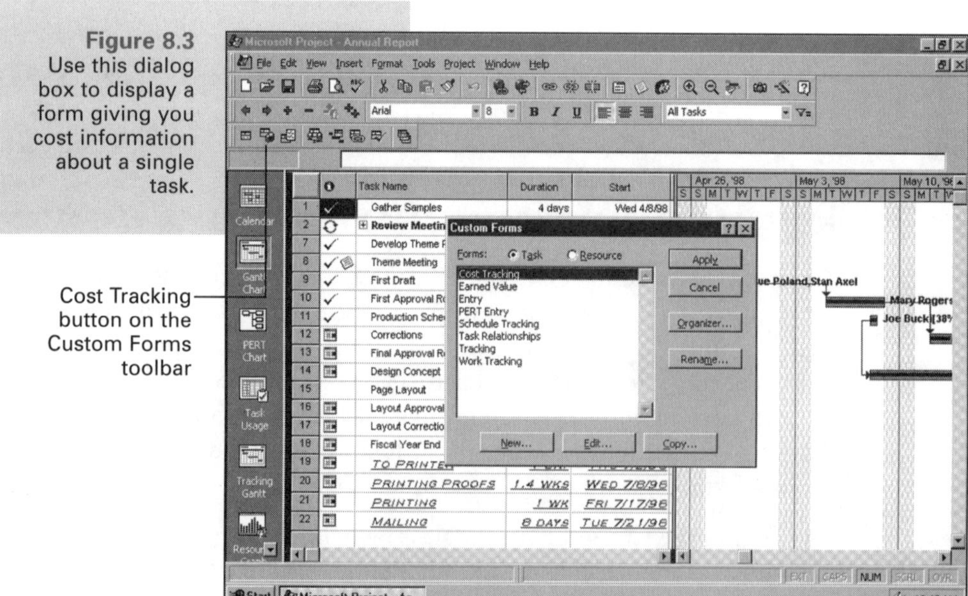

Figure 8.3 Use this dialog box to display a form giving you cost information about a single task.

Figure 8.4 This form displays cost information for a single task.

Cost Tracking

Name: Gather Samples

Cost

Total:	$320.00	Fixed:	$0.00
Baseline:	$320.00	Actual:	$320.00
Variance:	$0.00	Rem:	$0.00
Duration:	4d	% Complete:	100%
Work:	32h	% Work Complete:	100%

OK Cancel

Looking at Resource Costs

Chapter 5, "Resolving Overallocations and Overbooked Resources," covers how to identify when you've assigned too much work to a resource. Similarly, there might be situations where you want to review exactly how much each member or piece of equipment associated with your project costs. This information can help you make intelligent decisions about cost cutting, or can help tease your memory about invoices that are coming due as the project schedule progresses. As usual, Project gives you several options for precisely how to view resource costs. Each of these is covered next.

Note

If you haven't finished adding all the resources to your schedule, you can change the default standard hourly rate and overtime rate for new resources (so that it's no longer $0 for each). Do so using the General tab in the Options dialog box. Chapter 21, "Customizing Microsoft Project," covers setting this type of option.

Individual Resource Costs

The way you'll typically want to view resource costs is to view the total costs assigned to each resource. You can view this kind of information by adjusting the columns shown in the Resource Sheet, which Chapter 4, "Managing Resources," showed you how to use to add resources to your schedule. Here are the steps for displaying the Resource Sheet and displaying resource cost information in it:

1. If the Resource Sheet isn't currently onscreen, open the View menu and click Resource Sheet, or click the Resource Sheet icon on the View Bar. The Resource Sheet appears.
2. Open the View menu, point to Table, and click Cost. The Resource Sheet displays columns of cost information, as shown in Figure 8.5.

Note

To return to regular Resource Sheet view, open the View menu, point to Table, and click Entry.

Each column in the Resource Sheet contains a particular type of cost information, and most are self-explanatory. One that isn't so obvious is the Cost column, which contains the current total cost of the work scheduled for the resource, taking into account any task duration changes, as opposed to the baseline amount you initially planned. The cost information in all columns consists solely of calculated information; you can't edit any of these values. In fact, if you click on a cell in one of the cost columns, you'll see that the entry in the text entry box above the Resource Sheet appears "grayed out"—if you try to edit it, you can't.

Figure 8.5 You can adjust the Resource Sheet to display cost information, as shown here.

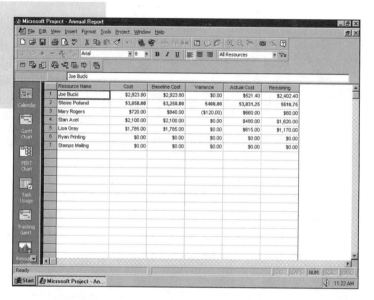

	Resource Name	Cost	Baseline Cost	Variance	Actual Cost	Remaining
1	Joe Bucki	$2,923.80	$2,923.80	$0.00	$521.40	$2,402.40
2	Steve Poland	$3,650.00	$3,250.00	$400.00	$3,031.25	$618.75
3	Mary Rogers	$720.00	$840.00	($120.00)	$660.00	$60.00
4	Stan Axel	$2,100.00	$2,100.00	$0.00	$480.00	$1,620.00
5	Lisa Gray	$1,785.00	$1,785.00	$0.00	$615.00	$1,170.00
6	Ryan Printing	$0.00	$0.00	$0.00	$0.00	$0.00
7	Stamps Mailing	$0.00	$0.00	$0.00	$0.00	$0.00

After you change the Task Sheet or Resource Sheet to display cost information, you can print the information. See Chapter 10, "Proofing and Printing a View," for more details.

Resource Group Costs

You might recall that one of the columns in the default version of the Resource Sheet is the Group column. In this column, you enter information to tell Project that a particular resource has something in common with other resources. For example, you might enter Comm in the Group column to identify each resource from the Communications department in your company. Or, you might enter Contract to identify each freelance or contract resource on the team. You might enter Equipment to distinguish nonhuman resources.

After you display resource cost information as just described, you can reduce the list to display only resources that are part of a particular group and associated costs for only those resources. (This is a filtering operation; you learn more about filtering in Chapter 9, "Working with the Different Project Views.") To do so, follow these steps:

1. Display cost information in the Resource Sheet as previously described.
2. On the Formatting toolbar, click the arrow beside Filter to display a drop-down list (see Figure 8.6).

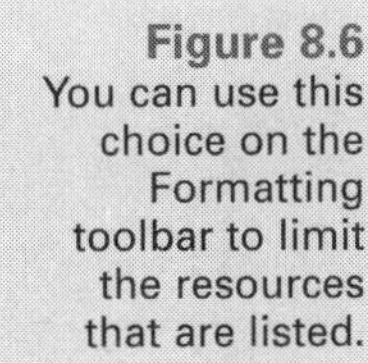

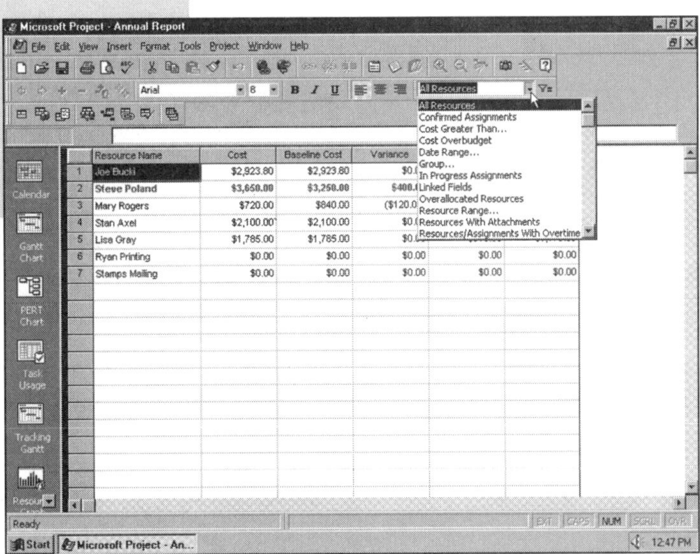

Figure 8.6 You can use this choice on the Formatting toolbar to limit the resources that are listed.

3. Click to select Group... from the Filter drop-down list. Project displays the Group... dialog box.
4. Enter the name of the group for which you want to view costs in the Group name text box (see Figure 8.7). You don't have to match the capitalization you used when you identified the resource group in the Group column (Project treats "comm," "Comm," and "COMM" as equivalent), but you do have to use the exact spelling.
5. Click OK to close the dialog box. The Resource Sheet displays cost information for only those resources that you identified as part of the specified group (see Figure 8.8).

If you want to return to displaying all your resources in the Resource Sheet, select All Resources from the Filter drop-down list on the Formatting toolbar.

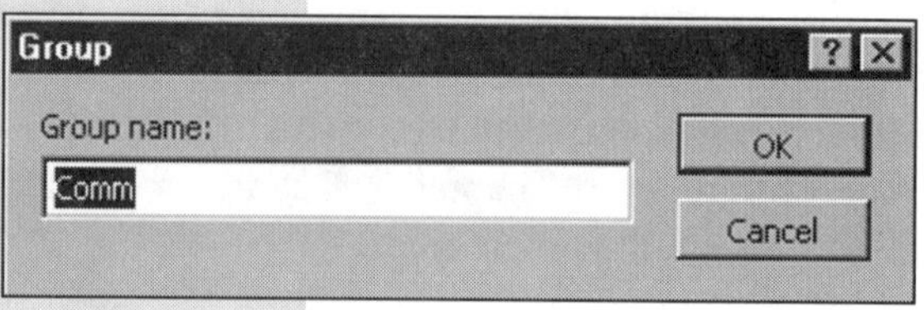

Figure 8.7 Specify a resource group for which you'd like to see cost information.

Figure 8.8 Here's the cost information for a group of resources.

	Resource Name	Cost	Baseline Cost	Variance	Actual Cost	Remaining
3	Mary Rogers	$720.00	$840.00	($120.00)	$660.00	$60.00
5	Lisa Gray	$1,785.00	$1,785.00	$0.00	$615.00	$1,170.00

Graphing Individual Resource Work and Costs

In addition to showing task information in graphical form with a Gantt or PERT chart, you can show some resource information in a chart. Although you'll learn more about adjusting various views in the next chapter, here's a quick look at how to display graphical information about resource costs:

1. Open the View menu and click Resource Graph, or click the Resource Graph icon on the View Bar. By default, Project shows a graphical representation of the work scheduled for the resource that was selected in the Resource Sheet.
2. Right-click the right pane of the view (where the graphical information appears), or open the Format menu and point to Details. On the shortcut menu (see Figure 8.9) or submenu that appears, click Cost or Cumulative Cost. Project adjusts the graph in the right pane to show the exact cost amounts on the dates when they accrue (see Figure 8.10), or a running total of the costs for the selected resource as they will accumulate (see Figure 8.11).
3. If you want to view a cost graph for another resource, use the scroll bar below the left pane where the resource name appears (refer to Figure 8.9) to move between resources. You also can press Page Up to display the graph for the previous resource, or Page Down to display the graph for the next resource. Pressing Alt+F5 displays the graph for the first resource in the Resource Sheet.

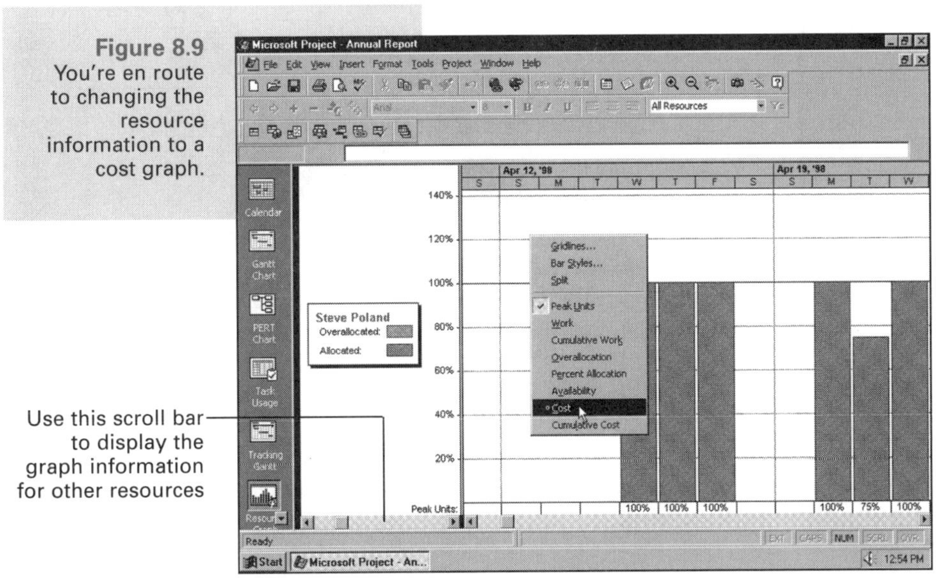

Figure 8.9 You're en route to changing the resource information to a cost graph.

Use this scroll bar to display the graph information for other resources

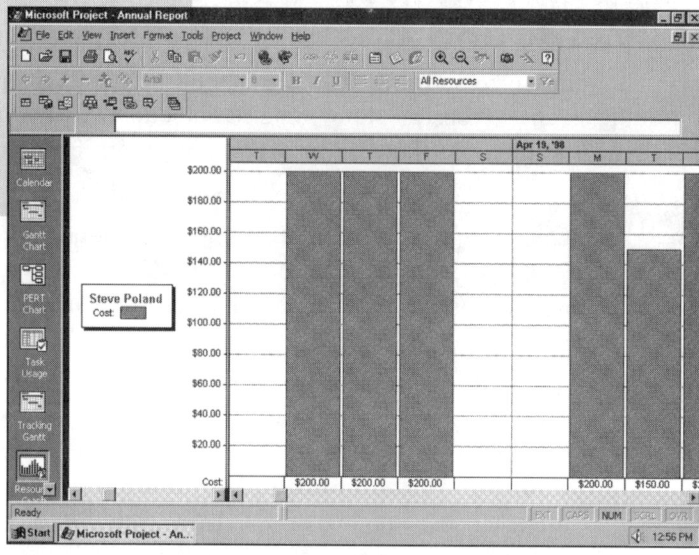

Figure 8.10 Here you're graphing the costs for a particular resource on particular dates.

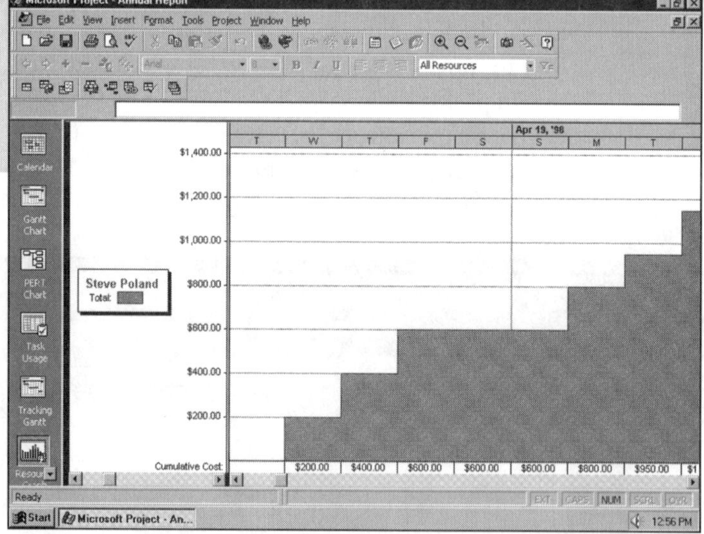

Figure 8.11 Here you're graphing how resource costs accumulate over time.

Viewing the Project Cost

In addition to viewing cost information about specific tasks or resources, you can view how costs are adding up for the entire project. Access information about project costs via the Project Information dialog box, which you've seen in a couple of earlier chapters in this book. To display total costs for your project, open the Project menu and click Project Information. In the Project Information dialog box that appears for your project, click Statistics.

The Project Statistics dialog box appears (see Figure 8.12). After you review the cost information, click Close to exit the Project Statistics dialog box.

A Word About Earned Values

The term *earned value* seems a bit misleading, because it's really a measure of whether particular tasks are on budget. In fact, when you view earned value information in either the Task Sheet or the Earned Value dialog box, you actually get to look at several statistics, which are listed in Table 8.1.

That's a lot of ways to slice up the information and might be more than you ever want to know about the costs associated with your tasks. (For many project managers, the most relevant figure is the final variance.) There are two places to view all this cost information: the Task Sheet or the Earned Value dialog box. To display earned value information in the Task Sheet, follow these steps:

1. If you aren't already in Gantt Chart view, switch to it by opening the View menu and clicking Gantt Chart.
2. Open the View menu, point to Table, and click More Tables. The More Tables dialog box appears.

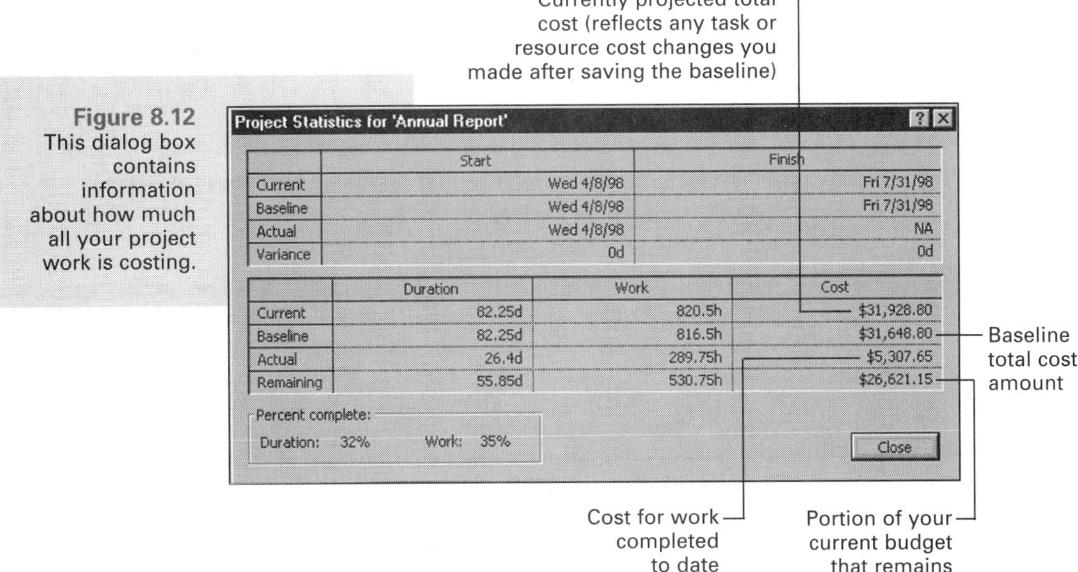

Figure 8.12 This dialog box contains information about how much all your project work is costing.

Table 8.1 Earned Value Statistics Tracked by Project 98.

Abbreviation	Description
BCWS	Budgeted Cost of Work Scheduled is the cost you budgeted for work scheduled up to the current date in your baseline plan.
BCWP	Budgeted Cost of Work Performed is calculated by multiplying the percentage of work actually completed on a task (as of the current date) by the cost you budgeted for the task in the same timeframe.
ACWP	Actual Cost of Work Performed calculates the cost for work performed to date on a task, based on the hourly, per use, and fixed costs you entered.
SV	Schedule Variance is the difference between BCWS and BCWP (BCWS-BCWP). This value compares the money you planned to spend (in your baseline) by the current date to the money you budgeted to spend for work performed by the current date. This figure simply shows how your budgeted costs have changed since you established the baseline. A positive SV value indicates that your current plan calls for spending more than your original plan did.
CV	Cost Variance shows how reality compares with the current budget; it subtracts BCWP from ACWP to tell you whether the work completed is over budget (indicated by a positive value) or under budget (indicated by a negative value).
BAC	Budgeted At Completion is the amount you budgeted for the complete task, including fixed costs, and per use costs. This amount is from your baseline plan.
EAC	Estimate At Completion is the amount presently budgeted for the complete task; it reflects any changes you made to the amount of work scheduled, hourly costs, fixed costs, or per use costs since saving the baseline plan.
Variance	Compares the FAC with the BAC to see whether you'll be spending more (indicated by a positive value) or less (indicated by a negative value) than initially planned to complete the task.

3. Make sure that the Task option is selected, and then double-click Earned Value in the Tables list (or click it and then click Apply). The Task Sheet shows all the earned value amounts.
4. Drag the vertical split bar to the right so that you can review as many earned value amounts as needed (see Figure 8.13).

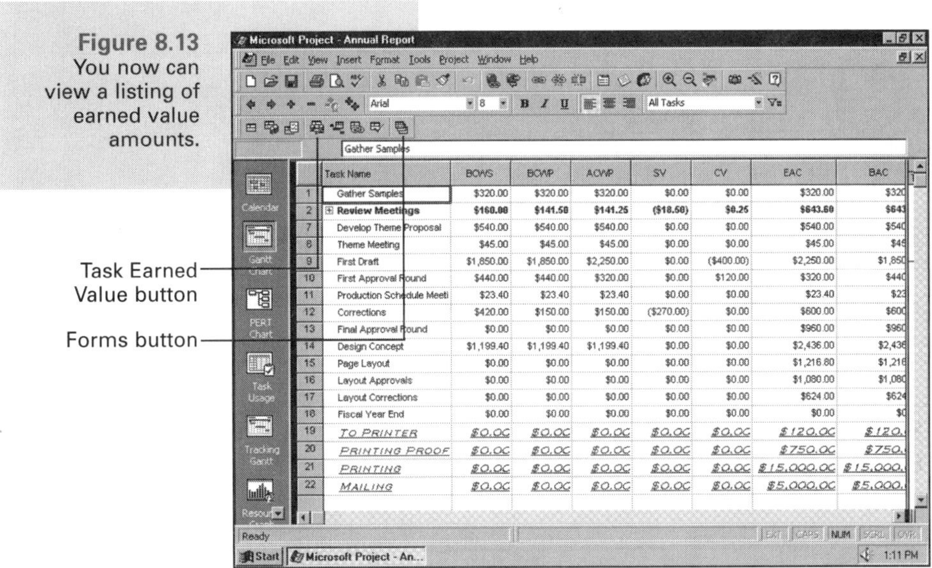

Figure 8.13 You now can view a listing of earned value amounts.

If you want to view the earned value information for a single task in a convenient format, click its task row in any view that includes the Task Sheet. Next, click the Task Earned Value button on the Custom Forms toolbar, if you've displayed that toolbar as explained earlier in this chapter. Alternatively, open the Tools menu, point to Customize, and click Forms, or click the Forms button on the Custom Forms toolbar. In the Custom Forms dialog box, make sure that the Task option is selected, and double-click Earned Value in the Forms list. Either way, the Earned Value dialog box appears (see Figure 8.14). When you finish viewing the earned value information, click OK to close the dialog box.

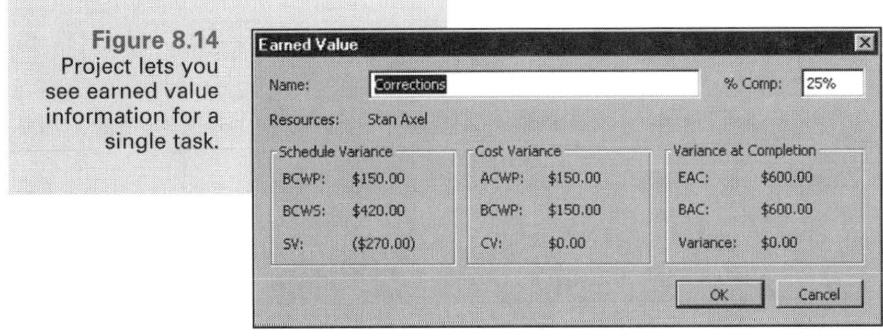

Figure 8.14 Project lets you see earned value information for a single task.

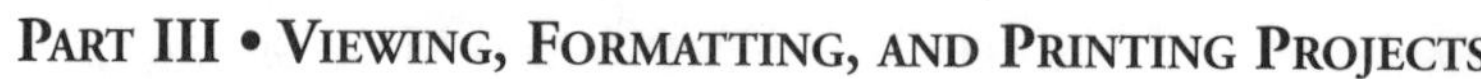

Note

If there's a Per Use cost for a resource in addition to an hourly cost, the Per Use cost always accrues when work begins on the task.

Previewing Cost Reports

Chapter 12, "Creating and Printing a Report," covers how to display, format, and print various reports in Project. These reports gather and calculate myriad types of data for you. Because budget information is so important to any project planning process, Project provides many types of cost and budgeting reports—five, to be exact. To display these cost reports, open the View menu and click Reports. In the Reports dialog box, double-click the Costs icon. The Cost Reports dialog box appears and offers icons for five different reports; select and compile a report by double-clicking its icon. Figures 8.15 through 8.19 show examples of the available reports. Click Print in any report display to print that report, or click Close to return to the Reports dialog box.

Figure 8.15 The Cash Flow report presents an update of how much you spent per task each week.

Microsoft Project - Annual Report

Page Setup... Print... Close Help

Cash Flow as of Mon 12/8/97
Annual Report

	4/5/98	4/12/98	4/19/98	4/26/98	5/3/98	5/10/98	5/17/98	5/24/98
Gather Samples	$240.00	$80.00						
Review Meetings								
Develop Theme Proposal	$180.00	$360.00						
Theme Meeting			$45.00					
First Draft		$900.00	$950.00	$400.00				
First Approval Round					$320.00			
Production Schedule Meeting					$23.40			
Corrections						$480.00	$120.00	
Final Approval Round							$480.00	$480.00
Design Concept					$112.40	$1,087.00	$862.00	$374.60
Page Layout								$93.60
Layout Approvals								
Layout Corrections								
Fiscal Year End								
To Printer								
Printing Proofs								
Printing								
Mailing								
Total	$420.00	$1,340.00	$995.00	$400.00	$455.80	$1,567.00	$1,462.00	$948.20

Page: 1 of 2 Size: 1 row by 2 columns NUM

Start Microsoft Project - An... 1:20 PM

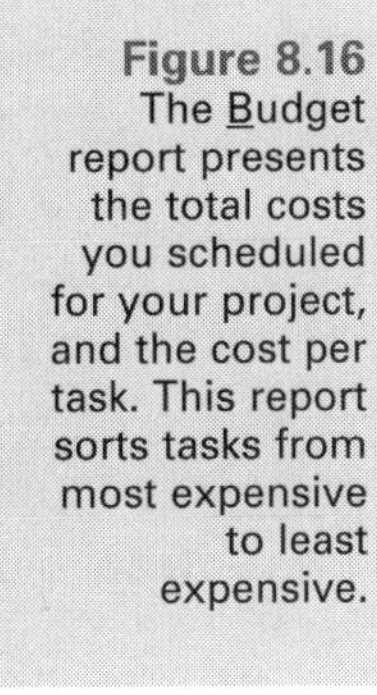

Figure 8.16 The Budget report presents the total costs you scheduled for your project, and the cost per task. This report sorts tasks from most expensive to least expensive.

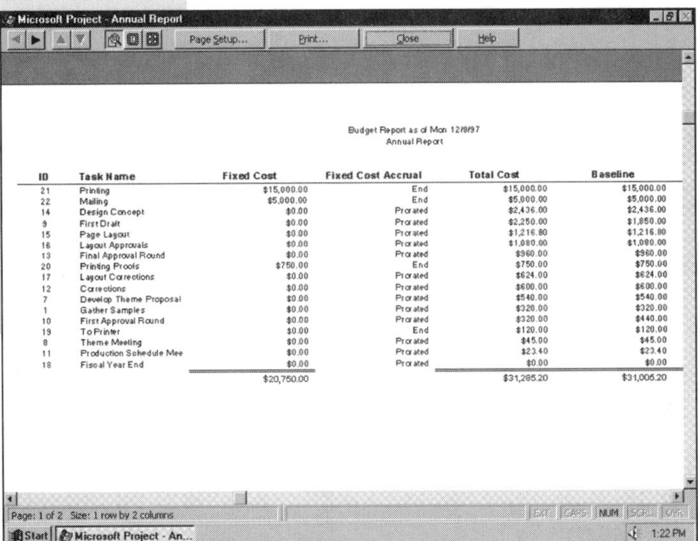

Budget Report as of Mon 12/8/97
Annual Report

ID	Task Name	Fixed Cost	Fixed Cost Accrual	Total Cost	Baseline
21	Printing	$15,000.00	End	$15,000.00	$15,000.00
22	Mailing	$5,000.00	End	$5,000.00	$5,000.00
14	Design Concept	$0.00	Prorated	$2,436.00	$2,436.00
9	First Draft	$0.00	Prorated	$2,250.00	$1,850.00
15	Page Layout	$0.00	Prorated	$1,216.80	$1,216.80
16	Layout Approvals	$0.00	Prorated	$1,080.00	$1,080.00
13	Final Approval Round	$0.00	Prorated	$960.00	$960.00
20	Printing Proofs	$750.00	End	$750.00	$750.00
17	Layout Corrections	$0.00	Prorated	$624.00	$624.00
12	Corrections	$0.00	Prorated	$600.00	$600.00
7	Develop Theme Proposal	$0.00	Prorated	$540.00	$540.00
1	Gather Samples	$0.00	Prorated	$320.00	$320.00
10	First Approval Round	$0.00	Prorated	$320.00	$440.00
19	To Printer	$0.00	End	$120.00	$120.00
8	Theme Meeting	$0.00	Prorated	$45.00	$45.00
11	Production Schedule Mee	$0.00	Prorated	$23.40	$23.40
18	Fiscal Year End	$0.00	Prorated	$0.00	$0.00
		$20,750.00		$31,285.20	$31,005.20

Figure 8.17 The Overbudget Tasks report points out where expenses are getting out of hand.

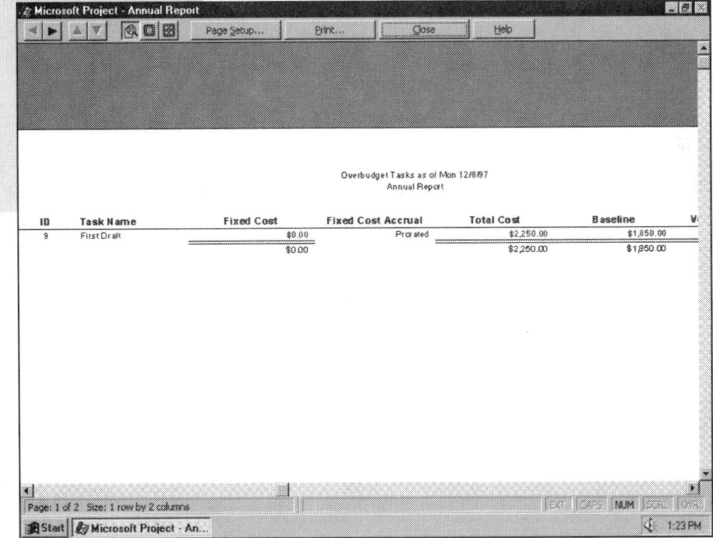

Overbudget Tasks as of Mon 12/8/97
Annual Report

ID	Task Name	Fixed Cost	Fixed Cost Accrual	Total Cost	Baseline
9	First Draft	$0.00	Prorated	$2,250.00	$1,850.00
		$0.00		$2,250.00	$1,850.00

Changing How Costs Add Up

When you added resources to the project file using the default view of the Resource Sheet, you used the Accrue At column to note when costs for work performed should be charged to the project as an actual cost. Most costs accrue

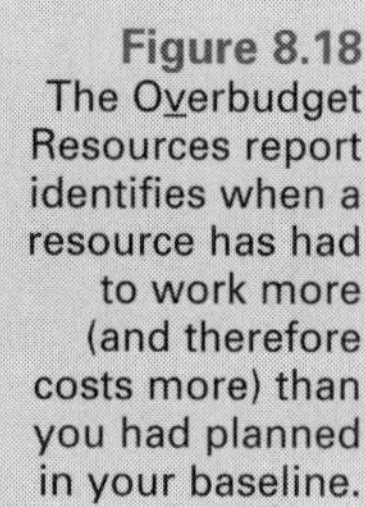

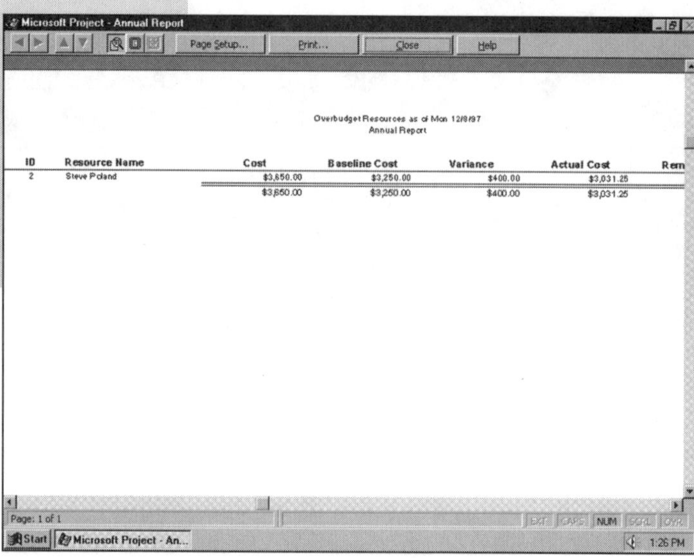

Overbudget Resources as of Mon 12/8/97
Annual Report

ID	Resource Name	Cost	Baseline Cost	Variance	Actual Cost	Rem
2	Steve Poland	$3,650.00	$3,250.00	$400.00	$3,031.25	
		$3,650.00	$3,250.00	$400.00	$3,031.25	

Figure 8.18 The Overbudget Resources report identifies when a resource has had to work more (and therefore costs more) than you had planned in your baseline.

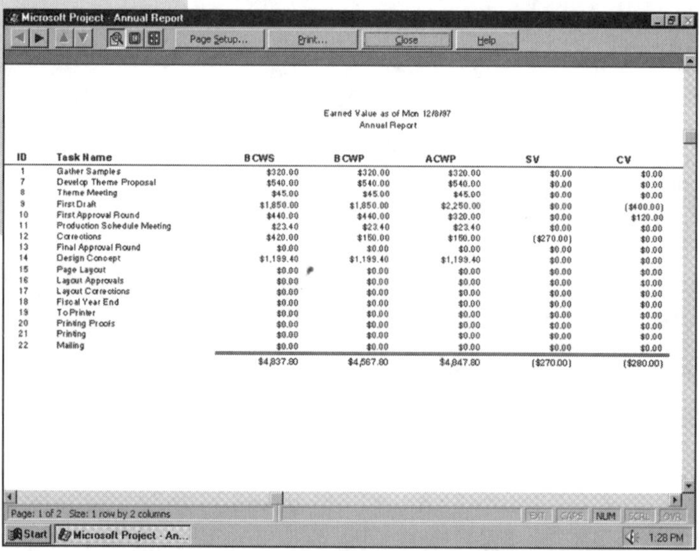

Earned Value as of Mon 12/8/97
Annual Report

ID	Task Name	BCWS	BCWP	ACWP	SV	CV
1	Gather Samples	$320.00	$320.00	$320.00	$0.00	$0.00
7	Develop Theme Proposal	$540.00	$540.00	$540.00	$0.00	$0.00
8	Theme Meeting	$45.00	$45.00	$45.00	$0.00	$0.00
9	First Draft	$1,850.00	$1,850.00	$2,250.00	$0.00	($400.00)
10	First Approval Round	$440.00	$440.00	$320.00	$0.00	$120.00
11	Production Schedule Meeting	$23.40	$23.40	$23.40	$0.00	$0.00
12	Corrections	$420.00	$150.00	$150.00	($270.00)	$0.00
13	Final Approval Round	$0.00	$0.00	$0.00	$0.00	$0.00
14	Design Concept	$1,199.40	$1,199.40	$1,199.40	$0.00	$0.00
15	Page Layout	$0.00	$0.00	$0.00	$0.00	$0.00
16	Layout Approvals	$0.00	$0.00	$0.00	$0.00	$0.00
17	Layout Corrections	$0.00	$0.00	$0.00	$0.00	$0.00
18	Fiscal Year End	$0.00	$0.00	$0.00	$0.00	$0.00
19	To Printer	$0.00	$0.00	$0.00	$0.00	$0.00
20	Printing Proofs	$0.00	$0.00	$0.00	$0.00	$0.00
21	Printing	$0.00	$0.00	$0.00	$0.00	$0.00
22	Mailing	$0.00	$0.00	$0.00	$0.00	$0.00
		$4,837.80	$4,567.80	$4,847.80	($270.00)	($280.00)

Figure 8.19 The Earned Value report shows earned value calculations for each task, as well as totals for the project.

in a prorated fashion, meaning that for each percentage point of the task that's marked as completed, a corresponding amount of the budgeted expense is charged as an actual cost. For tasks that have the Start setting in the Accrue At column, the total budgeted cost for the task becomes an actual cost as soon as any work is completed on the task. In contrast, for tasks where Accrue At is set to `End`, no actual costs accumulate until you mark the task as 100% completed.

In most cases, cash flow is as important to project management as the ultimate bottom line is. One of the biggest scams a consumer can fall prey to occurs when dealing with certain unscrupulous home repair contractors. The contractor gives the best estimate for a repair job, but asks for all or a large part of the money up-front. You hand over a check, and the contractor disappears into thin air without doing anything. Just as you'd certainly want to delay payments to a home repair contractor, it's in the interest of any business to delay project expenses until the work is completed to your satisfaction.

If you review task costs and it seems that too many have accrued too early in the schedule, look for tasks for which you can postpone accrued costs. (Negotiate with your resources, of course, to ensure that your changes reflect reality.) You want to be able to change as many tasks as possible to accrue at the end of work on the task. (Although this isn't the realistic choice for most internal resources, which cost your company as soon as you use them.) Where you can't have tasks accrue at the end, at least lobby for prorated cost approval and minimize the number of tasks that accrue at the start of work on the task. To review or change Accrue At information, display the Resource Sheet, and review or change your choice in the Accrue At field. Alternately, right-click a resource in the Resource Sheet, and then click Resource Information to display the Resource Information dialog box for that resource. On the Costs tab, change the entry in the Cost Accrual drop-down list box as needed.

Note

If you changed the Resource Sheet to display earned value or other information instead of the default entry information, you need to change it back to adjust how costs accrue. With the Resource Sheet onscreen, open the View menu, point to Table, and click Entry.

Changing a Fixed Task Cost

After work has been completed on a task, most external resources present you with a bill. Alternatively, your company's accounting department might inform you how much of an allocated (shared) cost your group or department has to pay for the completion of a task. Even though you usually aren't dinged for a fixed cost until the work on the task is completed, by default Project prorates fixed costs based on how much of the task work has been completed. If you want Project to add in entire fixed costs at the start or end of the work on the task, follow these steps:

1. Open the Tools menu and click Options. The Options dialog box appears, with many tabs.

2. Click the Calculation tab to display its options.
3. Open the Default Fixed Costs Accrual drop-down list and choose Start or End.
4. Click OK to close the Options dialog box. Your change takes effect immediately.

Whether the actual (fixed) cost for a task is higher or lower than what you budgeted in the Task Sheet, when you receive the actual bill or charge, you need to compare it with the Fixed Cost entry you made for the task and adjust the entry upward or downward. Follow these steps to enter the actual, final fixed cost for a task after work on the task has been completed:

1. If you're not already in Gantt Chart view, change to it by opening the View menu and clicking Gantt Chart.
2. Open the View menu, point to Table, and click Cost. The Task Sheet adjusts to show columns of cost information.
3. Click the Fixed Cost cell in the row for the task for which you want to enter actual data.
4. Click the task entry box above the Task Sheet, and then edit the entry (see Figure 8.20).
5. Click the Enter button or press Enter to finish your edit.

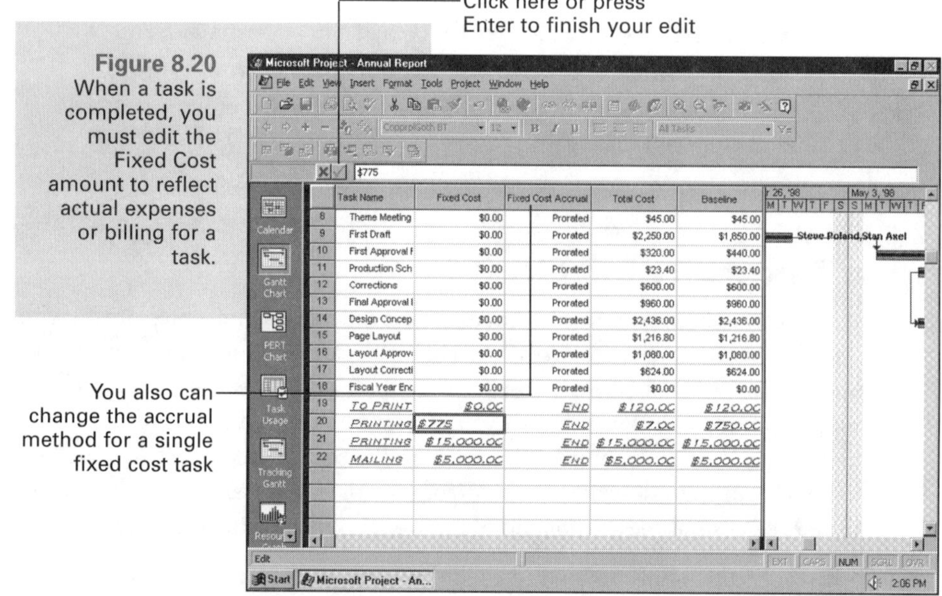
Click here or press Enter to finish your edit
You also can change the accrual method for a single fixed cost task

Figure 8.20 When a task is completed, you must edit the Fixed Cost amount to reflect actual expenses or billing for a task.

Note

If you want to change the accrual method for a single fixed cost rather than all of them, change the entry in the Fixed Cost Accrual column, as shown in Figure 8.20.

Overriding a Calculated Resource Cost

Just as your original Fixed Cost entry might not reflect the final, actual cost, a calculated expense based on the amount of hourly work completed by a resource might not reflect the final charge to you for that work. This might happen when a resource (particularly a freelance resource) has to work more hours or days than you estimated, but because of a contractual obligation, the resource only bills you the original amount; in such a case, entering all the hours the resource worked would make the calculated higher than the final bill. Other times, a resource might have reason to bill you more for a task than had been initially agreed upon, even if the days or hours of work completed remained consistent with your estimate.

In either case, you need to adjust the actual costs for the task without changing the number of hours or days worked on the task. There's only one way to do so, and it involves the following steps:

1. Open the Tools menu and click Options. The Options dialog box appears, with many tabs.
2. Click the Calculation tab to display its options.
3. Click to clear the check beside the Actual Costs Are Always Calculated by Microsoft Project option.

After you disable automatic calculation, be aware that turning it back on overrides actual costs you enter. Therefore, it's best to follow the steps listed here only after your project is finished. Project offers another approach for entering actual costs that's the best of both worlds. You can override a calculated resource cost after you mark a task as 100% completed and remaining costs (Rem. Cost) for the tasks are calculated as $0, without turning off automatic calculation.

Caution

4. By default, actual costs you enter are distributed (accrued) along the full duration of the task. If you want to spread the actual cost only through the project status date you entered, click to check the Edits to Total Actual Cost Will Be Spread to the Status Date check box.
5. Click OK to close the Options dialog box.
6. Switch to Gantt Chart view and click the task for which you want to enter an actual cost that's different from the cost calculated by Project.
7. Open the View menu and click More Views, or click the More Views icon on the View Bar. The More Views dialog box appears.
8. Scroll down the Views list and double-click Task Entry (or click it and click Apply). Project displays the Task Entry form in the lower pane.
9. Right-click the lower pane and click Resource Cost. The pane changes to display cost information about the resource.
10. Click the Act. Cost column and edit the entry as needed (see Figure 8.21).
11. Click OK to finish your entry.
12. (Optional) Use the Previous and Next buttons to display information about the resource work for other tasks, and repeat steps 5 and 6 to edit the Act. Cost entries.

To remove the lower pane and return to regular Gantt Chart view, open the Window menu and click Remove Split.

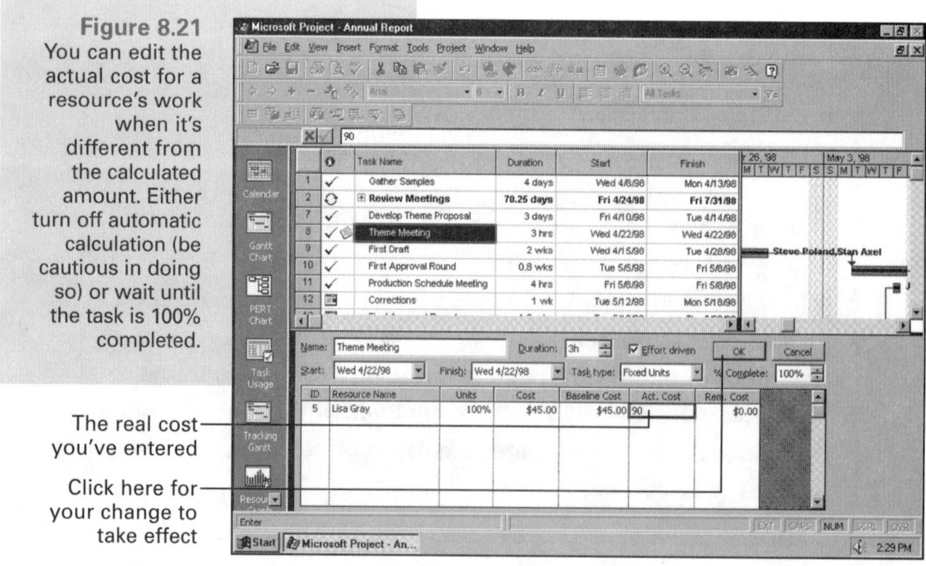

Figure 8.21 You can edit the actual cost for a resource's work when it's different from the calculated amount. Either turn off automatic calculation (be cautious in doing so) or wait until the task is 100% completed.

Entering Exact Daily Costs

You can use the Task Usage view to see and enter actual costs per day for an assignment. To do so, you must first turn off automatic calculation (refer to "Controlling Whether Costs Are Updated Based on Work Completed"), because you can't edit Act. Cost entries for a particular assignment even when work on a task is 100% complete. Then, follow these steps to see and edit daily costs for an assignment:

1. Switch to the Task Usage view. (The fastest way to do so is to click the Task Usage icon on the View Bar.)
2. Right-click the right pane of the view, or open the Format menu and point to Details. In the shortcut menu or submenu that appears, click Cost. This choice adds a row of Cost cells for each assignment to the right pane, showing the original calculated daily costs for each resource assignment.
3. Right-click the right pane of the view, or open the Format menu and point to Details. In the shortcut menu or submenu that appears, click Actual Cost. This choice adds a row of Act. Cost cells for each assignment to the right pane, showing the daily actual cost for each resource.
4. Display the assignment for which you want to enter actual cost information, and then click the Act. Work cell for the date you want in the right pane.

Note

The cells in the grid in the right pane of Task Usage or Resource Usage views are called *timephased fields* or *timephased cells*. That's because they let you focus in on a particular date and enter precise work and cost measurements for that date.

5. Type the new cost figure (see Figure 8.22), and then press Enter or click the Enter button on the entry box to finish your entry. Project updates the Act. Cost, and the cost information for the assignment for that date.

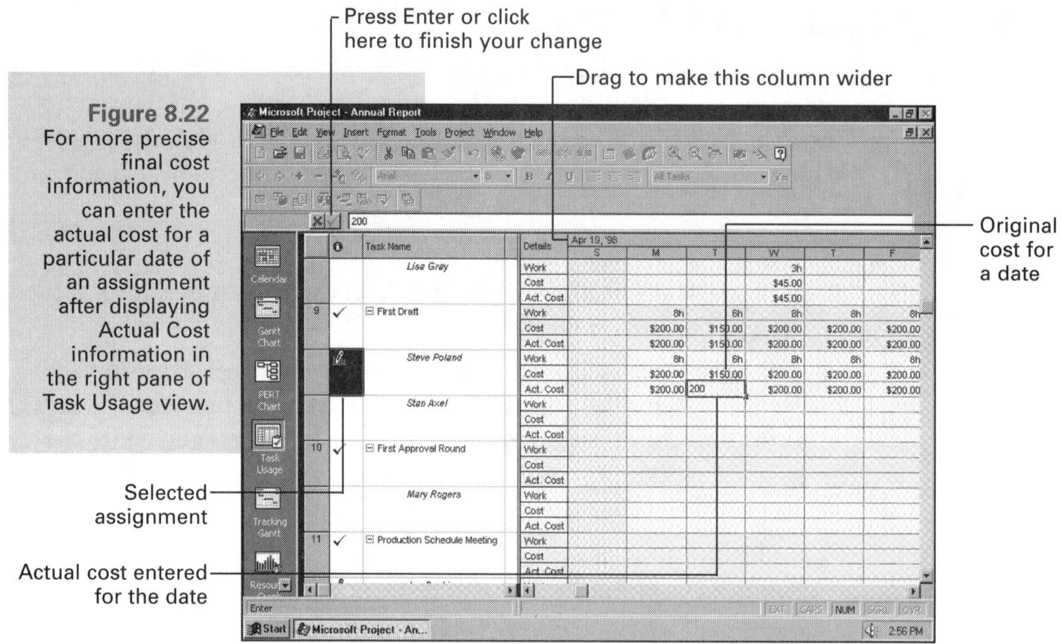

Figure 8.22 For more precise final cost information, you can enter the actual cost for a particular date of an assignment after displaying Actual Cost information in the right pane of Task Usage view.

Cutting Back Costs

When you're developing your overall project schedule, or after work is underway and you're seeing that some of your actual cost amounts are exceeding the amounts you budgeted, you might need to look for ways to cut back costs. Here are just a few ways that you can reduce your overall budget:

- Look at the schedules for more expensive tasks—the Budget report (refer to Figure 8.16) can help you identify these—and see if you can decrease the scheduled work for them or negotiate a more favorable fee or hourly rate.
- Cut back the working time allotted for later tasks.
- Return to your cost estimates, and see if you have time to substitute less expensive resources for more expensive ones.
- Cut back the amount of work handled by an expensive resource, perhaps by adding resources with lower hourly rates to share the expensive resource's workload.

Working with the Different Project Views

In This Chapter

- Reviewing the views
- Choosing a view
- Working with tables, including how to control table information by sorting and filtering
- Using Gantt ChartWizard
- Adjusting whether charted information is displayed on a weekly, monthly, or other timescale
- Creating your own views and organizing views

Project enables you to capture a huge amount of information about the tasks and resources associated with your plan. In theory, you could use a spreadsheet program or word processor instead of Project to store all these details. To a limited degree, those kinds of programs let you chart or display information in alternative formats, but they do not provide the same flexibility in viewing and presenting your information that Project does.

Project offers this variety to enable you to be efficient at entering schedule and resource information, and to be proficient at reviewing the schedule and gleaning key facts. The different ways that Project presents information are called views, and this chapter reviews the views.

Reviewing the Views

Earlier chapters in this book periodically explained how to change the view so that you could work with different kinds of information. The views used in earlier chapters included the Gantt Chart, Resource Graph, Resource Sheet, Task Usage, Resource Usage, and Task Entry views.

Project views can present information in a table or spreadsheet-like grid (as the Task Sheet and Resource Sheet do); in a graphical format (as Gantt chart bars do); or in a fill-in form format (where you select fields or text boxes and then enter the information you want to view). Some views use a single method to present information and some present information in various ways by having multiple panes onscreen. When a view uses only one method to organize information, such as a form, it's called a single-pane view.

Project prints information using the currently selected view. However, Project doesn't print information in forms, so a view comprised of only a form won't print at all. When printing is unavailable, the Print button on the Standard toolbar is disabled (grayed out).

In addition to thinking about how views appear onscreen, you need to select a view based on the type of information you want to work with. Some views primarily provide information about tasks, and other views primarily provide information about resources. Here are the predefined views you'll find in Project:

- **Bar Rollup, Milestone Date Rollup, and Milestone Rollup**—Use these views after running the Rollup_Formatting macro that comes with Project to roll up the Gantt bars for subtasks onto the summary task Gantt bar. Each view provides slightly different formatting for the

rolled up tasks. See the section "Using the Rollup Views" near the end of this chapter for a look at how to use these views.

- **Calendar**—This single-pane view (see Figure 9.1) displays tasks on a monthly calendar, using a bar and label to indicate each task duration.
- **Detail Gantt**—In this variation of Gantt Chart view, the Task Sheet includes Delay information, and the Gantt bars indicate slack time and any task slippage(changes in the task schedule since you saved the baseline). Figure 9.2 shows Detail Gantt view.
- **Gantt Chart**—This is the default view in Project; it includes the Task Sheet in the left pane and Gantt bars showing task durations and relationships in the right pane.
- **Leveling Gantt**—In this variation of Gantt Chart view, the Task Sheet includes a Leveling Delay column to indicate any tasks that Project delayed when you used automatic resource leveling (refer to Chapter 5, "Resolving Overallocations and Overbooked Resources," to learn more about resource leveling). In addition, the Gantt bars are split into two smaller bars. The upper bar shows the task's original schedule, and the bottom bar shows its current schedule, with darker shading indicating the percentage of work completed on the task.
- **PA_Expected Gantt, PA_Optimistic Gantt, PA_PERT Entry Sheet, PA_Pessimistic Gantt**—Use these views, covered later in this chapter under "Using PERT Analysis," to have Project calculate a best estimate for your project's schedule.

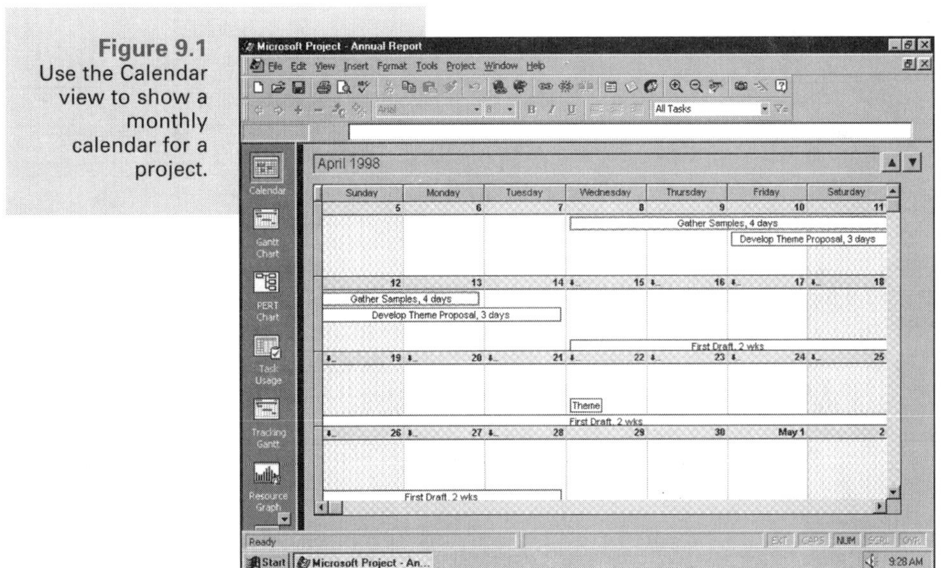

Figure 9.1 Use the Calendar view to show a monthly calendar for a project.

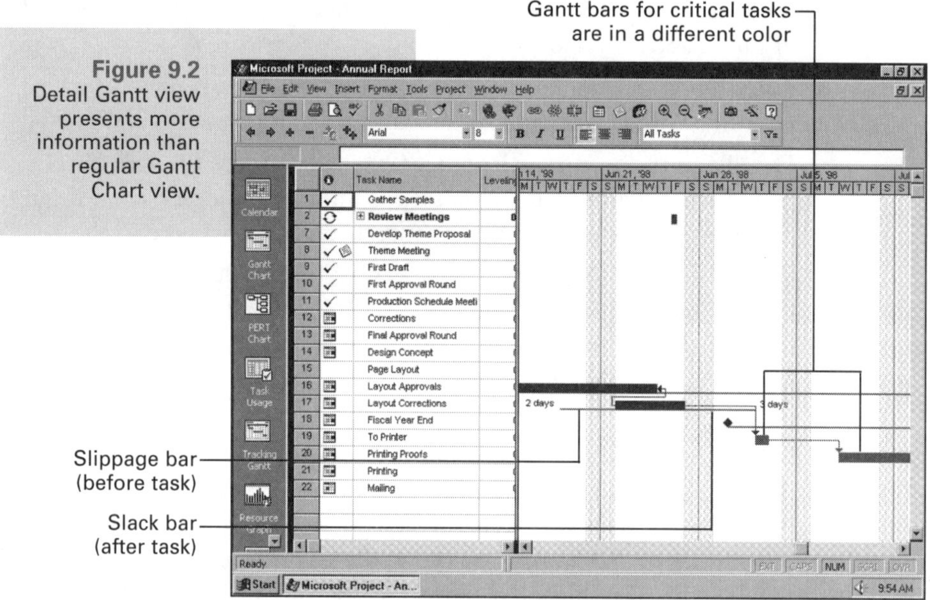

Figure 9.2 Detail Gantt view presents more information than regular Gantt Chart view.

- **PERT Chart**—This view displays tasks in a format resembling a flow chart (see Figure 9.3). You can drag to link tasks, or right-click a task and click Task Information to adjust the task schedule and resource assignments.

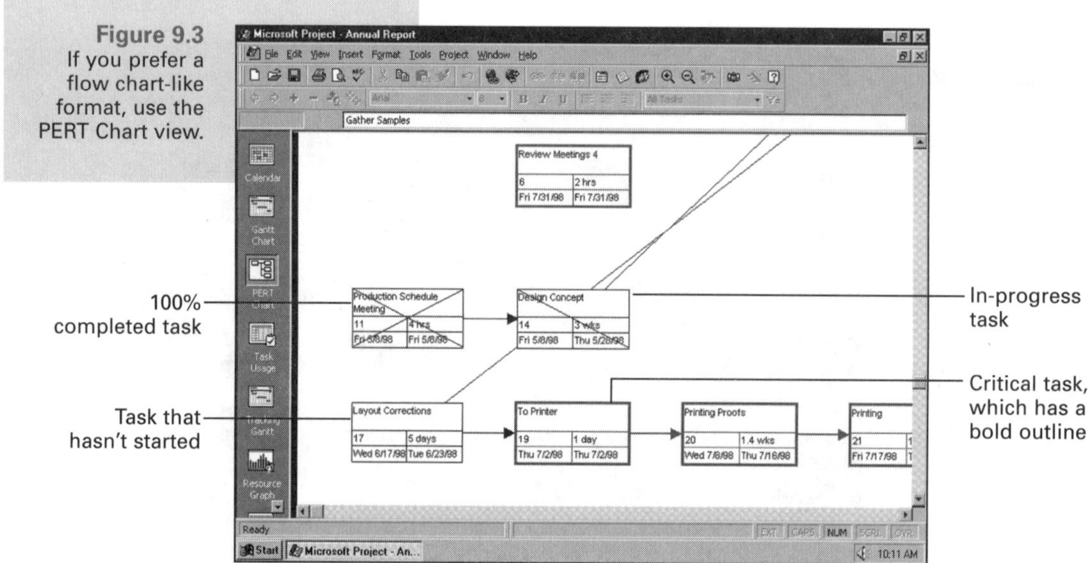

Figure 9.3 If you prefer a flow chart-like format, use the PERT Chart view.

Note

On the PERT chart, you can also drag to add new tasks to the schedule. Drag diagonally to create a box with the mouse. Right-click the new task box, and then click Task Information. Provide the details about the task in the Task Information dialog box, and then click OK. To delete a task in PERT Chart view, click the PERT chart box (node) to select it and press Delete. Or, to select multiple boxes, drag over an area that is larger than and surrounds the boxes to be deleted. When you release the mouse button, a gray selector appears around the boxes. Press the Delete key to remove the task boxes from the chart.

- **Resource Allocation**—This view presents the Resource Usage view in the upper pane and the Task Sheet and Gantt chart in the lower pane.
- **Resource Form**—This is a form you use to enter and edit information about a specific resource. It lists all the tasks assigned to that resource, resource cost information, and more (see Figure 9.4).
- **Resource Graph**—This view (examples of which are shown in Chapter 8, "Viewing and Managing Costs") can graph various information about a resource's daily and cumulative costs, scheduled work and cumulative

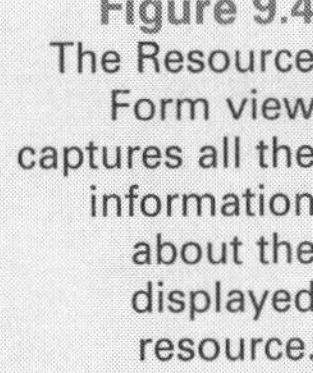

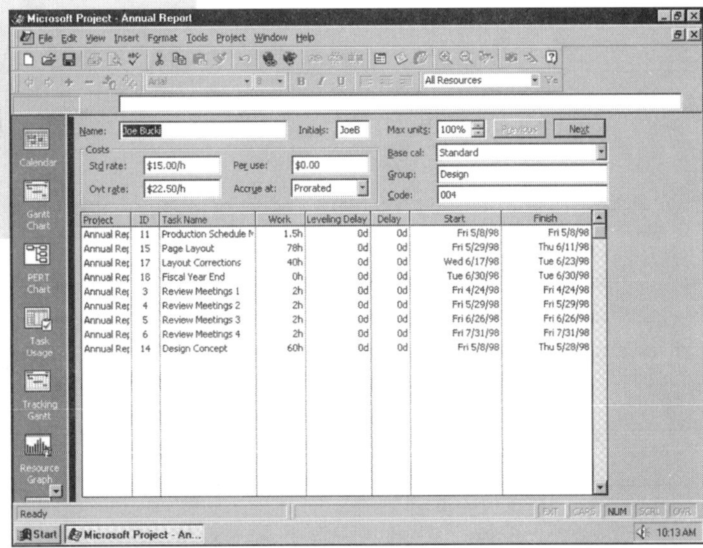

Figure 9.4 The Resource Form view captures all the information about the displayed resource.

work, overallocated times, percentage of work allocated, and availability. To change which information is graphed, right-click the chart area of the view and use the resulting shortcut menu to choose which information is charted.

- **Resource Name Form**—This abbreviated version of the Resource Form lists the resource name and its assigned tasks.
- **Resource Sheet**— This view provides a grid of cells you can use to add resources to your project file. Chapter 4, "Managing Resources," covers the Resource Sheet in detail.
- **Resource Usage**—This view, covered in various earlier chapters, combines the Resource Sheet on the left identifying the assignments for each resource, with a timephased grid on the right that you can use to enter daily actual costs, daily scheduled work and completed work, overallocated dates, and more. Right-click the right pane to choose which details you want to view or enter in it.
- **Task Details Form**—Similar to the Resource Form, this full-screen form displays task scheduling information, constraints, assigned resources, and more. You can view or edit information in this form, as you can in others.

You can right-click a blank area of any form to adjust what it displays.

- **Task Entry**—This view displays the Gantt chart in the upper pane and the Task Form in the lower pane. It lets you perform detailed editing of task information in the lower pane, so you can see how your changes affect the Gantt chart. You can right-click the Task Form to select which information it displays.
- **Task Form**—This form enables you to change the task name, schedule, work completion information, and assigned resource(s).
- **Task Name Form**—This is the simplest variation of the Task Details Form. It enables you to change the task name and assigned resource(s).
- **Task PERT**—In a format resembling a flow chart (see Figure 9.5), this view provides information about task links.
- **Task Sheet**—This view shows the Task Sheet at full-screen size rather than in combination with other view panes.

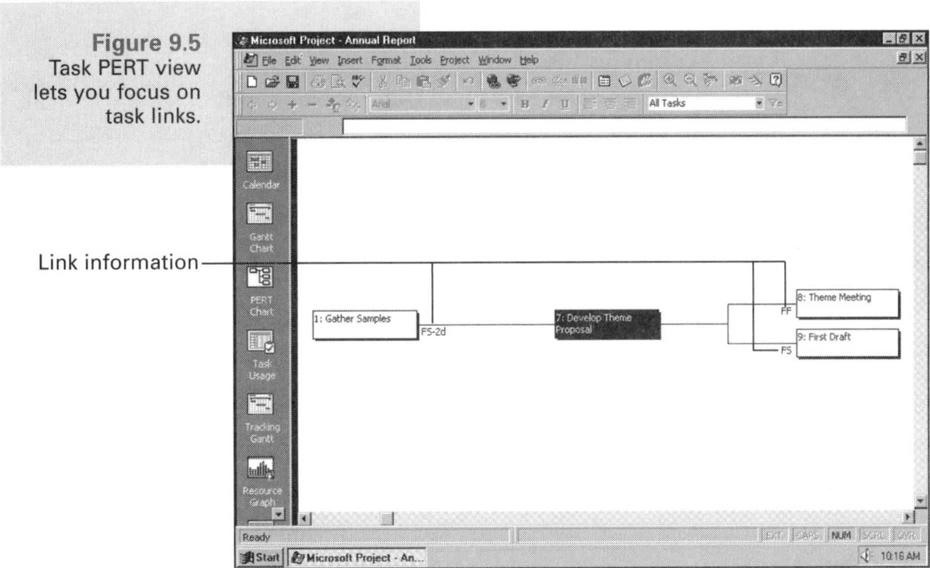

Figure 9.5 Task PERT view lets you focus on task links.

- **Task Usage**—Various chapters have already covered how to display and work with this view, which groups resource assignments by task. Use the timephased grid at the right to view and enter daily work and cost values. Right-click the right pane to choose what details you want to view or enter in it.
- **Tracking Gantt**—Chapter 7, "Comparing Progress versus Your Baseline Plan," discusses this variation of regular Gantt Chart view. In Tracking Gantt view, the Gantt chart bars are divided into upper and lower segments. The lower portion of each bar shows the task's original schedule, and the upper portion shows the task's current schedule.

Choosing a View

It's pretty obvious where to begin when you want to select a new view—the View menu. The top eight commands on this menu take you directly to the specified view: Calendar, Gantt Chart, PERT Chart, Task Usage, Tracking Gantt, Resource Graph, Resource Sheet, and Resource Usage. In addition, the View Bar at the left offers an icon for each of those eight views; click an icon to display the view it represents.

If you're changing from a combination view that includes more than one pane to a view that includes only a single pane, the extra pane often won't close on its own. To close it, open the Window menu and click Remove Split (or double-click the dividing line between the panes). If the bottom pane is a form, you also can right-click it, and then click Hide Form View. Finally, if you're changing from a split view to a single pane view, press and hold the Shift key when you select the new view from the View menu to both remove the split and display the selected view.

If you want to display a view that's not listed on the menu or the View Bar, follow these steps:

1. Open the View menu and click More Views, or click the More Views icon on the View Bar. The More Views dialog box appears (see Figure 9.6).
2. Scroll the Views list, if needed, to display the view you want.
3. In the Views list, double-click the name of the view you want to display (or click the name and click Apply).

In views that include upper and lower panes, click within the pane you want to work in to make that pane the active view, or press F6. The Active View Bar along the edge of the screen darkens to indicate which pane you selected to work in.

If you switch to any view that includes a Gantt chart and don't see *anything* in the pane, first make sure that Project hasn't scrolled the displayed dates before or beyond the schedule for the project. Try clicking the Go To Selected Task button on the Standard toolbar to scroll the display to the right area. Or, press Alt+Home to go to the project start task/milestone or Alt+End to go to the project end task/milestone.

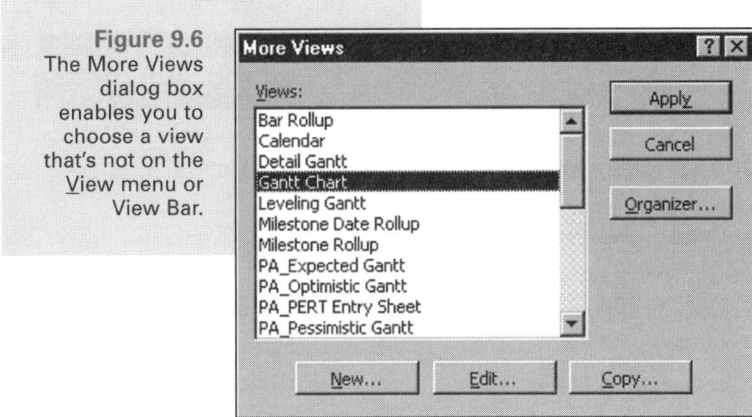

Figure 9.6 The More Views dialog box enables you to choose a view that's not on the View menu or View Bar.

Adjusting a Sheet

The Task Sheet and Resource Sheet present information in various columns (fields). Depending on the operation at hand, you may want to view columns that contain different information. For example, Chapter 8, "Viewing and Managing Costs," explains that you can display columns of actual and projected cost information in the Task Sheet. You also can control which rows appear in the current sheet and the order in which those rows appear. This section covers how to adjust the information presented in the Task Sheet or Resource Sheet.

Choosing a Table

In Project, each particular group of columns shown in a Task Sheet or Resource Sheet is called a table. To display one of the predefined sets of columns, therefore, you choose a different table for the currently displayed sheet. Of course, different tables are provided for the Task Sheet and Resource Sheet, as you track different information for tasks than you do for resources. When you select a particular table for a sheet and then print the view that includes the sheet, Project prints only the columns that are part of the presently selected table. Table 9.1 lists the many tables types that are available.

When you want to establish which table is used by a Task Sheet or Resource Sheet, first select the sheet. Next, open the View menu, point to Table, and click the name of the table you want. If the desired table is not listed, click More Tables. The More Tables dialog box appears (see Figure 9.7). If needed, select Task or Resource at the top of the dialog box to list the appropriate kinds of tables. Select a table from the Tables list by double-clicking it (or by clicking it and clicking Apply).

Table 9.1 Tables Available for a Task Sheet or Resource Sheet.

Table	Description
Task Sheet Tables	
Baseline	Displays the baseline schedule dates for tasks.
Constraint Dates	Lists key constraint dates you entered for tasks.
Cost	Shows fixed cost information you entered for a task, as well as calculated resource costs.
Delay	Tells you when a task has been delayed as a result of resource leveling.
Earned Value	Includes columns that identify planned costs versus actual costs, and more.
Entry	The default; provides columns that enable you to set up new tasks.
Export	When you export task data, Project uses this table, which includes all task fields.
Hyperlink	Displays links you created to Web pages or files on a network, such as a link to a memo file with more information about a task.
PA Expected Case	When you use PERT Analysis, enables you to view and edit the expected dates for tasks.
PA Optimistic Case	When you use PERT Analysis, enables you to view and edit the optimistic dates for tasks.
PA PERT Entry	When you use PERT Analysis, enables you to enter and view optimistic, expected, and pessimistic durations.
PA Pessimistic Case	When you use PERT Analysis, enables you to enter and view pessimistic dates for tasks.
Rollup Table	When you use the Rollup views, adds columns so you can control Gantt display features such as whether text appears above the rolled up bars.
Schedule	Presents task start and finish information, as well as information about slack time.
Summary	Presents scheduled task start and finish dates, percent of work completed, and budgeted cost and work hours.
Tracking	Presents information you entered about actual task start and finish dates, remaining duration, and actual costs.
Usage	Adjusts the table slightly to include the total work for each task, in hours.
Variance	Lists baseline start and finish dates along with the current dates, and shows the variance between the two sets of dates.
Work	Enables you to track work statistics, such as the baseline number of hours scheduled for a task, the actual hours worked, variance between the two, and so on.

Table 9.1 Tables Available for a Task Sheet or Resource Sheet.

Table	Description
Resource Sheet Tables	
Cost	Displays the baseline cost you estimated for a resource, the current scheduled cost, the cost actually incurred, and more.
Earned Value	Displays the calculated earned value statistics described in Table 8.1. For example, displays the Budgeted Cost of Work Scheduled (BCWS).
Entry	The default; provides columns that enable you to set up new resources.
Export	When you export resource data, Project uses this table, which includes all resource fields.
Hyperlink	Displays links you created to Web pages or files on a network, such as a link to a resource's Web page.
Summary	Includes information about hourly rates and work hours scheduled for a resource on a project, and more.
Usage	Displays the resource name and number of hours of work by that resource scheduled for the project.
Work	Lists scheduled and actual work hours by a resource, overtime work authorized, percentage of work completed, and more.

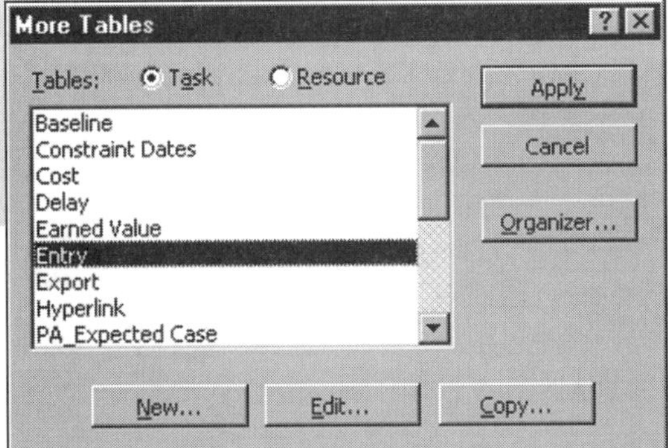

Figure 9.7 Here's where you choose a table that's not on the Table submenu.

If you try to display a table that's not available for a Resource Sheet, Project displays a message box telling you that you need to choose or create another table.

Filtering the Task Sheet or Resource Sheet

By default, each Task Sheet or Resource Sheet displays all the tasks or resources you entered for the project, no matter which table you've selected. There might be an occasion, though, when you want to see only some of the tasks or resources listed. For example, if you need to provide your boss with a list of tasks that have been completed, or a list of all resources from a particular resource group, you can filter the sheet to display only certain rows.

Filtering a sheet and then printing it is a "quick and dirty" method of creating a "report" about key facts from your schedule.

To filter the current sheet, use the Filter drop-down list on the Formatting toolbar (see Figure 9.8). The available Filter choices differ depending on whether a Task Sheet or Resource Sheet is currently displayed. (This figure shows the Task Sheet choices.) Some filter choices are followed by an ellipsis (...), which indicates that if you choose that particular filter, Project will ask you to supply more information to help it select the rows to display. For example, if you select Date Range..., Project displays the dialog box shown in Figure 9.9 asking you to enter a date to begin specifying the timeframe within which the displayed tasks must fall. In this case, you would enter a starting date, click OK, enter an ending date, and click OK again so that Project could filter the list.

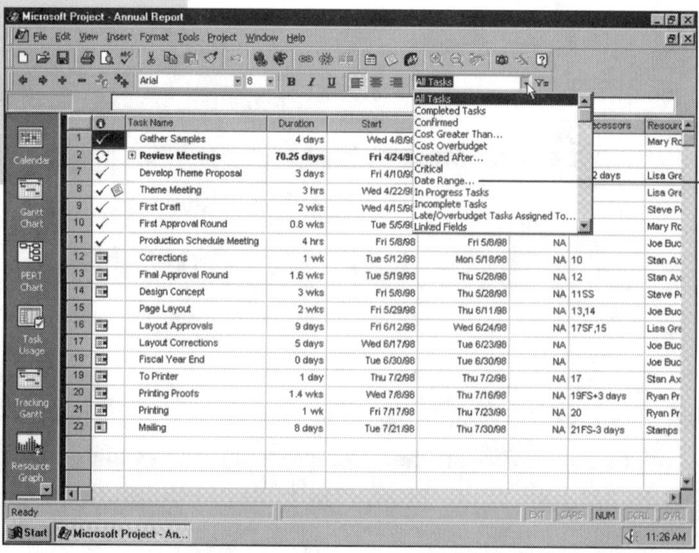

Figure 9.8 Use the Filter drop-down list to control which rows appear in a sheet.

The ellipsis (...) beside a filter means that Project will prompt you for details about which rows to select

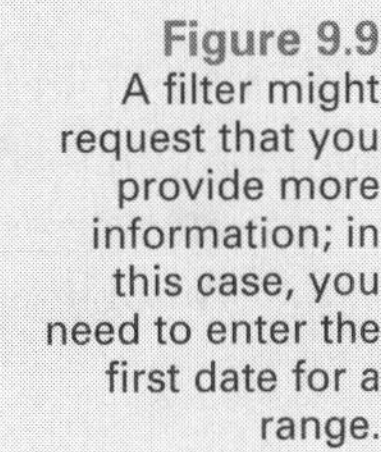

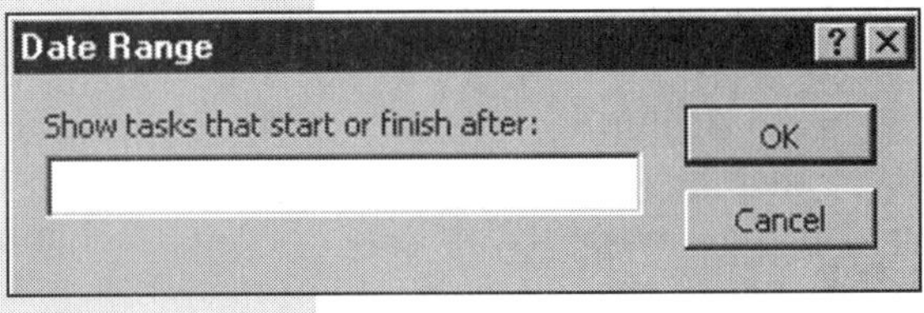

Figure 9.9 A filter might request that you provide more information; in this case, you need to enter the first date for a range.

To return to the full listing of tasks or resources after you're done with the filtered version, select All Tasks or All Resources from the Filter drop-down list.

If you prefer not to display the Formatting toolbar, but still want to filter tasks and resources, open the Project menu, point to Filtered For to display a submenu, and click the name of the filter you want. If the name doesn't appear, click More Filters to display the More Filters dialog box (see Figure 9.10). Use this dialog box to select the filter you want.

Note

Optionally, you can click the Highlight button in the More Filters dialog box to apply a highlight color to the filtered tasks or resources, rather than hiding the rows that don't contain the right type of information. If you do this, all rows are displayed onscreen, with the filtered tasks appearing in the highlight color. Or, hold the Shift key and select the filter from the Project, Filtered For submenu to apply a highlighted filter.

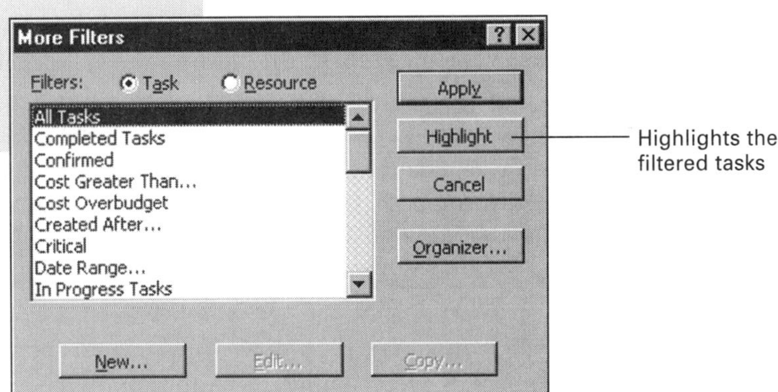

Figure 9.10 Access more filters via this dialog box.

Using AutoFilters

Project 98 offers yet another type of filtering, *AutoFilters*. Project AutoFilters work just like those in Microsoft Excel. Basically, you turn on the AutoFilters feature, and then choose an AutoFilter using the drop-down filtering arrow that appears on a Task Sheet or Resource Sheet column header. AutoFilters offer two advantages over the filtering just described:

- You can filter by any column, which you can't really do with regular filtering.
- You can choose specific criteria for filtering the list.

To apply AutoFiltering to a Task Sheet or Resource Sheet, open the Project menu, point to Filtered For, and then click AutoFilter. Alternately, click the AutoFilter button on the Formatting toolbar. An AutoFilter button appears on the header for every column in the displayed Task Sheet or Resource Sheet. Click the AutoFilter button for a column head to display the available AutoFilters for that column; the AutoFilters available depend on the type of information contained in the column. For example, because the AutoFilter list shown in Figure 9.11 is for a column that holds dates, you can choose to filter the Task Sheet to list only tasks that have a Start date that's This Week, This Month, and so on. The Duration column AutoFilters enable you to filter the list to show only tasks with a duration that's more than a week, only tasks with a duration that's less than a week, or other tasks with similar durations. If you want to only list the tasks being handled by a particular resource, choose one of the AutoFilters for the Resource Names column. To remove the AutoFilter from any column, open the AutoFilter drop-down list and click on the (All) choice.

You can create an AutoFilter that's more complex, by specifying your own filter criteria. To do so, open the AutoFilter drop-down list for the column that contains the information you want to use to filter the list. Choose (Custom...) to display the Custom AutoFilter dialog box. Open the first drop-down list, as shown in Figure 9.12, and then click an operator (test) choice. For example, to display all dates later than a particular date (in a date-oriented column), choose the Is Greater Than operator. Open the drop-down list that's at the right on the first row, and choose the entry representing the value that the operator should use to evaluate the list, such as the particular date the Is Greater Than operator should use. For a date field, for example, if you choose Is Greater Than, and then choose Fri 4/24/98, Project filters the list to display only tasks with an entry after Fri 4/24/98 in the filtered column. If the field entries must match two criteria, leave the And option button selected. If the field entries can match either of two criteria, click the Or option button. Choose the operator and value from the bottom two drop-down lists in the dialog box to specify the second criterion. Click OK to apply the custom AutoFilter for the column.

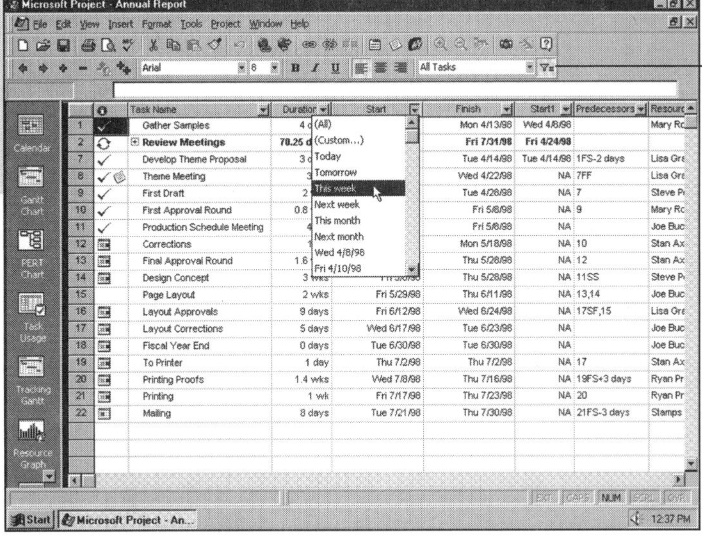

The AutoFilter button on the Formatting toolbar

Figure 9.11 After you turn on AutoFiltering, click to open an AutoFilter list, and then click an AutoFilter.

Note

Instead of clicking OK to apply a custom AutoFilter, click the Save button in the Custom AutoFilter dialog box; enter a Name for the AutoFilter in the Filter Definition in '(Current File)' dialog box, and click to enable the Show in Menu check box to have the AutoFilter appear on the Filtered For submenu. Then, click OK to save it. You also can use this dialog box to add even more criteria for a filter, by choosing entries in the And/Or, Field Name, Test (operator), and Value(s) column.

Figure 9.12 Enter criteria for your own AutoFilter in this dialog box.

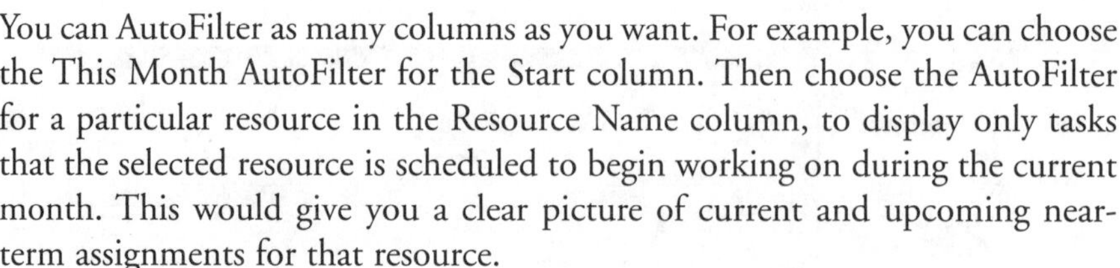

You can AutoFilter as many columns as you want. For example, you can choose the This Month AutoFilter for the Start column. Then choose the AutoFilter for a particular resource in the Resource Name column, to display only tasks that the selected resource is scheduled to begin working on during the current month. This would give you a clear picture of current and upcoming near-term assignments for that resource.

When you finish working with all AutoFilters, turn the AutoFiltering feature off (it toggles on and off). To do so, open the Project menu, point to Filtered For, and then click AutoFilter, or click the AutoFilter button on the Formatting toolbar. Project removes the AutoFilter buttons from the sheet column headers.

Sorting Information

By default, the information in your Task Sheet or Resource Sheet (and any accompanying charts in the view you selected) appears in the order in which you added it to the project. Even if you select a different table or filter, the basic order in which the rows appear remains static, unless you adjust that order. For example, you might want to sort the Resource Sheet by the name of the resource.

If you're sorting by name, keep in mind that Project, by default, sorts by the first letter listed, which is generally the first name if the resource is a person.

To sort a sheet, open the Project menu, point to the Sort submenu, and click the name of the field (column) to sort by. The fields listed vary depending on whether you're working in a Task Sheet or a Resource Sheet. For a Task Sheet, you can sort by Start Date, Finish Date, Priority, Cost, or ID. For a Resource Sheet, you can sort by Cost, Name, or ID. If the field you want to sort by does not appear on the Sort submenu, click Sort By. The Sort dialog box appears (see Figure 9.13).

Click to display the Sort By drop-down list, and then select the name of the field that contains the information you want to sort by. Select Ascending or Descending to specify whether the information should be sorted in lowest-to-highest order (A–Z) or highest-to-lowest order (Z–A). For example, when you sort tasks by the Cost field, Project by default reorders them from most expensive to least expensive; you might prefer to see the least expensive items first.

To sort by additional fields, as well, use the other drop-down lists provided in this dialog box. Click OK to complete the sort.

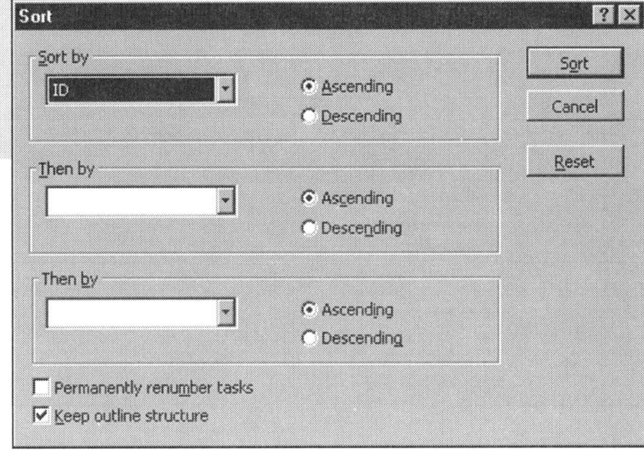

Figure 9.13 Use this dialog box to access more fields to sort by.

When you select the Permanently Renumber Tasks check box, Project changes the ID numbers for the sorted tasks and resources to reflect their new order. If you filtered tasks or resources already, or if you deselected the Keep Outline Structure check box in the Task Sheet, the permanent renumbering option is unavailable. If Keep Outline Structure is deselected, subtasks will not remain with their summary tasks after the sort.

Quick and Dirty Gantt Chart Formatting

Chapter 14, "Other Formatting," details all the options for formatting bars in a Gantt chart, as well as for formatting information in the Task Sheet and elsewhere. Right now, however, you might want a quick way to adjust the Gantt chart bars appearing in any view that includes a Gantt chart. To avoid the need to master the commands on the Format menu, you can use GanttChartWizard to walk you through the key steps for adjusting how the Gantt chart bars look. To start GanttChartWizard, click the GanttChartWizard button on the Standard toolbar (second button from the right), or open the Format menu and click GanttChartWizard. The GanttChartWizard—Step 1 dialog box appears. Click the Next button to display the GanttChartWizard—Step 2 dialog box (see Figure 9.14). In this dialog box, click to select the type of information you want to appear in your Gantt chart.

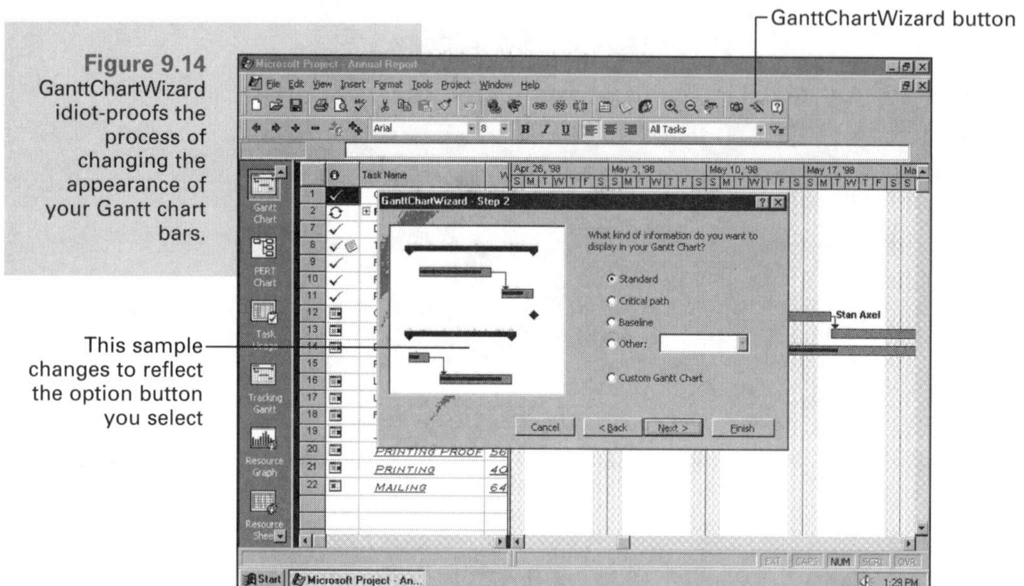

Figure 9.14 GanttChartWizard idiot-proofs the process of changing the appearance of your Gantt chart bars.

Note

If you select any custom option (listed last in each GanttChartWizard dialog box), the dialog box that follows enables you to specify details about the option. Obviously, the details you can specify vary depending on the particular option. Additionally, the step number of the subsequent dialog box varies depending on the dialog box from which you selected the custom option.

Make your selection, and click Next to continue. The GanttChartWizard—Step 9 dialog box appears, enabling you to indicate what kinds of labels you want to appear with the Gantt chart bars. (The step numbers on the dialog boxes are not sequential; they vary depending on the choices you make.) The default is to label the task bars with both the resources and dates assigned to the task, but you can change this. Specify your choice, and then click Next. The GanttChartWizard—Step 13 dialog box appears. Select whether you want Project to include lines indicating links between tasks in the Gantt chart, and then click Next. The GanttChartWizard—Step 14 dialog box appears so that you can finish the process. Click Format It, and Project formats your Gantt chart exactly as you specified. Then, click Exit Wizard.

Changing and Zooming the Timescale

The graphical portion of any view usually presents information in terms of a schedule. The schedule units used in that portion of the view, usually shown along the top of the view, are called the timescale. By default, Project uses a weekly timescale at the top of the graphical display; this is the major timescale. Below each week, the minor timescale slices the schedule into days.

Why would you want to change the timescale? Well, you might want to make the schedule more compact for easier printing (select a monthly timescale) or more extended to provide greater detail. To change the timescale, follow these steps:

1. Make sure that the pane that includes the graphical display is the active view.
2. Open the Format menu and click Timescale. The Timescale dialog box appears (see Figure 9.15). You also can right-click the timescale onscreen, and then click Timescale, or double-click the timescale on-screen.
3. Set up the major timescale in the Major Scale area. Use the Units drop-down list to adjust the measurement (days or months, for example). In the Count text box, enter a value to control how many of the timescale units are labeled. For example, 3 means that Project labels every third

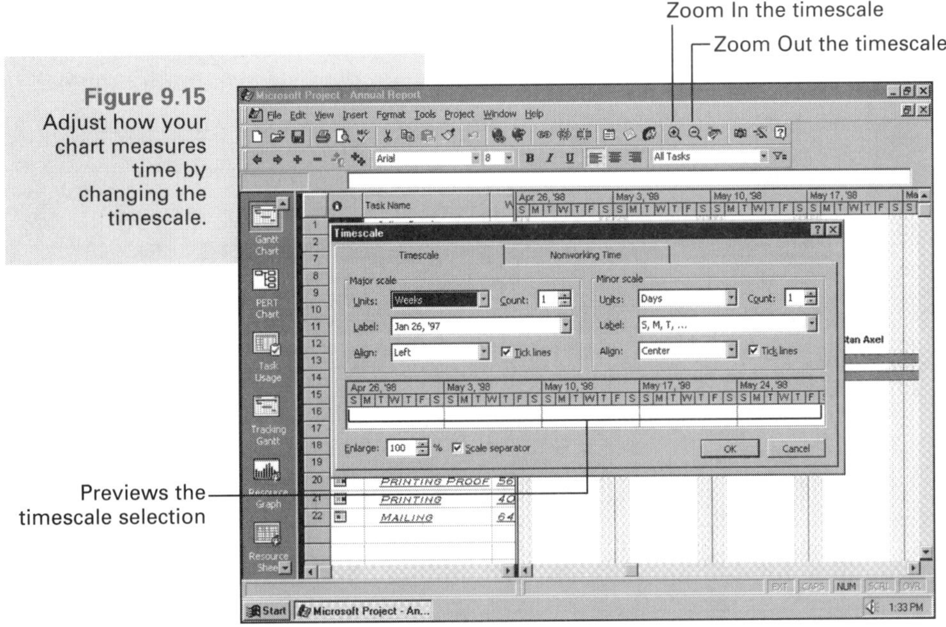

Figure 9.15 Adjust how your chart measures time by changing the timescale.

unit on the major timescale (the top row of time units, which shows the larger units of time you're displaying on the timescale). Select a date numbering style from the Label drop-down list, and use the Align drop-down list to specify how the labels will be aligned. Finally, select the Tick Lines check box if you want vertical dividing lines to appear between timescale units.

4. Set up the minor timescale in the Minor Scale area. (The minor timescale is the bottom row of time units, which shows smaller units of time to subdivide the major timescale. For example, if the major timescale is set to days, the minor timescale might show hours.) These settings work like the ones described in step 3.
5. If needed, adjust the percentage shown in the Enlarge text box to show more or less of the charted information in the same space.
6. The Scale Separator check box, when selected, adds a horizontal line to separate the major and minor timescales. Select or deselect this option as you prefer.
7. If the Nonworking Time tab is available for the selected Gantt chart, click that tab to display its options (see Figure 9.16). This tab enables you to control how nonworking time (such as holiday and weekend time) is charted. By default, nonworking time appears as gray vertical bars on the timescale.
8. You might want to change how the working time is charted for a calendar other than the Standard calendar. For example, you could specially highlight nonworking time for a particular calendar. In such cases, select the calendar to adjust from the Calendar drop-down list.
9. Use the Color and Pattern drop-down lists to specify the charted appearance of the nonworking time.

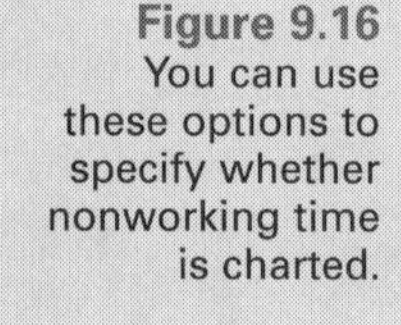

Figure 9.16 You can use these options to specify whether nonworking time is charted.

10. In the Draw area, select an option button to control how the charted nonworking time interacts with the charted tasks. Behind Task Bars means that Project always draws the task bars over the nonworking time. In Front of Task Bars means that the nonworking time "bars" appear in front of the charted task bars. Do Not Draw tells Project not to indicate nonworking time at all.

If you specify nonworking time in days, you must schedule the minor timescale in days or smaller units. Otherwise, Project is unable to chart the nonworking time.

11. Click OK to finish making your timescale settings. Your chart adopts a new appearance, as shown in Figure 9.17.

You can change the timescale in the Calendar view by right-clicking one of the day's names, and then clicking Timescale. For the Calendar view, the Timescale dialog box offers three tabs: Week Headings, Date Boxes, and Date Shading. Use the Week Headings tab to specify how the monthly, weekly, and daily headings appear on the calendar. You can specify whether each week displays 7 days or 5 days (the latter means that weekends are hidden). Also, select the Previous/Next Month Calendars check box if you want the calendar to include small thumbnail views of the months before and after the current month. Use the Date Boxes tab to control what appears in the gray shaded area along the top of each date box, or to display another shaded row (and control its contents) at the bottom of each date box. You specify what appears at the left or right side of each shaded area and can control the pattern and color of the shading. Finally, use the Date Shading tab to control the shading for working days, nonworking days, and other types of dates in the base calendar for the schedule or in resource calendars.

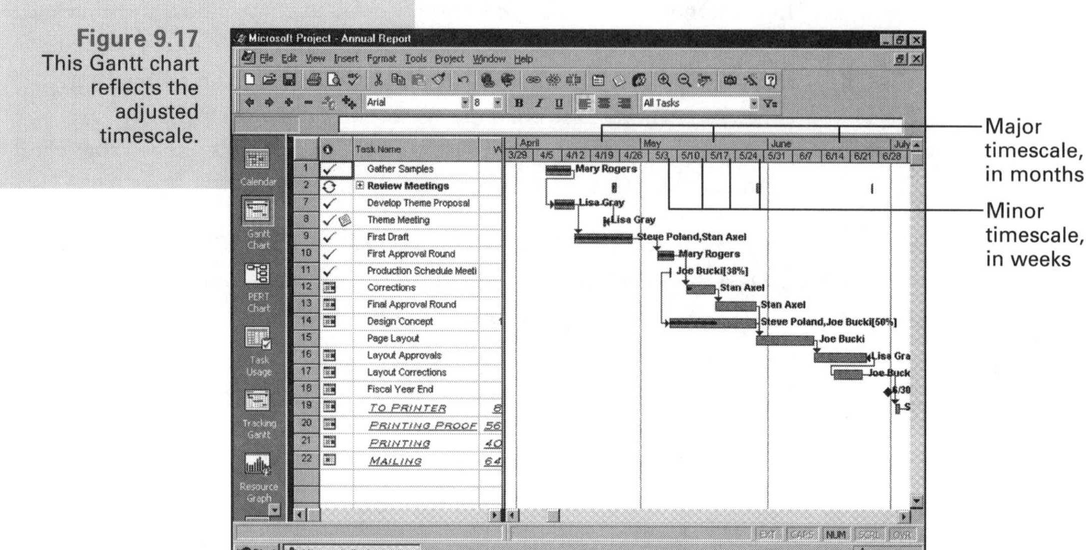

Figure 9.17 This Gantt chart reflects the adjusted timescale.

Creating a Table or Filter

The More Tables and More Filters dialog boxes each contain New and Copy buttons at the bottom. You can use these buttons to create tables and filters from scratch or based on an existing table or filter. For example, you might want to be able to quickly display a few added fields (columns) in a particular sheet. You also might want to create a set of fields completely different from the tables Project provides. (For example, you might want only the task name, resource initials, and remaining work for tasks.)

Note

You can use the Edit button in the More Tables, More Filters, or More Views dialog box to edit the selected table, filter, or view. Make changes using the dialog box that appears, and then click OK to finish. Also, it is not a good practice to edit a default table, filter, or view; rather, copy and rename it first, then edit the copy.

To create and save a custom table, follow these steps:

1. Display the More Tables dialog box. To do so, open the View menu, point to Table, and click More Tables.

2. (Optional) If there's an existing table similar to the table you want to create, click its name in the Tables list to select it.
3. Click the New or Copy button. No matter which button you choose, the Table Definition dialog box appears (see Figure 9.18).
4. Edit the Name for the table, if needed.
5. If you want the custom table to appear as a choice on the Table submenu, leave the Show in Menu check box selected. Otherwise, clear this check box so that the table is listed only in the More Tables dialog box.
6. To remove a row that appears (if you're working on a copy of an existing table), click the Field Name cell in that row; then click the Cut Row button.
7. To add a new field, click the Field Name cell in the first blank row. Next, click the field drop-down list arrow to display a scrolling list of all available fields. Click the field you want. If needed, edit the Align Data, Width, Title, and Align Title columns for the new field.
8. Continue adding and adjusting field rows. You can use the Copy Row, Paste Row, and Insert Row buttons to move selected rows, or to insert a new, blank row between existing rows.
9. If your table includes date fields and you want to change how they appear (for example, you want to spell out the month name), use the Date Format drop-down list to select a format.
10. If you want each table row to have more height (to make it more attractive or legible), increase the value in the Row Height text box by clicking and editing the existing entry.

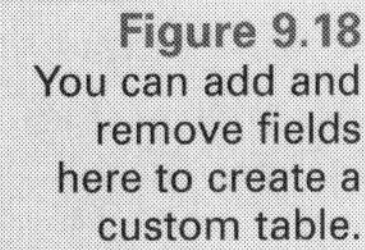

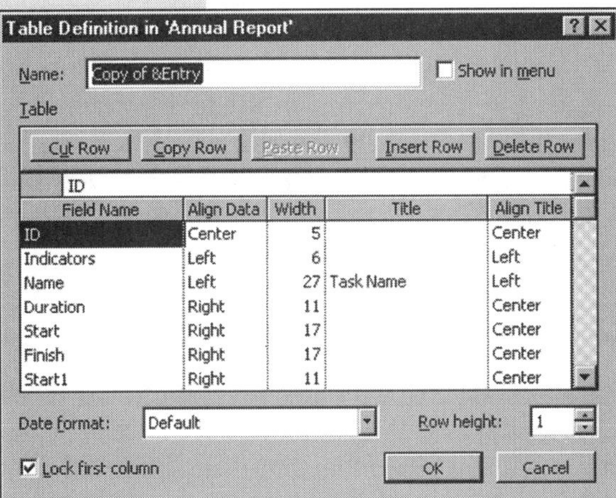

Figure 9.18
You can add and remove fields here to create a custom table.

11. The Lock First Column check box "freezes" the far-left column so that you can't edit it, and it won't scroll out of view. Clear this check box if you don't want either condition to apply.
12. Click OK. Project saves your table and adds it to the Tables list in the More Tables dialog box.
13. Click Close to exit the More Tables dialog box without applying the table, or click Apply to apply the new table to the current sheet.

Just as you can save a custom table, you can save a custom filter using a process very similar to the one just described. Open the Project menu, point to Filtered For, and click More Filters. In the More Filters dialog box, select the filter you want to use to create the custom filter, if any. Click on the New or Copy button. The Filter Definition dialog box appears.

I strongly recommend creating a custom filter by copying an existing filter because it's easier and faster to edit filtering criteria than to create new ones from scratch.

Edit the filter name and specify whether you want it to appear as a choice on the Filtered For submenu. Each row you edit or create in the Filter list area contains a single filter criterion. The Field Name cell for each row contains the name of the field you want to filter by. To specify a field, click the Field Name cell; then click the field's drop-down list arrow to display the list of field names. Click the one you want. Next, click the Test cell for this criterion. This holds the operator that Project uses to evaluate the selected field. To change the test, click the arrow to display the field box drop-down list, and click the operator you want.

Next, use the Value(s) column to specify which data the test will compare to the field contents. You can type a value or date in this column (see Figure 9.19), or use the field drop-down list to select another field to compare the data with. If you enter a value that involves a work amount or schedule amount, be sure to include a time abbreviation with your entry. For example, you might build a criterion with Remaining Work under Field Name, Does Not Equal under Test, and 0h under Value(s). Finally, if you want to filter by more criteria, use the And/Or column to specify whether the filtered rows must match all entered criteria (And) or just one of the entered criteria (Or).

Click the Show Related Summary Tasks check box to select it if you want the filtered list to display summary tasks that match the filter specifications. Click OK to finish creating the filter, and then close the More Filters dialog box by clicking Apply. Project applies your new filter to the current sheet.

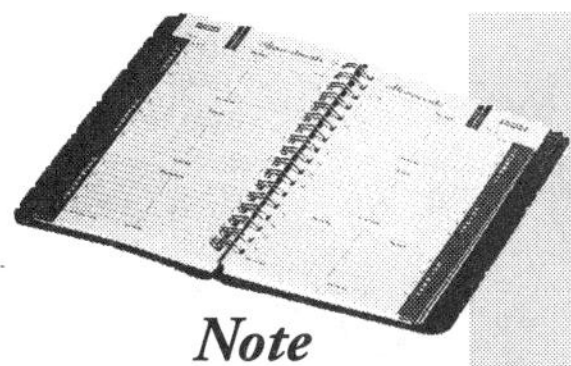
Note

You can create a filter that's *interactive*—meaning it displays a dialog box prompting you to enter the information to filter for—using the Value(s) column in the Filter Definition dialog box. Specify the And/Or, Field Name, and Test choices you want. Then, enter the message the dialog box should display, surrounded by quotes, with a question mark following the quotes. For example, you can create an interactive filter that prompts you to specify a percentage of work complete, then filters the list by the percentage you enter. To do so, choose % Complete from the Field Name drop-down list in the Filter Definition dialog box, and choose equals from the Test drop-down list. Then, click the Value(s) cell for that row, type "Enter percentage:"?, and press Enter. Click OK to finish creating the filter. Then, if you choose the filter from the More Filters dialog box, a dialog box appears, prompting you to Enter percentage. If you want the interactive filter to prompt you for a range of dates or values, choose is within or is not within as the Test, then enter "From:"?,"To:"? in the Value(s) cell. Using two sets of quotation marks, two question marks, and the comma tells the filter to prompt for two values. Note that you need to make sure that the prompt you enter in the Value(s) column needs to make it clear whether the reader should enter a value or a date. For example, if the Field Name the filter uses contains dates, prompting the user to enter a number or percentage would cause the filter not to work.

Creating a View

Unlike when you create a table or filter, it's often easiest to create a new view from scratch rather than edit an existing view. Project enables you to create and save a single-pane view that combines a specified table and filter. Thus, if you want to create a view that uses a custom table or filter, you need to create the custom table or filter first. To create a new single-pane view, follow these steps:

1. Open the View menu and click More Views, or click the More Views button on the View Bar. The More Views dialog box appears.

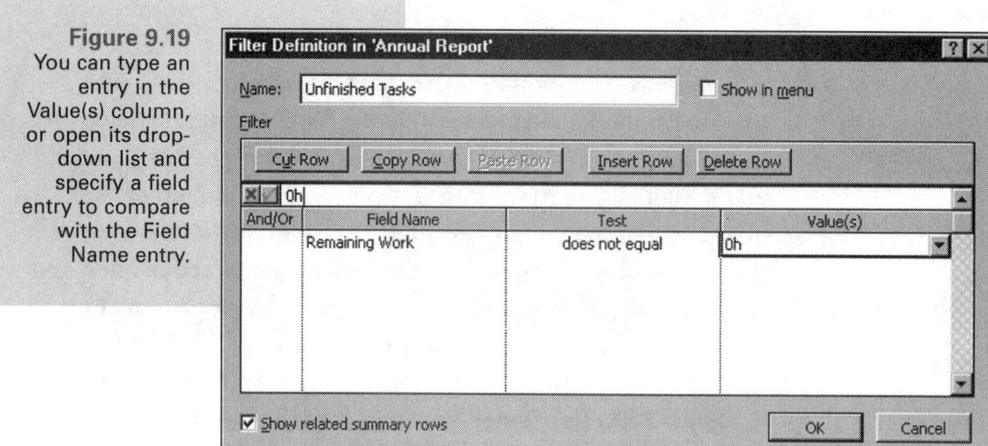

Figure 9.19 You can type an entry in the Value(s) column, or open its drop-down list and specify a field entry to compare with the Field Name entry.

2. Click the New button. Project uses the Define New View dialog box to ask if you want to create a Single View or Combination View. Leave Single View selected, and click OK. The View Definition dialog box appears (see Figure 9.20).
3. Enter a Name for your new view.
4. Use the Screen drop-down list to specify whether you want your view to offer a sheet, form, or chart. For example, select Task PERT to display task information in your view using the abbreviated form of the PERT chart.
5. If you selected a sheet style for your screen, use the Table drop-down list to specify a table that controls which columns of information appear in your view.
6. Use the Filter drop-down list to control which rows of information appear in your view.

View Definition in 'Annual ...'
Name: View 1
Screen: Gantt Chart
Table:
Filter:
Highlight filter
Show in menu
OK
Cancel

Figure 9.20 Project helps you view your schedule exactly as you want to.

7. If it's available, click Highlight Filter to highlight data that matches the filter, rather than hiding the data that doesn't match the filter.
8. Click the Show in Menu check box to select it if you want the new view to appear as a choice on the View menu or an icon on the View Bar.
9. Click OK to finish creating your view, and then apply the view by clicking Apply, or simply close the More Views dialog box by clicking Close.

A combination view displays two single-pane views in upper and lower panes onscreen. If you want a combination view to include a custom single-pane view, you need to create the single-pane view first and then create the combination view.

To create a combination view rather than a single-pane view, select Combination View in the Define New View dialog box (step 2 in the previous set of steps). The View Definition dialog box appears again, but this time it resembles Figure 9.21.

Type the Name you want for the view. Use the Top drop-down list to select the view that will appear in the upper pane, and use the Bottom drop-down list to select the single-pane view that will appear in the lower pane. Select the Show in Menu check box if you want the new view to appear as a choice on the View menu or as an icon on the View Bar. Then click OK to finish making the view and return to the More Views dialog box. Exit this dialog box as described in the previous set of steps.

Dealing with the Organizer

By default, the custom tables, filters, views, reports, and other items that you create are saved with the open, active project file only. This means that you can select one of these custom items only when that particular project file is open and active. If you want a custom view, filter, or other item to be available to other project files, you need to copy the custom item to the GLOBAL.MPT master file. To do this, you use the Organizer, which enables you to specify where custom items are stored.

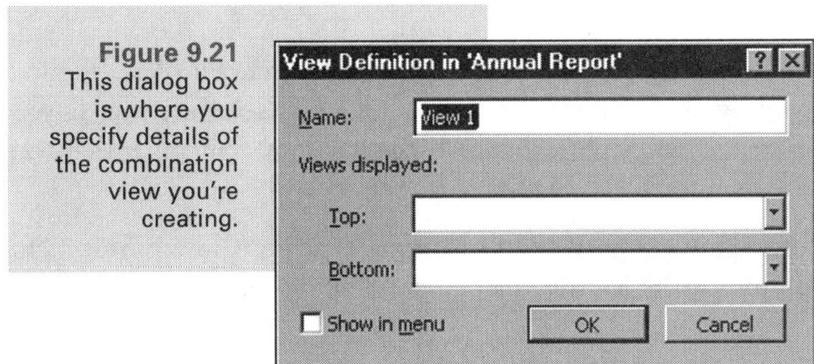

Figure 9.21 This dialog box is where you specify details of the combination view you're creating.

You might have noticed earlier in this chapter that the More Tables, More Filters, and More Views dialog boxes each contain an Organizer button. Clicking that button in any dialog box displays the Organizer dialog box (see Figure 9.22). You also can display the Organizer by choosing the Organizer command on the Tools menu. The tab that appears on top in this dialog box varies depending on which dialog box you were in when you clicked the Organizer button. For example, if you were in the More Views dialog box, the Views tab is selected when the Organizer dialog box opens. To deal with a different type of item, click the appropriate tab.

Each tab in the Organizer dialog box contains two lists. The list on the left shows the views (or tables, filters, or whatever) that are saved in GLOBAL.MPT. The list on the right shows the elements that are saved in the current project file. To copy an item from the list on the left to the list on the right (that is, from GLOBAL.MPT to the current project file), click the item name and then click Copy>>. To copy an item from the project file to GLOBAL.MPT, click the item name and then click <<Copy. If the file to which you're copying includes an item with the same name as the one you're copying, you'll be prompted to confirm that the copied file should overwrite the existing file.

Use the Views Available In drop-down list (in the lower-left corner of any tab in the Organizer dialog box) to control the file for which you're listing items on the left side of the tab. Similarly, use the Views Available In drop-down list (in the lower-right corner of the tab) to control the file for which you're listing items on the right side of the tab. If you want to copy a view or other item between two project files, rather than between a project file and GLOBAL.MPT, make sure that you change the Views Available In selection on the left to display the name of the second project file.

If you select an item from either list and then click Rename, Project displays the Rename dialog box. Type a new name, and click OK. If you select an item from either list and then click Delete, Project permanently deletes the item from the list for that file only, not from any other files that use the same item. Deleting an item from the GLOBAL.MPT file makes it inaccessible to all files, unless you previously copied the item to an individual schedule file. If you copied a custom item to multiple individual schedule files, remember that you need to remove it from each and every file to permanently delete it.

When you're finished working in the Organizer, click the Close button, and click Close again to exit the More... dialog box, if applicable.

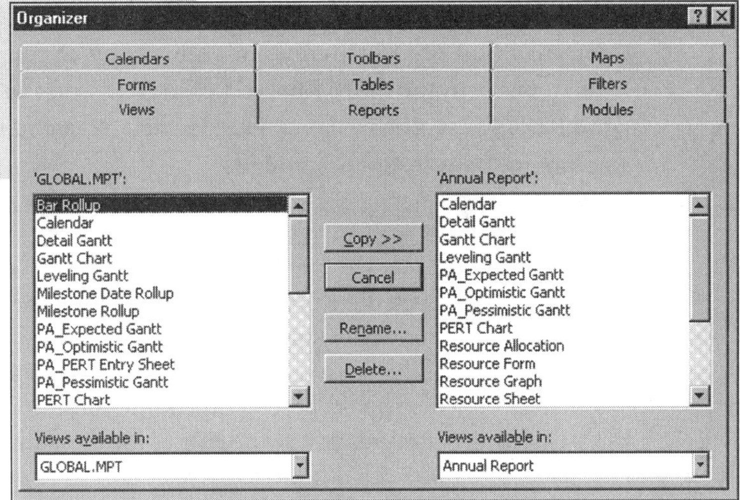

Figure 9.22 The Organizer enables you to move custom items between files.

To save an item such as a view or table that you added to any project file, be sure to save the file. When you exit Project, the application automatically saves changes that have been made to GLOBAL.MPT.

Using PERT Analysis

If you aren't confident that the timeline you're building for a project is accurate and you're not comfortable making an educated guess about the overall schedule, Project 98 offers special PERT analysis views to help do the job for you. You create your list of tasks and durations and enter resource information to evaluate whether the schedule can be completed in the timeframe you estimate. Then you enter Optimistic (best case), Expected (most likely), and Pessimistic (worst case) durations that could occur for each task. Then, you click a toolbar button, and Project creates a weighted average of the Optimistic, Expected, and Pessimistic duration for each task, and changes the task Duration to that average. You can then display the estimate in Gantt Chart view. You can display the optimistic, expected, and best case dates you entered in the PA_Optimistic Gantt (Optimistic Gantt), PA_Expected Gantt (Expected Gantt), and PA_Pessimistic Gantt (Pessimistic Gantt) views, respectively. Here are the basic steps for making PERT Analysis calculations:

1. Display the PERT Analysis toolbar, which offers you the best access to all the PERT Analysis views and other tools. To display the toolbar, right-click another toolbar and click PERT Analysis.

You can't undo a weighted average calculation, so use the Save As command on the File menu to create a copy of your schedule file. Then, perform the PERT Analysis calculation on the file copy, print the PERT Entry Sheet view showing the calculated results, and compare them to the original file.

2. (Optional) Click the PERT Weights button on the PERT Analysis toolbar. This button displays the Set PERT Weights dialog box, which you use to tell Project whether the Optimistic, Expected, or Pessimistic dates you enter should be given the most consideration (the heaviest weighting) in calculations. The entries for these three weightings must add up to 6; by default, the Expected entry is 4, weighting it the heaviest. To weight each date equally, you would enter **2** in the text box beside it. Make your entries, and then click OK.
3. Click the PERT Entry Sheet button on the PERT Analysis toolbar to display the Task Sheet for entering the Optimistic, Expected, and Pessimistic Dur. (Duration) for each task. (To enter these settings for a single task, select the task, click the PERT Entry Form button on the PERT Analysis toolbar, enter the durations, and click OK.) Your entries might look something like Figure 9.23.
4. Click the Calculate PERT button on the PERT Analysis toolbar. The Duration column changes to display the calculated weighted averages.
5. To display the estimated (calculated durations), switch to the Gantt Chart view. Or, click either the Optimistic Gantt, Expected Gantt, or Pessimistic Gantt button on the PERT Analysis toolbar to see the Gantt Chart with the dates you entered for the desired scenario. (You also can choose these views from the More Views dialog box; each will have "PA_" in front of its name.)

Using the Rollup Views

Three other views—the Rollup views that affect how subtasks look when rolled up to summary tasks—warrant special mention because you need to perform a preliminary step before you use one of these views. The Rollup views are as follows:

- **Bar Rollup**—Rolls up subtasks to the summary task bar and displays the Task Name for each task.

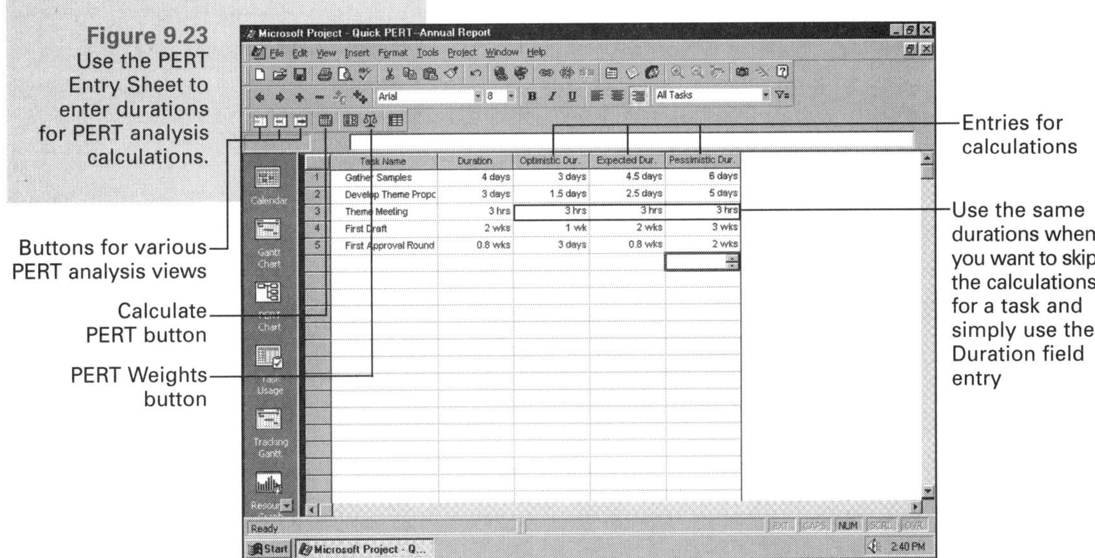

Figure 9.23 Use the PERT Entry Sheet to enter durations for PERT analysis calculations.

- **Milestone Date Rollup**—Rolls up subtasks to the summary task bar, displays each subtask as a milestone, and displays the Task Name and start date.
- **Milestone Rollup**—Rolls up subtasks to the summary task bar, displays each subtask as a milestone, and displays the Task Name only.

These views can be more helpful than simply rolling up subtasks to a summary task bar, because they enable you to show more information on the rolled up summary task. So, you can summarize your project, but still have a clear picture of which tasks it contains.

Before you display one of the Rollup views in the current project file, you have to rollup subtasks and run the Rollup_Formatting macro, as follows:

1. In the Task Sheet of the Gantt Chart view, select the subtasks to roll up.
2. Click the Task Information button on the Standard toolbar, click twice to check Roll Up Gantt Bar to Summary on the General tab, and then click OK.
3. Repeat steps 1 and 2 to roll up other groups of subtasks as needed. If you want to use the Rollup views for all summary tasks in your project, you'll need to use steps 1 and 2 to roll up all subtasks for each summary task.
4. Click Tools, point to Macro, and click Macros. The Macros dialog box appears.
5. Double-click Rollup_Formatting in the Macro Name list. The Rollup Formatting dialog box appears (Figure 9.24).

6. Click to specify whether to display rolled-up tasks as Bars or Milestones, and then click OK. The Task Sheet changes to display summary tasks only, and specially formatted (depending on your choice in this step) rolled-up Gantt bars appear in the Gantt chart at the right.
7. Click the More Views button in the View Bar, and then choose the Bar Rollup, Milestone Date Rollup, or Milestone Rollup view, as needed. Figure 9.25 shows the Milestone Rollup view applied to a rolled-up summary task.
8. You can choose Gantt Chart view to display regular Gantt bars but return to one of the Rollup views as often as needed during the current work session.

Figure 9.24 Specify whether you want your rolled up tasks to appear as Bars or Milestones on the Gantt chart using this dialog box from the Rollup_Formatting macro.

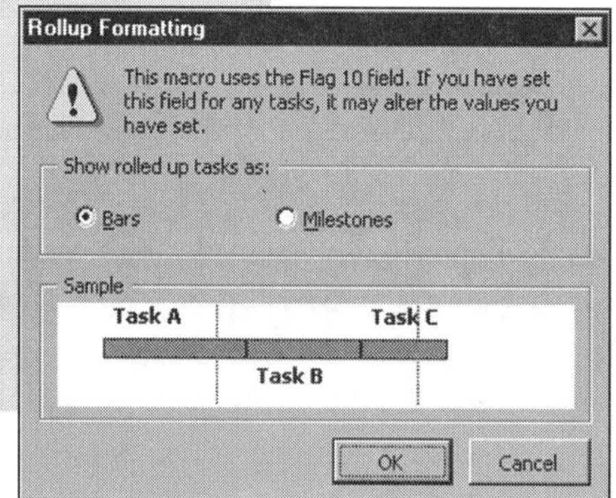

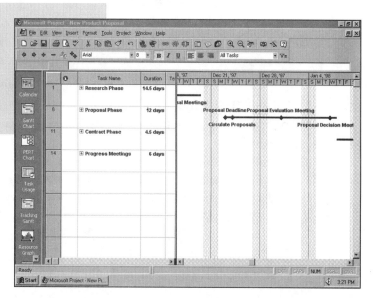

Figure 9.25 The rolled-up summary task at right displays milestones and Task Names in the Milestone Rollup view.

10

Proofing and Printing a View

In This Chapter

- Making sure that you've spelled everything correctly
- Replacing entries
- Telling Project and Windows which printer you want to use, and what settings it should use
- Setting up the appearance of the printed pages
- Adjusting which page information appears
- Getting a sneak preview of your printed document
- Printing your document

Unless you've developed telepathic capabilities or are connected to everyone involved with your project via a network or via e-mail, you're going to need some kind of method of sharing information. The most traditional method of sharing information is via printed hard copies. While "virtual" information sharing has its benefits, certain situations—such as meetings or bound proposals made for clients—call for printouts.

Like other Microsoft applications, Project 98 provides you with a great deal of control over what you print and how it appears in the hard copy. This chapter focuses on the steps you need to take to prepare and print information from your schedule

Spell-Checking the Project

Although a program's spelling checking capabilities can't take the place of your basic ability to come up with what appear to be words in English, spelling checkers provide an essential backup for your brain.

To put your best, most professional foot forward, you should always—I repeat, *always*—spell-check your files in Project and any other business documents you create.

Project's Spelling feature checks all the information in your schedule for correct spelling, starting from the first task in the Task Sheet and progressing through all your task information, no matter whether it's currently displayed. It even checks any information you entered as a Task Note or Resource Note. To spell check a project file, follow these steps:

1. Make sure that the file you want to check is the open, active file.
2. Open the Tools menu and click Spelling. Alternately, press F7 or click the Spelling button on the Standard toolbar. The spelling check starts, and when the spelling checker encounters a word it doesn't recognize, it displays the Spelling dialog box (see Figure 10.1).
3. Look at the Not In Dictionary entry to see which word Project doesn't recognize; then use one of the following methods to adjust its spelling, if needed:
   - If the word isn't misspelled, click on Ignore to leave it intact, or Ignore All if you know that the word is used several times in the file. For example, if "Blalock" is in your company name and appears several times in the file, you want the Spelling feature to ignore all uses of "Blalock," meaning that for the rest of the spelling check, it assumes "Blalock" is spelled correctly.

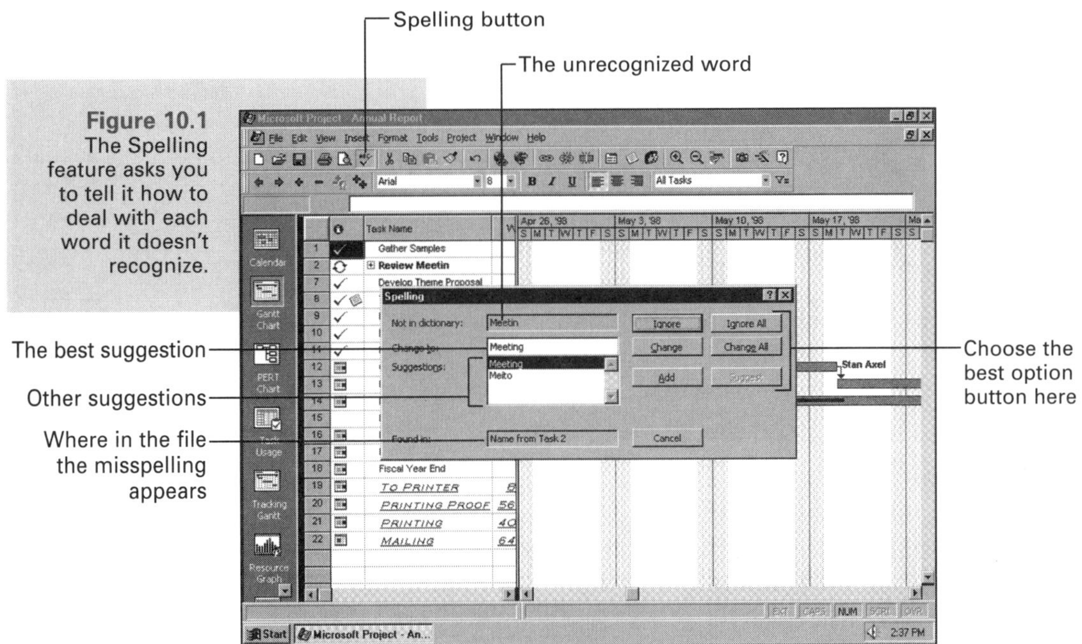

Figure 10.1 The Spelling feature asks you to tell it how to deal with each word it doesn't recognize.

- If the word is wrong and the spelling in the Change To text box is correct, click Change or Change All. Change corrects only the presently highlighted instance of the word, and Change All corrects it everywhere it appears in the Project file.
- If the word is wrong and the Change To spelling isn't correct either, you can edit the Change To text box entry, or click another spelling in the Suggestions list to place that spelling in the Change To text box. (If you specified that suggestions shouldn't automatically appear on the Spelling tab of the Options dialog box, which is described in Chapter 21, "Creating and Using Macros," click the Suggest button to display suggestions.) Then, click either Change or Change All.

4. After you tell Project how to adjust the unrecognized word, it displays the next unrecognized word so that you can adjust that one. Deal with each unrecognized word as explained in step 3.

Note

If you edit the Change To entry and want Project to remember that spelling as a correct word for future files, click the Add button to include the spelling in Project's dictionary.

5. When the Spelling Checker has reviewed the entire file, it displays a message alerting you that the spelling check is finished (see Figure 10.2). Click OK to close the dialog box.

Using AutoCorrect for Entry Accuracy

To learn to type, you had to learn the pattern of the letters on the keyboard. If you learned a particular pattern incorrectly, chances are that you'll make the same typographical error (typo) over and over for the rest of your typing career. Or, you might be a fine typist but would like a way to quickly enter certain words that you use often and are tricky to type. For example, you might not want to have to type "Blalock" each time it's needed in a file.

Project's AutoCorrect feature can help in either of these situations. In essence, you train Project to automatically replace your frequent typos (or abbreviations) with the correct (or full) terms you're trying to type. This ensures that certain terms are entered correctly in the first place, so you don't have to rely on the spelling checker to catch those errors. Use the following steps to create an AutoCorrect entry:

1. Click the Tools menu; then click AutoCorrect. The AutoCorrect dialog box appears (see Figure 10.3).
2. If you want Project to change the second letter in any word from uppercase to lowercase if you mistakenly type two capital letters, leave the Correct TWo INitial CApitals check box selected. Otherwise, clear this check box. You might want to clear it, for example, if you'll be typing a lot of state abbreviations.
3. If you want the first letter in the first word of each sentence (in Notes, primarily), leave the Capitalize the First Letter of Sentence choice checked. Or, clear the check box to capitalize new sentences only when you specify.

Figure 10.2 Project alerts you when it has checked the entire file.

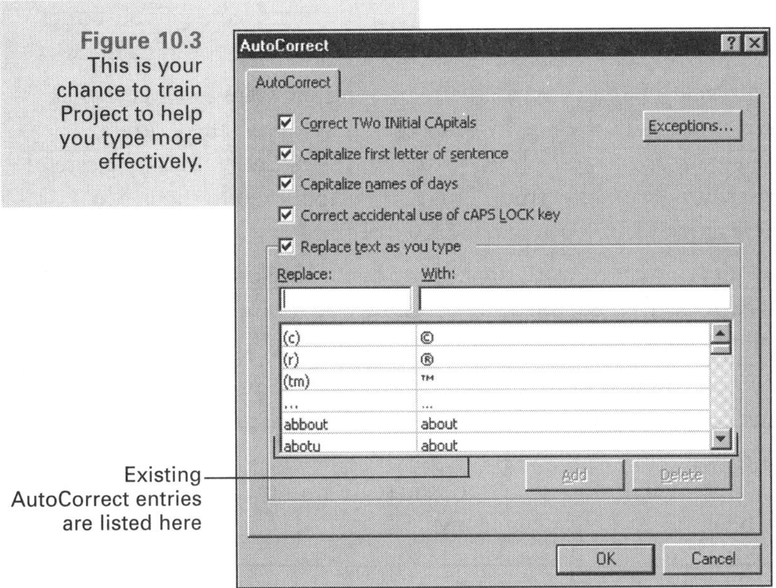

Figure 10.3 This is your chance to train Project to help you type more effectively.

Note

The option described in step 3 only works in fields that contain generic text entries, or in Task Names fields that contain task names with punctuation included. It doesn't work in any Notes fields, though.

Note

You can create exceptions that won't be corrected when you turn on the options described in steps 2 and 3. Click the Exceptions button in the AutoCorrect dialog box. To identify an instance when you don't want to capitalize the first word after a period (normally, this is after any abbreviation), type the abbreviation in the Don't Capitalize After text box on the First Letter tab, and then click Add. If a specialized term begins with two capital letters, as in "CSi," click the INitial CAps tab, type the term in the Don't Correct text box, and click Add. Click OK to finish creating your exceptions and return to the AutoCorrect dialog box.

4. Leave the Capitalize Names of Days check box selected if you want Project to automatically capitalize day names when you type them.
5. If you have a habit of accidentally pressing the Caps Lock key when you're aiming for the nearby Shift or Tab key, leave the Correct Accidental Use of cAPS LOCK Key check box selected to take care of the resulting capping errors. This feature applies in particular to Task Name entries and Resource Sheet entries.
6. For AutoCorrect to work, make sure that a checkmark appears beside the Replace Text As You Type check box. If this option is not checked, Project will not make automatic replacements.
7. To create a new AutoCorrect entry, type the typo or abbreviation you want Project to catch and replace in the Replace text box. For example, you might type bl as the abbreviation you want to use for "Blalock." You can't include any spaces or punctuation in the Replace entry, but it can be up to 254 characters long.

Note

AutoCorrect doesn't make the correction until you type a full word and press the spacebar. So, you don't have to worry if the typo or abbreviation you enter as the Replace choice is the beginning of other words. For example, even though "bl" is the beginning of words like "black" and "blue," you can still use "bl" as an AutoCorrect abbreviation.

8. In the With text box, enter the correction you want AutoCorrect to make (for example, Blalock).
9. Click Add to finish creating the AutoCorrect entry. Project adds this entry to the list of AutoCorrect entries, as shown in Figure 10.4.
10. Click OK to close the AutoCorrect dialog box. New AutoCorrect entries take effect immediately.

Replacing Entries

Other business changes might require that you make a correction to a term or entry that appears frequently in your project file. For example, a resource company may have changed names, or your company may have changed the accounting code used to track work by a particular department. In some cases you could run a spelling check to make the global correction, but doing so

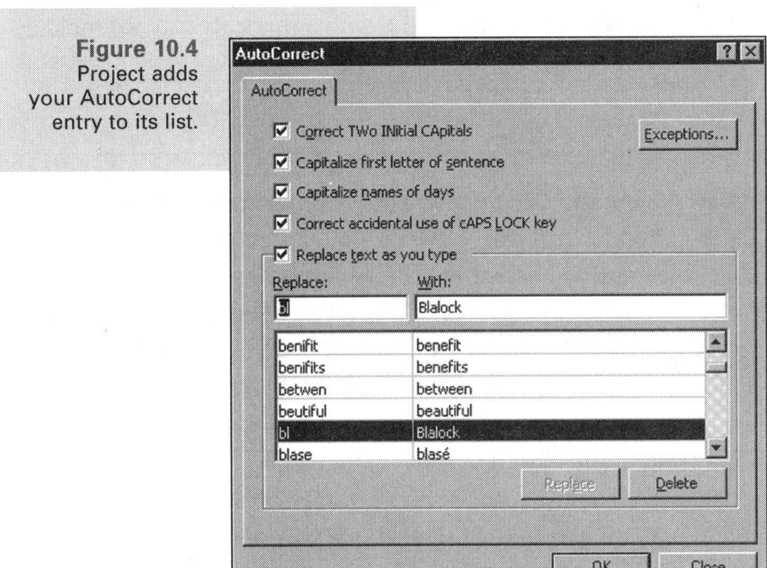

Figure 10.4 Project adds your AutoCorrect entry to its list.

would also mean you'd have to review and work with other unrecognized words, making the process slower than needed. If you already added the term to replace to the Spelling feature's dictionary, however, running a spelling check won't work, because the Spelling dialog box will never stop on that term.

Instead, you can use the Replace feature in Project to find one or more occurrences of a particular entry in a field and replace those occurrences with a new entry that you specify. Follow these steps to replace information in a field:

1. Display either the Task Sheet or the Resource Sheet, depending on which one contains the information to find and replace. If you want the search to begin with a particular row, click a cell in that row.
2. Click the Edit menu, and then click Replace, or press Ctrl+H. The Replace dialog box appears.
3. Type the entry to search for in the Find What text box.
4. Type the new entry that you want to use as the replacement for each found entry in the Replace With text box.
5. Choose the Task Sheet or Resource Sheet field that holds the entries to find and replace from the Look In Field drop-down list. (Choose Name to search the Task Name field in the Task Sheet or Resource Name in the Resource Sheet, depending on which you displayed before opening the Replace dialog box.)

6. If you want to use an operator in the Find What entry, for example if you're searching for all numeric entries over a particular number (is greater than), choose the operator from the Test drop-down list.

I recommend using the Contains Exactly choice in the Test drop-down list as often as you can. For example, if you only use the Contains choice and are searching for an entry like "004," Project would stop on entries like "1004," "A004," or "10040," too, resulting in many more entries to sort through. Plus, you could inadvertently make a replacement you don't want. Let's say you're finding "004" and replacing it with "A004." If the column already contains entries that read "A004" and you haven't specified Contains Exactly as the Test, each existing "A004" entry will be changed to "AA004," because Project replaces matching portions of entries, too.

7. Make a choice from the Search drop-down list to change the direction of the search. Project can search either Down or Up from the current row.
8. If you want each replacement to match the case (capitalization) of the entry it replaces, click to check the Match Case check box.
9. After you enter all the information to tell Project what entries to find and where to find them (see Figure 10.5 for and example), click the Find Next button. Project highlights the first instance of the entry you told it to search for.
10. You can handle the highlighted entry in one of three ways:
    - Click Find Next to skip the highlighted instance without changing it and highlight the next matching instance of the Find What entry.
    - Click Replace to change the matching instance to the Replace With entry, and then highlight the next instance.
    - Click Replace All to change all matching instances.
11. When Project finishes searching the field and making replacements, a message box appears to tell you the search is complete. Click OK to close the message box.
12. Click Close to close the Replace dialog box.

If you want to find an entry instead of replacing it, display the Find dialog box by choosing Find from the Edit menu (Ctrl+F). The Find dialog box is nearly identical to the Replace dialog box. The Find dialog box lacks the Replace

Figure 10.5 These choices find a particular Code field entry in the Resource Sheet, replacing each occurrence with a new code entry.

With text box (because you're not replacing anything) and the Replace All buttons. It does have a Replace button, which you can click to change the Find dialog box to the Replace dialog box. Otherwise, the Find dialog box offers the same options as the Replace dialog box, which you can use just as described in the preceding steps for a replacement operation.

Changing Printer Settings

If you're using Project in a small business or home office, you'll probably have only one printer attached to your computer system. If you work in a larger company, however, you might have access to multiple printers, for example, one in your office and one attached to your company network. In any environment, your computer also might have a built-in FAX/modem that you can "print" to, thereby faxing documents without making a hard copy; this is the same as having multiple printers.

If you have multiple printers attached to your system, you need a way to select the one you want to send your Project file to. In addition, each printer offers slightly different capabilities. For example, your laser printer might be capable of printing at 600 dots per inch (dpi), but for everyday printing you might want to print at 300 dpi to ensure faster printing. Similarly, many dot matrix and inkjet printers offer a choice between letter quality and draft modes.

Before you set up your printout pages in Project, you should first select the printer you want to use and set the options you prefer for that printer. Select and set up the printer first, if needed, because different printer capabilities might affect the page setup options available in Project. Note that you don't have to set up a document or open any project file to print before setting up the printer. After you adjust printer settings, they remain in effect until you change them or exit Project.

If you're using an older dot-matrix or inkjet printer, any Project printouts that include graphical information might not appear as crisp and clean as you desire, and printing might be slow. In addition, depending on the printer, Project might present fewer options for altering the page setup, based on the printer's limitations. If you need to print many Gantt or PERT charts, you should buy a quality laser printer, or even a color inkjet printer. Quality models are available for as little as $500.

To select and set up a printer, use the steps that follow. As there's quite a bit of variation between printers, and it's impossible to cover every option for every printer, This list covers the most important options.

1. Click to open the File menu; then click Print. Alternately, press Ctrl+P. (*Don't* click the Print button on the Standard toolbar, though. Doing so sends the current view to the specified printer, bypassing the Print dialog box.) The Print dialog box opens (see Figure 10.6).
2. Click the drop-down list arrow to display the Name selections in the Printer area. The printers listed here are ones that have already been installed to work with Windows on your system or with a Windows

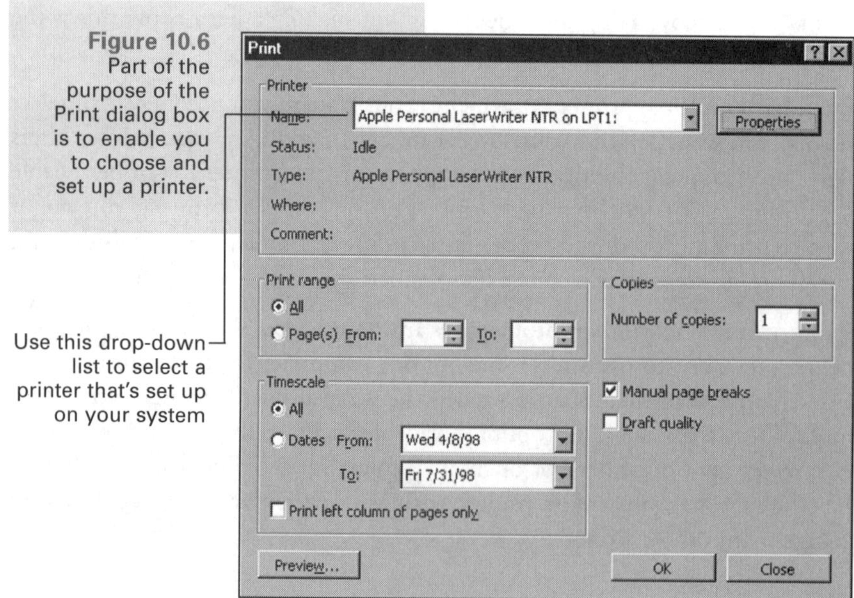

Figure 10.6 Part of the purpose of the Print dialog box is to enable you to choose and set up a printer.

NT network you're connected with. (To learn to set up a printer using the Windows Control Panel, see the Windows documentation or online help.) In this list, click the name of the printer you want to print your Project files to.

3. After you select the correct printer, click the Properties button beside it. If this is the first time you've worked with printer properties during the current Project work session, Project displays a dialog box alerting you that your printer settings will apply to all views you subsequently print—not just the currently displayed view.
4. Click OK to continue. The Properties dialog box for the selected printer appears onscreen, as shown in Figure 10.7.

In Windows, *properties* include information about a file, program, or piece of hardware, as well as the settings or options available for that file, program, or hardware.

5. On the first tab, you adjust settings for paper. Most printers enable you to control the following options:
   - Paper size—Use the scrolling list to display the size you'll be using, and click the appropriate thumbnail example to select it.

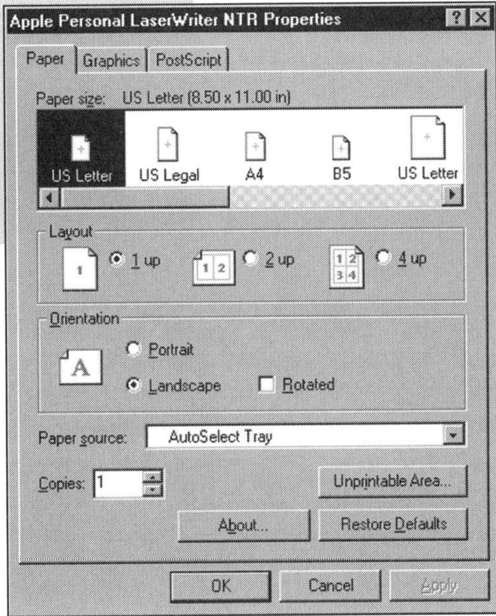

Figure 10.7 The Properties dialog box offers different options, depending on the capabilities of the selected printer.

- Orientation—Select whether you want to print in a format where the paper's taller than it is wide (Portrait) or wider than it is tall (Landscape). To print the information upside-down in a landscape orientation, click the Rotated check box. The thumbnail picture in the Orientation area shows you what effect your selection there will have on your document's printed layout.
- Copies—Change the entry here if you want Project to print more than one copy of each document (which is the default).
- Restore Defaults—This command button appears on each tab of the Properties dialog box. Clicking on it restores the tab's settings to the defaults for that printer.

If you need information about one of the Properties settings for your printer, click the question mark button near the right side of the Properties dialog box title bar, and then with the question mark pointer, click the item you want information about.

6. After you completed changing the settings you want on the Paper tab, click the Graphics tab to display its options (see Figure 10.8). The two options on this tab that are available for most printers are Resolution and Scaling. Adjust the Resolution setting, if needed, to adjust how "fine" the appearance of printed graphics will be. Adjust the Scaling setting to specify the size of the printed image as a percentage (from 25% to 400%) of the original size.
7. After setting the Graphics tab options, click the Final tab, which for PostScript printers is the PostScript tab, and for nonPostScript printers is the Device Options tab. This tab usually offers a single drop-down list. On the PostScript tab, it's the PostScript Output Format list, which offers options that let you print faster—or with higher quality—in PostScript format. On the Device Options tab, the single drop-down list is for Print Quality, enabling you to specify whether to print a document in draft or letter quality.
8. After you specify all the property settings for your selected printer, click OK to close the Properties dialog box and return to the Print dialog box.
9. At this point, you can click the Close button to return to Project and alter the Page Setup for your project file, as described in the next section. Or, you can use the Print dialog box to print your document, as described in the last section of this chapter, "Finishing the Print Job."

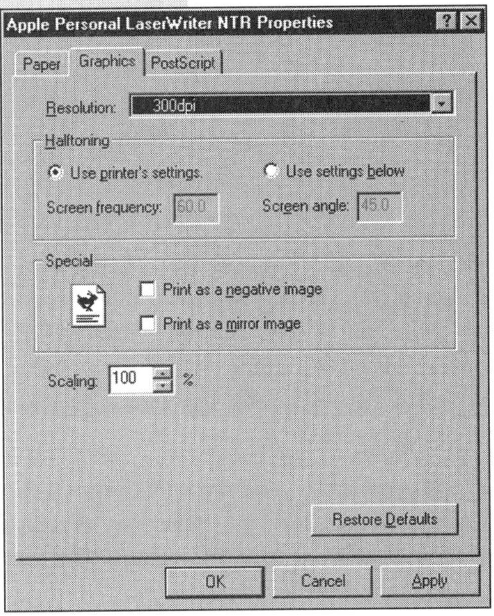

Figure 10.8 The Graphics tab offers options that are especially useful when you print a Gantt or PERT chart.

Controlling the Page Setup

In Project, the first step to determining what appears on your printout is to select a view. Project creates a printout of that view, so if you've displayed Gantt Chart view, the printout contains the Task Sheet Task Name and Duration columns at the left, and the Gantt chart bars on a schedule at the right. If you display only the Resource Sheet, Project prints the contents of the Resource Sheet. In a Task Sheet or Resource Sheet, you need to be sure that you display the correct table and filter the information, if needed, before printing. (See Chapter 9, "Working with the Different Project Views," to learn more about selecting and filtering a table.)

There are only a couple of limitations on what you can print. Project doesn't print any information or view pane that's a form. It also doesn't let you print the Task PERT chart, which is an abbreviated version of the standard PERT chart. In the selected view, you also need to specify formatting—such as adjusting the appearance of Gantt bars, changing the timescale, and changing column breaks (see the next section in this chapter)—to control how information appears in the final printout. The formatting changes you make appear both onscreen and in the printed document.

Note

Page Setup options are different from formatting changes, such as choosing a new font for text or adjusting how Gantt chart bars look. To learn more about formatting your project, see Chapter 14, "Other Formatting."

In contrast, the Page Setup options control only how the printed information appears. For example, you can adjust the header or footer that appears on each page of a printout, or can specify how many pages you want the printout to occupy. To adjust the Page Setup options before printing, click to open the File menu, and then click Page Setup to display the Page Setup dialog box for the selected view (see Figure 10.9).

The available options vary slightly, depending on the selected view. The choices for each option that Project suggests by default also differ, depending on the selected view (in Figure 10.9, for example, Project suggests printing the Gantt chart in the Landscape orientation). Finally, some of the settings you see in the Page Setup dialog box resemble the ones provided in the printer Properties dialog box. Remember that the printer Properties settings become the default for all Project files printed. Any Page Setup options you select for the current view take precedence over the Properties settings.

The remainder of this section describes the settings on each tab of the Page Setup dialog box. (Keep in mind that some of them might not be available in

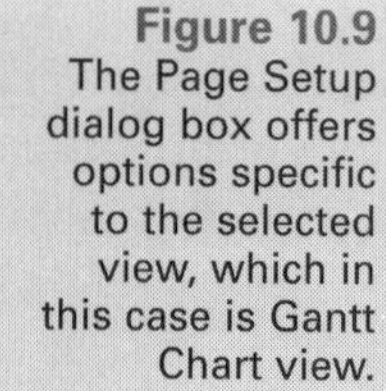

Figure 10.9 The Page Setup dialog box offers options specific to the selected view, which in this case is Gantt Chart view.

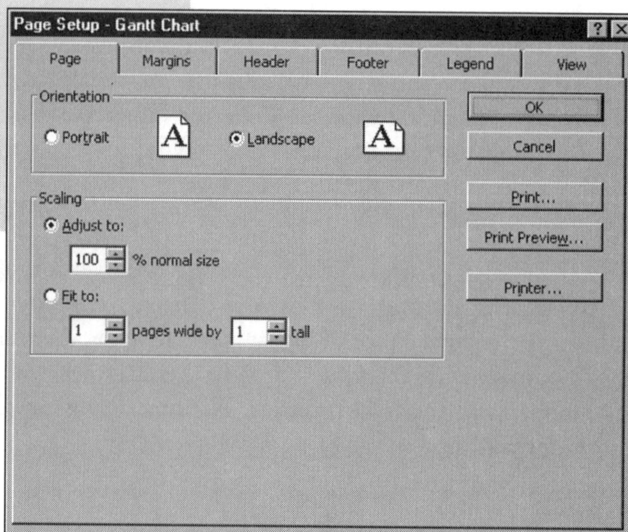

your selected view, in which case they'll be grayed out.) After you chose the settings you want from all tabs, click the OK button to close the dialog box and have your changes take effect. (Or, using one of the other option buttons, you can preview your print job or jump directly to the Print dialog box to finish printing. Each of these operations is described later in this chapter.)

Page Tab Settings

Figure 10.9 shows the first tab in the Page Setup dialog box, the Page tab. In the Orientation area of the dialog box, specify whether you want the printout to appear in Portrait (tall) or Landscape (wide) format. The Scaling options enable you to scale the printed view or report to a particular size or page count. When the Adjust To option button is selected, you can enter a percentage that makes the printed image smaller (down to 10%) or larger (up to 500%) than its original size. I prefer, however, to use the Fit To option, which enables you to enter values telling Project how many pages wide and tall to make the printout. This is my preference because it's more error-proof; otherwise, you might have to print at a few different percentages to get a printed document that fits your needs. In most professional situations, I prefer to have a printout that's one page tall but as many pages as needed wide, because it easier for an audience to understand if it's included in, for instance, a bound report. For a Task Sheet or Resource Sheet printout, on the other hand, you might prefer a result that's one page wide and multiple pages tall.

Margins Tab Settings

The second tab in the Page Setup dialog box is the Margins tab. Click the tab to display its options (see Figure 10.10). When you change the margin settings, you're changing the amount of white space that Project leaves around the information printed on a page. The Margins tab offers four text boxes— Top, Bottom, Left, and Right—where you can type the margin setting you want to use for your printout, in inches by default. To change one of the settings, double-click its text box and type the new value or use the spinner buttons (spinner arrows).

By default, Project also prints a thin border around the information on Every Page of the printout. If you wish, you can change that setting in the Borders Around area of the Margins tab. If the selected view is the PERT chart, you can click to select the Outer Pages option button, which prints a border around only the first and last pages of the printout. For other views, you can click the None option button to completely eliminate borders from the printout.

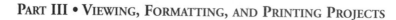

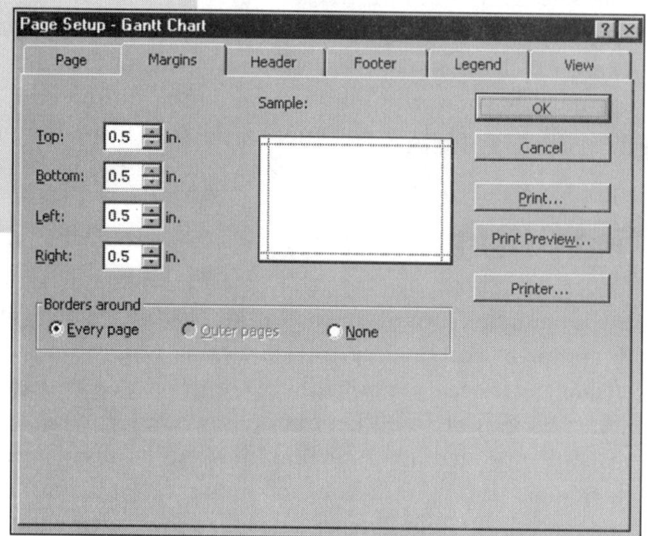

Figure 10.10 Use this tab to control the margins (white space) that appear around the information in your printout.

This sample shows how wide the specified margins will look

Headers, footers, and legends print within any border included on the printout.

Header Tab Settings

Moving on, you can click the Header tab in the Page Setup dialog box. A *header* appears at the top of a printout and provides information about the printout. A header can consist of any text you want to type in; for example, you might want to designate the printout as "First Draft" or something similar. Alternatively, you can build the header components using the tabs and buttons in the Alignment area of thc Margins tab.

Start by clicking a tab in the Alignment area to select whether the entered header information will align to the left, center, or right. (Note that you can designate header information to appear simultaneously in two—or even all three—of these tabs.) To enter information simply by typing, click in the blank area below the tab and type the information you want; it appears in the Sample area as you type.

As indicated in Figure 10.11, you can use several of the buttons in the Alignment area to enter calculated fields of header information. For example, suppose that you want your header to include the printout date. Click within any information already entered for the header to specify where the date should be inserted, and then click on the button that inserts the printout date. A code that identifies where the printout date will be positioned appears in the header (see Figure 10.11).

Project enables you to automatically insert other kinds of information, such as the schedule Start Date, in the header by using the drop-down list at the bottom of the Alignment area. First, click to indicate where you want the information inserted in the header. Click the drop-down list to see the kinds of information you can insert; click the name for the type of information you want to insert; then click the Add button beside the drop-down list. Project inserts a code for that kind of information in the header.

You can format the appearance of the text in any header area by dragging to highlight it, and then clicking the Formatting button in the Alignment area (this button is on the far left and has the letter "A" on it). Project then displays the Font dialog box, in which you can choose a new Font, Size, and so on for the selected text. Chapter 14, "Other Formatting," covers how to use the Font dialog box, which also appears when you format text in a Task Sheet or Resource Sheet. Suffice it to say here that you can make the changes you want, and then click OK to return to the Page Setup dialog box.

Figure 10.11 Build a header using a variety of techniques.

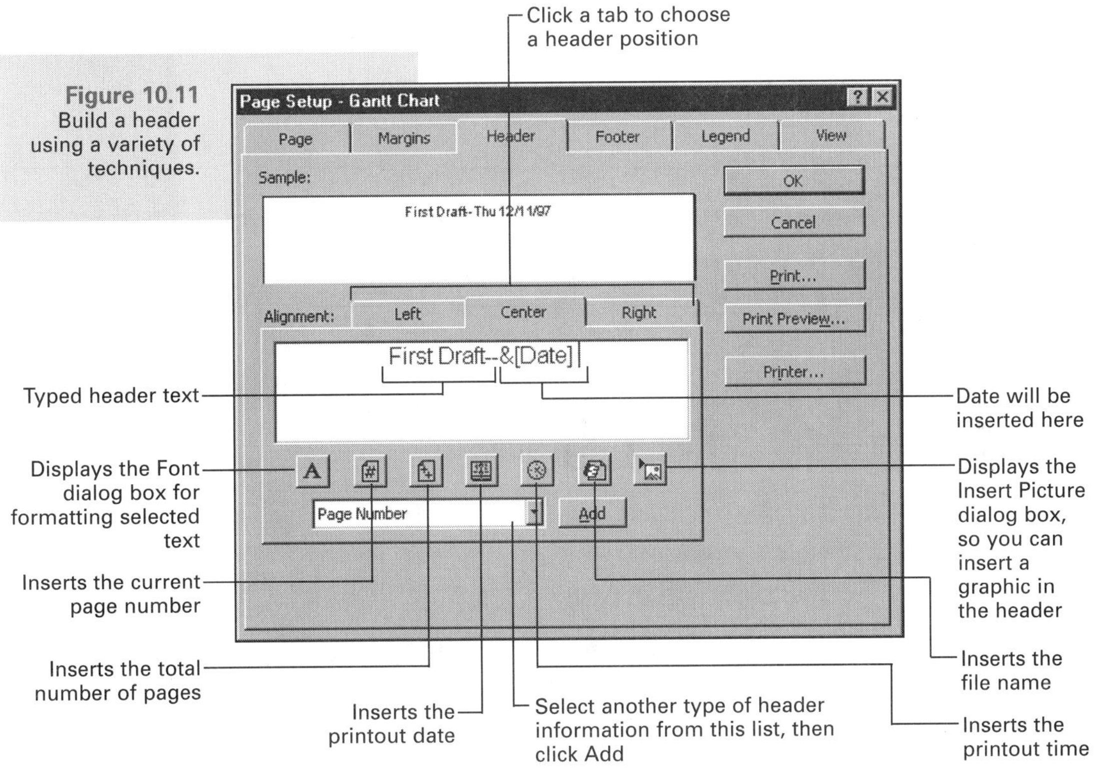

Click a tab to choose a header position
Page Setup - Gantt Chart
Page | Margins | Header | Footer | Legend | View
Sample:
First Draft-Thu 12/11/97
OK
Cancel
Print...
Print Preview...
Printer...
Alignment: Left | Center | Right
First Draft--&[Date]
Page Number
Add
Typed header text
Date will be inserted here
Displays the Font dialog box for formatting selected text
Displays the Insert Picture dialog box, so you can insert a graphic in the header
Inserts the current page number
Inserts the total number of pages
Inserts the file name
Inserts the printout date
Select another type of header information from this list, then click Add
Inserts the printout time

If you want your company logo to appear on every page of a printout, insert the logo graphic in the header or footer.

Footer Tab Settings

Click the next tab to move to the Footer options (see Figure 10.12). A *footer* resembles a header, but appears at the bottom of each printed page. You create a footer just as you would a header, so refer to the preceding information about creating a header to learn how to work with the Footer tab options.

Legend Tab Settings

You can insert a legend, which includes graphical information to explain what the graphical chart symbols mean, on your printouts. To specify whether or not a legend appears on your printout, click on the Legend tab in the Page Setup dialog box. The Legend tab options appear as shown in Figure 10.13.

Because a legend can include text, Project offers the kind of text formatting options available for creating headers and footers. Those settings work just like the ones on the Header and Footer tabs, so I won't explain them again here.

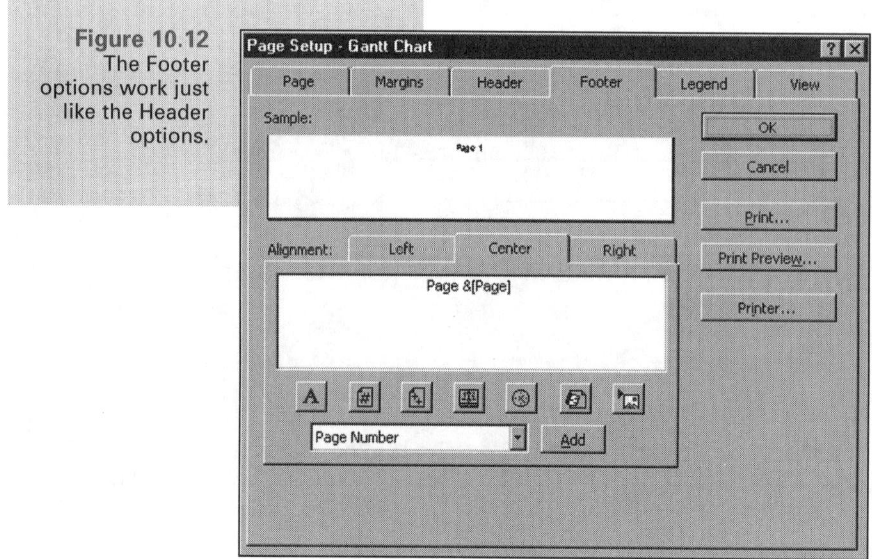

Figure 10.12 The Footer options work just like the Header options.

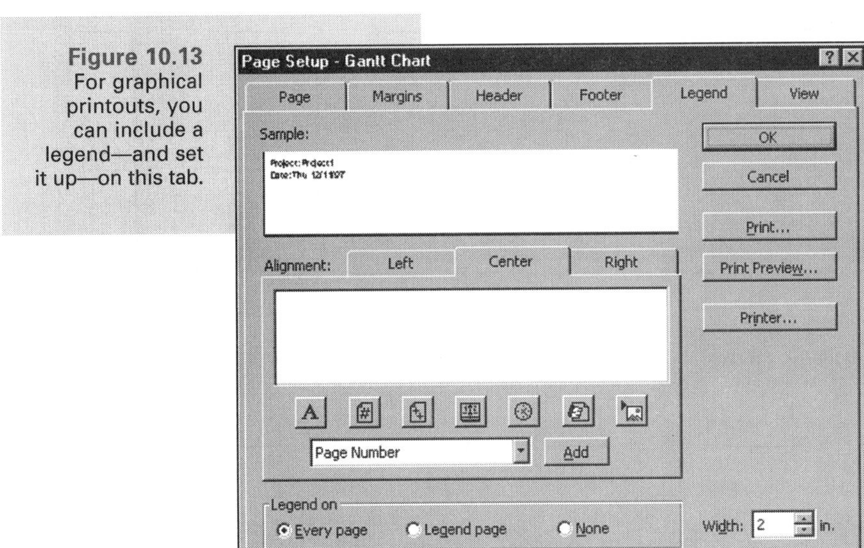

Figure 10.13 For graphical printouts, you can include a legend—and set it up—on this tab.

The Legend On area at the bottom of the tab enables you to control whether the legend appears. By default, Every Page is selected, meaning that the legend appears on every page of the printed hard copy. If you select the Legend Page option button, Project prints the legend on its own, separate page, so that there is more room for the schedule's graphical information on the other printed pages. The None option causes the printout to have no legend at all. You can control how wide the legend area is with the entry in the Width text box. If you need more room in the legend area—to include more detailed text in the legend, for example—double-click the Width text box and type the new setting you want to use.

View Tab Settings

In the Page Setup dialog box click the final tab, called the View tab, to set a few final options specific to the selected view. Figure 10.14 shows how this tab looks for Gantt Chart view. Here's how to work with each of the listed options, when they're available:

- Print All Sheet Columns—When a view contains a chart with a timescale, Project by default prints only the columns in the accompanying Task Sheet or Resource Sheet that appear onscreen. If you drag the split bar so that only one sheet column is visible, then only that column prints. Click to select the Print All Sheet Columns check box if you want to print all the sheet columns, not just the presently displayed columns.

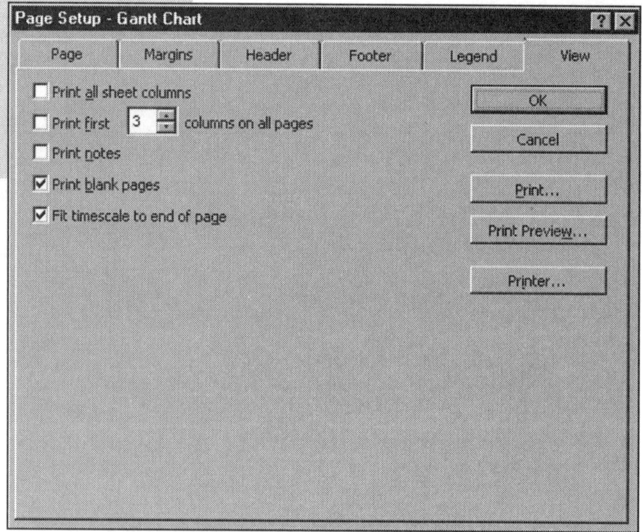

Figure 10.14 Fine-tune how your view prints by using the options on this tab.

- Print First... Columns On All Pages—If you want to choose exactly how many columns in a Task Sheet or Resource Sheet print, click to select this check box and then, in the accompanying text box, enter the number of columns to print. You can only use this option if you're printing a view that includes information charted on a timescale. This option doesn't always behave as you'd expect, however. If your printout is more than a page deep and more than a page wide, then all the far-left pages include the visible columns, not the number of columns you specify here. Thus, you ideally want to use this option only when you're sure that the printout will be one page deep but many pages wide. If you can't ensure that, then you'll have to drag the vertical split bar in the view to adjust the number of visible columns.
- Print Notes—When you click to select this option for the views where it's available, Project prints the notes you attached to a task or resource on a separate page at the end of the printout.
- Print Blank Pages—For some of the views that contain charted information, you might end up with pages that don't actually contain any data. An example is the lower-left page of any Gantt chart printout that's more than one page deep and one page wide. If you want to save paper by not printing these blank pages, clear the check mark beside this option. However, if you plan to assemble the multiple pages of your printout into a large, single chart—perhaps by taping them together and hanging them on the wall of your office—leave this option selected.

- Fit Timescale To End of Page—You saw earlier in this chapter that if your printer allows it, you can scale your printout by a certain percentage to control how small or large it prints. That's somewhat of an eyeball approach, and it doesn't ensure that your schedule fits neatly on the printed pages. You might end up, for example, with half a blank page at the end of your printout. If you want to ensure that the graphical portion of your printout (the timescale) takes advantage of all the available space on your pages, make sure that this check box is selected. Project then stretches the timescale (for example, by making each day take up slightly more space) to ensure that the graphical information fills the last printout page.

Controlling Page Breaks

You just learned that in any view that combines a Task Sheet or Resource Sheet with graphical or timescale information at the right side of the page, you must drag the vertical split bar to control how many columns of the sheet appear in the printout.

In addition, you might want to control which rows of task or resource information appear on each page of a printout. For example, you might know that you entered a milestone task in row 15 of your Task Sheet. You can control where the pages break in printouts of Gantt Chart view, Resource Usage view, and Task Sheets or Resource Sheets by inserting a manual page break. A manual page break tells Project to stop printing on the current page with a particular row and to begin the next page down with the information in the next row.

Manual page breaks don't affect how many pages wide your printout is. They only affect how many pages tall it is.

To add a manual page break, follow these steps:

1. Switch to the view you want to print.
2. In the Task Sheet or Resource Sheet, click to select a cell in the row that should be at the top of a new page. (You also can select the whole row by clicking its row number.) Project inserts the manual break above the selected row.
3. Open the Insert menu and click Page Break. Project inserts a dotted line in the sheet to show you where the page break will occur (see Figure 10.15).

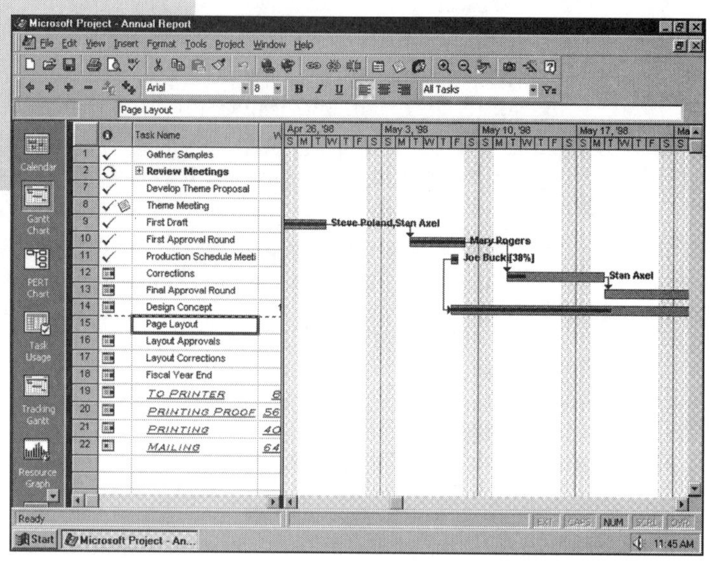

Figure 10.15 A manual page break appears as a dotted line above the row you selected.

Inserted page breaks can cause unexpected results in printed reports (see Chapter 12, "Creating and Printing a Report," for an in-depth look at reports). I recommend that you remove manual page breaks after you use them, unless you're sure that you won't be working with any reports.

To remove manual page breaks, either select the row just below the break by clicking its row number, or click the Select All button in the upper-left corner of the sheet. Open the Insert menu and click Remove All Page Breaks.

Previewing the Printing

You've been diligent. You selected the proper view to print and designated which table columns should print and where you want page breaks to appear. You chose the correct printer and adjusted its properties, and double-checked all the options in the Page Setup dialog box. Despite all this, you still might not have a good idea how your printout will look.

You can waste a lot of paper by repeatedly printing your schedule and then making adjustments to ensure that the final version is exactly what you want. However, you can preview the print job onscreen, make any necessary adjustments, and only create a hard copy when it's right. To switch to the print preview for the current view of your schedule, click the Print Preview button on the Standard toolbar. (It's the fifth button from the left and looks like a page with a magnifying glass over it.) Alternately open the File menu and click on Print Preview. A preview version of your printout appears onscreen, as shown in Figure 10.16.

At first, Print Preview shows you the first page of your printout in a reduced view that provides a look at the overall page layout. You'll see whether the printout includes a legend (the one in Figure 10.16 does), how the margin spacing looks around the data, where the headers and footers appear, and more.

If the printout includes more than one page, you can use the left and right arrow keys to move forward and backward through the pages. The up and down arrows only activate if there are too many rows to fit on a single page. You can use the up and down arrows to view the extra rows, which will be on separate pages when you print the hard copy.

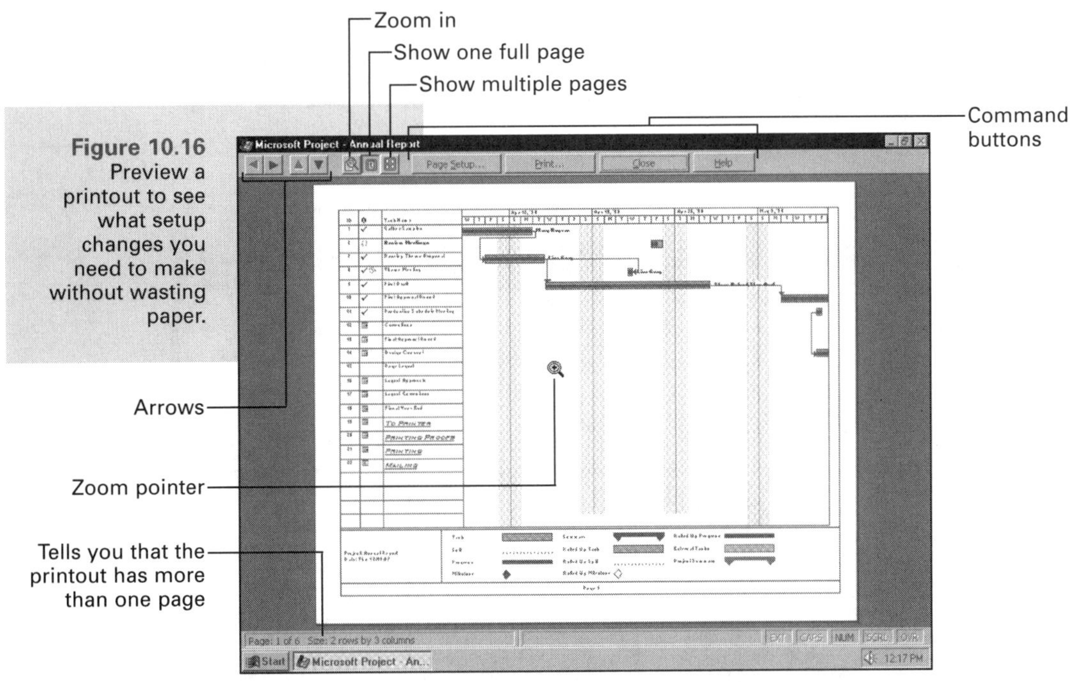

Figure 10.16 Preview a printout to see what setup changes you need to make without wasting paper.

You might, however, want to zoom in to read particular details in the printout before printing; for example, you might want to check to see if a heading you added looks the way you want it to. You can either click the Zoom button at the top of the preview to zoom in on the upper-left corner of the page, or use the zoom pointer to zoom in on a specific area. After you've zoomed in, you can click the button for displaying one full page (this button has a page on it) to return to the default view.

If the printout has more than one page and you want to view multiple pages, perhaps to see how the information is divided between pages, click the button that looks like a stack of papers. Project displays multiple pages of the printout onscreen, as shown in Figure 10.17. Again, to return to the default view, click the button for displaying one full page.

If the printout doesn't look the way you want it to, you need to make changes. For example, I want to move up the graphic in the lower-left page of Figure 10.17 to try to squeeze my printout onto three pages. To make such changes that require you to return to the normal schedule view (in this case, you can drag the graphic up on the Gantt chart), click the Close button to exit the print preview. Another example is if you think that you've squeezed the printout into too few pages, making the information small and difficult to read. If you need to change a page setup option in such a case, click the Page Setup button to display the Page Setup dialog box. If the preview meets with your approval, click on the Print button to go directly to the Print dialog box and complete the printout, as explained in the next section.

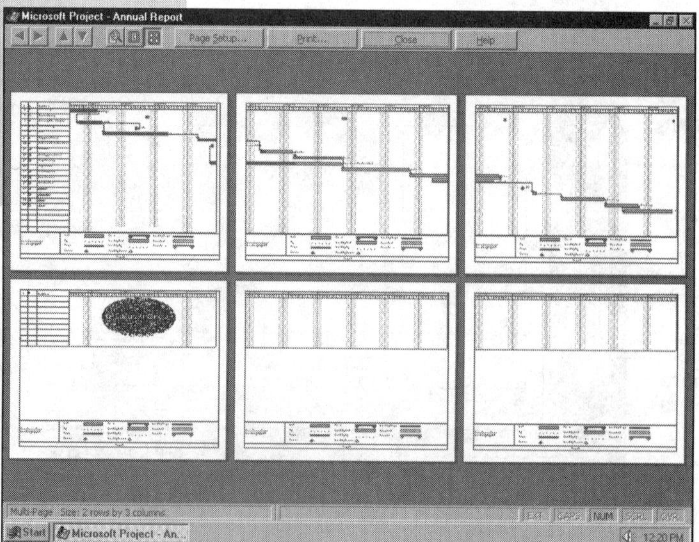

Figure 10.17 If the Printout has multiple pages, you can preview more than one page at a time.

Finishing the Print Job

Figure 10.18 shows the Print dialog box, which you saw earlier in this chapter when you learned to select and set up a printer. To display the Print dialog box, open the File menu and click Print (or press Ctrl+P).

If you want to print your schedule without going through the Print dialog box to specify final options, click the Print button on the Standard toolbar. When you print using this method, Project automatically prints with the current printer settings and current Page Setup options.

The settings in the Print dialog box override any settings you made elsewhere, such as when you initially set up your printer. Here's a review of the final choices you can make from this dialog box before sending your schedule to the printer:

- In the Print Range area, leave the All option button selected to print all the pages in your schedule. Or, if your printout includes more than one page and you don't want to print the entire document, click the Page(s) From option button, and then enter the page number of the first page you want to print. In the To text box, enter the page number of the last page you want to print.

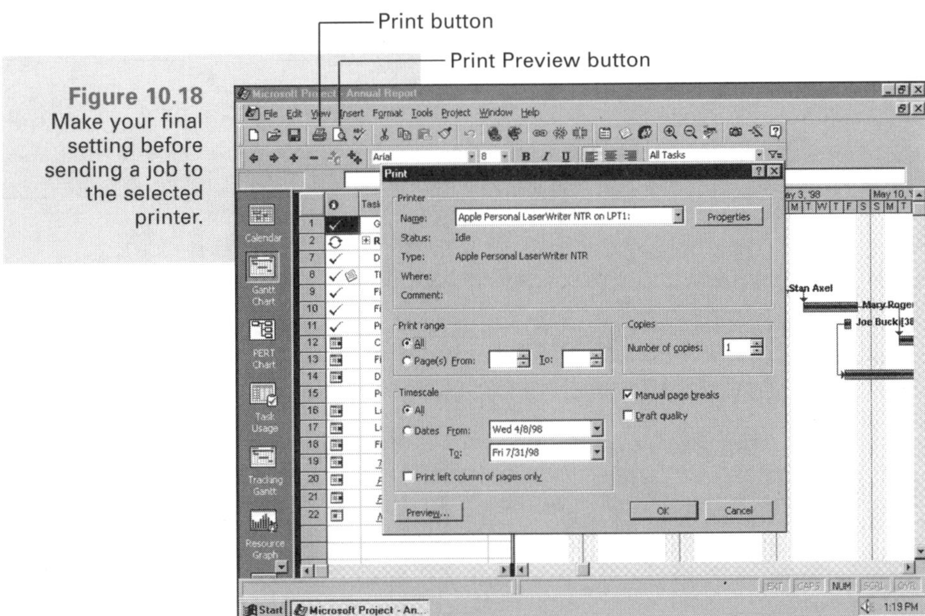

Figure 10.18 Make your final setting before sending a job to the selected printer.

- To print more than one copy, change the entry in the Number of Copies text box.
- You can use the Timescale options to control which tasks print. Leave the All option button selected to print all the tasks. To print only tasks starting within a particular range of dates, click the Dates From option button and enter the starting date for the range in that text box. In the To text box, enter the ending date for the range. If you want only one page's worth of Timescale tasks to print, click to select the Print Left Column of Pages Only check box.
- When the Manual Page Breaks check box is selected, the printout uses any manual page breaks you inserted. If you don't want to remove the page breaks you set up, but don't want Project to use them for this particular printout, clear the check box for this option.
- Click to select the Draft Quality check box if you want to print a quick-and-dirty version of your printout that might be less attractive, but will print faster and give you an adequate opportunity to review the information before printing a final version.

After you finish changing the Print dialog box settings as needed, click OK to send your schedule to the printer.

11

Working with Forms

In This Chapter

- Understanding forms
- Creating a custom form

In Chapter 9, "Working with the Different Project Views," you learned how to change the view that Project uses to display and organize your schedule information onscreen. You learned that some views include (either alone or with other types of information) forms that are intended to make it easier to enter and edit information.

This chapter shows you how to work with forms on their own, rather than working with them as part of a view.

Understanding Forms

Years ago, people had to communicate with programs run on large mainframe computers using punch cards. They would punch a pattern of numbers on a card, and the computer would read (and presumably understand) the data from the card. For obvious reasons, this was one of many factors that discouraged lots of people from working with computers—so that computing became a geeks-only affair.

Over time, many easier ways of communicating with programs have evolved. So far, you've seen, that in Project, you can enter information via spreadsheet-like tables or sheets, by dragging on a Gantt chart or PERT chart, via dialog boxes, and more. Forms are yet another method for entering data.

Forms resemble dialog boxes in that they include text boxes to let you enter and edit information and also display other information, such as calculated costs, that you cannot edit. Although some views consist solely of a large form—or include a form in a lower pane—you also can display a form in its own floating dialog box (see Figure 11.1).

Project offers some forms for resource information (see Figure 11.2) and others for task information. Table 11.1 lists the predefined forms available in Project.

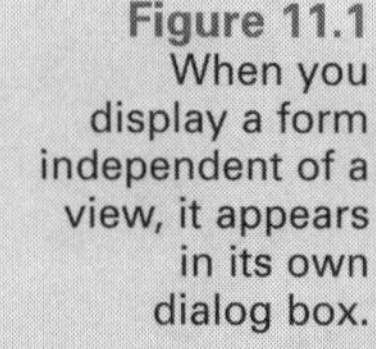

Figure 11.1 When you display a form independent of a view, it appears in its own dialog box.

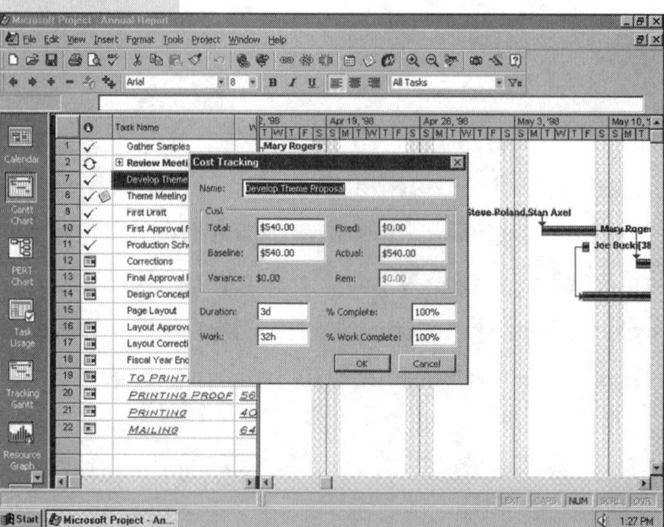

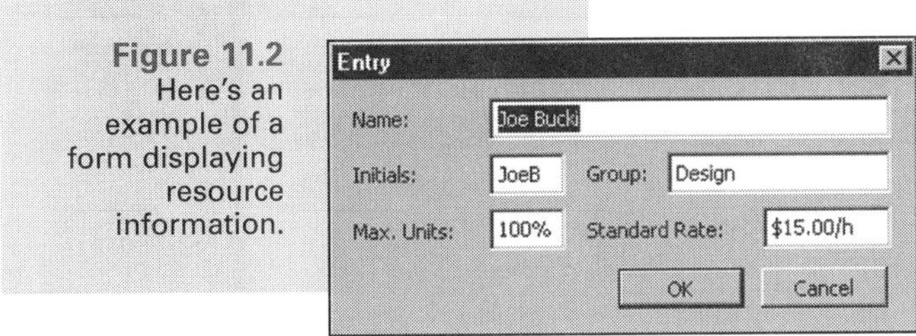

Figure 11.2 Here's an example of a form displaying resource information.

Selecting a Form

The process for selecting a form differs a bit from selecting some of the other types of view information, because there's no way to directly display a form via a menu or submenu choice. You have to use the Custom Forms dialog box, as described in the following steps:

1. Display the Task Sheet or Resource Sheet, and select the task or resource for which you want to display form information by clicking the Task Name or Resource Name cell in the appropriate row.

If you're working in a task view, you can't display resource forms, and vice versa. Thus, it's critical to select a task or resource to ensure that the correct form choices are available.

2. Open the Tools menu, point to Customize to display its submenu, and click Forms. The Custom Forms dialog box appears (see Figure 11.3).

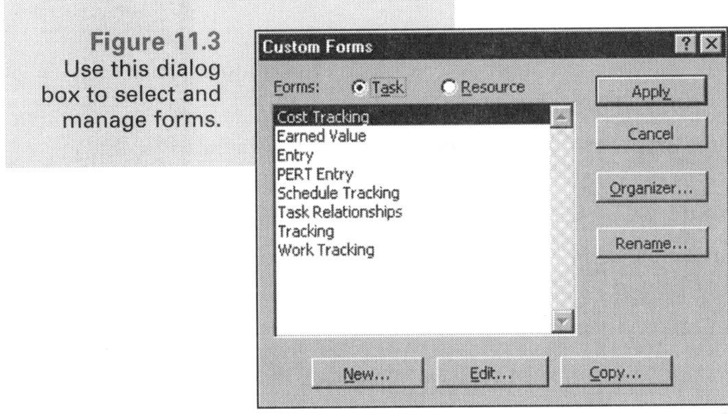

Figure 11.3 Use this dialog box to select and manage forms.

Table 11.1 Task Forms and Resource Forms in Project

Form Name	Description
Task Forms	
Cost Tracking	Displays cost information for the selected task, including baseline budget, current budget, and actual costs to the current date or status date based on work performed.
Earned Value	Displays earned value information, such as the variance between the originally budgeted cost and currently budgeted cost (see Chapter 8 to learn more about costs); only lets you edit the task name and completion percentage.
Entry	Enables you to enter or edit basic information about the selected task, including its name, duration, start date, and finish date.
PERT Entry	When you're using PERT Analysis, as described in Chapter 9, use this form to enter optimistic, expected, and pessimistic durations for the selected task.
Schedule Tracking	Shows the selected task's baseline and currently scheduled start and finish dates, and calculates the variance between the original and current dates.
Task Relationships	Displays and lets you edit the predecessors and successors linked to the selected task.
Tracking	Enables you to enter actual start and finish dates, as well as completion information, for the selected task.
Work Tracking	Enables you to enter actual start and finish dates, as well as completion information, for the selected task.
Resource Forms	
Cost Tracking	Displays cost information for the resource selected in the Resource Sheet, including baseline cost, total cost (currently budgeted), and actual cost for work performed to-date (or to the status date); none of these values can be edited.
Entry	Enables you to edit the basic information defining the resource, such as the resource's name, initials, and standard rate.
Summary	Summarizes the amount of work and budget for costs scheduled for the resource, such as the resource's name, initials, and standard rate.
Work Tracking	Displays the amount of work scheduled for a resource, the percentage completed, and variance in work completed to-date or to the status date; these calculations can't be edited.

3. In the Forms list, select the form to display by double-clicking its name (or by clicking the name once and then clicking Apply). Project closes the Custom Forms dialog box, and displays the form you selected onscreen.
4. If you need to edit any information in the form, and the form offers editable text boxes, double-click each text box and then edit its contents.
5. Click OK when you're finished displaying the form.

Creating a Custom Form

You might find that none of the custom forms in Project capture the information you want to show. For example, you might need a quick way to check actual task costs, along with the resource name and group, to keep an eye on how much work by another department in your company you'll need to pay for. That is, you may want to track the costs for work performed by resources from another group that are coming from your project budget.

Project enables you to create your own custom forms, and to do so you don't need any programming experience. You simply need to be able to click and drag. You can add text to your form, or you can add information from any field in the Task Sheet or Resource Sheet. If a field contains a calculated value that you shouldn't edit, Project automatically formats the field so that it can't be edited on your form.

While there's a nearly infinite number of custom forms that you can create, the following steps and the example shown with them should give you a good start. Afterward, you can experiment on your own to discover the combinations of form information you'll find most useful.

1. Open the Tools menu, point to Customize to display its submenu, and click Forms. The Custom Forms dialog box appears.
2. Click either the Task or Resource option button at the top of the dialog box to indicate whether your form will display information from the Task Sheet or Resource Sheet. This is a critical step, because your choice here affects which fields you can add to your form.
3. Click the New button. Project displays the Define Custom Form dialog box (see Figure 11.4).
4. Enter the form name in the Name text box. For example, if you're creating a form showing actual task cost, resource name, and resource group information, you might enter **Cost and Group**.

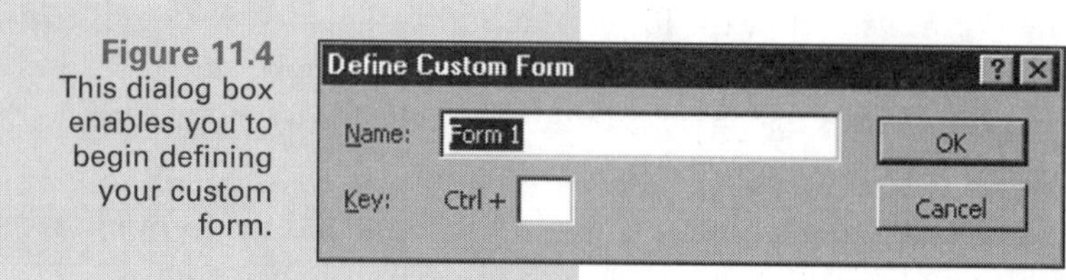

Figure 11.4
This dialog box enables you to begin defining your custom form.

5. If you want to be able to use a shortcut key combination to display the custom form, enter the second key for the combination in the Key text box. Project allows only letters here; you can't enter numbers, function keys, or special characters such as punctuation marks.
6. Click OK to continue defining the form. Project displays the Custom Form Editor, with a new blank form background, as shown in Figure 11.5. Notice that the toolbar tools have been hidden, and that the available menus have changed to reflect that you're working with the Form Editor functions.
7. By default, a dotted outline appears around the border of the blank form dialog box to indicate that this box is selected. (If this boundary outline doesn't appear, you can display it by opening the Edit menu and clicking Select Dialog.) If needed, you can change the size of the form by clicking and dragging the dotted line on any side of the dialog box, as shown in Figure 11.6.
8. Now, it's time to begin adding elements to the form. Usually, you'll want to add a text label for each field you display. To add a text label,

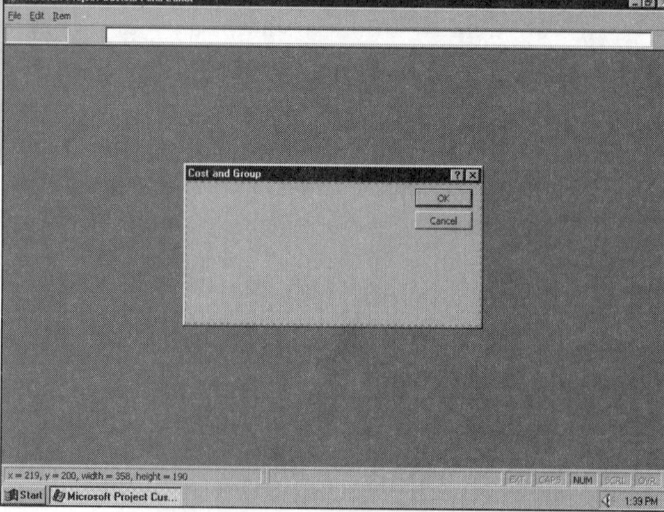

Figure 11.5
Create custom forms with the Custom Form Editor shown here.

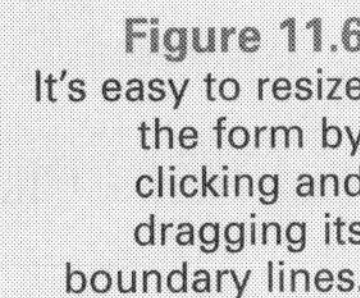

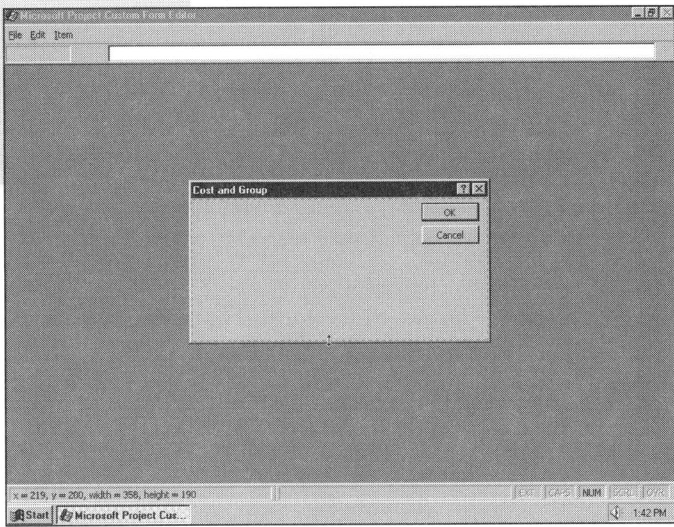

Figure 11.6
It's easy to resize the form by clicking and dragging its boundary lines.

open the Item menu and click Text. Project adds placeholder text to the form, surrounded by dotted boundary lines. If you point to this text and a four-headed arrow appears (see Figure 11.7), you can drag it to a different location. You can adjust the size of the text by dragging one of its boundary lines.

9. After you position and size the text placeholder, double-click it on the form (or open the Edit menu and click Information). The Item Information dialog box appears, as shown in Figure 11.8.

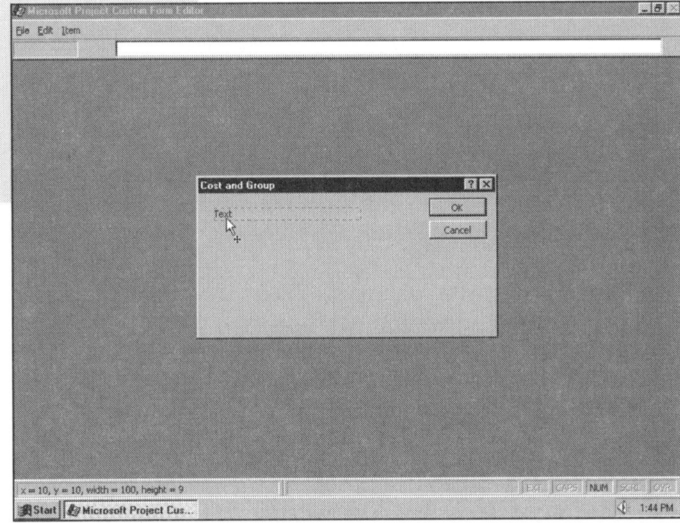

Figure 11.7
You can drag the text box placeholder into the position you prefer on the form.

10. You shouldn't need to edit any of the top four text boxes, because you already defined the placeholder's size and position in step 8. Simply double-click the Text text box, and then type the text you want to appear in that area of the form, for example, I'll type **Task Name**. Click OK to close the Item Information dialog box.
11. To add a field to the form, open the Item menu and click Fields. Project displays the Item Information dialog box immediately, because you have to specify which field to display.
12. Open the Field drop-down list, and click on the name of the field you want to appear on the form. For example, I'll select Name to display the task name, as shown in Figure 11.9.
13. If you know that a field typically appears in an editable format on forms—as the Name field usually does—then click to select the Show As Static Text check box if you want Project not to enable editing of the field information.
14. Click OK. The field appears on the form, ready for you to resize and drag into place (see Figure 11.10).

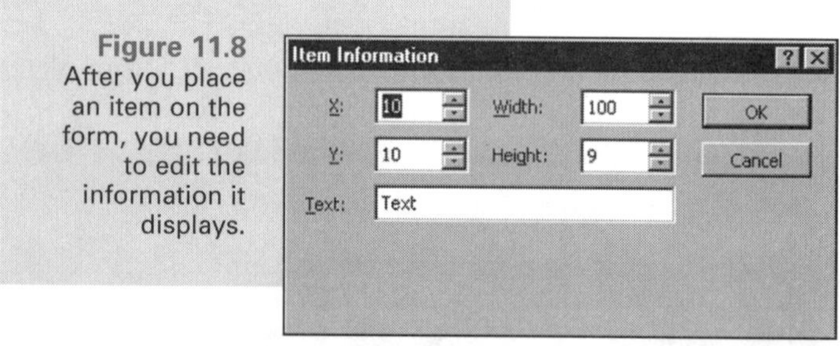

Figure 11.8 After you place an item on the form, you need to edit the information it displays.

Figure 11.9 Tell Project what field information you want displayed on the form.

To delete any item you added to a form, click the item once so that a dotted selection line appears around it, and then press the Delete key.

15. Continue adding items to the form, using the same general process of making a choice from the Item menu, displaying (if needed) the Item Information dialog box to define what the item displays, resizing the item, and dragging it into position. For example, Figure 11.11 shows my completed form. I've used the Group Box selection on the Item menu to create the Stats box.
16. Open the File menu and click Save to save your form with the name you provided in step 4.
17. Open the File menu and click Exit. Project closes the Form Editor, and returns to the Custom Forms dialog box. Your new form appears there, as shown in Figure 11.12.

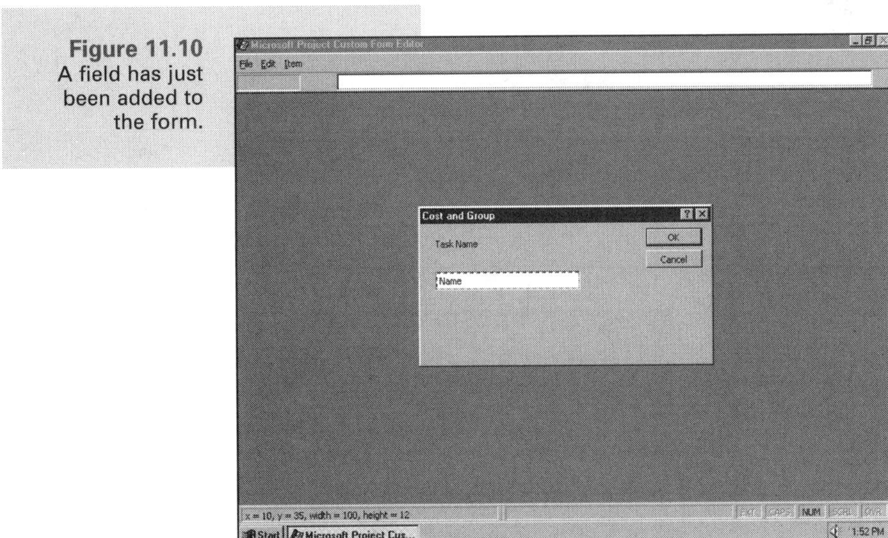

Figure 11.10 A field has just been added to the form.

Figure 11.11 Here's how the final form looks.

Cost and Group
Task Name
Name
OK
Cancel
Stats
Resource Initials
Resource Group
Actual Costs
Resource Initials
Resource Group
Actual Cost

Dimmed fields display as static text that you can't edit

18. At this point, if you displayed the appropriate sheet before creating the form, you can double-click the form name to display it. (If you're at the wrong sheet view, you have to close the Custom Forms dialog box, switch to the appropriate sheet, redisplay the Custom Forms dialog box, and then select your form.) Figure 11.13 shows how my custom form appears when displayed.

It takes a little practice, but soon you can create a variety of useful forms. Pay attention to every detail if you want to achieve professional results. For example, make sure that your text boxes and field boxes align at both the left and right sides of the form whenever possible, and make sure that information looks centered when you intend it to.

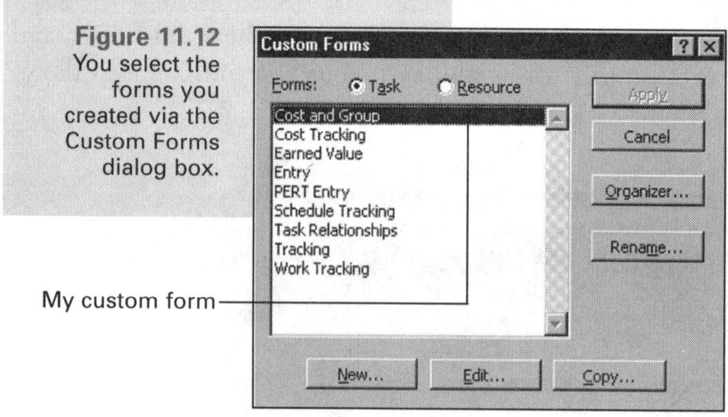

Figure 11.12 You select the forms you created via the Custom Forms dialog box.

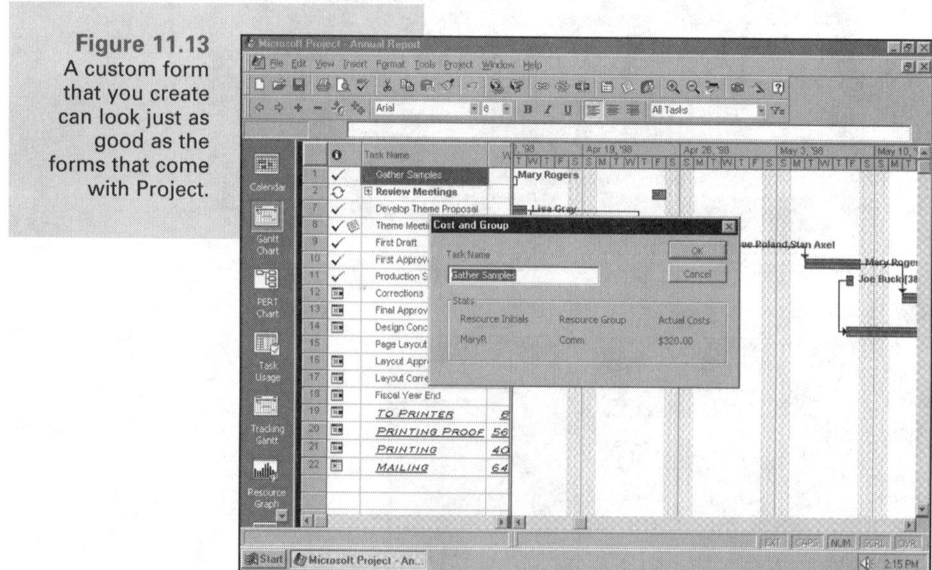

Figure 11.13 A custom form that you create can look just as good as the forms that come with Project.

Custom forms that you create are saved with only the current project file, until you either copy them to Project's GLOBAL.MPT master file or delete them. To make a form available to all files or to delete a form, click the Organizer button in the Custom Forms dialog box, and use the Forms tab of the Organizer to make your changes. Chapter 9, "Working with the Different Project Views," discusses working with the Organizer.

Creating a Toolbar Button or Menu Command to Display a Form

Note that each form only lets you display information about one task or resource at a time. Unlike forms used as part of a view, forms that you display on their own don't offer Previous and Next buttons to enable you to display information about other resources or tasks without closing the form. Because it can become tedious to use the Tools menu to display a form over and over, and a shortcut key can be difficult to remember, you might want to create a toolbar button or menu command that displays this form.

Here are the steps for adding such a toolbar button or menu command (see Chapter 21, "Customizing Microsoft Project," for an in-depth look at creating menu commands and toolbar buttons):

1. Open the Tools menu, point to Customize, and then click Toolbars, or, right-click any toolbar and then click Customize.
2. Click the Commands tab in the Customize dialog box.
3. Scroll down the Categories list on the tab; then click All Forms in the list.
4. In the Commands list on the tab, click the name of the form you want to create a button or command for; then drag the form from the Customize dialog box onto the appropriate toolbar or menu.

Although you can change an existing toolbar button so that it displays a form rather than executing its currently assigned command, I don't recommend doing so, because it might prove very difficult (or impossible) to recall what the button's original command was if you ever want to reinstate it.

5. Right-click the form you just dragged onto the toolbar to display a shortcut menu with options for customizing the button or menu command (see Figure 11.14). Chapter 21 explains how to use the commands on this shortcut menu to control such features as the icon that appears on a button, the menu command name, and more. Refer to that chapter for details about using the shortcut menu.
6. After you finished using the shortcut menu to make changes to the new button or command, click Close to finish creating the button and close the Customize dialog box. Figure 11.15 shows an example form button.

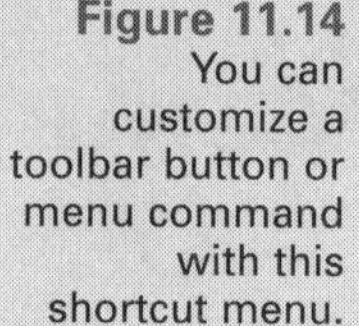

Figure 11.14 You can customize a toolbar button or menu command with this shortcut menu.

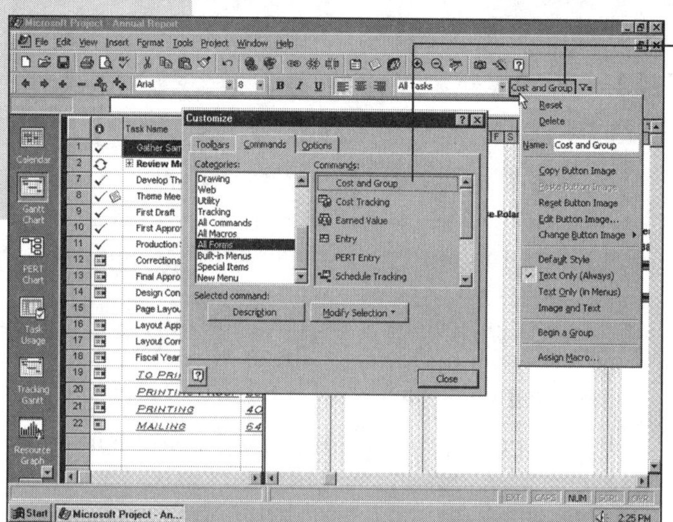

I dragged this form onto the toolbar

Figure 11.15 I've added a custom form toolbar button near the right end of the Formatting toolbar; its ScreenTip is displayed.

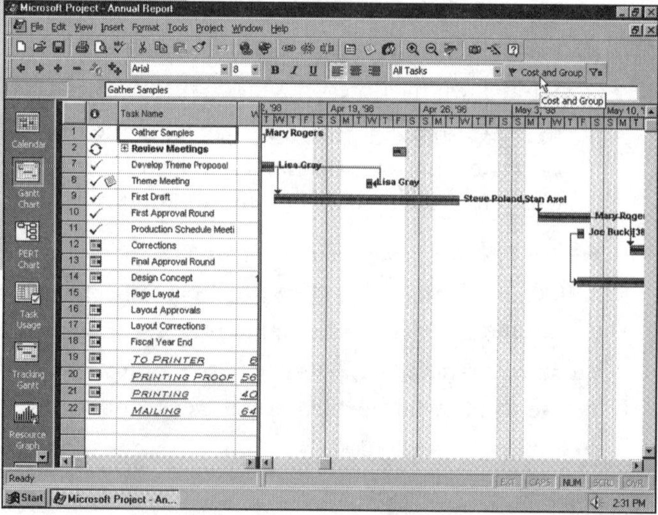

12

Creating and Printing a Report

In This Chapter

- Learning what predesigned reports Project offers
- Selecting the correct report
- Fine-tuning and printing a report
- Designing a unique report

Software developers have placed a good deal of emphasis on offering more ways to work with the information you gather in a particular program. That's because the typical businessperson needs to share information with a variety of audiences, and each audience needs only a particular subset of the information.

For a Project file, for example, you might need to prepare a weekly report of the current expenses for a project to give to your boss, a listing of upcoming tasks to give to the participants in a planning meeting, or a weekly to-do list for yourself, to tickle your memory about issues you need to follow up on.

Project can generate these kinds of reports (and more) automatically. This chapter introduces you to reporting in Project.

Understanding the Report Types

The predefined reports offered in Project provide the most common types of summary information that you might need to provide to others within and outside of your organization. In Chapter 10, "Proofing and Printing a View," you learn how to select and filter different views for printing and to control the information appearing in your printout. Although that method of selecting and printing information works fine in many cases, it has a few drawbacks:

- It frequently requires several steps to display just the facts you want to see.
- You often can't capture totals for data in the format you prefer.
- There are some kinds of lists you just can't print from a view, such as a list of working days for the schedule.

Project's reports address these issues for you, providing a streamlined approach for selecting and printing information. In addition, using a report rather than printing a view yields a printout with an attractive layout that's suitable for distribution to readers whom you need to impress. Finally, the reports capture information in key columns; there's no need for the reader to wade through extraneous data in a report printout.

To create reports in Project, you work with the Reports dialog box. To display the Reports dialog box, start from any view. Open the View menu and click Reports; the Reports dialog box appears (see Figure 12.1). This dialog box offers five icons (pictures) of different categories of reports: Overview, Current Activities, Costs, Assignments, and Workload. The sixth icon, Custom, enables you to create more unique reports, as described later in this chapter, in the "Creating a Custom Report" section.

To select a report category, click the icon for the category and then click Select (or simply double-click the icon). Project displays a dialog box showing the different kinds of reports available in that category, including an icon for each report that shows a thumbnail view of what the report looks like. Although there's not room in this book to show you a printout of every report type, the rest of this section introduces you to the reports in each category, via the dialog box for that category. The

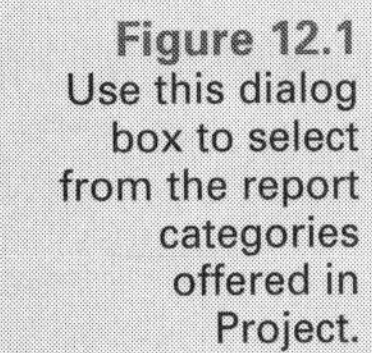

Figure 12.1 Use this dialog box to select from the report categories offered in Project.

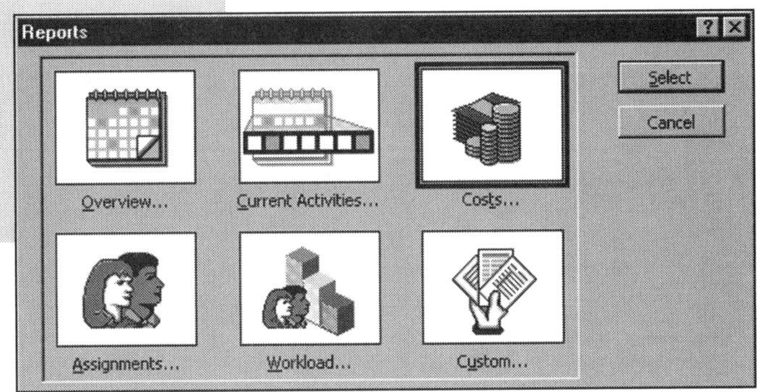

reports that work best for you will depend on what information you're required to report to others, as well as how concerned you are about having frequent updates on specific information, such as upcoming tasks or tasks that are underway. After you review the dialog boxes shown here for the various report categories, spend some time on your own experimenting to discover which reports you prefer to work with.

Clicking Cancel from any dialog box listing specific reports closes that dialog box and redisplays the Reports dialog box.

Overview Reports

When you select the Overview Reports icon in the Reports dialog box, Project displays the Overview Reports dialog box (see Figure 12.2).

Current Activities Reports

The next category of reports, Current Activities, appears in the Current Activity Reports dialog box (see Figure 12.3) that appears after you select Current Activities in the Reports dialog box.

Two of the report types in the Current Activities category, Tasks Starting Soon and Should Have Started Tasks, require you to enter dates. Whenever Project prompts you to enter a date, type it using mm/dd/yy format, and then click OK to continue.

Figure 12.2 Reports that provide project summaries at a glance.

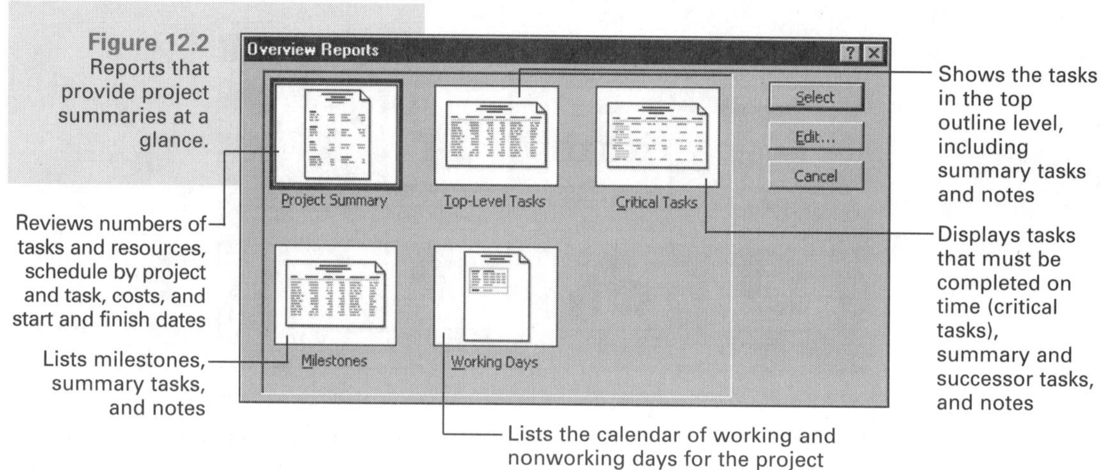
Overview Reports
Select
Edit...
Cancel
Project Summary
Top-Level Tasks
Critical Tasks
Milestones
Working Days
Shows the tasks in the top outline level, including summary tasks and notes
Displays tasks that must be completed on time (critical tasks), summary and successor tasks, and notes
Reviews numbers of tasks and resources, schedule by project and task, costs, and start and finish dates
Lists milestones, summary tasks, and notes
Lists the calendar of working and nonworking days for the project

Figure 12.3 Reports that provide project summaries at a glance.

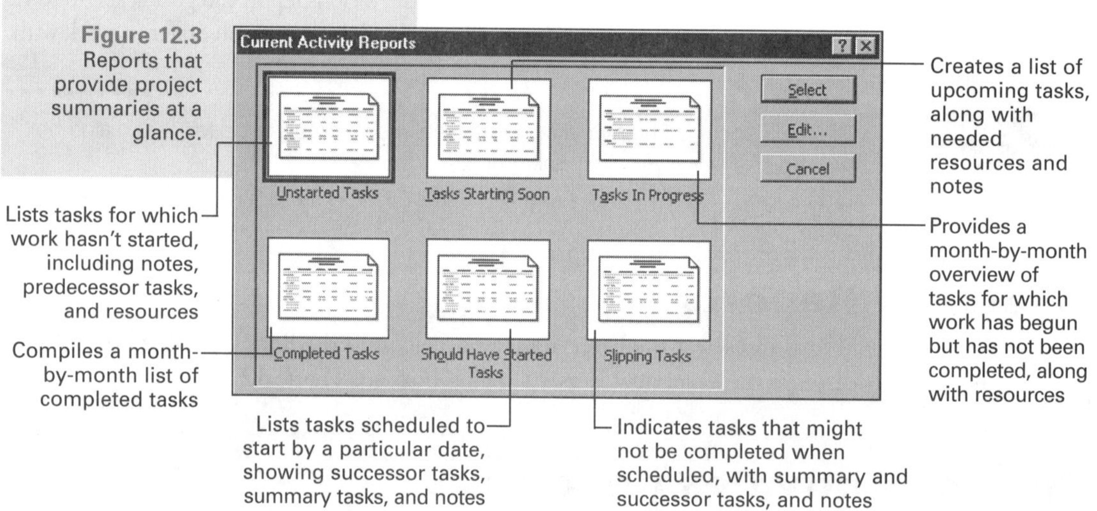
Current Activity Reports
Select
Edit...
Cancel
Unstarted Tasks
Tasks Starting Soon
Tasks In Progress
Completed Tasks
Should Have Started Tasks
Slipping Tasks
Creates a list of upcoming tasks, along with needed resources and notes
Provides a month-by-month overview of tasks for which work has begun but has not been completed, along with resources
Lists tasks for which work hasn't started, including notes, predecessor tasks, and resources
Compiles a month-by-month list of completed tasks
Lists tasks scheduled to start by a particular date, showing successor tasks, summary tasks, and notes
Indicates tasks that might not be completed when scheduled, with summary and successor tasks, and notes

Costs Reports

To take a look at the dollars and cents you're spending on your project, select the Costs category in the Reports dialog box to display the report types shown in Figure 12.4. It's likely that you'll get a lot of mileage from these report formats, as one of the key aspects of project management is monitoring the bottom line and adjusting planned expenditures as required. These reports not only compile the expenses you specify, but also total various expenses by column (category).

Figure 12.4 These reports track and sum up costs.

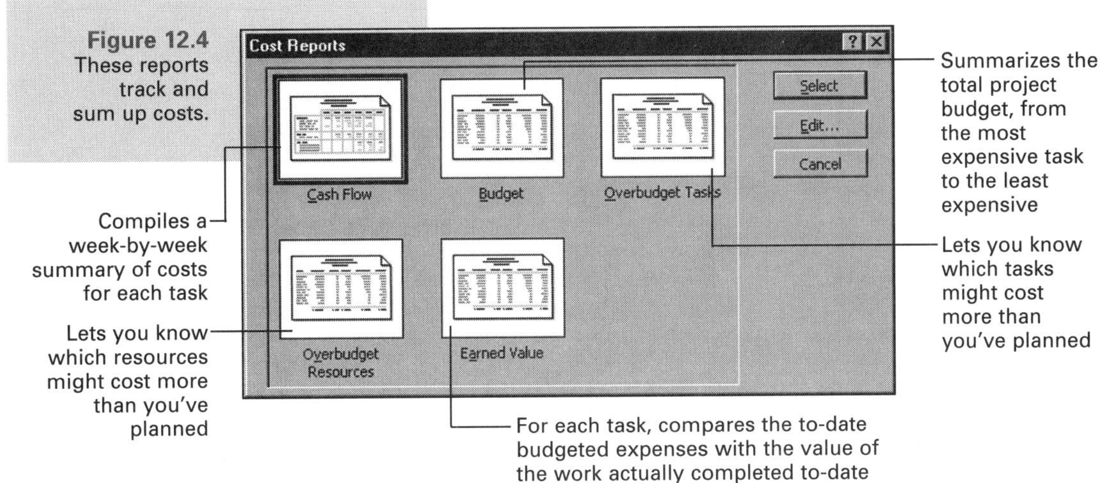
Cost Reports
Cash Flow
Budget
Overbudget Tasks
Overbudget Resources
Earned Value
Select
Edit...
Cancel
Compiles a week-by-week summary of costs for each task
Lets you know which resources might cost more than you've planned
Summarizes the total project budget, from the most expensive task to the least expensive
Lets you know which tasks might cost more than you've planned
For each task, compares the to-date budgeted expenses with the value of the work actually completed to-date

Assignments Reports

The Assignments selection in the Reports dialog box displays four report types in the Assignment Reports dialog box (see Figure 12.5). Although you can print much of the same information by printing a Gantt chart, the report formats summarize the information in a more accessible format that's suitable for presentation; For example, you can bind them as part of a project plan to be distributed at a meeting.

Two of these reports provide particularly valuable management tools. The To-Do List lets you prepare a list of all the scheduled tasks for a resource you select, when prompted, from the Using Resource dialog box. The Overallocated Resources report provides you with ammunition you might need to help you request more resources for a project—or for particular tasks—during a given timeframe, by showing when currently available resources have too many assignments.

Workload Reports

While the Assignments reports focus on enabling you to view work schedules by resource, the two reports available when you select Workload in the Reports dialog box enable you to examine the total workload scheduled during each day of the project. The schedule can be grouped by either Task Usage or Resource Usage (see Figure 12.6).

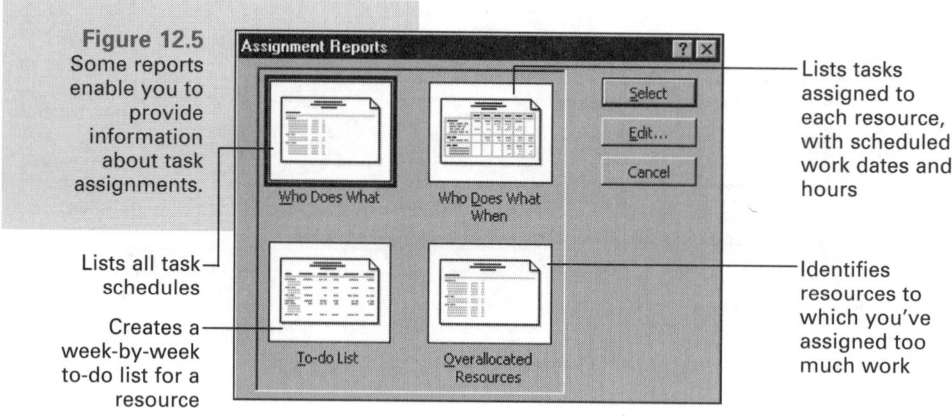
Assignment Reports
Select
Edit...
Cancel
Who Does What
Who Does What When
To-do List
Overallocated Resources
Lists tasks assigned to each resource, with scheduled work dates and hours
Lists all task schedules
Creates a week-by-week to-do list for a resource
Identifies resources to which you've assigned too much work

Figure 12.5 Some reports enable you to provide information about task assignments.

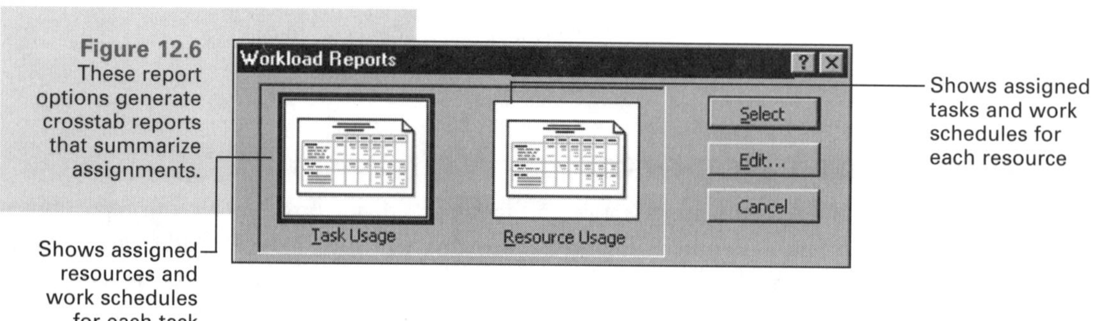
Workload Reports
Select
Edit...
Cancel
Task Usage
Resource Usage
Shows assigned tasks and work schedules for each resource
Shows assigned resources and work schedules for each task

Figure 12.6 These report options generate crosstab reports that summarize assignments.

Note

The Workload reports and some of the other reports you've seen are referred to as *crosstab reports* because they present information in rows and columns separated into specific cells of information by a grid. At the intersection of each row and column is a cell with specific information about the resource or task listed in that row, on the date indicated by the selected column.

Selecting, Setting Up, and Printing a Report

As noted at the beginning of this chapter, the report creation process begins with the Reports dialog box. After you select the report you want, Project compiles

the report information and displays the report onscreen in Print Preview mode. When the report is onscreen, you can make modifications to its layout before printing it out. This section describes how you can tackle all these tasks.

To select the report you want to work with and print out, open the project file that you want to create the report about, and then follow these steps:

1. Open the View menu and click Reports. The Reports dialog box appears onscreen.
2. In the Reports dialog box, select the category of report you want by double-clicking a category icon (or by clicking the icon once and then clicking Select). Project displays the dialog box for the report category you selected.
3. Select the thumbnail icon for the type of report you want to use. Do so by double-clicking the icon (or by clicking the icon once and then clicking Select).
4. Some report types require you to specify a date or resource name, and prompt you to do so with a dialog box (see Figure 12.7). If a date is requested, enter it in mm/dd/yy format. If the dialog box prompts you to select a resource, do so using the drop-down list that's presented. After you specify either a date or a resource, click on OK to finish. (Some report formats prompt you for another date; if this happens, enter the date and click OK again to finish.)

After you complete the preceding steps, Project compiles the report and presents it onscreen for viewing, fine-tuning, or printing.

You might encounter instances, however, when you have selected a report type that Project cannot compile, or have entered a date for which there's no data to report. For example, if you try to print a report about Slipping Tasks from the Current Activities category, and there are no tasks that are behind schedule on the date on which you try to print the report, Project displays the dialog box shown in Figure 12.8. Click on OK to close the message dialog box, and Project redisplays the Reports dialog box so that you can try again. Select a different report type, or try specifying a different date for the report you want.

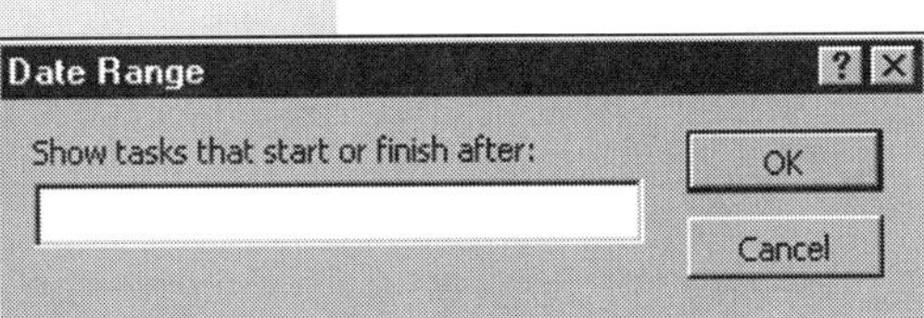

Figure 12.7 Project may prompt you to specify a date or select a resource to report about.

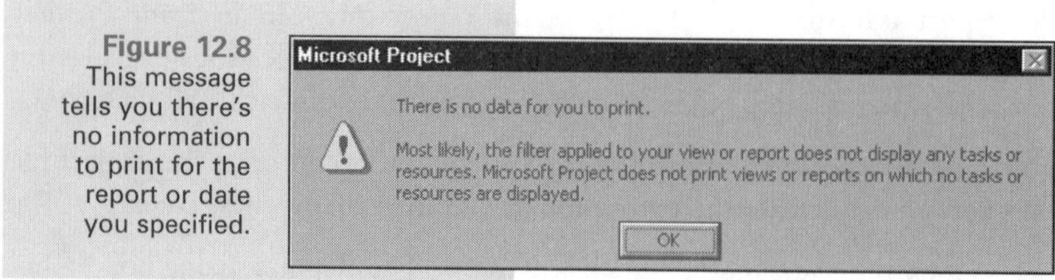

Figure 12.8 This message tells you there's no information to print for the report or date you specified.

At any time, to close the preview area where the report appears, click the Close button near the top of the screen. Project returns to the Reports dialog box. Click the Cancel button to put away that dialog box and return to the active view for the project file.

Navigating in the Report

The report you selected appears onscreen in a Print Preview view similar to the one you learned about in Chapter 10. This view offers a few special tools and icons that enable you to view different parts of the report, or to take a closer look at particular items in the report (see Figure 12.9).

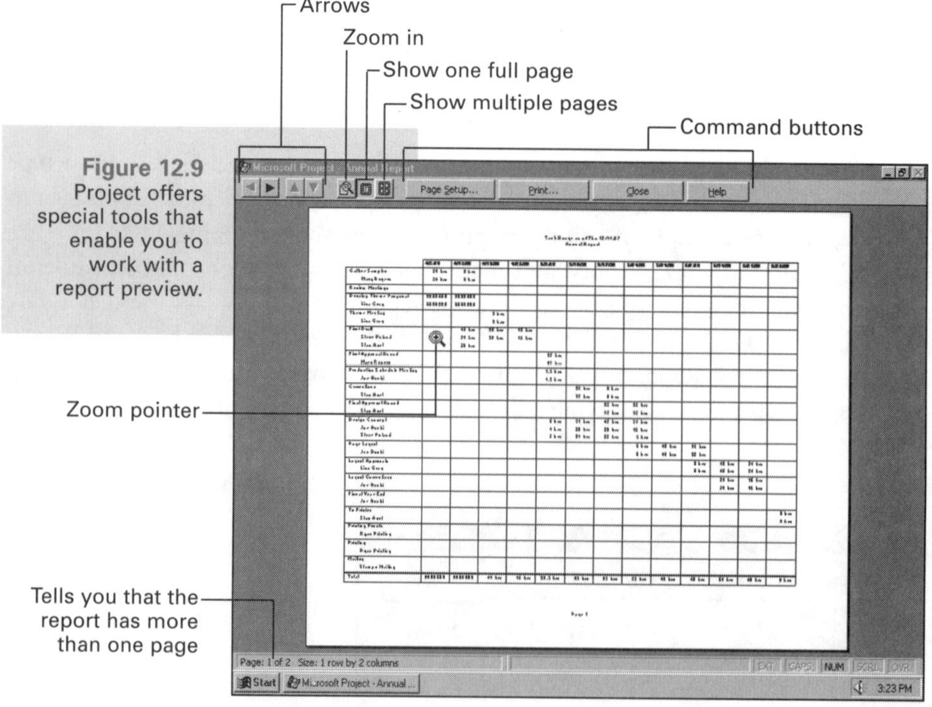

Figure 12.9 Project offers special tools that enable you to work with a report preview.

Use the left and right arrow keys to move forward and backward through the pages in the report. The up and down arrows are enabled only if there are too many rows to appear in a single report page. You can use the up and down arrows to view the extra rows, which appear on separate pages if the report is printed.

By default, you'll see one page of the report, shown in a size that keeps the whole page visible in the preview. You might, however, want to zoom in to read particular details in the report before printing. You can click the Zoom button at the top of the preview to zoom in on the upper-left corner of the report, or use the zoom pointer to zoom in on a specific cell. After you zoom in, click the button for displaying one full page (the button has a page on it) to return to the default view.

If the report has more than one page and you want to view multiple pages, perhaps to see how the information is divided between pages, click the button that looks like a stack of papers. Project displays multiple pages of the report onscreen. Again, to return to the default view, click the button for displaying one full page.

Obviously, you won't always want to print the reports you generate. Reports often are a fast way to check information such as the current budget total. You can generate the report, zoom in to check a detail or two, and then click the Close button to exit the preview and the Cancel button to close the Reports dialog box.

Viewing Setup Options

As you learned in Chapter 10, "Proofing and Printing a View," you have control over numerous aspects of how a printout appears. For example, you can adjust margins to allow for more or less space around printed data, or you can specify whether a page number appears on every page. You adjust these options using the Page Setup dialog box, which you display from the Print Preview view by clicking the Page Setup button at the top of the screen. The Page Setup dialog box for the report appears (see Figure 12.10).

Although the dialog box offers six tabs, two of them aren't available for many reports. These are the Legend and View tabs, which offer options that apply when you're printing certain charts and views. Additionally, other tabs may become disabled (grayed out) when you select a report type for which they don't apply. For example, you cannot adjust the header or footer for a Project Summary report.

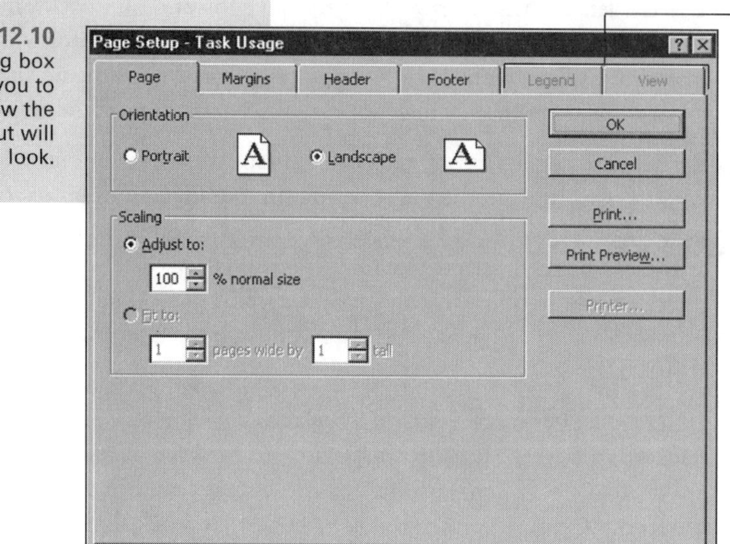

Figure 12.10 This dialog box enables you to adjust how the final printout will look.

As you learned in Chapter 10, to change a page setup option in the Page Setup dialog box, first click to select the tab that offers the option, make your changes, and then click OK to close the Page Setup dialog box (or click Print to send the report to the printer). The four tabs of available Page Setup options for reports are as follows:

- **Page**—Enables you to specify whether the printout is wide (landscape) or tall (portrait); also lets you scale the printed information by entering a size percentage or the desired number of pages for the printout.
- **Margins**—Enables you to enter a separate measurement for the margin for each of the four page edges, or to specify a printed border for report pages.
- **Header**—Enables you to edit the header that appears at the top of the report pages (see Figure 12.11), including what it contains (page number, company names, and so on) and whether it's centered or aligned left or right (see Chapter 10 for more information about creating printout headers and footers).
- **Footer**—Offers options similar to those found on the Header tab, but places the specified text at the bottom of each printed report page.

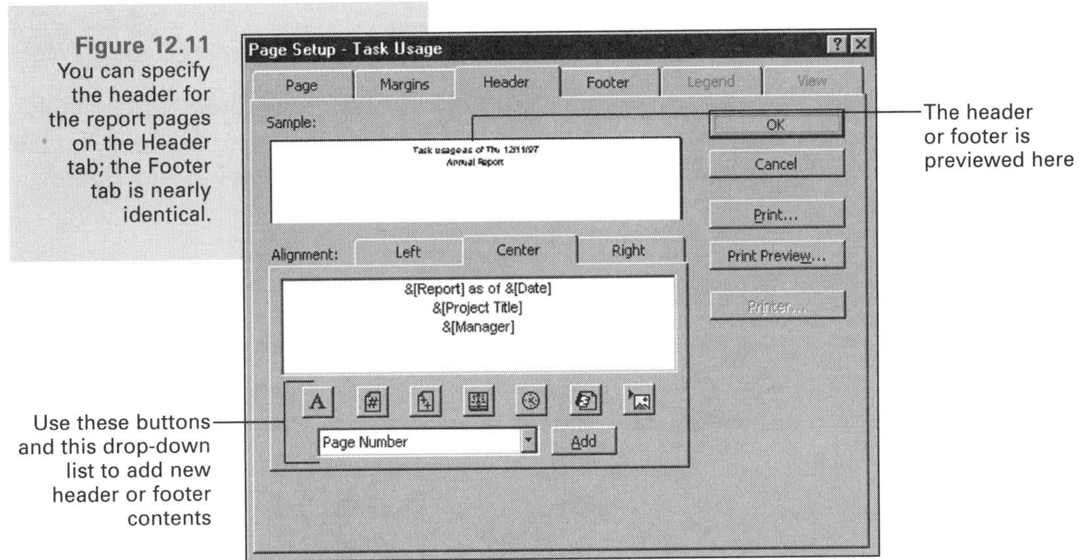

Figure 12.11 You can specify the header for the report pages on the Header tab; the Footer tab is nearly identical.

Printing

After you check to ensure that you chose the report you need and have made any changes you want in the Page Setup dialog box, you're ready to print your report. To initiate the print process, click on the Print button found in either the Page Setup dialog box or the Print Preview screen. The Print dialog box appears.

This dialog box is covered as part of Chapter 10's in-depth look at printing; however, a few options in the dialog box might be particularly attractive to you when you're printing reports. They are as follows:

- **Print Range**—By default, Project prints All pages in a report if the report has more than one page. You might, however, only want to print part of a report. To do so, click the Page(s) From option button in the Print Range area, then enter the starting page in the From text box and the final page in the To text box. For example, enter 4 and 5 to print only pages 4 and 5 of the report.
- **Copies**—To print more than one copy at a time (such as 10 copies to distribute at a meeting), change the Number of Copies text box by double-clicking the current entry, and typing a new entry (such as 10).
- **Timescale**—Normally, unless a report by default asks you for a particular timeframe, the report covers the full duration of the project schedule. If you want to print only the report pages that pertain to particular dates in the schedule, click to select the Dates From option button in the

Timescale area. Then enter the starting date in the From text box and the last date of the range you want to print in the To text box.

After you specify the options you prefer in the Print dialog box, click OK. Project sends the report to the printer, and closes the print preview for the report. To close the Reports dialog box, which reappears onscreen after printing, click Cancel.

Creating a Custom Report

The sixth category icon in the Reports dialog box, the Custom button, enables you to control various features of any available report, create a new report based on an already existing report, or start from scratch to build an entirely unique report to suit your needs. The report features you can change vary depending on the report you start working with. For some reports, such as the Project Summary report, you can only change the font and text formatting to adjust the report's appearance. For other reports, Project displays a dialog box enabling you to edit such elements of the report as its name, the time period it covers, the table it's based upon, filtering, and more.

To change, copy, or create a custom report, you work in the Custom Reports dialog box (see Figure 12.12). To display this dialog box, double-click the Custom option in the Reports dialog box (or click Custom once and then click Select). The scrolling Reports list in this dialog box enables you to select a report to customize, if needed.

From the Custom Reports dialog box, after you select a report in the Reports list, you can use the Preview button to display the selected report in Print Preview mode, the Setup button to go to the Page Setup dialog box for the report, or the Print button to go to the Print dialog box for the report. After selecting one of these buttons, you can work with the preview, setup, or printing options for the report just as described previously in this chapter. Click Cancel to close the Custom Reports dialog box, and then click Cancel to close the Reports dialog box.

Making Changes to an Existing Report

The fastest way to customize a report and arrive at both the report contents and formatting you need is to choose the report that most closely resembles what you want, then make changes to it. To start this process, click the name of the report to edit in the Reports list of the Custom Reports dialog box. Then click the Edit button.

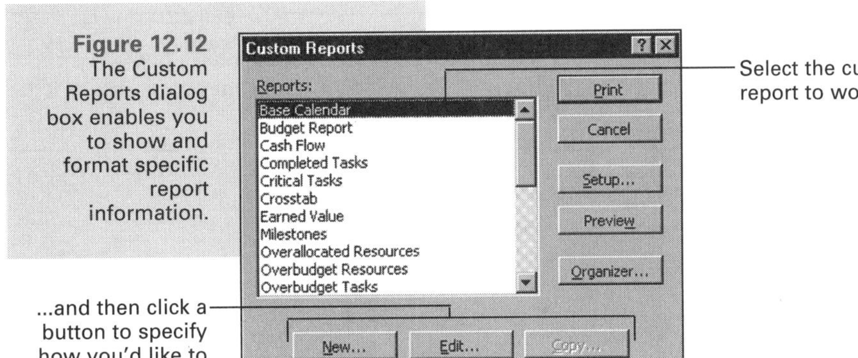

Figure 12.12 The Custom Reports dialog box enables you to show and format specific report information.

You also can click the icon for a report in the dialog box for that report category, and then click the Edit button (refer to Figures 12.2 through 12.6).

What happens next depends on the report you selected for editing. If you selected the Base Calendar or Project Summary report for editing, Project only enables you to change the fonts specified for the report, and thus displays the Report Text dialog box shown in Figure 12.13. Use the Item to Change drop-down list if you want the change to apply only to the Calendar Name or Detail information in the report; then use the Font, Font Style, and Size lists to select the text attributes you want. The sample area shows a preview of what your selections will look like when applied to text in the report. To underline the text, for example, select the Underline check box, and to specify a color for text, use the Color drop-down list. After you've made the desired font selections, click on OK to implement your changes and return to the Custom Reports dialog box. From there, you can preview or print the edited report.

After you make changes to a report offered in your project file, the changes remain in effect until you specifically return the report to its original format. There's always a chance, however, that you might forget what the original format was. If you're planning to make major changes to a report, you're always safer working from a copy of the original file as described next, rather than working from the original.

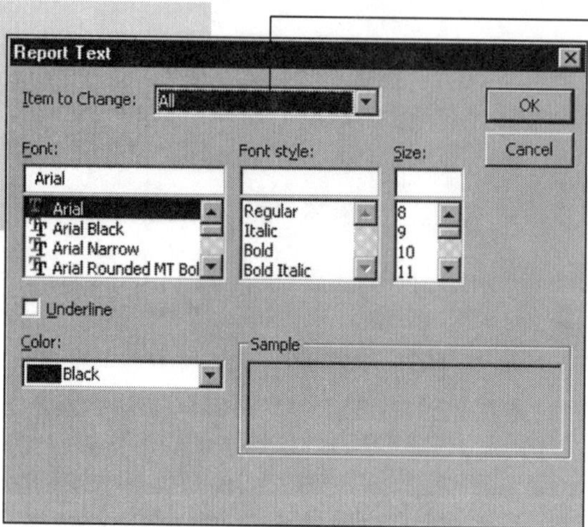

Figure 12.13 For some reports, you can change only the appearance of printed text.

For other reports you select from the Reports list, a different dialog box appears when you click the Edit button. Depending on the selected report type, the dialog box that appears is named Task Report, Resource Report, or Crosstab Report. Each of these dialog boxes has three tabs, but the tab contents vary slightly, depending on the report category (as described next). After you specify the options you want in one of these dialog boxes, click OK to implement your changes. From the Custom Reports dialog box, you then can preview, set up, or print the report.

Task Reports

A *task report* generally has the word "task" or "what" in its name in the Reports list of the Custom Reports dialog box. When you select one of these reports and then click the Edit button, the Task Report dialog box appears (see Figure 12.14). The first tab of this dialog box, the Definition tab, enables you to work with the most basic information about the report, such as the report name. You might want to change the report name to reflect your changes, perhaps calling it "Weekly Budget Report" instead of simply "Budget Report." This tab also enables you to control the timeframe for which information is reported and to specify whether or not to apply a filter to display only some tasks in the project (Chapter 9, "Working with the Different Project Views," covers filtering in detail).

After you set the project definition options, click the Details tab. The options on this tab (see Figure 12.15) control which details appear for the tasks you've chosen to display using the Definition tab.

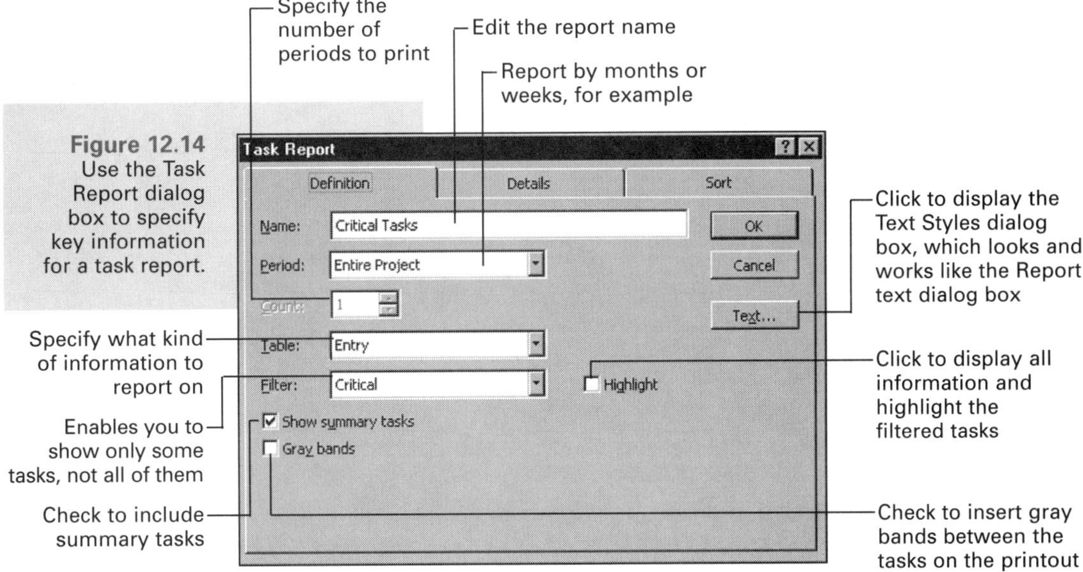

Figure 12.14 Use the Task Report dialog box to specify key information for a task report.

Finally, click the Sort tab to determine how to sort the tasks that appear in your report. Click to display the Sort By drop-down list to display it (see Figure 12.16). Then choose the name of the field that contains the information you want to sort by. Select Ascending or Descending to specify whether the information is sorted in A-Z (lowest-to-highest) order or Z-A (highest-to-lowest) order. For example, by default the Budget Report lists the most costly tasks first, but you might want to see the least expensive items first. To sort by other fields, as well, use the additional drop-down lists provided on this tab.

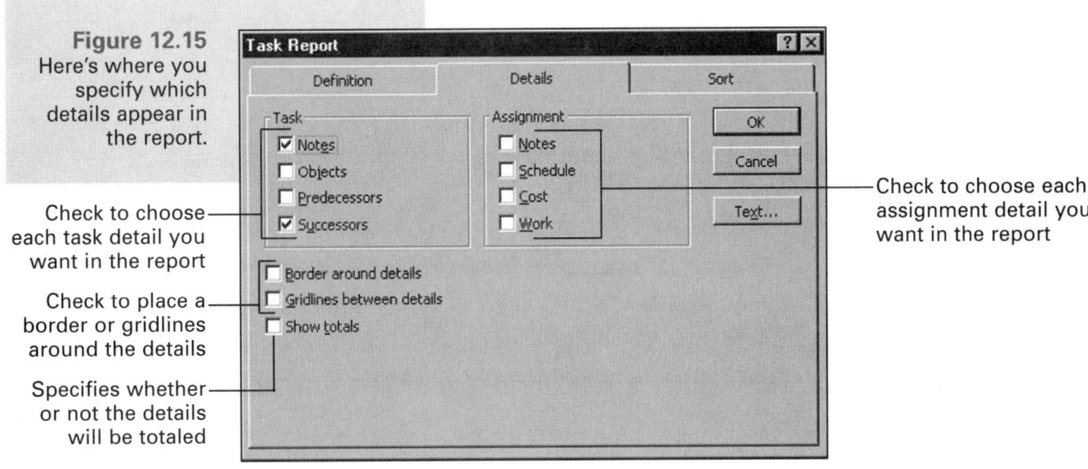

Figure 12.15 Here's where you specify which details appear in the report.

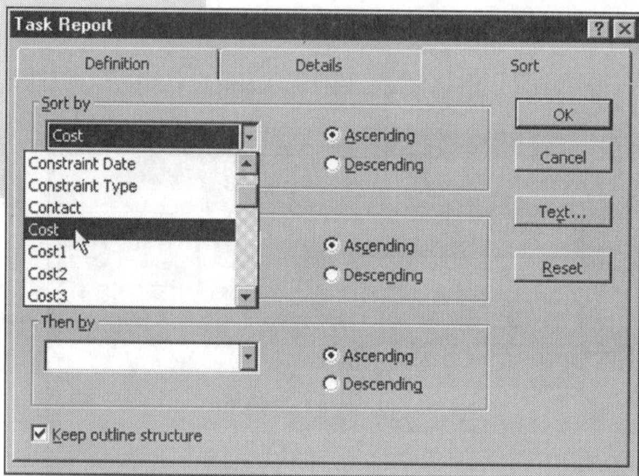

Figure 12.16 The final touch in organizing your report information is to sort it.

To specify that there's no field to sort by for one of the drop-down lists in the Sort tab, select the blank line at the top of the drop-down list.

Resource Reports

A *resource report* provides information about resources, and generally includes the word "resource" or "who" in the report name. For example, the "Overallocated Resources" and "Who Does What" reports are examples of resource reports. When you select a resource report from the Reports list in the Custom Reports dialog box and then click the Edit button, the Resource Report dialog box appears. This dialog box offers three tabs that look and work exactly like the tabs for the Task Report dialog box (refer to Figures 12.14 through 12.16).

You can edit a resource report so that it shows resource cost rate tables, and then print that report. To do so, click the Resource choice in the Reports list of the Custom Reports dialog box, and then click Edit. Click the Details tab to select it; then click the Cost Rates check box to select it. Click OK, and then click the Preview button in the Custom Reports dialog box to display the edited report onscreen.

Crosstab Reports

A *crosstab report* is the last type of custom report you might want to customize. These reports summarize information in a grid of rows and columns and include reports like Cash Flow. When you select a crosstab report from the Reports list in the Custom Reports dialog box and then click the Edit button, the Crosstab Report dialog box appears (see Figure 12.17). You'll notice that the first tab here differs from that for the two previous report types. Use the Row drop-down list to specify whether the rows contain task or resource information. In the Column area, type an entry for how many units of time to display, and then (if needed) change the time unit type to something like Months using the drop-down list beside your entry. These choices determine how many columns appear in the crosstab (for example, **4 weeks** or **2 months**). Then, in the drop-down list below your time selections, select what kind of information about the task or resource to display in each column below the date.

The Details tab also offers a couple of unique choices for crosstab reports. On this tab, click to select the Show Zero Values check box if you want to have zeros displayed rather than blank cells. Make sure that the Repeat First Column on Every_ Page option is selected if you want to repeat the names of the listed tasks or resources on every report page for easier reference. Finally, use the Date Format drop-down list to control the appearance of any dates listed for your crosstab report.

The Sort tab for crosstab reports works just like the Sort tab for the Task Report dialog box (refer to Figure 12.16).

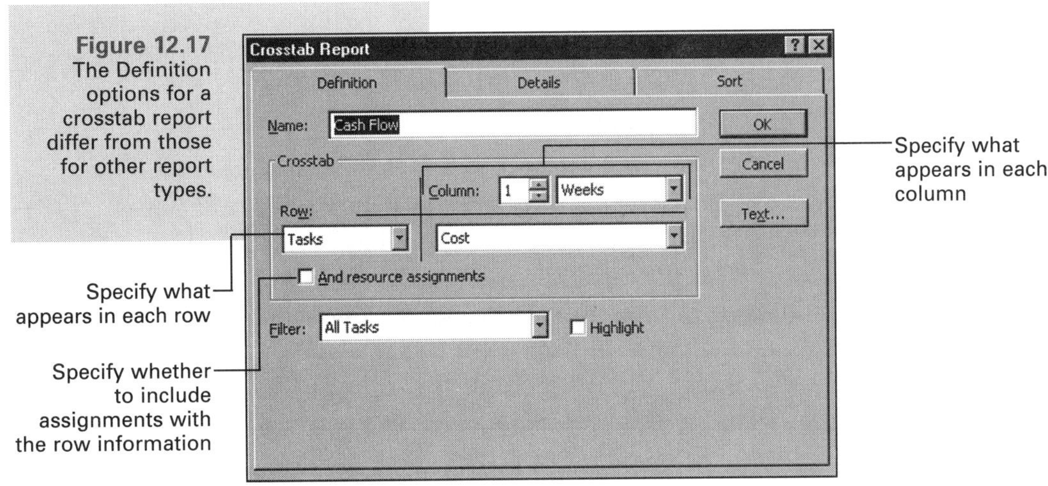

Figure 12.17 The Definition options for a crosstab report differ from those for other report types.

Creating a Report Based on an Existing Report

If you want to leave an existing report intact but create a new report based on it, follow these steps:

1. Display the Custom Reports dialog box.
2. In the Reports list, click to select the name of the report that you want to use as the basis for your custom report.
3. Click the Copy button. Depending on the type of report you selected, the appropriate Report dialog box (such as the Task Report dialog box) appears.
4. In the Name text box of the Report dialog box, Project shows "Copy of" plus the name of the report you selected in step 2. Be sure to edit this name to ensure that your custom report has a name you'll recognize. For example, you might edit it to read **Monthly Budget Report** if that's the kind of report you're creating.
5. Make any changes you desire to the various options in the three tabs of the Report dialog box, as well as any font changes using the Text button.
6. Click OK. Your custom report appears, with the name you gave it, in the Reports list of the Custom Reports dialog box (see Figure 12.18).

Saving a Unique Report

If you ever want to define a new report completely from scratch, to avoid the possibility of making an unwanted change to one of your existing reports, you can do so by clicking the New button in the Custom Reports dialog box. The Define New Report dialog box appears (see Figure 12.19).

Note

Custom reports that you create are saved with the current project file, until you either copy them to Project's GLOBAL.MPT master file or delete them. To make a report available to all files or to delete a report, click the Organizer button in the Custom Reports dialog box, and then use the Reports tab to make your changes. Chapter 9, "Working with the Different Project Views," discusses working with the Organizer.

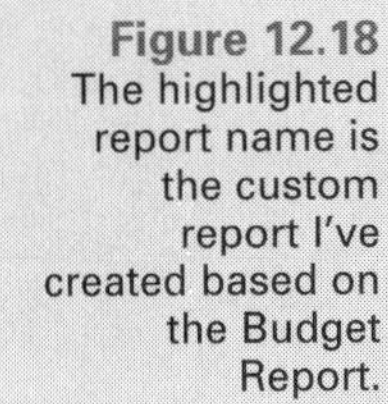

Figure 12.18 The highlighted report name is the custom report I've created based on the Budget Report.

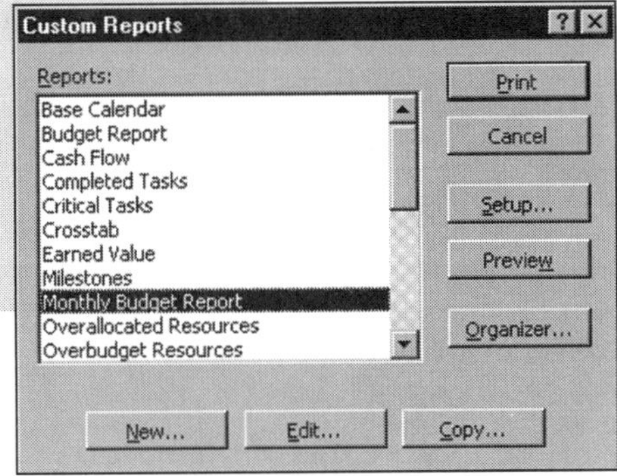

Figure 12.19 This dialog box enables you to build a report from scratch.

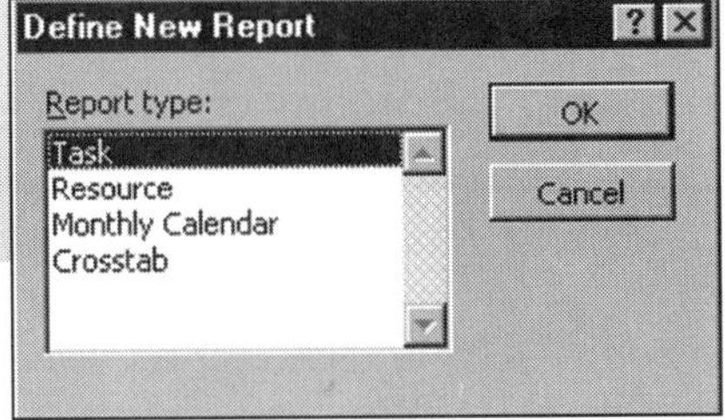

In the Report Type list, select the type of report you want to create, and then click OK. If you select Task, Resource, or Crosstab, Project displays the Task Report, Resource Report, or Crosstab Report dialog box, respectively. You work in any of these dialog boxes (refer to Figures 12.14 through 12.16) just as described earlier in this chapter when you learned how to edit different types of reports. Make sure to edit the report Name on the Definition tab (it starts out as "Report 1," "Report 2," or another sequentially numbered name) to make it more descriptive. Select any other options you want on the applicable tabs, and then click OK. Your report appears in the Reports list of the Custom Reports dialog box.

If you click the Monthly Calendar choice on the Define New Report dialog box, Project displays the Monthly Calendar Report Definition dialog box, as shown in Figure 12.20. Most of the options in this dialog box work just like options you've seen on various tabs of the Report dialog boxes. Some options, however, are unique to calendar formats.

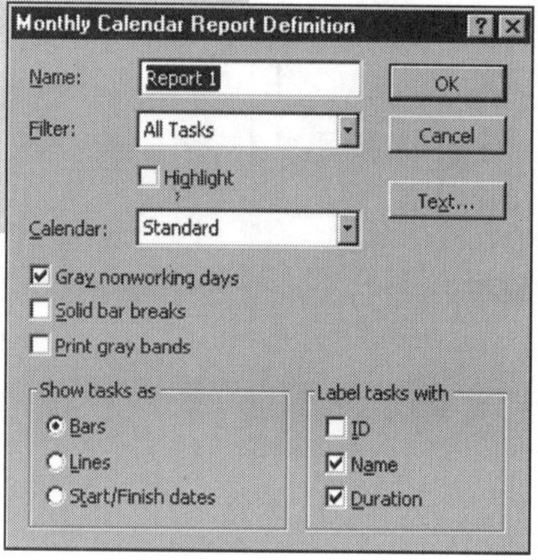

Figure 12.20 This dialog box offers some options particular to calendar reports.

For example, use the Calendar drop-down list to specify whether the calendar is based on one of the default schedule base calendars (Standard, Night Shift, or 24 Hours), or the calendar for a particular resource. Use the Solid Bar Breaks and Show Tasks As options to specify whether or not to gray out non-working days, and to control how the bars representing tasks appear on the report. Finally, use the Label Tasks With check boxes to specify whether each task is identified with its ID number, task Name, or task Duration (or any combination of these pieces of information). When you finish setting all these options, click OK to close the Monthly Calendar Report Definition dialog box and add your new calendar report to the Reports list of the Custom Reports dialog box.

13

Working with Outlining

In This Chapter

- Promoting and demoting tasks
- Controlling the outline display
- Using summary tasks

At one time many artists and writers used a particular style or method called stream of consciousness, which basically meant that the creator would sit down and just let the brushstrokes or words come out, leading where they would. The artist or writer made no effort to impose any type of structure on his or her output.

We humans, by nature, tend to prefer a more orderly approach to work of any kind—especially in the business world, where the most effective professionals excel at spelling out expectations and providing clear direction for what others need to do.

To help you become more orderly as you build your list of tasks, Project provides outlining capabilities. This chapter helps you learn how to outline.

What Outlining Does for You

Different project leaders definitely have different styles. Some fancy themselves "big picture thinkers" and like to sketch out overall plans first; such a leader might even hand a project off to someone else charged with "figuring out the details." Other leaders treat project tasks as a puzzle, first laying out all the pieces, then grouping together pieces for the edge, the sky, the grass, and so on before proceeding to put the puzzle together. No matter which approach best describes you, you'll find that Project's outlining features can accommodate you.

If you prefer to build a schedule using a top-down approach where you identify and arrange major, general tasks before filling in the details, you can enter those major categories and then break them down into more specific action items. Conversely, if you like to simply do a brain dump and list every possible task (the bottom-up approach), you can later group your list into logical areas.

When you use outlining in Project, the major tasks within your Task Sheet are called summary tasks, because they summarize a series of actions in a given timeframe. Each of the tasks that's part of the work required to complete a summary task is called a subtask. Because Project allows for thousands of outline levels (65,000 if your system has enough resources to handle it). Keep in mind that you can have summary tasks within summary tasks.

Project uses special formatting to help you identify summary tasks and subtasks onscreen, as shown in Figure 13.1. Summary tasks usually appear in bold text in the Task Sheet, and use a special summary Gantt bar. By default, an outlining symbol appears beside each summary task. (You can turn these symbols off as described later in this chapter under "Hiding and Showing Outlining Symbols." Subtasks are indented in the Task Name column of the Task Sheet; if a task is a summary task of a summary task, it's indented twice.

Summarizing work in this way not only gives you an idea of where major milestones in your project will occur, but also can help you make resource assignment decisions. For example, you may examine a particular summary task and

its subtasks, and decide to farm the whole mess out to a contractor who can provide multiple people to complete and add continuity to the summary task. Or, you may see that the start and finish dates for two summary tasks are about the same and realize that those tasks are creating a "crunch period" in your schedule, during which you'll need as many resources as possible, or to authorize overtime hours.

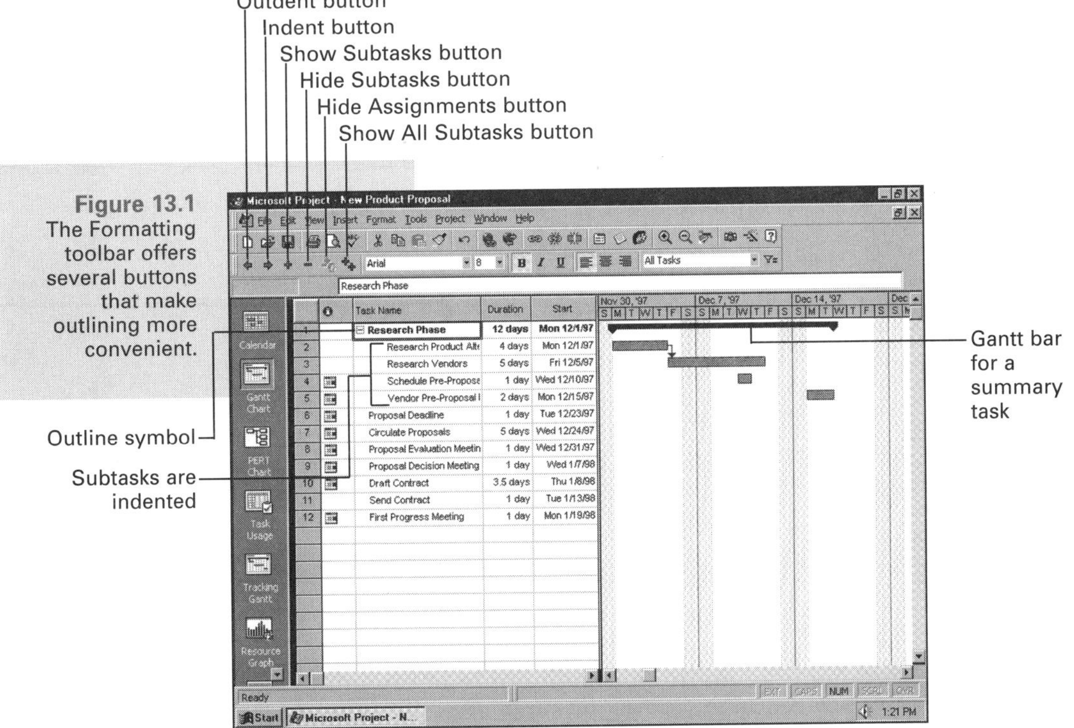

Figure 13.1 The Formatting toolbar offers several buttons that make outlining more convenient.

Outlining isn't a difficult technique, but most users need to learn about basic task and resource entry before bothering with Project outlining. So, I'm covering this technique later in the book, and using a different example file to illustrate. Keep in mind that you use the outlining techniques you'll learn about in this chapter with your existing schedule files. Just add in summary tasks as needed.

Microsoft Word 97 and Excel 97 also provide outlining features. Unfortunately, however, if you copy outlined information from Word or Excel and paste it into Project, Project does not recognize the outline levels you assigned in Word or Excel. You still save the time and effort of retyping the information.

You apply outlining in the Task Sheet for your schedule, from any view that includes the Task Sheet. The fastest way to work with outlining is to use the outlining tools on Project's Formatting toolbar. The Formatting toolbar appears onscreen by default, but if you need to display it, right-click any toolbar and then click Formatting. Refer to Figure 13.1 to identify the outlining tools.

Promoting and Demoting Tasks in the Outline

Whether you're using outlining for a list of existing tasks or using the outlining tools to organize a list of tasks that you're building, the process is generally the same. You select the Task Name cell (or entire row) of the task for which you want to define an outline level, then outdent (or promote) it to a higher level, or indent (or demote) it to a lower level.

To promote the selected task, use one of the following methods:

- Click the Outdent button on the Formatting toolbar.
- Open the Project menu, point to Outline, and click Outdent.
- If the task is a subtask and is not on the top level of the outline, select the entire task by clicking its row heading (row number). Then right-click the row, and click Outdent on the shortcut menu that appears.
- If the task is not on the top outline level, point to the first letter of the task name until you see the double-arrow pointer. Press and hold the mouse button, and drag to the left to move the task up a level, as shown in Figure 13.2. A vertical gray line appears to indicate the outline level to which the task is being promoted.

If a task is already at the top level of the outline, meaning that it does not appear indented in the Task Name column (keep in mind that there is some space to the left of task names by default), Project will not let you promote it.

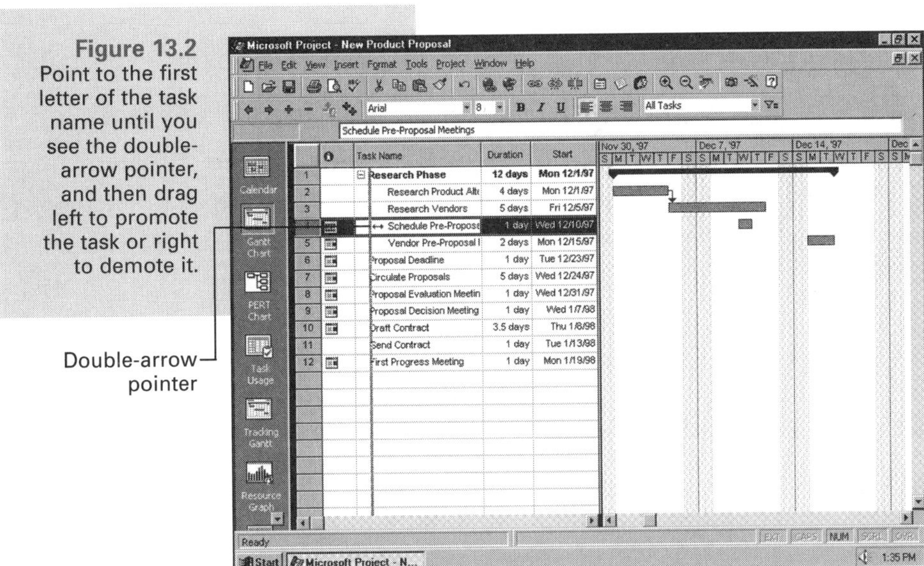

Figure 13.2 Point to the first letter of the task name until you see the double-arrow pointer, and then drag left to promote the task or right to demote it.

If the Planning Wizard is active when you attempt to promote such a task, Planning Wizard appears onscreen to inform you that the task can't be promoted (see Figure 13.3). Simply click OK to close the Planning Wizard dialog box. Project returns you to your Task Sheet without making any changes. When you promote a task, the tasks listed below it that were previously on the same level become subtasks of the promoted task, and the promoted task is reformatted accordingly.

To demote a selected task by one level (to the next lowest level), you have similar choices:

- Click the Indent button on the Formatting toolbar.
- Open the Project menu, point to Outline, and click Indent.
- Select the entire task by clicking its row heading (row number). Then right-click the row, and click Indent on the shortcut menu that appears.
- Point to the first letter of the task name until you see the double-arrow pointer, press and hold the mouse button, and drag to the right to move the task down a level. A vertical gray line appears to indicate the outline level to which the task is being demoted.

The demoted task is automatically formatted as a subtask, and the task above it is formatted as a summary task. Just as Project prevents you from promoting a task that's already at the top level of your outline, it prevents you from demoting a task if doing so would skip a level in the outline and result in some task ending up two outline levels below the task above it.

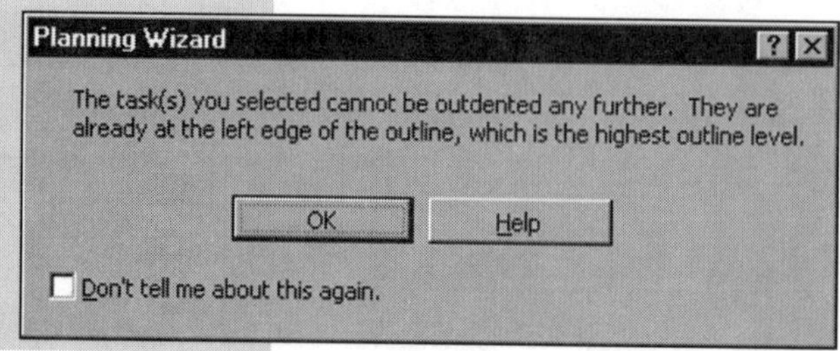

Figure 13.3 If you try to promote a task that is already at the top level, Planning Wizard tells you that it can't make the change.

You can select multiple tasks that are on the same outline level and demote them simultaneously. To do so, drag across the row numbers to select the group of tasks; then click the Indent button on the Formatting toolbar.

If you promote or demote a summary task, Project promotes or demotes its subtasks, as well.

Inserting a Summary Task

If you're using a bottom-up approach to building your schedule, you may have a list of tasks, into which you want to insert summary tasks. It would be nice if Project simply allowed you to simultaneously demote all the tasks you typed in and then insert higher-level tasks, but it doesn't work that way. Instead, follow this multistep process:

1. Insert a blank row above the tasks you want to summarize. To do so, right-click the row heading (row number) for the top task in the group you want to summarize; then click New Task in the shortcut menu.
2. Enter the Task Name for the new task. You don't have to specify any other task details, such as Duration. Project makes those entries for you when you define the subtasks for the summary task.
3. Drag over the row headings for the tasks you want to convert to summary tasks (to select those rows). Then click the Indent button on the Formatting toolbar. Alternately, you can open the Project menu, point to Outline, and click Indent, or right-click the selected tasks, and

then click Indent on the shortcut menu (see Figure 13.4). Figure 13.5 shows how the tasks in Figure 13.4 look when the indent operation is completed. A summary bar has been added in the Gantt chart for the newly designated summary task in row 6.

If the task above the inserted row is a subtask, you need to promote the inserted task before going on to step 3. Simply leave the Task Name cell for the new task selected, and click the Outdent button on the Formatting toolbar.

Inserting Subtasks

To insert a subtask, you need to insert a new row for it in the Task Sheet. As you learned in the preceding section, when you insert a new row into a Task Sheet, the task in that row adopts the outline level of the task above it. Therefore, one of two situations might develop:

- If the task above the inserted row is at a summary level, you need to enter the Task Name, and then demote the task in the newly inserted row.
- If the task above the inserted row is at the correct subtask level, just enter the Task Name. Notice that if you insert a new task row within a group of several subtasks, Project does not demote the tasks in rows

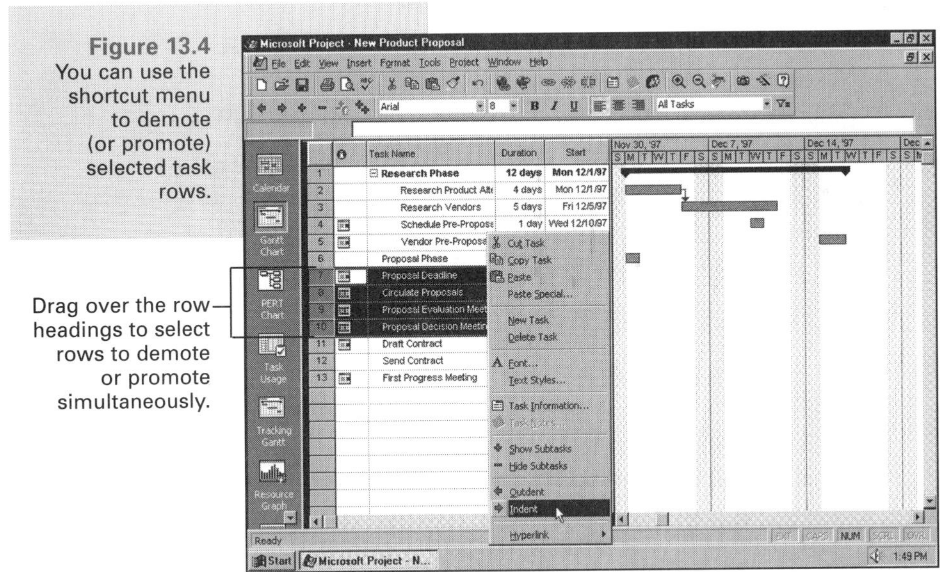

Figure 13.4 You can use the shortcut menu to demote (or promote) selected task rows.

below the newly inserted row to a lower outline level. Instead, Project assumes that all tasks in the group should remain at the same level until you tell it otherwise.

Similarly, when you're entering brand new tasks into blank rows at the bottom of the Task Sheet, Project assumes that each newly entered task should adopt the outline level of the task above it. For example, if I type a new Task Name into row 17 of the Task Sheet shown in Figure 13.6, Project assumes it to be a subtask of the row 14 summary task, just like the subtasks in rows 15 and 16.

Adjusting Subtask Scheduling and Moving Subtasks

If you experiment at all with outlining, you might notice that the summary task duration and summary task bar on the Gantt chart adjust to encompass the earliest task start date for any subtask of the summary task, and the latest task finish date for any subtask. For that reason, I think it's a little easier to create your entire list of tasks, apply the outlining you prefer, and then adjust the scheduling information as needed for all subtasks. If you enter dates for a task, convert it to a summary task, and then later demote it to be a subtask, you lose the original duration information you entered for the task.

You can change the schedule for a subtask by using any of the methods for rescheduling tasks that were described in Chapter 3, "Fine-Tuning Tasks." The

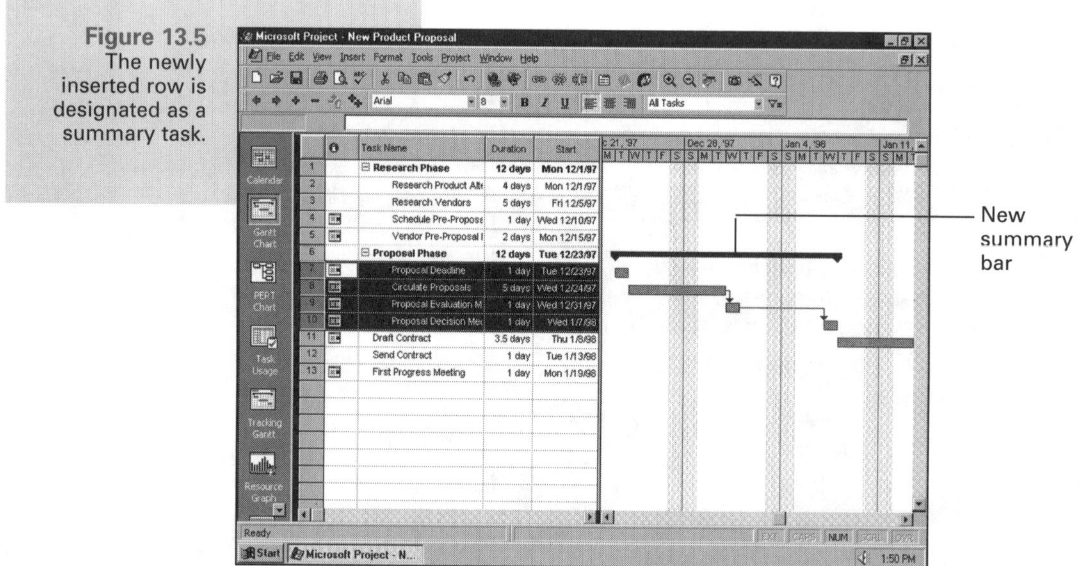

Figure 13.5 The newly inserted row is designated as a summary task.

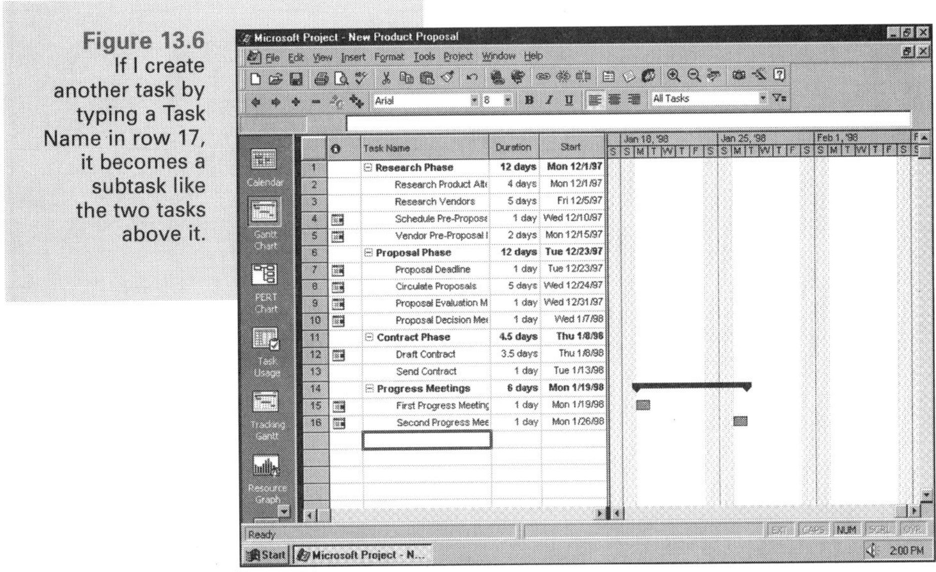

Figure 13.6 If I create another task by typing a Task Name in row 17, it becomes a subtask like the two tasks above it.

Duration, Start date, Finish date, and Gantt chart summary bar for the summary task all adjust automatically to reflect the change. Figures 13.7 and 13.8 show an example of how dragging to lengthen a subtask changes the summary task.

No creative process is perfect, and you might find that you incorrectly positioned several tasks, including a summary task and its subtasks, in the outline.

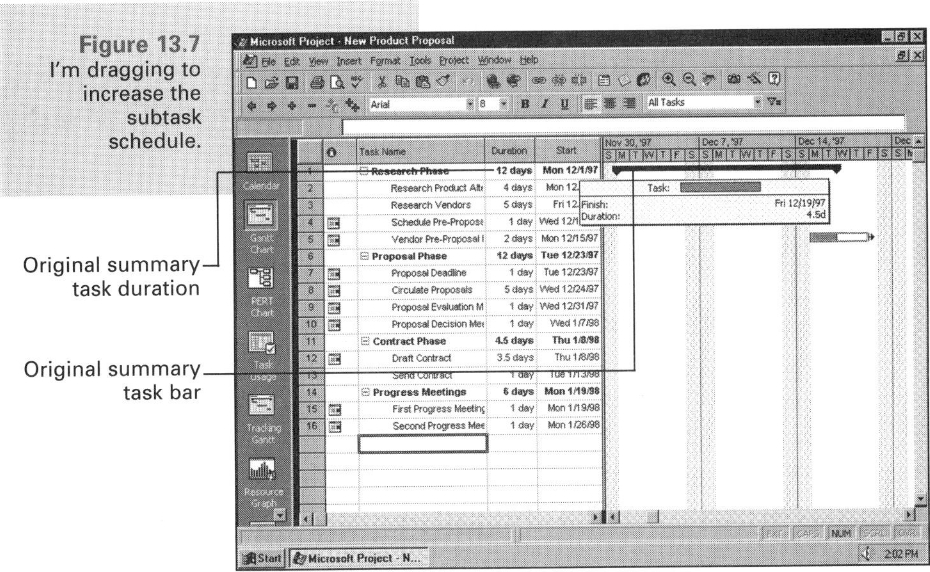

Figure 13.7 I'm dragging to increase the subtask schedule.

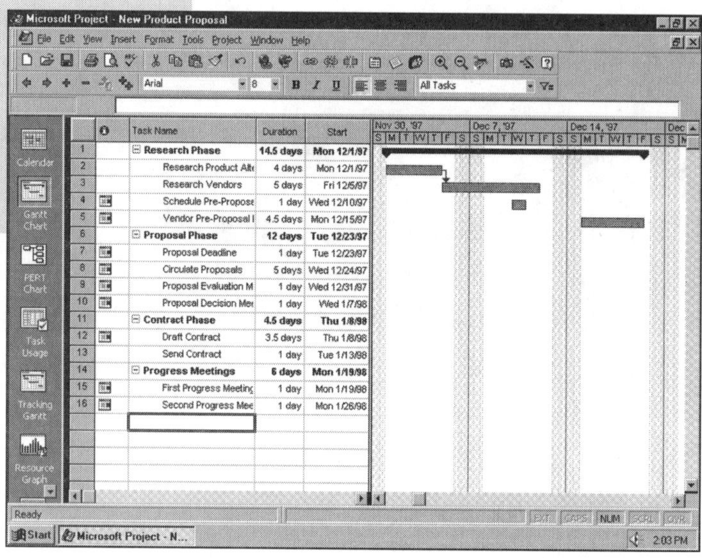

Figure 13.8 After I've rescheduled the subtask, notice that the summary task duration has changed.

Note

You can display the Task Information dialog box for a summary task. When this dialog box appears, it won't let you edit certain information, such as the summary task Duration. Don't assume that all the information you can enter for the summary task also applies to all subtasks of the summary task; it doesn't. For example, if you assign a resource to the summary task, such as a supervisor who'll manage all the resources handling the subtasks, that resource does not appear as a resource for each subtask. It's only a resource for the summary task.

When this is the case, you can move the tasks as usual, by dragging task rows. To move a row, click its row heading (row number). Point to a row border, and then press and hold the mouse button while you drag the row to its new location, dropping the row into place whenever the gray insertion bar reaches the location you want. There are, however, a couple of points to remember when dragging outlined tasks:

- **Subtasks travel with their summary task**—Therefore, if you drag a summary task to a new location in the task list, when you drop it into place, its subtasks appear below it.

- **Dragging tasks around can disturb links**—If you insert a group of subtasks linked by a series of Finish-to-Start links within tasks already linked by Finish-to-Start links, the results are unpredictable. This is yet another argument for nailing down your outline as much as possible before progressing too far with information about scheduling, resources, or links.

You can link a summary task to other tasks in many instances, by simply dragging between bars in the Gantt chart. The only restriction is that you cannot link a summary task to one of its subtasks.

- **A moved task adopts the outline level of the task above it**—When you move a task, Project assumes that you want the task to be on the same outline level as the task above it in its new location. If you move a summary task (and thus its subtasks) to a location that demotes the summary task, click the Outdent button on the Formatting toolbar to return the group of tasks to the proper outline level before proceeding. Project even demotes or promotes a moved task more than one level, if needed. For example, if you move a task to a Task Sheet row directly below a task that's two outline levels lower, Project demotes the moved task (and any subtasks that travel with it) two levels.

Work Breakdown Structure Information

The *work breakdown structure (WBS)* for a list of tasks is simply a method of hierarchically numbering tasks in a traditional outline numbering format. WBS numbers are also called outline numbers. Tasks at the top outline level are numbered sequentially. For example, the WBSs for the first 10 top-level outline tasks are numbered 1 through 10. Subtasks on the first level use the top-level number for their summary task plus a decimal value; for example, the first three subtasks of summary task 2 are numbered 2.1, 2.2, and 2.3. For the next outline level down, Project adds another decimal; for example, the first two subtasks under task 2.1 are numbered 2.1.1 and 2.1.2.

When you use outlining, Project assigns the WBS numbers automatically behind the scenes. As you move, promote, and demote tasks, Project updates the WBS numbers accordingly. Your company might follow a specific set of WBS numbers that you need to follow. If you need to assign a WBS to a task that's different from the WBS that Project assigns, click the task. Then click the Task Information button on the Standard toolbar (or right-click on the task, and then click Task Information on the shortcut menu). In the Task Information dialog box, click the Advanced tab. Double-click the entry in the WBS Code text box, and type the new entry you want, as shown in Figure 13.9. Click OK when you finish editing the entry.

You can add a field (column) to the Task Sheet to display WBS numbers, or can even sort by WBS numbers, if you want. You also can display WBS numbers along with the task name in the Task Sheet. To do so, open the Tools menu and click Options. On the View tab of the Options dialog box, click to place a check beside the Show Outline Number option and click OK. The assigned outline number appears to the left of each task name, as shown in Figure 13.10.

Note

If you copy the Task Name column into Word 97 as unformatted text (see Chapter 19, "Using Project with Other Applications,") the WBS numbers are not copied with the Task Name entries, even if the WBS numbers were displayed in Project. If you need to include accurate WBS numbers in documents in other applications, insert a WBS column into the Task Sheet by right-clicking a column heading, and then clicking Insert Column on the shortcut menu. In the Column Definition dialog box, select WBS as the Field Name, and then click OK. Then, make sure you also copy or export the WBS column information to Word.

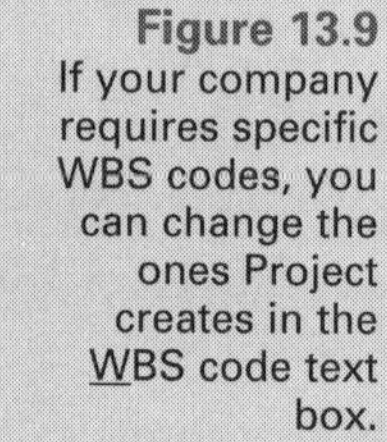

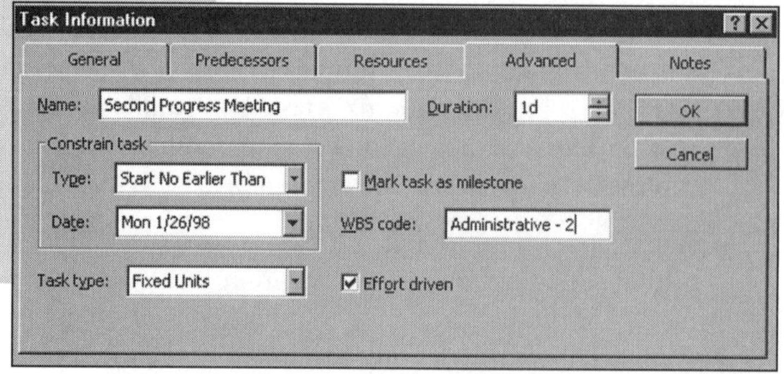

Figure 13.9 If your company requires specific WBS codes, you can change the ones Project creates in the WBS code text box.

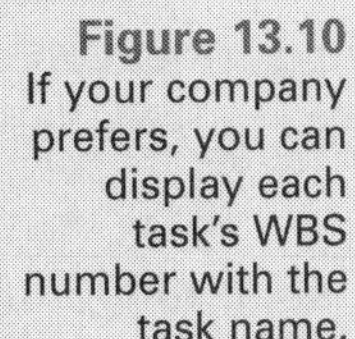

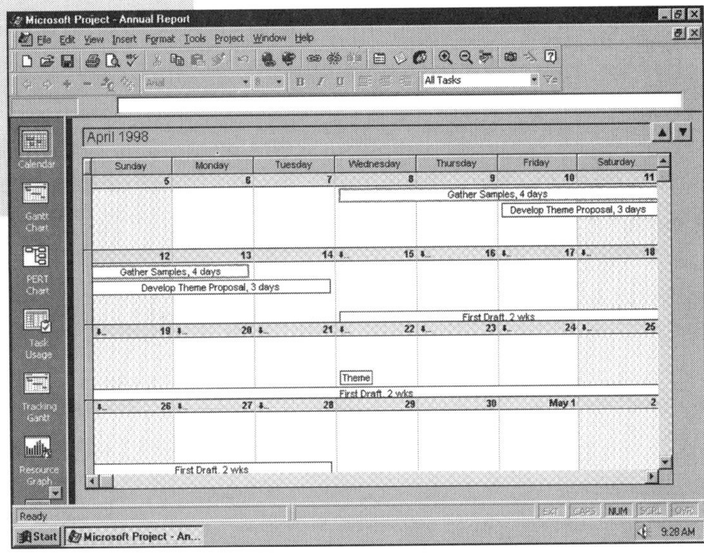

Figure 13.10 If your company prefers, you can display each task's WBS number with the task name.

Other aspects of how the outlined information appears are controlled on the View tab of the Options dialog box. For more information about setting Project options, see Chapter 20, "Customizing Microsoft Project."

Controlling the Outline Display

As when you're outlining in a word processing application or spreadsheet program, one of the advantages of outlining in Project is that outlining enables Project to give you visual cues about how you structured your outline. This can help you to make intelligent decisions about scheduling changes and resource assignments. This section explains how you can work with the outlining display features.

Hiding and Showing Outlining Symbols

Outlining symbols help you differentiate summary tasks from subtasks. Any task that has subtasks below it is considered a summary task, and is indicated with an outlining symbol to the left of the Task Name. When the summary task has a plus (+) outlining symbol beside it, its subtasks are hidden. When the subtasks for a summary task are displayed, the summary task has a minus

(–) outlining symbol beside it. If a task is as a summary task level (most often the top level of the outline) but has no subtasks, no outlining symbol appears beside it. By default, outlining symbols appear for all tasks in the Task Sheet, at the left of the task names.

To hide outlining symbols, click to open the Project menu, point to Outline, and then click Hide Outline Symbols. To redisplay the outlining symbols, click to open the Project menu, point to Outline, and then click Show Outline Symbols.

You can add a Show/Hide Outline Symbols button to any toolbar for your convenience. Chapter 21 explains how to customize toolbars. The Show/Hide Outline Symbols button is found on the Commands tab of the Customize dialog box; click Outline in the Categories list on the tab to display that button in the Commands list.

In Chapter 3, "Fine-Tuning Tasks," you learned how to create a recurring task, which behaves somewhat like a summary task. When you display outline symbols, they appear on a recurring task (and each of its subtasks) just as they do on real summary and subtasks. However, the Gantt chart bars for a recurring task never look like the Gantt chart bar for a summary task created via outlining.

Specifying Which Outline Levels Appear

Summary tasks wouldn't provide much of a summary if you could never view them without their subtasks. Consequently, Project enables you to hide subtasks from view for your convenience. There are a couple of reasons why you might want to hide some or all subtasks in your schedule. First, you might want to print the schedule and have the printout only include summary tasks, not the details shown in subtasks. Second, if you have a lengthy list of tasks in your project, you might find it easier to move up and down through the Task Sheet if you hide subtasks until you need to view or work with the information for a particular subtask.

The fastest way to hide and display subtasks for a summary task is to use the summary task's outlining symbol. Click the minus (-) outlining symbol beside a summary task to hide its subtasks or the plus (+) outlining symbol beside a summary task to redisplay its subtasks.

When you hide and redisplay subtasks using other commands, you do so for a single summary task by selecting that summary task first.

Then, to hide subtasks, click the Hide Subtasks button on the Formatting toolbar. Alternately, open the Project menu, point to Outline, and click Hide Subtasks. Figure 13.11 shows a Task Sheet with the subtasks for one summary task hidden. Notice that not only the subtask rows but also the corresponding Gantt bars are hidden, leaving only the summary task bar on the Gantt chart.

To redisplay subtasks for selected summary task(s), click the Show Subtasks button on the Formatting toolbar. Alternatively, open the Project menu, point to Outline, and click Show Subtasks.

If you want to redisplay all subtasks without taking the time to select particular summary tasks, click on the Show All Subtasks button on the Formatting Toolbar or choose Show All Subtasks from the Outline submenu of the Project menu. Alternately, first select the whole Task Sheet by clicking the Select All button in the upper-left corner, or select the whole Task Name column by clicking that column heading. Then use the Show Subtasks or Hide Subtasks button on the Formatting toolbar as needed.

You can right-click a summary task's row heading, and then choose Show Subtasks or Hide Subtasks from the shortcut menu as needed.

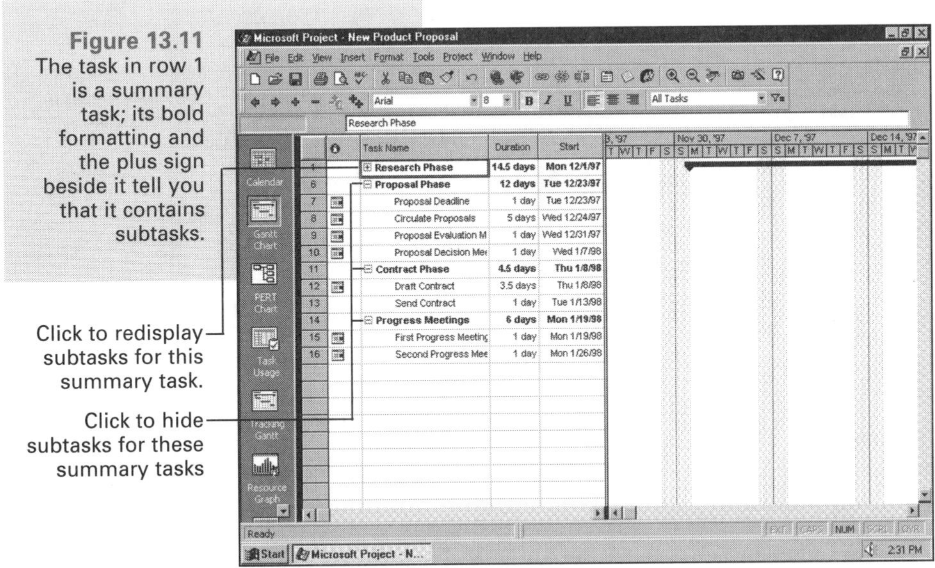

Figure 13.11 The task in row 1 is a summary task; its bold formatting and the plus sign beside it tell you that it contains subtasks.

Rolling Up Subtasks

If you have a long list of subtasks within a summary task, you might lose track of how a particular task compares to the summary schedule. Or, you might have a particular task near the middle of the summary task range that you want to highlight by having it appear on the summary bar as well as its usual location. To achieve this effect, you roll up the subtask to its summary task.

Click the row heading to select the summary task to roll up, and then press and hold Ctrl while you click to select the row heading for the subtask to roll up. Click the Task Information button to display the Task Information dialog box. On the General tab of this dialog box, click twice to place a check beside the Roll Up Gantt Bar to Summary option; then click OK. The subtask bar is then displayed on the summary bar, as shown in Figure 13.12. To remove the effects of a roll up, select the summary task and subtask, redisplay the Task Information dialog box, and clear the Roll Up Gantt Bar to Summary check box.

Do not select the Hide Task Bar check box in the General tab of the Task Information dialog box when you're rolling up tasks. If you do so, you won't be able to see the rolled up task or any text that accompanies it.

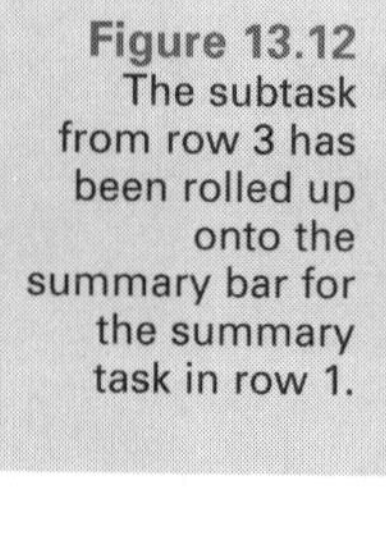

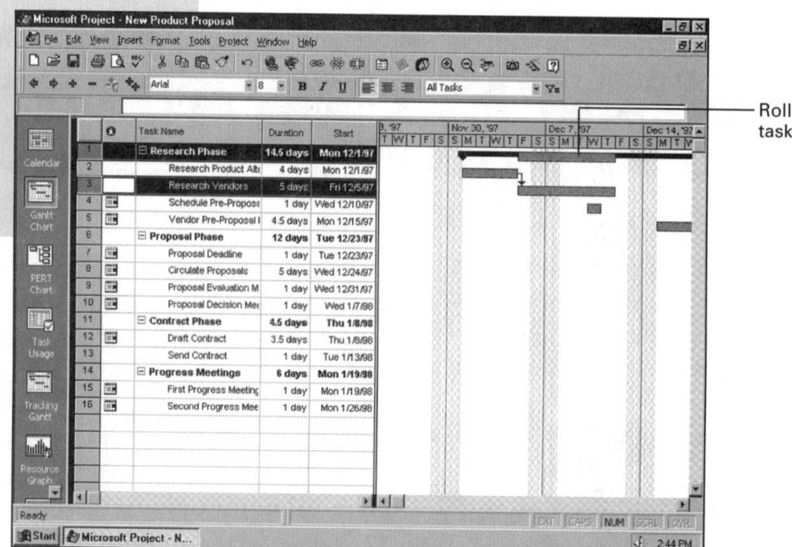

Figure 13.12 The subtask from row 3 has been rolled up onto the summary bar for the summary task in row 1.

If you want to roll up a summary task and several of its subtasks simultaneously, drag over the row numbers to select the rows. Display the Task Information dialog box, select the Roll Up Gantt Bar to Summary check box, and click OK.

You can reformat the bars for summary tasks so that they display dates or have a different appearance that makes them stand out more when rolled up. For example, you can make the Gantt bar for a particular subtask red so that it stands out when rolled up. To learn how to reformat a Gantt bar, see Chapter 14, "Other Formatting."

Using Summary Tasks to Reduce the Critical Path

As you learned in Chapter 6, "Optimizing the Schedule," the critical path for your schedule identifies tasks that can't slip without causing the overall project finish date to move. When you finish setting up all your schedule information, you might find that the schedule is longer than you want it to be. If that's the case, working with your summary tasks (perhaps hiding subtasks in the process) can help you to identify critical tasks. Here are a few ideas about how you can use summary task information to identify ways to condense the critical path:

- Look for ways to remove slack time between summary tasks.
- If none of your summary tasks overlap in timing, check to see if you can move up the schedules for some later summary tasks, so that some summary groups run concurrently.
- Create a Gantt bar style for bars that indicate both summary and critical path information. See Chapter 14, "Other Formatting," for more details about bar styles.

14

Other Formatting

In This Chapter

- Changing the appearance of selected text in a Task Sheet or Resource Sheet
- Working with a single chart bar or box
- Controlling progress lines and gridlines that appear on a chart
- Adjusting the appearance of a particular style of sheet text or a particular style of chart bar or box
- Controlling the display of details and choosing a layout for links
- Working with Project's drawing tools

When you're learning to use Project, the way that text and other elements look may be the farthest thing from your mind. At first, you worry about setting the schedules for your tasks, figuring out how different kinds of links work, determining how to allocate resources most effectively, and working out any kinks that unnecessarily extend your overall schedule.

After you set everything, however, you may begin to look at your schedule in a new light. You may become more interested in ensuring that your schedule not only is attractive, but also highlights key facts clearly. This chapter examines the tools that enable you to control the appearance of information in Project.

Formatting Selected Sheet Text

Fonts are different types of lettering used for text. Within Project, you can select a different font—along with a particular font size, color, and so on—for any cell, row, or column that you selected in a Task Sheet or Resource Sheet. The fonts you can choose depend on the fonts that you installed to work with Windows on your system. When you reformat selected text, the formatting changes appear both onscreen and in printouts, including the formatted text.

Font sizes are measured in *points*. Each point is 1/72 inch; 12 points equal 1/6 inch.

An easy way to apply formatting to selected text is to use the tools in the Formatting toolbar (see Figure 14.1). To display the Formatting toolbar if you've removed it from the screen, right-click any toolbar, and then click Formatting.

Note that the three alignment buttons—Align Left, Center, and Align Right—realign all cells in the sheet column, even if you have selected a single cell in the column. If you select a single row, and then click an alignment button, all columns in the sheet are realigned.

In addition to using the Formatting toolbar, you can format text by using the Font dialog box. Follow these steps:

1. Select the cell that contains the text that you want to format. Alternatively, click a column header to select the entire column, or click a row header to select an entire row.
2. Open the Format menu and click Font, or right-click and then click Font on the shortcut menu. The Font dialog box appears (see Figure 14.2).

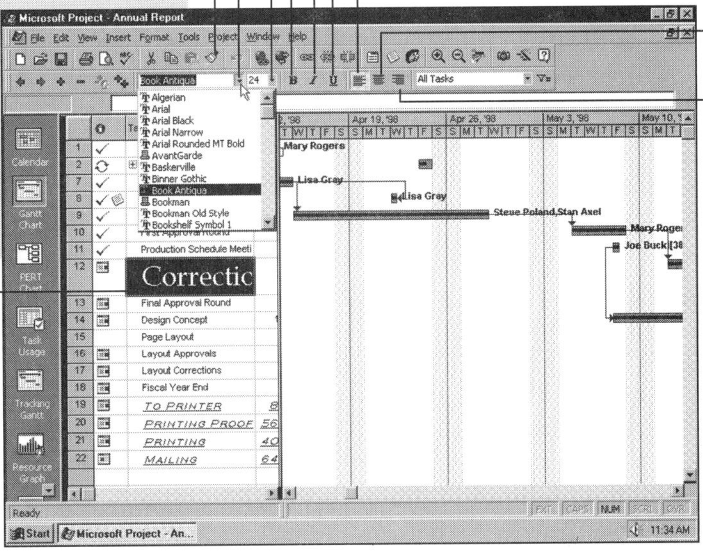

Format Painter button
Font drop-down list
Font Size drop-down list
Bold button
Italic button
Underline button
Align Left button
Center button
Align Right button
Text with a different, larger font; the row automatically becomes taller to accommodate the new size

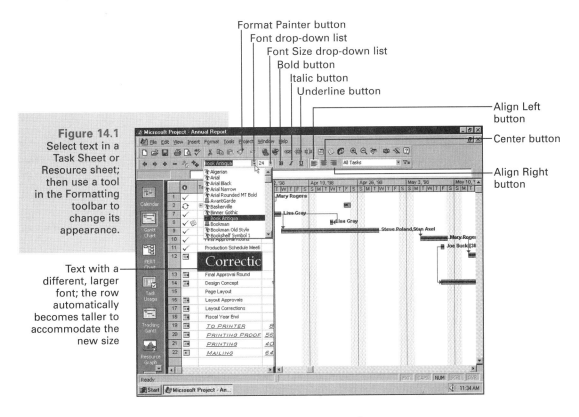

Figure 14.1 Select text in a Task Sheet or Resource sheet; then use a tool in the Formatting toolbar to change its appearance.

3. Scroll the Font list and select the font you want to use.
4. If you want to format the text with an effect such as bold or italic, select the effect from the Font Style list.
5. Scroll the Size list and select the font size you want to use, or double-click the Size text box, and type the appropriate size.

Font
Font:
Font style:
Size:
OK
Cancel
Book Antiqua
Regular
24
Bookman
Bookman Old Style
Bookshelf Symbol 1
Italic
Bold
Bold Italic
26
28
36
Underline
Color:
Black
Sample
AaBbYyZz
This is a TrueType font. This same font will be used on both your screen and your printer.
The effects of your selections appear here

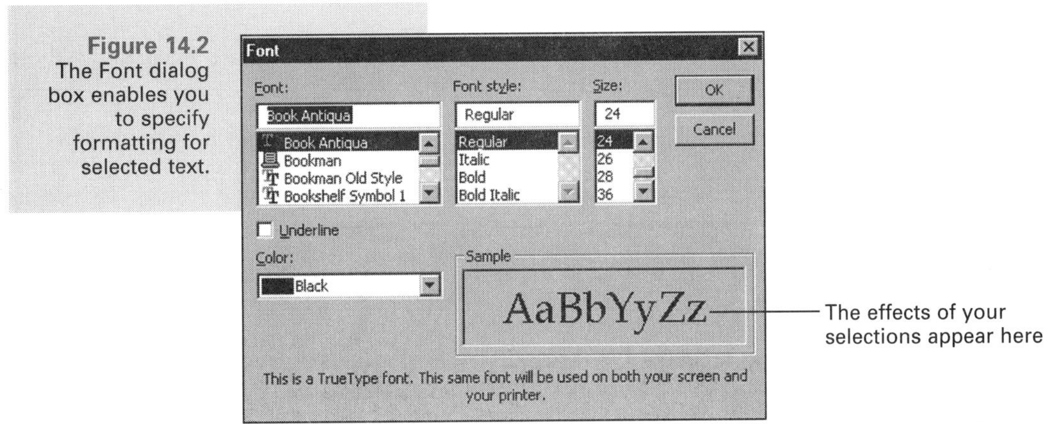

Figure 14.2 The Font dialog box enables you to specify formatting for selected text.

6. If you want to apply an underline to the selected text, click the Underline check box.
7. If you want to format the selected text with a particular color (perhaps to call more attention to it onscreen or in color printouts), select the color from the Color drop-down list.
8. Click OK to close the Font dialog box and apply your selections.

If you've added several formatting selections to some text, and you'd like to use those same settings for other cells in the sheet, you can quickly copy all the formatting selections to other cells with the Format Painter button. To do so, select the cell that holds the formatting to copy. Click the Format Painter button, and then click the cell to which you want to apply the formatting settings.

Formatting the Bar for a Selected Task

Just as you can use formatting selections to call attention to specific text in a Task Sheet or Resource Sheet, you can reformat the Gantt bars for selected tasks in your schedule. Suppose that you want to call attention to the Gantt bars for all the tasks that begin next week. You could make each of those bars yellow, so that they're brighter onscreen or in a printout. Alternately, you could include the text of a particular field of task information (such as the Actual Start date) in the Gantt chart bar.

Note

You can't reformat individual boxes in PERT Chart view or individual bars in Resource Graph view.

To adjust formatting options for one or more Gantt chart bars, follow these steps:

1. Click the Task Name cell to select the task you want to reformat, or select row headers (or adjoining cells) to select multiple rows.

If you want to skip step 1 and display the Format Bar dialog box to reformat a single Gantt bar, double-click the Gantt bar. If you've marked the task as partially completed, be sure to double-click the edge of the larger Gantt bar, not the smaller bar marking the completed work.

2. Open the Format menu and click Bar. The Format Bar dialog box appears (see Figure 14.3).
3. Click the Bar Shape tab, if needed, to display the Bar Shape options. This tab enables you to specify the appearance of the selected Gantt bar(s), including overall thickness, color, and ending shapes or symbols.
4. To add a symbol to the left end of the selected bar(s), select it from the Shape drop-down list in the Start Shape area. (If you leave this option blank, the Start Shape will be invisible.) Then use the Type drop-down list to specify the ending shape, such as Solid. Finally, to apply a color to the selected Start Shape, select that color from the Color drop-down list. Figure 14.4 shows some possible Start Shape selections.

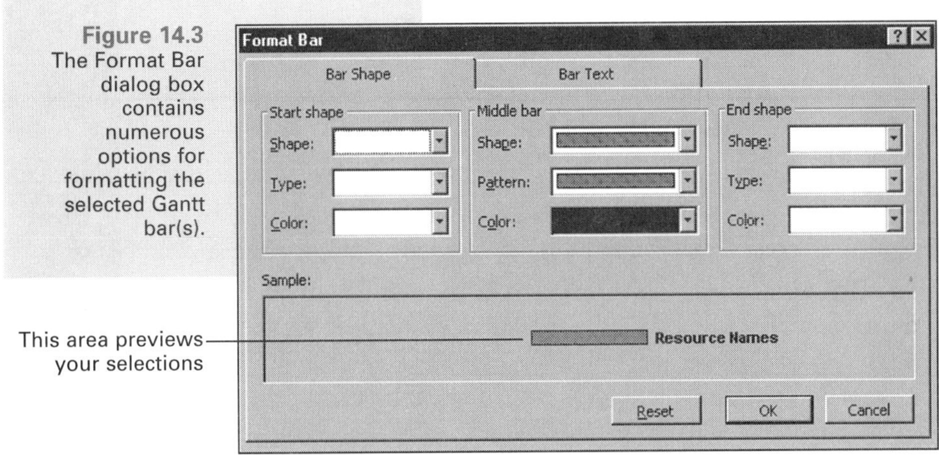

Figure 14.3 The Format Bar dialog box contains numerous options for formatting the selected Gantt bar(s).

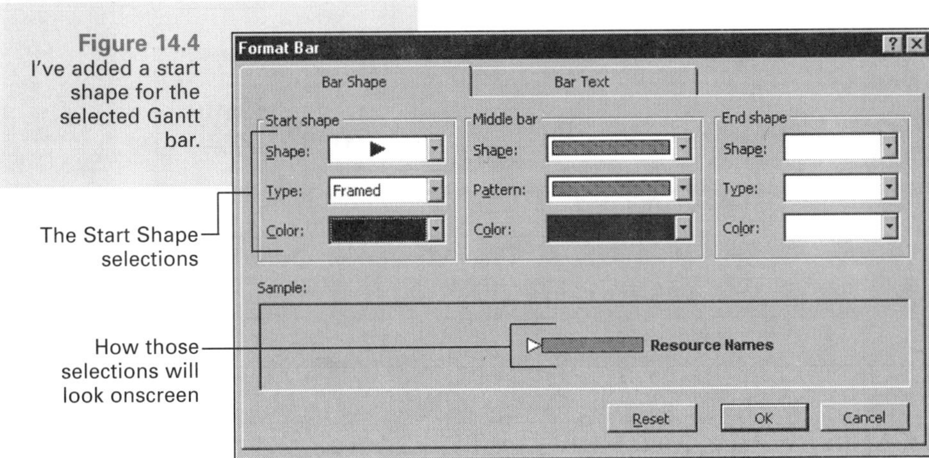

Figure 14.4 I've added a start shape for the selected Gantt bar.

5. In the End Shape area of the dialog box, use the Shape, Type, and Color drop-down lists to specify and format a shape for the right end of the selected Gantt bar(s). These options are the same as the corresponding options in the Start Shape area.

Note

The Start Shape and End Shape settings do not have to match.

6. In the Middle Bar area, specify how the center of the selected bar(s) will look. The Shape drop-down list enables you to specify how thick you want the bar to be and how you want to position it in relation to the start and end shapes—slightly up or down, or centered.
7. If the bar Shape that you specified is more than a thin line, use the Pattern drop-down list to adjust the relative density and hatching of the color used for the bar.
8. Select a Color for the bar. Figure 14.5 shows some selected bar shapes.
9. Click the Bar Text tab to display the Bar Text options. You use this tab to specify how you want to display text in relation to the selected Gantt bar(s): Left, Right, Top, Bottom, or Inside. The tab offers a separate line for each of these options; you can enter text in any of them or a combination of them. (By default, resource names are displayed to the right of each bar.)
10. To add text to appear with a particular part of the bar, click the cell beside the area name; then select the field from the drop-down list of fields (see Figure 14.6).

Figure 14.5 The final result of my bar color and shape adjustments.

If you want to remove text from a particular display area, highlight the existing field name, delete it, and then click the Enter button that appears in the upper-left corner of the tab.

11. Use the technique described in step 10 to edit any of the other text areas.
12. When you finish setting options in the Bar Shape and Bar Text tabs, click OK to close the Format Bar dialog box. (Figure 14.7 shows a sample formatted bar.)

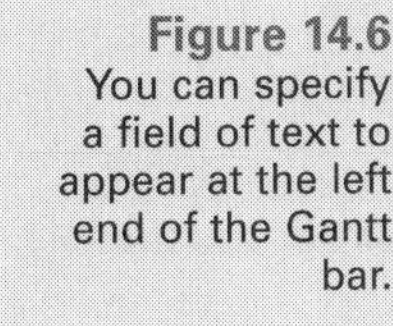

To return a Gantt bar to its default formatting, select the bar, display the Format Bar dialog box, and click the Reset button on either tab.

Formatting a Progress Line

Chapter 7, "Comparing Progress versus Your Baseline Plan," introduced a new feature in Project 98: *progress lines*. You add a progress line to a particular date on the Gantt chart to highlight in-progress tasks and provide a graphical representation of which tasks have not been completed by that date, or which are ahead of schedule. By default, the progress line for the current date or project status date, if you've displayed it, is red and has circular shapes at each point on the line. Progress lines for other dates are black and have no graphics. Because progress lines contribute to the appearance of your project, you'll want to be able to enhance them as needed for clarity and eye appeal. For example, you can change the pattern or color of a progress line.

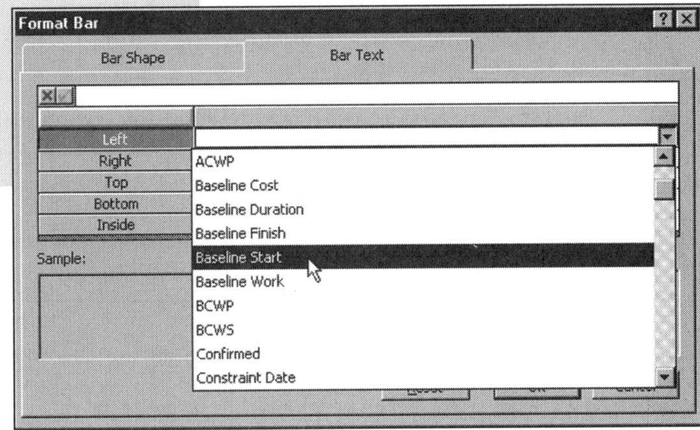

Figure 14.6 You can specify a field of text to appear at the left end of the Gantt bar.

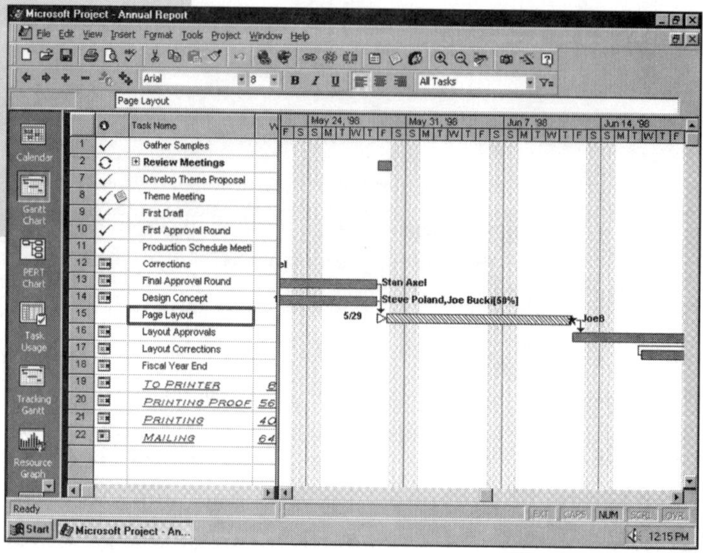

Figure 14.7 The Gantt bar for task 15 has new starting and ending markers, a patterned bar in the middle, and new labels.

Follow these steps to change the appearance of progress lines on your Gantt chart:

1. Right-click on the Gantt chart and click Progress Lines. The Progress Lines dialog box appears.
2. Click the Line Styles tab to display its options, as shown in Figure 14.8.
3. Click one of the designs shown in the Progress Line Type area to change the overall shape of the progress lines. The choices here enable you to specify whether the progress line points are sharp angles or blunted shapes. Also choose whether the progress line itself moves straight from point to point, or returns to travel along the progress line date.
4. The Line Style area offers four settings for the Current Progress Line or All Other Progress Lines (change the settings in the column that applies), some of which work like the similar settings you saw for formatting Gantt bars:
   - **Line Type**—Choose a dashed line style, or no line at all, for the actual line that travels between progress line points.
   - **Line Color**—Choose a color for the progress line.
   - **Progress Point Shape**—Choose a shape (or no shape) to appear at each progress line point.
   - **Progress Point Color**—Choose a color for the progress point shape you selected to make that shape stand out from its progress line or the Gantt bar to which it points.

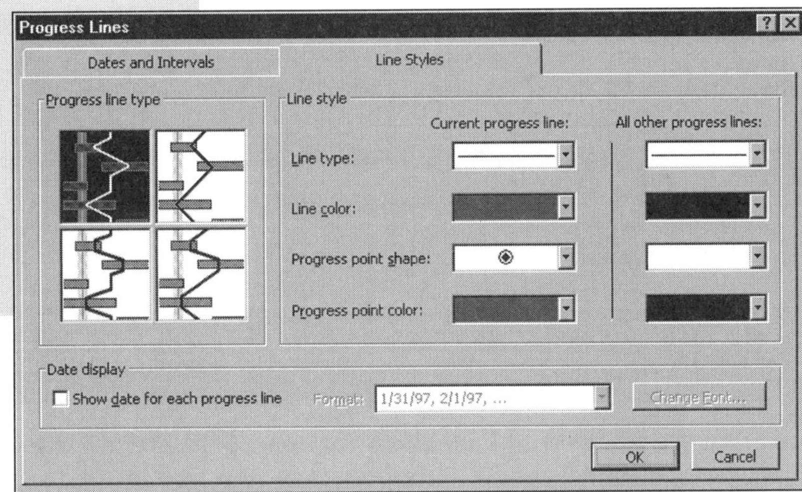

Figure 14.8 You can change the appearance of progress lines with the settings shown here; for example, you can choose a different color for progress lines.

5. If you want a date to appear at the top of each progress line to identify the progress date being charted, click to check the Show Date for Each Progress Line check box. Then, you can open the Format drop-down list to select another date format for the displayed date, such as **Jan 31, '97**. Click the Change Font button to display the Font dialog box and choose a different font for the displayed dates on the progress lines; this Font dialog box works as described earlier in this chapter.
6. Click OK to apply your changes and change the display of the progress lines. Figure 14.9 shows some example progress lines that I've reformatted.

Working with Gridlines

Gridlines in Project, like gridlines in other applications that display graphical information, help your eye determine whether objects line up or where particular measurements occur. If you add gridlines to separate Gantt bars, you can easily tell which Gantt bars align with which Task Sheet rows. By default, the timescale in Gantt Chart view shows vertical gridlines that identify the major columns, which generally represent workweeks.

Some gridlines are horizontal, such as those that identify Gantt bar rows. Other gridlines are vertical. Generally, if the items for which you want to add gridlines appear in rows, the gridlines will be horizontal; if the items for which you want to add gridlines are organized in columns, the gridlines will be vertical.

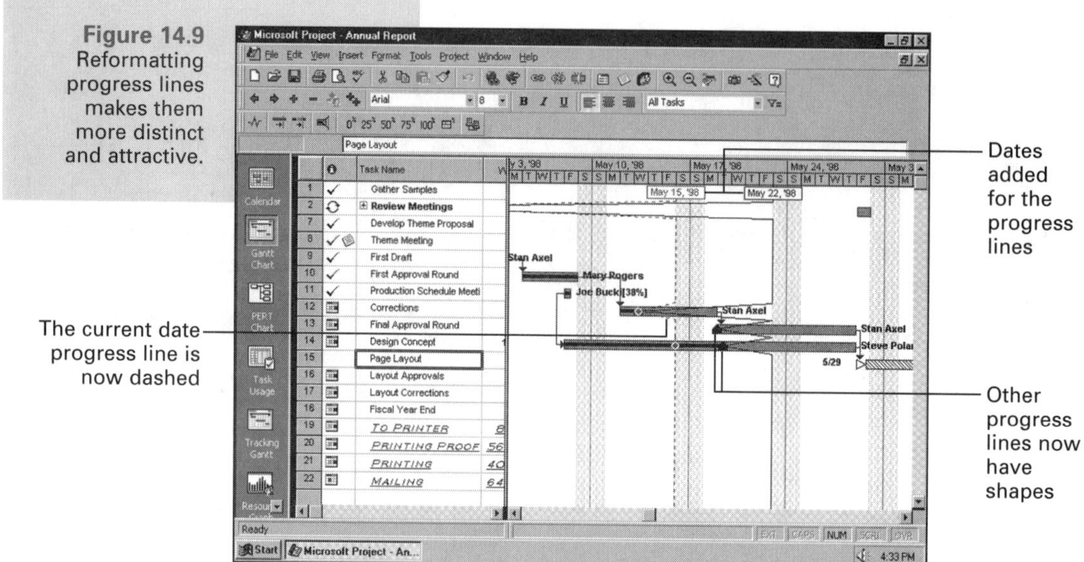

Figure 14.9 Reformatting progress lines makes them more distinct and attractive.

Note

The lines that separate the rows and columns in Task Sheets and Resource Sheets are also considered to be gridlines and can be removed or reformatted. These gridlines are identified as the Sheet Rows and Sheet Columns options in the Line to Change list of the Gridlines dialog box.

When you change gridline settings, your changes apply to the entire schedule file; you can't change only the gridlines that correspond to selected tasks.

To add gridlines to a graphical view in Project, follow these steps:

1. Open the Format menu and click Gridlines, or right-click the graphical area of the view (such as the Gantt chart) and then click Gridlines on the shortcut menu. The Gridlines dialog box appears (see Figure 14.10).
2. In the Line to Change list, select the item for which you want to add or edit a gridline. If the selected item already has some type of gridline applied, the specified formatting options for that gridline appear on the right side of the dialog box.
3. In the Normal area (the upper-right portion of the dialog box), specify the gridlines that you want for your Line to Change choices. Use the Type drop-down list to select the overall gridline appearance, such as dotted or dashed. Use the Color drop-down list to apply a color to the gridlines.

Figure 14.10 The Gridlines dialog box enables you to add gridlines to the Gantt chart area of your view.

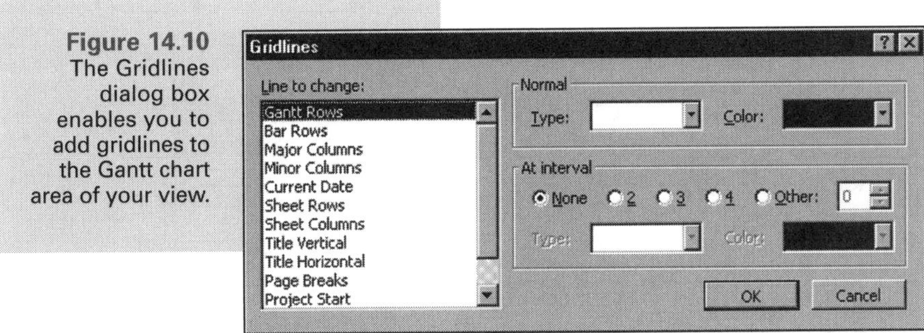

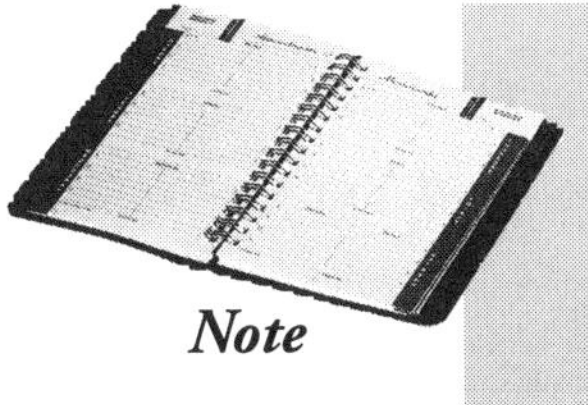

Note

If you want to remove displayed gridlines for the selected Line to Change item, select the blank option at the top of the Type list. If you want gridlines to appear at intervals and not for every column or row, make sure that no line Type is selected.

4. In the At Interval area, you can specify the appearance of gridlines at a specified interval. If the normal gridlines are black, for example, you may want every fourth gridline to be red. Click the 2, 3, 4, or Other option button (and edit the default Other value, if necessary) to specify which gridlines should use the alternative formatting. Then select the alternative gridline Type and Color.
5. Click OK to close the dialog box and display your gridlines.

Figure 14.11 shows dotted gridlines used to separate Gantt rows. Every fifth gridline is a solid red line.

Formatting Text Styles

Based on the information you add to your schedule, Project classifies certain tasks based on their impact. The program marks all tasks on the critical path as being critical tasks, for example, or treats summary tasks differently from subtasks. Even though Project can track task categories easily, tracking might be a bit more difficult for you. To make the job easier, Project enables you to apply special text formatting to any category of task or resource information in the Task Sheet or Resource Sheet. In Project, when you apply formatting to a particular category of information, you're defining a special text style.

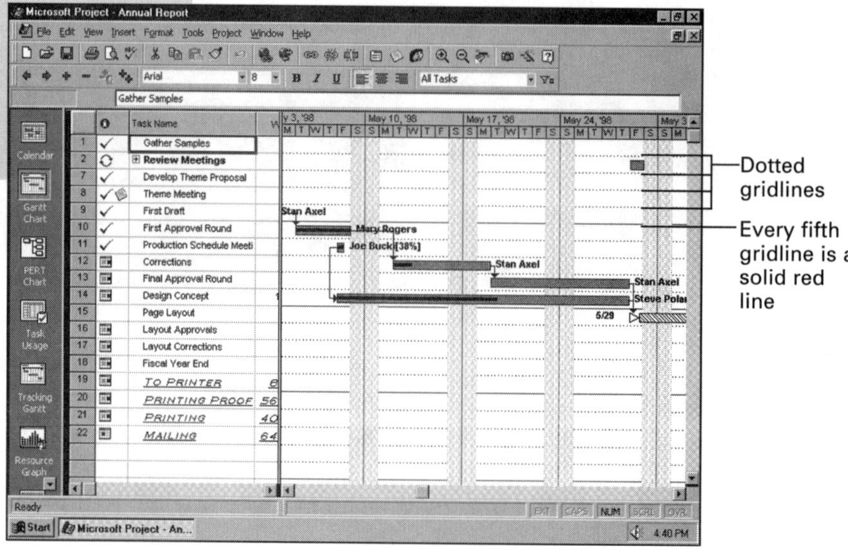

Figure 14.11 This Gantt chart shows gridlines separating the Gantt bar lines.

To work with a text style, follow these steps:

1. Display the view that includes the Task Sheet or Resource Sheet to which you want to apply the style.
2. Open the Format menu and click Text Styles. Alternately, select a column, right-click it, and then click Text Styles on the shortcut menu. The Text Styles dialog box appears.
3. Select the category of information for which you want to adjust formatting from the Item to Change drop-down list (see Figure 14.12). If you want to change the font size of summary tasks, for example, select Summary Tasks here.

Note

The Item to Change list contains such items as column and row heads. The list is rather long, so check out everything that you can change.

4. Specify the text-formatting options for this category of information, just as you did for selected sheet text in the "Formatting Selected Sheet Text" section earlier in this chapter. The text-formatting options here work just like those you saw in Figure 14.2.

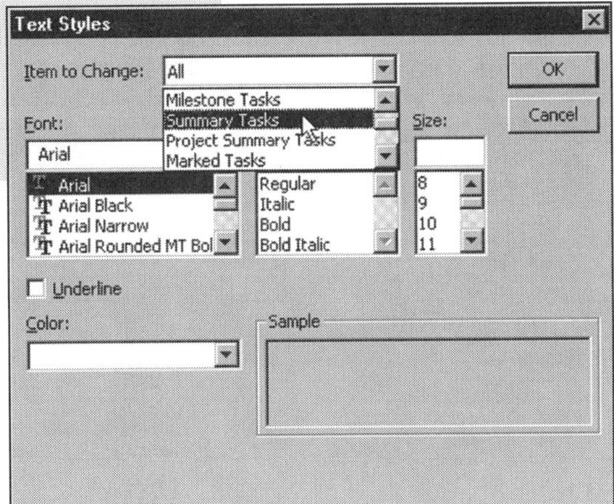

Figure 14.12 You select a style to change and then set its options.

5. (Optional) If you want to set the formatting for other categories of information, repeat steps 3 and 4.
6. Click OK to close the Text Styles dialog box and apply the styles. All text in that category displays your formatting changes. (Figure 14.13 shows an increased font size for summary tasks.)

Adjusting the Bar or Box Styles for Charts

Just as Project applies a particular style of text to different categories of tasks or resources, it applies a particular style of formatting to the corresponding charted information. The adjustments that you can make in charted information depend on the selected view in Project. The formatting options are different for Calendar view bars, Gantt Chart view bars, PERT Chart view boxes, and Resource Graph bars. The following sections provide an overview of the most important options for each type of display.

The formatting options that are available for bars and boxes vary, depending on whether the graphical information appears in a combination view or in a single pane. The options also might change based on the type of information displayed.

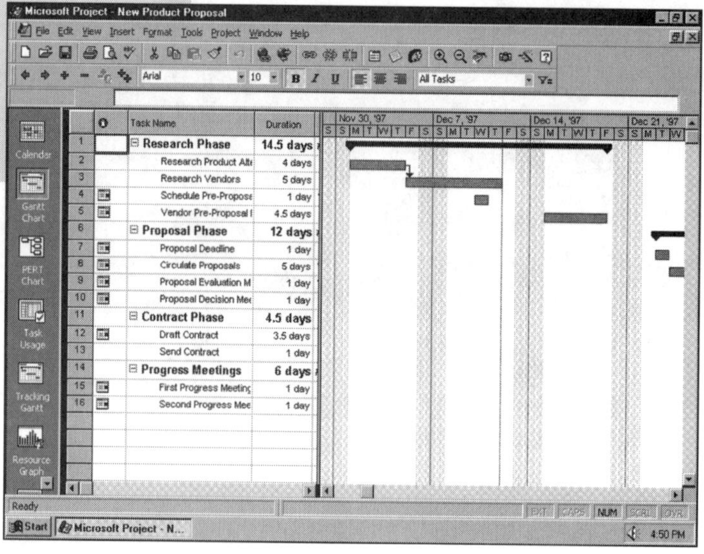

Figure 14.13 The summary tasks in rows 1, 6, 11, and 14 now appear in a larger font size.

For all views but Calendar view, you can display a dialog box that contains the appropriate bar, or box-formatting options, by double-clicking the chart area. For all charts, you can right-click the chart area and then click Bar Styles or Box Styles on the shortcut menu. If you prefer to use menu commands, open the Format menu and click Bar Styles (for Calendar, Gantt Chart, or Resource Graph view) or Box Styles (for PERT Chart view). After you make changes in one of these dialog boxes, click OK to close the dialog box and apply your selections to the appropriate bars and boxes.

Style Options in Gantt Chart View

Figure 14.14 shows the Bar Styles dialog box that appears in Gantt Chart view. To adjust a bar style, edit the column entries and Text and Bars tab settings. To add a new bar style, scroll down the list, enter the information for the style in each column, and then specify the Text and Bars tab options. To delete a style, select it in the Name list and then click on the Cut Row button near the top of the dialog box.

Figure 14.15 shows an example of the formatting possibilities for the summary task bars.

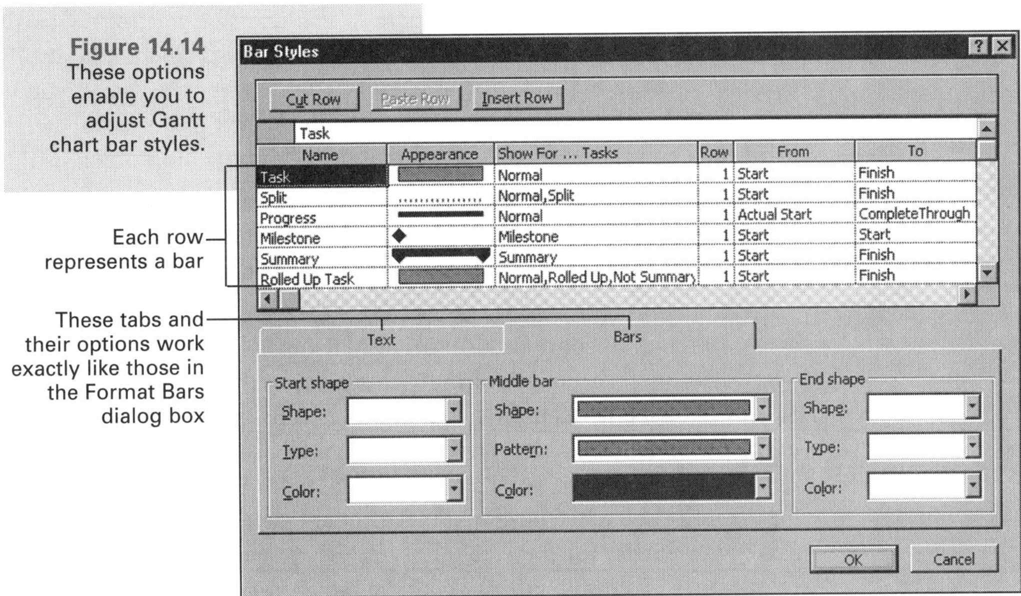

Figure 14.14 These options enable you to adjust Gantt chart bar styles.

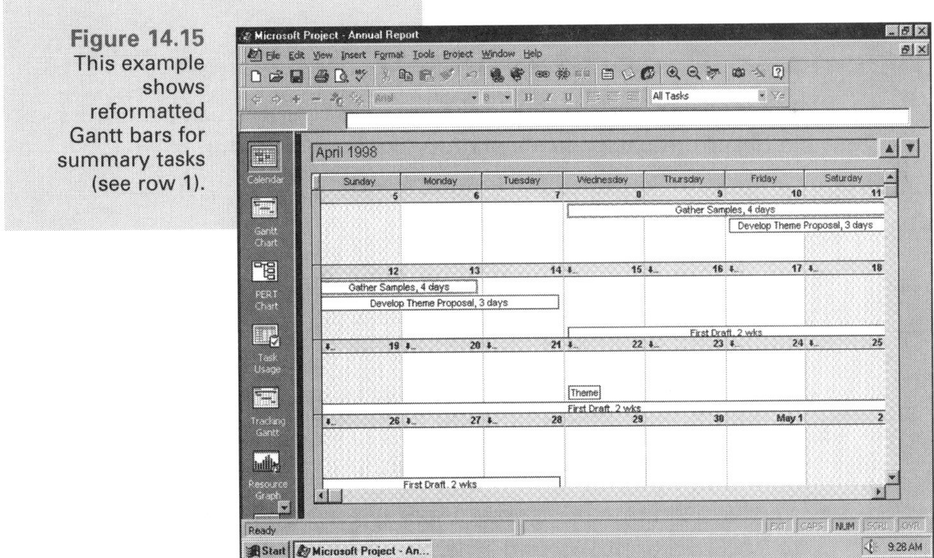

Figure 14.15 This example shows reformatted Gantt bars for summary tasks (see row 1).

Not all the style columns are self-explanatory, so the following list reviews them:

- The Name column displays the name you enter for the style.
- The Appearance column displays the style's settings, which you specify by using the Text and Bars tabs at the bottom of the dialog box.

- The Show For... Tasks column specifies which fields or types of tasks the bars represent. Use the drop-down list to select a field. (You could, for example, create a bar style that applies to tasks Not Started Yet.) If you want to add multiple fields, type a comma in the text box after the last listed field and then select an additional field from the drop-down list.
- If you want to display multiple bars for each task (as in Tracking Gantt view), enter a value other than 1 in the Row column for a style. If you create a new style for tasks Not Started Yet, for example, you might enter 2, so that the Not Started Yet bar appears below the task's default bar.
- The From and To columns also can display fields. The fields that you select determine the length of the Gantt bars for the style. For the Not Started Yet bars, for example, you might want to specify Baseline Start in the From column and Start (for the currently scheduled start) in the To column. Those options draw a bar that leads up to the default bar for the task. Use the drop-down list at the far right of the text box to make your entries for these columns. However, for milestones, the From and To columns should show the same time period; for example, From start To start.

Style Options in Calendar View

Select a Task Type from the list in the upper-left corner; then choose the various Bar Shape options (which work just like those for Gantt charts).

This dialog box offers a few options that are unique to Calendar view (see Figure 14.16):

- Use the Split Pattern drop-down list to specify whether you want a dashed, dotted, solid, or no line to appear between the bar segments for split tasks.
- If you choose the Shadow option, Project displays a drop shadow below bars of that style to provide a 3-D appearance.
- The Bar Rounding option makes bars of that style appear in full-day increments, even when an actual task's duration is less than a full day.
- The Field(s) box enables you to specify what field information is used to label bars of the selected style. You can select fields from the drop-down list at the far right of the box. Again, you can separate multiple fields in the text box with commas.
- The Align options enable you to specify where in the bars the specified text should appear.
- The Wrap Text in Bars option allows the specified text to occupy more than one line, if necessary.

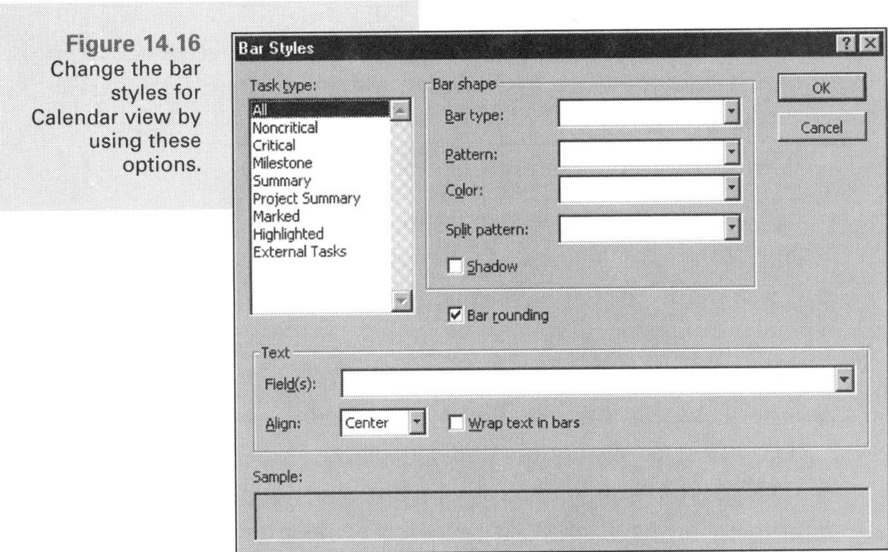

Figure 14.16 Change the bar styles for Calendar view by using these options.

Style Options in Resource Graph View

Figure 14.17 shows the Bar Styles dialog box for Resource Graph view.

The options available in this dialog box vary radically, depending on whether this graph appears by itself or in the lower pane of a combination view. The Filtered Resources options apply only to filtered resources when the Resource Graph appears by itself onscreen; otherwise, the settings apply to all resources. The Resource options apply to the displayed resource.

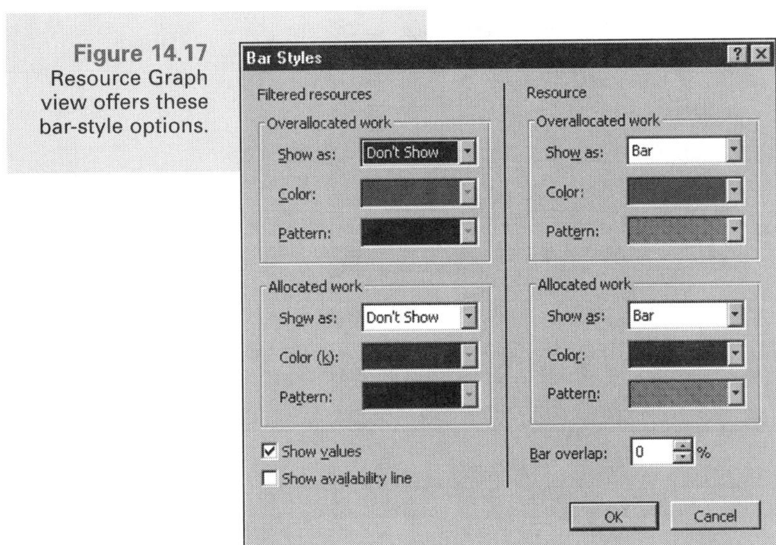

Figure 14.17 Resource Graph view offers these bar-style options.

Another factor that affects the options in this dialog box is which details you have chosen to display (see the "Working with Details" section later in this chapter). If you have chosen to display cost information in the graph, for example, the Bar Styles dialog box looks like Figure 14.18.

No matter which kinds of information you can format, the options are similar:

- Use any Show As drop-down list to specify whether the information appears as a bar, line, area, or other type of chart indicator.
- Select a color for the graphed information from the corresponding Color drop-down list.
- Select a pattern from the corresponding Pattern drop-down list.
- The Show Values option displays the values for the charted information at the bottom of the graph.
- The Show Availability Line option displays an indicator that shows whether the resource has any available working time. (This option is available when you're charting work information, as opposed to cost information.)
- If you want to display more than one type of bar for each time period in the graph, you can specify a Bar Overlap % option to allow the charted bars to overlap slightly, so that more information fits into less horizontal space. Figure 14.19 shows bars with a 25 percent overlap. The legend at the left side of the display shows what each style of charted information means.

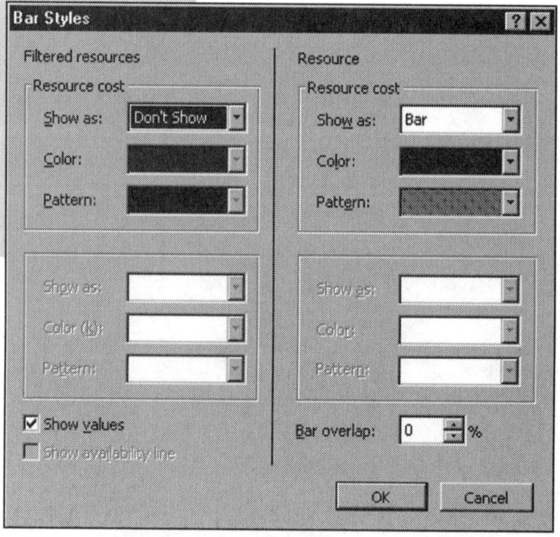

Figure 14.18 The Resource Graph bar-style options have changed because cost information now appears in the graph.

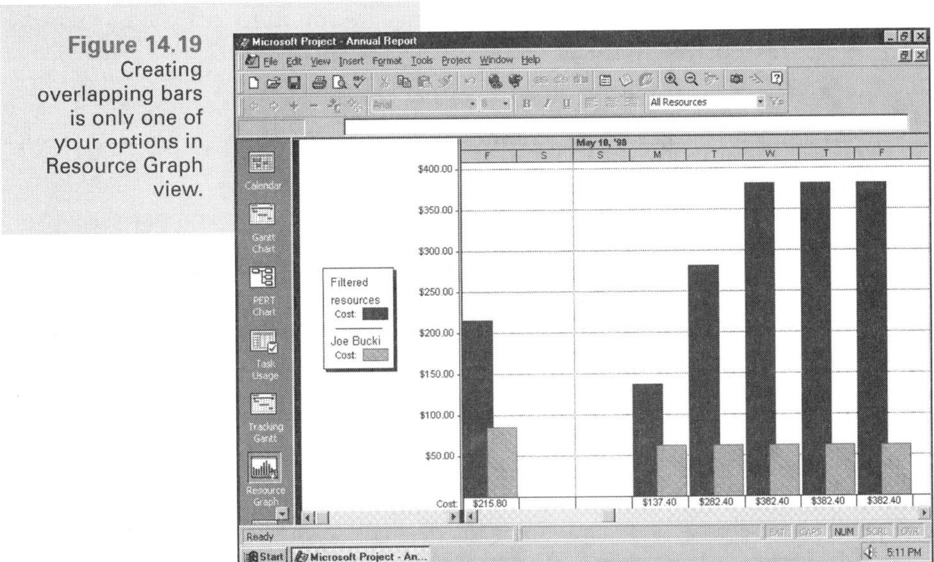

Figure 14.19 Creating overlapping bars is only one of your options in Resource Graph view.

Style Options in PERT Chart View

In PERT Chart view, you adjust box styles (instead of bar styles) by using the Box Styles dialog box shown in Figure 14.20.

When you display this dialog box, select the Boxes tab. This tab contains the following options:

- By default, each PERT chart box is divided into five cells. Drop-down lists 1 through 5 let you specify what field information appears in each cell.

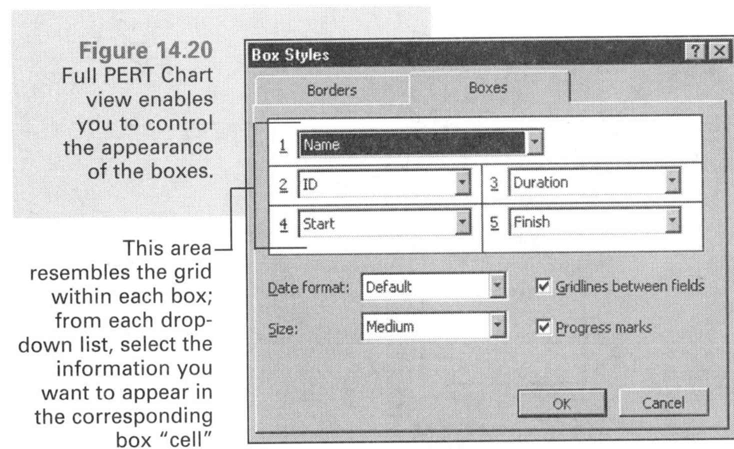

Figure 14.20 Full PERT Chart view enables you to control the appearance of the boxes.

This area resembles the grid within each box; from each drop-down list, select the information you want to appear in the corresponding box "cell"

- The Date Format drop-down list enables you to specify the way dates are displayed in the boxes.
- The Size list specifies the size of the boxes.
- When you select the Gridlines Between Fields option, lines separate the cells in the boxes.
- The Progress Marks option (selected by default) displays one diagonal slash through each in-progress task in the PERT chart box and crosses out completed tasks with an X.
- Clear the Progress Marks check box to prevent Project from indicating whether tasks are underway or completed.

Click the Borders tab in the Box Styles dialog box to display the options shown in Figure 14.21.

Select the style of box (for a particular type of task) from the Item to Change list; then select a Style and Color for that type of box. You subsequently can select other task types from the Item to Change list and adjust each box's Style and Color.

Working with Details

In the "Graphing Individual Resource Work and Costs" section in Chapter 8, you learned that you can right-click the graph area on the right side of Resource Graph view to display a shortcut menu, from which you select the information you want to view. You can select Percent Allocation, for example, to display a daily percentage of how much of the workday a resource will spend on a given task.

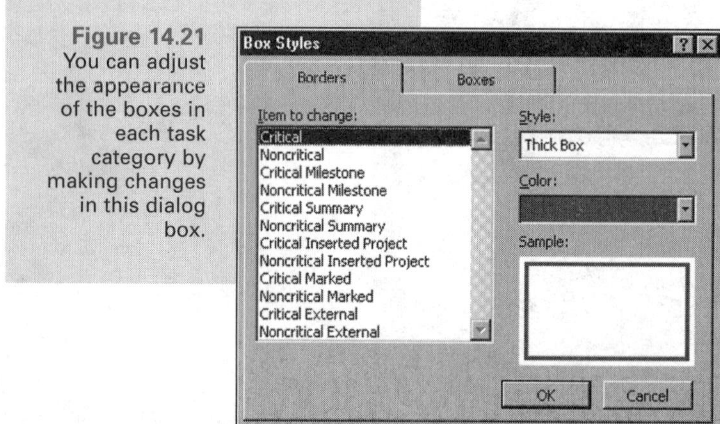

Figure 14.21 You can adjust the appearance of the boxes in each task category by making changes in this dialog box.

Similarly, you learned in Chapter 9 that you can right-click any form that's part of a combination view to display a shortcut menu that enables you to specify which information the form displays. In the lower pane of Task Entry view, for example, you can right-click the form and then click Predecessors & Successors on the shortcut menu. The form then displays information about all predecessor and successor tasks that are linked to the selected task in the Task Sheet.

The equivalent of these shortcut menus is the Details submenu of the Format menu (see Figure 14.22). This submenu becomes available only when you select a pane that can "morph" to display different information. The submenu options vary, depending on the nature of the selected pane. Simply select the type of information you want to display in the selected pane—the submenu closes, and the display changes accordingly.

Choosing a Layout

The layout features control how graphed bars appear in relation to one another in Calendar, Gantt Chart, and PERT Chart views. The layout options for bar and box styles vary, depending on the selected view. To display the layout options for one of these views, open the Format menu and click Layout, or right-click a blank space of the chart area and then click Layout on the shortcut menu.

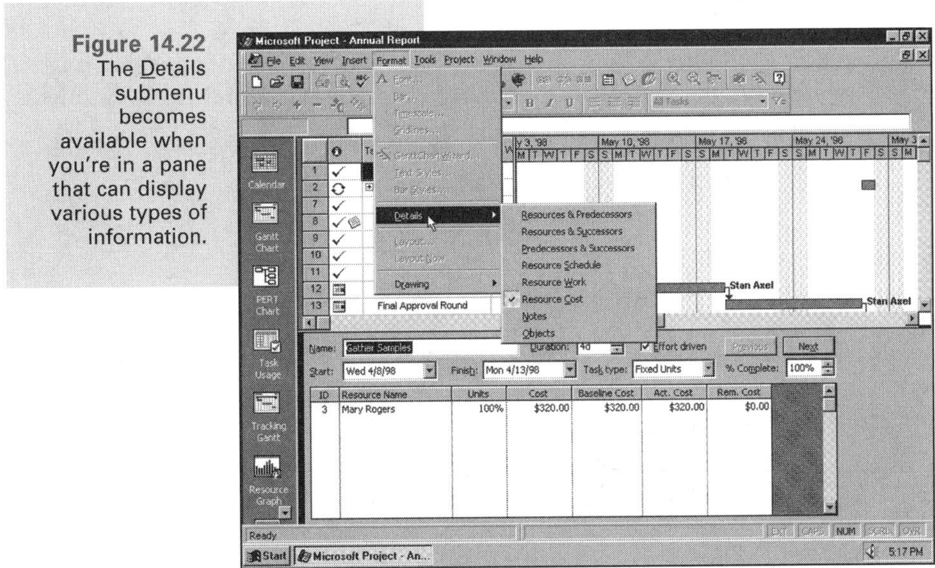

Figure 14.22 The Details submenu becomes available when you're in a pane that can display various types of information.

Layout Options in Calendar View

The layout options for Calendar view are simple, as Figure 14.23 shows. If you want each week to show more task information, select the Attempt to Fit As Many Tasks As Possible option. To ensure that bars for split tasks are divided into segments, make sure the Show Bar Splits check box is checked. Select the Automatic Layout option to tell Project to adjust the calendar to accommodate inserted and moved tasks.

Note

As you might surmise from the presence of the Automatic Layout option in the Layout dialog box, Calendar view doesn't update automatically when you move or reschedule tasks in Gantt Chart view; neither does PERT Chart view. If you need to update Calendar view or PERT Chart view to reflect the current schedule and task relationships, open the Format menu and click Layout Now.

Layout Options in Gantt Chart View

Figure 14.24 shows the Layout dialog box for Gantt Chart view.

This dialog box contains the following options:

- Select the Links option to specify how (and whether) you want task-link lines to appear.
- The options in the Date Format for Bars drop-down list enable you to control the display of any date information that accompanies Gantt bars.
- The Bar Height option enables you to make all bars (and their rows) larger or smaller.

Figure 14.23 The layout options are limited in Calendar view.

Layout

Method

Use current sort order

ID [Ascending]

Attempt to fit as many tasks as possible

Show bar splits

Automatic layout

OK

Cancel

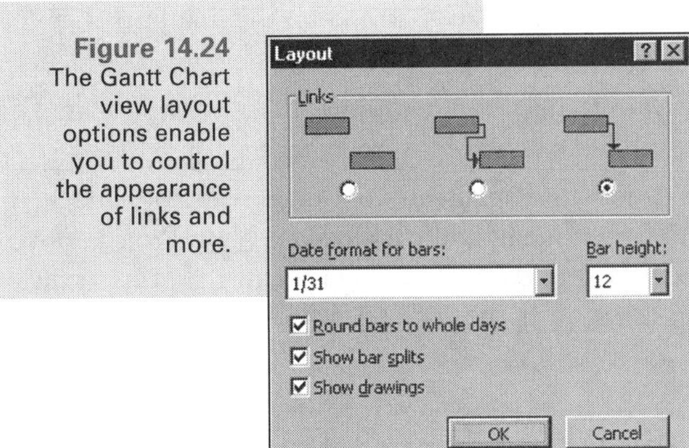

Figure 14.24 The Gantt Chart view layout options enable you to control the appearance of links and more.

- The Round Bars to Whole Days option enables you to format each bar as a full day—even for, say, a three-hour task.
- To ensure that bars for split tasks are divided into segments, make sure the Show Bar Splits check box is checked.
- If you added a drawing to the Gantt chart area, make sure that the Show Drawings check box is selected, so that the drawing appears. To hide the drawing temporarily (for printing, for example), clear this check box.

Layout Options in PERT Chart View

Figure 14.25 shows the Layout dialog box for PERT Chart view.

This dialog box contains the following options:

- As you can for a Gantt chart, you can use the Links option to specify how links appear on a PERT chart.

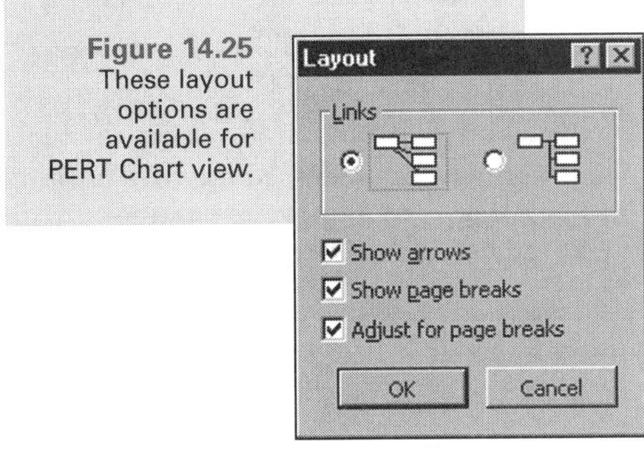

Figure 14.25 These layout options are available for PERT Chart view.

- Use the Show Arrows option to specify arrows on the link lines that indicate the flow of work.
- Select Show Page Breaks to display dotted lines in the view, so that you'll know which PERT boxes will print together on a page.
- Make sure that the Adjust for Page Breaks option is selected. Later, when you open the Format menu and click Layout Now, Project moves task boxes that appear on a page break to one page or the next, so that the box doesn't split in the printout.

Creating a Drawing in Project

In Chapter 15, "Using Information from Another Project or Application," you learn how to insert a drawing from another application into your Gantt chart as an object. Although Project is by no means a drawing application, it includes some basic drawing tools that you can use to add simple graphics to your Gantt chart. You might want to display a box with some text to call attention to a particular task, for example. If you have a great deal of time, you can be creative, layering numerous drawn objects for a nice effect. By default, the drawn objects that you add appear onscreen and in any printout of a view that contains your Gantt chart.

The drawing tools in Project work like those in Word, Excel, and many other Microsoft applications. Although an exhaustive discussion of drawing is beyond the scope of this book, this section shows you how to draw objects, select and format them, and position them in relation to the correct date or task in the Gantt chart. Follow these steps:

1. In Gantt Chart view, scroll the chart to display the blank area where you want to create the drawing.
2. Display the Drawing toolbar. To do so, open the Insert menu and click Drawing, or right-click any toolbar onscreen, and then click Drawing.
3. The seven buttons at the center of the Drawing toolbar—Line, Arrow, Rectangle, Oval, Arc, Polygon, and Text Box—enable you to create those objects. To use each of these buttons, you basically select the tool, and then click and drag. (There are two exceptions: to use the Polygon button, you have to click for each point and double-click to finish; to use the Text Box button, you have to type text.) When you finish drawing the object, release the mouse button (the object appears with black selection handles around it).

   Figure 14.26 shows an example of using the Oval tool.

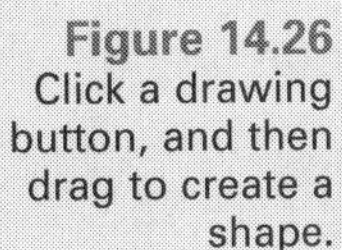

Figure 14.26 Click a drawing button, and then drag to create a shape.

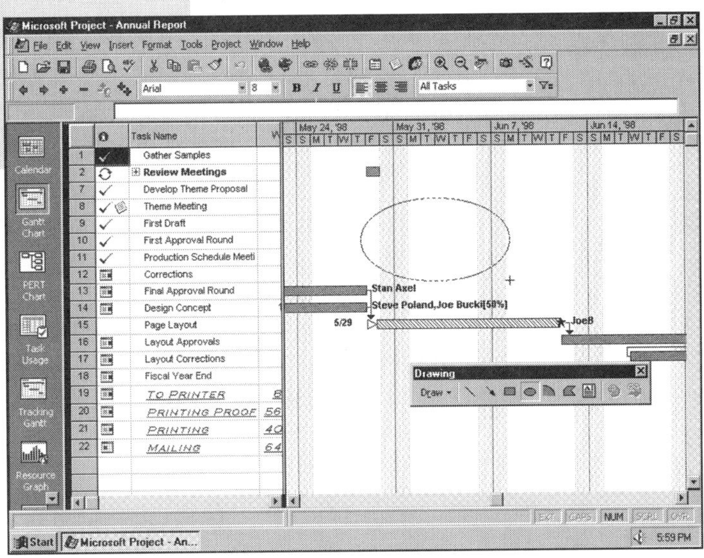

4. Double-click the object you just drew; the Format Drawing dialog box appears (see Figure 14.27). Alternately, click the object to select it (if it's not already selected), and then open the Format menu, point to Drawing, and click Properties.
5. Choose the Line and Fill options that you want to use. The Preview area shows the result of your choices.
6. Click the Size & Position tab, which contains the following options:
   - You probably don't need to worry about the Size options near the bottom of the dialog box, because you defined the size when you created the object.

Figure 14.27 Format an object with this dialog box.

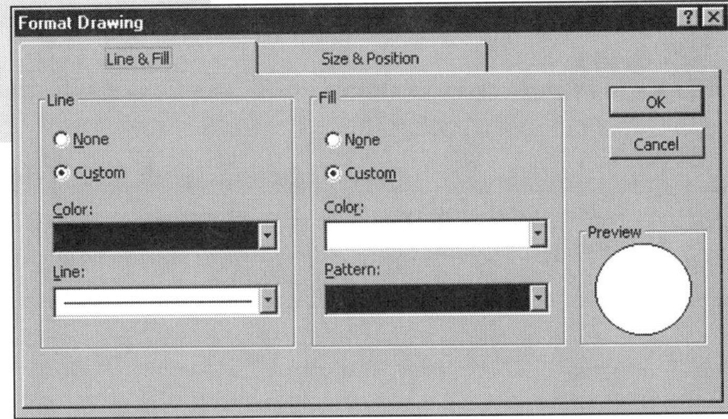

- The Position options enable you to attach the drawing to a particular date (the Attach to Timescale option button) or task (the Attach to Task option button) in the Gantt chart.
- By default, Attach to Timescale is selected, with the Date and Vertical entries reflecting the way that you positioned the object when you created it.
- The Attach to Task option attaches the drawn object (from its upper-right corner) to the Gantt bar for the specified task in the list. Enter the ID number for the Gantt bar to which you want to attach the graphic in the ID text box. Click an Attachment Point option button to specify whether the upper-right corner of the graphic should be positioned relative to the left or right end of the Gantt bar. Adjust the Horizontal and Vertical entries to control how close the upper-right corner of the graphic is to the specified end of the Gantt bar.

I find using the Horizontal and Vertical entries counter-intuitive. Entering higher values moves the graphic down and to the right of the Gantt bar. To move the graphic above or to the left of the Gantt bar, you need to enter negative values. For example, if you attach a graphic to the right end of the Gantt bar, you might need to enter -1.00 as the Vertical setting to position the graphic above the selected Gantt bar.

You also can attach an inserted graphic (see Chapter 19, "Taking Project Online") to a Gantt bar.

7. When you finish selecting options, click OK to close the Format Drawing dialog box.
8. Create another object, if you want. Figure 14.28 shows a newly created text box.

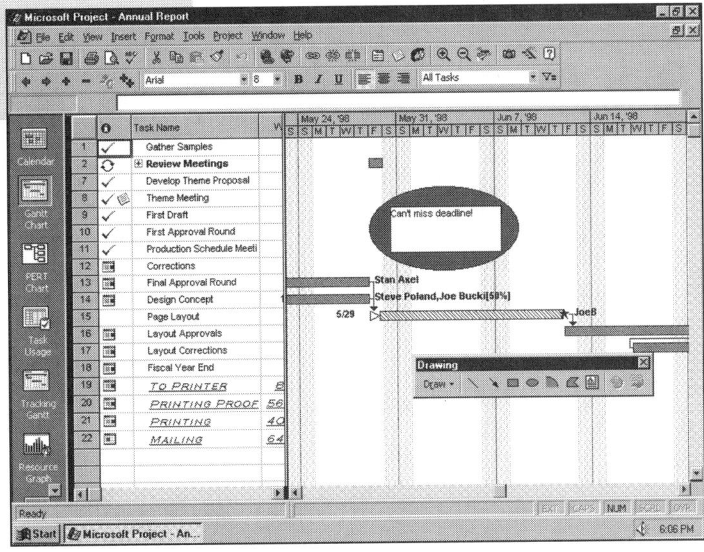

Figure 14.28
This is a second new object.

9. Double-click the new object to set its formatting options. If you're adding a text box over an oval and you want the text to look like part of the oval, choose None for both the Line and Fill Color options (on the Line & Fill tab) in the Format Drawing dialog box. Close the dialog box.
10. You have to use a special method to format the text in a drawn text box. Click the box to select it (you click to select any drawn object), and then drag over the text within the box to select (highlight) it. Next, open the Format menu and click Font; finally, use the Font dialog box to specify the formatting you want. Close the dialog box. Figure 14.29 shows the resulting text box.
11. Save the file to save your drawing on the Gantt chart. If you close the Project file without saving it, you lose your drawing.

The objects you draw appear in invisible layers, with the object drawn most recently appearing on the top layer. You can use the Bring to Front or Send to Back choices in the Draw menu on the Drawing toolbar to send the selected object to the top or bottom layer, respectively. If you want to move the selected drawing object up or back by a single layer, use the Move Forward or Move Backward commands.

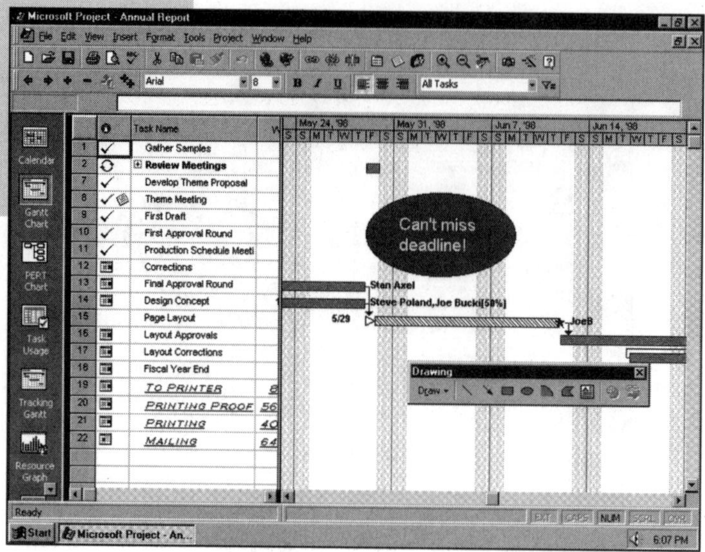

Figure 14.29 A text box layer over another object can be an attention-getting reminder.

Part IV
Handling Multiple Projects

15

Copying and Moving Project Information

In This Chapter

- Copying data between projects
- Moving data between projects
- Understanding how copying and moving affects tasks links

There's no shame in using shortcuts; in fact, smart businesspeople seek them out and use them as tools for repeating successes. If you wrote a new-sales-call follow-up letter that enabled you to close a sale, you'd be silly to write a new follow-up letter after the next call.

Instead, you'd reuse as much as you could of the letter that had already worked for you.

When you have invested a good deal of time entering information about resources and certain kinds of tasks in Project, and when you find that information to be valuable, you may want to reuse that information. If different projects that you manage have similar tasks or use some of the same resources, you can save time by copying or moving information between those projects.

Copying Information between Projects

When you copy or move information in Windows applications, Windows leaves the original information intact and places the copied information in the Clipboard—a holding area in your computer's memory. When data is in the Clipboard, you can paste it into a new location, or into several locations. The file or location from which you copy or move information is called the *source*, and the place where you paste the information is called the *destination*.

The following sections show you how to copy information between two Project files. The steps that you take vary a bit, depending on whether you're copying all the information about a particular task or resource, or only part of the information.

Note

You can copy and move information within a Project file as well. Simply select the information; cut or copy it, select another location for it in the Task Sheet or Resource Sheet, and then paste it into place.

Copying Task and Resource Information between Projects

When you select and copy an entire task row (or multiple rows), the entire set of information related to that task—the task name, resources assigned to that task, the duration, the start time, task notes, and so on—is copied. If you select two or more linked tasks and paste them into another project, the link information that connects the tasks is copied, too.

You also can copy resource information to other projects. Copying resource rows picks up all the fields defined in your Resource Sheet.

If you frequently copy the same resource information to new projects, choose Tools, Resources, Share Resources to create a common set of resources that are available to multiple projects. To learn more about shared resources, see Chapter 17, "Consolidating Projects."

To copy tasks or resources between projects, follow these steps:

1. Open the files for the two projects in question, select the same view in each project window (Gantt Chart view, for example), and arrange the project windows so a portion of each window is visible. You can open the Window menu and click Arrange All to tile the project windows automatically. Alternately, you can press Ctrl+F6 to toggle between the active files.
2. Select the entire task or resource row to copy by clicking the row number. To select multiple consecutive rows, hold down the Shift key and click each row. To select multiple nonconsecutive rows, hold down the Ctrl key and click each row.
3. Open the Edit menu and click Copy (Task) or Copy (Resource). Alternately, do any of the following: right-click the selection and then click Copy (Task) or Copy (Resource) from the shortcut menu; press Ctrl+C; or click the Copy button on the Standard toolbar. (The command name reflects the type of information that you selected—task or resource.)
4. If you're copying the information to another Project file, click a portion of the destination window (such as the title bar) to tell Project that you want to copy information to that file. Then select the first cell of the row in which you want to place the copied information.
5. Open the Edit menu and click Paste. Alternately, do any of the following: right-click the row to paste to, and then click Paste on the shortcut menu; press Ctrl+V; or click the Paste button on the Standard toolbar. The task or resource information is pasted into the selected row.

You also can use Project's drag-and-drop feature to copy task or resource rows between project windows. Follow these steps:

1. Open the project files, and arrange the windows so that the source and destination rows are visible.

2. Select the rows to copy by clicking the appropriate task or resource row numbers.
3. Position the mouse pointer on the border of the selected area. The pointer changes to an arrow.
4. Drag the selected information to the first cell of the destination row. As you drag, the pointer changes to an arrow and a plus sign, indicating that the copy operation is in progress.
5. Release the mouse button to drop the copied information in the new location.

Figure 15.1 shows the drag-and-drop operation in progress.

If you try to paste a copied or cut row of information between existing rows, Project inserts a new row for the pasted information. Otherwise, when you're pasting cells or column selections, Project pastes the information over any information that currently appears in the destination location. When you paste information, make sure that you're not pasting over other information that you need.

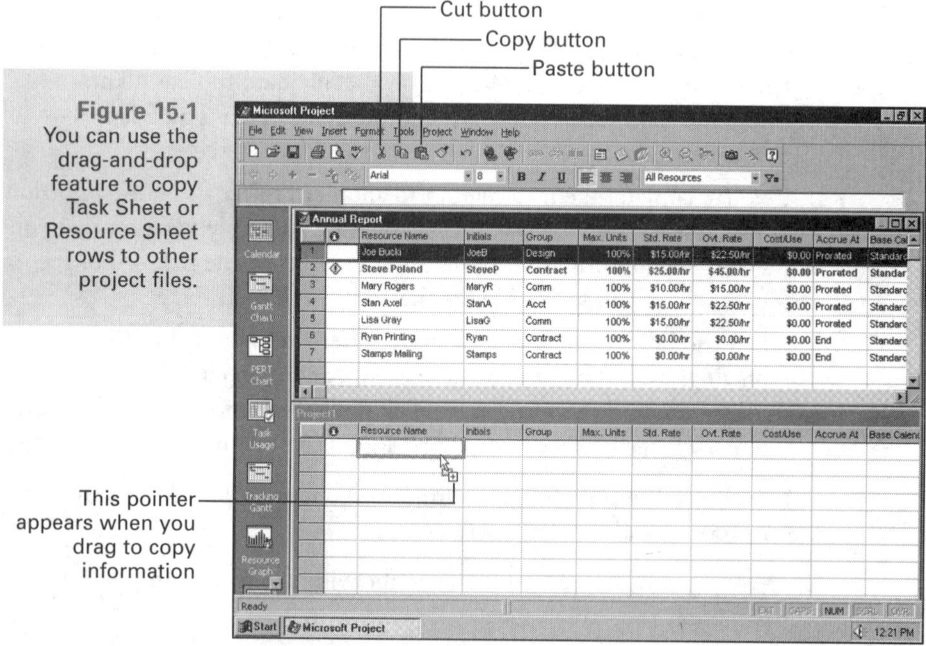

Figure 15.1 You can use the drag-and-drop feature to copy Task Sheet or Resource Sheet rows to other project files.

Copying Cell and Column Information between Projects

In some cases, you want to copy selected information about tasks or resources from one Task Sheet or Resource Sheet to another. You can copy a list of task names only, for example, or you can copy the hourly and overtime rates for one resource to the corresponding cells for another resource.

When you copy information from cells, all the original information for the task or resource is left behind; only a copy of the cell contents is placed in the destination project. When you copy partial task or resource information to another project, the default values for Duration and Start Date (tasks), Accrue At and Baseline (resource), and so on are assigned to the task. You can edit those settings as necessary.

Keep the field (column) format types in mind when you copy information between Task Sheets or Resource Sheets. Typically, you should copy only between fields of the same type—from a Task Name field to a Task Name field, for example. Otherwise, you may get unexpected results. In some cases, if you try to paste an entry into a cell that needs a different kind of data (if you're trying to paste a name into a cell that contains an hourly rate, for example), Project displays a warning, as shown in Figure 15.2. Also, Project does not allow you to paste information into any calculated field.

To copy cell information between projects, follow these steps:

1. Open the two projects between which you want to copy information; select the same view in each project window, and arrange the project windows so that a portion of each is visible.
2. Select one or more cells to be copied. To select multiple consecutive cells (a range or block of cells), select the upper-left cell of the range, and then hold down the Shift key and click the lower-right corner of the range (see Figure 15.3). To select multiple nonconsecutive cells, hold down the Ctrl key and click each cell that you want to copy.

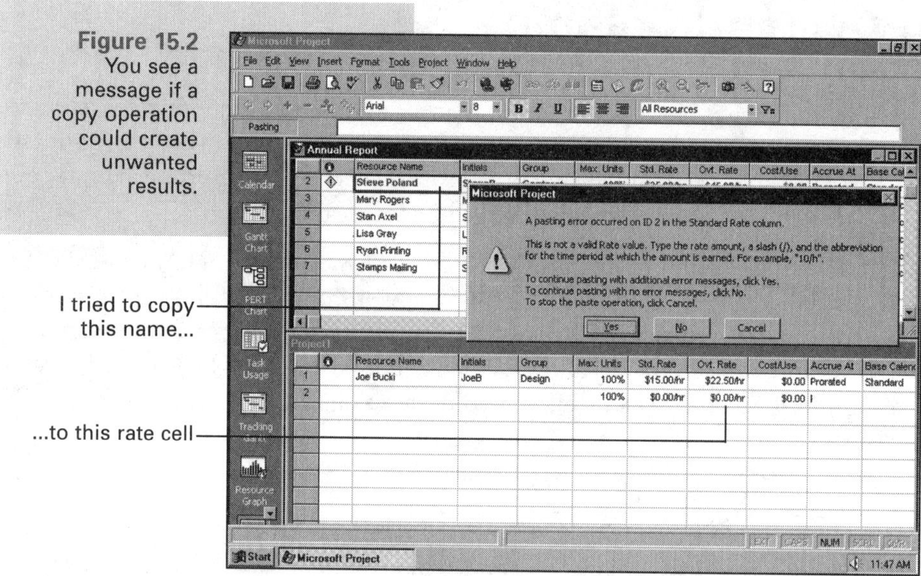

Figure 15.2 You see a message if a copy operation could create unwanted results.

Figure 15.3 You can select a range of cells.

Annual Report

	Resource Name	Initials	Group	Max. Units	Std. Rate	Ovt. Rate	Cost/Use	Accrue At	Base Cal
1	Joe Bucki	JoeB	Design	100%	$15.00/hr	$22.50/hr	$0.00	Prorated	Standarc
2	Steve Poland	SteveP	Contract	100%	$25.00/hr	$45.00/hr	$0.00	Prorated	Standar
3	Mary Rogers	MaryR	Comm	100%	$10.00/hr	$15.00/hr	$0.00	Prorated	Standarc
4	Stan Axel	StanA	Acct	100%	$15.00/hr	$22.50/hr	$0.00	Prorated	Standarc
5	Lisa Gray	LisaG	Comm	100%	$15.00/hr	$22.50/hr	$0.00	Prorated	Standarc
6	Ryan Printing	Ryan	Contract	100%	$0.00/hr	$0.00/hr	$0.00	End	Standarc
7	Stamps Mailing	Stamps	Contract	100%	$0.00/hr	$0.00/hr	$0.00	End	Standarc

Click this cell...

...then hold down the Shift key and click this cell

3. Open the Edit menu and click Copy (Cell). Alternately, right-click your selection and click Copy (Cell) on the shortcut menu; press Ctrl+C; or click the Copy button on the Standard toolbar. (The command name reflects the type of information that you selected—in this case, a cell.)
4. If you're copying the information to another Project file, click a portion of the destination window (such as the title bar) to tell Project that you want to copy information to that file; then select the first cell of the row in which you want to place the copied information.
5. Open the Edit menu and click Paste. Alternately, do any of the following: right-click the selection you're pasting to, and then click Paste on the shortcut menu; press Ctrl+V; or click the Paste button on the Standard toolbar. The cell information is pasted in the selected area.

As you would expect, you can use the drag-and-drop feature to copy cell information between projects. Select the cells that you want to copy; point to the selection border so that you see the arrow pointer; drag the information to the destination, and release the mouse button to drop the information in place.

You also can copy and paste entire columns of information from one project to another. Suppose that you are creating a new project that has all the same tasks as an existing project, but the associated Duration, Start, and Finish entries—and the resources—are different.

To copy the Task Name entries from the existing project to the new one, click the column heading (Task Name, in this case) to select the entire column. Then do any of the following: open the Edit menu and click Copy (Cell), press Ctrl+C, or click the Copy button on the Standard toolbar. In the window for the new project file, click the Task Name column heading. Then do any of the following: open the Edit menu and click Paste, press Ctrl+V, or click the Paste button on the Standard toolbar. The entire list of task names is pasted into the new project.

If you often work with multiple projects at the same time, you can save the open projects and window positions as one unit. Save each of the open projects individually, and then open the File menu and click Save Workspace. Give the workspace a meaningful name, and click OK to save the workspace. The next time you open the workspace file, the project windows open in the place where you last left them. Chapter 1, "Getting Started with Project," covers saving a workspace in more detail.

Finally, you can make entering information in a single column easier by filling—an operation that's similar to copying. Start by selecting the cell that contains the information you want to copy to other cells that are lower in the list. Next, hold down the Shift key and click the bottom cell of the group of cells that you want to fill, or hold down the Ctrl key and click other noncontiguous cells lower in the column. Then open the Edit menu and click Fill Down (or press Ctrl+D). Project fills all the selected cells with the information that appears in the first cell that you selected.

Moving Information between Projects

In addition to copying, you can move information between Task Sheets or Resource Sheets in open Project files. Moving information is almost identical to copying, except that you cut the information from the source file, leaving the selected row, column, or cells empty, rather than leaving the information in place, as you do when you copy. Then you paste the information where you want it.

As in copying, the moved information replaces existing information unless you're moving an entire row, in which case the moved information is inserted between existing rows. Finally, moving an entire row of information carries all the task or resource information for that row, except for linking information.

To ensure that the information you're moving doesn't overwrite existing entries in your destination Task Sheet or Resource Sheet, open the Insert menu and click New Task or New Resource before you perform the move. Project inserts a new row in the location of the currently selected cell and moves existing rows down in the sheet.

The possibilities for moving information are almost endless. You may want to move information if you have more than one project under way and decide to move a resource from one project to another. In such a case, you need to move the contents of the row that contains that resource from the Resource Sheet of the first project file to the Resource Sheet of the second project file.

To move information between two Task Sheets or Resource Sheets, follow these steps:

1. Open the files for the two projects in question, select the same view in each project window (Gantt Chart view, for example), and arrange the project windows so that a portion of each is visible. You can open the Window menu and click Arrange All to tile the project windows automatically.
2. Select the task or resource row, column, or cells that you want to move.
3. Open the Edit menu and click Cut (Task) or Cut (Resource). Alternatively, do one of the following: right-click the selection, and then click Cut (Task) or Cut (Resource) on the shortcut menu, press Ctrl+X, or click the Cut button on the Standard toolbar. (The command name reflects the type of information that you selected—task or resource.)

   Cutting removes the information from its original location and places the information in the Windows Clipboard.

Information stays in the Clipboard only while your computer is on. If you shut off the computer, or if it loses power for some reason, the Clipboard empties. Also, if you cut or copy anything else to the Clipboard, the new information wipes out the existing Clipboard contents. Therefore, make sure that you paste information as quickly as possible after cutting it.

4. If you're moving the information to another Project file, click a portion of the destination window (such as its title bar) to tell Project that you want to move information to that file. Then select the first cell of the row in which you want to place the moved information.
5. Open the Edit menu and click Paste. Alternatively, do any of the following: right-click the selection you're pasting to, and then click Paste on the shortcut menu; press Ctrl+V; or click the Paste button on the Standard toolbar. The task or resource information is pasted into the area.

To use the drag-and-drop feature to move information between projects, you use a process that's similar to copying. First, select the information that you want to move. Next, point to the selection border so that you see the arrow pointer, hold down the Ctrl key, and drag the information to the destination. Release the mouse button to drop the information in place, and then release the Ctrl key.

Affecting Links When You Copy and Move Information

Many of the tasks in the Project files that you create are part of a series of tasks linked via Finish-to-Start (FS) links. The tasks are strung together like beads on a string. If one of the beads cracks and falls off, the remaining beads slide together to fill the gap.

When you copy or move a group of linked tasks from one project file to another, the links stay intact within the group. If you move or copy a single task, linked information doesn't travel with the task.

By default, when you move a task that's linked, via FS links, to a series of other tasks within a Project file, Project adjusts the linking information so that the linked tasks still flow continuously. If you move the linked task to a location that's higher or lower in the Task Sheet list, the links update to reflect all new task predecessors and successors.

In Figure 15.4, for example, the tasks in rows 1 and 4 are linked via an FS link, as are the tasks in rows 2 and 3. If you drag the task from row 1 to a location between tasks 2 and 3, the links rearrange, as shown in Figure 15.5. If the linking change would create a scheduling problem, Planning Wizard warns you (by default), as shown in Figure 15.6.

Pasting a copied task within a series of linked tasks also can disturb the linking relationships. If you want to be able to move tasks that are linked by FS relationships without changing the links, click to open the Tools menu, and then click Options to display the Options dialog box. Click the Schedule tab, clear the Autolink Inserted or Moved Tasks check box, and click OK. Otherwise, you can avoid screwing up links simply by not moving or pasting tasks within a series of linked tasks, or by moving only tasks that aren't connected to a predecessor or successor via an FS relationship.

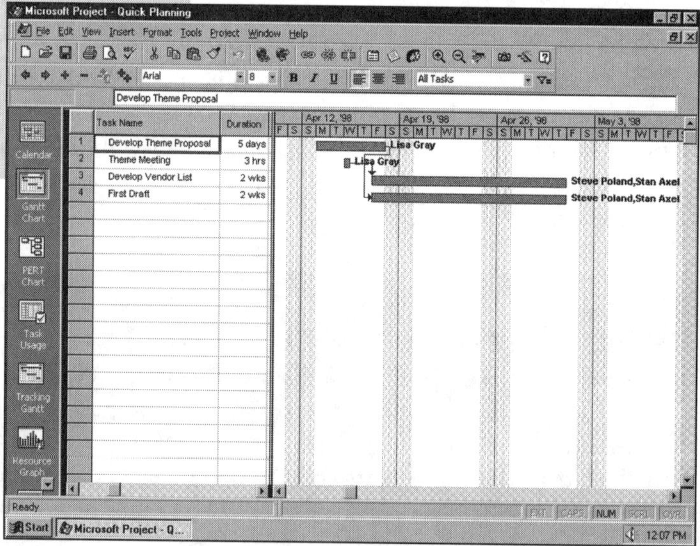

Figure 15.4 These two pairs of tasks are linked via Finish-to-Start (FS) links.

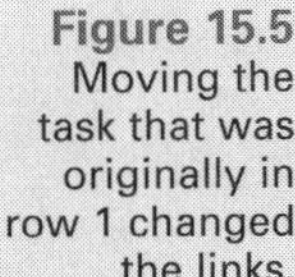

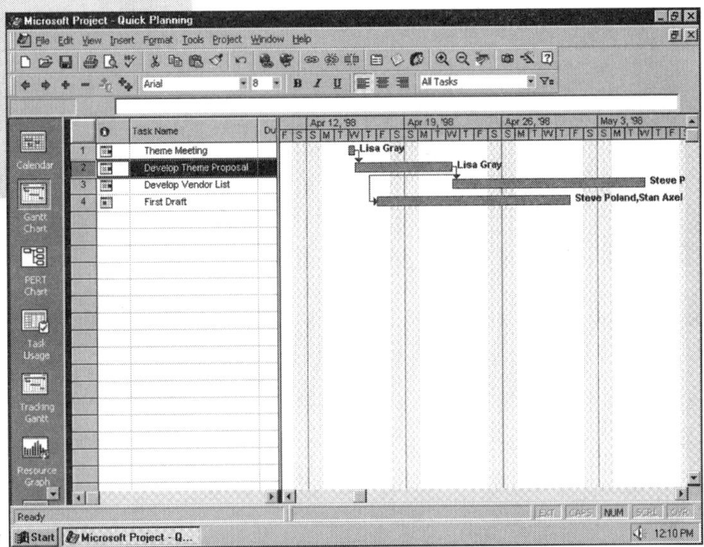

Figure 15.5 Moving the task that was originally in row 1 changed the links.

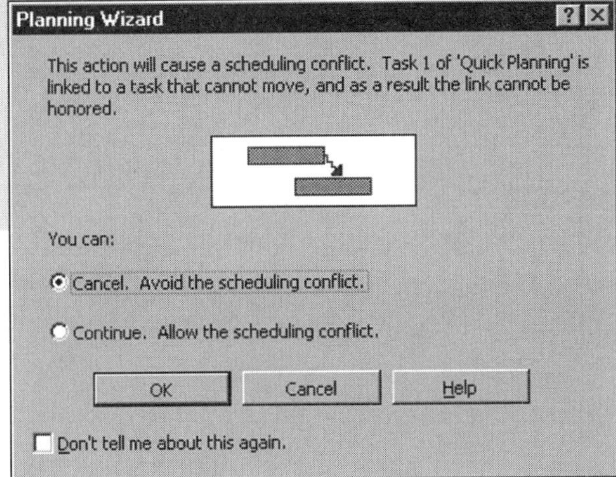

Figure 15.6 If moving or copying tasks would cause a linking problem, Planning Wizard warns you.

16

Working with Templates

In This Chapter

- Understanding benefits templates provide
- Reviewing templates that come with Project
- Creating a new file from a template
- Creating a new template from a file
- Finding other template files

Clothing makers a century or two ago had to have strong powers of visualization. Unless one had an old garment to take apart and copy the pieces from, he or she had to envision how each piece of fabric should be shaped to come together into a garment.

Then, some genius determined that you could make a prototype for a garment out of cheap muslin, and the muslin pieces could be copied as a paper pattern to use when cutting fabric for duplicates of the garment.

The pattern does the grunt work, freeing the user to focus on improvements and fine-tuning, and that's exactly what a *template* file does for you in Microsoft Project 98. You'll learn, in this chapter, how to put a template to use.

Why Templates Can Save Time

When you save a file in Project 98, it's saved by default as a regular Project or schedule file, and includes all the task and resource information you entered. When you open the file, it opens the one and only copy of that file, and when you save the file, it saves changes to that file.

In this scenario, it's not necessarily convenient to reuse all the information stored in your Project file. If you have a similar project and want to save the trouble of reentering all the information, you'll have to do some careful saving (and saving as) to reuse the information you want without overwriting the original file.

A better way to make your basic task and resource information available for reuse is to save that information as a template file. The template file is like a pattern of project tasks and resources that you can use as many times as you want. Using a template saves you the trouble of entering similar task and resource information over and over.

The template file sets up your basic task and resource information for you. Then you can edit it to fine-tune it for the unique requirements of your current project. Before I launch into describing the templates Project provides and how to work with them, here are a few situations where you might want to create a template:

- You have a project, such as a newsletter or publication that recurs on a regular basis.
- You have a schedule file into which you've entered a tremendous amount of task or resource information, and you think you might have other similar projects.
- You want to create an example file of how numerous links work, so you don't have to create the links again.
- Members of your company's sales force need a basic tool for plotting out schedules for customers, and you want to provide a schedule blueprint with typical task durations.

- You're training others to manage a particular type of project in your company, and you want to provide a framework to help them with planning and to ensure that they don't miss any steps.

Using a Template

When you install the typical Project features, the Setup process copies a number of predesigned templates to your system. Although you can create your own templates (as you'll learn later in this chapter), and the process for using one of your own templates is the same as the process for using a template provided with Project, it's worth reviewing the templates that come with Project in the hopes that some will be useful to you. Table 16.1 lists the templates that ship with Project 98.

Table 16.1 Templates Installed with Project 98

Template	Description
Aerospace	Offers a detailed plan for developing an aerospace product; this plan could be adapted for other manufacturing environments and products.
Event Planning	Maps out a plan for planning, publicizing, and running a special event; uses outlining, summary tasks, and linking to clearly organize tasks, and contains suggested task durations.
Intranet	Establishes a complete framework for planning, designing, testing, implementing, and supporting a corporate intranet; includes extensive notes about tasks and outlining to provide added guidance for running the project.
ISO 9000	Provides a plan for implementing ISO 9000 quality standards and management in a company, including documenting the process, setting up the internal audit process, training, and company education.
Renovation	Plans for all the phases of a major workplace renovation, including selecting an architect and designer, preparing the site for renovation, performing the construction and systems improvements, furnishing, and reoccupying the space.
Software Launch	Maps out the process of launching new software, covering areas including market planning, advertising and public relations, developing relationships with vendors and customers, and the product release announcement; this plan could potentially be adapted for other products.

You can use one of Project's templates to create a "practice" file that you can use to learn to work with Project features. That way, you only risk messing up sample information, not vital schedule information that you had to spend your own time entering.

The previous version of Project (for Windows 95, also sometimes called version 4.1) offered several more templates. These were found in the folder \Msoffice\Project\Library by default. If you didn't delete your old version of Project and installed Project 98 to a new folder, you may be able to access the old template files. Be aware, though, that if you open an older template file, Project 98 may make slight scheduling changes, because Project 98 handles some scheduling details differently than the previous version.

Project and Windows identify template files with an MPT file name extension (which normally is hidden) instead of the MPP extension used for normal Project schedule files. Because the template files are identified differently "behind the scenes," opening a template file is slightly different from opening a regular Project file.

To open a template file—one that you created or one that comes with Project—follow these steps:

1. Open the File menu and click Open (or press Ctrl+O). Alternately, click the Open button on the Standard toolbar (second from the left and has an open file folder). The File Open dialog box appears.
2. Click to open the Files of Type drop-down list; then click Templates, as shown in Figure 16.1. After you make this selection, the Look In list in the dialog box adjusts to list only folders and template files.
3. Use the Look In drop-down list and the folder icons to navigate to the folder that holds the template you want to use. To access the templates that come with Project, navigate to the \Program Files\Microsoft Office\Templates\Microsoft Project folder (refer to Figure 16.1) to display the templates that come with Project shown in Figure 16.2. (If you didn't install Project 98 to the default folder for it and other Office applications, you'll need to navigate to the appropriate template folder on your system.)

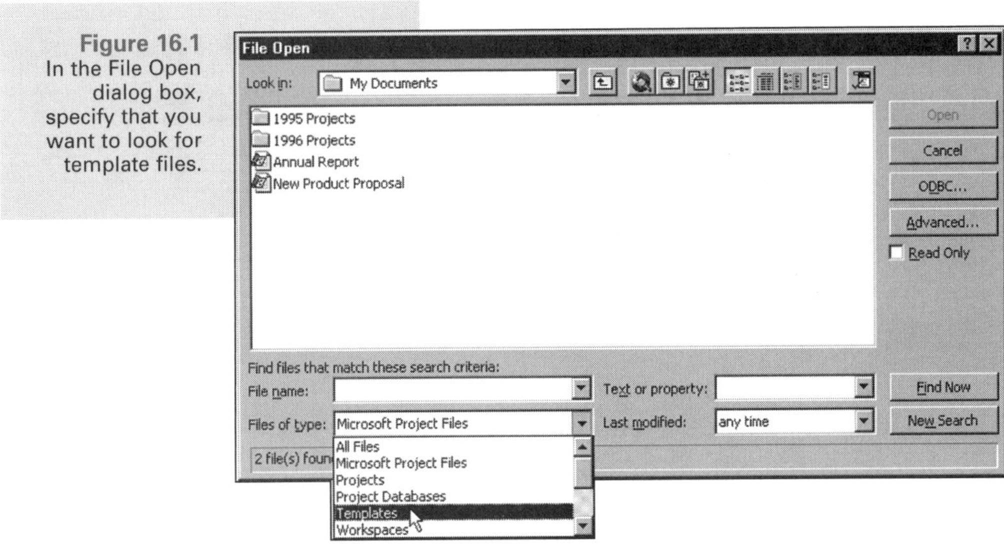

Figure 16.1 In the File Open dialog box, specify that you want to look for template files.

4. In the Look In list, double-click the name of the template file you want to open, or click the file name once, and then click the Open button. The template opens onscreen. Figure 16.3 shows an example of how one of Project's templates, the Event Planning template, appears when it's opened.

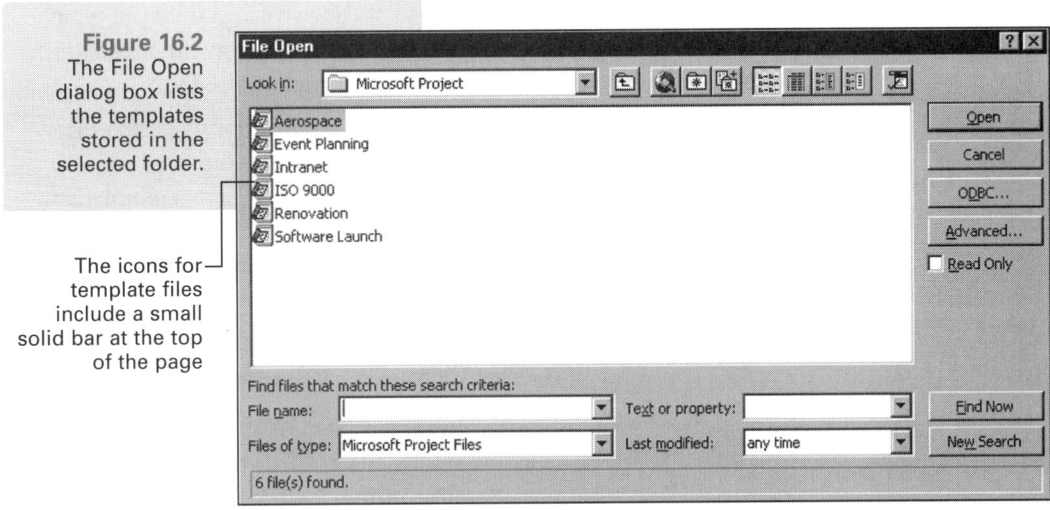

Figure 16.2 The File Open dialog box lists the templates stored in the selected folder.

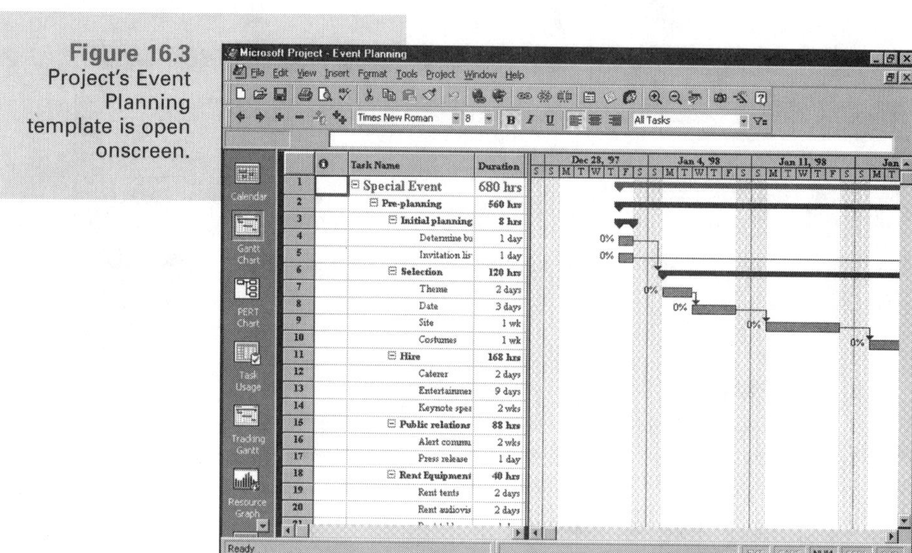

Figure 16.3 Project's Event Planning template is open onscreen.

5. Before you make any changes, I recommend immediately saving the template as a Project file. By default, when you try to save a template file, Project assumes you want to save a copy of the template file as a regular Project file. To start the save, open the File menu and click Save (or press Ctrl+S). Alternately, click the Save button on the Standard toolbar. The File Save dialog box appears.
6. In the File Save dialog box, navigate to the drive and folder in which you want to save the file using the Save In list. (To avoid confusion, you shouldn't save the file in the default templates folder.)
7. In the File Name text box (see Figure 16.4), edit the suggested file name to save the file with a name that's different from the template name—one that's more descriptive of your project. For example, you might include the name of the product you're marketing in the file name for your copy of the Event Planning template, as in **98 Sales Conference Banquet Event Plan**.
8. Click Save to finish saving your file. Planning Wizard, if enabled, asks whether you want to save the file with a baseline (see Figure 16.5).
9. I recommend saving the plan without a baseline, because you haven't yet entered your real schedule information. Click to select the Save '(Current File)' Without a Baseline option button, if needed; then click on OK.

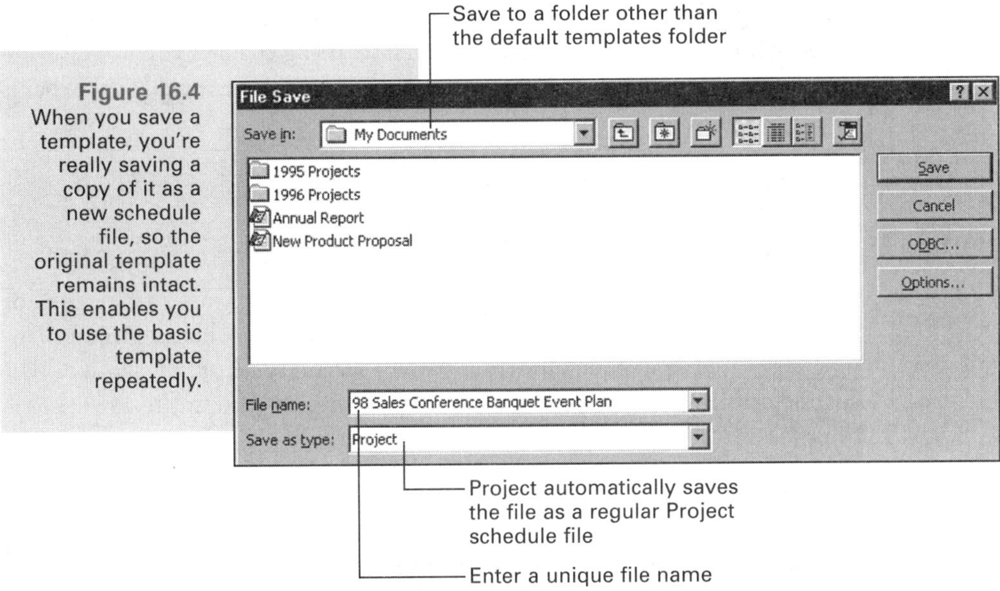

Figure 16.4 When you save a template, you're really saving a copy of it as a new schedule file, so the original template remains intact. This enables you to use the basic template repeatedly.

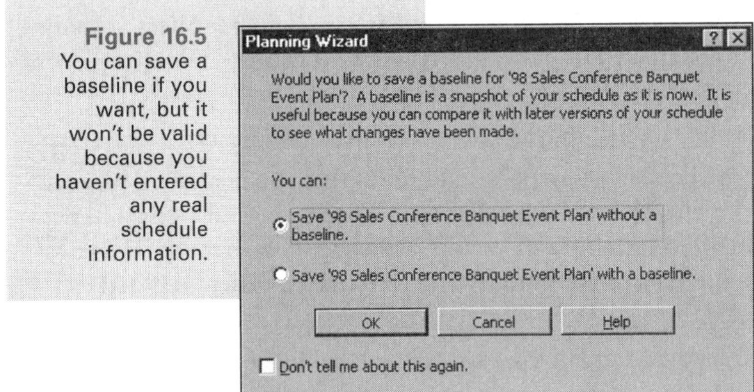

Figure 16.5 You can save a baseline if you want, but it won't be valid because you haven't entered any real schedule information.

After you open the template you want, and save a copy of it as a regular file, you can begin editing it to include your actual schedule information. The types of edits you need to make and the available bells and whistles vary, depending on the contents of the template. For example, the Event Planning template (refer to Figure 16.3) provides a suggested list of tasks and a suggested duration for each task. Therefore all you need to do is to enter correct start dates for tasks in the Task Sheet and assign resources. In the Event Planning template, the text and Gantt bars are already attractively formatted and color-coded (the top summary task is in red) to make them easy to tell apart. Other templates might include special tables and views you can apply, or other kinds of formatting. Simply make the edits and formatting changes you want, saving and printing when needed. After you save your copy of the template, it behaves as other Project files do.

Creating a Template

Because a template works like a pattern, it can consist of just a few pieces, or as many pieces as are needed to create the final product. Thus, a Project planning template can include numerous pattern pieces (types of information) that anyone opening the template can use. Any template you create can include these kinds of information and tools, among others:

- Lists of tasks in the Task Sheet, including suggested durations and links.
- Lists of resources in the Resource Sheet; for example, if a particular project always requires a resource, such as a shipping company that charges a per use and hourly rate, include information about that resource (especially its costs) with the template.
- Text formatting applied in the Task Sheet or Resource Sheet, including formatting applied to individual cells as well as Text Style changes for categories of information.
- Formatting applied to chart elements, such as Gantt bars.
- Custom views, tables, reports, and filters that you created and stored with the file using the Organizer (see "Dealing with the Organizer" in Chapter 9 to learn how to use the Organizer to save special elements with a file rather than in the default Project template, GLOBAL.MPT), if needed.
- Macros and custom toolbars or toolbar buttons (see Chapter 21 for more information about macros) that you saved with the file or added to the file using the Organizer.

To build your own template, start by opening a new file and creating all the elements you want the template to include, such as the types of elements just listed. If you want to use a project file you previously created as a template, open that file. For example, if you created a New Product Proposal schedule that worked well for you, such as the one shown in Figure 16.6, you can save it as a template.

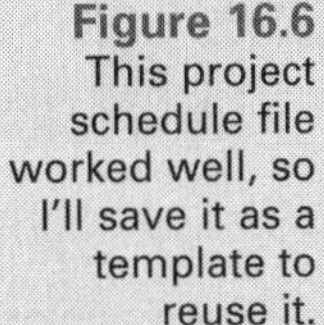

Note

Make sure that you include as much file Properties information and as many Task Notes and Resource Notes with your template file as possible. This information will remind you and other users how to correctly use the template and will help you recall what particular entries mean.

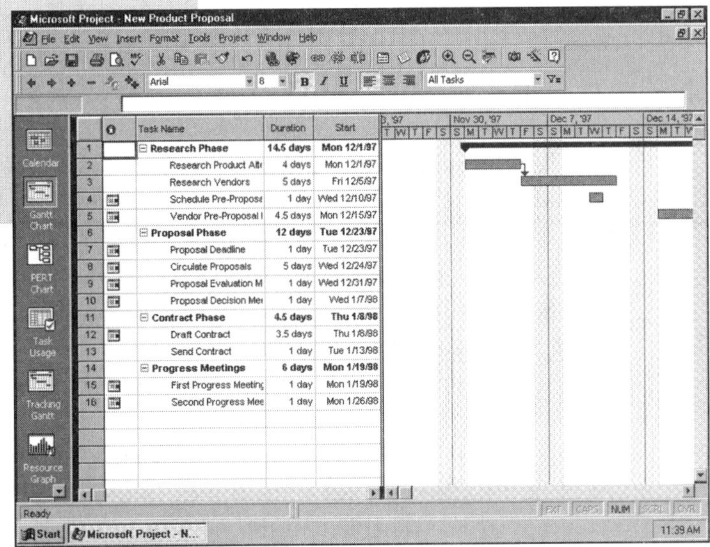

Figure 16.6 This project schedule file worked well, so I'll save it as a template to reuse it.

Next, follow these steps to save your creation as a template:

1. Use the Organizer to ensure that you save all custom elements, such as views, reports, macros, and toolbars to the file that you want to save as a template (see "Dealing with the Organizer" in Chapter 9). If you don't do so, those elements won't be available in your template.
2. Open the File menu and click Save As. The File Save dialog box appears.
3. Use the Save In list to navigate to the folder where you want to store the template file. If you want to store your custom template along with Project's templates, select the \Program Files\Microsoft Office\Templates\Microsoft Project folder.
4. Click to open the Save As Type drop-down list; then click on Template.
5. Edit the File Name entry to make it easy to see that the file is a template, as shown in Figure 16.7.

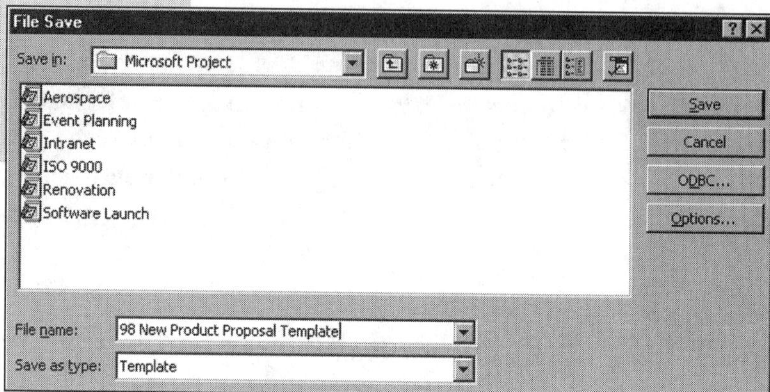

Figure 16.7 Edit the File Name entry to clarify that the file's a template.

6. Click the Save button. Planning Wizard, if enabled, asks whether or not you want to save the file with a baseline.
7. I recommend that you save the template without a baseline so as not to interfere with baseline calculations for schedule files based on the template. Click to select the Save '(Current File)' Without a Baseline option button, if needed; then click OK to finish saving the template. The title bar for the file changes to indicate that the currently opened file is a template file.
8. Open the File menu and click Close. This removes the template file from the screen. At any time, you can reopen the template file and save a copy of it as described in the previous section to begin working with the copy.

Sometimes you might want to make changes to one of your custom template files, or one that came with Project. Say, for example, that you have a template file in which you included resource information, and you discover that the standard hourly rates and overtime rates for several of the resources have increased. You can open the template file, edit the template, and resave it as a template file. Here are the steps:

1. Open the template file, as described in steps 1 through 4 of the previous section, "Using a Template."
2. Make any changes you want to make in the template.
3. Open the File menu and click Save As.
4. In the File Save dialog box, select Template from the Save As Type drop-down list. Leave all other settings intact to ensure that your changes are saved within the same template file.

5. Click Save. Planning Wizard, if enabled, asks if you want to save the template with a baseline.
6. Click to select the Save '(Current File)' Without a Baseline option button, if needed; then click on OK to finish saving the template.
7. You then should open the File menu and click Close to close the template file. If you want to use it immediately to create a schedule, reopen it and save a copy.

Finding More Templates

Software publishers, such as Microsoft, now have a better way to help keep users up-to-date about product developments and to provide example files, macros, and—yes—templates users can work with to save time. Microsoft does offer a Web site that includes not only support for Project (see Chapter 19, "Taking Project Online," to learn more about online support), but also template and example files you can download free of charge. When you see a link to a file to download, simply click the link to initiate the download process.

The Web page for Project 98 downloads is **http://www.microsoft.com/project/software/software_templates.htm.** As of this writing, the templates posted there focus mostly on setting up Project 98 to work in conjunction with other applications (Office 97) or in particular networked (NT Server) or data sharing (SQL Server) environments.

The download page for the previous version of Project, however, is still available, and contains a number of files, templates, and examples for download. Although Project 98 may make slight scheduling changes when you open one of these files, for the most part they can serve as a good starting point for your work. (Many of these files will probably be updated for Project 98 and posted to the 98 Web download page in the near future.) The Web page for downloads for the previous version of Project is **http://www.microsoft.com/project/software/software_prev_temp.htm.**

The previous version download page offers templates both from Microsoft and third-party sources, and these templates run the gamut from computer development and business topics to personal topics. For example, there are four Template Packs (numbered 1-4), which offer templates for engineering projects, oil drilling, negotiating and signing a commercial lease, publishing a magazine, and planning a wedding. You can download other individual templates, such as the holiday planning template pictured in Figure 16.8.

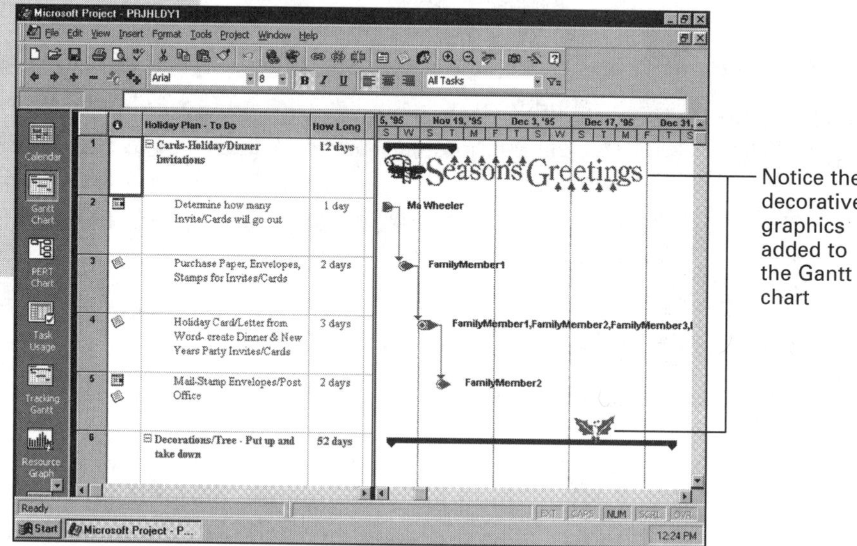
Notice the decorative graphics added to the Gantt chart

Figure 16.8 I downloaded this holiday planning template, designed for the previous version of Project, from the Project Web site.

Caution

If you search the Web or look at various forums on CompuServe and America Online, you may find additional Project files and templates created by other users or third-party software developers. Be aware of two things when you download files created by unfamiliar sources. First, some of these files aren't free; you either must provide a credit card number to purchase them or are expected to mail in a shareware fee (an honor-system fee that compensates the author for developing the file). Second, files that contain macros may also contain macro viruses. Make sure you have Project's macro virus protection feature turned on (as described in Chapter 21), and use caution if you open an unfamiliar file with macros enabled.

17 Consolidating Projects

In This Chapter

- Consolidating projects
- Using and adjusting the consolidated information
- Linking individual tasks between projects
- Sharing resources between projects that aren't consolidated

After you become a Microsoft Project guru (I know you will with this book in hand), you'll use it to manage more forms of work than you could have imagined.

You can have two, three, or more schedules running simultaneously. In such a situation, the challenge for you as the project leader becomes to understand and prioritize work *between projects*, as well as to understand and prioritize work between tasks in a project.

This chapter shows you how to better manage all of the work on your plate by consolidating information from multiple project files.

When to Combine Projects

If you need a single printout of the tasks from two projects, you can print them out separately, trim the excess, tape the two together, and make a photocopy so that you have a single, solid document. This solution, however, is clearly inelegant and forces you to do the dirty work rather than having your computer do it.

Project offers a workaround for situations like this; it's called consolidating projects. When you consolidate two or more schedule files, Project places all the information from each of the selected files (sometimes called *subprojects* or *source projects*) into a single, consolidated file (sometimes called the *master project*). Then you can change the view, print, and otherwise work with the combined information. You can consolidate up to 1000 different project schedules (assuming your system has the horsepower to do so) in a single consolidated file.

Here are just a few situations in which you might want to consolidate projects into a single file:

- You're managing multiple projects and you want a list of in-progress tasks to jog your memory about tasks that you need to follow up on. You consolidate the tasks, and then filter the Task Sheet so that it lists only the in-progress tasks.
- You want to display a list of all the tasks in your projects that will start in the near future. You can print them before a meeting with your boss, so the two of you can discuss shifting priorities and identify some tasks to reschedule.
- You want to print a list of all the resources you're using for all projects.
- You have two projects using the same resources, and you want to see if there are any resource overallocations. You can consolidate the files and switch to Resource Usage view to find overallocations.

Combining Projects

Consolidating schedule files places all the information from the specified individual files into a new file that is the consolidated file. You can save a consolidated file in order to reuse the information it contains. When you save it, you can assign it a unique name of your choosing. Alternately, you can insert other schedule files into the current file to consolidate them; the current file then becomes the consolidated file. The rest of this section explains the details of creating and working with a consolidated file.

Consolidation Methods

Consolidated files can work in two different ways. The consolidated file can exist independently of the files from which its information came, or remain linked to the original source files. The first situation is fine if you want to work with the consolidated file on a one-time basis only. If, however, you want to reuse the consolidated file over a period of days, weeks, or longer, the schedules for the individual, original project files might change, making the consolidated file obsolete—unless you link it to the original files when you create it.

Using the first method described next, you can create consolidated files with or without links. The second method is faster and can only be used when you want to consolidate project files with links.

Inserting a Project to Consolidate Files

The primary method for consolidating files in Project 98 is to insert a schedule file into a row in an existing project file, which then becomes a consolidated or master project file. Each inserted source project or subproject file is linked to a single Task Sheet line in the master project. At first, you don't see all the tasks for the inserted subproject; instead, you see a single summary task and Gantt bar summarizing the inserted project. By default, the start date entered in the inserted subproject file is the same date it uses in the master project file; when the files are linked, you can change the start date in either file to update it for both. The duration of the full schedule for the inserted subproject file becomes the duration for the subproject summary task entry in the master project Task Sheet. So, if all the tasks listed in the subproject will take 95 days to complete, the master project shows **95d** as the duration entry for the subproject task, and you can't edit that entry.

There will be times when you need to readjust the start date for a subproject. See the "Controlling Dates in Consolidated Projects" section later in this chapter for more details.

You have to create the source or subproject files before adding them to the consolidated project file. You can't insert a file that doesn't exist, after all. You don't, however, have to initially create the tasks within the subproject file. You can simply open and save the file with the name you want, and then close it and add it to the consolidated master project. You can reopen the subproject file at any time to enter its tasks.

The approach just mentioned works best in many cases, because it ensures that you don't have to go back and manually update a subproject start date.

To insert a project (source project or subproject) within an existing project file (which becomes the consolidated or master project), follow these steps:

1. Create and save the subproject files.
2. Create or open the file where you want to insert other files. This file will become the consolidated or master project file.
3. Click the Task Name cell for a blank Task Sheet row in which you want to insert another project. Or, click on a cell in the row above where you want to insert the project. (Actually, you're specifying the row where the summary task representing the inserted task will appear).

You can insert a project at any outline level or later demote or promote it by demoting or promoting the summary task that represents it.

4. Open the Insert menu and click Project. The Insert Project dialog box appears, as shown in Figure 17.1.

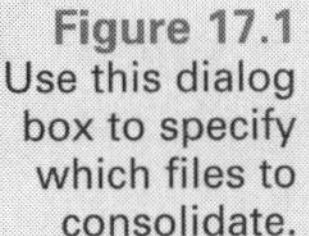

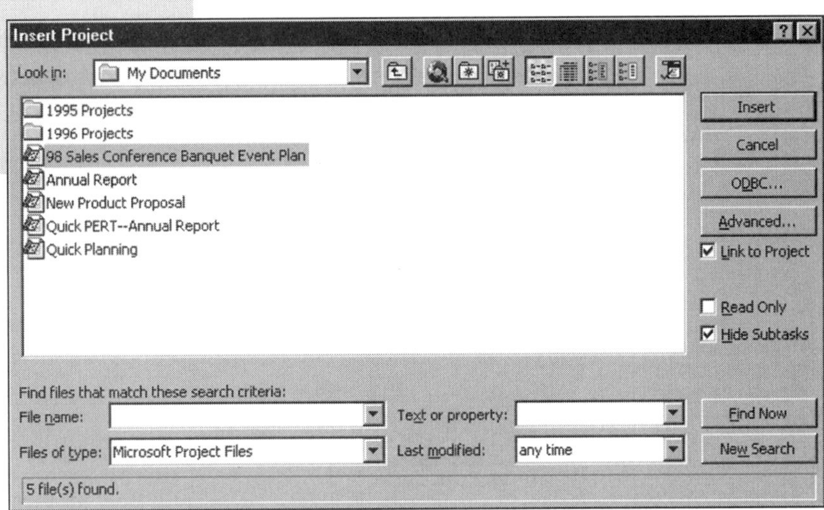

Figure 17.1 Use this dialog box to specify which files to consolidate.

5. If needed, use the Look In drop-down list to navigate to the drive and folder holding the file to insert.
6. Click the file you want to insert. If you want to insert more than one file and they're both stored in the same drive and folder, you can click the first file; then press and hold Ctrl and click additional files to select them.
7. By default, the inserted subproject file is linked to the consolidated (master project) file, so the Link to Project check box will be checked. If you do not want the files to be linked (meaning changes you make in one of the files will not appear in the other), clear the Link to Project check box.
8. If you want the inserted (subproject) file information to appear in the consolidated file but you don't want to be able to edit the subproject information from the consolidated file, click the Read Only check box. (When the project is inserted as a read-only file, you can still edit the separate subproject file; changes you make there show up when you open the consolidated file.)
9. By default, the inserted file appears as a summary task, with its subtasks hidden. To display all the subtasks when the project is inserted, click the check beside Hide Subtasks to clear it.
10. Click Insert. The inserted (subproject) task appears in the file, as shown in Figure 17.2.

If the inserted file name doesn't display correctly or you want to use another way to identify the inserted file in the consolidated file, change the Title for the file on the Summary tab of the Properties dialog box (File, Properties).

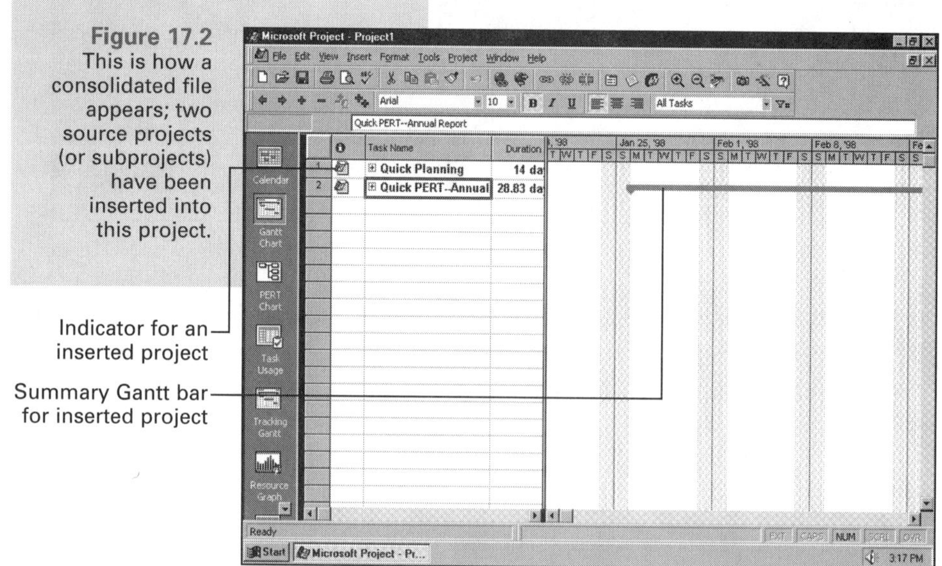

Figure 17.2 This is how a consolidated file appears; two source projects (or subprojects) have been inserted into this project.

11. Save the master project file to save the links to subprojects.

You can use the preceding steps to link other subprojects to the master project file.

Combining Multiple Projects in a New Window

There is a somewhat faster way to create a consolidated file, but as usual with such matters, you have to give up a little flexibility to save time. To use this method, begin by opening each of the files you want to consolidate. Make any changes you want to the files, and save them. Open the Window menu and click New Window. The New Window dialog box appears. In the Projects list, click the name of the first file to consolidate. Press and hold down the Ctrl key; then click additional files to select them (see Figure 17.3). Click OK, and Project compiles the consolidated file onscreen into a brand new file. (By default, the consolidated file is linked to the original subproject or source files. In addition, the resource pools for the individual files are not consolidated.) You then can save and work with the consolidated file. The source files remain separate and intact on disk. So, with this method, you're creating a brand new file rather than altering an existing one.

Working with Your Consolidated Information

When you're working with the consolidated file, you can do everything that you can do in an individual Project file. You can change any entries you want, or change the view. For example, open the View menu and click Resource Sheet or click the Resource Sheet to view the Resource Sheet for a consolidated project file. If you are sharing the resource pools for the consolidated files (sharing resource pools is described later in this chapter), any resource overallocations are highlighted in bold, red text. Also, if you have combined resource pools, you can open the View menu and click on Resource Graph or click the Resource Graph icon in the View Bar. When you display a resource that's assigned to more than one project, the overallocated hours for that resource are graphed (see Figure 17.4).

Another thing to note is that when you're working with the information in a consolidated file, the name for each of the subproject or source project files you inserted appears as a numbered summary task row in the Task Sheet of any view that includes the Task Sheet (such as Gantt Chart view). When you consolidate multiple files into a new window, these rows are treated by Project as summary tasks at the highest level of the outline (see Chapter 13, "Working with Outlining," to learn more about outlining). The top-level tasks from the source files appear as subtasks of the source files. All tasks that were subtasks within the original project files are hidden, and all individual project tasks

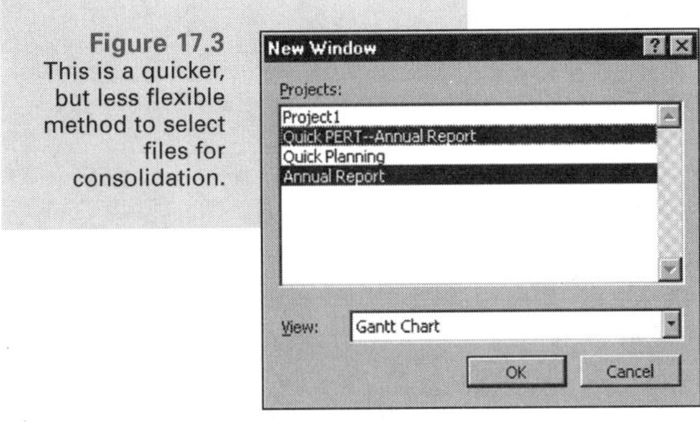

Figure 17.3 This is a quicker, but less flexible method to select files for consolidation.

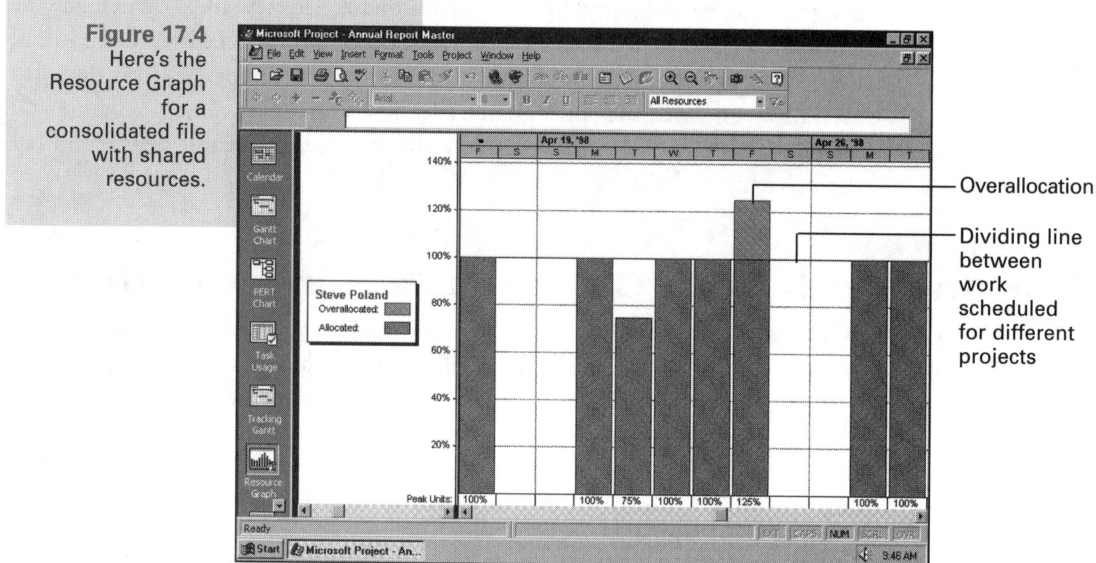

Figure 17.4 Here's the Resource Graph for a consolidated file with shared resources.

holding subtasks appear in bold (see Figure 17.5). However, if you consolidated the file by inserting a file, the summary task for the inserted file appears at the same outline level as the task below which it was inserted.

If you click the Task Name column and then click the Hide Subtasks button on the Formatting toolbar, the Task Sheet displays only the names of the consolidated files (see Figure 17.6).

Figure 17.5 Project provides cues to help you identify which tasks came from which subprojects (source files) and which tasks include subtasks.

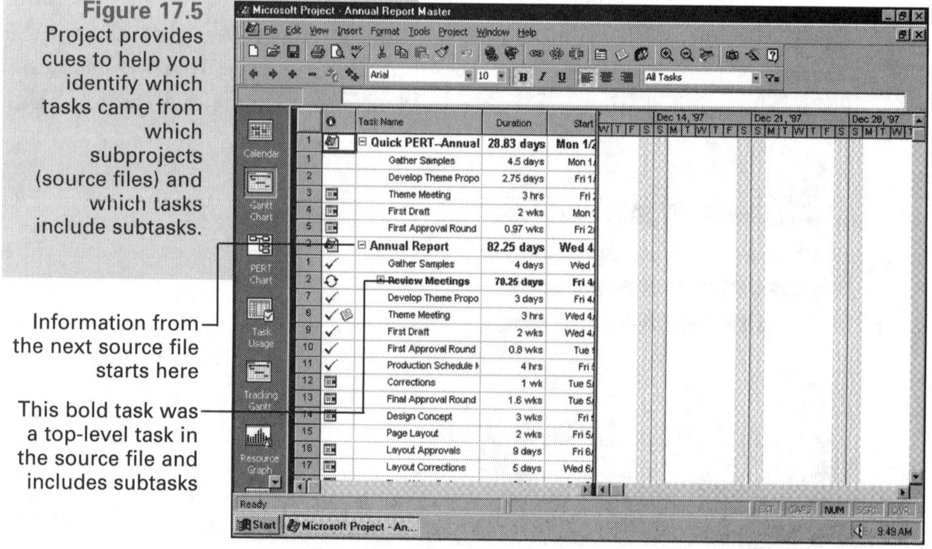

Information from the next source file starts here

This bold task was a top-level task in the source file and includes subtasks

By now, you get the idea. The consolidated file behaves much like other project files in terms of how you can change its contents.

Opening Subprojects

Even though the subproject files and consolidated (master project) file remain as separate entities on disk, by design they share information so that they always reflect the same dates. For example, if you reschedule several tasks in a subproject to make the total subproject duration longer, you'll want the new duration to be reflected in the master project file. It helps to understand how this automatic updating occurs; it takes place through opening files.

To update subproject and consolidated project information, open each subproject file as normal, update its contents, and save it. Then you open the consolidated (master project) file, which is automatically updated to display the latest information you added into each subproject file. Make sure that you then save the consolidated file to save its changes.

When you save or close a consolidated file in which the individual files share resource pools, you might be prompted to save the resource pool as a separate file. Follow the prompts to do so.

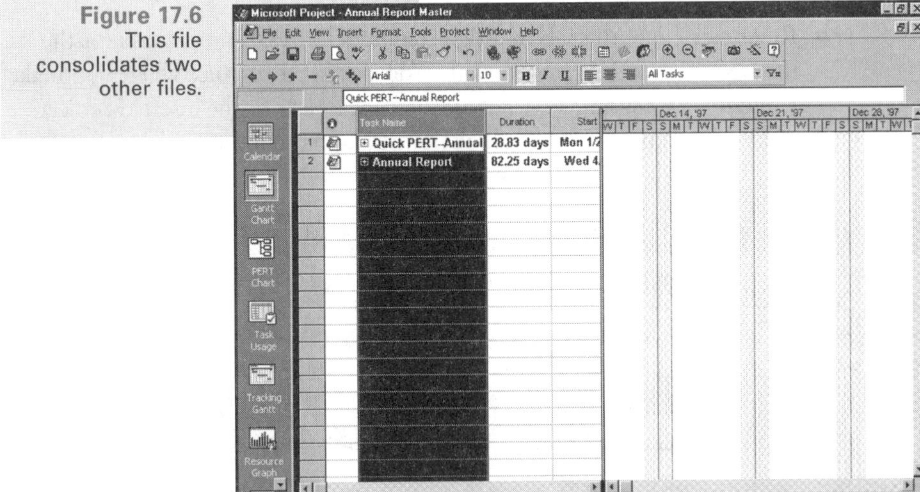

Figure 17.6 This file consolidates two other files.

Working with Subprojects

In most cases, working with an inserted subproject is identical to working with other summary tasks and subtasks. You can expand and collapse the inserted task's subtasks, or update information, such as actual start dates and work completed for any subtask. However, you'll need to use some unique steps when you're working with the inserted subproject's summary task, covered in this section.

Changing Subproject (Inserted Project) Information

When you double-click the summary task for an inserted subproject, or click the task and then click the Task Information button on the Standard toolbar, the Inserted Project Information dialog box appears. In most respects, this dialog box resembles the Task Information dialog box. It offers the same five tabs, which in most cases have identical options:

- **General**—The General tab appears in Figure 17.7. You can use it to change the inserted project's summary task Name and Priority, or to control the display of the summary tasks Gantt bar and any rolled-up subtask bars.
- **Predecessors**—Use this tab to link the inserted project's summary task to another task in the consolidated file. For example, if two inserted projects need to finish by the same date, you could create a Finish-to-Finish relationship between their summary tasks. The settings on this tab work just like those for a regular task.
- **Resources**—Use this tab to assign resources to the summary task for the inserted subtask. You might want to do this in an instance where you make a resource responsible (a supervisor) for all aspects of the inserted project. Again, the settings on this tab work just like those for a regular task.

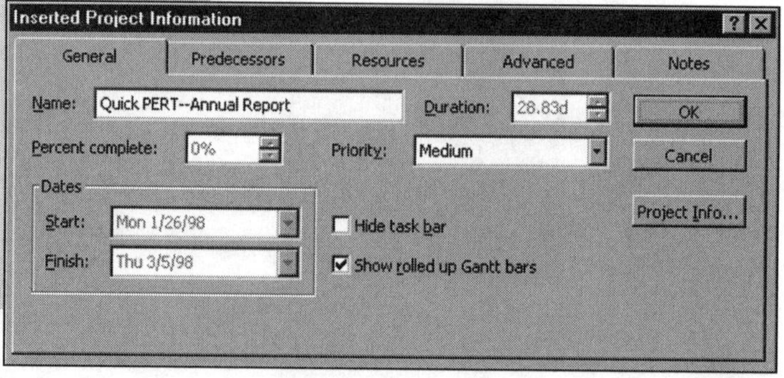

Figure 17.7 Some options on the General tab of the Inserted Project Information dialog box are dimmed, meaning you can't edit them.

- **Advanced**—This tab (Figure 17.8) differs most significantly from the corresponding tab in the Task Information dialog box for a regular task. In the Source Project area of the dialog box, you can specify whether the inserted subproject is linked to the consolidated project (Link to Project), and if so, whether the link is read-only. If you want to verify the name of the inserted file, it appears in the text box in the Source Project area. To insert another subproject file, instead, in the same location in the Task Sheet, click the Browse button to redisplay the Inserted Project dialog box to choose a different file to insert.
- **Notes**—Use this tab to insert, format, and edit a note for the inserted task's summary task. Use the same techniques on this tab that you would use on the Notes tab for an individual task.

The lower-right corner of each tab in the Inserted Project Information dialog box displays a Project Info button. Click that button to display a Project Information dialog box similar to the one shown in Figure 17.9. You can use this dialog box to change such key features as the Start Date for the inserted project or the Calendar it uses. Its options work just like those for the regular Project Information dialog box, which you can display in the open subproject. If you want to change the same information for the inserted subproject without opening the subproject file, display the Project Information dialog box by clicking the Project Info button in the Inserted Project Information dialog box.

Deleting a Subproject

If you want to delete the source project or subproject, right-click its row number, and then click Delete Task. If it's enabled, the Planning Wizard displays a dialog box (Figure 17.10) asking you to confirm the deletion. To finish the deletion, leave the first option button selected, and click OK. If you made changes to any of the inserted project's information in the consolidated project file, you'll

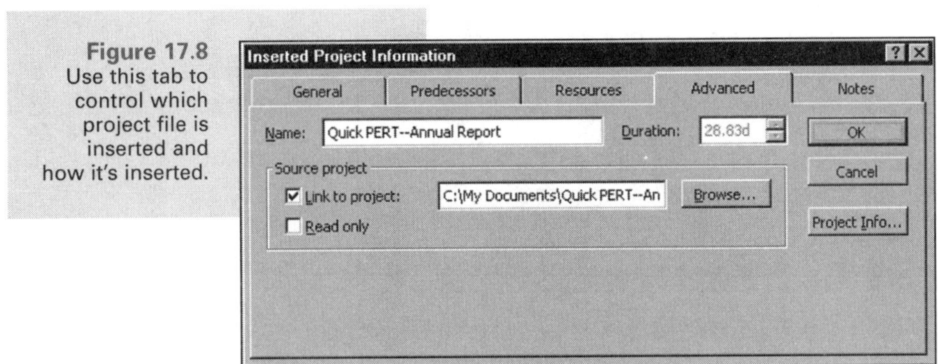

Figure 17.8 Use this tab to control which project file is inserted and how it's inserted.

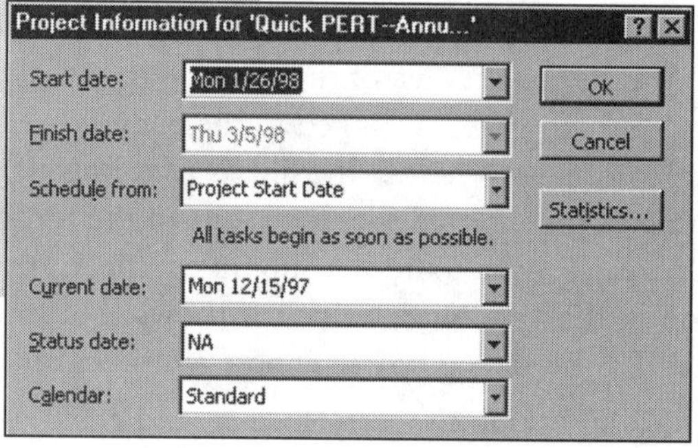

Figure 17.9 Use this dialog box to change overall schedule information for the inserted project.

also be prompted to specify whether or not to save those changes to the subproject file before the subproject is removed from the consolidated project. Click Yes to do so, or No to remove the inserted subproject without saving changes.

Controlling Dates in Consolidated Projects

Sometimes you'll need to make manual adjustments to ensure that the schedules in your subproject files and master project file are in sync.

For example, an inserted subproject file might include old schedule information, so you might need to adjust its start date to match the master project's start date. This would happen, for example, if you create the subproject file on April 7, so that its original project Start Date was April 7, but didn't create the master project file until April 8, and accepted that date as the master project's Start Date. You'd then need to change the inserted project's start date to April 8 to make sure its schedule falls within the consolidated master project schedule.

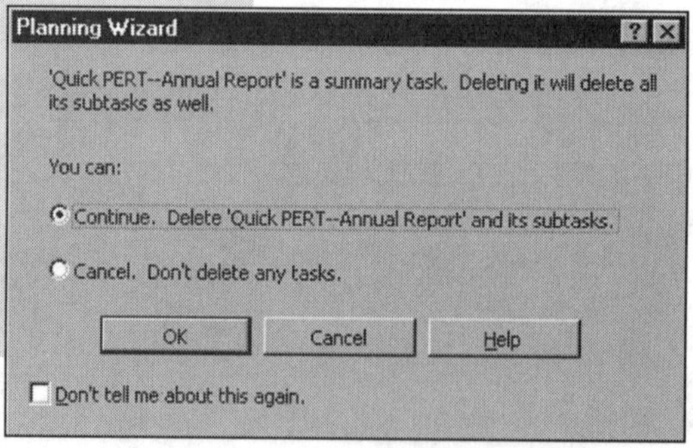

Figure 17.10 Planning Wizard asks you to verify whether to delete the inserted project summary task.

Simply updating the inserted project's start date doesn't fully work because the schedules for individual subtasks of the inserted project's summary task don't generally update correctly. To update a subproject file so that its start date reflects the start date you entered in the master project and so that the work for all its subtasks is correctly rescheduled, use these steps:

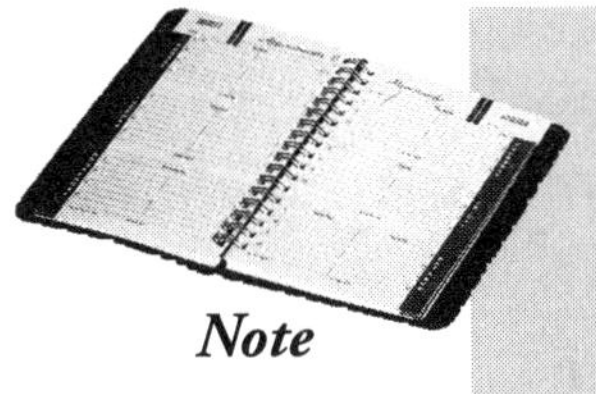

Note

Keep in mind that the following steps also reschedule the start date and scheduled work in the individual subproject (source project) file if the files are linked. Changes you make in the subproject file appear in the consolidated file, and vice versa, for linked files.

1. Open the master project file.
2. In the Task Sheet, display the summary tasks for the inserted subproject. (Click the plus beside the inserted project's summary task, or click the summary task and click the Show Subtasks button on the Formatting toolbar.)
3. Drag over the row headers for the inserted project's summary task and all the display subtasks to select all the task rows.
4. Click to open the Tools menu; point to Tracking, and click Update Project. The Update Project dialog box appears.
5. Click to select the Reschedule Uncompleted Work to Start option button (Figure 17.11). Click the drop-down arrow for the date text box shown beside that option button; then use the calendar that appears to select the new start date (which should be the start date for the consolidated master project).
6. Click the Selected Tasks option button to ensure you don't inadvertently reschedule tasks that aren't subtasks of the inserted project.
7. Click OK. If automatic recalculation is on, Project reschedules the inserted subproject to start on the adjusted dates. The subtasks are rescheduled accordingly, with each subtask's duration, link, constraint, and other settings controlling exactly how it's rescheduled. If the inserted subproject and its subtasks don't move automatically, press F9 to recalculate the schedule.

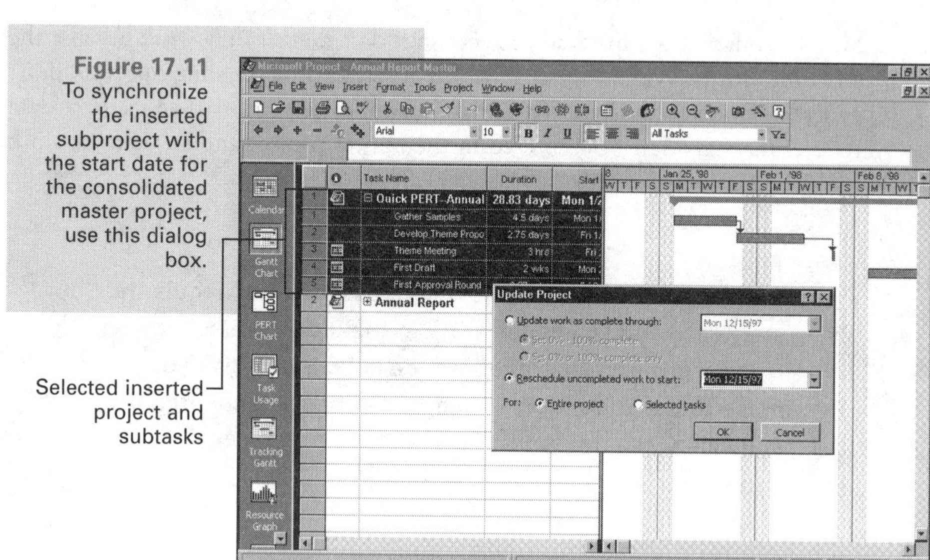

Figure 17.11 To synchronize the inserted subproject with the start date for the consolidated master project, use this dialog box.

Although links stay intact, you should review the moved tasks to ensure that they still make sense in light of the newly scheduled dates. For example, if a task is rescheduled during a period when a resource is on vacation, the task duration might've been greatly increased, so you might want to move the task manually or select another resource for it.

In some cases, task constraints will interfere with your ability to move out one or more tasks. For example, if a task has a Must Start On, Must Finish On, Finish No Later Than, or Start No Later Than constraint entered in the Constrain Task area of the Advanced tab in the Task Information dialog box, and the associated constraint date is earlier than the date you want to reschedule the task to, Project warns you that there's a scheduling conflict when you try to move the task. Click OK to continue; then remove the task's constraint, or select another constraint type, such as As Soon As Possible, As Late As Possible, Start No Earlier Than, or Finish No Earlier Than. (Remember that you can display the Task Information dialog box simply by double-clicking the task.)

Another problem occurs if you try to move out a single linked task rather than all the tasks. If you move a task and the link creates a scheduling conflict, you can remove the conflict by clicking the Task Name for the successor task, and then clicking the Unlink Tasks button on the Standard toolbar.

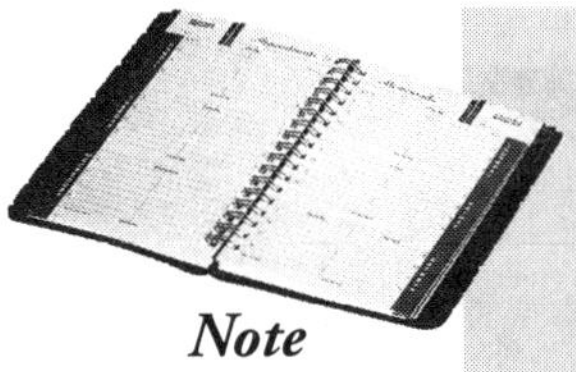

Note

If the subproject contains work already marked as completed, and the start date for that work precedes the start date you specified for the master project file, you can remove the conflict by removing the work specified as completed. To do so, open the Tools menu, point to Tracking, and click Update Tasks. Edit the % Complete entry to be 0; then click OK. Or, if the work really has started for the task, move the start date for the subproject entry in the master project to an earlier date, and also change the start date for the master project (choose Project, Project Information to display the proper dialog box) so that it begins earlier.

Linking Tasks between Projects

Another reason to consolidate files using the New Window command on the Window menu is to create a Finish-to-Start link between two tasks in different (separate) schedule files. Such a link enables you to ensure that the tasks happen in the proper order, even if they're in different project files. For example, you may have an external resource scheduled to handle both tasks, and you might want to link them to have a clear picture of what the impact is on both projects if the resource begins to run behind. Follow these steps to create a link:

1. Open the files holding the tasks to link. Make any needed changes to the files; then save the files.
2. Click to open the Window menu; then choose New Window.
3. In the Projects list of the New Window dialog box, press the Ctrl key and click the names of the files to consolidate.
4. Click OK to consolidate the files.
5. In the task list, click the Task Name cell for the earlier task, which will be the predecessor task for the link.
6. Press and hold the Ctrl key, and click the Task Name cell for the second task to link, which will be the successor task.
7. Click the Link Tasks button on the Standard toolbar. Project links the tasks. Project adjusts the schedule for the successor task and any tasks linked to it as needed to honor the new link. Figure 17.12 shows such a link.

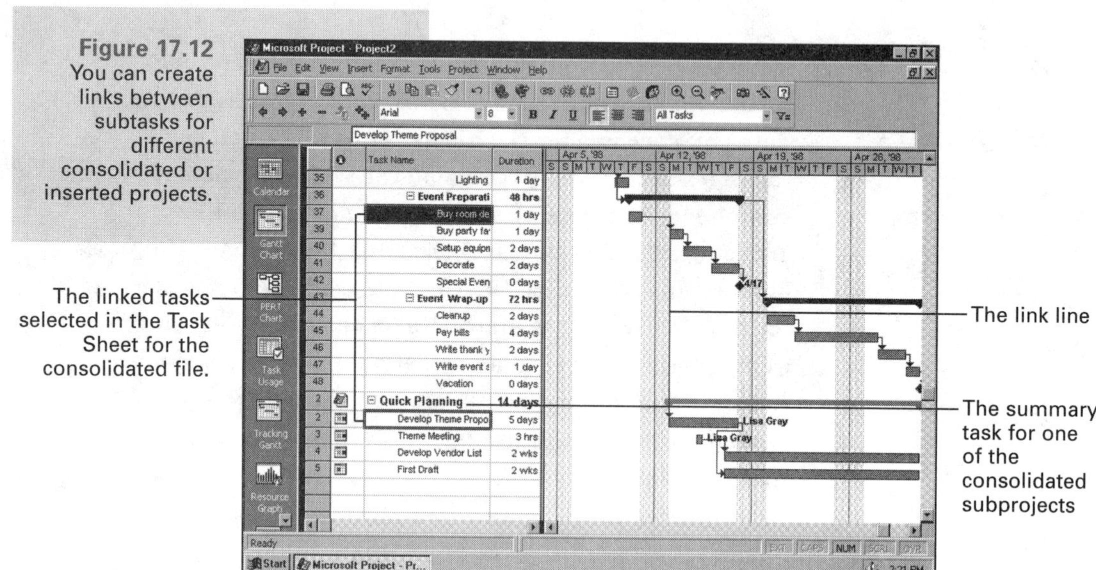

Figure 17.12 You can create links between subtasks for different consolidated or inserted projects.

If you then open one of the subproject (source) files, you'll see that a special task has been inserted to identify the external *predecessor* or *successor* task. For example, Figure 17.13 shows the external predecessor task for one of the consolidated files linked in Figure 17.12. Note that the external task's name is dimmed, meaning that you can't edit it. Its Gantt bar is gray as well because you can't move or otherwise reschedule the task. When you open the subproject file that holds the successor linked task, the task row displays a special Predecessor field entry that points to the full path and file name for the file holding the predecessor task, followed by a backslash and the task ID number. If you want to link tasks between two files without first consolidating them, simply open the file that holds the successor task to link, and make an entry in the Predecessor column for that task. That entry should give the full path and file name, followed by a backslash and the ID number, for the predecessor entry, as in **C:\My Documents\Work\Budget.mpp\14**.

If you want to break the link between tasks in different files, you can clear the Predecessor field entry in the file that holds the successor task. Or, redisplay the consolidated file if you saved it. Click a cell in the successor task row, and click the Unlink Tasks button on the Standard toolbar.

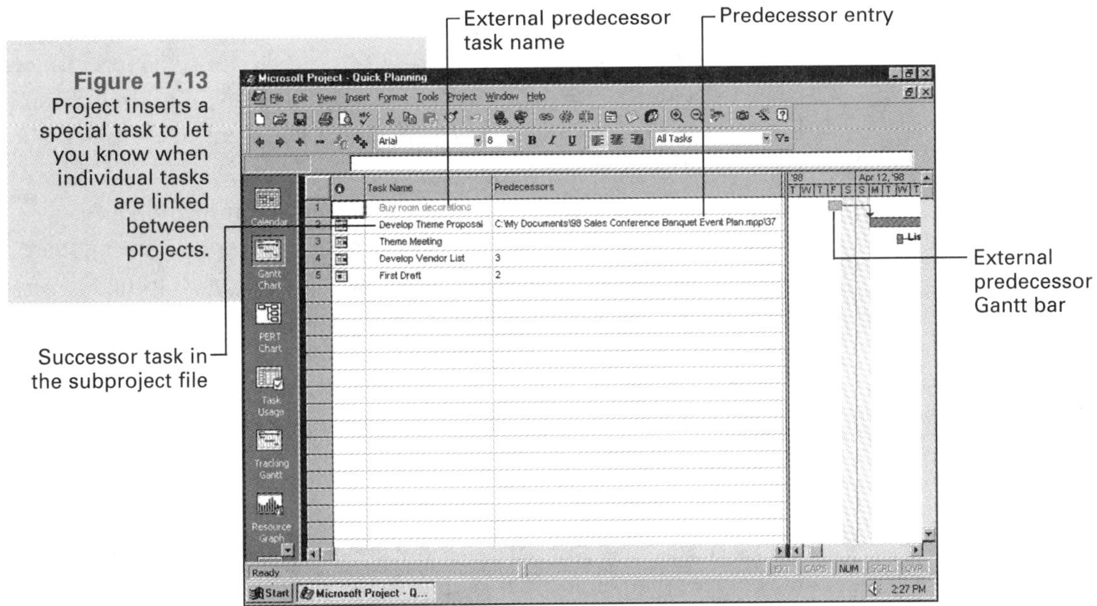

Figure 17.13 Project inserts a special task to let you know when individual tasks are linked between projects.

Working with Resource Pools (Sharing Resources)

Another name for the list of resources you create in the Resource Sheet for a particular project is the resource pool. You can assign any of the resources in that pool to any task in the project file. Each list of resources is saved along with the project file where you created it. It's important to realize, though, that any Project file can access the resource pool that's saved with another file.

When you start a new project file and want to use the entries in the Resource Sheet saved with another file, rather than typing in a whole new list of resources, you can do so by sharing resources. Here are the steps, which assume that you've already created and saved the Project file containing the resources you want to reuse:

1. Open the file in which you've already created and saved the resource information that you want to reuse. This is an important initial step because only those files that are open, and using their own resources, will appear in the Use Resources From drop-down list in the Share Resources dialog box.
2. Open or create the file that will share the existing resource information.

3. Open the Tools menu, point to Resources, and click Share Resources. The Share Resources dialog box appears.
4. Click the Use Resources option button; then use the From drop-down list to select the file containing the resources you want to share (see Figure 17.14).
5. In the On Conflict With Calendar Or Resource Information area, select Pool Takes Precedence (meaning that Project will adjust resource assignments in a way that makes sense for all the projects using the pool) or Sharer Takes Precedence (meaning that Project will adjust to accommodate any assignment change you make in a particular consolidated file).
6. Click OK to finish sharing the resources. The resource pool from the file you specified is now used for the current file. Save the current file to save the resource sharing information.

When you save and close a file that uses the resource information from another file, Project saves that "link." When you reopen the file containing the "link" to resource information, Project must open the other file. It displays a dialog box asking if you want to open the resource pool, open the resource pool and all other files using those shared resources, or not to open any other files. Make your choice and click OK. If you've made changes to the Resource Sheet in the file you're sharing information from and specified that the resource pool should open, those changes appear in the file that shares the information.

Conversely, if you reopen the file where you originally entered the resources, Project presents a few options. You can open the resource pool as read-only, open the resource file normally so that you can make changes to it (although if you choose this option and your files reside on a network, others users won't be able to change the resource pool), or open the file with the resource pool and any other files using the resource pool.

Figure 17.14 Select the file containing the resource pool you want to reuse.

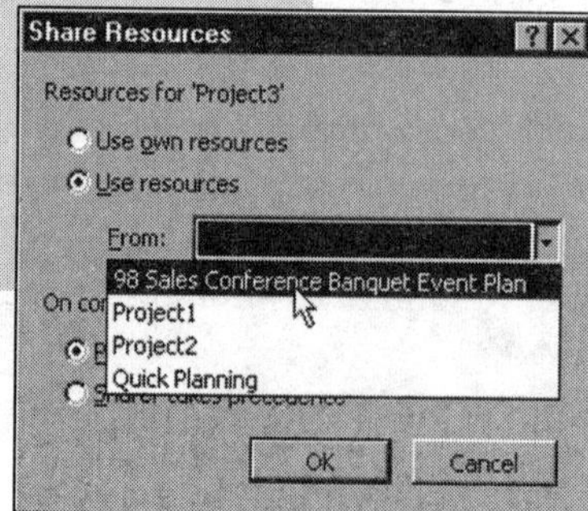

Note

If one of the files in a consolidated file holds the resource pool for all the consolidated files, you'll see both the options for opening a file that uses shared resources and for opening a file that holds the resource pool.

You can make changes such as rate changes to the resource information in the file that holds the resource pool and then simply open the other files that also use that resource pool to update the resource information for those files, too. However, if the resource pool file is stored on a network and others can make changes to the pool, and you have left a file using that resource pool open for several hours, your resource information won't be up to date. You can refresh the resource information (to get the latest information) without closing and reopening your file. Instead, open the Tools menu, point to Resources, and click Refresh Resource Pool. Conversely, if you make changes in any file that uses the resource pool on the network and want the pool to be updated with those changes, open the Tools menu, point to Resources, and click Update Resource Pool.

If you open a file that uses resource information from another file, you can edit the resource "link" information. To do so, redisplay the Share Resources dialog box by opening the Tools menu, pointing to Resources, and clicking Share Resources. In this dialog box, make the changes you prefer (such as selecting another file to use resources from, or opting not to use resources from another file at all), and then click OK. Project closes the dialog box, and your resource sharing changes take effect. Make sure that you save the current file to save these changes.

Note

In practical terms, this means that you can create a project file that's strictly for listing resources. For example, if you use the same resources over and over, you can create a single file, named Resources, where you store every resource you use for every project. You then can specify that every other schedule file you create uses the resources stored in the Resources file.

Part V
Sharing and Publishing Project Information

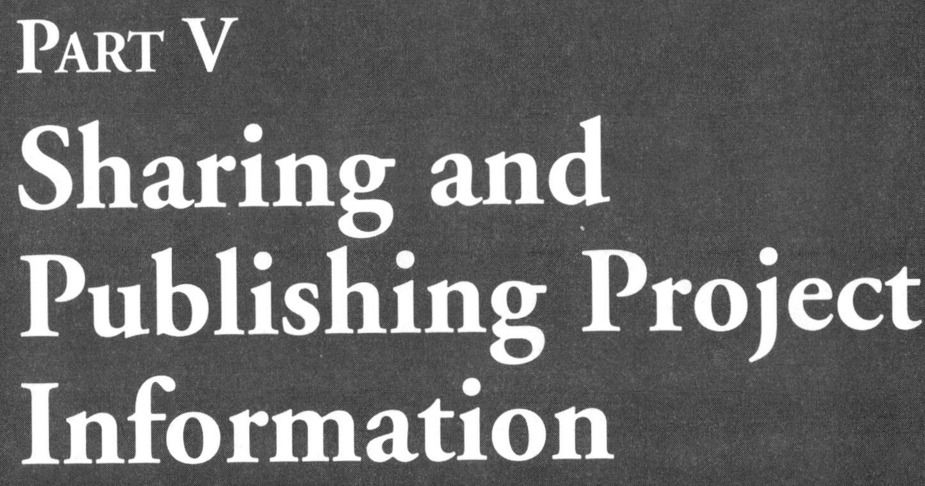

Microsoft Project 98

18

Using Project with Other Applications

In This Chapter

- Enhancing a project's Gantt Chart views with graphics from other applications
- Copying Gantt charts and other Project images into other applications
- Using OLE objects to create dynamic links between applications
- Importing and exporting Project data

No one software program can handle all your business functions, even though different applications can work with similar information.

You may need to use features from one application to accent your work in Microsoft Project 98. Or, you may have to share information with a colleague who doesn't use Project. This chapter covers features that let you share tools and data between Project and other applications.

Using Text and Graphics from Another Application

As a companion to the Microsoft Office suite of applications, Project was designed with information-sharing in mind. All Office applications (and many other Windows applications) are built to enable you to share information between applications easily. You can create information in one application and then copy and use that information in another application.

Suppose that your boss types a list of key operations for a project in a word processing program—say, Microsoft Word. The list is about three pages long. If you're not a skilled typist, typing such a list could take you an hour or more. If you have Word installed on your computer, however, and if your boss e-mails you a copy of the file that contains the list, you can get the job done in minutes by copying the list from the Word file to a file in Project.

Every time you retype information, you have the potential to make errors. When information has already been spell-checked or proofed for errors, always copy it rather than retype it.

Following are just a few other examples of text and graphics from other applications that you can copy and paste into Project:

- You can convert a to-do list created in Word to a list of tasks in Project.
- You can use a list of committee members who are assigned to a project as the foundation of a Resource Sheet list.
- You can paste the names of people in your department from a spreadsheet to a Resource Sheet.
- You can include graphic images, such as company logos, in a Gantt chart to make the printouts more attractive and informative.
- You can paste electronic images of product designs or chart images of product information in the Objects box of the Task Form for particular tasks.

- If you have scanned in photos of colleagues or of equipment to be used to complete a task, you can add those images to the Objects box for the resources in the Resource form.

The procedures for copying text and graphics are different, so the following sections cover the procedures separately.

Note

When you paste information into blank rows in a Task Sheet or Resource Sheet, Project automatically creates new tasks or resource entries in those rows and adds the default settings for fields (columns) into which you do not paste information. If you paste a to-do list in the Task Name column of a Task Sheet, for example, Project adds a default duration of 1d (one day) for each task and sets the defaults for remaining columns.

Using Lists from Other Applications

You can copy information from any application that supports OLE (see "Working with OLE Objects," later in this chapter) and enables you to create lists; this includes most Windows-based word processing and spreadsheet programs—and then paste that information into a Project file. When you paste, you're restricted to pasting the information into a Task Sheet or Resource Sheet. Therefore, you can paste information into any view that shows the Task Sheet or Resource Sheet, or into any table that's a variation on those sheets.

Keep in mind that if you're copying cells from a spreadsheet program (such as Excel), Project tries to paste to an area that's similar in shape—say, three columns wide by two rows deep. Also, no matter what kind of application you're pasting from, Project won't allow you to paste a type of information that's inappropriate for the destination. You can't paste text information into a cell that calls for an hourly rate, for example.

In most cases, you probably will simply paste a one-column list into the Task Name or Resource Name column of the Task Sheet or Resource Sheet.

To copy text information from an application and paste it into a Project sheet, follow these steps:

1. Open the document that contains the text that you want to copy to Project.

Text information that you paste replaces any information that's in the selected destination cells. Be sure to select only a blank area of the Task Sheet or Resource Sheet if you don't want to wipe out any existing information.

2. Select the text; then open the Edit menu and click Copy (or click the Copy button, if available). Figure 18.1 shows an example.
3. Open or switch to the Project application. You can press Alt+Tab or click the Project button on the Taskbar to switch to Project. If Project isn't open, use the Windows Start menu to start Project.
4. Select or open the Project file into which you want to paste the copied information.
5. Select the view that you want to use, such as Gantt Chart or Resource Sheet.
6. Select the upper-left corner of the range of cells into which you want to paste the information. To paste a list of tasks, for example, you could click the top cell of the Task Name column.
7. Open the Edit menu and click Paste. Alternately, do any of the following: right-click the selection to paste to, and then click Paste on the shortcut menu; press Ctrl+V; or click the Paste button on the Standard toolbar. The text is pasted into the selected cells.

Figure 18.1 You can copy information from a word processing program.

The Copy button

When you copy and paste specially formatted text from another application into Project, be prepared to lose the special formatting. For example, if you copy an outline from Word and paste it into Project, you end up with simple text that lacks the outline formatting.

Figure 18.2 shows the text copied from Figure 18.1 pasted into the Task Sheet.

Using Graphics to Enhance Your Project

You can copy graphics—such as electronic images of company logos, products, and charts—created in other applications into Microsoft Project graphic areas. These graphics can range from purely decorative (an image that you use to jazz up a Gantt chart) to purely informational (a graphic of a resource that enables widely separated team members to recognize one another). Although Project offers drawing capabilities, you may want to use a graphic that was created in another application or that may need to be created with tools that Project doesn't offer (as with scanned images). For these reasons, Project enables you to use graphics copied from other graphics applications.

You can copy a graphic to any view that shows a Gantt chart, such as Gantt Chart view (see Figure 18.3). When you paste a graphic into a Gantt chart,

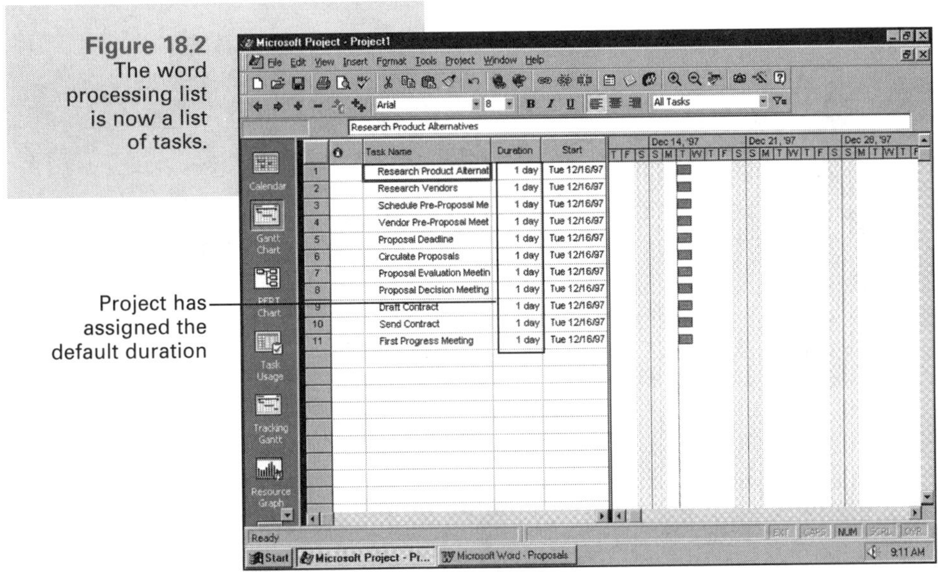

Figure 18.2 The word processing list is now a list of tasks.

Project enables you to format the graphic just as you would format a drawing that you created in Project. (For more information on formatting, refer to Chapter 14, "Other Formatting.")

You also can paste a copied graphic into the Objects box of the Task Form or Resource Form, or into any view that offers one of these forms. The Task Form, for example, appears as the bottom pane of Task Entry view.

To display the Task Form or Resource Form, open the View menu and click More Views to display the More Views dialog box; then double-click Task Form or Resource Form in the Views list. To display the Objects box for the form, right-click the form and then click Objects on the shortcut menu. The Objects box is the big blank area at the bottom of the form. Figure 18.4 shows a graphic pasted into the Task Form.

To copy a graphic image from another application, follow these steps:

1. Start the application that contains the graphic object that you want to copy to Project. (All Windows users have at least one graphic program, called Paint, for working with graphic images.)
2. Open the file for the graphic image, or create the new image.
3. Select the image (or any portion of the image) that you want to use in Project, using the program's selection method. (Many programs offer a Select All command on the Edit menu to enable you to quickly select the full image.) Figure 18.5 shows a graphic selected in Paint.

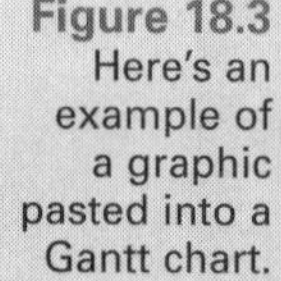

Figure 18.3 Here's an example of a graphic pasted into a Gantt chart.

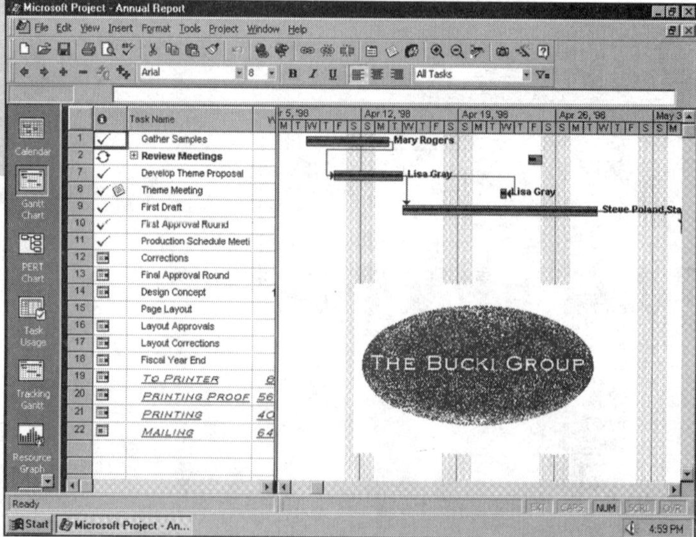

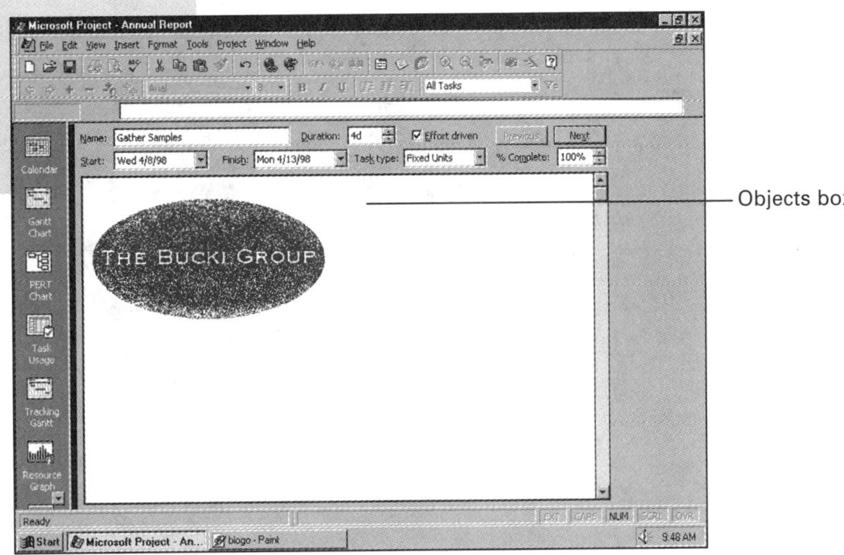

Figure 18.4 Here's an example of a graphic pasted into the Task Form.

Note

Graphics files can be rather large. If you'll be sharing your Project files with other people via e-mail or floppy disks, adding numerous graphics to your project files can make transfer more time-consuming and difficult. Under such circumstances, you should use graphics files sparingly.

4. Open the Edit menu and click Copy to copy the graphic to the Clipboard.
5. If this object is the only one that you need to copy, exit the application.
6. Open or switch to the Project application. (You can press Alt+Tab or click the Project button on the Taskbar to switch to Project.) Then use the Start menu to start Project.
7. Select or open the Project file into which you want to paste the copied information.
8. Select the view that you want to use, such as Gantt Chart view; or display either the Task Form or Resource Form to paste the information into the Objects box on the form.
9. In a Gantt chart, scroll to the section of the view where you want the graphic to appear. In a Task Form or Resource Form, click the Objects box.

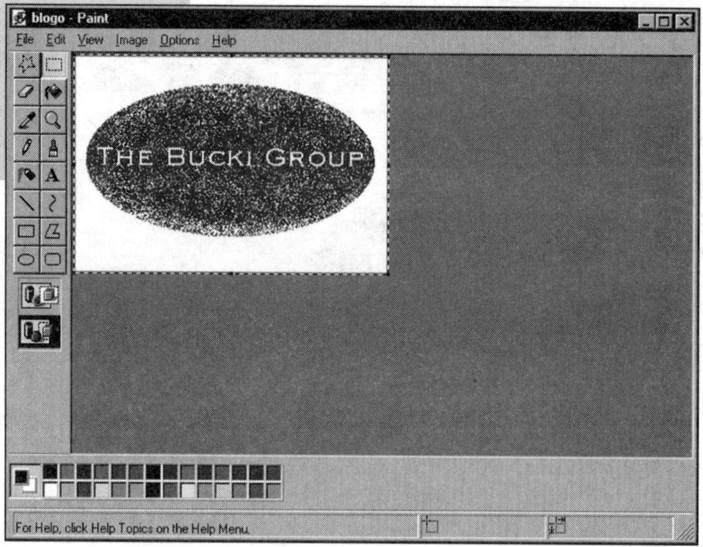

Figure 18.5 The dotted line borders the selected area that will be copied.

10. Open the Edit menu and click Paste. Alternately, right-click the selection to paste to, and then click Paste on the shortcut menu (or press Ctrl+V). The graphic object is placed in the upper-left corner of the Gantt chart area or Objects box.

If you don't like the location of the graphic in the Gantt bar chart area, you can drag the object to the exact position you want. Place the mouse pointer on the object. A four-headed arrow is attached to the selection pointer, indicating that you can drag the object to a new location. Click outside the object when you finish moving it to deselect it. In an Objects box, however, you can't move an object after it's been placed.

Using Project Information in Other Applications

You can copy almost all the information and views in Project to other applications. Copying information into Project saves time and reduces errors; copying information from Project and using it elsewhere does the same thing. Following are a few examples of how you can use Project information in other applications:

- You can copy Gantt chart timelines as pictures (graphics that can't be edited) and paste them into a weekly status report in Word.

- You can copy resource cost tables, showing how much time various people have spent on the project, and paste that information into a spreadsheet.
- You can paste a list of tasks from Project into a project-update memo for company executives.
- If you added the e-mail addresses field to your Resource Sheet, you can copy resource names and addresses into a note for distribution to all team members.

Project enables you to copy information as straight text, as an object (for more information on objects, see "Working with OLE Objects" later in this chapter), or as a picture. Information that appears in the timescale area on the right side of a view, such as the Gantt-chart portion of Gantt Chart view or the schedule portion of Resource Usage view, can be copied only as a picture or an object, not as text. In addition, the table information that appears to the left of the charted information is always copied as well. You can't copy a picture of a few Gantt chart bars without copying a picture of the accompanying task information.

Copying Project Information as Text

When you paste to most programs, such as a spreadsheet program like Excel or a word processing program like Word, Project assumes (by default) that you're pasting the information as text. The pasted cell entries will appear in spreadsheet cells or as entries separated by simple tab characters in a word processor.

If you select the task or resource row before copying, the entire set of task or resource fields is copied and pasted at the destination. If you want to copy only some fields (columns) from the Task Sheet or Resource Sheet, select the individual cells that you want to copy and paste.

Note

The text in Calendar and PERT Chart views cannot be copied to other applications. These views can be copied only as picture or Microsoft Project objects.

To copy information from Project as text, follow these steps:

1. Select the Project view that contains the text that you want to copy to another application.

2. In the Task Sheet or Resource Sheet, select the task or resource row or the individual cells that you want to copy.
3. Open the Edit menu and click Copy (Task), Copy (Resource), or Copy (Cell). Alternately, right-click the selection, and then click the appropriate command on the shortcut menu (or simply press Ctrl+C). The command name on the Edit or shortcut menu reflects the type of information you selected: task, resource, or cell. The text is copied to the Windows Clipboard.
4. Exit Project, if this is the only copy operation you need to perform.
5. Open or switch to the destination document.
6. Select the area in which you want the Project text to appear. In a spreadsheet application, select the upper-left cell of the range of cells in which you want to paste the text. In a word processing application, position the insertion point where you want to paste the text.

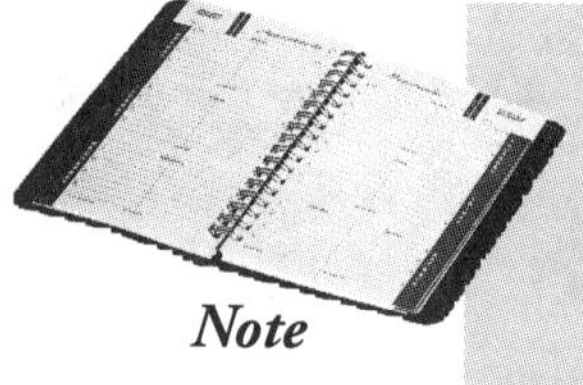
Note

As in any copy-and-paste operation, make sure that you have room for the information that you want to paste. Pasting into some applications, such as word processing programs, inserts the pasted information. In other applications, such as spreadsheet programs, pasting overwrites (or replaces) existing text.

7. Click to open the Edit menu and click Paste; or click the application's Paste button if one is offered. The text appears in the document as unformatted text.

Figure 18.6 shows some resource information pasted into Excel.

If a simple paste operation using the Paste button on the Standard toolbar pastes as Microsoft Project Graphic objects (not as text) in an application, you must use the Paste Special command on the Edit menu. In the Paste Special dialog box that appears, click the Text or Unicode Text option in the As list, and then click OK to finish pasting as text.

Pasting a Picture of Project Information

Pasting a picture of Project information enables you to insert that image into the destination application as a graphic. This method can be a good way to go

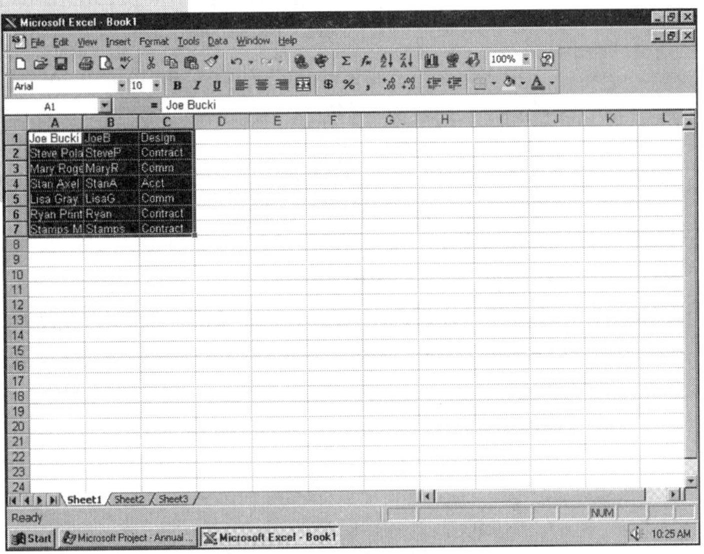

Figure 18.6 Resource information pasted into Excel appears where you specify.

if you won't need to edit the information in the destination application; if you don't want to reformat any text after pasting; and if you want to include Gantt bars, PERT charts, or timescale information in the destination application.

To copy Project information as a picture of the information, rather than text that can be edited, follow these steps:

1. Select the Project view that contains the information that you want to copy.

Note

When you copy and paste Project information as a picture-formatted object (a noneditable graphic), only the portion of the current view that corresponds with the selected Task Sheet or Resource Sheet information is copied. Whether you are in Calendar view, Gantt Chart view, or any of the Resource views, be sure to scroll to the appropriate section of the view and select the right rows in the table before using Copy or Cut.

2. Select the task row, resource row, or PERT chart area that you want to copy. In a view like the Gantt Chart view, if you've selected whole task rows, you also should adjust the vertical split bar between the Task Sheet and the Gantt area at right so that the Task Sheet displays only the columns that you want to appear in the linked object.

3. Click the Copy Picture button on the Standard toolbar. The Copy Picture dialog box appears (see Figure 18.7).
4. If you want to copy only the information in the same size as the current screen view, leave For Screen selected. If you want to copy a larger view, select For Printer. If you want create a .GIF graphic file of the image (perhaps to include it in a Web document), click the To GIF Image File option button. The path and suggested name for the graphic file appear in the accompanying text box; if you want to change either, use the Browse button.
5. If you've copied from some views like the Gantt Chart view, the Copy and Timescale options near the bottom of the dialog box are enabled. In the copy area, you can select Rows On Screen to copy all the information currently displayed, or keep Selected Rows as the choice if you selected specific rows of information to copy in Step 2. Similarly, you can copy the Timescale portion of the view As Shown on Screen. Or you can choose a specific period of the timescale to include. To do so, click the Date From option button; then use its drop-down calendar and the To drop-down calendar to specify the time period for which you want to show timescale information.
6. Click OK to copy the Project view to the Windows Clipboard (or create the GIF file, in which case you don't have to perform further steps).
7. Switch to (or open) the document into which you want to paste the picture.

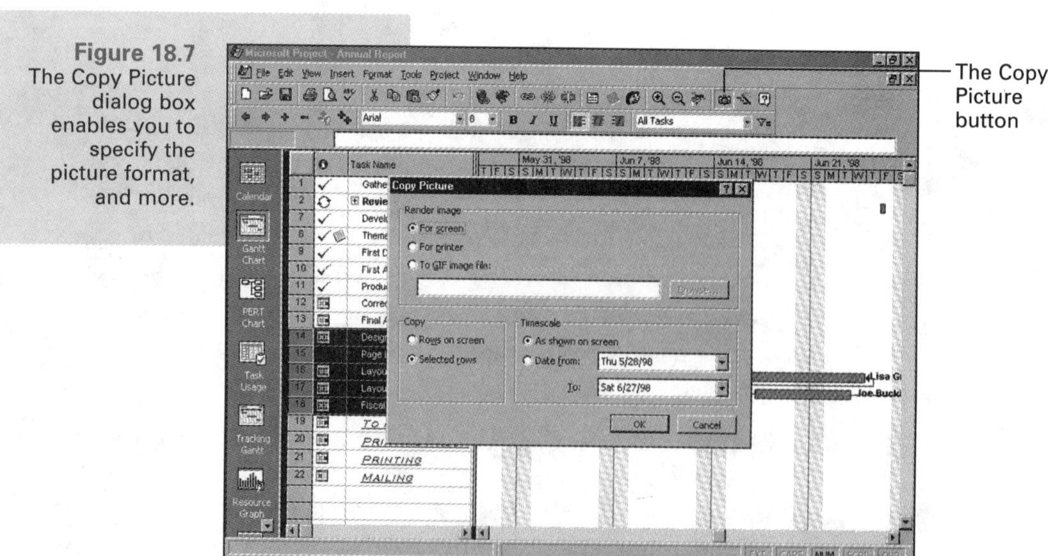

Figure 18.7 The Copy Picture dialog box enables you to specify the picture format, and more.

8. Place the insertion point where you want the picture to appear.
9. Open the Edit menu and click Paste. Alternately, press Ctrl+V or click the Paste button on the Standard toolbar. The Project picture appears in the document.

Figure 18.8 shows a PERT chart selection copied to a Word page.

Working with OLE Objects

Object linking and embedding (OLE) allows applications to share information dynamically. Basically, the information is created with the source application or its tools; then that information is displayed in the container application.

If the information in the container application is linked to the original information in the source application, you can make changes in the source document, and those changes show up in the linked information in the destination document.

Embedding enables you to edit an object that was created in another application within the current application. You can edit a chart created in Excel and embedded in a Word document by using the menus, commands, and other features of Excel from within Word. You don't have to exit Word, start Excel, edit the object, cut or copy the object, and paste it back into your Word document.

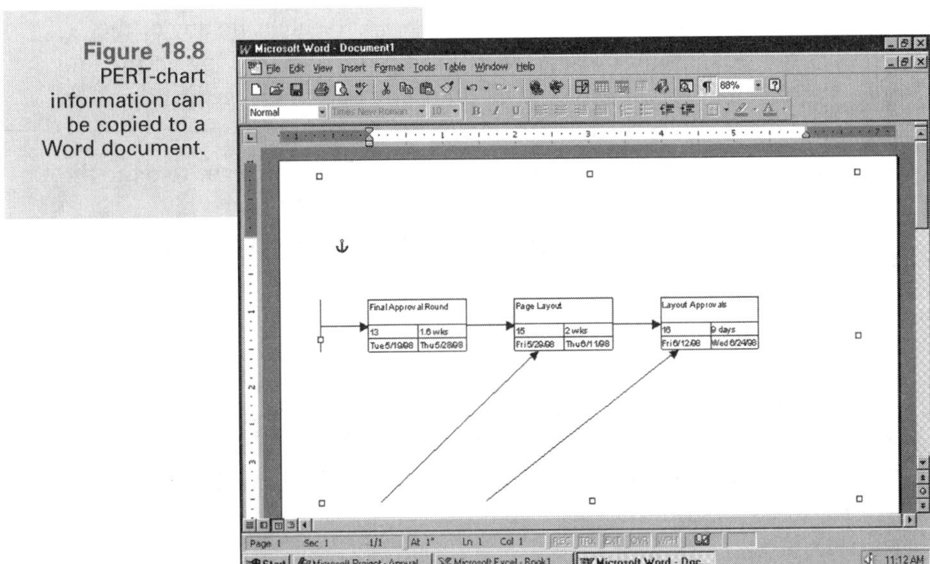

Figure 18.8 PERT-chart information can be copied to a Word document.

Numerous books cover OLE and the various ways that you can put it to work for you, so detailed descriptions of all the possibilities are beyond the scope of this book. The following sections cover the basic procedures for creating linked and embedded objects.

The steps described in the following sections explain how to create linked and embedded objects based on Project data. Keep in mind that you can do the reverse—link and embed information from other applications in Project files.

Creating a Linked Object

When you link information from a view, the linked object looks like a picture in the container document. Thus, the linked object can include Gantt bars and timescale information.

To link information from Project to a document in a container application, follow these steps:

1. Select the information that you want to place in another document. The information can be from a Task Sheet, a Resource Sheet, or even a PERT chart. In a view like the Gantt Chart view, if you've selected whole task rows, you also should adjust the vertical split bar between the Task Sheet and the Gantt area at right so that the Task Sheet displays only the columns that you want to appear in the linked object.
2. Open the Edit menu and click Copy. Alternately, do any of the following: right-click the selection and then click Copy on the shortcut menu; press Ctrl+C; or click the Copy button on the Standard toolbar. Project copies the information to the Windows Clipboard.
3. Open or switch to the document into which you want to paste the linked Project object.
4. Position the insertion point where you want the linked object to appear.
5. Open the Edit menu and click Paste Special. The Paste Special dialog box appears (see Figure 18.9).
6. Click the Paste Link option.
7. In the As list box, select Microsoft Project 8.0 Project Object. You also can select the Picture object type in the As list box if you want to paste the object as a bitmap graphic. The bitmap object will still be linked to the Project document.

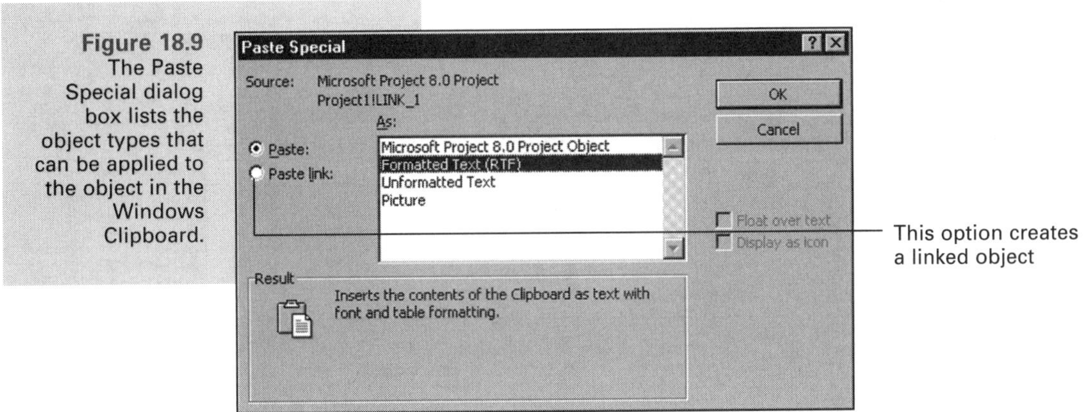

Figure 18.9 The Paste Special dialog box lists the object types that can be applied to the object in the Windows Clipboard.

Note

Working with the paste options for a particular application may take some experimentation. Excel's options, for example, include weird looking items called BIFF, BIFF3, and BIFF4. These options represent different kinds of Excel text and will paste the copied information into a group of cells, for example.

8. Click OK. The Project information appears in the destination document, as shown in Figure 18.10.

Managing a Link's Update Setting

By design, a linked object is updated each time the object's source document is changed or updated. By using the Links command, you can specify when the changes in the source document are reflected in the linked object. You have two choices of link-update timing. You can update the linked object automatically each time the source document changes, or you can update the object manually by making menu and dialog-box choices.

To select a link's update setting, follow these steps:

1. Open the document that contains the linked OLE object.
2. Click the linked object to select it.

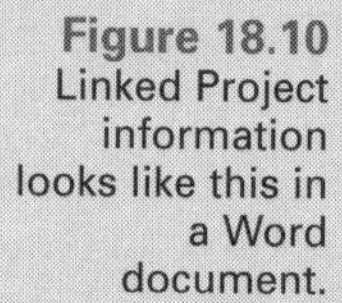

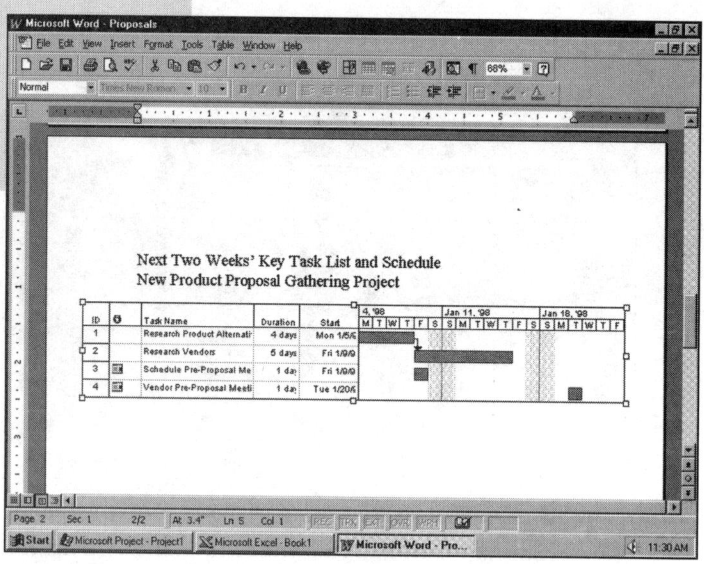

Figure 18.10 Linked Project information looks like this in a Word document.

3. Open the Edit menu and click Links. The Links dialog box appears, displaying a list of linked objects in the document.

   The dialog box lists the link name and the path name of the source document, and indicates whether the link is set to update automatically or manually. Also, the name of the object that you selected in step 2 is highlighted.

4. Click to select the Manual option button at the bottom of the dialog box.
5. Update the link by clicking the Update Now button. The object is updated with any changes that have taken place in the object's source document.
6. Click OK. The Links dialog box closes, and the link is set for manual updating.

With the link set for manual updating, you must open the Links dialog box and click the Update Now button to update the object with the latest changes in the source document. In some cases, depending on the application and document holding the linked information, you can right-click the linked object, and then click Update Link on the shortcut menu.

Using Other Linking Options

The Links dialog box contains a few other buttons that enable you to manage the links to objects in your documents:

- The Open Source button opens the source document of the currently selected link. With the source document open, you can make changes in the source object, investigate surrounding information, or just refresh your memory as to the name and location of the source file.

You can open any OLE object's source application without displaying the Links dialog box. To do so, double-click the linked object.

- The Change Source button displays the Change Source dialog box, which enables you to select a new file as the source document for the linked object.
- The Break Link button removes the link information to the selected object. If you click this button, a dialog box appears, asking whether you are sure that you want to break the link to the selected object. If you are sure, click OK; otherwise, click Cancel. After you break a link, you must perform a cut-and-paste operation to reestablish the linked object.

Creating Embedded Objects

The process of creating an embedded Project object is similar to the process of creating a linked object, but the connection between the source document and the destination document is different. The information in the embedded object does not depend on the source document; that is, you can make changes in the embedded object that don't show up in the source document.

Unlike the situation with a linked object, when you embed an object, Project copies all the tasks or resources in the selected Task Sheet or Resource Sheet. This means that after you open the Edit menu and click Paste Special to place the embedded information in the container document, click the object and then drag the black resizing handles to control how much of the information appears.

To create an embedded Project object, follow these steps:

1. Select the view that you want to use to create the embedded object. If the view includes a Task Sheet or Resource Sheet, click any cell in the sheet, and drag the vertical split bar to control which sheet columns appear (the same ones will appear in the embedded object).
2. Open the Edit menu and click Copy. Alternately, do any of the following: right-click the selection and then click Copy on the shortcut menu; press Ctrl+C; or click the Copy button on the Standard toolbar.
3. Open or switch to the destination document.
4. Position the insertion point where you want the embedded object to appear.
5. Open the Edit menu and click Paste Special. The Paste Special dialog box appears (refer to Figure 18.9), listing the available paste options.

   The default Paste Special options are set up to create an embedded object. The Paste option should be selected, and the object type Microsoft Project 8.0 Project Object should be highlighted in the As list. Notice that the Results area of the dialog box indicates that the selected settings enable you to use Microsoft Project 8.0 (Project 98) to edit the object.
6. Click OK to paste the object. The object appears at the insertion-point location.

You cannot create an embedded object from an image that you copied by using the Copy Picture button on the Standard toolbar. The Copy Picture button creates a bitmap image of the selected area; it does not maintain the information that is necessary for embedding.

Editing an embedded object is a simple, straightforward process and one in which the primary advantage of embedding comes into play, because you do not have to recall the name and location of the source document that created the object. You simply double-click the object, and the source application (Project) tools appear, enabling you to edit the object.

When you finish making changes in the object, click outside the object. The source application tools close, and you return to the container document and application. (In some applications, you may have to open the File menu and click Exit to close the source application.)

Importing Other Project-Management Files

Project enables you to work with information stored in a variety of file formats. If you need to bring in information from an application that saves information in tabular format (such as a spreadsheet or database program), you can import that information rather than copy it. Table 18.1 lists some of the file formats that you may be able to import.

Table 18.1 The Most Common File Types That Project Can Read

Application	File Format
Microsoft Project	MPP, MPX, MPT
Microsoft Project Database	LDB
Microsoft Excel	XLS
Microsoft Access (as well as FoxPro, dBASE III and IV, which share the same format)	DBF
Plain Text (ASCII)	TXT
Comma-separated values	CSV

Note

The data that you import needs to be properly formatted in order for Project to recognize it. For example, the first row in an Excel workbook file must contain field names that match the field names that Project uses: ID, Task_Name, Duration, and so on. Use an underscore rather than a space for two-word field names. If you have any questions about how the type of data you want to import needs to be set up in its source application, export some test data from Project into that format (including choosing the corresponding export map, if needed). Then open the exported file in its source application to see how Project set the file up, named fields, and so on. Exporting is covered later in this chapter.

If your software (especially other project planning software) isn't listed in Table 18.1, see whether the program enables you to use its Save As command to save files in one of the listed formats.

The procedure for importing a file is similar to the procedure for opening a file that you learned in Chapter 1, "Getting Started with Project." Follow these steps:

1. Open the File menu and click Open; press Ctrl+O; or click the Open button on the Standard toolbar. The File Open dialog box appears.
2. In the Look In drop-down list, select the drive where the file that you want to import is stored.

Select Network Neighborhood in the Look In drop-down list if the file is on a drive that is connected to another network.

3. Double-click a folder to display the contents of that folder. (You may need to double-click subfolder icons to display the file that you want to open.)
4. In the Files of Type drop-down list (see Figure 18.11), select the format for the file that you want to import.
5. When the file that you want to open appears in the list, double-click its name, or click it and then click Open to load the file into Project. The Import Format dialog box appears. Examples of this dialog box appear in Figure 18.12.
6. The type of file you chose to import in Step 4 determines which of the two option buttons is active in the Import Format dialog box:
   - For database formats, such as the Microsoft Project Database format, the top option button, for importing the Entire Project, is enabled. If the imported file has information for more than one project, select the correct project to open from the Name of the Project in the Database to Import drop-down list.
   - For importing files in other formats, the Selective Data option button is selected. The Import/Export Map to Use for Importing list displays "maps" that specify which fields of information to import. For example, the Default Task Information choice imports ID, Task_Name, Duration, Start_Date, Finish_Date, Predecessors, and Resource_Names fields. Click the map to use the list.

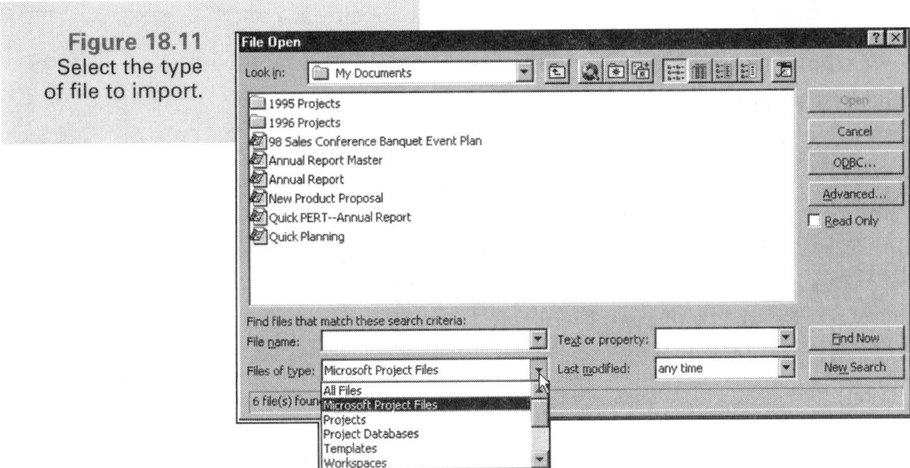

Figure 18.11 Select the type of file to import.

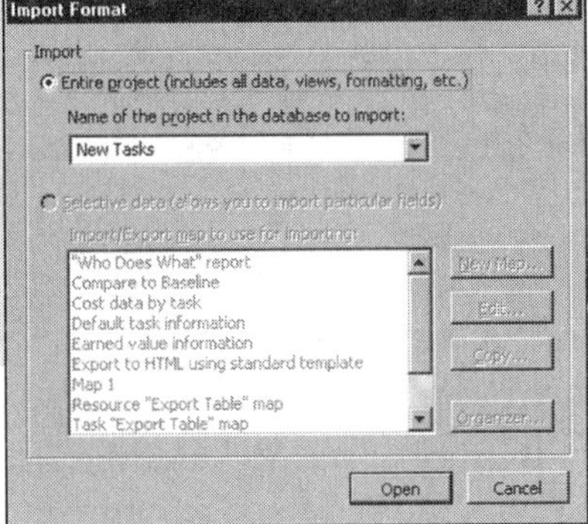

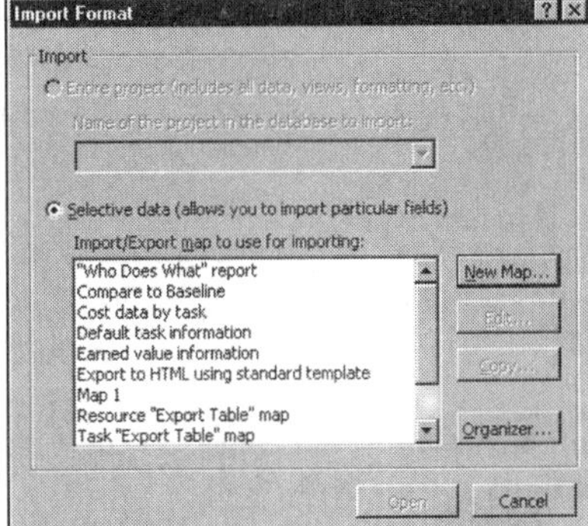

Figure 18.12 The Import Format dialog box provides different options, depending on what type of file you're trying to import.

7. Click Open to finish the import operation.

If necessary, Project adds default information for columns that are not filled in by the imported information, such as the Duration column.

Exporting Project Files

The flip side of importing is exporting. When you export information from a Project file, you save it in a format that another application can use. The formats to which you can export generally are the same as the import formats listed in Table 18.1 earlier in this chapter, with two exceptions. You also can export project information as an Excel PivotTable (a dynamic table that you can reorganize by dragging categories on a grid) or an HTML file (a Web page).

An export operation resembles a Save As operation. Follow these steps:

1. Open the File menu and click Save As. The File Save dialog box appears.
2. Navigate to the drive and folder where you want to save the file, using the Save In drop-down list and the folders that appear below it. (Double-click a folder icon to open that folder so you can store the file there.)
3. In the File Name text box, type the name you want to give the file.
4. Use the Save as Type drop-down list to specify the file format to which to export.
5. Click the Save button. The Export Format dialog box appears (see Figure 18.13 for examples).

If you're saving to some database formats, you can append additional tables to an existing database file. To do so, navigate to and select the file in the File Save dialog box, so that its name appears in the File Name text box. Select the file type from the Save As Type drop-down list. After you click Save, a dialog box appears to warn you that you've chosen an existing file. Click the Append button, and then enter a unique name for the project in the Name to Give the Project in the Database text box, as described in the next step.

6. The type of file you chose to export in Step 4 determines which of the two option buttons is active in the Export Format dialog box:

- For database formats, such as the Microsoft Project Database format, the top option button, for exporting the Entire Project, is enabled. Specify the name to use for the project in the new or existing database file in the Name to Give the Project in the Database text box.

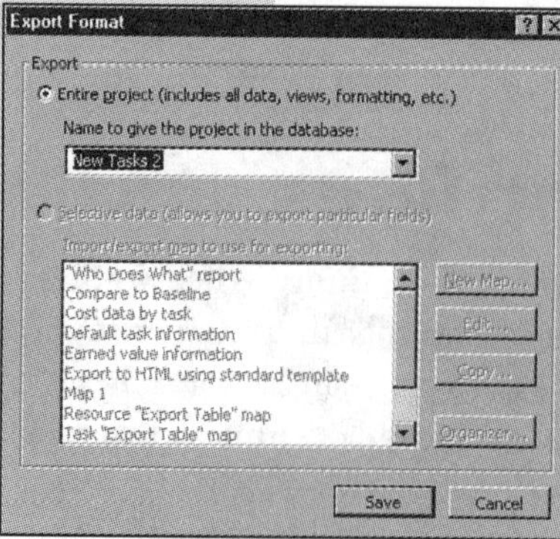

Figure 18.13 Use the Export Format dialog box to control which information is saved in a new file.

- For exporting files to other formats, the Selective Data option button is selected. Click the map you want in the Import/Export Map to Use for Exporting to specify which fields of information to export.

7. Click Save. Project exports the file, saving it with the name and format you specified.

Sharing Project Data with ODBC Databases

Project also can share information with database programs that are ODBC-compliant, meaning that those databases can communicate in a particular way. For this feature to work, ODBC drivers need to be installed on your system using the 32-bit ODBC icon in Windows Control Panel. (Describing how to do this is beyond the scope of this book; chances are that if your company requires you to work with its central databases, your company's computer support staff will already have set up this capability for you.). This means that you can save Project data in a database from any other ODBC-compliant database application that your system is set up to save to, or use information from those databases in Project.

To work with ODBC database information, you click the ODBC button in the File Save or File Open dialog box, depending on whether you want to export data to an ODBC database or open it from one. You also might want to display the Workgroup toolbar by right-clicking on any toolbar, and then selecting Workgroup. This toolbar offers the Save To Database As and Open From Database buttons, which are equivalent to the ODBC button in the File Save and File Open dialog boxes, respectively.

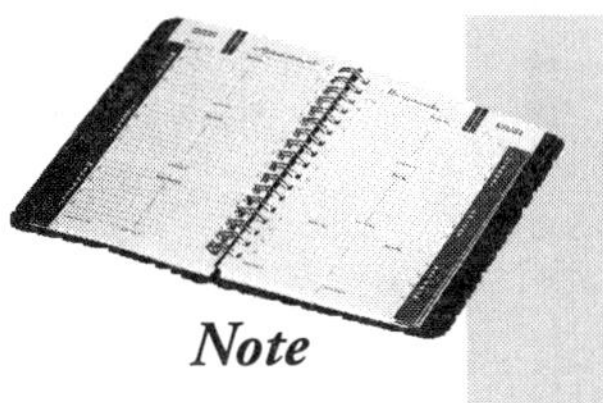
Note

Only text or numerical information from the project is stored in the database, such as task names, start and finish dates, resource names, and resource assignments. No formatting or graphical information is stored.

Saving Project data to an ODBC database requires two general operations. First, you have to create the *data source* if it doesn't already exist. The data source tells Project which ODBC driver to use to create and work with the database. Next, you save the Project data as a database in the data source. Use the following steps to accomplish both operations:

1. Create and save your schedule information in Project.
2. Click to open the File menu; then click Save As in the File Save dialog box, and click the ODBC button. Rather than displaying the File Save dialog box, you can click the Save To Database button on the Workgroup toolbar.
3. In the Select Data Source dialog box that appears (see Figure 18.14), type a name for the data source file in the DSN Name text box, and then click New.
4. In the Create New Data Source dialog box that appears, select the database driver you want in the list of drivers (the list will vary depending on what drivers have been installed on your system); then click Next.
5. Type a name for the data source in the text box of the next Create New Data Source dialog box. (This assigns a name to the data source you're creating to hold the database file; use the same name you entered in the DSN Name text box.) Then click Next.
6. Review your choices in the final Create New Data Source dialog box that appears, and then click Finish.
7. In the ODBC...Setup dialog box that appears, click the Create button to display the New Database dialog box, as shown in Figure 18.15.

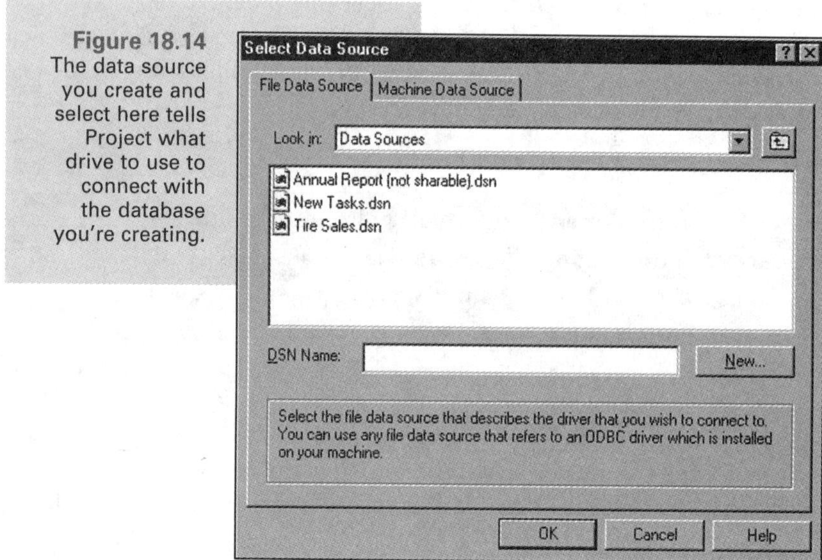

Figure 18.14 The data source you create and select here tells Project what drive to use to connect with the database you're creating.

Figure 18.15 At this point, specify a name for the database file itself.

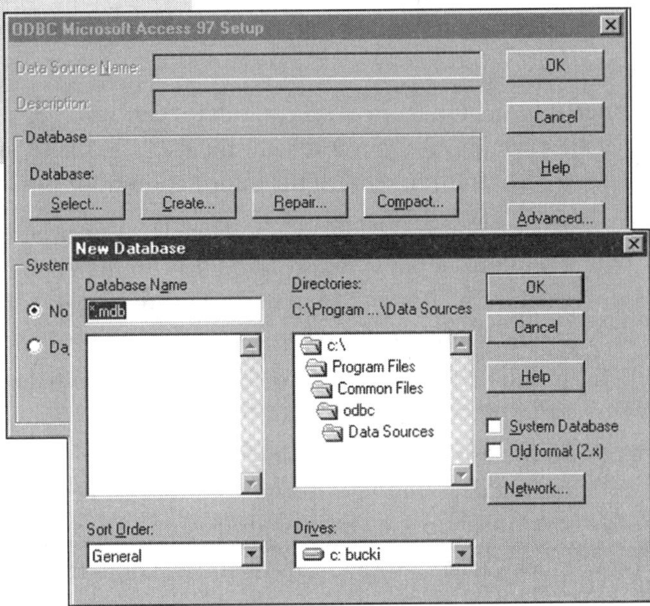

8. Type a name for the database file in the Database Name text box. If necessary, use the Directories and Drives lists to specify a different location for saving the database file. Click OK.
9. When a message box informs you that the database file has been created, click OK again.
10. Click OK again to exit the ODBC… Setup dialog box.
11. In the Select Data Source dialog box, click the name of the data source you just created from the Look In list, and then click OK.
12. The Export Format dialog box appears (refer to Figure 18.14), with the Entire Project option button selected. Type a name to use for the project information in the Name to Give the Project in the Database text box; then click on Save.

Note

Some ODBC drivers are for spreadsheets, like Excel. If you use such a driver, the bottom option button in the Export Format (and Import Format dialog box for opening the database) will be selected instead. Use it as described earlier in the chapter.

13. The Planning Wizard may appear to ask you whether or not to save the information with a baseline. Click the option you want, and then click OK. Project saves the database.

After information from a schedule has been saved as an ODBC-compliant database, you need to open it from the database file to use it again in Project. Follow these steps to retrieve the information from the file:

1. Click to open the File menu; then click Open, or click the Open button on Project's Standard toolbar. In the File Open dialog box, click the ODBC button. Alternately, click the Open From Database button on the Workgroup toolbar.
2. In the Look In list of the Select Data Source dialog box, click the name of the data source you created when you saved the file. Click OK.
3. In the Import Format dialog box, click the title you assigned to the project data (in step 12 of the previous set of steps) in the Name of the Project in the Database to Import drop-down list.
4. Click Open. Project opens the information from the database file.

19

Taking Project Online

In This Chapter

- Working with Web features such as Help and links to Web pages and files
- Publishing or posting your schedule online
- Creating resource workgroups and entering e-mail addresses
- Sending a TeamAssign message to assign work
- Sending a TeamUpdate message to tell resources about changes in a task schedule or work completion status, or send a note about a task
- Requesting a status update for one or more tasks with TeamStatus
- Responding to and using workgroup message information
- Setting up your Web workgroup

Like most other business-oriented applications, Project 98 has evolved to enable you to work with information on the Internet. These new features enable you to connect quickly to information you need, or to make schedule information easily available to your colleagues and contacts.

In addition, Project 98 offers paperless, automated project management alternatives through its workgroup message-handling capabilities. Workgroup messaging works in conjunction with e-mail in Windows to enable you to automatically send assignment and update information—and receive status reports—to and from resources that you communicate with via e-mail.

This chapter walks you through using project's Web and workgroup messaging features.

Web Basics

With tens of millions of users worldwide, the *Internet* (a global network of connected networks) has become one of the most important communication tools in the business world. Different *sites* (individual server computers) on the Internet organize and handle different types of information. Most users work with at least two different types of sites or information on the Internet: e-mail and Web (which displays information graphically, in linked *pages)*. This section explains how to use Project 98's new features for working with the Web. The next section explains how to use e-mail along with workgroup features to manage project progress.

Note

The Web coverage in this chapter assumes that your system is set up to connect to the Internet and that you have a Web browser program (which enables you to display Web pages) installed and configured to launch when needed.

Getting Help on the Web

Although software publishers do provide manuals and online help along with software, the help that comes with the software itself has become slimmer. To supplement the help that ships with its products like Project, Microsoft provides a number of Web sites and pages providing additional help about Project, Microsoft Office and the Web, and even Microsoft itself. You can easily access

this online help using the commands on the Microsoft on the Web submenu of the Help menu in Project, shown in Figure 19.1. For example, clicking the Online Support choice on the submenu displays the Web page shown in Figure 19.2.

When you click one of the commands on the Microsoft on the Web submenu, your Web browser program (such as Internet Explorer or Netscape Navigator) launches. Depending on how your system is configured to connect to the Internet, you may see a dialog box like the Connect To dialog box used to connect with dial-up connections with Internet Service Providers (ISPs); this dialog box prompts you to connect to the Internet. Click the Connect button (or the correct button for your configuration) to connect and display the page in your Web browser.

Each Web page is identified by its URL (Uniform Resource Locator) address, which represents its specific location on the Internet. Figure 19.2 identifies what the various parts of a URL mean. The Web page shown in Figure 19.2 is for an .ASP (*active server page*) Web page, identified by the .ASP extension embedded in the file name; other pages, called HTML (*hypertext markup language*) pages, have an .HTML or .HTM file name extension. Web pages provide dynamic features. As illustrated in Figure 19.2, many offer drop-down lists, text boxes, and buttons you can work with to ask for or submit information. Web pages also contain *hyperlinks*, which are links to other pages of information. A hyperlink can appear either as underlined text or an underlined URL, or as some type of onscreen graphic that you can click. Clicking a hyperlink displays another Web page with other information you might want to read.

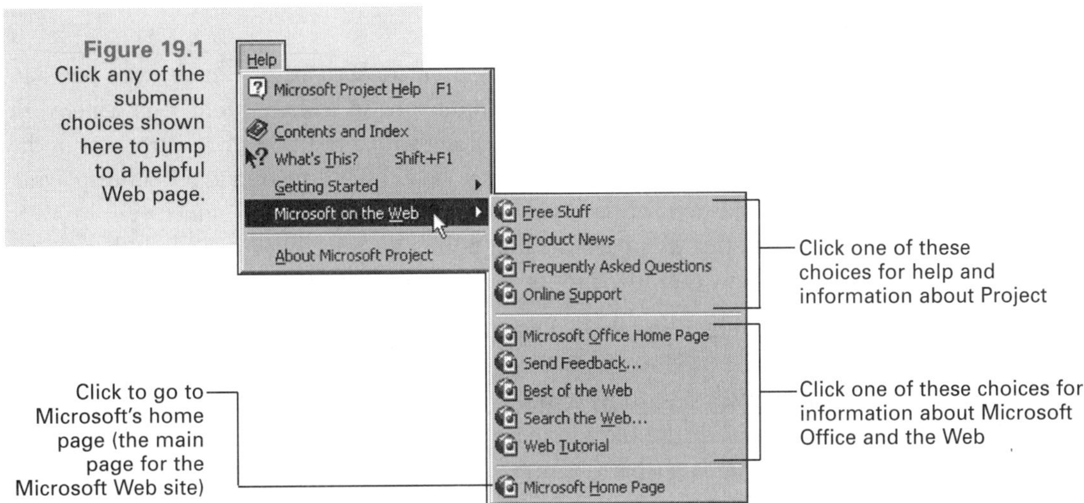

Figure 19.1 Click any of the submenu choices shown here to jump to a helpful Web page.

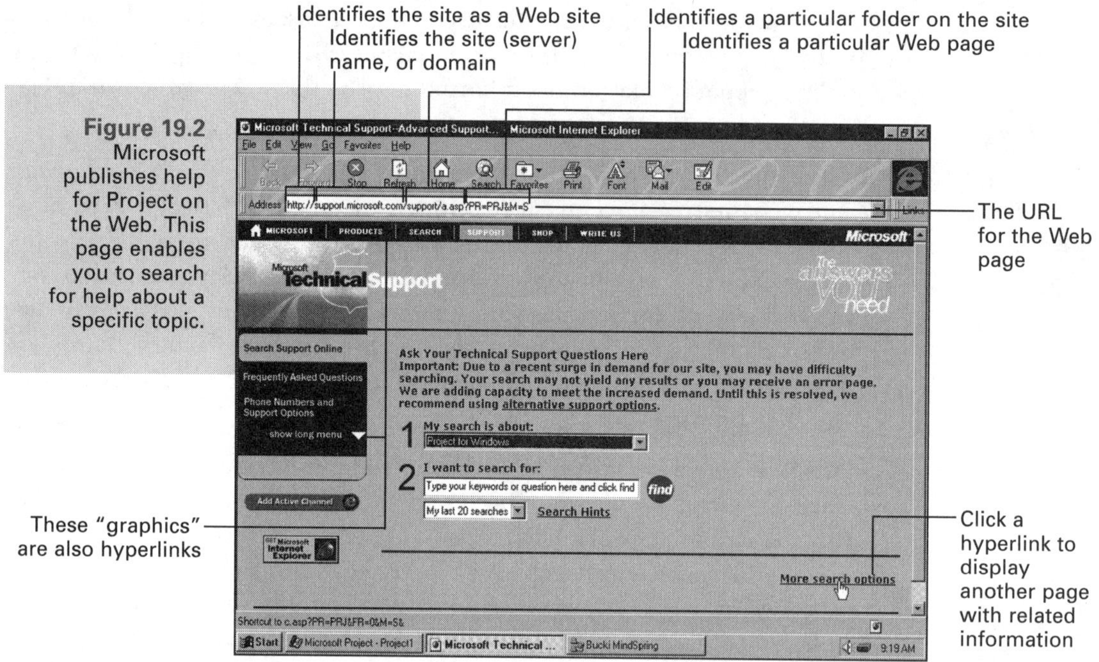
Identifies the site as a Web site
Identifies the site (server) name, or domain
Identifies a particular folder on the site
Identifies a particular Web page
The URL for the Web page
These "graphics" are also hyperlinks
Click a hyperlink to display another page with related information

Figure 19.2 Microsoft publishes help for Project on the Web. This page enables you to search for help about a specific topic.

Most Web browsers offer features you can use to capture and review information. For example, you can print a Web page after it's fully displayed. Or, you can save a copy of many Web pages to your hard disk, so you can open those pages at a later time (without connecting to the Internet), and read or print them.

Embedding a Hyperlink

In Project, hyperlinks can not only point to Web pages but also can point to files stored elsewhere on your computer or in a shared folder on a network server. You can embed a hyperlink along with a task row or resource row in the Task Sheet or Resource Sheet of any view. Then, if you add a field displaying the hyperlinks to the Sheet, you can click the hyperlink to launch your browser and display the Web page the link points to. Selecting a hyperlink that points to a file opens that file, and its application, if needed.

As an example, if an external resource has a Web site that you want to view to find updated product pricing information, you could add a hyperlink for that resource's Web site to the resource's entry on the Resource Sheet. Or, you may want to consult the file for another project that's on your company network before you update a particular task, so you could create a hyperlink to that file.

To create a hyperlink to a path on your hard disk, use the full path, file name to identify the file, as in **C:\My Documents\NewProduct.mpp**. You can use the same format if a file is stored on a *mapped network drive*; basically, a mapped drive is a particular storage area on the network that has a particular drive letter assigned, usually H:. For other networks, you may instead need to enter the *UNC (Universal Naming Convention)* address to point to the file on the network server. Enter the UNC address in the format **\\Server\Share\Path\FileName.ext**, where *Server* is the name of the network server computer and *Share* is the named of a shared area or partition that network users can access. If you've worked at all with files on your company's network, you probably have experience with which method to use to name and access network files, and should use the same method for creating hyperlinks.

To insert a hyperlink and display one or more columns for the hyperlink, follow these steps:

1. Display the view with the Task or Resource Sheet holding the task or resource for which you want to add a hyperlink.
2. Click to open the Insert menu and click Hyperlink (Ctrl+K), or click the Insert Hyperlink button on the Standard toolbar. The Insert Hyperlink dialog box appears.
3. In the Link to File or URL text box, enter the Web page or file address. If you're creating a link to a file on your hard disk, you can click the Browse button to display a dialog box for selecting that file. Figure 19.3 shows an example network link address entered in a file.

Note

If the file the hyperlink opens is in the same folder as the file in which you're creating the hyperlink, you can check the Use Relative Path for Hyperlink check box, and then enter only the file name in the Link to File or URL text box. Otherwise, the hyperlink will always refer to the absolute path you enter with the file name.

4. If the file you're opening uses easily referenced labels like cell addresses (spreadsheets), bookmarks (word processors), or task ID number (Project file), enter the name of such a location in the Named Location in File (Optional) text box. For example, if the hyperlink opens a project file, you could enter **20** to have the cell selector jump to task 20 in the file when it opens.

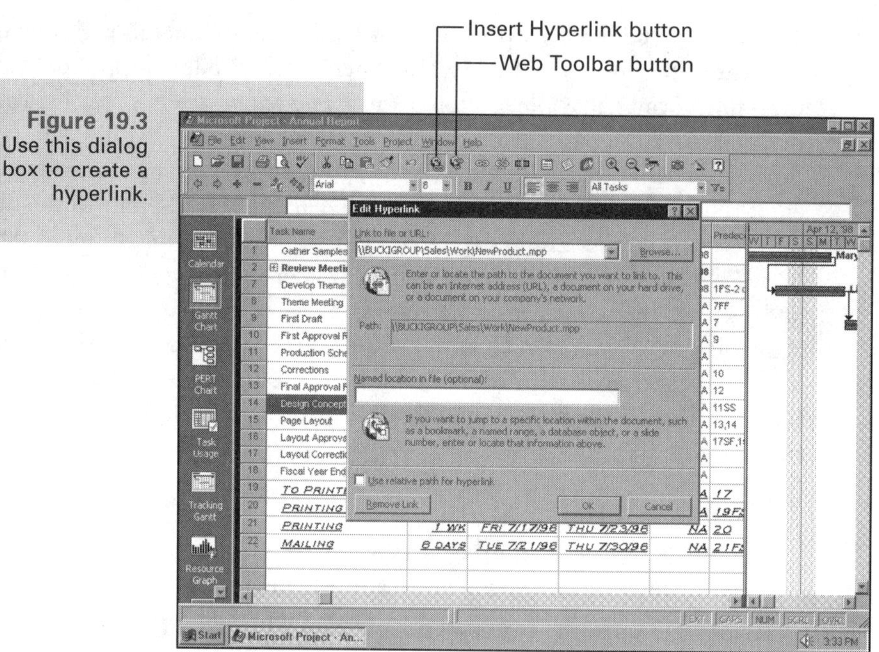

Figure 19.3 Use this dialog box to create a hyperlink.

5. Click OK to finish creating the hyperlink. An indicator for the hyperlink displays in the indicator column.
6. (Optional) To insert a column showing the hyperlink address, right-click the column head that's in the position where you want the new column to appear and click Insert Column. In the Column Definition dialog box, select Hyperlink Address from the Field Name drop-down list; then make any other changes you want to the settings for the field. Click OK to add the field.
7. (Optional) If you want to display and use a shorter name for the hyperlink (called a *hyperlink representation*), insert the Hyperlink column using the techniques described in step 6. Then, click a cell adjoining the Hyperlink for the task or resource, use an arrow key to select the cell (you can't click it), type a new name to represent the hyperlink, and press Enter.

Your hyperlink is now complete. To display the Web page or document that the link points to, click the hyperlink indicator, the Hyperlink Address, if you added that column to the sheet, or the representation you created if you added the Hyperlink column. Figure 19.4 shows an example hyperlink, with the indicator and the new columns.

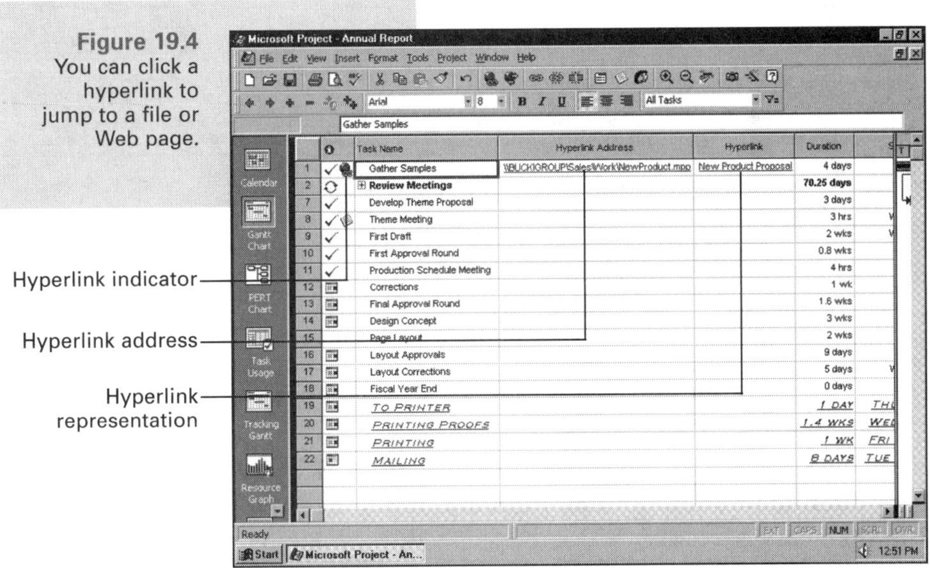

Figure 19.4 You can click a hyperlink to jump to a file or Web page.

If you need to change the location for the hyperlinked page or file, or want to remove the hyperlink, you can display the Edit Hyperlink dialog box, which has options nearly identical to those in the Insert Hyperlink dialog box shown in Figure 19.3. To change or remove a hyperlink, click a cell in the row for the task or resource that holds the hyperlink. Click the Insert Hyperlink button on the Standard toolbar. In the Edit Hyperlink dialog box, change the text box entries as needed. Or, to remove the link, click the Remove Link button. Click OK to close the dialog box.

Note

By default, the entries in the Hyperlink Address columns are blue and underlined when you first create the link. After you click a link to display the linked document, those entries turn purple.

Using the Web Toolbar to Surf

When you click a hyperlink to open the linked document, the Web toolbar appears near the top of the screen, just under the Formatting toolbar. You also can display the Web toolbar at any time by right-clicking another toolbar and then clicking Web or clicking the Web toolbar button on the Standard toolbar. Figure 19.5 shows the Web toolbar.

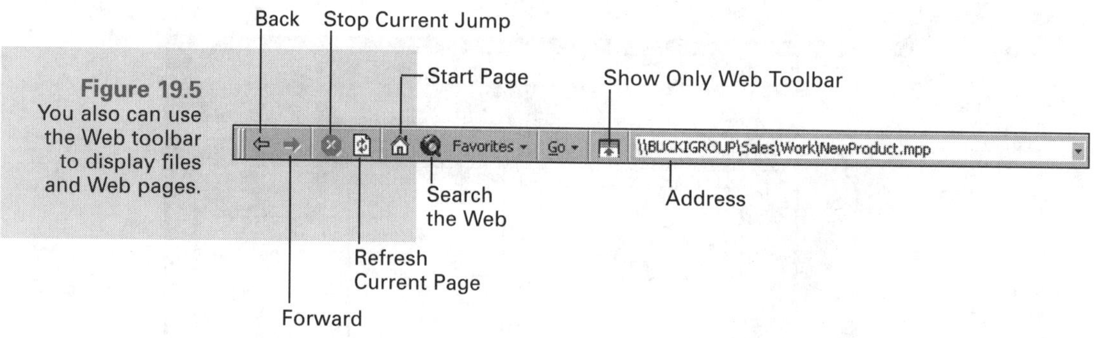

Figure 19.5 You also can use the Web toolbar to display files and Web pages.

The Web toolbar offers buttons you can click to display particular Web pages or hyperlinked files. Many of the buttons on this toolbar work just like buttons in your Web browser. For example, the Back and Forward buttons move back and forward through pages and files you displayed during the current project work session. Click the Stop Current Jump button to stop loading a hyperlinked file, or click the Refresh Current Page button to update the Project files that are currently open.

The Start Page button launches your Web browser and displays the start page (the first Web page your browser has been set up to display). The Search the Web button also displays your browser and a page with tools and links for searching the Web for a particular topic. Clicking the Favorites button opens a drop-down list naming the pages you've added to the Favorites list in your Web browser; click a page name to launch your browser and jump to the page. The Go menu offers commands that correspond to some of the buttons already described, as well as Set Start Page and Set Search Page for changing the Web page that either of those Web toolbar buttons display. Click the Show Only Web Toolbar button to hide or display other onscreen toolbars.

Finally, you can enter a Web address or file path and name in the Address text box, and then press Enter to display the linked page in your Web browser, or the linked file. To jump back to a previously displayed page, click the drop-down list arrow beside the Address text box, and then click the name of the link to follow.

Saving Project Information as a Web Page

The section called "Exporting Project Files" in Chapter 18 noted that one of the formats you can select for exporting data is the HTML format. You can use the File, Save As command and choose HTML Document from the Save As Type drop-down list in the File Save dialog box, and then continue exporting the file as described in Chapter 18.

In addition, the File menu includes the Save As HTML command. Choosing that command displays the File Save dialog box with the HTML Document choice already selected, as shown in Figure 19.6. Project suggests the name of the original schedule file as the File Name. You can edit that name or the location to which the file will be saved. Click Save to continue the export process. The Export Format dialog box appears. In the Import/Export Map to Use for Exporting list, click a Map to specify which fields of information from the Project file will appear in the Web document. Click Save to save the document as the HTML Web page.

After you create the Web page, you should copy it to the Web (http://) server folder (on your company's Internet or intranet Web site), where other users can access it. If your Web site is on an ISP or configured in certain ways, you may need to use a program like CuteFTP to transfer the file. You can then build hyperlinks in other documents (Web and otherwise) to display the Web page from the folder where you posted it. Figure 19.7 shows an example of information from the Annual Report.mpp schedule file shown in many figures in this book exported as a Web document and displayed in a Web browser.

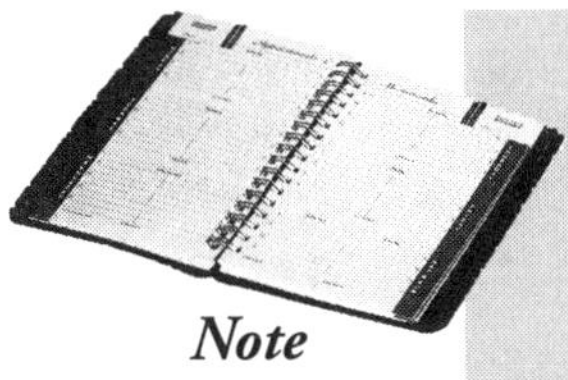

Note

If you have a program that lets you open HTML documents, you can use it to edit the exported Project Web page, adding graphics or changing fonts. For example, you can open any HTML (or HTM) file in Microsoft Word 97 and use Word to improve its look and layout.

Figure 19.6 Choose the HTML Document type to save the current Project file as a Web page.

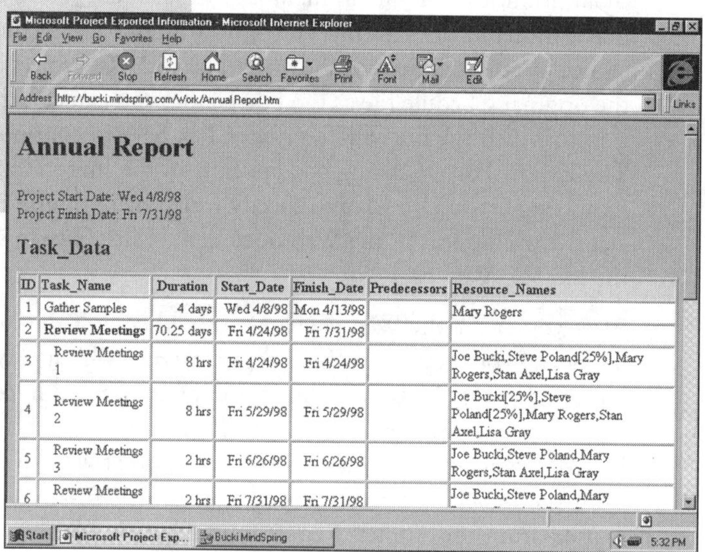

Figure 19.7 Project data saved as a Web page includes title information and a table of fields.

You also can open the HTML file in your browser without copying it to a Web site directory. To do so, double-click the file in the Windows Explorer. I suggest doing this to preview the HTML Document before incorporating it into your Web site.

Preparing to Communicate with a Workgroup

The workgroup for a project includes all the resources you've entered in the resource sheet. You can use workgroup features in Project to send automatic messages to the workgroup, via e-mail or via a Web Server that you, as project manager, set up for the project. (See "Setting Up the Web Server," later in this chapter.)

Chances are, you'll communicate with the bulk of the resources for your project in the same manner. So, you should first select the default workgroup communication method; then, you can enter e-mail addresses for individual workgroup members and specify whether that particular resource requires a communication type other than the default you specified.

The e-mail system used with workgroup e-mail features must be 32-bit, MAPI-compliant. Depending on whether you have Windows (either the original release or OSR-2, which released in Fall of 1996), Windows NT, or Microsoft Office 97 installed, you'll have a different e-mail program: Microsoft Exchange, Windows Messaging, or Microsoft Outlook 97. Or, your company might be using another compliant e-mail system. The figures in this book show examples only from Microsoft Outlook 97.

Follow these steps to set the defaults for communicating with the workgroup:

1. Click to open the Tools menu; then click Options. The Options dialog box appears. Click the Workgroup tab, if necessary.
2. In the Workgroup Messages Transport for '(Current File)' area of the dialog box, click to open the Default Workgroup Messaging for Resources drop-down list; then click the choice you want. The None choice means you want to disable workgroup messaging. Choose Email if you'll be communicating with resources via e-mail only, or Web if you created a Web workgroup site and will use that method for sending messages. If you'll be using both e-mail and a Web workgroup site for communicating, depending on the settings for individual resources, choose Email and Web.
3. If you chose either Web or Email and Web in the preceding step, you need to make entries in the Web Server URL (for Resource) and Web Server Root (for Manager) text boxes. In the former text box, enter the URL for the Web server and folder you established to serve the workgroup. In the latter text box, enter the UNC address for the shared folder on the Web server that will hold the workgroup messages; Project will set up special files and folder in that location. Figure 19.8 shows example entries in these text boxes. Remember, URL and UNC addresses are usually case-sensitive, as the figure illustrates.
4. If you want Project to check your Web Inbox every 10 minutes and then notify you when new messages arrive, click to check the Notify When New Web Messages Arrive check box.

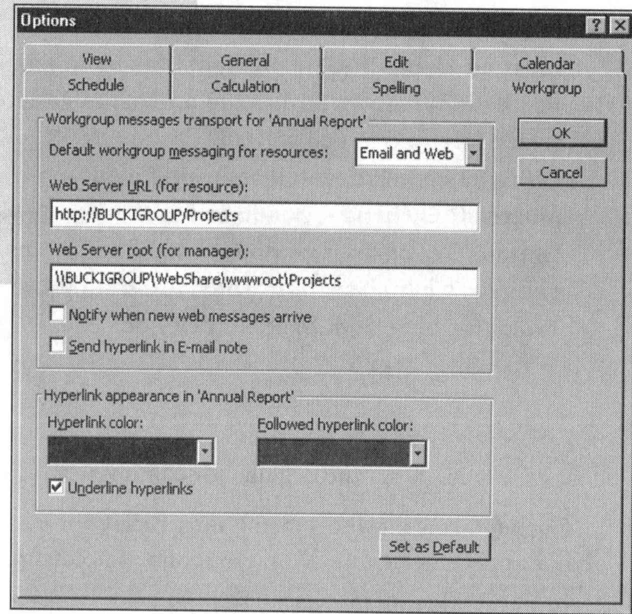

Figure 19.8 If you want to use a Web workgroup site for messaging, enter the locations where Project should set up messaging folders.

5. Each time you sent a message to the Web workgroup site, Project can send each resource an e-mail message containing a hyperlink that the resource can click to jump to the new message on the site. This ensures that the resources will check workgroup messages in a timely fashion. To enable this capability, select the Send Hyperlink in E-mail Note check box.
6. If you want your messaging settings to apply to all of your schedule files, click the Set as Default button. Otherwise, your changes apply only to the currently opened file.
7. Click OK. If you specified that a Web workgroup site will be used for workgroup messages, a dialog box appears telling you that Project needs to copy files to the server location. Click Yes to finish specifying your workgroup messaging settings. (Insert your Microsoft Project 98 CD-ROM in your computer's CD-ROM drive.)

Just as you have to address paper mail or regular e-mail, you need to tell Project what each resource's e-mail address is to ensure that Project properly addresses the messages you send. You also need to specify whether a resource uses the same type of messaging you specified in the preceding steps, or another method, to ensure Project sends the message correctly.

If the recipients of your workgroup messages don't have the full Project 98 program installed, at the very least each recipient must install workgroup messaging capabilities, by running the WGSETUP.EXE file found on the Project 98 CD-ROM in the \Wgsetup\ folder.

To tell Project what a resource's e-mail address is and what message method the resource uses, follow these steps:

1. Switch to the Resource Sheet view (open the View menu and click Resource Sheet, or click the Resource Sheet icon in the View Bar).
2. Double-click the Resource Name for the resource for which you want to specify the e-mail address.
3. On the General tab of the Resource Information dialog box, enter the e-mail address in the Email text box. Figure 19.9 shows an example.
4. (Optional) If you want to add the resource's e-mail address to your Personal Address Book (for Microsoft Exchange, Windows Messaging, or Outlook), click the Details button. The Properties dialog box for the e-mail recipient appears. Click the Personal Address Book button beside Add To:. Click OK.

Figure 19.9
Enter an e-mail address in the Resource Information dialog box.

5. Click to open the Workgroup drop-down list, and then choose the type of messaging to use: None, Email, Web, or Email and Web.

You definitely want to disable workgroup messaging for nonhuman resources. To do so, double-click the resource entry in the Resource Sheet, open the Workgroup drop-down list in the Resource Information dialog box; then click None.

6. Click OK to finish creating the address and setting the messaging method to use.
7. Repeat steps 2–6 if you want to specify an e-mail address and messaging method for another resource.

Sharing Information with the Workgroup

After you specify how to communicate with resources, you can use the commands on the Workgroup submenu of the Tools menu to send different types of messages to the workgroup members. This section covers how to use those features, as well as how to send and route files.

E-Mailing or Routing a Project File

There are instances, such as when the project schedule is finalized or when you receive a request from a superior to review the schedule, when you might want to send your entire project file as an attachment to an e-mail message. Of course, doing so assumes that the recipient of the message also has Microsoft Project installed, so that he or she can open and review the file.

The WorkGroup toolbar offers buttons for sending files and other workgroup messages. To display this toolbar, point to any toolbar onscreen, right-click, and then click WorkGroup.

When you send a file, it's sent to your e-mail program's Outbox. You then have to launch your e-mail program and send the message from there, as described in the later section titled, "Finishing the Send."

To send a project file as an attachment to an e-mail message, use these steps:

1. Open the file you want to send, make any last-minute changes you want; then save the file.
2. Open the File menu, point to Send To; then click Mail Recipient or click the Send to Mail Recipient button on the WorkGroup toolbar. If Exchange or Windows Messaging prompts you to specify a Profile, select a different one from the drop-down list, if needed, and click OK to continue. The e-mail message window appears, with the project file already inserted as a file attachment, as shown in Figure 19.10.
3. If you didn't add the resource's e-mail to your Personal Address book, you can type the recipient's e-mail address in the text box beside the To button. Otherwise, click the To button to display the Select Names or Address Book dialog box, depending on the e-mailing system you're using. Click a name in the list at the left; then click on To to add the name to the list of Message recipients. Add other names as needed; then click OK.
4. If you want to include text—perhaps to describe what the file contains or to ask the recipient a specific question—click in the message area below the file icon, and then type your message (see Figure 19.11).
5. Open the File menu and click Send. Alternately, click the Send button at the left end of the top toolbar. The message with the file attachment is sent to your e-mail Outbox. When you later open your e-mail program and send and receive messages, the message will be mailed to the recipient.

You can route a message including a file to a number of users and have a copy automatically come back to you when the last recipient closes the file after working with it. You can send the message to all recipients at once, or set it up so that it goes to the first recipient, who then must forward it to the next recipient, and so on.

To route a file, open the File menu, point to Send To, and click Routing Recipient, or click the Sent to Routing Recipient button on the WorkGroup toolbar. The Routing Slip dialog box appears. Click the Address button to display the Address Book dialog box. Click a name from the list at the left; then click To to add this name to the list of recipients at the right. Add all the names you want, and then click OK to close the dialog box and return to the Routing Slip dialog box.

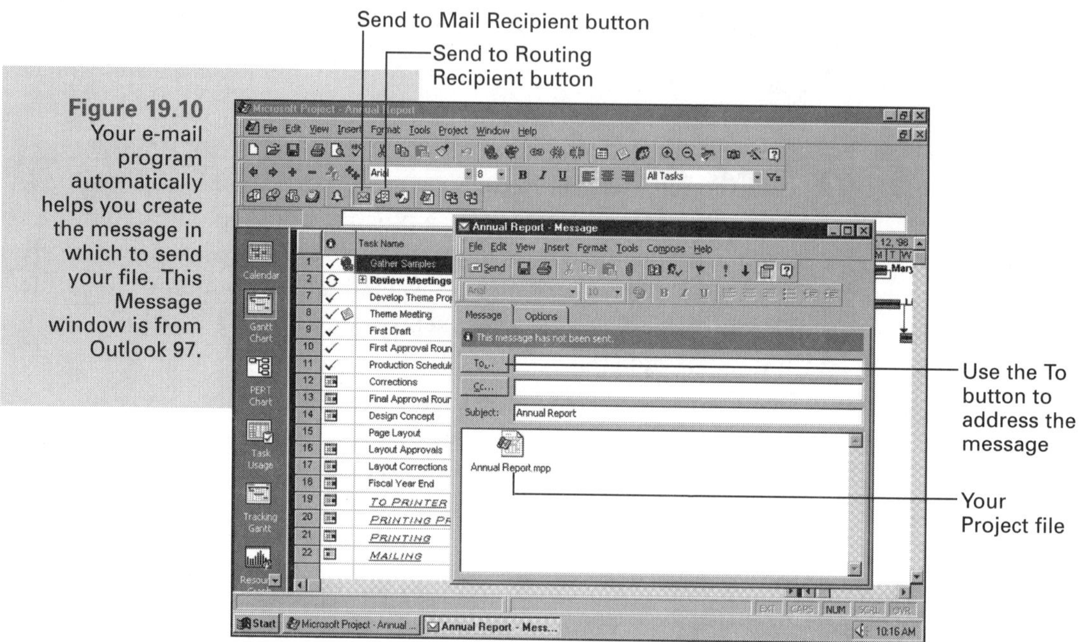

Figure 19.10 Your e-mail program automatically helps you create the message in which to send your file. This Message window is from Outlook 97.

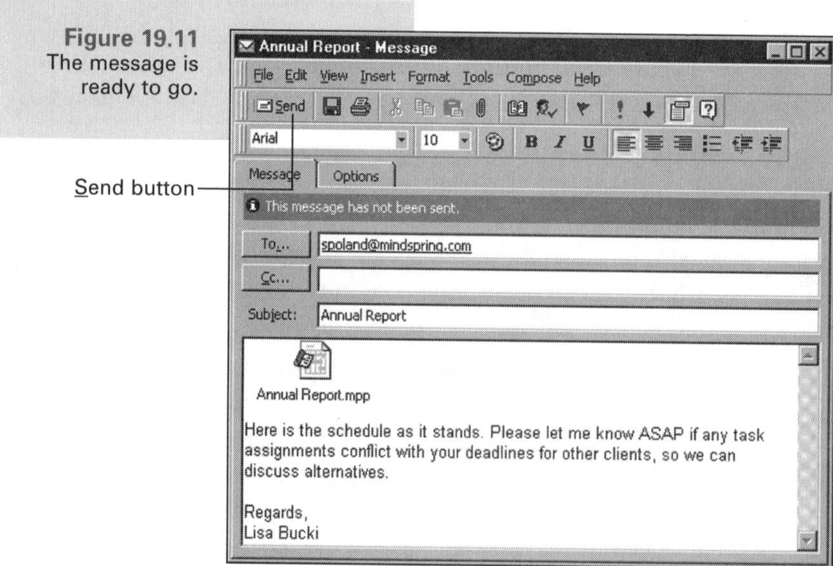

Figure 19.11 The message is ready to go.

The Routing Slip dialog box shows the routing order (see Figure 19.12). If needed, click a name in the To list and click one of the Move arrows to change the selected name's position in the list. Click and enter any Message Text you want to appear. In the Route to Recipients area, tell your e-mail system and

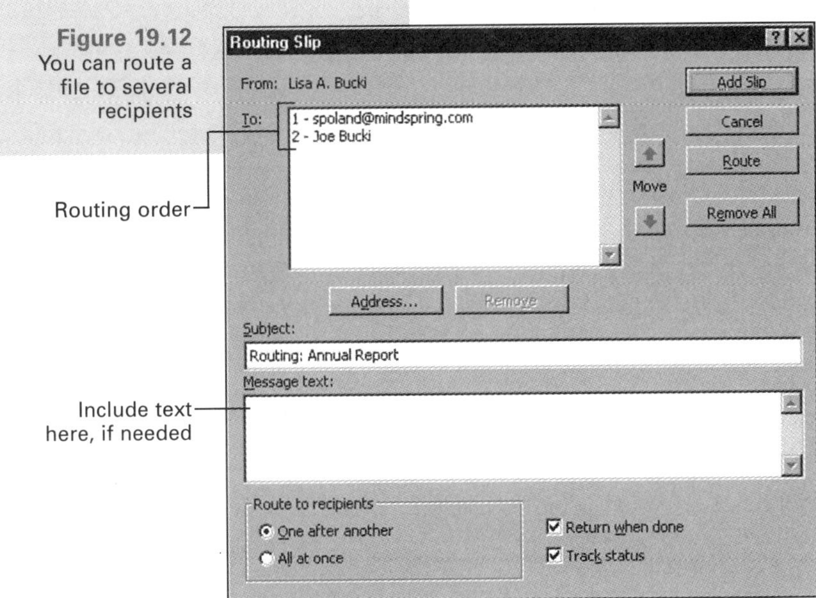

Figure 19.12 You can route a file to several recipients

Project messaging whether you want the message to be routed to the listed recipients One After Another or All at Once. Make sure that there's a check mark beside the Return When Done option if you want to automatically receive a copy of the routed file back after the last recipient in the list works with the file and closes it. The Track Status feature, when checked (and when you're routing the file from one recipient to the next), generates a notification message to you when each recipient on the list forwards the file to the next recipient. Click Route after you specify all the settings you want; this sends the routed file to your e-mail Outbox. You can then launch your e-mail program and send and receive messages to forward the routed message.

Sending Assignments, Updates, and Status Requests

The TeamAssign, TeamUpdate, and TeamStatus commands on the Workgroup submenu of the Tools menu all work in concert with your e-mail program to enable you to share task information with the resources assigned to particular tasks. These Workgroup commands take advantage of the workgroup messaging features that come with Project. Selecting any of these commands generates a special message in the workgroup messaging format, which is then sent to your e-mail Outbox as an attachment to a regular e-mail message or to the TeamInbox on the Web workgroup site, which recipients can display and log on to with a Web browser. (See the section titled "Using the TeamInbox" in this chapter to learn how to open and work with Web workgroup messages.)

The workgroup message lists the resource(s) you're sending the message to and key data about each of the tasks you selected to send or request information about. It includes suggested message text, so you don't even have to type instructions if you don't want to. It lists the task name, start date, number of work hours completed, and number of work hours remaining. It also offers a comments column for each task. The recipient of each workgroup message can make changes to the task information and then automatically return the message to you via their Exchange Outbox.

Each of these commands has a particular purpose, so I'll review each of them in turn:

- TeamAssign—This type of message asks a resource to verify that he/she has accepted an assignment, as well as the schedule you've sent for it, as shown in Figure 19.13.
- TeamUpdate—A message of this type (see Figure 19.14) enables you to report changing task information, such as a revised start or finish date. In order for this to work, you have to have previously sent information about tasks and incorporated resource replies into these tasks (as you'll learn to do later in this chapter). Otherwise, Project tells you that there are no tasks in the schedule to update.

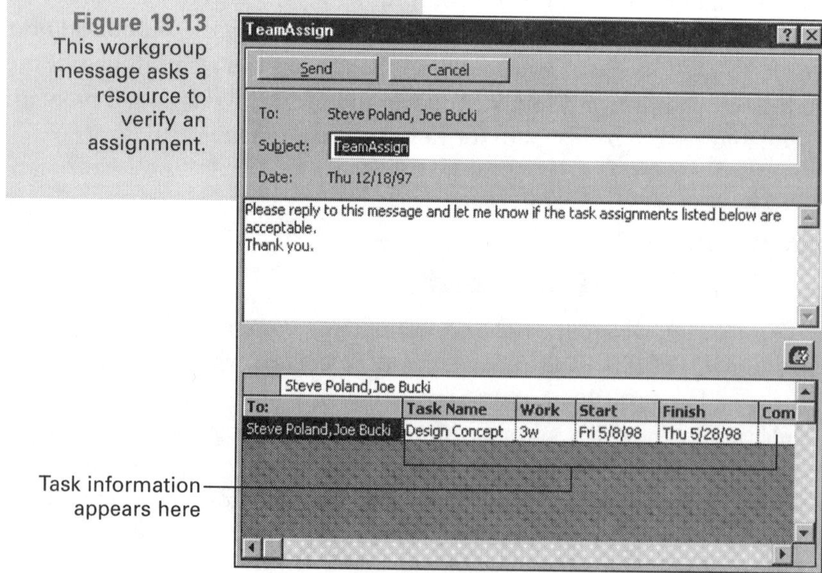

Figure 19.13 This workgroup message asks a resource to verify an assignment.

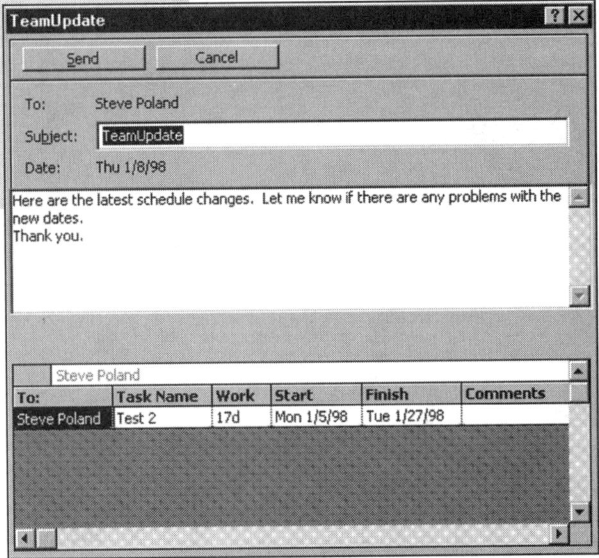

Figure 19.14 Workgroup messaging makes it easy to communicate an update to a team member.

- TeamStatus—This type of message queries the recipient to tell you how work is progressing on a task (see Figure 19.15).

The steps for sending each type of workgroup message are similar and are as follows:

1. Update information in the schedule in Gantt Chart view, and save your file. (Messaging features don't work in other views, such as the Resource Sheet.)
2. If you want to send a workgroup message about a particular task or group of tasks, click to select a single task; then hold down Ctrl while clicking any additional tasks you want to select.
3. Open the Tools menu, point to Workgroup to display a submenu, and click TeamAssign, TeamUpdate, or TeamStatus. Alternately, click the TeamAssign, TeamUpdate, or TeamStatus button on the WorkGroup toolbar.

Note

Depending on which e-mail system you're using or whether or not you're presently logged onto your e-mail program, you might or might not be prompted to specify a profile when you send messages of any type. Make the appropriate selection, if prompted, and then click OK to continue.

Figure 19.15 You can ask resources to report to you about progress on tasks.

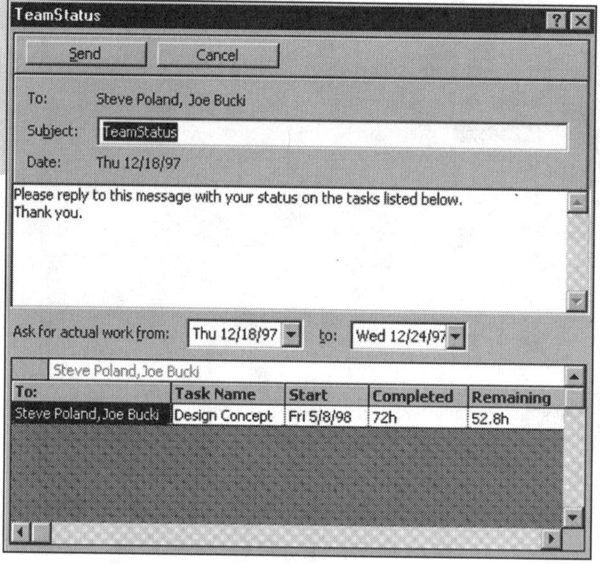

4. The Workgroup Mail dialog box appears (see Figure 19.16). Click to specify whether to send the message regarding All Tasks or the Selected Task, and then click OK.
5. The workgroup message appears onscreen. Edit any of the information you want, such as the Subject or text of the message; then click the Send button at the top of the message. The message is sent to your e-mail Outbox or the Web TeamInbox. You'll learn shortly what to do with it from there.

Sending Notes to the Team

Project can automatically set up an e-mail message for you, building the recipient list based on options you specify and enabling you to select whether the attached file should hold your entire schedule file or just a graphic picture (.BMP file) of any tasks you selected in the Task Sheet. This kind of note can be sent to e-mail addresses that you specify.

To send an automatically formatted message like this, follow these steps:

1. Update information in the schedule in Gantt Chart view, and save your file.
2. If you want to send a note message about a particular task or group of tasks, you need to select the task or tasks. Click to select a single task, then hold down Ctrl while clicking any additional tasks you want to select.

Figure 19.16 Specify whether you want to send a message for all tasks.

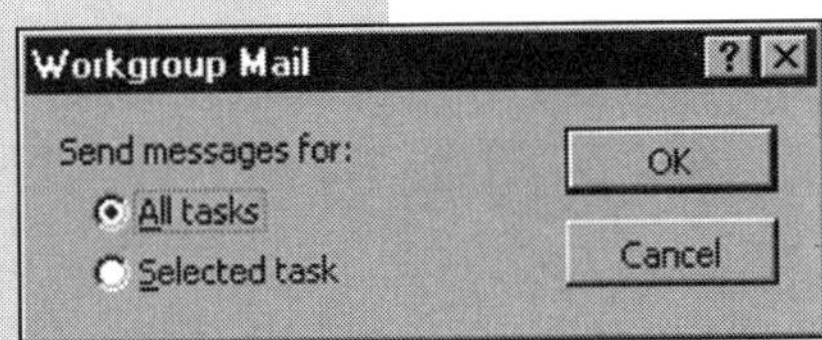

Note

You might use Outlook 97 to remind you of appointments and tasks. You also can use it to remind you before a task is set to begin, so you can either begin the task (if you're assigned to it) or check in with resources. In the Task Sheet, select the tasks for which you want reminders by dragging over the row headers. Choose Tools, Workgroup, Set Reminder. In the Set Reminder dialog box that appears, use the settings to tell Outlook when to display the reminder (they're self-explanatory); the default is 15 minutes before the start of the task. Click OK to finish setting the reminder.

3. Open the Tools menu, point to Workgroup, and click Send Schedule Note. The Send Schedule Note dialog box appears, as shown in Figure 19.17.
4. In the Address Message To area, specify the recipients for the message and whether the list should include the Resources and Contacts from the Entire Project or Selected Tasks.
5. In the Attach area of the dialog box, specify whether the attachment message should be the entire File or just a Picture of Selected Tasks.
6. Click OK. If you haven't included an e-mail address for any of the selected recipients and one is needed, you're prompted to do so. Specify the needed address(es) as described earlier in this chapter. (You may be prompted to choose a profile; do so, and then continue.) The message appears onscreen, as shown in Figure 19.18.

You can delete the attached file from the message if you want. All your addressing information remains intact. To delete the attachment, click its icon, and then press the Delete key.

7. Type a Subject for the message; then click in the message area below the attached file, and type the note you want to send.

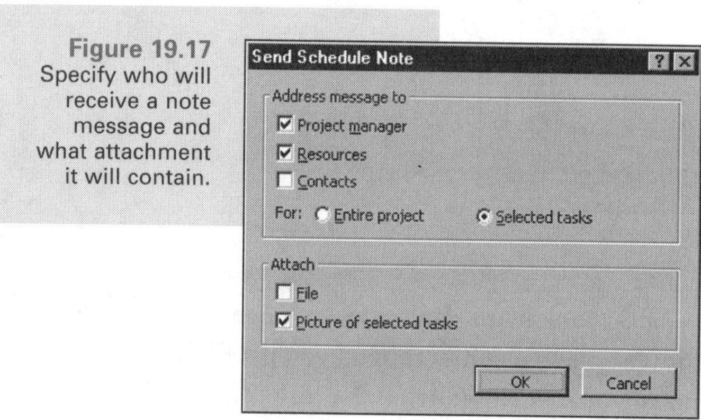

Figure 19.17 Specify who will receive a note message and what attachment it will contain.

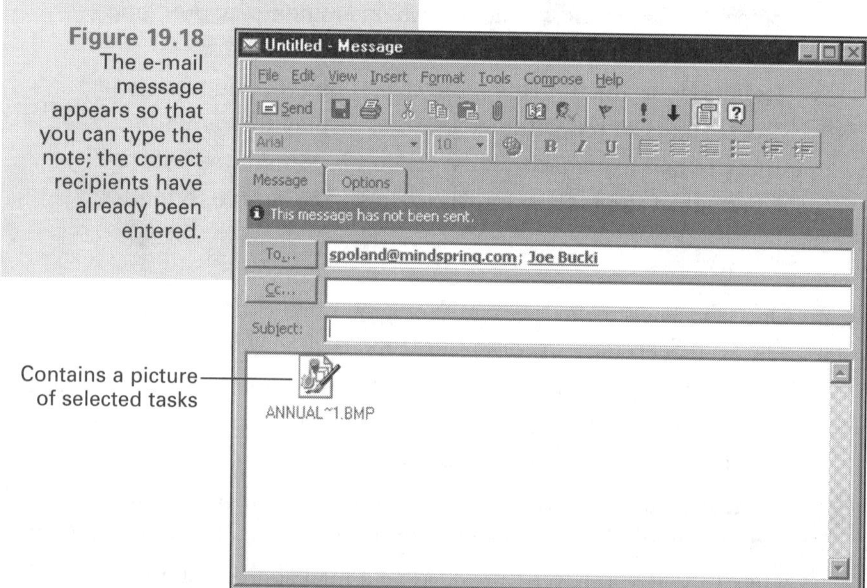

Figure 19.18 The e-mail message appears so that you can type the note; the correct recipients have already been entered.

8. Open the File menu and click Send. Alternately, click the Send button at the left end of the top toolbar. The message with the file attachment is sent to your e-mail Outbox, from which you can later send it.

Finishing the Send

All the workgroup messages you've learned to create so far in this chapter were sent from Project to your Outbox folder within your e-mail program (or to the TeamInbox if you're using Web messaging). This makes sense, because Project and the workgroup messaging features aren't e-mail programs; they simply prepare your information to be sent via e-mail.

Now, you need to send your messages from the Outbox to the intended recipients. To send the messages from an e-mail program, you use whatever method you normally would use to send messages from the Outbox. For example, to send messages from Outlook 97, follow these steps:

1. Go to your Windows desktop and double-click the Microsoft Outlook icon to start Microsoft Outlook 97. Alternatively, click on the Start button on the Taskbar, point to Programs, and click on Microsoft Outlook. Outlook loads and appears onscreen, with your Inbox folder open.
2. (Optional) Click the Outbox folder icon to open it and show outgoing messages (see Figure 19.19).
3. Open the Tools menu and click Check for New Mail.
4. Outlook connects to your mail system (an Internet Service Provider, for example, or your company's e-mail server) and delivers the messages, keeping you informed onscreen as the messages are delivered. It also checks for incoming e-mail messages and places them in your Inbox.

Note

If you need to take any steps to retrieve regular messages from your e-mail system to get those messages to appear in your Inbox, then you'll need to do the same for workgroup messages.

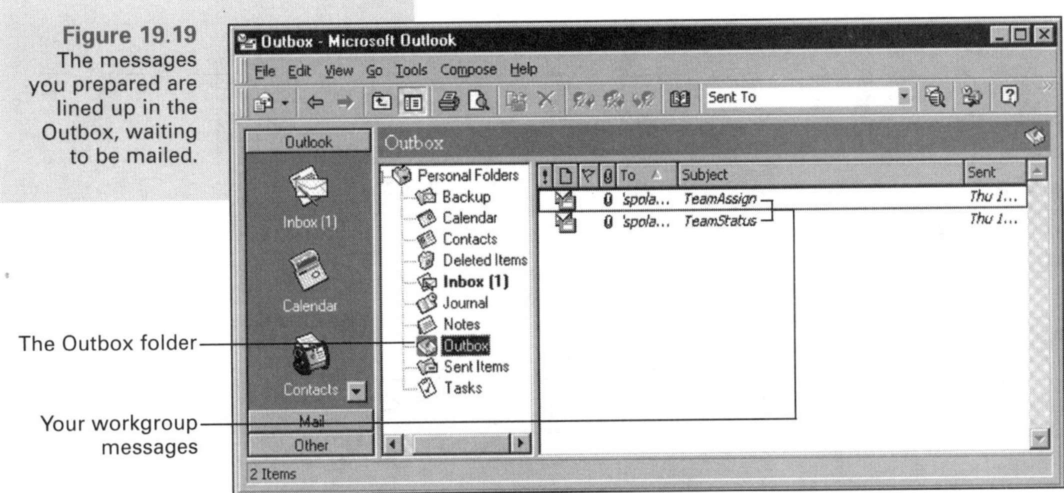

Figure 19.19 The messages you prepared are lined up in the Outbox, waiting to be mailed.

Responding to Assignments and Updates

When you're on the receiving end of workgroup messages, they appear in your e-mail Inbox folder along with other, normal e-mail messages. To read a workgroup message, double-click it. If you sent a project file as a message attachment, routed the file, or sent information as a schedule note, the message simply opens like a normal e-mail message. If you're opening a TeamAssign, TeamUpdate, or TeamStatus message, Project's messaging features launch and opens the message, which appears in a special message dialog box onscreen (see Figure 19.20).

Click the Reply button to prepare your response to the message. The window automatically adjusts to enable you to reply, and RE: appears beside the window title and in the beginning of the Subject text. An insertion point appears in the Message area; type your overall reply there. In your reply, enter work completed on a particular day for the Report Period being shown, in one of the blank cells. To make an entry, click in the cell; then type your entry and press Enter. Figure 19.21 shows some example entries. Click the Send button to send the reply to your e-mail Outbox. From the Outbox, send the reply to the project manager using the steps outlined in the preceding section.

If you're a project manager, your resources will send replies to your assignment and status requests. Such responses appear in your e-mail Inbox (or the Web Inbox, which you'll learn about later), and you can double-click each one to open it. For example, the response shown in Figure 19.21, after being sent to the project manager, resembles Figure 19.22 when the project manager opens it.

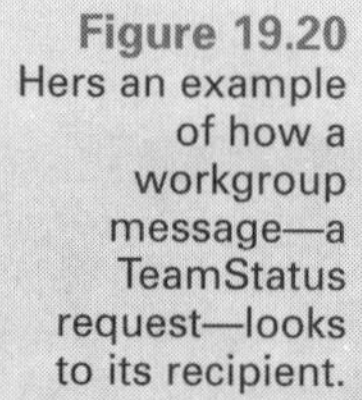

Figure 19.20 Hers an example of how a workgroup message—a TeamStatus request—looks to its recipient.

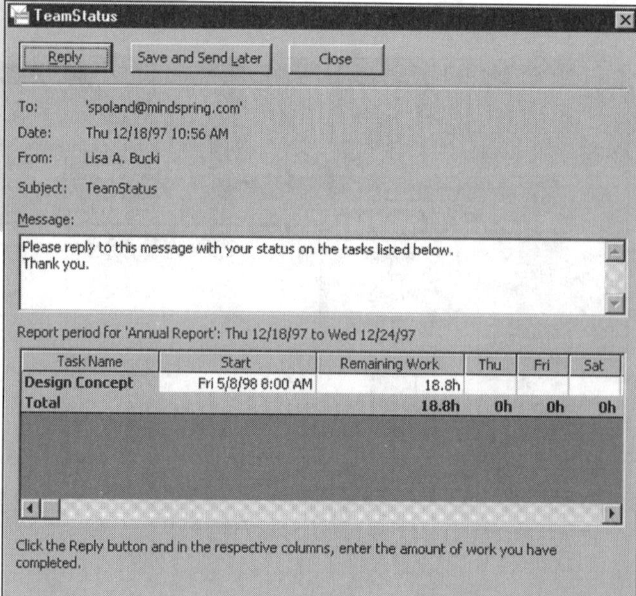

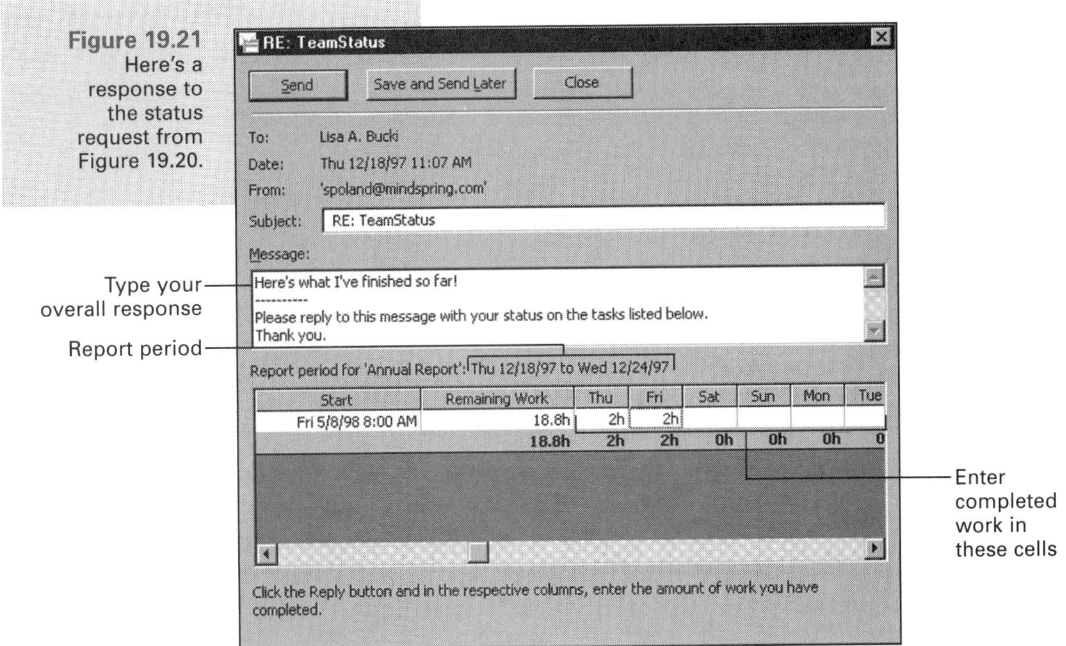

Figure 19.21 Here's a response to the status request from Figure 19.20.

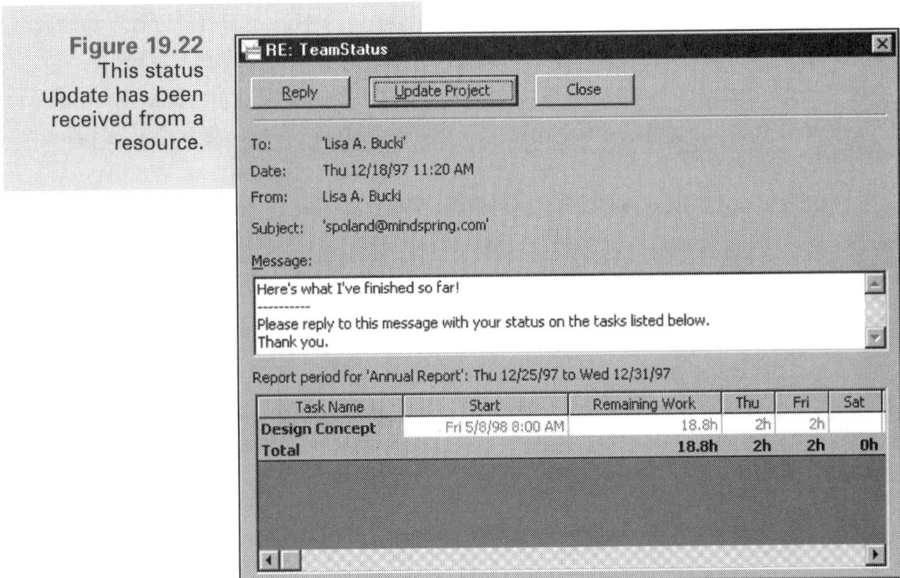

Figure 19.22 This status update has been received from a resource.

If the resource's response isn't satisfactory, click the Reply button to send a reply message. If the resource simply confirmed the existing schedule, you can click the Close button to close the message, and click No if you're asked whether to update the Project file. If the response suggests some schedule changes or reports completed work and you want to enter these changes into your project file, click the Update Project button. If Project isn't open, it starts and the file opens for updating. The schedule changes are made to the appropriate task in the schedule, and the status update message closes. Save your project file to keep these changes.

Creating a Web Workgroup

If you want to use a Web server on the Internet or your company's intranet to communicate with members of the workgroup, you must set up the Web server for the workgroup. You can do this either in a specific, shared folder on your company's network server computer (check with your system administrator if you need authorization to do this), or on your desktop PC that's connected to the network. However, whether you can directly set up a Web server by creating folders on your company's network server computer. This section provides an overview of how to set up the Web server for your workgroup and introduces you to how to access messages in the TeamInbox and Web Inbox.

If you connect to the Internet via a dial-up connection to an Internet Service Provider, you really can't practically use a Web server to communicate with the workgroup, because your computer would have to be on and connected to the Internet 24-hours a day, a practice that ISPs don't allow. If it's essential that you use a Web workgroup, consult your ISP for alternatives to get it done.

Creating and managing a Web site under any circumstances can get complicated. This section covers the general premises, but you may have to take additional steps to make the Web server work in your computing environment.

Setting Up the Web Server

If your company's network (or your computer connected to the network) runs on Windows NT 4.0 Server or later, it already has Web server software called

IIS (Internet Information Server) built in. On such a computer, you need to set up the folder (directory) that will serve as the workgroup Web site (this is the Web Server Root, with an example shown in Figure 19.8—\\BUCKI-GROUP\WebShare\wwwroot\Projects). You also need to make sure that all users can access the folder, and that IIS is set up to both read and execute data. As this is a more advanced topic, consult Project's online help system and your IIS documentation to learn more.

If your company's network doesn't have IIS, uses an earlier version of NT, or uses nonMicrosoft software, read the **Pjread8.txt** file stored in the folder that holds Project (C:\Program Files\Microsoft Office\Office, if you installed Project to the default folder on your computer).

If you're using a Windows 95 (or later) system connected to your company's network, and you want the server to be stored on your hard disk rather than your network, you need to install the Personal Web Server program that comes with Project. (If you choose this method, your computer must remain on and logged on to the network, and the Internet or intranet.) To do so, run the **Pws10a.exe** file in the \ValuPack\PWServer folder on the Microsoft Project 98 CD-ROM. Follow the onscreen instructions for completing the installation. Next, open the Windows Control Panel (double-click the Control Panel icon in the My Computer window), and then double-click the Personal Web Server icon.

Click the Administration tab; then click the Administration button. Your Web browser launches and you're prompted to connect or log on, if needed. An Administration page loads. Click the WWW Administration hyperlink. On the WWW Administrator-Directory page that displays, click the Directories tab. Look down the list to find the C:\WebShare\wwwroot directory in the list, and then click the Edit hyperlink beside it. Scroll down to the Access area, and click the Execute check box. Click the OK button at the bottom of the page. (If the Security Information dialog box appears, click Continue.) You can then close your browser and log off or disconnect, as needed.

You then need to share the hard disk folder C:\WebShare\wwwroot (as well as any alias you created to hold the workgroup information) so that other users can access it, without necessarily accessing everything else on your computer. To do so, navigate to the folder to share in either Windows Explorer or a My Computer window. Right-click the folder, and then click Sharing. On the Sharing tab, click the Shared As option button. Leave the default Share Name text box entry as is. In the Name list, press and hold Ctrl, and click the name of each workgroup member. If some users are on other domains, click the correct domain under Obtain List From. Click Full Access, and then click OK. Click the Web Sharing button. Click to check the Share Folder for HTTP, Read Only, and Execute Scripts check boxes. Click OK twice to close both Properties dialog boxes and enable sharing.

Using the TeamInbox

Whew! Now the Web server is ready to be selected (as described earlier under "Preparing to Communicate with a Workgroup") and workgroup members can access the TeamInbox to check for workgroup messages (TeamAssign, TeamUpdate, and TeamStatus) and respond to them. Here's how to log on to TeamInbox:

1. Start your Web browser and connect or log on to the Internet or intranet if prompted.
2. In the Address box or applicable location to enter the URL for the page to display, enter the URL to the Web workgroup server, followed by the startup command **mspjhttp.exe** and a question mark, as in **http://BUCKIGROUP/Projects/mspjhttp.exe?**. The Workgroup Login page loads, as shown in Figure 19.24.
3. Open the User Name drop-down list and click your name. Enter a Password (only if you've previously created one), and then click the Go! hyperlink button. A list of your messages appears, as shown in Figure 19.25.
4. Click the closed envelope icon beside any message to open it. The message appears, automatically set up for you to reply. Enter your responses (see Figure 19.26), and then click Send to send the response to the Web Inbox, which is used by the project manager who set up the workgroup Web site to send and receive information. (If you click Delete to delete a message, you'll be asked to confirm the deletion.)
5. Respond to other messages as needed.
6. If you want to send an update about work you've completed on a particular task, click the Task List button. Click to place a check beside any and all tasks that you're sending an update about; then enter information about the work yet to be done or completed in the cells to the right (see Figure 19.27—if there were more uncompleted tasks, more would appear on the list). Click Send to send the update to the project manager's Web Inbox.
7. Click the Logoff hyperlink at the left side of the screen to return to the Login page. This is an essential step—you don't want to leave your connection open if a project is confidential and you need to step away from your computer.
8. You can either browse other Web sites, or close down your browser and connection.

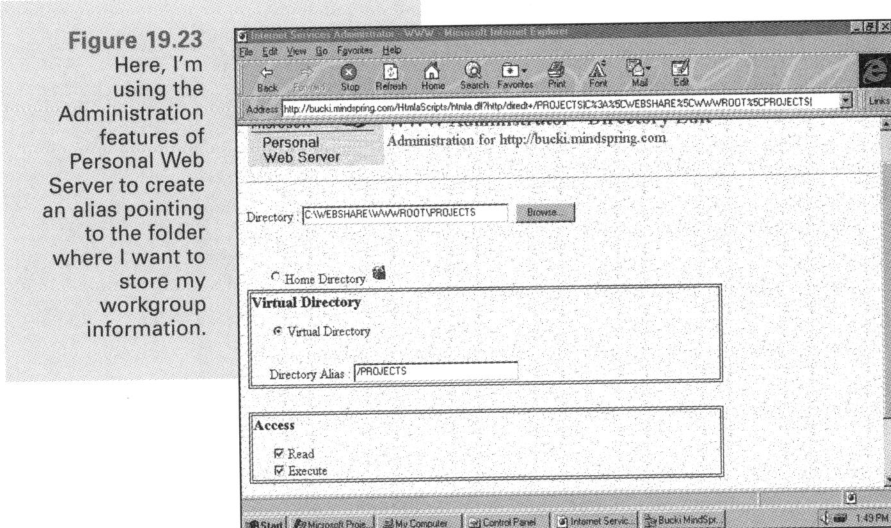

Figure 19.23 Here, I'm using the Administration features of Personal Web Server to create an alias pointing to the folder where I want to store my workgroup information.

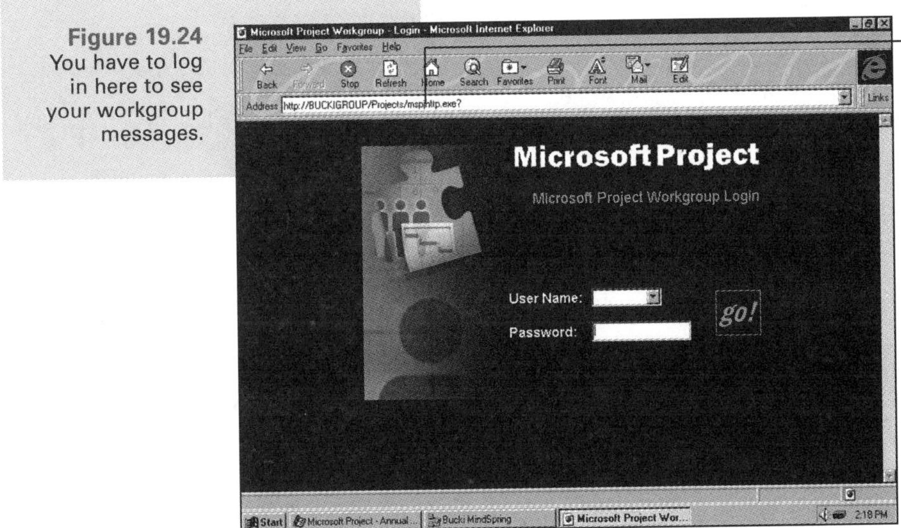

Figure 19.24 You have to log in here to see your workgroup messages.

Reviewing Responses with the WebInbox

Unlike the TeamInbox, you can launch WebInbox within Project, because the Web information is either stored on your hard disk (if you installed Personal Web Server) or a network location you can access. Follow these steps to launch the WebInbox:

1. Click to open the Tools menu, point to Workgroup, and choose WebInbox, or click the WebInbox button on the Workgroup toolbar. The WebInbox appears, as shown in Figure 19.28.

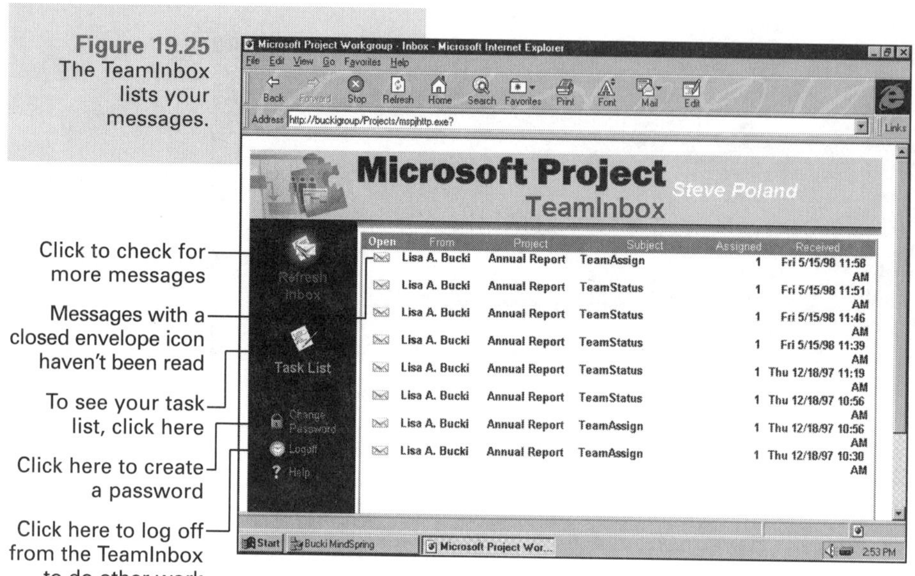
Microsoft Project Workgroup - Inbox - Microsoft Internet Explorer
Microsoft Project
TeamInbox
Steve Poland
Refresh Inbox
Task List
Change Password
Logoff
Help
Click to check for more messages
Messages with a closed envelope icon haven't been read
To see your task list, click here
Click here to create a password
Click here to log off from the TeamInbox to do other work

Figure 19.25 The TeamInbox lists your messages.

Caution

If you don't want to store your workgroup Web in C:\WebShare\www-root, and want instead to use another folder, you'll need to use the Add hyperlink on Directories tab on the WWW Administration-Directory page to create an *alias* for the folder. The alias is an alternate name that represents the folder in the URL. For example, if your computer is identified by the name BUCKIGROUP when connected to the network, your site's name will resemble something like http://BUCKIGROUP/, and the default startup page (Default.htm) for that site is stored in C:\WebShare\wwwroot (its UNC might be \\BUCKIGROUP\WebShare\wwwroot). Let's say you want instead to use a subfolder called C:\WebShare\wwwroot\Projects (it's UNC would be \\BUCKIGROUP\WebShare\wwwroot\Projects, and would be the Web Server Root address you'd enter in the dialog box shown in Figure 19.8). After you create and enable sharing for the C:\WebShare\wwwroot\Projects folder, create an alias for it called /Projects. Make sure that both the Read and Execute choices are checked in the Access area as shown in Figure 19.23. Afterwards, workgroup members will be able to access files (and the workgroup information, if you set it up there as described earlier under "Preparing to Communicate with a Workgroup,") via a URL combining the root and the alias, as in http://BUCKIGROUP/Projects/.

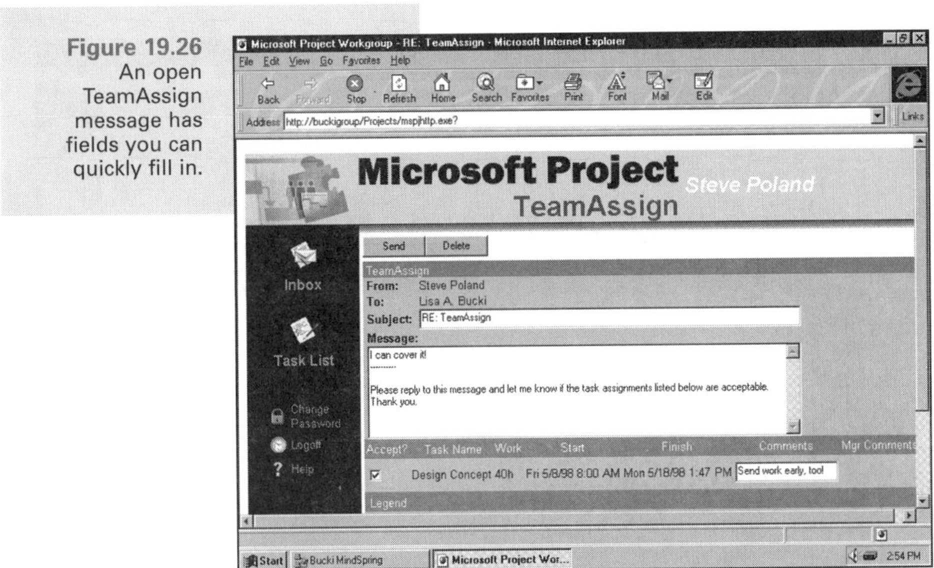

Figure 19.26 An open TeamAssign message has fields you can quickly fill in.

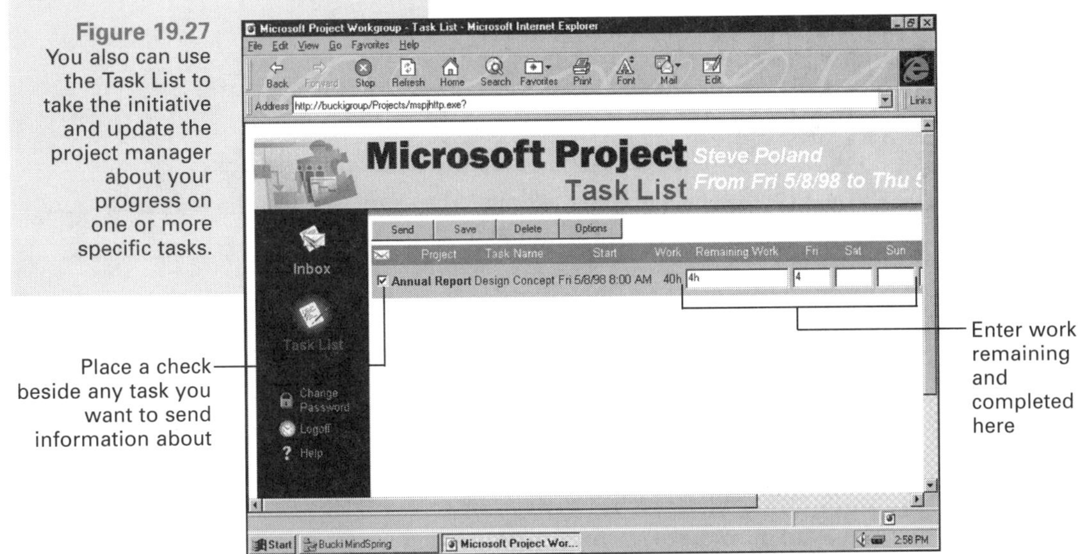

Figure 19.27 You also can use the Task List to take the initiative and update the project manager about your progress on one or more specific tasks.

2. To view a response, click it in the list; then click the View button. The message opens in a TeamMessage window, which looks like one of the other workgroup messages (TeamAssign and so on).

Figure 19.28 When a user responds to your messages from the TeamInbox, those responses appear here.

3. Click Update Project to add any schedule or work completed changes from the message into the schedule file and close the message, or just click Cancel to close the message.

Note

If you choose to update the schedule file at any point and the schedule file isn't currently opened and shares resources, you'll be prompted to specify how the resource information and related files should open.

4. To update the schedule with information from the message without opening the message, click the message in the list; then click Update Project. Or, click Update All to add the information from all the messages to the schedule.
5. To delete a message, click it and click Delete.
6. If you want to see only messages of a particular type, click TeamAssign or TeamStatus rather than All Messages.
7. When you finish working with messages, click Close to close the WebInbox.

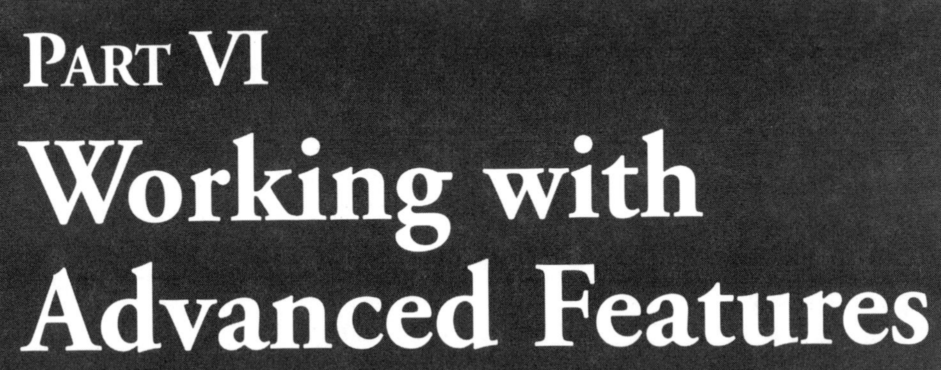

Part VI
Working with Advanced Features

20

Customizing Microsoft Project

In This Chapter

- Making adjustments to menus
- Hiding and displaying toolbars, and working with toolbar tools
- Working with the Options dialog box

Throughout the book, I've noted numerous situations where you need to tweak how Project 98 reacts to your commands, or even how you communicate with Project to give it commands. This chapter provides an overview of all the customization options available to you in Project.

It explains how to make Project look and work the way you want it to.

Creating a Custom Menu

Early on, many computer programs deserved the reputation of being difficult to learn. Each program used its own terms for particular operations, such as opening a file (which was also called "getting," "retrieving," and so on). Moreover, each program had different menus that grouped commands differently. From one program to the next, you never knew exactly how to navigate. While software publishers have come a long way toward standardizing terms and menus so that what you learn in one program applies in another, they've been kind enough to leave in plenty of flexibility for controlling how menus appear.

In fact, in Project and many other applications, you can create custom menu bars, custom drop-down menus, and custom menu commands to suit your needs and working style. The commands you create can execute standard program commands, macros that come with the programs, or macros you create. To work with menus in Project, open the Tools menu, point to Customize, and click Toolbars. Or, right-click the menu bar, and then click Customize. The Customize dialog box (see Figure 20.1) displays the list of menu bars and toolbars available in Project. (In Project 98, you use similar steps to create menu bars and toolbars.) Each menu bar offers a list of menus, which in turn list commands. To display a different menu onscreen, click its check box in the Toolbars list of the Toolbars tab in the dialog box, and then click Close to close the dialog box. If you no longer want a particular menu to appear onscreen, click to clear the check box beside its name before closing the dialog box.

To display a menu bar you've created, right-click an onscreen menu bar or toolbar, and then click the name of the menu to display in the shortcut menu.

You also can use the Customize dialog box to add a new command to a menu, to add a new menu to a menu bar, or to create an entirely new menu bar. For example, to create a new menu bar, click the New button on the Toolbars tab in the Customize dialog box. The New Toolbar dialog box appears. Type a name for the menu in the Toolbar Name text box, preferably a name that distinguishes the new bar as a menu bar rather than a toolbar. Click OK, and the new menu bar appears onscreen as a small, blank, floating toolbar.

Figure 20.1 Work with menus and toolbars using this dialog box.

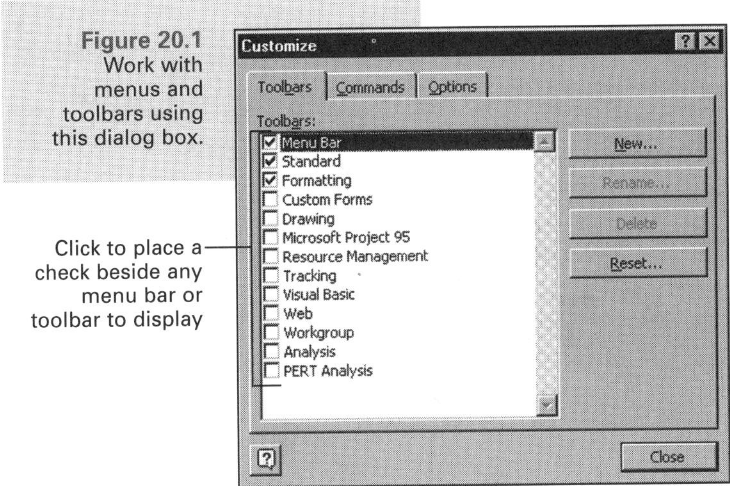

Next, you want to create the first menu on the menu bar. Click the Commands tab in the Customize dialog box. Scroll down the Categories list; then click New Menu in the list. A New Menu choice appears in the Commands list at the right side of the dialog box. Drag the New Menu choice from the dialog box onto the new menu bar. A New Menu placeholder appears on the menu bar. Right-click the placeholder or click it and then click the Modify Selection button in the Customize dialog box. Then, in the Name text box, type a menu name, such as Favo&rites (see Figure 20.2). Press Enter. Project knows that you intend the entry to be a menu name, and automatically formats it in bold. The ampersand (&) before the r is how you tell Project to format the letter "r" as a selection letter; for your custom menu, pressing Alt+R opens the Favorites menu.

Note

For obvious reasons, you can't use the same selection letter for two menu names on the same menu bar, or for two commands on the same menu. You also should be careful not to duplicate selection letters in menu names, if you plan to display more than one menu at a time.

Tip

You also can add a menu to any toolbar that's displayed onscreen by dragging the New Menu placeholder onto the toolbar rather than onto a menu bar.

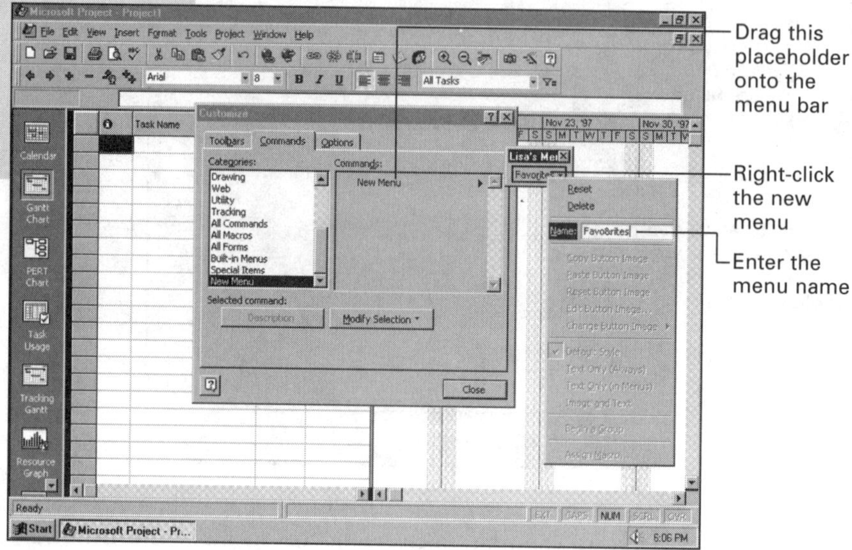
Drag this placeholder onto the menu bar
Right-click the new menu
Enter the menu name

Figure 20.2 You can create a completely new menu on a menu bar.

On the Commands tab of the Customize dialog box, scroll through the Categories list and click the category that holds the first command or macro you want to add to the menu. If you're not sure what category to choose, click the All Commands or All Macros choice. Then scroll down the Commands list until you see the command you want to add to the menu. Drag the command from the Commands list to the new menu name on the menu bar; when the blank menu opens below the menu name, drag the command onto the menu and release the mouse button. The command appears on the menu, which remains open. If you want to rename the command or change its selection letter, right-click the command or click it and click the Modify Selection button in the Customize dialog box. Edit the Name text box entry, and press Enter. To add each additional command to the menu, simply click the Categories choice you want, and drag a command from the Commands list to the position on the menu where you want it to appear. Then drop it into place as shown in Figure 20.3.

Note

You have to leave the Customize dialog box open to make all your menu changes. Otherwise, the techniques described in this section won't work. If you need to redisplay the Customize dialog box, click to open the Tools menu, point to Customize, and click Toolbars.

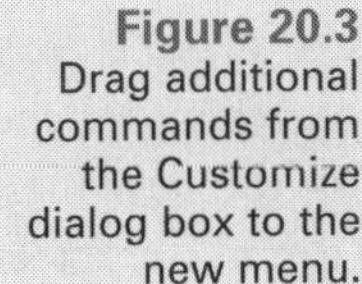

Figure 20.3 Drag additional commands from the Customize dialog box to the new menu.

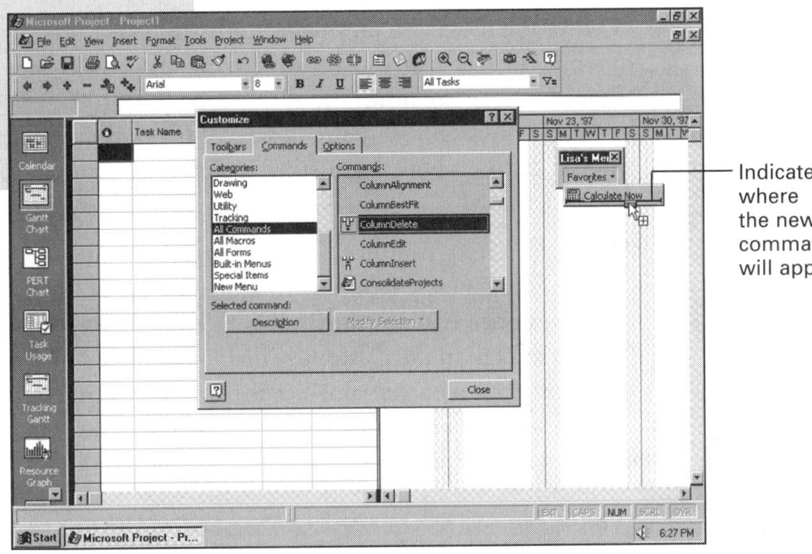

If you want to create a command to display a submenu, select New Menu in the Categories list of the Commands tab of the Customize dialog box, and then drag the New Menu choice onto a menu. Name the submenu just as you would name a menu. Then, select command categories from the Categories list, and drag commands from the Commands list onto the submenu you added to the menu.

You might want to be able to group commands on your menu for easier access. You can do so by inserting a separator line. Open the new menu, and then click the command above which you want the separator line to appear. Click the Modify Selection button in the Customize dialog box or right-click the selected command. Click the Begin a Group choice to insert the separator line. To remove the separator, redisplay the shortcut menu for the selected command, and click the Begin a Group choice to toggle it.

Continue using the techniques just described to add additional commands to your menu. Any time you want to start a new menu on the menu bar, click the New Menu choice in the Categories list, and then drag the New Menu placeholder from the Commands list to the desired position on the menu bar. If you make a mistake and add an unwanted menu bar or command, simply drag the menu or command from the menu bar or command where it resides over the Project work area, and release the mouse button. Alternately, you can drag a menu name to change its position on a menu bar, or drag a command to move it up or down in a menu. For example, if you're right handed, you may want to move the file menu on the default menu bar to the right, to make it easier to work with. When you finish making all of your menu bar changes, click Close to close the Customize dialog box. Then, you can drag the new menu bar to the position you desire onscreen. If you drag it to the top of the screen, you can drop it above an existing toolbar or menu bar to "dock" it in a horizontal position.

Although starting from scratch when creating a menu is fine, you may be better off adding a copy of an existing menu to your menu bar and modifying it to suit your needs. Click the Built-In Menus choice in the Categories list of the Commands tab in the Customize dialog box. Then drag the name of the menu that most approximates your needs from the Commands list to the appropriate position on a menu bar or menu. Then, make changes to the menu and commands as needed.

If you make changes to the Standard menu bar and later want to undo the changes, display the Customize dialog box, click Menu Bar in the Toolbars list of the Toolbars tab, and click the Reset button.

Your custom menu bars and toolbars are stored by default with the Global.mpt file where Project settings are stored. If you want to e-mail a schedule file and have it offer the custom menu bar or toolbar, you need to copy the custom menu bar or toolbar, as well as any macro modules holding macros for commands or toolbar buttons, to that particular file. Use the Organizer choice on the Tools menu to display the Organizer, which enables you to copy the custom feature. See Chapter 9, "Working with the Different Project Views," to learn more about the Organizer.

Working with Toolbars

Toolbars are as easy to customize as menu bars, and most users find toolbars easier to use. You've seen numerous instances elsewhere in this book where displaying different toolbars or working with particular toolbar buttons can help you get the most out of certain Project features. This section shares more information about how you can work with Project's toolbars.

Displaying and Hiding Toolbars

Every toolbar is accessible via the other toolbars. You can right-click on any toolbar to display a shortcut menu. Then click the name of another toolbar you want to display or click the name of a toolbar that's already onscreen that you want to hide. Similarly, you can click to open the View menu and point to the Toolbars choice to display a submenu listing toolbars and menu bars; click the toolbar you want to hide or display.

An alternative method of choosing which toolbars appear onscreen and which don't, as well as accessing other commands for working with toolbars, is to open the Tools menu, point to Customize, and click Toolbars. The Customize dialog box appears (refer to Figure 20.1). To display the Customize dialog box using the mouse, right-click any toolbar; then click Customize.

Click the check box beside any toolbar you want to display in the Toolbars list of the Toolbars tab. If you want to hide a toolbar that's onscreen, simply click its check box in the Toolbars list to remove the check mark. Click the Close button to close the Customize dialog box and finish making your choices.

Customizing the Buttons on a Toolbar

You can make any changes that you want to the contents of a toolbar. The process for doing so is very similar to creating and editing a menu, which you learned about earlier in the chapter. You can remove buttons, add buttons, or edit the function of any button. To add and remove buttons on a toolbar, use the following steps:

1. Display the toolbar that you want to edit onscreen.
2. Open the Tools menu, point to Customize, and click Toolbars. Alternately, you can right-click any toolbar, and then click Customize. The Customize dialog box appears.
3. To add a button to one of the displayed toolbars, click the Commands tab to display it. Click one of the Categories list choices to display the available buttons and commands in that category. Then drag a button or command from the Commands list onto the toolbar in the position you want, as shown in Figure 20.4. Release the mouse button to drop the new toolbar button into position.

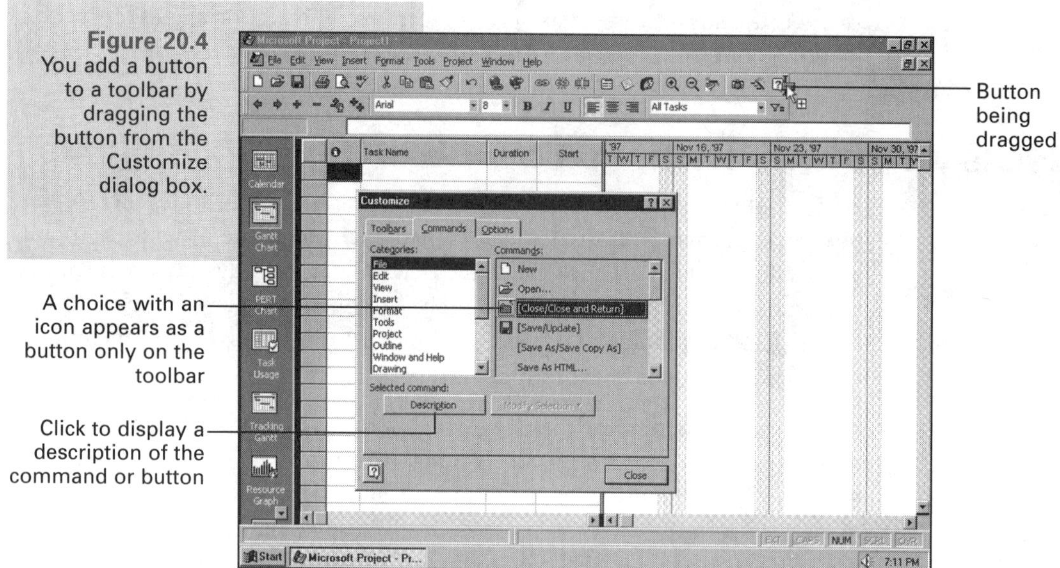

Figure 20.4 You add a button to a toolbar by dragging the button from the Customize dialog box.

To add a toolbar button or menu command for a macro you created, select All Macros from the Categories list box of the Commands tab in the Customize dialog box. Then drag the macro from the Commands list to a menu bar or toolbar.

The Commands list of the Commands tab in the Customize dialog box clues you in as to whether a command you add to a toolbar will appear as a picture button only or a text command only. A choice that has an icon will appear as a picture button when you drag it onto a toolbar. If a choice lacks an icon, the command name will appear on the added toolbar button.

4. To move an existing toolbar button to a new position on the same toolbar, which you must do while the Customize dialog box is open, just drag the button and release the mouse to drop it into the new location.
5. To remove a button from a toolbar, which you must do while the Customize dialog box is open, drag it off of the toolbar and release the mouse button. (Make sure that you don't accidentally drop it on another toolbar.)

6. When you finish dragging buttons onto, off of, and around on toolbars, click Close to close the Customize dialog box.

The buttons available in the Customize dialog box are, for the most part, buttons that already exist on a Project toolbar or menu. If you want to place a custom button image on a toolbar button, display the toolbar and the Customize dialog box. Right-click the toolbar button to change. Then point to Change Button Image to display a palette of available button images, as shown in Figure 20.5. Click the image you want to apply to the button. (You also can use this technique to add an image to a menu command.)

If you can't find a button that's exactly what you need, click a button that's close in appearance. Then right-click the toolbar button with the image to edit and click Edit Button Image in the shortcut menu that appears. The Button Editor appears onscreen, as shown in Figure 20.6. Click a color or Erase in the Colors area; then click a square (called a pixel) on the Picture to change that pixel to the selected color. Click OK when you're done making changes. The edited image appears on the toolbar button.

You can change the command or macro assigned to a button or its status bar description using the Customize Tool dialog box. (This technique applies to menu commands, too.) With the Customize dialog box open onscreen, click the toolbar button (or menu command); then click Modify Selection on the Commands tab or right-click the toolbar button. In the menu that appears, click Assign Macro. The Customize Tool dialog box appears. To change the existing

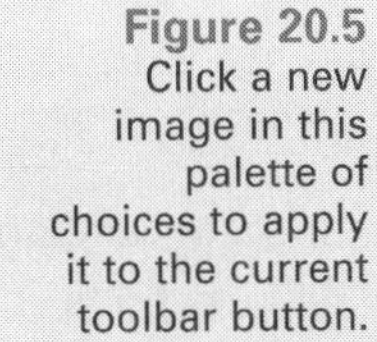

Figure 20.5 Click a new image in this palette of choices to apply it to the current toolbar button.

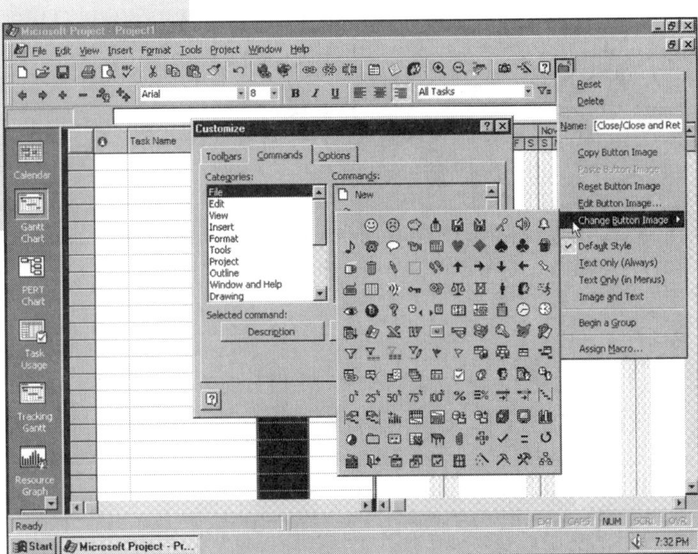

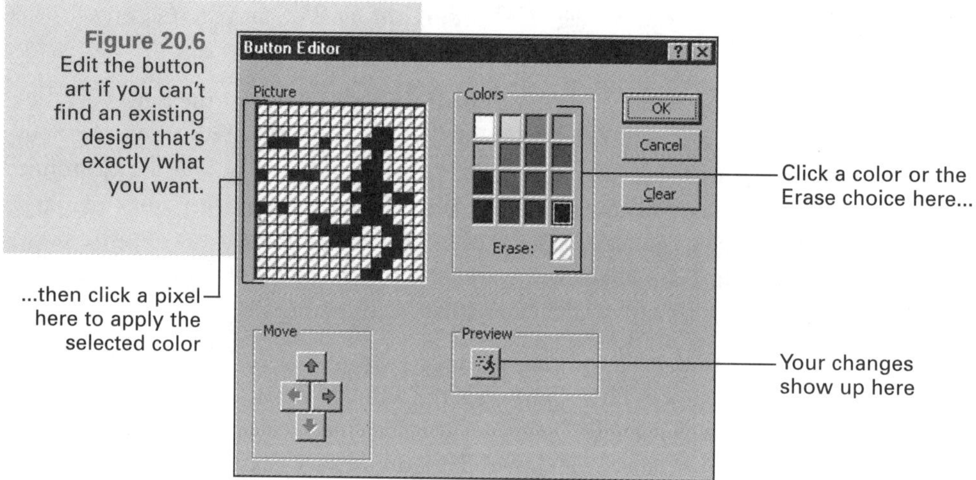

Figure 20.6 Edit the button art if you can't find an existing design that's exactly what you want.

command, macro, or custom form assigned to the button (or menu command), click the drop-down list arrow beside the Command text box. Scroll through the list, and click the selection you want to assign to the button. (Forms and macros are listed under "f" and "m" respectively; for example, a custom form might be listed as *Form "Summary"* and a macro as *Macro "Adjust_Dates"*.)

Click the Name text box and type or edit the button name, which will pop up as a ToolTip to describe the button whenever you point to the button with the mouse. Then, click the Description text box and type a description for the button, which will be used to explain the button in the status bar whenever you point to the button. Figure 20.7 shows some sample entries. Click OK to finish editing the toolbar button, and then adjust other buttons or close the Customize dialog box.

If you want to display the Customize Tool dialog box to make changes to any button on any toolbar without displaying the Customize dialog box, press and hold the Ctrl key, and then click the button. Make any adjustments you want in the Customize Tool dialog box, using the same techniques just described for creating a custom button; then click OK.

Creating a Custom Toolbar

You can create a brand new toolbar or one that's based on an existing toolbar. To do so, right-click a toolbar, and then click Customize. Alternately, click the Tools menu, point to Customize, and click Toolbars. The Customize dialog box appears. On the Toolbars tab in the dialog box, click the New button, type

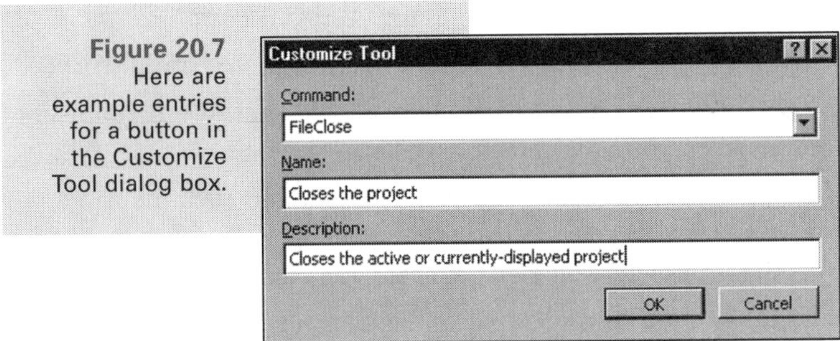

Figure 20.7 Here are example entries for a button in the Customize Tool dialog box.

a Toolbar Name in the New Toolbar dialog box, and click OK. This displays a new, blank toolbar onscreen.

After the new toolbar appears onscreen, click the Commands tab in the Customize dialog box to add or remove toolbar buttons, as described earlier. You also can right-click any individual button on the toolbar to display a menu of commands for modifying that button.

Deleting a Custom Toolbar or Menu Bar

Project does not let you delete any menu bar or toolbar that comes with the program. You can, however, delete the custom menu bars or toolbars you create. To delete a custom menu bar or toolbar, right-click any menu bar or toolbar onscreen, and then click Customize to display the Customize dialog box. In the Toolbars list of the Toolbars tab, click to select the name of the custom menu bar or toolbar you want to delete. Then click the Delete button. Project asks you to confirm that you want to delete the menu bar or toolbar. (You're warned because you can't undo the deletion.) Click OK to do so; then click Close to close the Customize dialog box.

Customizing Workgroup Message Fields

Chapter 19, "Taking Project Online," explains how to send specialized messages called workgroup messages from Project to make resource assignments, send task updates, and request status reports from resources. In each of these messages, Project lists certain fields for each task you're communicating about, such as Task Name or Remaining work hours. You can customize the fields that appear for tasks listed in these messages by using the following steps:

1. Open the Tools menu, point to Customize, and click Workgroup. The Customize Workgroup dialog box appears, as shown in Figure 20.8.
2. To add a new field, scroll through the Fields list and click the name of the field above which you'd like to insert the new field. Click the Add button. The Add Field dialog box appears (see Figure 20.9).
3. From the Field drop-down list, select the name of the field to include. In the Title text box, type the name of the column title you want to use for the selected field. Clear the check mark for the Include in TeamStatus Messages option only if you want to restrict the inclusion of the new field to TeamAssign and TeamUpdate messages. If the Let Resources Change Field option is available, use it to specify whether you want resources to be able to change the field when replying to you. Click OK when you're done working with these options.
4. Back in the Customize Workgroup dialog box, use the Fields list to click any field you want to move to the left in the message columns; then click Move Up. Similarly, to move a field to the right, click it in the Fields list, and then click Move Down.
5. To remove one of the custom Fields you added, click it, and then click Remove.

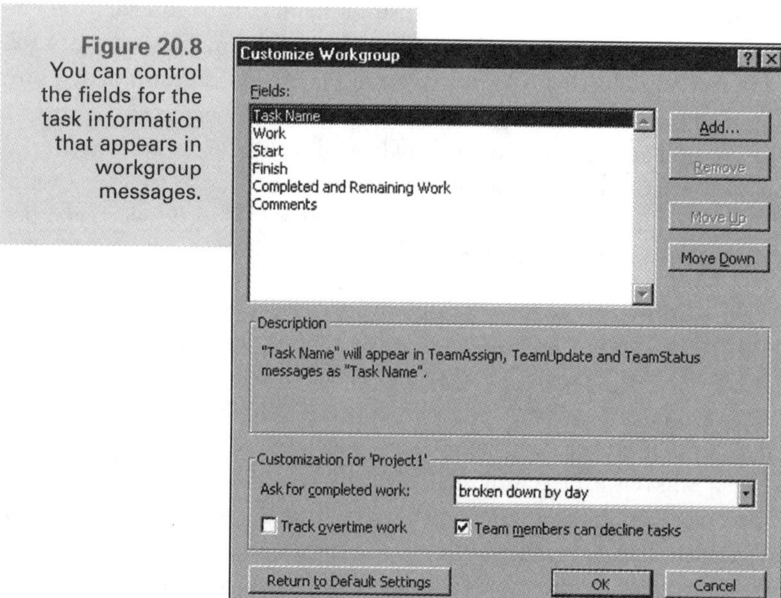

Figure 20.8
You can control the fields for the task information that appears in workgroup messages.

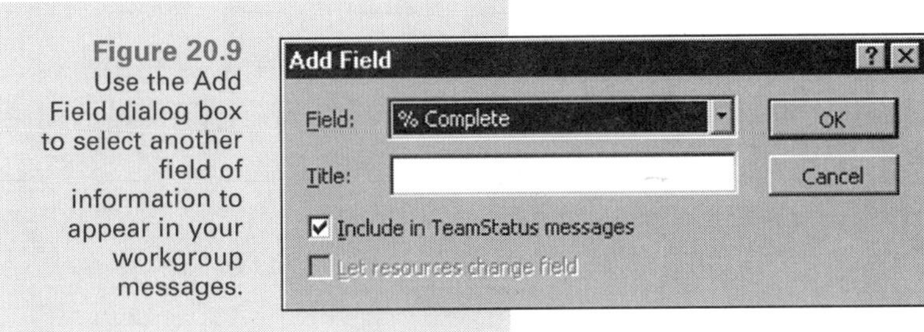

Figure 20.9 Use the Add Field dialog box to select another field of information to appear in your workgroup messages.

6. If you'll be sending TeamStatus messages to the resources assigned to some tasks in your project, make a choice from the Ask for Completed Work drop-down list. Your choice here adds a field telling each resource how quickly you expect to receive a status report via e-mail in response to your TeamStatus message.
7. Click to check the Track Overtime Work check box if you want your TeamStatus messages to include a field prompting recipients to report actual overtime hours worked via e-mail in response to your TeamStatus message.
8. If you want to include a field enabling recipients to decline tasks (via e-mail) you assign via TeamAssign messages, click to check the Team Members Can Decline Tasks check box.
9. If at any point, you're not satisfied with the Fields list or the other changes you made, click the Return to Default Settings button.
10. When you're done specifying the custom fields for your workgroup messages, click OK.

Setting Project Options

As with most other application programs today, Project offers dozens of options that you can set for the entire program, to control how it looks and behaves. To set options for the Project program, open the Tools menu and click Options. The Options dialog box has eight tabs, each of which relates to a particular functional area of Project. Each of the tabs and its choices are described next. Click a tab to display its options; then make the changes you want on that tab. When you finish specifying your choices for all of the tabs in the Options dialog box, click OK to close the dialog box and put your changes into effect.

View Options

The first tab in the Options dialog box, the View tab (see Figure 20.10), specifies how Project looks onscreen when you run it. Here are the choices you have there:

- Default View—Choose a view from this drop-down list to specify the view Project uses for the current schedule when you start the program.
- Date Format—Your selection from this drop-down list specifies how dates appear in the Task Sheet for any column holding date information.
- Show—In the Show area, you specify which of the following window features of Project should appear—Status Bar, Scroll Bars, OLE Links Indicator, and Entry Bar. Click to place a check mark beside each feature that you want to appear.
- Cross Project Linking Options for (current file)—If you linked tasks between files or consolidated projects (see Chapters 15 and 17), use these options to control whether and how the links appear. Click to check either the Show External Successors and/or Show External Predecessors if you want tasks linked to other projects to appear in the current project file; clear these check boxes to hide the linked tasks. Click to check the Show Links Between Projects Dialog on Open check box if you want Project to prompt you about whether or not to update links when you open a file that contains linked tasks. When that check box is cleared, you can click to check the Automatically Accept New External Data check box to have project update the tasks without displaying a dialog box. Alternately, clear both check boxes to simply open the file without updating the linked tasks.
- Currency (under View Options for (current file))—In the Symbol text box, specify the currency symbol, if any, that should appear to the left of columns containing cost information. The Placement drop-down list lets you control how the specified currency symbol appears in relation to the currency value. In the Decimal Digits text box, enter how many decimal places should appear after whole numbers in currency values. For example, enter **0** to see whole currency values only.
- Outline Options (under View Options for (current file))—If you clear the check mark beside the Show Summary Tasks option, summary tasks won't appear in the Task Sheet, so you won't be able to use outlining features. The Project Summary Tasks option works in a similar fashion for consolidated files (see Chapter 17, "Consolidating Projects," to learn more about consolidated files). When the Indent

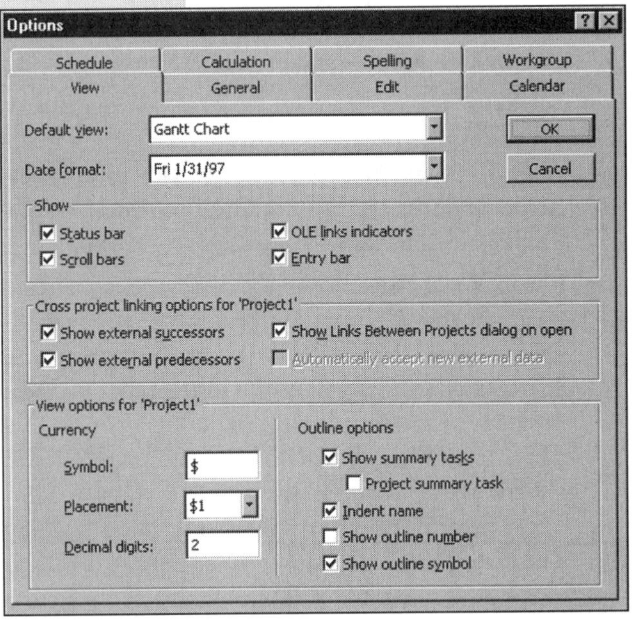

Figure 20.10 Project offers options for controlling its onscreen appearance.

Name check box is selected, any tasks you indent move to the right in the Task Name column. When the Show Outline Number check box is selected, Project displays an outline number that you can't edit beside each task in the Task Name column of the Task Sheet. You can use the Show Outline Symbol check box to turn on or off the display of the outlining + (summary task) and – (subtask) symbols.

General Options

Click the General tab to display the options shown in Figure 20.11. Here's what you can do with each of these options:

- Show Tips At Startup—Click to place a check mark beside this option if you want to see a Tip dialog box when you start Project.
- Show Welcome Dialog at Startup—When this option is checked, Project displays a special dialog box when you start the program, enabling you to view various forms of interactive help.
- Open Last File on Startup—Click to place a check mark beside this option to tell Project to automatically reopen the last schedule file you worked in when you restart Project.

- Prompt for Project Info for New Projects—Click to place a check mark beside this option to have Project ask you for Project schedule information when you create a new project.
- Set AutoFilter on for New Projects—When checked, this option automatically turns on the AutoFilter feature in all new project files. As you learned in Chapter 9, AutoFilter arrows appear on Task Sheet and Resource Sheet column headings, providing a speedy way for you to display only entries with similar information in a particular field.
- Macro Virus Protection—Macro viruses are a relatively new phenomenon that applies to particular applications; opening a file with a macro virus installs the virus on your system so it infects and usually damages other files you create in the program. Many Microsoft programs, including Project 98, offer the built-in capability to warn you when a file, particularly a file from an unfamiliar source, contains macros. Click to check this option if you want Project to display a dialog box informing you that a file you're opening contains macros. The dialog box gives you a few options. The Disable Macros choice opens the project file without making the macros active. The Enable Macros choice opens the file and its macros; you should only click this choice if you're familiar with the person or company that sent the file. You also can choose not to open the file at all.

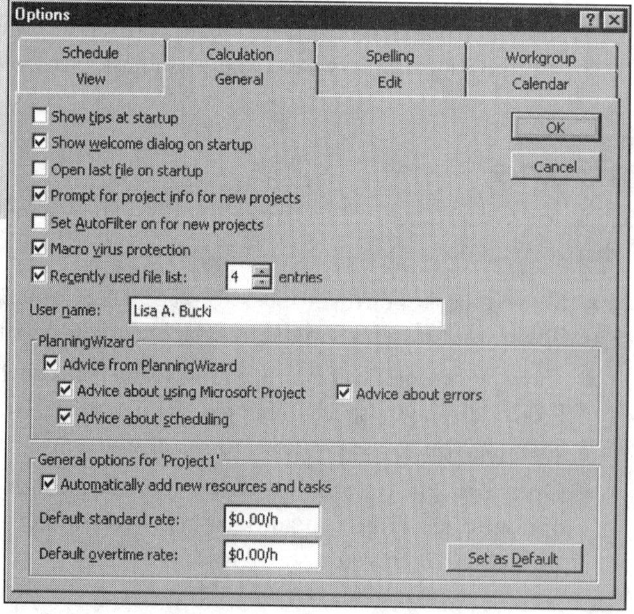

Figure 20.11 Control the most common Project options in this tab of the Options dialog box.

- Recently Used File List—Enable this check box to specify that the names for files you worked with recently appear at the bottom of Project's File menu. Use the spinner buttons beside the Entries text box to tell Project how many file names should appear on the File menu; clicking one of those file names on the menu quickly opens the file.
- User Name—Type your name in this text box.
- PlanningWizard—When no check mark appears beside the Advice from PlanningWizard option, no PlanningWizard choices are available. You can click to place check marks to determine whether you want Project to display Advice About Using Microsoft Project; Advice About Scheduling (asks whether you want to create links where they're possible, and so on); or Advice About Errors (informs you when your changes will create a scheduling conflict or other problem).
- General Options for (current file)—A check mark beside the Automatically Add New Resources and Tasks option means that any name you type in the Resource Name column of the Task Sheet becomes a row entry in the Resource Sheet; otherwise, Project prompts you for resource information. If Automatically Add New Resources and Tasks is selected, you can specify a Default Standard Rate and Default Overtime Rate in the text boxes below.
- Set As Default—If you want to make the changes on this tab the defaults for Project, click this button.

Edit Options

The Edit tab enables you to specify which editing features you want to use in Project. Click this tab to display it, as shown in Figure 20.12. When a check mark appears in the box beside any of the options here, that option is available; otherwise, you can't use the specified editing technique.

The first option, Allow Cell Drag and Drop, controls whether you can drag to move information in the Task Sheet or Resource Sheet. Move Selection After Enter means that the cell selector moves down to the next row after you press Enter after making an entry in the Task Sheet or Resource Sheet. Ask to Update Automatic Links means that Project prompts you about links if you update a file that's linked to task or resource information in another file. The options under For Time in (current file) Show enable you to choose how time measurements are displayed in the Task Sheet and Resource Sheet. You can use the five drop-down lists to control how the labels (abbreviations) for minutes, hours, days, weeks, and years appear. In addition, click to check the Add Space Before Label check box to insert a space between the number and label for any time value in the Task or Resource Sheet. Click the Set as Default button to make your time label setting change the defaults for Project.

Calendar Options

The Calendar tab of the Options dialog box (see Figure 20.13) enables you to specify the default base calendar for the current schedule file. Use the top two drop-down lists to specify the start of each work week and fiscal year in your calendar for the current schedule file. Depending on which month you select from the Fiscal Year Starts In drop-down list, the Use Starting Year for FY Numbering check box becomes enabled. Use that check box to tell Project which year to use to label your company fiscal years. Click the check box to label the fiscal year according to the starting year (calling it fiscal '97 if the fiscal year spans 1997 and 1998). Clear the check box to label the fiscal year according to the ending year (calling it fiscal '98 if the fiscal year spans 1997 and 1998).

The choices in the Calendar Options area affect only the current file; they work as follows:

- Default Start Time—The time you enter here is the time of day Project uses for new tasks you add to the Task Sheet, unless you specify otherwise.
- Default End Time—Sets the time of day when Project cuts off work on tasks for the day, unless you specify otherwise for a particular task or its assigned resource.
- Hours Per Day—When you enter durations in terms of days, this entry determines how many working hours each day contains.
- Hours Per Week—As with the preceding option, the number of hours you enter here is reflected in the schedule. If you enter 35 hours, each work week contains 35 hours by default.
- Set As Default—Click this button to make your changes in this tab the default settings usc by Project.

Schedule Options

The default scheduling options, displayed by clicking the Schedule tab of the Options dialog box (see Figure 20.14), control how Project responds when you enter information in the Task Sheet. The first option is Show Scheduling Messages. When this option is checked, Project warns you if you make a mistake that will cause a scheduling error. This tab offers numerous key settings for the current file, as well:

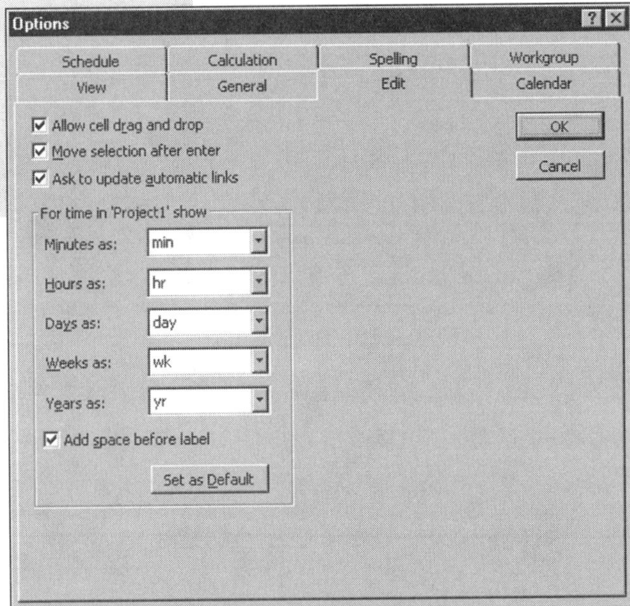

Figure 20.12 Project offers numerous editing features, and here you choose whether to use them.

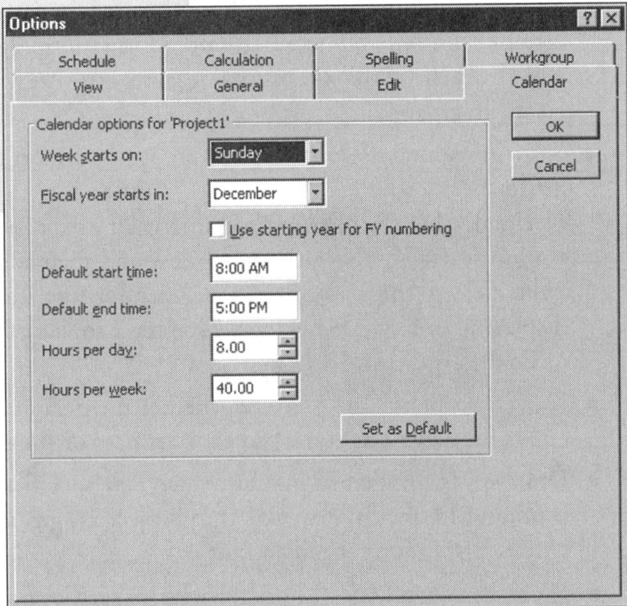

Figure 20.13 Use the Calendar tab to establish the default calendar for the current schedule file.

Figure 20.14 This tab enables you to specify how Project handles scheduling choices.

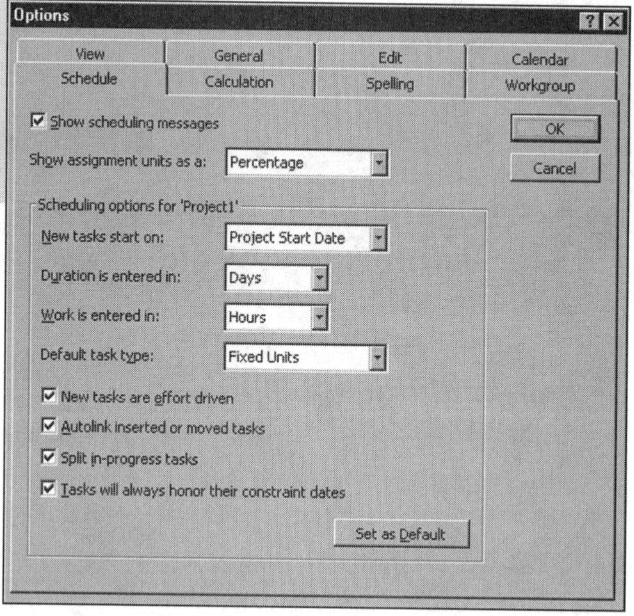

- Show Scheduling Messages—Project can't prevent you from making certain errors when you enter date information in the Task Sheet, but when you check this check box, it can warn you when an entry will create an error.
- Show Assignment Units As A—Choose an option from this drop-down list to specify whether Assignment Units appear as a Percentage or Decimal value. To display Assignment Units for individual assignments, you must display the Task Usage view and then add the Assignment Units field to the Task Sheet. (See Chapter 9 to learn more about displaying different views, and Chapter 2 to learn how to add a column or field to the Task Sheet in a view.)
- New Tasks Start On—Choose whether the default start date Project enters for new tasks is the project start date or the current date.
- Duration Is Entered In—Your choice here specifies the time units (minutes, hours, days, weeks) that Project assigns to Duration column entries if you don't specify a unit.
- Work Is Entered In—Your choice here specifies the time units (minutes, hours, days, weeks) that Project assigns to Work column entries if you don't specify a unit.

- Default Task Type—Your choice from this drop-down list specifies whether tasks in the active project have a Fixed Duration, Fixed Units, or Fixed Work. Fixing one of these choices means that its value remains constant, even if you change the other two values. For example, if you select Fixed Duration here and then double the work allowed for a task, Project cuts the units value in half to ensure the duration stays the same. Any change you make in the Task Type choice of the Task Information dialog box for a particular task takes precedence over the Default Task Type choice on the Schedule tab.

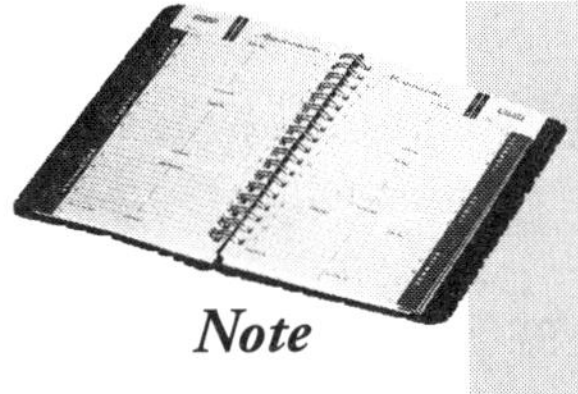
Note

The *duration* is the time between the start and finish dates that you enter. *Units* represent the total number of resources assigned to the task—two resources full-time for example. *Work* stands for the number of person-hours required to complete the task.

- New Tasks Are Effort Driven—This check box controls whether or not adding resources to a task or removing them from a task effects the task duration by default. Check this option if you want task durations to adjust when you add or remove resources.
- Autolink Inserted or Moved Tasks—If you insert or move tasks within a series of tasks linked by Finish-to-Start (FS) relationships and this option is checked, Project links the inserted tasks within the group of linked tasks. If you reschedule tasks, Project automatically asks whether you want to create links where they're possible.
- Split In-Progress Tasks—When this option is checked and you automatically reschedule uncompleted work, uncompleted work on in-progress tasks is rescheduled, in addition to work scheduled for tasks that haven't yet begun.
- Tasks Will Always Honor Their Constraint Dates—This check box controls the behavior of tasks with negative total slack (that is, tasks that cannot slip or move out without delaying the entire project's finish date). When this option is checked, tasks will honor their constraints and not move to correct the negative slack situation. If you prefer that tasks move according to their links to help compensate for negative slack, clear this check box.
- Set as Default—Click this button if you want your choices on the Schedule tab to apply to all new project files you create.

Calculation Options

Calculation options (Figure 20.15) indicate whether Project automatically updates all calculated values (such as actual cost figures that equal actual hours worked multiplied by hourly rates). In the Calculation area of this tab, specify whether calculation should be Automatic or Manual. If calculation is set to Manual, you can display this tab and click the Calculate All Projects button to recalculate all values in all open projects. Alternately, you can click the Calculate Project button to simply update the values in the currently open schedule file.

The following settings in the Calculation Options for (Current Project) area of the dialog box apply to the currently open schedule file:

- Updating Task Status Updates Resource Status—Select this check box if you want information you enter into task views to be reflected in calculated fields in resource views. For example, if you enter an actual task completion amount, it's reflected in terms of actual hours worked and costs for a particular resource.
- Edits to Total Task % Complete Will Be Spread to the Status Date—Check this option if you want your percent Complete entries to spread to the next status date set for the schedule or the finish date for the task. For example, if you enable this check box and your project has a status date of 4/15/98 and the finish date for a task is 4/30/98. Marking the task as 100% complete marks it complete only through 4/15/98.

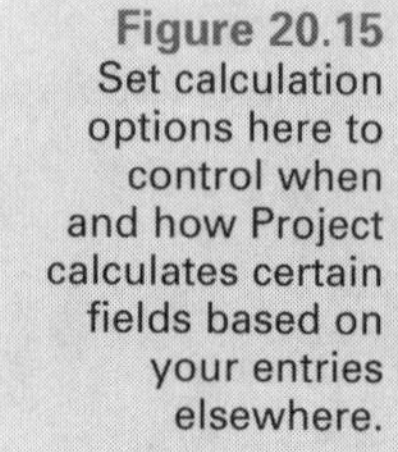

Figure 20.15 Set calculation options here to control when and how Project calculates certain fields based on your entries elsewhere.

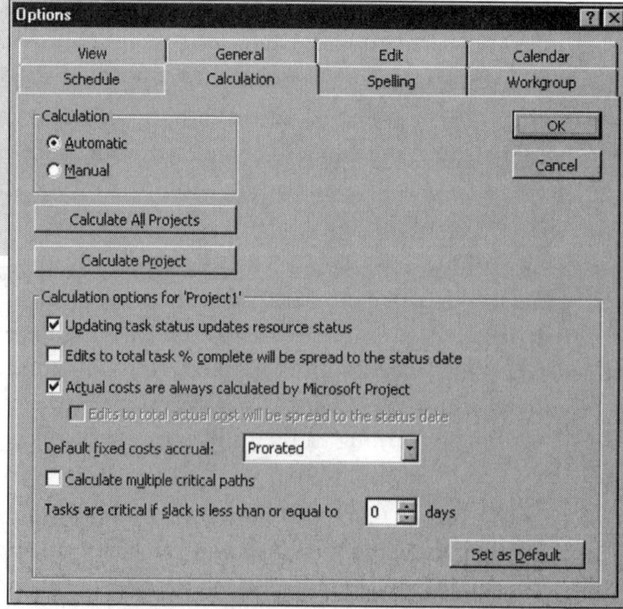

- Actual Costs Are Always Calculated by Microsoft Project—Check this option to have Project calculate actual costs for each task until it is marked as 100% complete, at which point you can then enter a differing actual cost value. This ensures that you won't enter an actual cost value prematurely; however, if you already entered an actual cost, don't turn on this check box unless you want to re-enter that information.
- Edits to Total Actual Cost Will Be Spread to the Status Date—When the preceding check box is cleared, this check box becomes active. Clicking it then specifies that actual cost information you enter for a task applies only through the status date of the file, not through the task finish date.
- Default Fixed Costs Accrual—Your choice from this drop-down list tells Project when and how to add cost information for new tasks with fixed costs into the actual costs calculated for the task and project. For example, if you want to assume the task's fixed cost is spent as soon as the task begins, such as a non-refundable retainer fee you pay in advance, click Start. If you won't pay a resource at all until a task is finished and you inspect and accept the work, click End. If you agreed to pay the resource a partial fee even if the resource doesn't complete its work or are paying a monthly fixed fee for the resource's work, you can choose Prorated.
- Calculate Multiple Critical Paths—If you have a few different groups of linked tasks that span your project duration rather than a single string of linked tasks, you can enable this check box to have Project calculate multiple critical paths. The effect is that more tasks will be marked as critical, so you'll be able to identify all the tasks that could potentially delay the project finish date if they slip out.
- Tasks Are Critical if Slack Is Less Than or Equal To—Enter a value here to control how many tasks are considered critical tasks (are part of the critical path). Higher values mean that fewer tasks are marked as critical.
- Set as Default—Click this button if you want your choices on the Calculation tab to apply to all new project files you create.

Spelling Options

By default, the spelling checker in Project reviews most task and resource text information. Using the options on the Spelling tab (see Figure 20.16), you can speed up the spelling checker by selecting which information it checks; you also can specify other options related to the spelling checker.

To tell the spelling checker not to review information in a particular task or resource field, click to select the field in the Fields to Check list. Then click the drop-down list arrow in the right column and click No.

The next options on the Spelling tab are the Ignore Words in UPPERCASE check box and the Ignore Words with Numbers check box. When these options are checked, the spelling checker does not check the spelling for words typed entirely in uppercase (such as IN) or words including numbers (such as Qtr1), respectively. Always Suggest, when checked, means that the spelling checker displays a list of suggested corrections for any unrecognized word it finds. Suggest From User Dictionary, when checked, means that the spelling checker includes corrections from your user dictionary with the suggestion list.

Workgroup Options

Click the Workgroup tab to display options for controlling how some online features work by default (Figure 20.17). Chapter 19, "Taking Project Online," discusses how to work with online features in more depth.

The options in the Workgroup Messages Transport for (Current Project) area of the tab enables you to specify defaults for workgroup messages you send, such as TeamAssign messages. You can set the following options for those messages:

- Default Workgroup Messaging for Resources—Your choice from this drop-down list controls how Project attempts to send e-mail message. The Email choice sends messages to the Outbox of your e-mail program, so you can then launch the e-mail program and send the messages. The Web choice sends the messages to a Web server on the Internet or your internal company intranet. You also can choose to send each message in both ways.
- Web Server URL (For Resource)—If you're using a Web server to communicate with team members and chose Web or Email and Web as your choice for the preceding option, enter the URL for the Web server in this text box. For example, if you've set up a Web site on your computer, which is connected to your company's network, your URL might be something like this: http://BUCKIGROUP/Projects.
- Web Server Root (for Manager)—Again, if you're using a Web server to manage messages to workgroup members, type the address of the shared folder (either on your computer that's connected to the company network or the netwok server) that serves as the Web server root here. For example, the shared address for a folder on your system that's connected to a network might resemble \\BUCKIGROUP\WebShare\wwwroot\Projects.

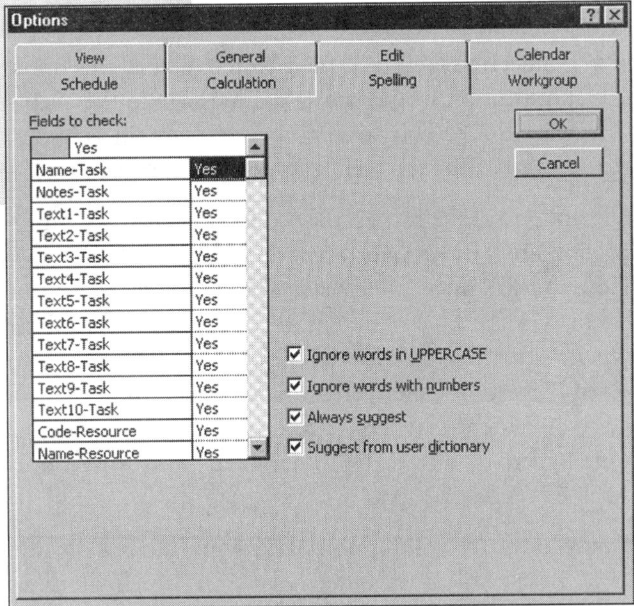

Figure 20.16 If you don't want the spelling checker to review particular fields, specify them here.

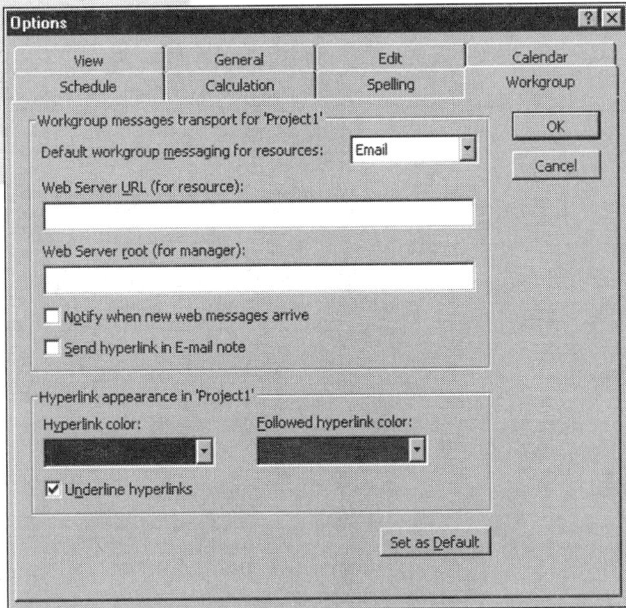

Figure 20.17 Control how some online features work and look with these options.

- Notify When New Web Messages Arrive—Tells Project to display an onscreen message if it checks the Web InBox and finds a new message.
- Send Hyperlink in E-mail Note—Check this option to provide better notification when you send a message to the Web server for the workgroup. This "teaser" message contains a hyperlink to the Web server, so the recipient can double-click it to look for the message.

The options in the Hyperlink Appearance in (Current Project) area of the dialog box are very straightforward, and control how hyperlinks look in Task Sheet and Resource Sheet fields that hold hyperlinks in the current file. Click a choice in the Hyperlink Color drop-down list to determine what color the hyperlink text has before you click the link. Similarly, your choice in the Followed Hyperlink Color drop-down list determines how hyperlink text appears after you click the hyperlink to display the file or Web page it links to. If you want hyperlink text to be underlined, make sure the Underline Hyperlinks check box holds a check.

Finally, if you're comfortable with your choices on the Workgroup tab and want those choices to apply no matter which file is open, click the Set as Default button.

21

Creating and Using Macros

In This Chapter

- Recording and playing back macros
- Changing macro information, such as the shortcut key
- Making changes in or removing macros
- Finding more help about VBA
- Creating your own command or button for a macro
- Looking at a few last ideas about macros

Every company's needs and projects are unique. Even seasoned temporary workers need a bit of on-site training to conform with the specific processes of a new client company.

While company A might want temps to organize files and information by project name, company B might want the information to be ordered by job number. Although such differences seem to be trivial, misunderstanding the requirement or making filing mistakes can create hours of work down the line for someone else who is searching for particular files.

Like temporary workers, Project can conform to your unique needs in building schedules. Project does so by enabling you to create macros, which are mini-programs that you create to perform certain tasks.

Creating Macros

Macros store a series of commands or steps as a single entity, so that you can execute the entire series via the single step of selecting the macro. In earlier computer applications, macros had to be created manually via scripting, which was a "user-friendly" euphemism for programming. Thus, most people didn't use macros, because macros were too difficult to create.

Today's applications, including Project, enable you to record macros. You don't have to be a whiz to create a macro. All you need to know is how to start the macro recorder and how to execute the commands that you want to save as a macro. Unless you specify otherwise, a recorded and saved macro becomes available to all the files that you work with in Project.

Note

The macros you record in Project are built behind the scenes with Visual Basic for Applications (VBA) commands, a macro programming language used in all the Microsoft Office applications as well. Each macro is stored in a VBA Macro *module*, which is like a single sheet that can hold multiple macros. By default, the modules and macros are saved with the GLOBAL.MPT file, a read-only file that saves your default information for Project. You can use VBA programming to develop more powerful macros; however, programming with VBA is beyond the scope of this book.

In two basic situations, you should record macros to automate a task:

- **When the task is lengthy and requires many steps**—Creating a macro to store such a process helps other users to work with the file, particularly if the file is stored on a network. If several users need to create and print a particular report, for example, you can create a macro for that purpose, rather than try to teach each person all the steps that are involved.
- **When the task is repetitive**—Even though formatting the text in a cell as red takes only a few steps, you might regularly need to format cells in red; if so, you'll save time with a macro that does the job for you.

Project enables you to record and work with macros by means of commands in the Tools menu or tools in the Visual Basic toolbar (see Figure 21.1). To display that toolbar, right-click any toolbar onscreen, and then click Visual Basic.

To record a macro, follow these steps:

1. Take whatever preparatory steps are necessary to bring you to the point at which you want to begin recording the macro. If you want to record a macro that formats a selected cell's text in red, for example, go ahead and select a cell in the Task Sheet.
2. Open the Tools menu, point to Macros, and click Record New Macro, or click the Record Macro button on the Visual Basic toolbar. The Record Macro dialog box appears, as shown in Figure 21.2.

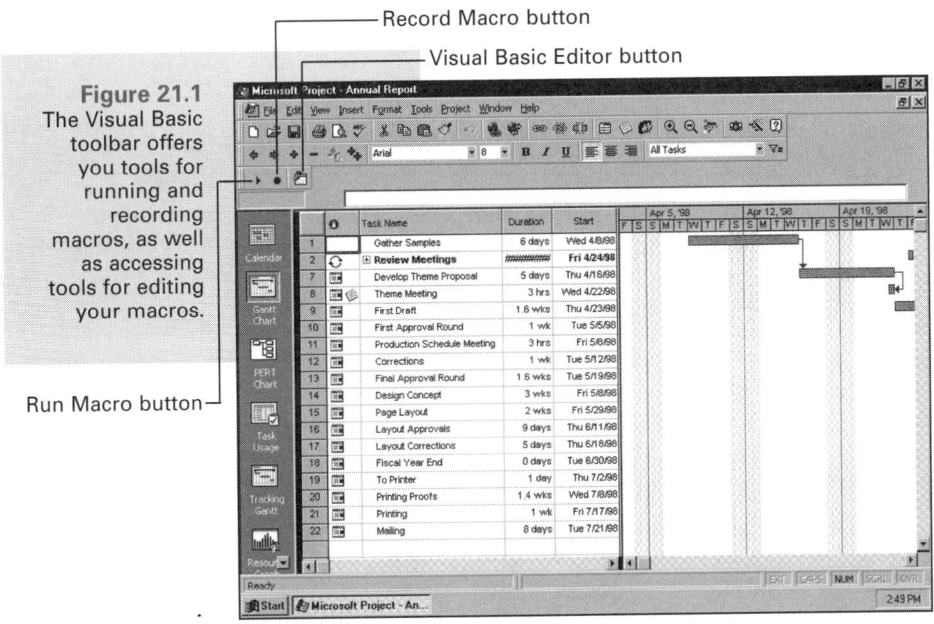

Figure 21.1 The Visual Basic toolbar offers you tools for running and recording macros, as well as accessing tools for editing your macros.

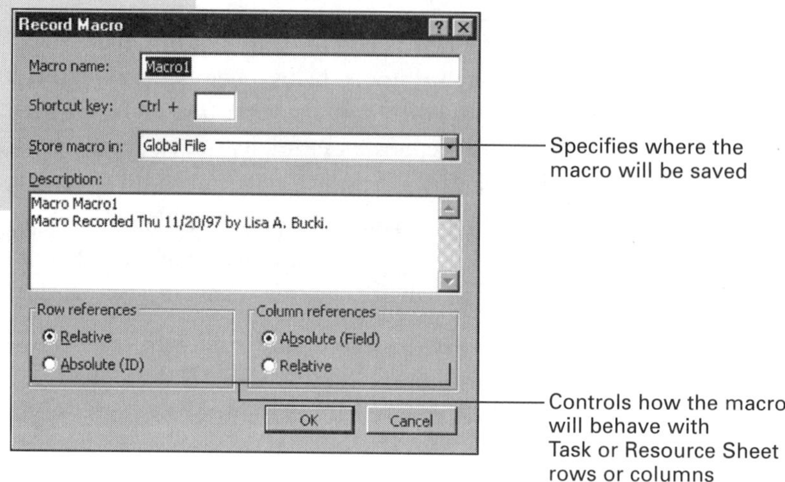

Figure 21.2 Assign a name and settings for your macro after you start the recording process.

3. In the Macro Name text box, enter a unique name for the macro. The name can include an underscore character but can't include spaces or punctuation. Red_Text, for example, is an acceptable name.
4. If you want to be able to run the macro by pressing a shortcut key, click in the Shortcut Key text box, and enter the second keystroke for the combination in the Ctrl+ text box. You can enter any A–Z keyboard character. You can't use numbers, punctuation marks, or function keys.

Note

Avoid specifying a shortcut key that's already assigned to a command in Project, such as Ctrl+X (the Cut command). If you attempt to specify such a key, Project later asks you to choose another shortcut key (see step 9).

5. If you want the macro to be stored only with the currently open file (not recommended, because you might need to use the macro in future files), click to open the Store Macro In drop-down list. Then click the This Project choice. If you leave Global File selected, instead, Project stores the macro in GLOBAL.MPT, the file that stores macros, forms, and settings, and other default and custom information you specify for Project.

Note

You need to select the This Project option if you'll be saving the open project file as a template file and want the macro to be part of that file.

6. If you want, edit or add more detail to the Description of the macro.
7. The options in the Row References area control the way that the macro interprets row selections in Task Sheets and Resource Sheets, and the way that it handles those selections during playback. Select one of the following options:
   - Relative means that during playback, the macro selects rows based on the location of the selected cell. Suppose that you selected three rows or cells in three rows (such as rows 1–3) when you recorded the macro, and that before you played back the macro, you selected a cell in row 4. The macro selects rows 4–6, or the specified cells in those rows, during playback.
   - Absolute (ID) means that during playback, the macro always selects the same rows (by row number) that were selected when the macro was recorded.
8. The options in the Column References area control the way that the macro interprets column selections in a Task Sheet or Resource Sheet, and the way that it handles those selections during playback. Select one of the following options:
   - Absolute (Field) means that during playback, the macro always selects the same field (by field or column name) that was selected when the macro was recorded.
   - Relative means that the macro selects columns based on the location of the selected cell. Suppose that you selected two columns or cells in two columns (such as the Start and Finish columns of the Task Sheet) when you recorded the macro, and that before you played back the macro, you selected a cell in the Predecessors column. The macro selects the Predecessors and Resources columns (or the specified cells in those rows) during playback.
9. After you make all your selections, click on OK to begin recording the macro.

   If, in step 4, you specified a shortcut key that's already assigned, Project displays a warning (see Figure 21.3). Click OK, specify another shortcut key, and click OK in the Record Macro dialog box to continue.

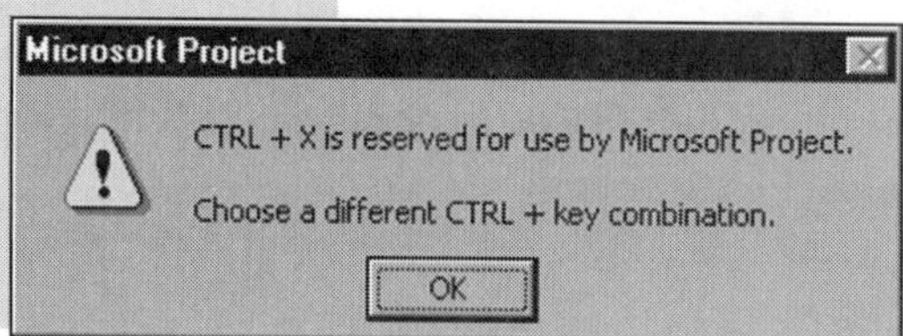

Figure 21.3 Project warns you when the shortcut key you specified isn't available.

10. Perform the steps that you want to record in your macro.
11. When you finish performing all the steps, stop the macro recording by clicking the Stop Recorder button on the Visual Basic toolbar, or by opening the Tools menu, pointing to Macro, and clicking Stop Recorder.

If you're creating a macro and want to select only the range of cells in the Task Sheet or Resource Sheet that currently contains entries, select the cell in the upper-left corner of the range. Then press Ctrl+Shift+End. This method is better than selecting the entire sheet. This method also is the one to use when you might end up running the macro on different sheets or filtered lists of differing lengths because it ensures that the macro highlights all the rows that contain entries, not just the number of rows that was correct during macro recording.

Project automatically saves all macros in GLOBAL.MPT (global macros) when you exit the program, but not macros saved in a particular schedule file. If, in step 5, you specified that the macro will be saved in the current file, make sure that you save the file immediately after you record the macro, just for safety.

Running a Macro

After you create a macro, it's immediately available for use. Running a macro is sometimes referred to as playing back the macro. To play back any macro, follow these steps:

1. Perform whatever preparatory tasks you need to complete before running the macro. If your macro applies red formatting to text in Task Sheet or Resource Sheet cells, for example, select the row(s), columns(s), or cell(s) to which you want to apply the formatting.

2. Use one of the following methods to execute the macro, depending on how you set up the macro when you created it:
   - Press the shortcut key combination that you created for the macro.
   - Click the Run Macro button on the Visual Basic toolbar, or open the Tools menu, point to Macro, and click Macros. The Macros dialog box appears. If you want the Macro Name list to display only macros contained in a particular file (which narrows the display and may make the macro you want easier to find), click to open the Macros In drop-down list. Then click the name of the file you want. Select the name of the macro in the Macro Name list (see Figure 21.4). Then click the Run button.

Changing Macro Options

The information and options that you specify when you create and store a macro aren't carved in stone. If you initially don't assign a shortcut key to the macro, for example, you can go back and add one. If you want to change the description for a macro, you can do that, too.

To adjust the options for a macro, follow these steps:

1. Open the Tools menu, point to Macro, and click Macros. Or, click the Run Macro button on the Visual Basic toolbar. The Macros dialog box appears.

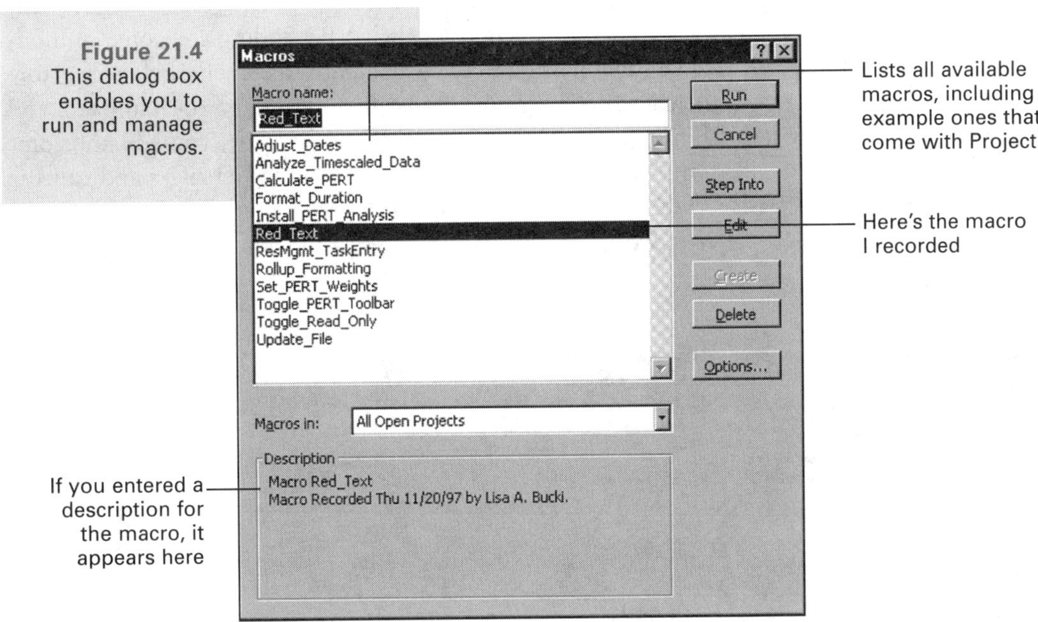

Figure 21.4 This dialog box enables you to run and manage macros.

2. In the Macro Name list, select the name of the macro for which you want to change the options. If you don't see the macro you want, click to open the Macros In drop-down list. Then click the name of the file that holds the macro. The macro appears in the Macro Name list so that you can select the macro.
3. Click the Options button. The Macro Options dialog box appears, as shown in Figure 21.5.
4. Edit the Description and Shortcut Key options as needed , by using the techniques described earlier in the steps for creating macros.
5. Click OK to close the Macro Options dialog box.
6. Click Close to close the Macros dialog box and activate your new macro options.

Editing Macros

Unless you have time to learn VBA programming, you probably don't need to learn how to edit macros, especially if the macros are fairly simple. In such cases, the fastest way to make changes in a macro is to delete the macro (as described in the following section) and re-record it. In other cases, however, making a change or two in a macro is much speedier than creating it again from scratch.

This section explains the basics of macro editing, so that you can experiment if you are inclined to do so. Macros and their VBA coding are stored in modules, which are like pages in the Project Global.mpt file. Each module can store numerous VBA macros. You use the Visual Basic Editor to open a macro and display it (within its module) for editing. In the module, you edit the commands just as you would edit text. When you save your changes and exit the Visual Basic Editor, Project returns you to Gantt Chart view (or whichever view you prefer to work in) and your changes to the macro take effect.

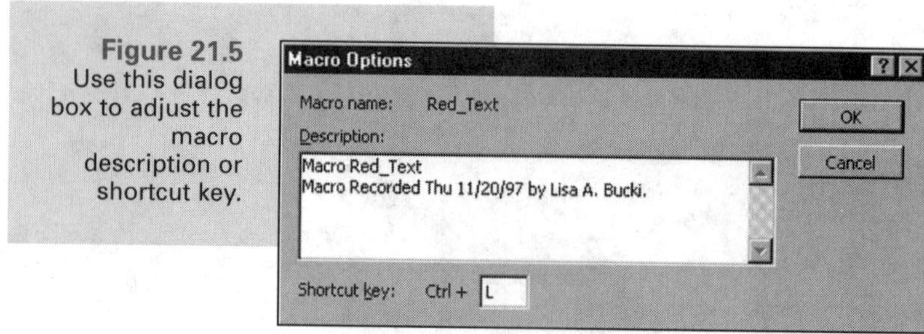

Figure 21.5 Use this dialog box to adjust the macro description or shortcut key.

Note

Even if you are experienced in editing VBA code, there's always the chance of introducing an error that really fouls up the macro. As a precaution, print the original macro code before you make any changes, so that you have a record of what the macro's contents were when the macro worked. To print macros in Project, simply click the Print icon on the Standard toolbar when the macro is displayed in the Code (Module) window.

Project and the Visual Basic Editor can provide help about using specific Visual Basic for Applications and VBA commands in Project, but this help doesn't installed by default. Therefore, before you begin editing macros, re-run the Project 98 Setup program to install Visual Basic Help. Use these steps to do so:

1. Close Project 98 and any other open applications.
2. Click Start on the taskbar, point to Settings, and then click Control Panel. The Control Panel window opens.
3. Double-click the Add/Remove Programs icon. The Add/Remove Programs Properties dialog box appears.
4. Click Microsoft Project 98 (in the scrolling list at the bottom of the Install/Uninstall tab in the dialog box). Then click Add/Remove.
5. Insert your Project 98 CD into your CD-ROM drive when prompted, and then click OK. Microsoft Project 98 Setup starts and searches your system for installed components.
6. When a dialog box appears with four buttons for setup options, click the Add/Remove button.
7. In the Microsoft Project 98—Maintenance dialog box that appears, click Help in the Options list; then click the Change Option button.
8. In the Microsoft Project 98—Help dialog box that appears, click as many times as needed to place a check beside Help for Visual Basic, and then click OK.
9. Click Continue to have Setup install the Help.
10. At the message that tells you that Setup is complete, click OK. Then you can restart Project 98 and resume your work.

After Visual Basic Help is installed, you can use online Help within Project to learn more about the overall process of VBA programming with Project, and use online Help within the Visual Basic Editor to learn more about specific VBA commands, syntax, and more.

After you make Help available and review key topics, you'll definitely be ready to try to basic macro editing. Suppose that you created a macro that enters a new task—named Monthly_Meeting"—in the Task Sheet and assigns the task a duration of 2h (two hours). Later, you decide that you no longer want to have a monthly meeting; you just want to prepare and distribute a monthly report. Accordingly, you want the macro to specify the task name as "Monthly_Report." To make this change, follow these steps:

1. Open the Tools menu, point to Macro, and click Macros. Or, click the Run Macro button on the Visual Basic toolbar. The Macros dialog box appears.
2. In the Macro Name list, select the macro that you want to edit—Monthly_Meeting, for this example. If you don't see the macro you want to edit, click to open the Macros In drop-down list, click the name of the file that holds the macro. The macro appears in the Macro Name list so that you can select the macro.
3. Click the Edit button to display the Visual Basic Editor, with the module for the macro displayed in its Code window. The Code window for the Montly_Meeting macro appears in Figure 21.6.

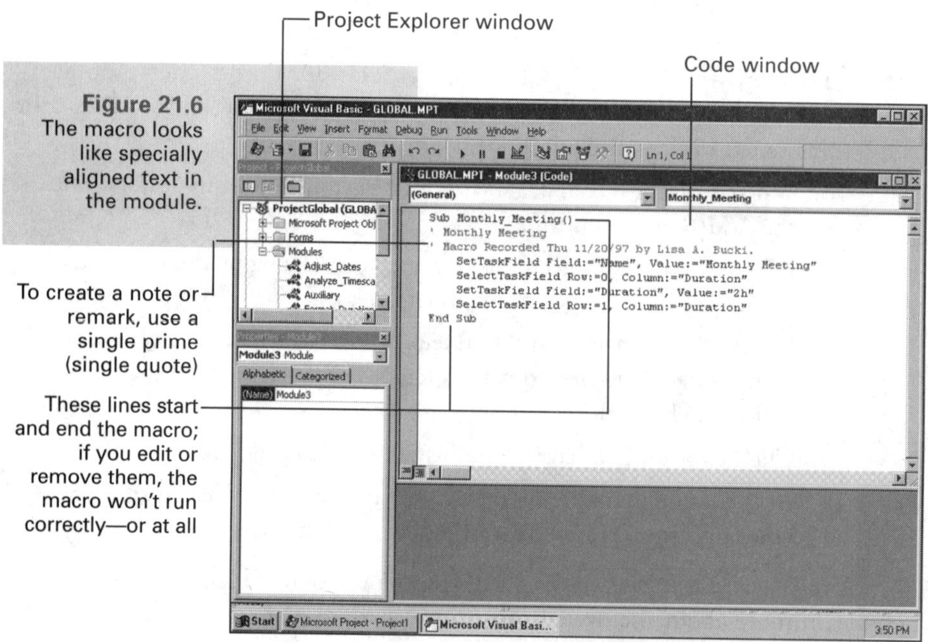

Figure 21.6 The macro looks like specially aligned text in the module.

4. Make your changes in the macro's contents, using the same editing techniques that you would use in a typical word processing program, such as WordPad or Word 97.

   For this example, because you want to change the task name, first look for the line that defines the Name column (TaskField) and then look for the value assigned there, which is what you want to change. You can double-click the word Meeting to select it, as shown in Figure 21.7, being careful not to select the quotation marks. Then simply type **Report** to replace the selection.
5. When you finish making your changes, open the File menu and click the Save (File Name), to ensure your macro changes are saved. To close the Visual Basic Editor and return to Project, click to open the File menu again, and then click Close and Return to Microsoft Project.
6. Test the macro to ensure that your changes work correctly.

Project comes with numerous macros, which provide a good illustration of how to structure VBA code. These macros are excellent learning tools for would-be macro gurus. If you want to see how one of these macros is written, select it in the Macro Name list Macros dialog box, and then click Edit. Alternately, if the Microsoft Visual Basic window is already open, double-click a macro in the Project Explorer window to display the macro's contents in a code window.

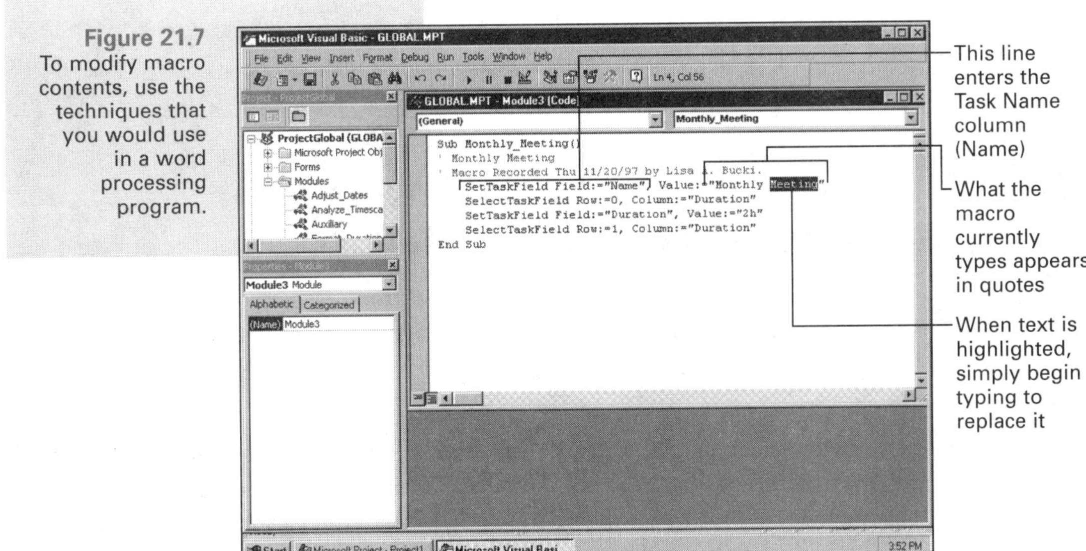

Figure 21.7 To modify macro contents, use the techniques that you would use in a word processing program.

When the Visual Basic Editor is open, you can open code windows for multiple modules (holding macros), by double-clicking each module to open in a file's Modules folder in the Project Explorer. Then, you can cut, copy, and paste code between macros, switching between Code windows with the Window menu.

Deleting Macros

When you no longer need a macro, you can simply delete it from the Macro Name list in the Macros dialog box. If you use many macros, it's good practice to occasionally review and delete the macros you no longer need, just to keep your macro modules and Global.mpt file slim and trim.

To delete a macro, follow these steps:

1. Open the Tools menu, point to Macro, and click Macros. Or, click the Run Macro button on the Visual Basic toolbar. The Macros dialog box appears.
2. In the Macro Name list, select the macro you want to delete. If you don't see the macro you want to delete, click to open the Macros In drop-down list, and then click the name of the file that holds the macro. The macro appears in the Macro Name list so that you can select it.
3. Click the Delete button. Project asks you to verify that you want to remove the macro (see Figure 21.8).
4. Click Yes to delete the macro.
5. Click Close to close the Macros dialog box.

Creating a Menu Command or Toolbar Button for a Macro

Although you can create shortcut keys for the macros you create, remembering shortcut keys can be as difficult as remembering the exact names of macros.

In Chapter 20, "Customizing Microsoft Project," you learned the general steps for editing Project's menus and toolbars. You can use that knowledge to add, to any Project menu bar, a menu that lists all your macros. This procedure not only provides quick access to your macros but also provides more room for listing macros than the Tools menu does. In addition, you can add a command for an individual macro to any menu, or add a button for any macro to a toolbar.

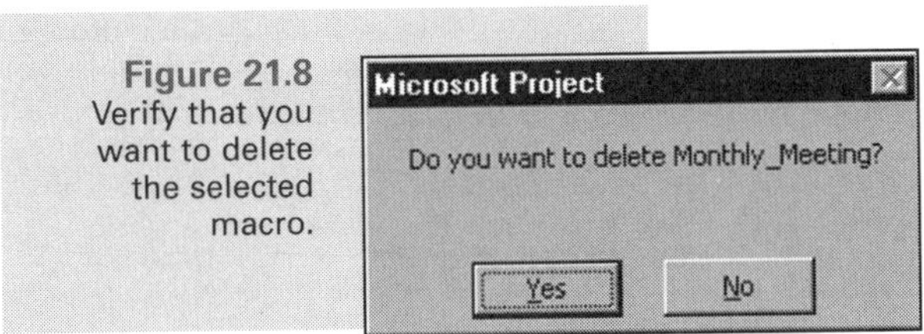

Figure 21.8 Verify that you want to delete the selected macro.

Adding a Menu Listing All Macros

If you want to be able to run any macro simply by selecting its name from a menu, you can add a special menu listing all the macros available in the GLOBAL.MPT file in Project. You can add this menu to Project's default menu bar, or to any toolbar. To create a menu for your macros, follow these steps:

1. If you want to add the macro menu to a toolbar, display that toolbar.
2. Click the Tools menu to open it, point to Customize, and click Toolbars. Alternately, right-click any onscreen menu bar or toolbar and click Customize. The Customize dialog box appears.
3. Click the Commands tab to display its options.
4. Add a brand new menu for the macros to the menu bar or toolbar where you want the macros menu to appear, as described in Chapter 20, "Customizing Microsoft Project." Briefly, scroll down the Categories list and click the New Menu choice. Drag the New Menu placeholder from the Commands list to the menu bar or toolbar that will hold the menu, and then drop the placeholder into the appropriate location, as shown in Figure 21.9.
5. To rename the placeholder for the new menu, right-click it, edit the contents of the Name text box in the menu that appears, and then press Enter. Remember, if you want the menu name to have an underlined selection letter, insert an ampersand (&) before that letter in the menu name.
6. In the Categories list of the Commands tab in the Customize dialog box, click the Special Items choice.
7. In the Commands list, scroll down to display the [Macros] choice, and then drag that choice onto the new menu, as shown in Figure 21.10. Release the mouse button to drop it onto the menu.
8. Click Close to close the Customize dialog box.

   When you open the new menu later, it lists available macros, as shown in Figure 21.11.

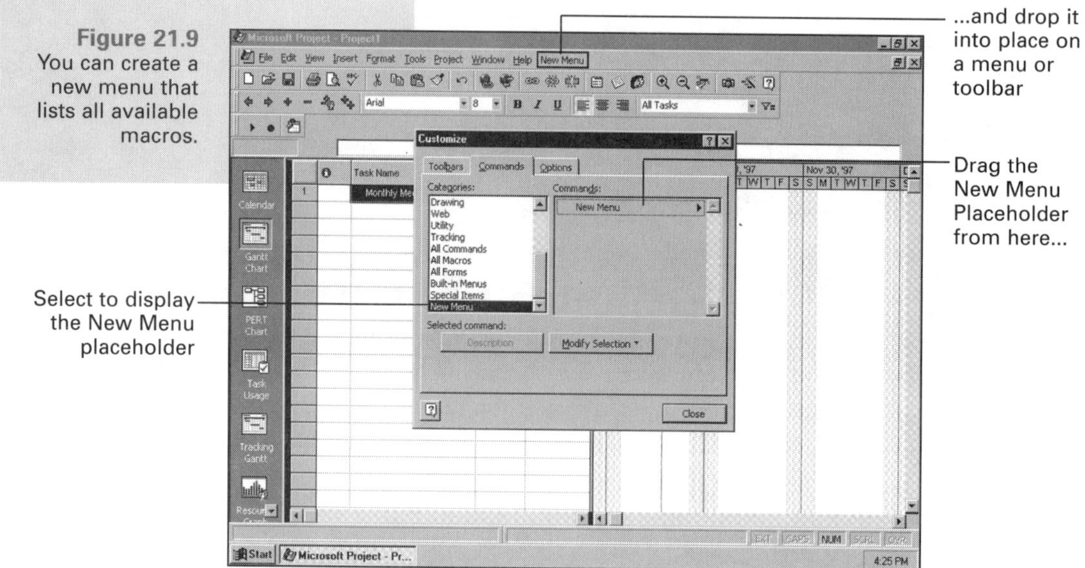
...and drop it into place on a menu or toolbar
Drag the New Menu Placeholder from here...
Select to display the New Menu placeholder

Figure 21.9 You can create a new menu that lists all available macros.

Adding a Macro Command or Button

Although adding a menu for macros as just described gives you easy access to all your menus, it can be cumbersome if you created dozens of macros. Such a menu displays a slowly, and you still have to take the time to scan through the menu to find the macro you need. For the ultimate in easy access to the macros

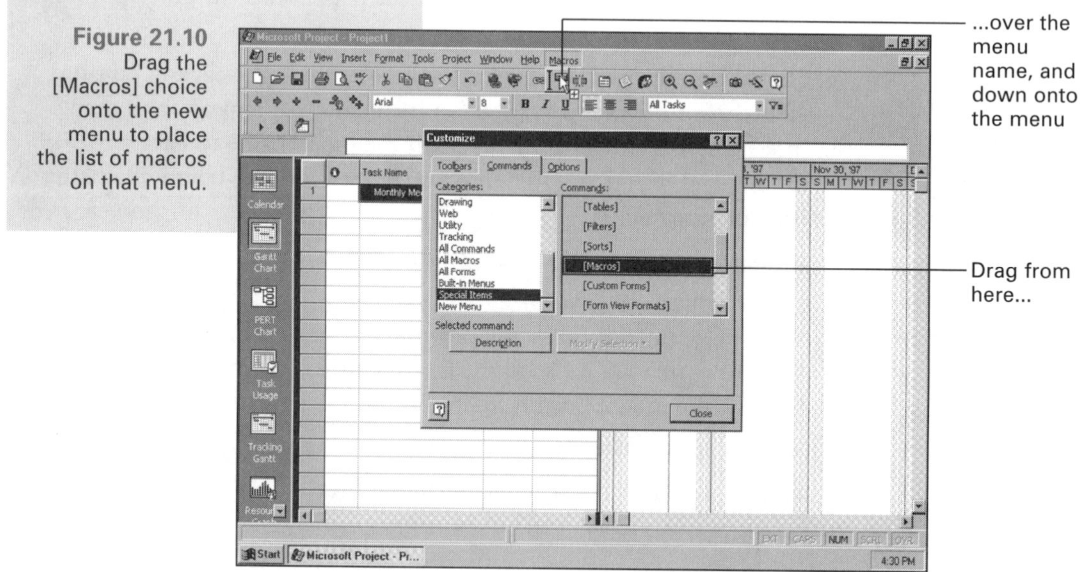
...over the menu name, and down onto the menu
Drag from here...

Figure 21.10 Drag the [Macros] choice onto the new menu to place the list of macros on that menu.

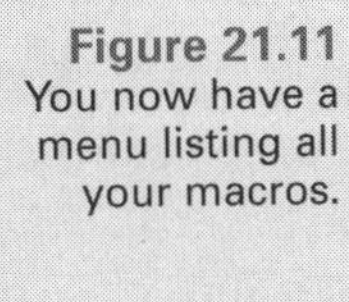

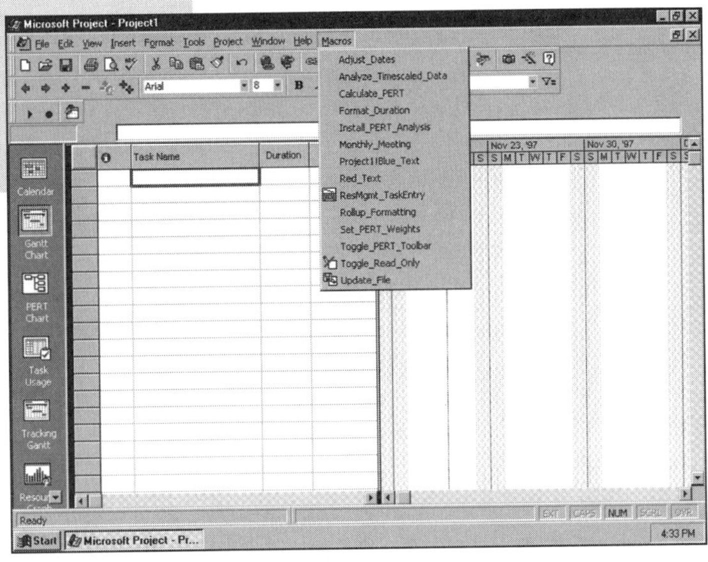

Figure 21.11 You now have a menu listing all your macros.

that you create, add a custom menu command or toolbar button for the macro to any menu or toolbar. Then you can execute your macro simply by selecting its name from a more streamlined menu or by clicking its toolbar button.

Although you can assign a macro to an existing toolbar button, replacing the command that was originally assigned to that button, this procedure is not recommended. It would be difficult to recall what the button's original command was, should you want to reinstate it.

To create a menu command or toolbar button for a macro, follow these steps:

1. As you learned in Chapter 20, start by displaying the menu bar or toolbar that you want to hold the command or button.
2. Display the Customize dialog box. To do so, click the Tools menu to open it, point to Customize, and click Toolbars. Alternately, right-click any toolbar or menu bar and click Customize.
3. Click the Commands tab to display its options.
4. Scroll down the Categories list and click the All Macros choice. The Commands list then lists all the macros available in Project.

5. Scroll down the Commands list until you see the macro for which you want to create a menu command or toolbar button.
6. Drag the macro from the Commands list to the menu or toolbar that will hold the menu; then drop the macro into the appropriate location. Note that if you drag the macro over a menu and drop it into place on the menu, it becomes a menu command. If you drop the macro directly onto a toolbar, it becomes a toolbar button. See Figure 21.12 for an example of each.
7. Click the Close button to close the Customize dialog box and finish your menu and toolbar edits.

Adjusting the Macro Command or Button

After you add your menu command or toolbar button for a macro, you might want to fine-tune it a bit. For example, you might want to display an icon rather than the macro name on a toolbar button, or change how the macro command reads on the menu.

Chapter 20 covers how to make changes to a command or button in more detail, but review these steps for a refresher.

1. Display the menu bar or toolbar that holds the command or button you want to edit.

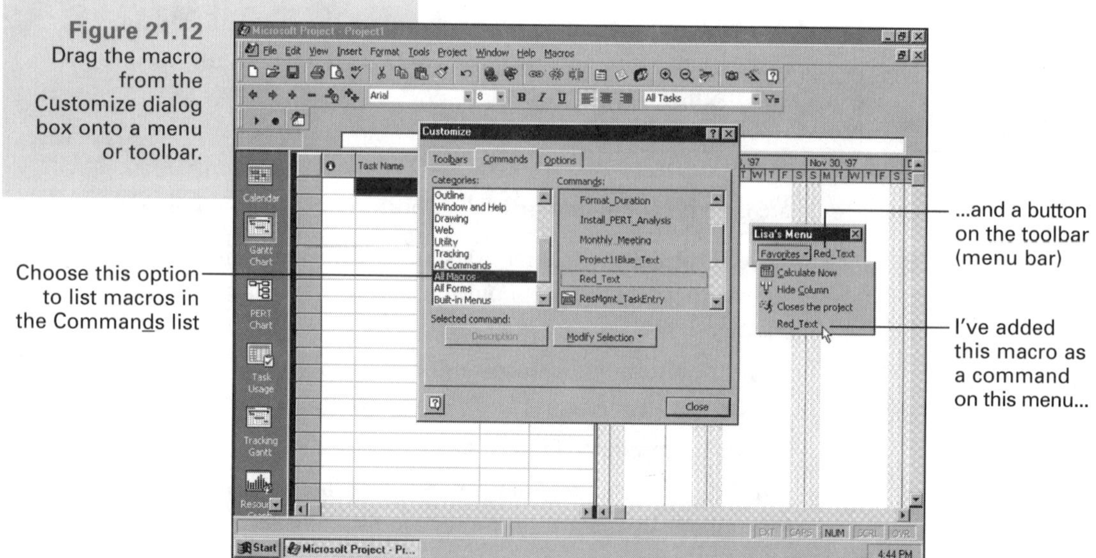

Figure 21.12 Drag the macro from the Customize dialog box onto a menu or toolbar.

2. Click the Tools menu to open it, point to Customize, and click Toolbars. Alternately, right-click any toolbar or menu bar and click Customize. The Customize dialog box appears.
3. Right-click the menu command or toolbar button to edit. A shortcut menu of commands appears, as shown in Figure 21.13.
4. To make changes to a menu command (or text that you want to appear on the toolbar button), edit the Name text box contents and press Enter.
5. If you're working with a toolbar button and want it to display an icon only, right-click the button and then click the Default Style option in the shortcut menu to toggle that choice on. (The default for buttons is to show only an icon.) Then, right-click the blank button to redisplay the shortcut menu, point to the Change Button Image Choice, and click an icon in the pop-up palette that appears. Figure 21.14 shows the toolbar button for the Red_Text macro, changed to display only an icon.
6. If you're working with a menu command or toolbar button and want it to display text and an icon, right-click the command or button. Then click the Image and Text option in the shortcut menu to toggle that choice on. Then, right-click the menu command or toolbar button to redisplay the shortcut menu. Edit the contents of the Name text box. (Do not press Enter.) Point to the Change Button Image Choice, and click an icon in the pop-up palette that appears.
7. Click Close to close the Customize dialog box and finish making your changes.

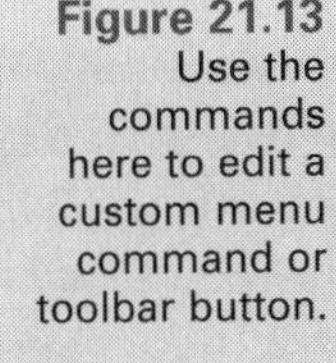

Figure 21.13 Use the commands here to edit a custom menu command or toolbar button.

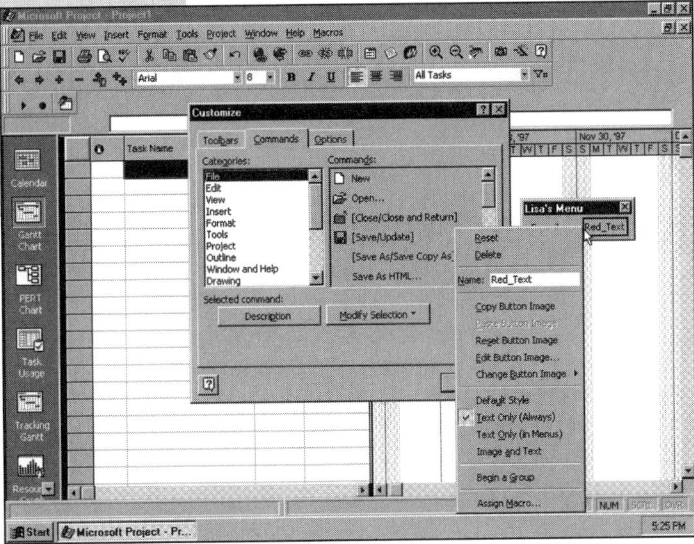

Figure 21.14 You can display a custom button with an icon only.

A Few More Macro Ideas

This chapter—the final one in the book—has shown you how to create macros to make your work in Project faster and more efficient. Here are a few other ideas about how to use macros to get the most out of Microsoft Project:

- Create a macro that inserts a new task—with a particular name and duration—that you want to use more than once. Assign a shortcut key to run the task.
- Create a macro to format summary commands in a way that calls even more attention to them. The macro can apply a particular font, color, or emphasis (such as italic). Add a button for the macro to the Formatting toolbar.
- Create a macro that inserts your company logo where you specify (such as in a Gantt chart), so that the logo appears on printouts you send to clients.
- Record macros that change the active view or display a particular Task Sheet table. Create a shortcut key or button for each macro.
- If you supervise a team of people and use Project to manage multiple tasks, create a macro that assigns each person (as a resource) to the currently selected task. Then you can assign a task to a particular worker with a single shortcut key, reducing the time that you spend making assignments.
- If you regularly need to print a particular form or report, create a macro that automates the process, and assign the macro to a toolbar button.

Planning Wizard
Microsoft Project - Annual Report
Start

Index

A

B

C

D

F

H

I

K

L

M

N

O

P

S

T

U

V

W

Z

Prima's *fast & easy*™ Series

Relax, learning new software is now a breeze. You are looking at a series of books dedicated to one idea: To help you learn to use software as quickly and as easily as possible. No need to wade through boring pages of endless text. With Prima's FAST & EASY series, you simply look and learn.

Microsoft® Office 97
0-7615-1162-8
$16.99 (Can. $23.95)

Microsoft® Word 97
0-7615-1007-9
$16.99 (Can. $23.95)

Microsoft® Excel 97
0-7615-1008-7
$16.99 (Can. $23.95)

Internet Explorer 4.0
0-7615-1191-1
$16.99 (Can. $23.95)

ACT!™ 3.0
0-7615-1175-X
$16.99 (Can. $23.95)

Lotus® 1-2-3® 97
0-7615-1193-8
$16.99 (Can. $23.95)

SmartSuite® 97
0-7615-1192-X
$16.99 (Can. $23.95)

Windows® 95
1-55958-738-5
$19.95 (Can. $27.95)

Also Available

Access 97
0-7615-1363-9

Netscape Navigator® 4.0
0-7615-1382-5

WordPerfect® 98
0-7615-1083-4

WordPerfect Suite® 8
0-7615-1188-1

Coming Soon

Windows® 98
0-7615-1006-0

Outlook 98
0-7615-1405-8

Publisher 98
0-7615-1513-5

FrontPage® 98
0-7615-1534-8

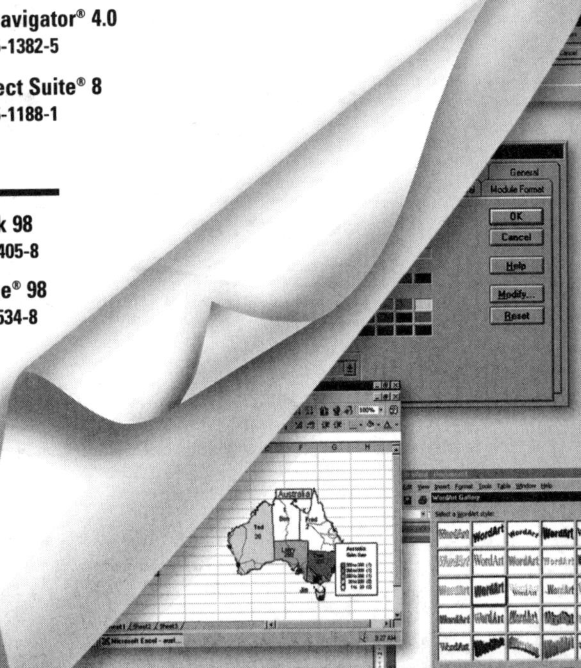

PRIMA

www.primapublishing.com

Call now to order
(800)632-8676, ext. 4444